HEINEMANN

INTERMEDIATE
HEALTH AND SOCIAL CARE

SECOND EDITION

GENERAL EDITOR: NEIL MOONIE

RICHARD CHALONER

KIP CHAN PENSLEY

MARGARET HILTON

KAREN HUCKER

BERYL STRETCH

Heinemann

Heinemann Educational,
a division of Heinemann Publishers (Oxford) Ltd
Halley Court, Jordan Hill, Oxford OX2 8EJ

OXFORD LONDON EDINBURGH
MADRID ATHENS BOLOGNA PARIS
MELBOURNE SYDNEY AUCKLAND SINGAPORE
TOKYO IBADAN NAIROBI HARARE
GABORONE PORTSMOUTH NH (USA)

© Richard Chaloner, Kip Chan-Pensley, Margaret Hilton,
Karen Hucker, Beryl Stretch, Neil Moonie

First published 1995
99 98 97 96
10 9 8 7 6 5 4 3 2 1

A catalogue record for this book is available from the
British Library on request

ISBN 0 435 45252 5

Typeset by TechType, Abingdon
Printed in Great Britain by The Bath Press

Front cover
Designed by: Tad Kasa
Photograph by Format Partners

Contents

Preface to the second edition

This book has been written to support students who are working to the 1995 national standards for Intermediate Health and Social Care.

The book aims to help students to gain Merit or Distinction grades by providing:

- An introduction to GNVQs including:
  - levels of awards
  - GNVQ standards and structure
  - grading criteria
  - portfolios
  - tests.
- The knowledge, skills and values associated with each of the four GNVQ mandatory units:
  1. Promoting health and well-being
  2. Influences on health and well-being
  3. Health and social care services
  4. Communication and interpersonal relationships in health and social care.
- The knowledge and skills associated with the core skills of Information Technology, Communication and Application of Number at level 2.
- A section on interviewing skills, included in the Communication chapter, to support evidence collection for the mandatory units.

Special features of the book

- Icons are used to link theory with practice. Icons are provided to suggest areas for:

 Reflection (*Think it over*)

 Practical experience (*Try it*).

 Meeting evidence requirements (*Evidence collection point*)

Icons are also suggested as a way of labelling work.

- Multiple-choice questions will help you to prepare for tests and to check personal understanding.
- Fast Facts will also help you to prepare for tests and provide a quick reference section for key concepts.
- Case studies show how theory links to practice. They explain ideas and guide evidence collection.
- Diagrams, drawings and cartoons are used throughout the book to explain concepts and to make sections easier to refer to and remember.

How to use this book

This book is designed to be used as a source of knowledge and ideas. It can be read from beginning to end, but it is also designed so that you can go directly to a section on a particular element. Fast Facts are listed alphabetically at the end of each unit so that concepts can be checked quickly. You may wish to use the book in a very different order from the way it is set out.

In particular, you may want to study the core skills chapters on Communication and interviewing, Application of Number and Information Technology before studying all the mandatory units.

Core skills interlink with the mandatory units and evidence for them should be gathered with evidence for the units. You will probably wish to dip in and out of these chapters as you study each of the units.

Each reader will have his or her own needs and purposes for this book. For this reason it has been designed with easy reference headings and icons, so that it can be used flexibly – in keeping with the ideas behind GNVQs.

Acknowledgements

The authors and publishers would like to thank the following for permission to reproduce photographs and other material:

Age Concern
British Standards Institution
Cancer Relief Macmillan Fund
Health Education Authority
Robert Harding
Science Photo Library
Winged Fellowship Trust

Every effort has been made to contact copyright holders of material published in this book. We would be glad to hear from unacknowledged sources at the first opportunity.

Introduction to GNVQ

This section covers:

- What are GNVQs?
- Levels and pathways to qualifications
- What does a GNVQ Caring qualification lead to?
- How GNVQ Health and Social Care is made up
- GNVQ standards – an explanation
- GNVQ assessment
- Meeting evidence indicators – things that count as evidence
- Collecting evidence
- Reflection
- Assignments
- Grading criteria for Intermediate GNVQ
- The portfolio
- Tests
- Self-assessment of knowledge about GNVQs
- Answers to self-assessment quiz
- Fast Facts

What are GNVQs?

GNVQs are a new system of qualifications designed to fit into a national pattern of 'levels'. GNVQs are also designed to allow students to have some choice in the work that they do. This introduction explains how the national system works and how *you* can manage your own learning while working on a GNVQ programme. GNVQs are not intended to be simple, but this section will help you to manage your own study of GNVQ at Intermediate Level in Caring.

This introduction contains a range of *theory* and *advice*. Before starting it, it may be worth checking what you need to know. Use the list above as a guide to what is on offer. If you know very little about GNVQs then start at the beginning.

Getting a GNVQ qualification may be a bit like learning to drive a car or learning to ride a bicycle. It takes time and, most importantly, it takes *practice*. What is said here will make more sense when you are actually working to get the GNVQ award. Like learning to drive, there is a limit to how much *theory* you might want to learn in one go. It may be best just to read parts of this section as you need them.

When you have finished the introduction you might like to test your understanding with the questions at the end. Another idea is that you look at the questions to begin with and decide whether you need to know about these things. If you just need to understand a technical word, look up Fast Facts.

You are in charge of your own learning, so please see this section as something to explore. Different people might want to use this introduction in different ways and at different stages of their GNVQ programme.

A note on change and development in GNVQs

Learners develop their skills by constantly building on their experience. Good learners are open to change – they drop things that don't work well in practice, and fine-tune behaviours that do seem to work, in order to get the best outcomes.

General NVQs are still new. The detail of how to achieve a GNVQ will almost certainly continue to build on experience and develop over the next few years. The advice and guidance in this introduction is based on the GNVQ system as it was in the spring of 1995. Fine detail on issues like grading, revising for test questions and portfolio design may continue to develop. You are therefore recommended to check whether new details or new regulations have come about. It is worth checking the latest information with a tutor or teacher if you are enrolled on a GNVQ programme.

GNVQs involve exploring ideas and developing skills in using information and knowledge. You should use your skills to check that the information has not become dated!

The meaning of GNVQ

GNVQ stands for General National Vocational Qualification:

- **General** means that the qualification is not just for a particular job. General qualifications are broad; they are designed to enable people to move on to higher qualifications or to get jobs in a wide range of employment.

- **National** means that the qualification is valuable nationally. The qualification has the same value everywhere in the 'nation'.
- **Vocational** means that the qualification focuses on areas of employment. A vocational qualification in caring provides the knowledge and understanding a person needs to go on to work in many different caring jobs. The study involved also means that people with Intermediate Level will be ready to take A levels or an Advanced GNVQ if they want to.
- **Qualification** means that an individual has passed at a definite standard. Intermediate Level is equivalent to good GCSE passes at an academic level and is also equivalent to work skills which would enable a person to perform some complex and individually responsible jobs.

Levels and pathways to qualifications

There is now a national system of qualifications at five levels, as shown in Figure 1. *Level 1* is the starting point for foundation qualifications. *Level 2* (Intermediate) covers jobs that are more complex, and academically it is worth GCSE at good grades. *Level 3* covers jobs that involve high responsibility and complexity, perhaps including supervising others. This level is designed to provide vocational A levels. *Levels 4* and *5* cover professional and management jobs and are designed to be degree and post-graduate equivalents.

As well as the five levels, there are three *pathways* to qualifications. The first pathway – the 'academic' one – has been around for many years and has worked well for some people. But in 1986 the government decided to set up the National Council for Vocational Qualifications (NCVQ) so that there would be new ways to obtain qualifications. To begin with, the NCVQ designed qualifications called National Vocational Qualifications (NVQs).

NVQs are designed to provide qualifications for particular jobs or professions. Sometimes NVQs can be studied at college, but many of these qualifications are easier for people to get if they already have a job. For many individuals, NVQs opened up the possibility of getting a recognised qualification for the skills and 'know-how' they had already learned at work. NVQs meant that people could become qualified at work without necessarily having to start at the beginning with their studies again.

The third pathway or ladder is a GNVQ. GNVQs first began in 1992 and their original purpose was to

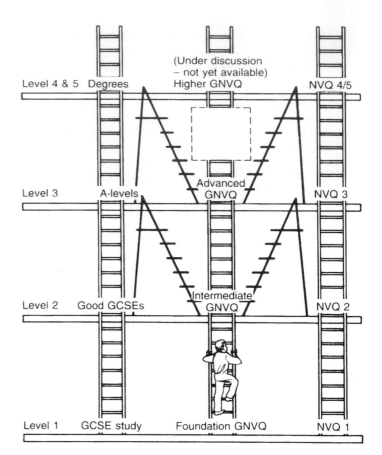

Figure 1 How the ladders work

provide a 'middle way' between academic and work-based qualifications.

GNVQs are based on standards in a similar way to NVQs. GNVQs cover a much broader range of knowledge and understanding than NVQs.

There is increasing interest in new types of qualification that will allow students to combine units of GNVQ with units of other qualifications. In the future, the three ladders may become merged. It may even be possible for you to take a mixture of GNVQ units and A level, or BTEC, or Open College units at Advanced level. You may even be able to climb the ladders using footholds across the ladders.

What does a GNVQ caring qualification lead to?

At present, a person with GNVQ Intermediate has three options:

1 He or she can decide to stay with the GNVQ ladder and go on and achieve an Advanced GNVQ.

2 He or she can decide to switch to A level studies.
3 He or she can decide to look for employment in health or in social care.

Chapter 9 explores some of the jobs available in health and social care. When studying this chapter you will be able to explore the opportunities available to people with an Intermediate GNVQ qualification.

If you take a job in health or social caring you might be offered the chance to collect an NVQ at Level 2 or even Level 3. An Intermediate qualification will provide much of the knowledge that you would need for an NVQ at Level 2. Your GNVQ experience might help you to understand NVQ assessment systems.

You might take an Intermediate GNVQ simply out of personal interest. Some people take GNVQ qualifications while they are working in health or social care jobs. Intermediate GNVQs should open up a wide range of future career and learning opportunities.

In the future you may be offered more complicated choices of Advanced level study. Ask your tutor or teacher about current opportunities.

How GNVQ Health and Social Care at Intermediate Level Is made up

All GNVQs are made up of **units**. Making a qualification up of units is a useful idea because a unit can be 'passed' and then awarded to the person who has achieved it. GNVQs can be 'passed' bit by bit, unit by unit. If a person leaves a GNVQ course, he or she still keeps the units passed. This means that it is possible to start again without having to go right back to the beginning. The whole qualification consists of **nine** units. The nine units are made up of four mandatory (no choice), two options and three core skills units.

Mandatory units

Optional units

Core skills units

This book is designed to cover the knowledge you will need for the four mandatory units and the three core skills units required to gain a GNVQ Intermediate award. The book does not cover the optional units because the awarding bodies such as BTEC, City and Guilds or RSA offer different optional units.

To pass mandatory units 1, 2 and 3, you have to pass a test set by your awarding body. Unit 4 and the optional units are not expected to be tested.

Core skills units are different from mandatory units or optional units. This is because they are meant to be studied *with* the other units. The evidence needed to 'pass' core skills is meant to be collected with the evidence to pass the mandatory and optional units.

The idea of core skills is that communication, number and information technology skills are needed in *all* work situations. GNVQs will probably cover many areas of work in the future. Core skills *standards* will be the same across all the areas, but the *evidence presented* will be different because it will be linked to practical assignment work for each qualification. In health and social care, evidence opportunities for core skills such as information technology may link with assignment work in caring.

Only core skills units in communication, number and information technology have to be assessed and awarded to obtain a GNVQ qualification. However, there are three other areas of core skills: problem solving, working with others and improving own learning and performance. These core skills are worth including in a portfolio of evidence for two reasons: first, they can be recorded in your National Record of Achievement; and, secondly, they help towards evidence for Merit and Distinction grades.

An Intermediate GNVQ in Caring will usually take one year of full-time study for you to complete all the work and evidence collection.

GNVQ standards – an explanation

To collect GNVQ units and qualifications, candidates have to demonstrate that they have achieved a defined standard of work. GNVQ standards are definitions of what is required in order to 'pass' and be awarded the qualification. Because standards are definitions, they are not always easy to understand. This part explains the technical detail of units, elements, performance criteria, range statements and evidence indicators.

The whole set of standards for a qualification runs to many pages. Most people who sit down and read standards will say that they are boring. Many people will say they cannot really understand them!

Why are standards so complicated?

Standards are difficult for three reasons:

1 Standards are a system for defining outcomes.

Because standards define things to be understood or done, they become a bit like legal statements. Standards try to give exact details of what is required rather than discuss ideas about what would be useful. Standards end up being technical rather than interesting simply because they are definitions. Definitions are necessary because they have to be applied in the same way across the country. Standards are a guide to assessment; they explain what has to be done in order to pass the GNVQ. Standards don't really explain what has to be studied; rather, they define what has to be achieved in order to get the qualification. So standards are like goal-posts in football – they define the goal that has to be reached. Standards do not explain how to get there!

2 The value of a qualification will depend on the definition of standards.

There are two kinds of qualifications. One kind is based on what people can do or understand, and the other kind is based on who comes first in a

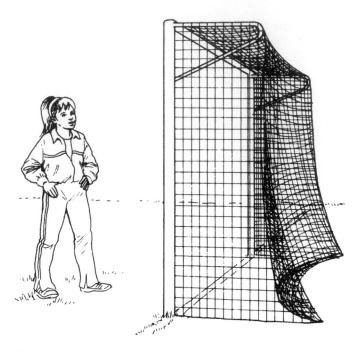

Figure 2 It is boring just standing looking at the goal.... it is much more fun if you are doing something with it!

competition. Many qualifications have exams, which are like a competition or a race. The people who run the fastest get to the end first – these people pass. In a running race, the people who come in last are not so good; in the exam, the people with the lowest marks fail. Not all exams are marked in terms of top and bottom, but they all have some degree of competition about them. Standards allow a different way of qualifying – instead of doing better than others in an exam, the candidate has to show what he or she can do or prove that he or she knows the details needed for the qualification.

Exams give people qualifications because they have come in the top group. Standards give people qualifications because those individuals have proved they can do what is needed. The problem with standards qualifications is that the qualification is only as good as the standards. If standards are not well defined, or if they don't cover much, then the qualification is not worth a lot. Standards need to define complicated details carefully if the qualification is going to be worthwhile in the end.

3 Standards are impossible to understand without the knowledge of the area they are about.

Because standards define areas of skill, values and knowledge, they are impossible to understand without the necessary knowledge. At the beginning

Figure 3 Climbing to the top is like achieving a standard – you can do it in your own way at your own pace. Running a race is different – you have to beat the others!

of a course of study, the standards will be difficult because people will not know all the terms and detail involved. As a person learns about the issues, so the standards should become easier to understand. When a candidate's work is ready for assessment, the standards should be clear.

Figure 4 It looks a long way up from the bottom!

The way standards are written

Standards are written for guiding the assessment of GNVQs. They start with units.

- **Units.** GNVQ qualifications are split into units. Units cover particular areas of knowledge, values and skill. For example, Unit 1 covers knowledge on how to maintain and improve personal health, how to present advice on health, and how to identify risks to health and deal with emergencies. A person who achieves Unit 1 will have a very wide range of practical knowledge which will help him or her to care for others. Unit 1 isn't a whole qualification, but it is the first part of an Intermediate GNVQ in Health and Social Care.

- **Elements.** Each GNVQ unit is split into elements. Unit 1: Promoting health and well-being is split into three elements. Each element defines an area of knowledge. Elements are the smallest areas to be assessed, and *evidence* has to be presented for each element. When there is enough evidence, an element can be 'passed', but a person has to provide evidence for all the elements in a unit before the unit is awarded. Elements are not awarded.

  Elements have a title such as '1.1 Investigate personal health'. This may be a good definition, but it is not easy to see exactly what it means or how it should be assessed. To explain this definition, elements have performance criteria.

- **Performance criteria.** Performance criteria define what is required to pass the element. They help to explain what the element title is all about. When evidence is gathered to 'pass' an element, that evidence has to meet the requirements explained in performance criteria.

  The element title gives the focus of what has to be done, and the performance criteria help to explain this focus. However, range is also needed to explain what the evidence has to cover.

- **Range.** Range explains the area that performance criteria cover. The word *range* comes from archery or perhaps from shooting ranges. If something is in range, then it is within your area of study. If an issue is not in range, then you would not be expected to know about it when you come to take tests or present assignments.

  Each element also has evidence indicators.

- **Evidence indicators.** Evidence indicators explain exactly what your assignment or final portfolio of

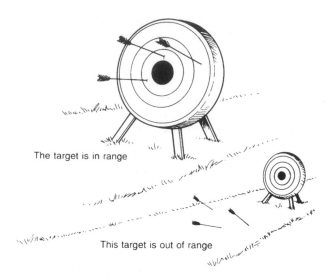

The target is in range

This target is out of range

evidence needs to cover. You will need to check that any written reports or assignments have covered everything that was asked for in the evidence indicator section of the standards. You may want to check that you understand these requirements when you design your action plans. You may need to check that your work has covered the evidence indicators before handing it in for assessment.

Reports or assignments can cover more than just one element's evidence indicators. You do not have to cover evidence indicators in the order in which they are written. There are often a number of possible ways of choosing to cover evidence indicators. You might choose to write a report on a video you have seen, or you might go out and interview people in order to collect evidence. The way in which you cover the demands of the evidence indicators may be up to you.

Standards also contain amplification and guidance sections.

■ **Amplification.** Amplification increases the amount of detail about the performance criteria. Amplification is intended to make the meaning of performance criteria clearer and to prevent misinterpretations.

■ **Guidance.** Guidance provides ideas to help teachers and tutors to cover the issues identified in the performance criteria and range.

Element 1.1 means Unit 1, Element 1. The element has six performance criteria which describe what the title 'Investigate personal health' has to cover. The range explains what the terms in the performance criteria cover. For example, a balanced lifestyle means

---

PERFORMANCE CRITERIA

A student must:

1 explain the importance of a **balanced** lifestyle
2 explain risks and benefits associated with **aspects of lifestyle**
3 identify how the body uses each dietary **component**
4 describe a **healthy diet** for an **individual**
5 describe the **effects** of use of substances on health and well-being
6 explain good practice in maintaining **hygiene**

RANGE

Balanced: in terms of activity (work, recreation), rest (sleep, inactivity)

Aspects of lifestyle: exercise, diet (adequate, balanced), sufficient rest, smoking, alcohol, sexual behaviour including celibacy

Components: protein, carbohydrate, fat, vitamins (C, D), minerals (iron, calcium), water, fibre

Healthy diet: types of food eaten, amount eaten, eating patterns

Individual: active, sedentary, child, elderly person, pregnant women

Effects: physical, social, emotional, intellectual

Substances: use of drugs intended as medical treatment, misuse of drugs intended as medical treatment, use of drugs which have no accepted use in medical treatment, misuse of solvents

Hygiene: personal (teeth, skin, hair), in public areas (food preparation, eating, medical treatment)

EVIDENCE INDICATORS

A report which:

■ explains the importance of a balanced lifestyle
■ explains risks and benefits associated with aspects of lifestyle for all aspects indicated in the range.

A description of a healthy diet for a child, an elderly person, and a pregnant woman, at least one of whom is active and at least one of whom is sedentary. This should include a description of how the body uses each of the dietary components in the range for one of the individuals.

A description of how using and misusing substances affects health and well-being covering

■ all categories in the use of substance range
■ all relevant categories in the effects range.

An explanation of good practice in maintaining hygiene in personal routines and in one public area.

Figure 5 An example: Element 1.1 Investigate personal health

a balance between activity and rest, a balance of work, recreation, sleep and inactivity. Without 'range' the term, 'balanced lifestyle', might be taken to mean all sorts of different kinds of balance. It could have applied to balanced relationships, balanced diets, balanced mental interests, and so on.

The evidence indicators explain what you really have to do. If you turn to Chapter 1 of this book you will be able to review the knowledge needed for Element 1.1 and a summary of ideas which may help you to meet the evidence indicators for 1.1.

Each element of each unit has to be assessed before the unit is awarded. Assessment takes place when there is enough evidence to be assessed. In order to know what counts as enough evidence, candidates need to have their own assessment skills. Self-assessment of evidence is necessary in order to achieve good grades on GNVQ.

The individual working for a GNVQ qualification will go through a process of action planning, assignment work, checking and submitting the work for assessment. This is not the whole story, however. When work is submitted or 'given in' for assessment, a whole system comes into operation.

GNVQ assessment

In the past, work was given to teachers or tutors, who marked it. This approach was often much simpler than in GNVQ. Now when work is given in, it is more than just 'work'. Assignments are now designed to provide evidence. Evidence has to be judged to decide if there is enough, and if it is the right quality to show that a standard has been reached. The person who decides whether there is enough quality evidence is called an **assessor**. Often the people who act as assessors will be teachers or tutors, but when they collect in the work, they become assessors.

Assessors have to have qualifications and knowledge in the field in which they work. They also have to understand fully the standards for which they are checking evidence. Assessors will have gained an NVQ award which shows that they understand the GNVQ assessment process. All these checks are required to try to ensure that the quality of GNVQ assessment is fair and works properly. But it is more complicated still. The assessments themselves have to be checked.

Assessments have to be checked by an **internal verifier**. 'Internal' means internal to, or inside the centre (inside the college or school, etc). 'Verifier' means that the person checks the correctness of assessment. Internal verifiers will look at samples of assessment work and check that evidence is being correctly and fairly measured in relation to standards. If candidates don't think their work is being fairly assessed, they can appeal to the internal verifier to look at their work, and re-check it. All the assessor's decisions can be checked by the internal verifier.

There is also an **external verifier**. 'External' means outside, from outside the centre (a school or college, etc). External verifiers are appointed by the awarding body. An awarding body is BTEC, City & Guilds, or RSA. The awarding body checks the overall quality of the centre's assessment. The external verifier checks the quality of both the assessor's and the internal verifier's decisions. The idea of all this checking is to ensure that standards *really work* – what is accepted as evidence must not become too simple or too complicated. A qualification gained at one college or school should require the same amount and quality of evidence as elsewhere.

Meeting evidence indicators – things that count as evidence

In order to pass your GNVQ you will need to provide evidence that you have done everything that the evidence indicators require you to do. Very often the evidence indicators ask for an assignment or a report which explains certain issues. At the end of your GNVQ programme (or course) you may have collected other evidence in a portfolio (a portable folder). Both assignments and portfolios might include the following examples of evidence:

Practical demonstration of skills can be watched by an assessor or they can be videoed or tape-recorded (with everyone's permission).

Reports can provide evidence of knowledge, records of practical work and projects. Many units will require some report writing.

Past records of achievement and qualifications can count as evidence towards GNVQ units. For instance, GCSE work might count towards core skills assessment.

References from other people such as placement supervisors or employers can provide evidence of practical caring skills and core skills.

Notes: not all written work needs to be put together into assignments – notes will often be enough to provide evidence for knowledge, or perhaps evidence of planning skills.

Log books or record books are a way of providing evidence to meet grading criteria standards. Log books may be easier to use than loose notes.

Photographs of placement work, perhaps of events organised by a candidate, can sometimes count as evidence towards achieving standards. Photos can often make assignments more interesting.

Other work such as computer printouts, can provide evidence of skills and knowledge. Computer printouts will sometimes need to be 'certified' by an appropriate person to prove that they were done by the candidate.

Collecting evidence

Each element suggests a way of getting the necessary evidence in the 'evidence indicators' section. Usually, tutors will provide more information and ideas on practical ways in which evidence can be gathered. Here are some points to remember:

- **Permission.** It is *always* necessary to have other people's permission before written details about them can be used. For instance, written details of a conversation can give evidence of conversation skills, but things other people have said must not be written down without their permission and knowledge of what is written. Where someone is unable to understand, perhaps because he or she is too young, then their parents or guardians have to give permission.

- **Confidentiality:** If you use written or taped evidence that involves other people, it is important that their confidentiality is respected. One of the most effective ways of keeping material confidential is to keep details anonymous. This means that you should not write the names or any identifying personal details of people you have worked with on your finished work. If you interview people for evidence, you should *not* explain who they were in your assignment, logbook or portfolio of evidence. Instead, you might say that you worked with a friend, a relative, or a tutor or supervisor. Any personal details such as age, place of work, or detailed description of appearance should not be recorded.

So as well as asking for permission to use interviews or group work, you should also keep your reports confidential. If this is not possible, for example, if you have video evidence where it is obvious who the people are, you should show the video to all the people involved in it and ask for written permission before you can use it as evidence. This might be agreed simply if you are all students. If you video clients on placement, you might need to get written permission from them and from parents or managers – after they have checked your material – that the material may be used as your evidence. This kind of agreement may sometimes be difficult to get.

Of course all written details, tapes or videos should be kept safely and used only as part of your GNVQ work, unless you have special arrangements.

- **Group work.** Working with other people is often the best way to plan to collect evidence. Sometimes a group project can meet the evidence requirements for an element. The only problem is that each individual's work has to be separately recorded or noted, so that each has individual evidence of planning and achievement for their portfolio. Naturally, the general outcome can be recorded as well.

■ **Evidence from others.** Evidence of skills used on placements is really valuable, but it will need to be confirmed by a manager or supervisor in the work setting. Usually the supervisor will also have to explain that he or she has watched practical work, and give reasons for agreeing with claims for evidence. Sometimes a report or reference will be needed.

Quality of evidence

Being assessed involves convincing an assessor that your evidence is good enough. Usually, candidates will get a lot of help and guidance to make sure the evidence is all right.

The process of assessment will probably start something like this:

1 Teachers or tutors suggest a project, assignment or demonstration to provide evidence for particular evidence indicators. Written guidelines are given out.
2 Candidates discuss the guidelines, probably with a tutor, and think of ways of planning practical work.
3 Each individual designs an 'action plan' for the assignment or project.
4 Each individual discusses the action plan with a tutor.
5 The individual 'monitors' the implementation of the action plan, i.e. he or she checks and revises ideas as the assignment gets going.
6 Candidates do the practical work and write about it.
7 The written work is checked by an assessor. If it is all right, then it counts as evidence. If not, then further work can be done until the evidence is right.
8 When there is enough evidence for an element, it is accredited as complete.

At the start of a GNVQ programme, tutors and teachers will probably help with action plans and other practical work. As the programme progresses, candidates will have to do this work without help in order to gain Merit and Distinction grades.

Reflection

Planning to collect evidence can be interesting. It involves a special skill called **reflection**. Think of a mirror. When a person looks in a mirror, his or her image is being bounced back – reflected – from the mirror. Reflection is the bouncing back of the

original image. In social care, reflection means the same sort of thing; except here we are thinking about thoughts and ideas rather than images. Thoughts and ideas get bounced backwards and forwards between people.

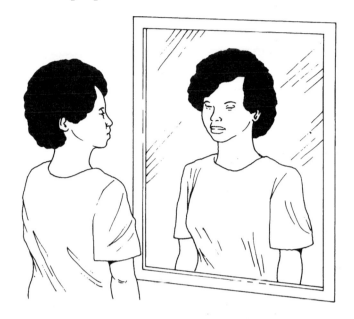

Reflection can be very useful. When people look in a mirror, they can see what they look like, they can change their hairstyle or appearance until it looks right. The same idea goes for thoughts. If an individual can have his or her thoughts mirrored or reflected by another person, then the individual has a chance to change or alter his or her thoughts. Like changing hairstyle, reflection allows individuals to experiment until their ideas are good.

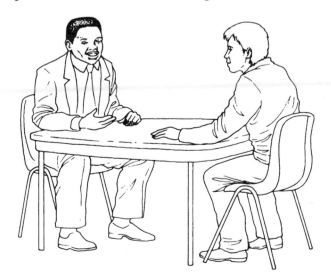

Providing reflective listening is a special skill that is explained in Chapter 10. People who can help others to reflect have a very useful skill. When people get very good at reflecting with others, they can sometimes reflect in their own mind – alone. This becomes a powerful learning skill as people can adapt their own thoughts using an internal mirror, rather than using another person. Reflection is also needed in order to plan the collection of evidence.

Assignments

Evidence for mandatory and optional units will mostly be found in assignment work. Assignments will probably contain most of the evidence for the core skills units, spread across the mandatory and optional units.

Most people will need to discuss how they plan to write assignments or do practical work. The act of talking a project through often helps to clarify ideas. Usually, ideas on assignment writing will need to be reflected on with a tutor. Ideas can be 'bounced' between people until the ideas grow more practical and useful.

Before starting any practical or written work it will be important to construct an **action plan** to help find the necessary information and evidence opportunities. Action plans can be monitored for progress. Keeping notes on progress may help to organise a project. Monitoring may also boost confidence when it comes to sitting down and writing an assignment. Planning involves self-assessment. Monitoring progress with evidence collection involves being in control of personal work. Self-assessment and control of work should provide a very useful starting point for getting a GNVQ qualification.

Action plans

Action plans are records of the ideas that go into getting ready for assignments and evidence collection. They record ideas for the following:

1 *Finding information*

- looking up books for information and ideas
- asking people for their opinions
- asking tutors, learning advisers, librarians for advice on how to find information.

2 *Reflecting on ideas*

- discussing with tutors, with other candidates

- discussing with placement supervisors
- working out what information is needed in order to do assignments, etc.

3 *Preparing to gather evidence – plans:*

- for practical activities
- to get evidence during placement
- for doing assignments
- for what to include in notes and written work.

4 *Self-assessment and monitoring*

- self-assessment of evidence before it is formally assessed
- self-checking of own progress
- checking of ideas against assignment guidelines
- checking own study patterns and use of time.

Many people like to use a form to help record their ideas. Forms are useful because they can focus attention on what needs to be done. They also keep a record of planning activities which can fit neatly into a portfolio. Records of planning are needed in order to get Merit and Distinction grades.

Forms are just one way of organising and recording a 'plan for action'. Some people prefer to write everything down in notes or to use notes to go with their forms. Others like to make 'pattern notes' to help display things visually.

Suppose you want to collect information to help with your work on Element 1.1 Investigate personal health. Pattern notes might help you to identify the information that you need. By looking at the demands of the evidence indicators, you could produce a pattern like the one shown in Figure 6.

Pattern notes can be used for both action planning and for identifying information needs. You may find pattern notes particularly useful for identifying information needs.

Planning and information seeking are usually required before you will be able to write assignments or produce work to meet the evidence indicators. Planning and information seeking are also part of the grading criteria for the full GNVQ award.

Grading criteria for Intermediate GNVQ qualifications can be awarded at a Pass, Merit or Distinction grade. At present, these grades are awarded when a student's final portfolio of work is assessed at the end of the programme.

To achieve a Merit or Distinction grade, Intermediate students have to be able to demonstrate that they have followed a process of planning, information seeking and information handling and evaluation – in at least one-third of their work. Students must also

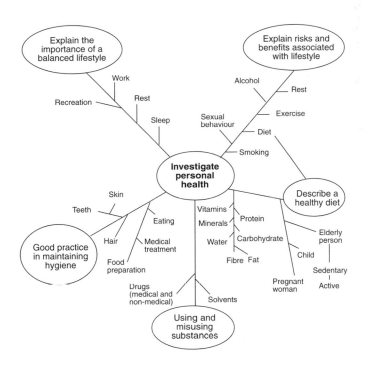

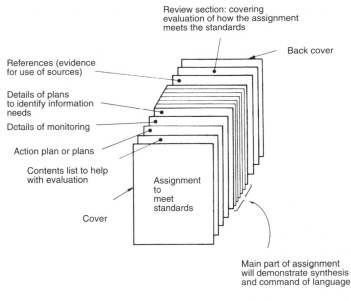

Figure 6 Information needs for Element 1.1

demonstrate 'quality' in the final one-third of their work. The quality of outcomes theme requires that students can use appropriate skills, knowledge and understanding, and link skills, knowledge and understanding effectively when presenting assignment work. Students must also be able to demonstrate their use of the ideas and concepts involved in appropriate units.

The process of evidence collection

The process of preparing to meet evidence indicators should always start with planning. Sometimes this planning stage might involve identifying information needs and where this information can be obtained. It is important to monitor your plans and your collection of information. You should reflect on whether your plans are working – are you collecting the information that you need? Finally, you should self-assess or check your work before handing it in. Did your work meet the evidence indicators? This is **evaluation**. You should always evaluate your work before handing it in.

When you design assignments they may be laid out something like this:

Outcome of your work

When your assignment work is received, it will be judged to see whether it shows a synthesis (combination) of skills, knowledge and understanding, and whether it demonstrates the right command of language.

If your work demonstrates the right process and outcomes you can be awarded a Merit or Distinction grade.

The grading criteria in more detail

The National Council for Vocational Qualifications has published a guide to grading, and your GNVQ Centre may provide you with up-to-date detailed guidance on the criteria by which your work will be judged.

These notes are intended to explain more about the process and outcomes you are aiming for. You will need to refer to the formal definitions of the grading criteria in order finally to judge your work.

To get Merit and Distinction grades you must:

 Action Plan: Independently draw up action plans for tasks that 'prioritise' or explain the order of activities to meet deadlines. At Distinction grade, this has to cover complex activities rather than just individual tasks.

Monitor: Independently work out where monitoring skills need to be used. This might involve monitoring action planning, revising and changing action plans where necessary. Revision may be made with guidance from a tutor. At Distinction grade, students have to demonstrate that they can make revisions independently.

Identify information needs: Independently identify the information required to do pieces of work. At Distinction grade, students must independently identify information needed to do whole assignments or complex pieces of work.

Use sources: Independently find and collect information needed for pieces of work. Students might get help with identifying some additional sources of information. At Distinction grade, students collect information for whole assignments or complex pieces of work. As well as this, students have to use a range of different sources of information and explain why they choose them.

Evaluation: Judge outcomes against plans or against evidence indicators or other criteria. Identify other criteria that could have been used to judge the success of activities and justify work. At Distinction grade, students have to justify their work in detail and explain alternative ways in which work could be done; and improvements that could be made to their work.

Synthesis: The work has to show an understanding and linking of skills and knowledge related to pieces of work. At Distinction grade, this understanding and synthesis has to cover complex work such as whole assignments.

Command of language: The work has to show an effective use of terms, ideas and concepts used in health and social care language. At Distinction grade, the work has to demonstrate a fluent use of concepts and terminology.

Your work needs to demonstrate the process of planning, action and reviewing. It then needs to demonstrate quality in terms of knowledge and command of language.

Collecting evidence for the grading criteria might begin with each piece of written work, each report or assignment that you design. As you begin to pass a number of units, you will need to think about the presentation of your work in a final portfolio. The overall design of your portfolio might also be something which could be evaluated and reviewed to provide extra evidence of your skills.

The portfolio

A GNVQ portfolio is your collection of evidence for the award of the qualification. Evidence for the qualification will probably be contained in:

- assignments
- a record or log book
- extra notes and forms.

Evidence has to cover:

- mandatory and optional units
- core skills units
- grading criteria.

Assignment work

Evidence for mandatory and optional units will mostly be found in assignment work. There may be one or more assignments per element or sometimes assignments might run across elements. Assignments may be straightforward to present at the end of the course. They will also probably contain most of the evidence for core skills units. However, the evidence for core skills will probably be spread *across* assignments.

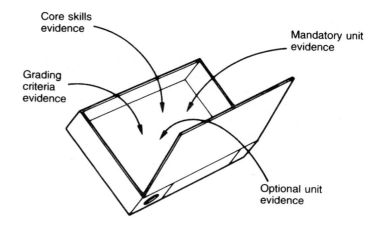

Figure 7 Grading criteria – the process

Figure 8 Grading criteria – the outcome

Record or log book

Another way of collecting evidence for the unit standards, core skills and the grading criteria, is to use a log book. By keeping a diary of study activities, it may be possible to provide evidence for the process grading criteria. A log book used on placement might provide evidence of communication, information technology and even use of number core skills. Placement activities might often provide opportunities for demonstrating skills. Records of performance might need to be signed by a supervisor or manager before they can count as evidence.

Notes

Sometimes candidates might prefer to use action plans forms for planning. Core skills in information technology might be demonstrated by designing action plan forms, or other record sheets. These sheets might be separate from the assignments or from other log books or notes.

What the portfolio might look like

By the end of the GNVQ programme, there could be a great deal of evidence to be reviewed for the award of the qualification.

All this evidence could be collected together, dumped in a bag and given to the assessors and verifiers. But no-one would be able to understand it all. A disorganised portfolio will not communicate quality, nor will it suggest good planning, monitoring or evaluation. So a portfolio is more than a bag of bits!

Think it over

Imagine your assessor checking the quality of assignment evidence. What sort of things will he or she be looking for?

If you can use your imagination to reflect on and visualise this situation, then you have the planning skills to organise a good portfolio of your work.

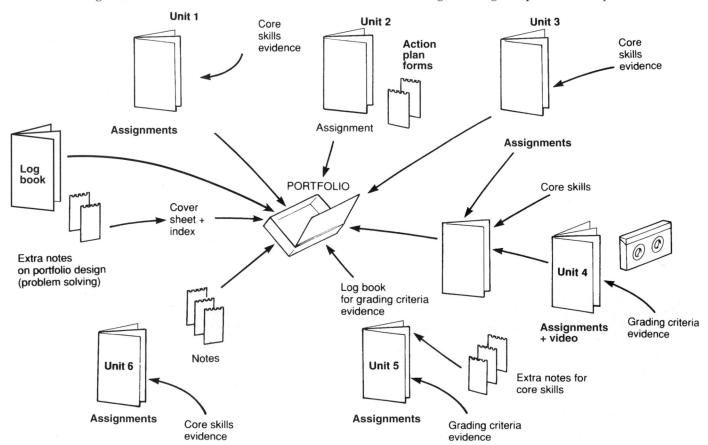

Figure 9 A visual map of evidence

Portfolios need to be carefully planned and organised. The planning of the portfolio might provide evidence for the grading criteria.

The portfolio might be a ring binder, an envelope folder or a file of some sort. The portfolio at the end of the programme might need more than one folder. What matters is that there is an explanation of how the evidence in the portfolio meets the standards for GNVQ, and the standards for a Merit or Distinction grade if this is claimed.

So, looking inside the folder there might be:

1 A *title sheet* stating the student's name, the centre's name (school or college) and the name of the qualification (Intermediate GNVQ in Health and Social Care).
2 An *index of assignments, evidence and assessments* which have already been made.
3 A *statement* or *claim* explaining that the assignment work meets the unit standards and has been assessed as meeting the standards (dates of assessment and forms might be included here).
4 Photocopies of the *unit standards* which the work claims to demonstrate (or workbook containing the standards).
5 An *index of core skills evidence*. This index would explain where evidence could be found for information technology, application of number and communication skills. Page numbers in assignment work might be quoted. Notes would be placed in order in the portfolio and numbered. Core skills demonstrated by other records (floppy disk, video, etc.) would also be noted, and disks and boxes labelled.
6 An *index of evidence for the grading criteria*. Most of the evidence would probably be in project reports, assignments or on forms. Page numbers should be quoted.

You do not have to supply evidence for the core skills of problem solving, working with others and improving own learning. It could still be worth putting in for these units, however, as the grading criteria often require problem solving and improving own learning skills. Health and social care assignment work often links with working with others. To design a really good portfolio you will need to self-assess your own learning. A high-quality portfolio might supply evidence to claim the additional core skills linked to achieving Merit or Distinction grades.

So, in summary, the portfolio will include indexing, the standards and the evidence. The portfolio can also contain explanations and arguments which support the claim for a Merit or Distinction grade.

Using icons to organise the portfolio

 One idea to make indexing easier is to use symbols or 'icons' to label your evidence. A range of icons appears at the back of this book – these can be photocopied for use with GNVQ evidence, free of copyright restrictions. After photocopying, they can be cut out and stuck to notes or pages of assignment or log-book work. When an icon is stuck next to a piece of writing, or on a tape box, etc. it means that evidence is being claimed. An icon states, 'Look, this is evidence'.

Portfolio design

Designing a portfolio to achieve a Distinction grade will involve a good deal of self-assessment work. Usually, this work will have to be started *early* in the programme and developed as the programme goes on. Good grades may be difficult to achieve if portfolio design is left until the end of the programme.

Designing a portfolio of evidence will eventually require you to self-assess your own evidence. You will have to be able to show that:

1 The work is your own.
2 There is enough work to cover the evidence indicators.
3 There is enough evidence to meet the grading criteria.
4 There is enough evidence to meet core skills standards.

Doing all this involves using imagination and checking ideas with tutors or assessors. Designing a good portfolio is a major learning task.

As you gradually put together your design for your portfolio, you will have opportunities to include new evidence to meet unit standards, to cover core skills or to meet the grading criteria. You are putting your own book together! The portfolio is the final record of your achievements. It can be more than just a box of assignment work. The portfolio can be the final review of all your learning. The indexing and the claim statements can make an argument for the grade of qualification that you are seeking.

Designing a portfolio is the final check that all the necessary evidence has been collected. The grade of the GNVQ qualification will be awarded in relation to the quality of the portfolio and its contents.

Getting started

Imagine trying to learn to drive a car by reading a book. Very few people could do it. To drive a car you have to *practise* doing it. Collecting evidence and designing projects, assignments and portfolios, will be the same kind of learning – try it, imagine how to do it better, listen to advice.... or listen to advice, imagine it and then try it. The order is not important. What can't be done is to learn the whole idea in one go and then do it.

Evidence collection will look very complicated at first – there is so much that can go into a portfolio. It is important to get some ideas, think about them, try them out in practice and then get advice. If this is done over time, it should become much easier. Like driving a car, it gets easier once you have tried it for real.

Some of the ideas here might make more sense after evidence for the first assignment has been collected. So, if you are reading this before starting your GNVQ, why not plan to read it again in a month's time or in two months' time? Some of the ideas about assignment and portfolio design will make more sense when they are tried in practice.

Tests

Three mandatory units were tested in 1995. Tests provide evidence that all the detail involved in the units has been covered. Some people think that test evidence will mean that GNVQ qualifications will be more valued and respected by the public and by future employers.

The GNVQ test should usually be taken after all the other evidence collection work for a unit has been

done. Tests will ask a number of short questions about the unit and will probably last about one hour. Tests have to be passed in order for a unit to be awarded. If a test is not passed first time, it can be taken again. Indeed, it should be possible to take the test several times if necessary. Fear of failing often worries people when they have to take tests. GNVQ tests *shouldn't* cause fear because the tests can be retaken.

You will probably have achieved lots of practical learning for the unit before you take a test. You will have planned evidence collection, reviewed your own knowledge, reflected on knowledge with others in discussion and written assignments or notes. All this work will have been assessed. It should mean that there is not a lot of extra work and revision to do for the test.

Before doing the test, it might be worth organising discussion sessions with others so that practical work and information can be shared. *Talking* about knowledge can be one of the best ways of learning to remember it for a test.

The knowledge contained in this book should help cover the needs of the test. Fast Facts won't always cover every question possible for a unit, but they should cover many. Use Fast Facts for revision.

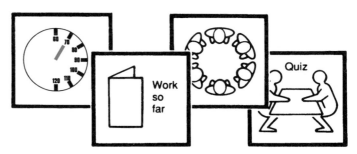

Another idea is to combine group discussion and Fast Facts to make up your own quiz game, along the lines of 'Trivial Pursuit'. Making revision fun can provide a good way of checking learning. Turning revision into a game may also remove anxiety.

Preparing for tests

You will need a lot of knowledge in your head to pass the test. Sometimes people imagine that getting this knowledge is like filling up a mug with water. The idea is to keep learning until the mug is full. Big mugs hold lots of water, little mugs can't hold so much. Sometimes people try to stretch their memory to hold lots of information – they try to become big mugs.

This idea of stretching memory is usually unnecessary and it makes taking a test a very unpleasant experience. In caring, it should not be necessary to 'strain' your memory.

For example, a student starting a placement may have lots of clients' and colleagues' names to remember. One idea could be to stretch the memory and go around trying to list all the names over and over again until they stick. Usually, carers do not do this. An alternative idea is to talk to each person and to get to know them one by one. After a while it becomes easy to remember all sorts of details about people. Their names become easy – and sometimes automatic – to remember, because names link to all the other details about the people. This kind of automatic knowledge feels natural; sometimes people feel that it just happens to them. It may be that this kind of learning is 'deeper' than the kind where a memory gets 'full up'.

GNVQ tests won't be as natural as remembering people on placement, but the ideas about learning may still work. If you have done project work, written assignments, shared ideas with other people, taken notes from other people's explanations and so on, then learning may feel more real and natural. This deeper learning may be interesting. It could even make the tests feel like a fun challenge, rather than an unpleasant pressure.

Whatever the test feels like, it is important to avoid 'overfilling' the memory – cramming things into it for a test. It is usually a better idea to learn from practical experience and then to use Fast Facts to help revise. Fast Facts probably won't work very well as starting points for learning. They should not be crammed into the memory for the test. One way that they might be useful is helping you to recognise

things that you already know. When you look at a Fast Facts list, the words should prompt thoughts. The thoughts should link with the details under each 'fact' heading. Experience of studying Fast Facts may make it easier to recall detail when actually taking a test for a unit.

Self-assessment of knowledge about GNVQs

1 What are 'standards'? Why are standards used in assessment?
2 Why are standards sometimes difficult to understand at the beginning of a GNVQ programme?
3 Why is it necessary to produce evidence in order to be awarded GNVQ units?
4 What are action plans? Why is it important to keep records of action plans?
5 Can a person plan to get a Distinction or Merit grade and be confident of getting it?
6 What is needed in order to get a Merit or Distinction grade?
7 What is a portfolio? When should work on a portfolio start?
8 How might students prepare to take a GNVQ test?
9 Why is it important for GNVQ candidates to assess their own learning?
10 Why is 'reflection' useful when learning in health and social care?

Answers to these questions can be found on the next page.

Getting there: the Health and Social Care Intermediate GNVQ Game (see page xxvii)

Goal

The object of the game is to get to Distinction grade as quickly as possible and in as few moves as possible. If you feel competitive you can try to get there before other players. If you want a short game you can aim for just a Merit grade or even for just a Pass grade.

Rules

1 Place your marker on the Start square.
2 Use only one six-sided die.
3 Throw the die and move up or sideways to the exact number thrown. You may choose to move in any up or sideways line, provided you stay on the board and you finish on the exact square that your die throw indicates.

4 'Skills squares' give you an extra free go, and you can move diagonally to any square that is counted by your die number. You may only move diagonally from a 'skills' square.

5 You must keep a list of the 'evidence' you collect, and which squares you landed on to collect that evidence. Other players must be able to check and see what you are recording; they are the 'verifiers' of your achievement.

6 Empty squares don't provide 'evidence' – try not to land on them.

7 Hazard squares cause you to miss a turn – try not to land on them.

8 You have to collect evidence for each element of every unit that you will need for the six unit programme. So you will need to land on three squares (marked 'M') for each numbered mandatory unit, and three squares (marked 'O') for your two options. You will also need to land on four element squares for 'Information Technology (IT), four element squares for Communication (C), and three element squares for Number (No).

9 Only when you have recorded landing on all these squares can you get through the 'pass' barrier.

10 You must land on the seven different grading criteria squares marked Merit in order to get a Merit.

11 You must land on the seven different grading criteria squares marked Merit, and the seven different grading criteria squares marked Distinction to get a Distinction.

12 As soon as you have all the evidence for Merit or Distinction grade, and all the evidence for the necessary units, you have to throw a number that will take you across the 'pass' barrier. You have then won.

In real life the game is a little more complicated and usually takes one year to play!

Answers to self-assessment quiz

1 Standards are definitions of what has to be demonstrated and assessed in order to get GNVQ awards and qualifications. Standards don't explain what has to be studied – only what gets assessed. Standards provide an alternative to exam-based qualifications. Exam-based qualifications are like a competition; only the people who come top do well. With standards, it only matters if people can demonstrate what's needed.

2 Standards often contain technical words and descriptions. People will need to know a great deal about an area before standards for that area can be easily understood. At the beginning of a programme, people often do not have the knowledge to understand what is meant by particular element and performance criteria statements. Understanding standards are part of the learning goals for GNVQ.

3 Assessment to standards requires evidence. The standards define what is needed for an award; evidence is the information that shows that individuals have done what was needed. They have reached 'the standard'. When all the appropriate standards have been reached, individuals have qualified.

4 Action plans enable individuals to work out how they will collect evidence to meet 'evidence indicators'. Action plans can also be used to plan assignments, practical demonstrations and placement and project work. Action plans might be useful in helping candidates to meet standards requirements. Action plans are necessary for Merit and Distinction grades, as candidates have to show skills in planning and in monitoring courses of action. Records of planning will be needed to provide evidence of planning and monitoring skills.

5 Yes! Candidates can work out what is needed and, provided they do the work and submit the necessary evidence, they should be able to guarantee the grade they want. GNVQs are not a competition – grades do not depend on some final assessment of group results. Candidates can get advice and guidance as they go through the programme, to ensure that they have the necessary evidence for Merits or Distinctions.

6 Evidence of independent action planning, monitoring, identifying information needs, using sources, evaluation, synthesis and command of language.

7 A portfolio is a portable collection of evidence, including assignment work, which aims to demonstrate that national standards have been met. The portfolio will, therefore, include an index of assignment evidence, core skills and grading evidence. This will be used by assessors and verifiers who will check the quality of a candidate's work.

The portfolio will be complicated and work on it should start early in the programme. Leaving the design of the portfolio to the end of the

Getting there: the Health and Social Care Intermediate, GNVQ Game

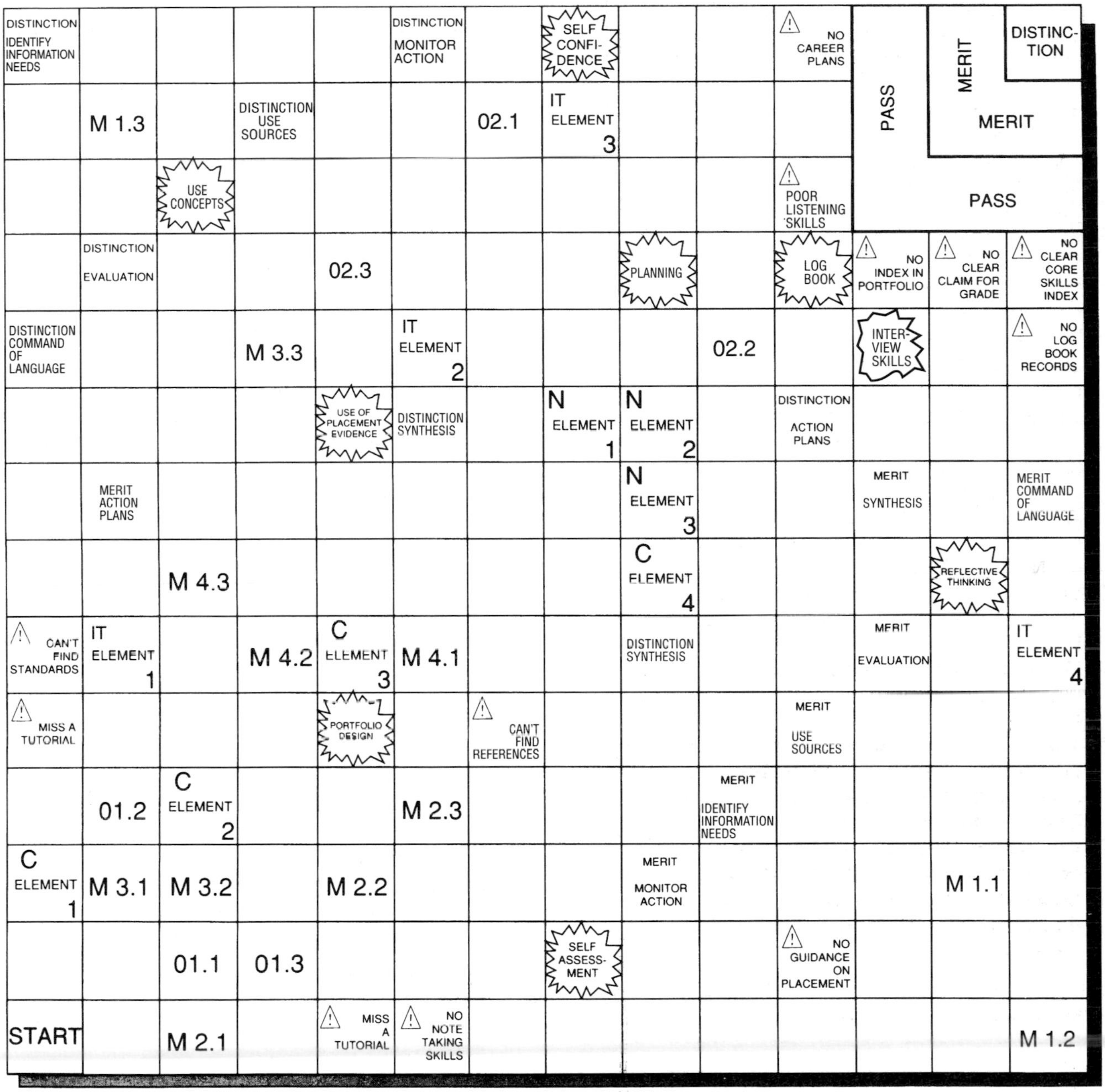

DISTINCTION IDENTIFY INFORMATION NEEDS				DISTINCTION MONITOR ACTION		SELF CONFI-DENCE (skills)			⚠ NO CAREER PLANS	MERIT / PASS	DISTINC-TION
	M 1.3		DISTINCTION USE SOURCES		02.1	IT ELEMENT 3				PASS	MERIT
		USE CONCEPTS (skills)							⚠ POOR LISTENING SKILLS		PASS
	DISTINCTION EVALUATION			02.3			PLANNING (skills)		LOG BOOK (skills)	⚠ NO INDEX IN PORTFOLIO	⚠ NO CLEAR CLAIM FOR GRADE	⚠ NO CLEAR CORE SKILLS INDEX
DISTINCTION COMMAND OF LANGUAGE		M 3.3		IT ELEMENT 2				02.2	INTER-VIEW SKILLS (skills)		⚠ NO LOG BOOK RECORDS
			USE OF PLACEMENT EVIDENCE (skills)	DISTINCTION SYNTHESIS		N ELEMENT 1	N ELEMENT 2		DISTINCTION ACTION PLANS		
	MERIT ACTION PLANS						N ELEMENT 3			MERIT SYNTHESIS	MERIT COMMAND OF LANGUAGE
		M 4.3					C ELEMENT 4				REFLECTIVE THINKING (skills)
⚠ CAN'T FIND STANDARDS	IT ELEMENT 1		M 4.2	C ELEMENT 3	M 4.1		DISTINCTION SYNTHESIS			MERIT EVALUATION	IT ELEMENT 4
⚠ MISS A TUTORIAL			PORTFOLIO DESIGN (skills)		⚠ CAN'T FIND REFERENCES			MERIT USE SOURCES			
	01.2	C ELEMENT 2			M 2.3			MERIT IDENTIFY INFORMATION NEEDS			
C ELEMENT 1	M 3.1	M 3.2		M 2.2			MERIT MONITOR ACTION			M 1.1	
	01.1	01.3				SELF ASSESS-MENT (skills)			⚠ NO GUIDANCE ON PLACEMENT		
START	M 2.1		⚠ MISS A TUTORIAL	⚠ NO NOTE TAKING SKILLS							M 1.2

Key:
- M = Mandatory unit
- 0 = Optional unit
- C = Communication (core skill)
- IT = Information technology (core skill)
- N: = Application of number (core skill)
- ⚠ = Hazard square
- (skills) = Skills square

programme may make it difficult to achieve Merit or Distinction grades. If the collection of evidence is regularly 'self-assessed' or checked, then candidates can change their work to ensure that it meets the requirements for these grades.

If the records are not kept, or not checked, then it may become too late to do the right kind of work at the end of the programme.

8 They should revise their own portfolio of evidence and assignments for the unit, discuss unit content with other people and make notes of their work! Discussion might help memory. Use the Fast Facts sections of this book as an aid to recognising concepts and ideas.

9 Good grades on GNVQ depend on reflection and self-assessment. Students have to provide enough evidence to meet the grading criteria. A good way to make sense of all this work is to self-assess the evidence before presenting it. The development of self-assessment skills would cover much of what is needed to meet the grading criteria.

10 Reflection is a skill which enables people to experiment with their ideas until the ideas work in a useful way. Reflection is a skill that will enable self-assessment and evidence collection.

 ## Fast Facts

Action planning Evidence has to be collected in order to pass a GNVQ. The collection of evidence needs to be *planned*. What action will produce enough evidence to demonstrate (pass) the standard? Action plans are the same as plans to get evidence. Evidence of good action planning helps towards Merit and Distinction grades.

Assessors These are the people who assess evidence to decide whether it meets the requirements of national standards. In other words, they assess work to see if it should pass. Assessors will also assess the grade of a GNVQ qualification when the portfolio is presented for assessment. Assessors will often be tutors or teachers.

Assignments Assignments are one way of collecting evidence to demonstrate (pass) an element or unit of GNVQ. Assignments should be planned and negotiated with an assessor or tutor.

Awarding body City & Guilds, BTEC or RSA will check the quality of courses and candidates' work. They award the GNVQ qualification (the National Council for Vocational Qualifications does not award qualifications – it designs and checks the national system).

Candidates People who collect evidence to get GNVQs are called candidates – they are candidates for assessment. Colleges call all people who study 'students', and 'students' and 'candidates' are the same.

Command of language To achieve Merit or Distinction grades, students must demonstrate an effective or fluent use of the terminology, ideas and concepts used within health and social care.

Concepts Concepts are ways of thinking which enable people to understand and make sense of the world.

Core skills The skills of communication, application of number and information technology are needed to get the GNVQ qualification. They are assessed using evidence gathered to pass mandatory and optional units. Core skills of problem solving, improving own learning and working with others can also be assessed.

Criteria Criteria are standards by which things are judged, i.e. measured.

Elements The smallest parts of standards to be assessed. *Units* are usually made up of between three and four elements. Once an element is 'passed', it has to be collected with other elements to pass a unit.

Evaluation An Intermediate grading criterion. Evaluation will require the ability to judge or self-assess work in relation to criteria. Evidence should be *evaluated* by candidates in order to check that it meets the standards.

Evidence This is the key to passing a GNVQ and getting good grades. Evidence is information which confirms that a standard has been reached. Evidence can be gathered in assignments. There are many ways in which evidence can be presented, such as by video or tape recordings. Demonstration of skill can be observed and recorded to provide evidence. Tests also provide evidence of knowledge.

Evidence indicators Part of GNVQ standards. Each element concludes with evidence indicators, for which evidence must be produced, but different assignments or projects may be designed to cover the indicators in different ways.

Grading GNVQs are graded Pass, Merit or Distinction. GNVQs cannot be failed, but they are not awarded or 'passed' until all the necessary units are passed. Merit or Distinction grades depend on extra evidence of performance to grading criteria standards.

Grading criteria At Intermediate level, candidates have to demonstrate the processes of action planning, monitoring, identifying information needs, use of sources and evaluation. Students' work has to demonstrate synthesis and command of language.

Identifying information needs A necessary part of all practical and assignment work. It is necessary to identify information needs in order to meet the grading criteria for Merit or Distinction grades.

Knowledge The work covers information, facts, concepts, theories and also the way people use their ideas to guide their work. GNVQs in Health and Social Care will involve using knowledge in practical situations. Just remembering things won't be enough for most units.

Levels Both GNVQ and NVQ qualifications are structured in five levels: Level 1 is Foundation; Level 2 is Intermediate and equal to good GCSE qualifications; Level 3 is Advanced Vocational A level; Levels 4 and 5 are graduate and post-graduate equivalents.

Mandatory unit Mandatory units are a fixed part of the GNVQ qualification. They have to be achieved or passed to get the GNVQ.

Methodology The approach taken, or methods used to organise or design outcomes.

Monitoring Monitoring means checking what's happening. In GNVQs plans have to be monitored, or checked, and developed, in order to achieve Merit and Distinction grades. Monitoring links with self-assessment, where individuals check their evidence before having it assessed. A log book or notes will often be needed to provide evidence of monitoring.

NCVQ The National Council for Vocational Qualifications. The Council controls the national framework of GNVQ and NVQ qualifications.

NRA A National Record of Achievement.

NVQ National Vocational Qualifications are more narrowly focused than GNVQs. They are structured in different units, but designed with the same qualification levels as GNVQs.

Optional unit Intermediate GNVQs have two optional units. These are not formally tested.

Performance criteria These define the performance necessary to reach the standard (or criteria) necessary to achieve an element. Performance criteria explain what is to be covered.

Planning A necessary part of all practical and assignment work. Independent planning forms part of the grading criteria for Merit and Distinction grades.

Portfolio A portable folder (or collection) of evidence. Action plans lead to the collection of evidence to meet unit requirements. All the evidence should be put together into a folder – or perhaps a file box if photos, tapes and videos are included. The portfolio can then be assessed and verified.

Programmes GNVQs are usually called programmes because units can be taken in any order, and passed in any order. Individuals could – at least in theory – take difference pathways to achieving a GNVQ.

Qualification The whole Intermediate GNVQ in Health and Social Care. GNVQ units are *not* qualifications.

Range Range provides details of what should be covered when providing evidence for an element.

Reflection A skill which helps in the process of evidence collection, self-assessment and planning. It is also a skill necessary in health and social care work.

Self-assessment Achieving Merit or Distinction grades will require candidates to monitor and evaluate their work. These skills require candidates to assess their own work before formal assessment takes place.

Skills Abilities which people can demonstrate and do. GNVQ standards cover instances of knowledge, skills, understanding and values.

Standards The basis for assessment – national standards are all the unit, element, performance criteria, range and evidence indicator descriptions for GNVQ areas. Standards don't explain what must be studied, but they do explain what is to be assessed.

Synthesis Means putting things together to make a whole. In GNVQs, knowledge, understanding and skills have to be synthesised, or put together in order to achieve Merit or Distinction grades.

Tests Three mandatory units are tested at present. Tests last about one hour, and involve multiple-choice questions.

Tutorials A term for the discussions with a tutor or teacher which will guide action planning, evidence gathering and project work.

Understanding Deep or thorough knowledge and skill that can be used in many different circumstances and settings; also, practical knowledge that can be used to solve problems. GNVQ evidence will often show that concepts can be used in practice, or in practical situations.

Units The building bricks of qualifications. Units are the smallest part of a GNVQ to be awarded. They can be recorded in the NRA. Units are made up of *elements*.

Using sources Students must identify relevant information for projects and assignment work. Identifying and using sources represents one of the grading criteria for Merit or Distinction grades.

Values Viewpoints which are the foundation of professional practice. Values are part knowledge and part skill. They are partly a skill because they have practical applications in decision making. In health and social care, values are emphasised because other caring skills cannot work without them.

Verifier A person who checks assessments. When assessments are made of people's evidence, these assessments themselves have to be checked. The *internal verifier* checks a sample of tutors' assessment work within a GNVQ centre. The *external verifier* checks the operation of systems in GNVQ centres on behalf of the awarding body.

Chapter 1

Personal health

Keeping healthy

Not everyone is lucky enough to be healthy, and many factors affect a person's quality of health. Poor health can sometimes be due to factors outside a person's control such as inherited diseases. For many people, good health is dependent on their lifestyle choices and habits. When you choose to do something that affects or changes your lifestyle, you need to understand the possible risks that may be involved.

This chapter looks at aspects of life that affect health, including diet, exercise, rest, personal hygiene and substance use/abuse, and the risks connected with poor choices in each case.

Think it over

How healthy is your lifestyle?

1 Think of aspects of your life which you would describe as
- **a** health promoting
- **b** unhealthy.

2 How healthy do you think an older relative or friend's lifestyle is?

3 What differences are there between your lifestyle and the older person's? Think about the reasons for the differences you have noted.

Work, rest and play

A **healthy lifestyle** may be thought of as a **balanced lifestyle**, one which includes the right amounts of activity – work and recreation – and rest – inactivity and sleep. Each person is different and we all live happily on differing amounts of work and rest. As life changes a person's work and rest patterns change. Take for example, the lifestyle of many young students. Their course may be considered their 'work'; they may also have a part-time job.

Work may take up five days per week and possibly some evenings for the job. Younger students may spend much of their time working. They relax by

going out in the evenings after work and may survive on 5 hours' sleep a night. The younger student may be able to cope with this balance.

Another type of lifestyle is that of an older care assistant who may work an 8-hour shift each day for five days of the week, with the remainder of the time spent on leisure activities, sleep and socialising. This may represent a balance which meets the needs of the older person.

Think it over

Think about how much of your time each week is spent working, resting and at leisure.

Are there any changes you would like to make to your use of time? Is it a balanced use of time?

Why are sleep and rest important?

The human body is like a rechargeable battery. It cannot keep going without recharging itself. The body does this through sleep. During sleep the body is in a state of unconsciousness which allows the individual to cope with the activity of the day. If a person is not getting enough sleep, they are less able to cope with day-to-day life and are more prone to accidents and psychological problems such as stress.

Another way that the body recharges is through rest or inactivity. Doing very little physically, such as watching the television or reading, can also promote health for people who lead physically active lives.

Exercise and health

Taking exercise is an important part of keeping healthy, and there are many different and enjoyable ways to do so. A person can become fit by exercising about three times a week for 20 minutes. Exercise can range from walking to water-skiing, or from a gentle game of badminton to a hard work-out in a gym.

Exercise should make use of the muscles. You should always warm up before any exercise, no matter how fit you are. You should also cool down as part of the routine.

Most forms of exercise can be taken at different paces and levels. It is important to make sure that the pace and level are chosen to suit the fitness of the individual.

Most exercise is a combination of **anaerobic** exercise, which stretches muscles, and **aerobic** exercise, which works the heart and lungs.

The benefits of exercise

Regular exercise has many benefits. It helps you feel good and can also make you more relaxed, confident and able to cope with the strains of life. Exercise also develops:

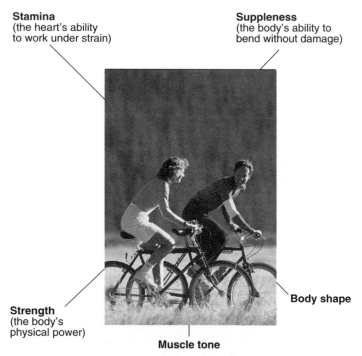

Stamina
(the heart's ability to work under strain)

Suppleness
(the body's ability to bend without damage)

Strength
(the body's physical power)

Muscle tone

Body shape

Exercise can also be a way for people to meet new friends. It can have a role in developing cooperative skills, especially in children.

The benefits of each form of exercise are often rated on how much it improves stamina, suppleness and strength (see Figure 1.1).

Exercise	Strength	Stamina	Suppleness	Kcal/min.
Badminton	**	**	***	5–7
Cycling (hard)	***	****	**	7–10
Golf	*	*	**	2–5
Dancing (disco)	*	***	****	5–7
Ballroom dancing	*	*	***	2–5
Swimming (hard)	****	****	****	7–10
Walking briskly	*	**	*	5–7
Climbing stairs	**	***	*	7–10
*Fair **Good ***Very good ****Excellent				

Figure 1.1 How each exercise rates

Costs of leisure

Unfortunately, not all sports and leisure activities are easily accessible to everyone, as some cost money. Because of this, a person's income and economic circumstances can affect the leisure activities that they choose.

However, this should not be an excuse for avoiding exercise as there are many cheap and even free ways to do so. Walking is one example. It suits most people and can be done at a person's own pace. Cycling is free once you have a bike. If the cost of the bike is divided by the number of times it is used, it is still a cheap way to exercise, and of course, you can use the bike instead of the bus or train!

Belonging to expensive leisure and fitness clubs and wearing all the right gear will not necessarily mean you get fit any quicker.

Think it over

Think of a variety of exercises to suit different client groups. Choose one activity from your list. Think of the benefits it has for the client group.

Food and health

A balanced diet is an important part of a healthy lifestyle.

Diet is a basic human need. We need food in order to live and this must be met above all other needs.

Food is the 'fuel' of the body. A lack of 'fuel' or the wrong type of 'fuel' can result in poor body performance and as a result less effective work and play.

The type of food we eat contributes to the health of the body in two ways:

1 Nutrients in the food allow the body to grow and function correctly.
2 A wise choice of food can help prevent some diet-related conditions.

Nutrients in food

There are five main nutrient groups in food – protein, fat, carbohydrates, vitamins and minerals. Each helps to keep our bodies healthy.

Protein

The main role of protein in the diet is to enable the growth and repair of body cells in children and the repair and maintenance of body cells in adults. It is also a secondary source of energy, which means that when the body does not have enough fat and carbohydrates to provide the necessary energy requirements, it uses protein for energy rather than for growth, repair and maintenance.

Protein foods are made up of units called amino acids. There are twenty-two amino acids, although only eight are essential to adults. The essential amino acids cannot be made in the body and have to be provided by the diet. Non-essential amino acids can be made in the body from the essential amino acids.

Protein foods are classified according to biological value. One group is known as **high biological value** (HBV) and these contain all the essential amino acids and tend to be of animal origin. The other group is known as **low biological value** (LBV) and do not contain all the essential amino acids. These foods tend to be of vegetable origin. An exception to this is soya which, although of vegetable origin, contains all the essential amino acids and is therefore a good course of high biological value proteins, especially for vegetarians.

Fat

Although health experts often recommend that we cut down the amount of fat in our diet, it should never be removed as it has many vital functions. These include:

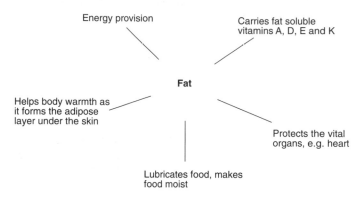

Energy provision

Carries fat soluble vitamins A, D, E and K

Fat

Helps body warmth as it forms the adipose layer under the skin

Protects the vital organs, e.g. heart

Lubricates food, makes food moist

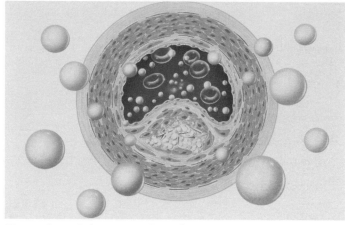

Illustration of the narrowing of an artery due to high levels of cholesterol

Fat comes from two main sources: **animal** and **vegetable.** We should keep to a minimum the animal sources of fat in our diet as these contain high levels of saturated fat and cholesterol. **Cholesterol** is a substance which gradually lines and clogs the arteries, so restricting blood flow and contributing to diet-related illnesses such as coronary heart disease. Animal sources of fat include butter, lard and suet.

Vegetable sources are high in polyunsaturated fats, which are believed to help reduce cholesterol levels in the blood. Corn oil, sunflower margarine, soya oil and olive oil are all examples of vegetable sources.

Vitamin	Function	Sources	Deficiency
A Retinol Carotene	Aids night vision – develops visual purple in retina which enables vision in dim light. Keeps mucous membranes free from infection.	Retinol – milk, cheese, butter, oily fish. Carotene – carrots, apricots, watercress, spinach.	Inability of eyes to adjust to dim light. Retarded growth in children. Dry skin and mucous membrane.
B complex Thiamin B1 Riboflavin B2 Niacin	Helps release energy from carbohydrate foods. Needed for normal nerve functions.	Cereals, especially wholegrain, yeast and yeast products, meat, eggs, milk.	Sores at corners of mouth. Anaemia. Nerve cell degeneration.
C Ascorbic acid	Needed to make connective tissue in cells. Helps absorb iron. Helps maintain skin and linings of the digestive system. Needed for the production of blood and blood vessel walls.	Fresh fruit and vegetables, especially blackcurrants, oranges, lemons, broccoli, cabbage, potatoes (potatoes are not particularly rich in vitamin C but because we eat so many in different forms, they are an important source).	Bleeding gums. Connective tissue not made or maintained healthily. Cuts and wounds take longer to heal. Blood vessels weaken and break resulting in small red spots under the skin.
D Cholecalciferol	Needed for strong bones and teeth in conjunction with calcium and phosphorus – helps the absorption of calcium and phosphorus.	Dairy products, margarine (added by law), oily fish. Sunlight on the skin is an important source as this converts a substance in the skin (dehydrocholesterol) to vitamin D, which is then stored in the liver until required.	Weak bones and teeth which may deform under the body's weight – known as rickets in children, osteomalacia in adults. Children's growth is retarded.

Figure 1.2 The role of vitamins

Carbohydrates

Carbohydrates also provide the body with energy. They are divided into two types:

1 Simple carbohydrates are found in sugar sources, such as cakes, biscuits and syrup. Sugar does not provide the body with any useful nutrients, only energy, and is often referred to as 'empty calories'.
2 Complex carbohydrates are found in starch sources, including potatoes, bread, rice and pasta. The starch sources of carbohydrate are also important providers of **fibre** which, although it is not a nutrient, is essential for the functioning of the digestive system.

Vitamins

Vitamins are an essential part of our diet and a lack of these can cause a range of health problems (see Figure 1.2).

Minerals

Minerals are another vital nutrient group. They are needed in very small amounts for body building, control of body functions and as part of body fluids.

The body requires some minerals in larger amounts such as iron, calcium, phosphorus, sodium, potassium and magnesium. Others are necessary in smaller amounts – 'trace elements' – such as zinc and iodine.

Figure 1.4 on the next page describes the role played by minerals in our bodies and in which foods they can be found.

Fibre and water

Our bodies also need water and fibre to keep them healthy.

Fibre comes from starch found in carbohydrates in the diet. Some parts of the starch cannot be digested and these form 'bulk' which absorbs water to make the faeces soft.

Fibre aids **peristalsis**, the muscular movement of the digestive system (from mouth to anus) which moves the food along the system. A lack of fibre slows this movement and causes constipation. As the food remains longer in the digestive system, there is also an opportunity for cancer-producing substances (carcinogens) to act, with the possibility of bowel cancer.

Fibre can be found in fresh fruit, and vegetables, wholegrain cereals, brown bread, rice etc.

Water is essential for life. Seventy per cent of the human body is water. It is part of all body fluids such as saliva and mucus, keeps the linings of the mucous membranes moist and lubricates joints. Health experts recommend that you drink 6–8 pints of liquid per day. You can live longer without food than you can without water.

Healthy eating

Once you know which foods provide each of the nutrients, you can plan a healthy diet.

In 1983 the National Advisory Committee for Nutrition Education (NACNE) produced five dietary goals to follow when planning meals. These goals were also recommended by the Committee on Medical Aspects of Food Policy (COMA).

1 Reduce your overall fat intake, but when you do eat it make sure that it is polyunsaturated, not saturated.
2 Eat less salt.
3 Reduce intake of sugar.
4 Eat more fibre.
5 Drink less alcohol.

Figure 1.3 shows the health risks if you do not follow these goals. It also makes some suggestions about changing to a healthier diet.

Goal	Health risk	Change from	Change to
Eat less fat	High cholesterol Heart disease Obesity	Animal fats, e.g. lard	Vegetable oil, e.g. corn
Eat less sugar	Tooth decay Obesity	Sweet puddings	Fresh fruit
Eat less salt	High blood pressure	Seasoning with salt	Using herbs or spices
Eat more fibre	Constipation Bowel cancer	White bread	Wholegrain bread
Drink less alcohol	Liver damage Stomach disorders	Alcoholic drinks	Low-alcohol drinks

Figure 1.3 Dietary goals

Iron
Found in haemoglobin of red blood cells; used to carry oxygen. Stored in liver (important in babies). Lack of iron in diet causes anaemia. Needs are greatest in children, pregnant and menstruating women. Most iron in diet comes from meat, but also from offal, apricots, cornflakes and cocoa.

Phosphorus
Main sources are milk, bread and meat products. Uses are:
a with calcium, in bones, teeth
b in proteins
c release of energy from food
d part of nucleic acids in nucleus.
High levels in newborn babies may be linked to low levels of calcium, producing muscular spasm.

Calcium
More of this than any other mineral, stored with phosphorus in bones, teeth and also found in a different form in blood and muscle. Used for clotting of blood, enzyme action and contraction of muscles. Vitamin D helps body to absorb calcium. In UK the main sources are milk, cheese and bread (added), so it is very important that children and pregnant and lactating women get plenty of these foods to enable the growth of healthy bones.

Fluorine
Required for healthy bones and teeth – helps prevent tooth enamel decay. Important sources are drinking water (variable amount), tea and seafoods. In areas of fluorine deficiency, some groups of individuals may add fluoride to their diet through treated drinking water, toothpaste or fluoride drops.

Zinc
Needed for enzyme action and wound healing. Like calcium, zinc salts are difficult to absorb, particularly if large quantities of whole cereals are eaten, so vegetarians could suffer from a lack of zinc. Zinc is usually linked to protein foods such as meat and dairy products. It has a role in the metabolism of insulin. Most zinc is stored in bones.

Figure 1.4 Minerals are needed for a healthy diet

Think about it

What other changes could be made to the diet to meet each of the goals? If changing to a healthier diet is so easy and the benefits so clear, why doesn't everyone follow it?

Many people have a poor diet not because they cannot afford to eat well but because they choose the wrong sorts of food. They eat cakes, biscuits, processed foods, fast foods, fried foods and other convenience foods because they are quick and easy to prepare and fit in with a busy lifestyle. However, these foods are often low in vitamins, minerals and protein, but high in fat and sugar. Such diets can contribute to diet-related disorders such as tooth decay, obesity and coronary heart disease. In many cases, symptoms are not immediately obvious, but appear in later life.

Some people choose not to follow a healthier diet for a number of reasons.

First, they may not like the taste and texture of higher fibre/lower fat and sugar foods. They will need to become used to the change.

Second, healthier options are sometimes more expensive than their less healthy alternatives. This means that less well-off people are unlikely to change to a healthier diet because their money for food will not go as far.

Third, depending on where you shop, foods may not be easily available. The large supermarkets are able to stock a wider range of products than the local corner shop.

As care workers are often responsible for preparing food for their clients, it is important that they are aware of the individual's nutritional needs and the best sources of food to provide these nutrients.

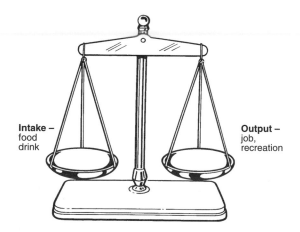

Intake – food drink

Output – job, recreation

Energy needs

The amount of energy needed by individuals is linked to their levels of activity. Although each of us requires a different amount, there are general recommendations for every age group. It is important to balance your food intake to match your energy needs.

Otherwise

1 too little exercise + too much food = weight gain
2 too much exercise + too little food = weight loss.

Think it over

Which of the following are likely to affect energy intake?

1 **Basal metabolic rate** is the amount of energy required for your body to function when lying down still and warm. It is lower for women (1440 kcals) than men (1680 Kcals) because women tend to have smaller body masses. Any movement increases the number of calories needed.
2 **Occupation** – different jobs require different levels of energy output and therefore the calories needed to sustain them. Occupations are classified into groups:
   a Sedentary – office workers, teachers, pilots, shop workers.
   b Moderately active – postmen/women, nursery assistants, care assistants, hospital porters.
   c Very active – coal miners, farm labourers, builders.
3 **Activity outside work** – the amount of exercise you take affects energy needs. Here are some examples of energy use of different types of exercise:

Average estimated kcals per hour

Sitting (watching TV)	85
Standing	90
Tennis	350
Cycling	400
Swimming	575
Household tasks	200

4 **State of body** – certain conditions such as pregnancy and breast feeding (lactation) require an increase in energy intake to cope with the extra demands placed on the body.
5 **Age** – young children require more energy for their body size than adults as they are growing rapidly and also tend to be active all of the time. On the other hand, aging people require less energy as activity levels often slow down along with the general slowing of the body processes.

Which foods provide energy?

All food provides some energy, but the amount per 100 g depends on the nutrient content of the food. Energy comes from four sources:

- protein – 4 kcal/g
- fat – 9 kcal/g
- carbohydrate – 3.75 Kcal/g
- alcohol – 7 kcal/g

Most foods are a combination of nutrients. Some calorie values of common foods are shown in Figure 1.5.

Food	kcal per 25g
White bread	68
White flour	100
Butter	226
Sugar	112
Roast beef	109
Cod (steamed)	23
Apples	13
Cabbage	5
Crisps	159
Chips	68
Boiled potatoes	23
Sweet biscuits	158

Figure 1.5 Some common foods and their calorie values

As can be seen from Figure 1.5 a balance of input and output is complicated by the calorie values of food. A person's choice of foods can affect whether they achieve the right balance. An inactive person on a high-fat diet of chips, fried food, cakes, etc. would soon eat more than his energy needs. Excess calories taken into the body are stored as fat in the adipose layer under the skin which can lead to obesity.

Do all client groups need the same nutrients?

Everyone needs a balanced diet which contains all the nutrients. However, some groups have particular needs because of their lifestage.

Children

There are some tips for feeding children:

- This is a time of rapid growth so they need plenty of protein, vitamin D and calcium to develop strong bones.
- They also need fluoride to ensure strong enamel on teeth to protect from decay and iron for red blood cells.
- Milk is important, so if children do not like to drink it, give plenty of milk in food.
- Children have small appetites, so give small portions and think about different ways to serve food attractively, for example, making faces in food might encourage a child to eat.
- Do not encourage children to eat sweets and snacks between meals as they will fill up on these and lose their appetite at mealtimes which results in an unbalanced diet.
- Do not encourage eating sweet food between meals as this can contribute to tooth decay and obesity.

This advice continues right through until adolescence.

Pregnancy – 'eating for two'

It is essential that a pregnant woman eats a healthy balanced diet to ensure the health of both herself and her baby. Research has shown that a healthy diet is also vital before conception to help prevent foetal disorders and ensure the woman's body is in the best condition to cope with the demands of pregnancy.

It is a myth that a pregnant woman should eat for two; this only leads to extra weight gain which may be difficult to lose after the birth. However, the intake of some nutrients does need to increase to meet the needs of the growing foetus. If the diet is lacking in any required nutrient, the body adjusts to ensure the baby has priority and the woman may suffer.

During pregnancy energy requirements increase as do the needs for certain minerals and protein.

Calcium is required for the development of the skeleton of the foetus. If there is not enough calcium to meet this demand, then this will be removed from the mother's bones, which will then weaken and could develop osteomalacia. To help absorb the calcium, a greater quantity of vitamin D is also needed.

Iron is essential to the foetus as it develops its own blood supply. The baby also needs to build up a store of iron for its first three months of life as milk, either breast or formula, contains little iron.

It is also important that the mother's haemoglobin levels remain high as blood can be lost in delivery and a good iron level can help speed recovery. Iron tablets are often prescribed to pregnant women as iron in the diet is not always readily absorbed. One traditional source of iron, liver, should be avoided as high amounts of vitamin A have been linked to spina bifida. However, iron tablets tend to cause constipation and an increase in fibre in the diet to prevent this is also needed.

Increases in energy requirements should come from healthy sources such as pasta and bread not sugar and fats.

Current dietary goals (see above) should be followed throughout pregnancy, and in particular alcohol consumption should be reduced. This is because alcohol crosses the placenta and can be harmful to the baby. Often, however, when pregnant, a woman finds she no longer likes certain foods such as tea, coffee and alcohol, all foods which could damage the foetus, but has cravings for other foods such as red meat and tomatoes. It is often suggested that these cravings are a result of deficiencies in the diet and are the body's way of getting the nutrients needed.

Older people

- As activity slows, the amount of calories eaten should be reduced to prevent obesity.
- The digestive system often slows, so food chosen needs to be easily digested, such as fish.
- Poor teeth may cause problems with eating, so softer well-cooked foods should be chosen.
- It is wrong to say that older people do not like, or need to avoid spicy foods. Ageing can dull the taste buds so some older people like spicy foods for flavour.

- Diets should be high in calcium and vitamin D to help prevent decalcification – removal of calcium – from the bones and teeth. A loss of calcium can also lead to osteoporosis which results in weaker bones more prone to fractures and breaks.
- Protein is important to maintain and renew cells.
- Fibre levels need to be increased as the slowing of the digestive system, along with reduced mobility, may cause constipation.
- Iron is needed to prevent anaemia.
- The NACNE food goal recommendations should be followed.

Social factors also play a part in the quality of diet of an older person, especially if living alone. Research has shown that older people living on their own often do not eat properly because it is 'not worth the bother of cooking for one'. In cases where a partner has died, the remaining person may become disorientated while grieving, and so miss meals and not eat properly. This can also happen if a person begins to suffer memory loss.

Physical difficulties may affect diet. For example, lack of mobility may mean that it is difficult for an older person to go to a supermarket where there is more choice of healthy foods and food is cheaper. They may be restricted to shopping close to home in a corner shop. Level of mobility may also affect an older person's ability to cook, and this can also affect the quality of diet. A person with arthritis may have difficulty preparing fresh vegetables and so rely on frozen varieties, which may contain fewer nutrients.

Evidence collection point

As we saw above, different people have different nutritional needs. However, often a range of age groups lives together and menus need to cater for all.

Plan a day's menu for three people who live together – a 3-year-old child, a pregnant woman and her 70-year-old grandparent, who is inactive.

1 Explain the factors you need to consider when planning meals to include each of these three people.
2 Suggest how your chosen menu meets the needs of each individual.
3 For one member of the group, explain how the body uses each nutrient in your menu.

Risks to health and well-being

It is easy to maintain a healthy lifestyle but there are many risks to health in modern-day life. Usually, the individual makes a conscious choice to take those risks. The following section looks at the risks related to alcohol, drugs, smoking and sexual practices, and explores the effect on health and well-being and ways to reduce the risks.

Effects can be:

- physical – affecting the functioning of the body
- emotional – affecting people's feelings about things, others and themselves
- social – affecting relationships with friends and family
- intellectual – affecting the brain's ability to function.

All of these will be covered as each risk is discussed.

Alcohol

Alcohol is very much part of our lifestyle. One way we celebrate achievement or good news or seal an agreement is to 'have a drink' or 'drink a toast'. Alcohol is really a drug, yet we often fail to see it as one.

Alcohol in small amounts is unlikely to be harmful to most healthy people. There is even some evidence that a glass of red wine a day actually has health benefits. There are, however, recommended maximum weekly intakes for alcohol: women, 14 units; men, 21 units.

A unit is roughly equivalent to one glass of wine, one measure of spirit or half a pint of beer or lager. If you frequently drink over the recommended levels, there may be a risk to health.

The speed at which alcohol takes effect on the body after being consumed depends on a number of factors:

1 If there is food in the stomach this slows the absorption of alcohol.
2 The physical size of the individual – if two people drink the same amount of alcohol, the smaller person (having less blood) will feel the effects first, as the concentration in the bloodstream is higher.
3 Gender – women are generally smaller and have less fluid in their bodies than men. Woman therefore feel the effects of alcohol quicker.
4 The amount and the time over which the alcohol is drunk – the more that is consumed over the shorter space of time, the greater the effect.

The effects of excess alcohol on health

1 It slows the functioning of the brain. Things become fuzzy. You misjudge distances, which can result in accidents.
2 Very heavy drinking causes inflammation of the brain which makes it shrink. This may reduce intelligence.
3 It is a depressant. Although, at first, alcohol seems to cheer people up, its depressant nature means that excess alcohol eventually has the opposite effect.
4 Liver damage – cirrhosis of the liver – is a common effect of heavy drinking. The liver enlarges as it copes with the excess alcohol and eventually becomes inflamed. The liver hardens and the cells die, no longer able to function.
5 Heavy drinking may weaken the body's immune system, making it susceptible to disease.
6 Alcohol damages the stomach lining and can lead to stomach disorders.
7 Alcohol can cause weight gain as it is high in calories.
8 Alcohol interferes with nutrient absorption and can contribute to nutrient deficiencies.
9 Heavy drinking reduces sexual performance.
10 Drinking in pregnancy, particularly in the early months can damage the development of the foetus.
11 A person can become dependent on alcohol.

Besides the effects it has on the body, alcohol also contributes to many lost working days due to sickness and headaches caused by a 'heavy' night out. It is also connected with many road accidents where people 'drink and drive', with crime, and with violence both between individuals and within the family.

Think it over

Classify each of the above effects into physical, social, emotional and intellectual. Does alcohol affect the whole person or just certain aspects of life?

Why is drinking alcohol so popular?

There are many suggestions why people drink, some of which relate to social influences.

1 Drinking is a sociable thing to do. It is common to go out for a drink or to have a drink with a meal.

2 As alcohol is such an accepted part of society, some people believe it is difficult to refuse a drink – you are viewed as 'strange' if you don't drink.

3 Friends may encourage you to drink and, to remain part of the group, you do so. This is called peer pressure.

4 Some people believe it helps reduce stress.

5 It is enjoyable.

How to reduce the risk from drinking too much alcohol

There are a number of ways to reduce the risks from excess alcohol:

1 Cut down on the number of units consumed each week – stay within the recommended limits.

2 Consume more low-alcohol/alcohol-free drinks. There are many of these now available in pubs, supermarkets and off licences.

3 Drink soft drinks occasionally instead of alcoholic ones.

Smoking

Smoking, like alcohol, has been very much part of our society. It also has health risks associated with it, but unlike alcohol, smoking is now much less acceptable. This could be because the dangerous effects of smoking both on the smoker and the non-smoker have been greatly publicised. There have also been a number of court cases brought against employers by employees who have developed cancer from working in smoky areas, and employers now have to provide a safe, healthy environment for their workers.

This publicity has resulted in a fall in the numbers of people who smoke and fewer public places and work situations allowing smoking. Some cases are completely 'non-smoking' while others have places where people may smoke.

Risks to health caused by smoking are increased according to the number of cigarettes smoked a day.

The effects of smoking on health

1 Smoking can cause cancer of the nose, throat and lungs. Cigarettes contain several substances which cause cancer, one of which is tar.

2 Smokers are more prone to chest and throat infections, including bronchitis and emphysema, where small bronchi in the lungs are destroyed.

Section of the lung of a heavy cigarette smoker, showing black tar deposits

3 Pregnant women who smoke produce smaller babies than the non-smoker. As the babies are smaller, they are also weaker and more prone to infections. It is also suggested that there is a higher rate of stillbirths and miscarriages among pregnant women who smoke.

4 Smoking contributes to the risk of heart disease, as smoking together with a diet high in cholesterol leads to furring and hardening of the arteries (atherosclerosis). This causes the heart to work harder to pump blood around the body. If a clot forms in one of the coronary arteries, it causes a heart attack.

5 Carbon monoxide is also inhaled from a cigarette. This can attach itself to haemoglobin instead of oxygen and reduces the blood's capacity to carry oxygen around the body. To compensate for this, the body produces more haemoglobin, but this increases the risk of clotting. At the same time, the heart works harder to pump blood around the body to provide oxygen, putting stress on the heart.

6 Nicotine thickens the blood. This can contribute to clotting in the arteries if they become constricted. This condition is known as thrombosis and can result in limbs having to be amputated.

Besides these risks to physical health, the nicotine in cigarettes causes a yellowing of the teeth and fingertips which looks unsightly.

Smokers are sometimes thought to smell unpleasant as the smoke lingers in their hair and clothes. Also, a smoker's breath can smell, and physical contact may be unpleasant to a non-smoker. Besides all this, it is an expensive habit!

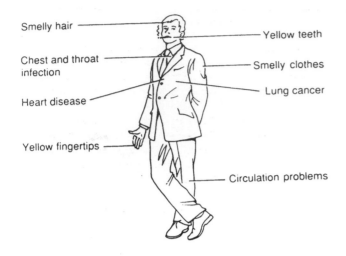

Smelly hair

Chest and throat infection

Heart disease

Yellow fingertips

Yellow teeth

Smelly clothes

Lung cancer

Circulation problems

Figure 1.6 Cigarette smoking – the drawbacks

Think it over

If smoking is connected to all these drawbacks, why do people smoke?

Smoking relaxes some people. The nicotine in cigarettes is a drug which slows down nerve impulses – this gives the feeling of relaxation. As a result, it gives some people more confidence.

As with alcohol, there is **peer pressure** – particularly in adolescence when smoking is often first tried. More adolescent girls smoke than boys. Nicotine, like alcohol, is a drug. People who have been smoking for some time find it difficult to give up.

Passive smoking

Research has shown that non-smokers are also at risk, together with smokers. The 'passive' smoker breathes in smoke which has not been filtered through the tip of a cigarette, and so the content of tar, nicotine and other substances is high. Evidence shows that only about one-sixth of the smoke goes into the smoker, the rest goes into the air!

The foetus of a pregnant woman is a passive smoker, receiving the drug by way of the women's blood stream. This can produce dependency later on.

How can the risks of smoking be reduced?

Risk reduction has to be considered for both the smoker and the non-smoker.

For the smoker, the only sure way to reduce the risks is to smoke less or to stop smoking. This is only possible if the smoker really wants to do it. The smoker should:

- over a period, cut down on the number of cigarettes smoked per day (some people find it difficult to stop suddenly)
- use a substitute such as nicotine gums or 'patches'
- try 'low-tar' cigarettes
- tell friends and family and ask for support and encouragement
- smoke only in certain places or at certain times of the day (this will reduce the opportunity to smoke)
- give themselves rewards for achievement (for example, money saved to buy themselves a treat).

Non-smokers must realise the risks they are taking by being in an atmosphere that is constantly smoky. They should avoid smoky areas as far as possible.

Parents, especially those who smoke, should avoid smoking around the children as it has been shown that children who are in constant contact with a smoky atmosphere are more prone to chest infections and pneumonia.

Drugs and health

As you saw above, alcohol and nicotine are both drugs. In Britain and many other countries they are available to those who can afford them, and they are, within limits, 'socially acceptable'. Other drugs are illegal to use (such as ecstasy and cannabis). Some drugs are prescribed by doctors as medicine, for example tranquillisers, but these can be just as dangerous to health *if used incorrectly*.

It is also important to distinguish between **drug abuse** and **drug misuse**. Drug *abuse* relates to the taking of a drug that is not socially acceptable. Drug *misuse* relates to the taking of a socially acceptable drug, but in an unacceptable way.

Prolonged use of any drug can be dangerous to health. The way the drug is used can also vary in safety; for example, injecting can be more dangerous than smoking a drug. Also, people vary in their reactions to the same amount of the same drug. This is due to individual factors such as body weight,

Drug	Form	How used	Effects	Health risks
Cannabis ('pot'/'hash')	Resin in form of solid brown mass	Smoked – usually crumbled and mixed with tobacco	■ Relaxation and talkativeness ■ Lightheadedness ■ Possible hallucinations ■ Confusion	■ Psychological dependency for enjoyment/coping with life ■ Bronchitis, lung cancer, heart disorders ■ Could lead to use of stronger drugs
Ecstasy ('E')	Tablet or capsule – white, brown, pink or yellow	Swallowed – effects begin in 20 minutes	■ Calmness with raised awareness of colour and sound ■ Loss of coordination ■ High doses result in anxiety and confusion	■ Prolonged use can reduce sleep ■ Those with high blood pressure, heart conditions, epilepsy or mental illness are at risk due to stimulant effects ■ Possible death
Amphetamines and cocaine ('coke')	White powder	Usually sniffed, but can be injected	■ Stimulate nervous system ■ Breathing and heart rate increased, pupils dilated ■ Person feels alert, energetic, cheerful and confident ■ Tiredness reduced for a time ■ Appetite reduced	■ Poor sleep, loss of appetite, bodily itching leading to scratching and anxiety ■ Lower resistance to disease ■ Damaged blood vessels ■ Heart failure ■ Damage to nose membranes ■ Depression and suicidal thoughts
LSD ('acid')	Impregnated into small sheets, like blotting paper	Dissolved on tongue	■ Affects perception – can be visions of joy and beauty, or nightmares ■ Confusion and disorientation	■ Accidents due to confusion ■ Can be a damaging experience to those with mental illness
Heroin ('H'/'horse')	White or brown powder	Sniffed or injected	■ First alertness, then drowsiness and drunkenness ■ Overdose results in unconsciousness	■ Dependency ■ Poor health due to inadequate diet ■ Risk of AIDS if needles shared
Solvents	A range of forms easily available, e.g. paint, glue, lighter gas, petrol	Sniffed	■ Similar to drunkenness ■ Disorientation and loss of control ■ 'Hangover' effects following use, e.g. headache, tiredness, paleness ■ Possible unconsciousness	■ Injury/death due to accidents while confused ■ Possible weight loss and depression ■ Physiological dependence possible

Figure 1.7 Analysis of some common drugs

tolerance of the body to the drug, and state of health.

As an individual's body becomes dependent on a drug, the money needed to finance the habit increases. In turn this has adverse effects on diet, housing, and the ability to cope in a job. A vicious cycle of dependency and lack of coping is set up. It has been shown that people often turn to crime to finance a drug habit.

Figure 1.7 outlines some of the common drugs and their effects on the body.

Think it over

Why do you think people become involved in drug abuse?

There are many reasons why people take drugs, and again these include some of the social influences covered earlier in this chapter. Drugs are seen as a way to escape temporarily from life's problems. They may be a way to relieve boredom, which may itself result from lack of opportunities.

Drug taking is seen by young people especially as daring and exciting, partly because of the risks involved. There is peer pressure, and opportunity.

People who lack confidence are less inhibited temporarily when they have taken drugs (as with alcohol).

Finally, and perhaps most seriously for the individual, people take drugs because they have developed a dependency.

How to spot drug taking

There are a number of signs which are linked to drug taking, but they can also be linked to other causes (such as stress or worry). These signs include:

- loss of interest in hobbies, friends and job
- mood changes
- irritability
- disorientation
- loss of appetite
- over-excitement or over-relaxation
- odd tablets, powders or smells.

Reducing the risk from drugs

The only way to reduce the risk from drugs is not to take them at all. However, the way this message is put across is crucial: straight education, merely providing the facts, does not always work.

When talking to people about drugs, it is important to keep an open mind and to remember the following points:

1 Be sure you are clear about the facts concerning drugs and their use.
2 Develop good communication with the group/individual concerned. They need to value your opinion if they are to accept it.
3 Try not to act hastily, but consider how to approach problems. Acting on the spur of the moment without fully thinking through the consequences of an action may well have an adverse effect.
4 Develop positive values. Encourage a strong self-image in the group/individual so they do not feel they have to use drugs to prove themselves and they are able to resist peer pressure.

Professional help is offered through a range of agencies in the health and social care services. These professionals often work together in a multi-disciplinary approach to help the client in a planned way. This ensures all needs are addressed – social, physical, psychological and emotional.

Solvents

Solvents are often classified in the same grouping as drugs. The term **solvents** covers a range of products, including household products which give off gases or fumes such as glue, lighter fluid, aerosol sprays, petrol and correction fluid.

Solvents are either sniffed through the nose and mouth, usually from bags (*huffing*), or sprayed directly into the mouth. Some solvents, such as thinner, may be sniffed from a cloth or coat sleeve in a similar way to how nasal decongestant is used for a cold. Because solvents are portable, sniffing can occur anywhere but often people go to remote or isolated places to abuse solvents.

The effects of abusing solvents

The effects of glue sniffing are very similar to the effects of alcohol, but the 'drunkenness' occurs more quickly. This is because the vapour is inhaled into the bloodstream through the lungs and not through the stomach, which delays the effect (depending on what else is present). As the vapour is inhaled through the lungs, the effects also wear off quickly and so a sniffer has to keep sniffing to maintain the effect. People who sniff may experience hallucinations; unconsciousness is also possible.

The risks from abusing solvents

Possibly the greatest risk from solvent abuse is from what happens when the person who sniffs is 'intoxicated'. They may not be realistic or 'aware' and may take risks they would not take normally. In the same way abusers may be unable to react to danger. Accidents as a result of this represent risk.

Sniffing solvents also has an effect on the heart and any physical effort or a fright following sniffing can result in death. If the solvent is sprayed directly into the mouth, this has been shown to cause a swelling of the throat tissues which can result in suffocation. It has also been shown that people who sniff can die from choking on their own vomit. As they often go to isolated places to sniff solvents, there may be no one around to help them.

Most of these risks are immediate and are directly connected to the sniffing of the solvent or the short-term intoxicating effect.

Why do people sniff solvents?

Solvent abuse is often thought to be a young person's habit. However, research has shown that only about one in ten secondary pupils try sniffing and many do not carry on the habit for very long. As with the other 'drugs', people sniff solvents for various reasons, including the following.

- It is an alternative to other drugs.
- Solvents are cheap and easily available. Although the law makes it an offence (under the Substance Supply Act 1985) to sell a young person under 18 a substance if they believe it will be used 'to achieve intoxication', this is very difficult to prove, and there have been few prosecutions under this Act.
- It can be exciting; and some people like the hallucinations that go with it.
- It might shock those seen as authority figures, such as parents and teachers.
- It is enjoyable.
- It helps to avoid or blot out problems.

Sexual behaviour and health

Sex is a natural part of life. It is the way in which people reproduce themselves and this ensures that the species continues. It is also a way of showing love and affection as well as a way of giving and receiving pleasure and excitement.

Whether sex is part of a short or long-term relationship, infectious diseases can be transmitted and it important to know how to limit the risks. Such diseases are known as STDs – sexually transmitted diseases – although doctors now call them GU or **genito-urinary** as they affect the genital area as well as the bladder and urethra.

Anyone can contract an infection – men and women, heterosexuals and homosexuals. Getting an infection is not dependent on having a lot of sexual partners. Sometimes infections can lie dormant for a time and then come out. Some infections can be a result of poor personal hygiene. The more partners a person has the greater the risk of catching or passing on an infection.

There are many different types of sexually transmitted diseases – see Figure 1.8.

STD	Cause	Symptoms	Treatment
Gonorrhoea	Bacteria which live in warm moist internal linings of the body	■ Discharge from vagina or penis ■ Irritation or discharge from anus ■ Pain in lower abdomen in women ■ Pain on passing urine	Antibiotics
Thrush	Yeast called 'Candida albicans'	■ Thick white discharge from vagina ■ Itching around genitals ■ Soreness and pain on passing urine	Pessaries and/or cream
Genital warts	Virus	■ Warts of varying sizes around genitals	Ointment
Genital herpes	Herpes simplex virus	■ Small painful blisters in genital region ■ Tingling or itching in genital area ■ Flu-like symptoms (headache, backache) ■ Pain or tingling on passing urine	
Pubic lice	Small lice living in pubic hair	■ Itching and small eggs on pubic hair	Special lotion
Hepatitis B	Virus in blood and body fluids, resulting in liver inflammation	Two stages: 1 Two to six months after contact with infection: flu-like symptoms, including sore throat and cough. Feeling of fatigue, loss of appetite and joint pain. 2 Jaundice stage: skin and eyes take on yellowish tinge. Stools become grey and urine brown. Abdomen is sore.	Bed rest and healthy food. Vaccinations are available for people in certain risk situations

Figure 1.8 Sexually transmitted diseases

HIV and AIDS

One of the most publicised sexually transmitted diseases of recent years is infection by HIV – Human Immunodeficiency Virus. This virus attacks and damages the body's defence mechanisms, preventing it from effectively fighting certain infections or illnesses. It lives in body fluids – blood, semen and vaginal secretions particularly.

AIDS – Acquired Immune Deficiency Syndrome is the end stage of a chronic infection by HIV. (A syndrome is a collection of illnesses.) An individual cannot 'catch' AIDS, only HIV. AIDS is said to be present if an HIV positive individual (i.e. after laboratory tests, an individual found to have HIV antibodies in the bloodstream) develops a particular infection or specific cancer with no apparent cause. AIDS first appeared in the 1970s, but was not recognised until 1981. There is as yet no cure for HIV or AIDS. The virus attacks and destroys certain types of white blood cells known as lymphocytes. It enters an uninfected individual through a break in the skin or pink lining tissue (mucosa).

How HIV is passed on

Although the virus is known to occur in saliva, tears, breast milk and urine, the 'normal' routes by which it spreads are via blood, genital tract secretions or from mother to baby via the placenta. The main ways HIV is spread are listed below.

1 Sexual transmission – because semen and vaginal fluid carry the virus. The greatest risks are male homosexual and heterosexual anal and vaginal intercourse, especially if a person has ulcerations. According to the World Health Organisation, nearly half of all newly infected adults are women. Anyone can contract HIV from unsafe sex (intercourse without protection of a condom).

2 From mother to foetus before birth, at delivery or soon after through breast feeding. At present 20 per cent of babies born to infected mothers will have the virus. As more women become infected so the number of babies born with HIV will rise.

3 By the sharing of equipment between injecting drug users – particularly syringes and needles. This is because they might receive contaminated blood from the equipment. The government, through the 'Health of the Nation' document (1993) set targets for reducing the numbers of drug users who report sharing injecting equipment by at least 50 per cent by 1997 and by at least a further 50 per cent by 1997 and by at least a further 50 per cent by the year 2000. This would leave a maximum of 5 per cent of drug users who practise this habit.

In the UK blood and blood products have been screened for HIV since October 1985, so both the receiving and the donating blood in this country are safe. All equipment for this purpose is sterilised. Most developed countries in the world share these safe practices, but this may not apply to all countries. (Advice can be obtained from the Medical Advisory Service for Travellers Abroad (0171 631 4408.)

In the early years of the disease, many haemophiliacs contracted HIV and AIDS because their blood

transfusions were not screened for the virus as they are now.

The virus is fragile and cannot live outside the body for long. It is also inactivated by disinfectants such as alcohol, bleach, peroxide, etc. This means that the virus cannot be passed on by:

- eating food prepared by an HIV-infected individual
- being in the same room as or by coughs and sneezes from an infected person
- swimming in the same water
- mosquito or other insect bites
- casual contact such as touching, kissing, hugging
- using the same cutlery or crockery as an infected individual
- giving first-aid treatment providing safe hygienic practices are carried out, for example, disposable gloves, disinfecting body fluids, etc.

How do HIV and AIDS affect the body?

Many people infected with HIV are not aware they have the virus and carry on a normal working life, feeling healthy and well.

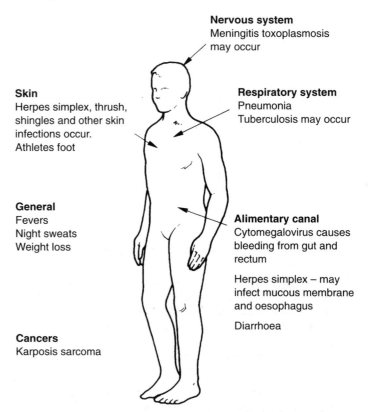

Nervous system
Meningitis toxoplasmosis may occur

Respiratory system
Pneumonia
Tuberculosis may occur

Skin
Herpes simplex, thrush, shingles and other skin infections occur.
Athletes foot

Alimentary canal
Cytomegalovirus causes bleeding from gut and rectum

Herpes simplex – may infect mucous membrane and oesophagus

Diarrhoea

General
Fevers
Night sweats
Weight loss

Cancers
Karposis sarcoma

Figure 1.9 AIDS-related illnesses

There is no evidence that rest, exercise or sensible nutrition stops transmission or progression of the infection.

One of the longest studies so far carried out suggests that about half the number of HIV positive individuals will develop AIDS within 10 years, and eventually 99 per cent will contract it. How long it takes to develop depends on the individual. When AIDS develops, some people die, but others can stay well for a long time if they have good care. Even if an individual becomes seriously ill, he or she can often be nursed back to better health for a while. After several years during which the virus gradually destroys the lymphocytes, the body's defence system is unable to cope with certain infections and these are responsible for 90 per cent of deaths from AIDS.

Ways to limit the spread of HIV

At present there is no treatment or vaccination to prevent HIV infection, but the disease can be controlled by behavioural changes.

1 Screening of blood – already implemented:
 a high-risk individuals excluded from blood donations
 b blood donors screened for antibodies against HIV
 c manufacturing processes for blood products incorporate heat treatment to inactivate HIV.
2 Education programmes in schools, colleges and for the general public have raised awareness about the need for changing behaviour in homosexual, and heterosexual males and females and intravenous drug users.
3 Safer sex recommendations include:
 a limiting the number of sexual partners
 b use of (kitemarked/British Standard) condoms to create barrier between body fluids
 c encouraging non-penetrative sexual acts between partners such as kissing, touching, etc.
 d practising celibacy (not having penetrative sex).
4 Providing support and counselling to intravenous drug abusers to end practice but to take advantage of syringe exchange schemes if they persist.
5 Treatment of other sexually transmitted diseases.
6 Safe hygienic practices associated with any procedures involving body fluids.

The government set up a programme of anonymous surveys to seek up-to-date information on HIV and AIDS.

Figures apply up to March 1992 in England	HIV infection	AIDS
Number of reported cases	15 133	5 366
Number of deaths		3 336

Location of surveys	Incidence rate
Antenatal clinics (London)	1 in 500 infected
Genito-urinary medical clinics for:	
■ Homosexuals and bisexually orientated males	1 in 5 infected
■ Heterosexually orientated males and females	1 in 100 infected

Important points to note about the above data are:

1 The figures show only *reported* cases and many people are unaware that they are infected with HIV virus.
 a Blood tests for HIV antibodies are unreliable until at least three months after the date of infection. The body takes a few months to produce antibodies for HIV.
 b The actual figures will be very much higher.
2 Experts agreed that new HIV infection and AIDS cases among gay men would probably peak in 1993 or 1994. This was providing safe sex behaviour continued to be practised. There was some concern that this may not be the case with the younger generation of gay men.
3 Each year until 1997, nearly a hundred HIV positive haemophiliac cases will develop AIDS.
4 Heterosexual cases of HIV are steadily increasing – this is the fastest growing section of the community. Around 25 per cent of current HIV infections arise from heterosexual contact:
 a 73 per cent from exposure overseas
 b 13 per cent from high-risk partners.
 Now the virus is in the heterosexual community the infection will increase. About 7000 men and women in Britain have become infected by HIV through heterosexual intercourse (excluding drug users). It is thought by some researchers that as many as 80 per cent of the infected heterosexuals have no idea that they are carrying the virus.

If you think you may have contracted the virus, it can take at least three months or longer to be sure

17

because the blood has to be checked for HIV-antibodies. The body can take a few months to produce these.

Therefore, people who contract HIV and AIDS and their families need a lot of support. Carers need to understand fully the nature of AIDS to be able to provide support effectively.

To protect yourself from the risk of HIV and AIDS you should:

■ always practise safer sex or celibacy
■ limit the number of sexual partners you have or defer sexual behaviour until you have a permanent partnership
■ always use disposable gloves when dealing with any body fluids
■ always use disposal gloves when dealing with other people's wounds, no matter how small
■ wipe surfaces with a disinfectant immediately after dealing with any body fluids or blood.

Think it over

What precautions should be taken by staff who work in care homes in order to protect themselves from hepatitis and HIV?

Personal hygiene

Good personal hygiene is essential for everyone. Carers particularly need to understand the importance of good personal hygiene and routines to maintain it because:

■ they have to work closely with people and poor personal hygiene is unpleasant
■ they are in a position to promote the personal hygiene of others
■ ill health and disease can be caused by poor personal hygiene.

Using deodorants and perfumes does not hide poor hygiene. The body needs to be clean before these products are used.

Good hygiene includes:

■ washing thoroughly every day, for example, taking a bath or shower
■ washing after exercise
■ using a cleansing products, such as soap, to remove sweat, dirt and sebum (oil produced by the skin)

■ using an antiperspirant/deodorant
■ regular teeth cleaning to reduce the risk of decay.

Bacteria which are present naturally in the mouth act on the food eaten, especially sugar, to produce acid. This acid attacks the enamel on the teeth, reducing its resistance to decay. In addition, plaque, a sticky substance, builds up in the mouth attacking the teeth and gums and causing disease. Regular brushing and the use of dental floss reduce the build-up of plaque and remove any food left on the teeth and gums so the bacteria have less to feed on. Dentists recommend that you clean your teeth at least three times day, especially after every meal. Decay is reduced considerably if you only eat sweet foods such as chocolate and confectionery at meal times – it is not the quantity of sugar eaten that affects the amount of decay but the frequency.

Hygiene in public areas

Food hygiene regularly receives the attention of the media. It is essential that all food is cooked and served under strict hygiene regulations to ensure food safety and minimise the risk of food poisoning. Food poisoning can result in unpleasant symptoms such as nausea, vomiting, headache, fever and diahorrea. It can be caused by a number of different strains of bacteria, depending on the source.

To reduce the risk from food poisoning a few simple steps should be followed:

■ Always wash your hands after using the toilet.
■ Always wash your hands before preparing or serving food.
■ Never prepare cooked and raw meat on the same board or using the same utensils, in order to prevent contamination of cooked food.
■ Always wear clean overalls for food preparation.
■ Cover cuts or wounds with a clean dressing. Plasters should be blue so you will notice immediately if one comes off.
■ Do not prepare food if suffering from a cold, cough or a stomach upset.
■ Do not cough or sneeze near food.

Evidence collection point

Provide an explanation of routines that promote personal hygiene and food hygiene. One way to do this might be to design an information leaflet aimed at one client group. Justify your choice of topic and group.

Medical treatment

Hygiene is also an important issue in medical care to avoid the transmission of bacteria (see Figure 1.10). When dealing with any body fluid, the advice given above on HIV and AIDS should be followed.

In areas where medical treatment is provided either **sterilise** or **disinfect** the premises. Sterilisation kills all bacteria preventing growth; disinfection slows bacterial growth, but does not always kill the bacteria.

Hygenic practice	Reason
Hands should be thoroughly washed: ■ after going to the toilet ■ after touching raw meat ■ before touching any food.	Salmonella bacteria live in human, animal and poultry intestines.
Wash all equipment including knives and chopping board after using with raw meat.	Raw meat may be contaminated.
Thaw meat and poultry thoroughly before cooking. Do not allow the water to drip over surfaces or other food.	Colder parts of meat will not reach the high temperatures needed to kill any bacteria present. Water will be contaminated from intestines.
Do not drink or use unpasteurised milk.	Harmful pathogenic bacteria will be present.
Cook meat, poultry and eggs thoroughly.	High temperatures kill the bacteria.
Avoid products containing raw or only lightly cooked egg, e.g homemade mayonnaise, mousse, meringues, ice cream.	Any bacteria present will not be killed.
Avoid cooking or preparing food if ill with intestinal upset.	Any bacteria present may be transferred to food and may infect others.
Never return to an occupation working with food after intestinal illness, however mild, until you have been officially cleared by laboratory testing.	You might have become a carrier without knowing it.

Figure 1.10 Personal and kitchen hygiene measures

Evidence collection point

1 Prepare a report which explains the importance of a balanced lifestyle and explains the risks and benefits associated with aspects of lifestyle, including exercise, diet, rest, smoking, alcohol and sexual behaviour.
2 Describe a healthy diet for a child, an older person and a pregnant woman, where one person is active and another is inactive (or sedentary). For one individual you should include a description of how the body uses each of the dietary components of protein, carbohydrate, fat, vitamins (C, D), minerals (iron, calcium), water and fibre.
3 Write a description of how using and abusing substances affects health and well-being. Your report should cover the use of drugs and solvents and their effects on people in physical, social, emotional and intellectual terms.
4 Produce a report explaining good hygiene practice in personal routines and in one public area (which could include food hygiene).

This chapter will provide you with the information needed to complete these reports.

These reports will contribute to the evidence indicators required for Element 1.1.

Presenting advice on health

When offering health advice to others, it is important that any advice you give is based on an analysis of other people's situations. It must be possible for others to achieve targets that you set. In order to do these things successfully, there are a number of stages to follow.

Assessment of an individual's current health status

Assessment might include gaining an overview of one or several areas of the individual's lifestyle. Areas might include diet, regularity and type of exercise, patterns of sleep and rest, the demands of the person's job and what they can afford. The important thing is to gain as much relevant information as possible, so that accurate advice can be given.

Besides being aware of the individual's lifestyle, it is also important to be aware of other factors such as social arrangements, likes and dislikes, job patterns and finance. There is no point suggesting a regular game of squash to improve fitness if the individual does not like racket sports, does not have a partner to play with, cannot afford the court and hire of rackets and works nights and weekends. The local squash courts may be unavailable in the day because schools use them! This individual would lose motivation straight away. Health advice often involves trying to change habits which have been a pattern for a long time and habits can be difficult to alter. For habits to change, targets must be achievable with relative ease, particularly in the early days.

Collecting information about other people's needs

Once you are aware of the health concerns of another person, it is important to decide what you need to know in order to provide an accurate assessment and achievable targets for change. It is

important that you find out as much information as you can. It may be worthwhile devising a simple sheet to help you to do this. Therefore, if you were looking specifically at a diet-related concern, your sheet might look like the following.

Diet record sheet			
Day/date:			
Time	**Amount**	**Food/drink**	**Reason for eating**
Breakfast			
Snack			
Lunch			
Snack			
Dinner/tea			
Snack			
Other			

Other questions might be:

- What are your current eating patterns? For example, do you have a snack lunch, and a hot dinner?
- Who decides what you eat? Who does your shopping and cooking?
- Does the person who cooks have a good knowledge of nutrition and food preparation?
- What facilities are available for food preparation?
- How far do you think you would be willing to change your cooking/eating habits?
- Is there anyone else to cook for?
- How much do you usually spend on food each week?
- What are your eating arrangements at work?
- Are there any foods you do not/cannot eat?

Questions such as these would support the diet analysis and enable you to give more realistic advice to suit the individual.

Evidence collection point

Choose an individual who fits into one of the target groups listed below, and for whom you can develop a plan to provide a balanced lifestyle which will benefit health and well-being.

Target groups: children, pregnant women, elderly people, disabled people.

Devise an assessment sheet to enable you to collect the information required.

Using standard measures

There are a number of **standard measures** which are used to assess a person's state of health and fitness. A standard measure means an accepted guide which is used as an indication of the 'norm' or average. Obviously, everyone will be different and a lot of factors will affect a person's level of health and fitness, so these measures should be seen as providing a starting point for assessment and advice.

Temperature

The accepted normal body temperature for a healthy individual is around 36–37°C. Even where the temperature of the environment changes, for example, a cold winter's day or a hot summer's day, the body's internal temperature should always remain within this range. This is maintained by balancing the heat lost from the skin with the heat produced by the body when burning food and the amount of clothing worn.

One indication of ill-health would be where the body temperature rises above or falls below the accepted range. The body's temperature often rises as it fights infection. Any excessively high or low temperatures should always be brought to the attention of a doctor or supervisor if at work.

How to take a temperature

A thermometer especially developed for taking human temperatures should always be used. There are four main types: forehead, clinical, digital and disposable thermometers.

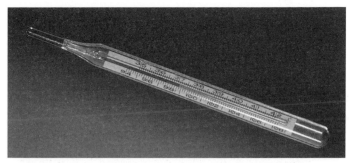

A clinical thermometer with a tube of mercury

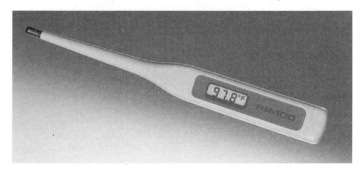

A clinical thermometer using liquid crystal technology

Which thermometer is used and how the temperature is taken will depend on the patient and the circumstances.

Some ways for taking a temperature are:

- resting the thermometer under the tongue for three minutes
- resting the thermometer under the armpit.

Occasionally, rectal temperatures are taken. With babies and children, it is most common to use a forehead thermometer (although these are not so accurate) or if using one of the other types, to take the temperature under the armpit. The thermometer is not placed in the mouth in case the child bites it.

With clients who may have fits or epilepsy or are unconscious or confused, the armpit method should also be used.

Temperatures can be taken over a certain period of time, at regular intervals, as an indication of change.

Whenever you are taking a temperature, ensure you read the thermometer's instructions carefully, and be as accurate as possible in recording the individual's temperature.

Pulse rates

Pulse rates can be taken as an indication of physical fitness. When the heart pumps blood, it surges into the circulation system with a wave-like motion. This is the pulse, and you can feel it at any point in the body where an artery crosses a bone just below the skin's surface. Typical places where a pulse can be easily taken are on the wrist (radial artery) or in the neck (carotid artery).

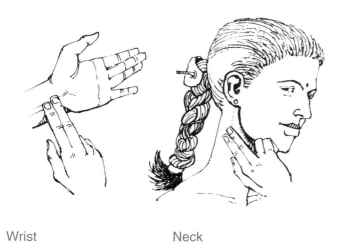

Wrist   Neck

To take a pulse, place two fingers on the neck or wrist as shown in the pictures. If you cannot find the pulse at once, you may need to change your position slightly or increase the pressure of the fingertips. Once you find the pulse, you need to note rate, rhythm and strength.

An adult pulse rate varies between 60 and 80 beats per minute; a baby's pulse is higher, at 140 beats. The rhythm should be regular.

A rise in pulse rate may be caused by exercise. A raised pulse can also be a sign of stress or an indication of infection, shock or heart disease.

Pulse rate as an indication of fitness

Pulse rate can be used as an indication of fitness. It is generally accepted that the slower the pulse, the fitter the individual. The pulse rate immediately after exercise and pulse rate one minute after the exercise has stopped, are used as an indicator of fitness. This is called the **recovery rate**.

To check recovery rate:

1 Find the pulse using your fingers on the neck or wrist. Count how many beats you can feel in 10 seconds, then multiply this by six to get a figure for the rate in 60 seconds.
2 Carry out some exercise, such as walking up and down flights of stairs for three minutes or jogging around the block.
3 Take the pulse again. The closer it is to the pulse when resting, the fitter the individual.
4 Take the pulse after one minute as an indication of the recovery rate. Fitness levels are indicated by how quickly the pulse returns to the resting state.

Height/weight charts

These are commonly used to indicate the acceptable weight range for individuals, depending on their height. They are sometimes in table form or presented as a chart – an example of each is given in Figures 2.1 and 2.2. There is usually an acceptable weight range for each height to take account of bone mass and build.

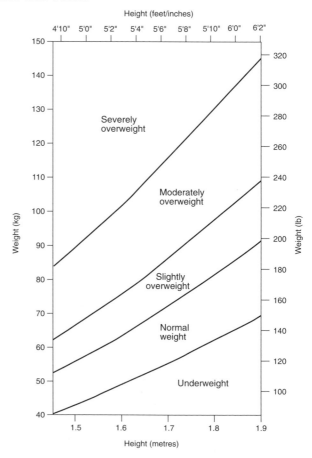

Figure 2.1 Example of a height/weight chart

The chart is based on weight-to-height ratio; it works for men and women. Find your height in metres or inches on the horizontal, and trace up to your weight in kg or lbs.

Severely overweight – weight is dangerous. Medical help is needed.

Moderately overweight – an increased chance of suffering from weight-related diseases such as heart disease, high blood pressure, and diabetes. Consult doctor and try to lose weight.

Slightly overweight – a slightly increased chance of suffering from weight-related disorders. Use a gradual, sensible diet for weight loss. Increase exercise.

Normal weight – no need to slim. To improve body shape, increase exercise to tone up.

Underweight – being underweight is also a health risk. Try a weight-gain plan through your doctor.

Body mass index

This is a more complicated measure of an individual's health according to weight. Using this would offer some evidence of core skills – application of number.

The formula to calculate the Body Mass Index (BMI) is:

$$\frac{\text{weight kg}}{\text{height metres}^2} = \text{BMI}$$

Ranges are different for males and females:

Female – less than 18   underweight
                18–20   lean
                20–22   average
                26–28   plump
                30–36   moderately obese
                40+   severely obese

Men

Height (in shoes)			Small frame						Medium frame						Large frame					
m	ft	in	kg kg	st	lb		st	lb	kg kg	st	lb		st	lb	kg kg	st	lb		st	lb
1.575	5	2	50.8–54.4	8	0	–	8	8	53.5–58.5	8	6	–	9	3	57.2–64.0	9	0	–	10	1
1.6	5	3	52.2–55.8	8	3	–	8	11	54.9–60.3	8	9	–	9	7	58.5–65.3	9	3	–	10	4
1.626	5	4	53.5–57.2	8	6	–	9	0	56.2–64.7	8	12	–	9	10	59.9–67.1	9	6	–	10	8
1.651	5	5	54.9–58.5	8	9	–	9	3	57.6–63.0	9	1	–	9	13	61.2–68.9	9	9	–	10	12
1.676	5	6	56.2–60.3	9	12	–	9	7	59.0–64.9	9	4	–	10	3	62.6–70.8	10	12	–	11	2
1.702	5	7	58.1–62.1	9	2	–	9	11	60.8–66.7	9	8	–	10	7	64.4–73.0	10	2	–	11	7
1.727	5	8	59.9–64.0	9	6	–	10	1	62.0–68.9	9	12	–	10	12	66.7–75.3	10	7	–	11	12
1.753	5	9	61.7–65.0	9	10	–	10	5	64.4–70.8	10	2	–	11	2	68.5–77.1	10	11	–	12	2
1.778	5	10	63.5–68.0	10	0	–	10	10	66.2–72.6	10	6	–	11	6	70.3–78.9	11	1	–	12	6
1.803	5	11	65.2–69.9	10	4	–	11	0	68.0–74.8	10	10	–	11	11	72.1–81.2	11	5	–	12	11
1.829	6	0	67.1–71.7	10	8	–	11	4	69.9–77.1	11	0	–	12	2	74.4–83.5	11	10	–	13	2
1.854	6	1	68.9–73.5	10	12	–	11	8	71.7–79.4	11	4	–	12	7	76.2–85.7	12	0	–	13	7
1.88	6	2	70.8–75.7	11	0	–	11	13	73.5–81.6	11	8	–	12	12	78.5–88.0	12	5	–	13	12
1.905	6	3	72.6–77.6	11	4	–	12	3	75.7–83.5	11	13	–	13	3	80.7–90.3	12	10	–	14	3
1.93	6	4	74.4–79.4	11	8	–	12	7	78.1–86.2	12	4	–	13	8	82.7–92.5	13	0	–	14	8

Women

Height (in shoes)			Small frame						Medium frame						Large frame					
m	ft	in	kg kg	st	lb		st	lb	kg kg	st	lb		st	lb	kg kg	st	lb		st	lb
1.473	4	10	41.7–44.5	6	8	–	7	0	43.5–48.5	6	12	–	7	9	47.2–54.0	7	6	–	8	7
1.499	4	11	42.6–45.8	6	10	–	7	3	44.5–49.9	7	0	–	7	12	48.1–55.3	7	8	–	8	10
1.524	5	0	43.5–47.2	6	12	–	7	6	45.8–51.3	7	3	–	8	1	49.4–56.7	7	11	–	8	13
1.549	5	1	44.9–48.5	7	1	–	7	9	47.2–52.6	7	6	–	8	4	50.8–58.1	8	0	–	9	2
1.575	5	2	46.3–49.9	7	4	–	7	12	48.5–54.0	7	9	–	8	7	52.2–59.4	8	3	–	9	5
1.6	5	3	47.6–51.3	7	7	–	8	1	49.9–55.3	7	12	–	8	10	53.5–60.8	8	6	–	9	8
1.626	5	4	49.0–52.6	7	10	–	8	4	51.3–57.2	8	1	–	9	0	54.9–62.6	8	10	–	9	12
1.651	5	5	50.3–54.0	7	13	–	8	7	52.7–59.0	8	4	–	9	4	56.8–64.4	8	13	–	10	2
1.676	5	6	51.7–55.8	8	2	–	8	11	54.4–61.2	8	8	–	9	9	58.5–66.2	9	3	–	10	6
1.702	5	7	53.5–57.6	8	6	–	9	1	56.2–63.0	8	12	–	9	13	60.3–68.0	9	7	–	10	10
1.727	5	8	55.3–59.4	8	10	–	9	5	58.1–64.9	9	2	–	10	3	62.1–69.9	9	11	–	11	0
1.753	5	9	57.2–61.2	9	0	–	9	9	59.9–66.7	9	6	–	10	7	64.0–71.7	10	1	–	11	4
1.778	5	10	59.0–63.5	9	4	–	10	0	61.7–68.5	9	10	–	10	11	65.8–73.9	10	5	–	11	9
1.803	5	11	60.8–65.3	9	8	–	10	4	63.5–70.3	10	0	–	11	1	67.6–76.2	10	9	–	12	0
1.829	6	0	62.6–67.1	9	12	–	10	8	65.3–72.1	10	4	–	11	5	69.4–78.5	10	13	–	12	5

Figure 2.2 Example of height/weight table: desirable weights (in indoor clothing) for adults

Male – 18–19 lean
21–22 average
24–25 ideal
32–33 obese
40+ severely obese

The Body Mass Index helps to indicate if weight loss is needed.

Food intake

Food intake is another standard measure. If you are interested in either the quality of food eaten; the nutrients an individual is eating; or calorie intake for weight loss, it is useful to analyse food intake against the suggested amounts. In doing this, you can also see where calories are coming from and whether a diet is healthy. This will help you to make recommendations for change. Figure 2.3 shows the recommended calorie and nutrient intakes for different age groups, including some special stages of life. Refer back to Chapter 1 to remind yourself of all the factors which affect the energy an individual needs and therefore the calorie intake they require. This will also tell you why different nutrients are needed in the body and the problems which might arise if they are lacking.

Other measurements against which diet can be measured include amounts of each nutrient eaten. The following are suggested:

Protein – 1 g per kg of body weight per day.
Fat – no more than 30–35 per cent of total calories from fat.
Fibre – 30 g per day (NACNE recommendations).
Salt – 9 mg per day (NACNE recommendations).

You can calculate an individual's dietary intake by noting down everything he or she eats in a day, *but you must take accurate weights* – guessing amounts of food portions can be very deceptive and lead to inaccurate results. You then need to use books such as the *Manual of Nutrition* to calculate nutrient and calorie values, or you could use a computer program. Once you have an accurate calculation, recommendations can be made.

Age ranges (years)		Body weight (kg)	Energy		Protein Recom-mended	Protein Minimum requirement	Calcium	Iron	Vitamin A (retinol) equivalent	Thiamin	Riboflavin	Nicotinic acid equivalent	Vitamin C	Vitamin D
			mj	kcal	g	g	mg	mg	ug	mg	mg	mg	mg	mg
Infants														
Under 1		8	3.3	800	20	15	600	6	450	0.3	0.4	5	15	10
Children														
1		10	5.0	1200	30	19	500	7	300	0.5	0.6	7	20	10
2		12	5.9	1400	35	21	500	7	300	0.6	0.7	8	20	10
3–4		13.5	6.7	1600	40	25	500	8	300	0.6	0.8	9	20	10
5–6		16	7.5	1800	45	28	500	8	300	0.7	0.9	10	20	2.5
7–8		20	8.8	2100	53	30	500	10	400	0.8	1.0	11	20	2.5
Males														
9–11		32	10.5	2500	63	36	700	13	575	1.0	1.2	14	25	2.5
12–14		46	11.7	2800	70	46	700	14	725	1.1	1.4	16	25	25
15–17		60	12.6	3000	75	50	600	15	750	1.2	1.7	19	30	2.5
18–34	sedentary		11.3	2700	68	45	500	10	750	1.1	1.7	18	30	2.5
	modern active		12.6	3000	75	45	500	10	750	1.2	1.7	18	30	2.5
	very active	65	15.1	3600	90	45	500	10	750	1.4	1.7	18	30	2.5
35–64	sedentary		10.9	2600	65	43	500	10	750	1.0	1.7	18	30	2.5
	moderately active		12.1	2900	73	43	500	10	750	1.2	1.7	18	30	2.5
	very active	65	15.1	3600	90	43	500	10	750	1.4	1.7	18	30	2.5
65–74		65	9.8	2350	59	39	500	10	750	0.9	1.7	18	30	2.5
75+		63	8.8	2100	53	38	500	10	750	0.8	1.7	18	30	2.5
Females														
9–11		33	9.6	2300	58	35	700	13	575	0.9	1.2	13	25	2.5
12–14		48	9.6	2300	58	44	700	14	725	0.9	1.4	16	25	2.5
15–17		55	9.6	2300	58	40	600	15	750	0.9	1.4	16	30	2.5
18–54	most occupations		9.2	2200	55	38	500	12	750	0.9	1.3	15	30	2.5
	very active	55	10.5	2500	63	38	500	12	750	1.0	1.3	15	30	2.5
55–74		55	8.6	2050	51	36	500	10	750	0.8	1.3	15	30	2.5
75+		53	8.0	1900	48	34	500	10	750	0.7	1.3	15	30	2.5
Pregnant, 2nd and 3rd trimesters			10.0	2400	60	44	1200	15	750	1.0	1.6	18	60	10
Lactating			11.3	2700	68	55	1200	15	1200	1.1	1.8	21	60	10

Figure 2.3 Recommended daily intake of nutrients

Evidence collection point

Analyse the findings of the assessment plan you devised against appropriate standard measures and draw conclusions.

Producing a plan of health advice

Once you have identified patterns and measured them against standard measures, you can identify goals or targets to improve people's health. These goals or targets could be major changes which are going to take place over a period of time. In this case, small steps towards the goals or targets may need to be identified to make the task seem more achievable to the other person.

A long-term goal might be to stop smoking; a short-term goal might be to cut down to two cigarettes per day.

It may also be necessary to work out an order of priority for the changes so that where a major change requires a number of small steps, some are given priority. This will help the individual to choose which steps to take if making all the changes at once seems too much for him or her.

All targets and goals need to be reviewed regularly so that people stay motivated and to ensure that targets remain realistic. This may involve reassessment of your original measures, for example, fitness rate, diet. Circumstances do change, and they may affect any plan you make.

Evidence collection point

Identify and discuss proposed changes to the lifestyle of your chosen subject. Identify both short-term and long-term goals or targets, and priorities within the proposed changes.

Presenting the advice to others

The way in which you present your advice to other people will vary from person to person. The aim is to bring about change, so the format must be one that each person finds easy to follow. Formats might include:

- **Written** – explained in detail, but requiring a certain level of literacy. It is also worth remembering that some people are 'turned off' by lots of writing.

- **Diagrammatic form** – some people find it easier to follow a diagram. Information could be given wholly in diagrammatic form or as a support to written work. Diagrams can have limited information on them.
- **Pictorial** – pictures or photographs can be used to support written suggestions and may help to explain a point more fully. This could be useful for people with limited literacy skills.

These three formats can be combined to produce an effective leaflet or booklet.

- **Audio-visual** – use of equipment such as videos, slides, films. These can sometimes help clarify points being made. However, they must be relevant to the group for maximum effect, for example, a video of older people dying as a result

Figure 2.4 Examples of ways of presenting advice

of smoking will not have much effect on teenagers as they may think old age is a long way off and 'believe it won't happen to me'.

Any advice given should have a beginning (to set the scene), a middle (the main advice) and an end (a brief summary or conclusion). Your summary or conclusion is likely to be a recap of the key points.

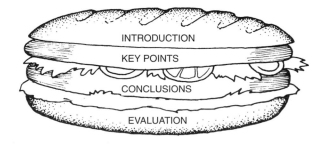

Figure 2.5 The presentation sandwich

25

A presentation should have clear sections: rather like a sandwich, with the bread being the introduction and the evaluation, and the filling being the key points and conclusions.

Advice should be given clearly and be appropriate to the audience. Speak slowly, allowing time for others to take in what you say and note it down as required. It is often helpful to note down key points on flashcards to remind you of these. It is easy to rush a presentation because of nervousness. A practice run, timing the presentation, will help overcome this. Make sure that any audio-visual aids, whether videos or overhead projections, are clear, especially for those at the back of the room. Also ensure the video is at the appropriate starting point before you begin. It is worth double-checking equipment you are likely to use before starting. This will avoid holdups. Above all, you need to be fully prepared for any presentation in order to give the appearance of being skilled.

Evidence collection point

Devise a method for presenting your advice to others. Justify your choice of method. Present your advice to the group and monitor their responses.

Monitor the impact of advice

You can find out how successful your advice has been by monitoring the effect it has on individuals at whom it is aimed. The immediate impact can be measured by evaluating the presentation, and then acting on feedback. This will help you to change the presentation in future in order to make it more successful.

Ways to collect this information may include a verbal or written questionnaire given at the end of the presentation.

A **written evaluation** need not be long or require much writing by others as long as it is designed to get the information you need (see Figure 2.6).

A **verbal evaluation** can suit those who are unable to express ideas well on paper. It can also save time. A group could discuss a number of points regarding the value of the presentation and its effect on them. An elected spokesperson could feed back the view to the presenter without saying which individuals hold particular views.

Evaluation: session on diet improvement

Please tick one box

I found this session   very useful ☐
useful ☐
not useful ☐

The most valuable part was:

The least valuable part was:

Please tick appropriate box

The session has motivated me to act on the advice ☐

The session has been interesting, but not relevant to me ☐

The session has will not affect my behaviour ☐

Ideas for improving the session:

Figure 2.6 Example of a written evaluation

Evaluation forms can be designed to meet the needs of different groups, for example, requests for written answers could be replaced by tick boxes with faces depicting feelings about the presentation.

Evidence collection point

Write a short report on the effect your advice has had on the others and how the session could be improved. Include a brief description of the way plans could be adapted and presented to different groups of people such as children, pregnant women, elderly people, people with disabilities, and very active or very sedentary people.

Chapter 3

Reducing the risk of injury and dealing with emergencies

A hazard is a risk or a danger to human beings. While most of us are aware of dangers associated with roads, railways, rivers and canals, we tend not to think of our homes and gardens as dangerous because they are familiar places. Despite this, our homes are dangerous places, perhaps because we often act without thinking and take short cuts with safety. We often use the word 'accident' to describe a mishap, especially if someone has been injured. Many people argue, however, that the word means a happening by chance or fate – but most 'accidents' (about 95 per cent) occur because of human error or failing. This means that we can take steps to prevent injuries and the word 'accident' should not be used if it is taken to suggest bad luck. For this reason the word is not used in the element specification – it only talks of hazards which could affect health.

Hazards in the home

Falls

The most common kinds of accident in the home are falls. People often climb on furniture such as a chair to reach high objects instead of using a stepladder.

Older people may be unsteady on their feet as a result of arthritis, strokes or dizziness and this frequently causes falls.

Babies and young children are naturally curious and when they cannot see above their head height, they pull themselves up on anything within their reach, unaware of any danger. Active babies may try to climb out of prams, high chairs and cots, especially if they can see or hear something interesting.

Young children and older people have a poor sense of balance and tripping over things left on the floor often leads to a fall. If young children or older people fall they are less likely to be able to save themselves than agile older children or younger adults. Older people may be more prone to injury as a result of a fall because they tend to have weak muscles and brittle bones – one-third of falls in the over-74 age group results in fractured spines, thigh bones (femurs) or wrists. Death may follow such injuries if complications arise.

Stairs, slippery floors and loose rugs can be the downfall of any person, but particularly of the young and the old. Bathrooms with slippery surfaces and wet floors are also hazardous places.

Falls of all types account for approximately 45 per cent of accidents in the home.

Falling objects

A further 12 per cent of home accidents are caused by objects falling on individuals. People often pull on the edges of articles without realising that other objects might fall as well. Objects can also fall if they have not been put away safely, or if there are too many items crowded into a cupboard.

One common accident involves toddlers who, unaware of the dangers, pull on an overhanging tablecloth, bringing down hot liquids or sharp knives.

Cuts

People suffering cuts account for 19 per cent of home accidents. These can occur through people

mishandling sharp tools, falling through glass doors and coming into contact with jagged edges of tin cans, broken crockery, mirrors or glass objects. Although children and older people are particularly prone to this type of accident all age groups are at risk.

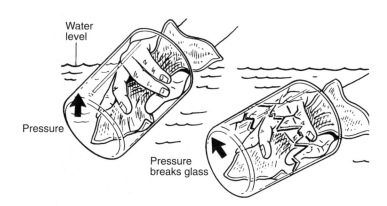

Water level

Pressure

Pressure breaks glass

One common accident is to push a dishcloth into a thin glass while washing up.

The dishcloth pressurises the water in the glass causing it to break. The person washing up is unaware that the glass has broken as there is no sound. They then run their hand across the jagged glass, which cuts like a knife.

Use and misuse of appliances

Accidents occurring from using or misusing appliances and equipment are also common. Rotating machinery (machines with parts that go round and round) is dangerous if people have long hair or trailing clothing as these can get caught in the moving parts.

Appliances that give out heat such as cookers, pressure cookers and irons can cause burns and scalds if mishandled. This type of hazard accounts for 6 per cent of all accidents in the home.

Electric shocks

Electric shocks account for a further 0.1 per cent, although many accidents of this kind are probably unrecorded. Power sockets, lamps without bulbs, televisions and radios are all very tempting to toddlers who delight in sticking fingers or nails, skewers and knitting needles into the small holes.

Toys

Toys and play equipment are frequently featured in news items if they are proved to be unsafe. Damage and faults in toys can also appear during vigorous play.

Dangerous substances

Dangerous substances may be simple household cleaning materials, drugs or medicines, or inflammable materials left close to a source of heat. They could also be pet droppings, hot liquids or just spills that no one has bothered to wipe up.

Although everyone is at risk from these, children and older people are more vulnerable as they may not be aware of the dangers, not see them due to poor eyesight or because they are confused and forgetful.

The main hazards from dangerous substances are poisoning, choking and asphyxia. Some client groups, mainly children, teenagers and young adults, are at risk from substance abuse involving sniffing aerosols, and glues, and inhaling, swallowing or injecting non-prescribed drugs.

 Try it

Examine Figure 3.1 which shows examples of hazards in the home and make a list of these.

Hazards in the garden

The garden should be a happy place for leisure and relaxation, but all too often it is a hazardous place leading to accidents and even death.

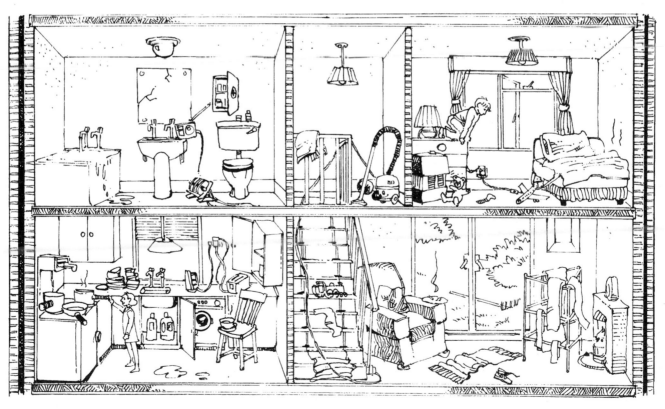

Figure 3.1 Potential hazards in the home

Even a few centimetres of water in a pond can be hazardous for small children who might fall, strike their head and become unconscious, so drowning in a small depth of water. Deeper water is obviously even more dangerous. Every year in the UK 350 people, mostly males, die through drowning. In addition to the risk of drowning, small children may inhale dirty water into their lungs which can cause pneumonia or a chest infection. Water invites attention, particularly that of curious children.

Garden equipment is very often sharp, dirty and heavy and it can cause serious injuries. Children love to copy their parents' activities, so garden equipment must be stored safely. Garden chemicals such as weedkiller should also be stored out of reach of children and animals. Most of these chemicals are designed to kill some form of life, for example, garden pests, and many can be fatal in small doses – even when absorbed through the skin.

Others may cause serious illness. All should be handled carefully, following the instructions on the label.

The garden should be kept free of rubbish, broken glass or plant pots, tools and poisonous plants and trees.

Figure 3.2 Poisonous plants in the garden

Hazards on the road

Road collisions

In the UK an average of 16 people are killed in road accidents every day and over 900 people are injured.

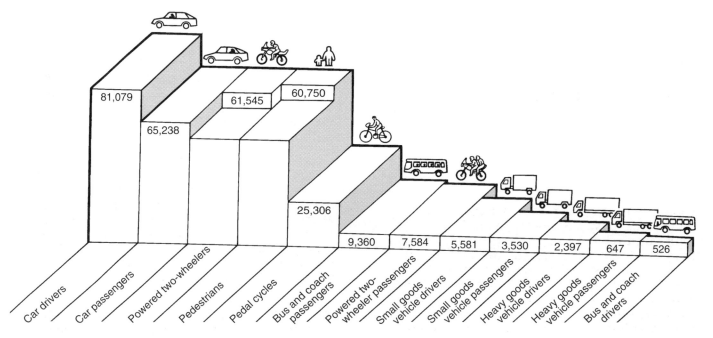

Road user	Casualties
Car drivers	81,079
Car passengers	65,238
Powered two-wheelers	61,545
Pedestrians	60,750
Pedal cycles	25,306
Bus and coach passengers	9,360
Powered two-wheeler passengers	7,584
Small goods vehicle drivers	5,581
Small goods vehicle passengers	3,530
Heavy goods vehicle drivers	2,397
Heavy goods vehicle passengers	647
Bus and coach drivers	526

Figure 3.3 Number of road-user casualties

Once again, we tend to talk about road 'accidents' meaning mishaps, when we really mean collisions.

Victims are of all ages, but the young are the most vulnerable. One victim in seven is a child under 15 years. Each type of road user has the most accidents in the earliest age group. For example, most pedestrian accidents occur in the 5–9 year old group; cyclists tend to be in their early teens, motorbike riders are in their late teens; and car drivers are in their late teens and early 20s. Only in the pedestrian category does the number of casualties rise again as people grow older.

Try it

You could use the information in Figure 3.4 to construct a pie chart to show the number of different road users who became casualties in 1982 (see Core skills – application of number, Chapter 14).

Think it over

Research has shown that most road collisions occur in the area close to the victim's home. Why do you think this is the case? It certainly cannot be because we do not know the area!

Two startling facts

- Sixty per cent of children under 5 years who are injured in accidents are less than 100 metres from home.
- Seventy-five per cent of drivers in collisions are within 10 miles of home. Most of these victims are injured during the morning or evening rush hours.

Road safety training

Road safety training is essential for children to help them to cross busy roads safely. With the increase in motor car travel, however, fewer parents walk any distances with their children, so that the time spent and the opportunities for training decrease. Some parents view the importance of teaching road safety as a low priority, and it is often left to school teachers or road safety officers, who have little opportunity to influence children in such matters. Good road sense taught in childhood will help to keep us safe as adults.

As people grow older they become more vulnerable to traffic because their reactions are slower, speed becomes difficult to estimate and their senses are not as good as when they were younger. This means that we should be aware of older pedestrians and try to protect them in busy traffic areas.

Cyclists

Cyclists generally wear little protective clothing such as a helmet and are exposed to other road users particularly motor vehicles. This means that cyclists are frequently involved in collisions, especially where road lanes turn, for example at junctions and roundabouts, and when being overtaken. Turning right at a junction and overtaking stationary vehicles can often be hazardous for cyclists as they have to leave the side of the road to travel towards the centre.

Cyclists who fail to make sure that they can be seen at night by fitting lights and reflectors to their machines put themselves in great danger.

Other accidents result from machines that are in poor condition and not regularly maintained. Children learning to ride tricycles and bicycles can be dangerous to other road users on pavements and roads.

Cars and motorbikes

Many people want to learn to drive either a motorbike or a car. Driving is a complicated skill so there is a sense of achievement, and it can lead to far greater independence. Expert tuition is expensive, but there is no substitute for learning the right way.

Motorbikes are far more hazardous than cars, as national statistics show. There has been considerable concern about the number of deaths and injuries among motor-cyclists. Special rules relating to the age and type of motorbike, licences and driving tests have been introduced in an attempt to lower the casualty rates. Once again, a well-maintained machine is essential, to ensure that any faults are detected before they become serious and cause an accident.

Motor-cyclists should watch their speed and the road conditions, and avoid an irresponsible attitude towards drinking alcohol (see Figure 3.4).

Drinking and driving

*T*he legal limit for driving is 80 milligrams of alcohol in 100 millilitres of blood, or 35 micrograms in 100 millilitres of breath. But there's no sure way of telling how much you can drink before you reach this limit. It varies with each person depending on your weight, your sex, your age, if you've just eaten and what sort of drinks you've had. Some people reach their limit after about 3 units.

In fact, your driving ability is affected by just one or two drinks. And, even if you're below the legal limit, you can still be prosecuted if a police officer thinks your driving has been affected by alcohol.

The only way to be sure you're safe is not to drink at all.

Facts

Alcohol is a major cause of accidents. More than half of the people breathalysed are over twice the legal limit.

One in three of the drivers killed in road accidents have levels of alcohol which are over the legal limit.

Most drinking and driving accidents happen within one mile of the driver's home.

Young people are affected more quickly by drinking than older people. So if you're young, its especially important not to drink and drive.

If you drink a lot in the evening, you might still be over the limit the next morning. And, if you've had a few drinks at lunchtime, another one or two drinks in the early evening may well put you over the legal limit. Remember that only time can remove the alcohol from your bloodstream.

Health Education Authority, *That's the Limit: A Guide to Sensible Drinking*, 1989. Reproduced with permission.

Figure 3.4 Some facts about drinking and driving

Car drivers should beware of the following hazards:

1 cushions, dangling mascots and toys which prevent the driver having a clear view of the road ahead and behind
2 awkward situations such as badly parked cars, drivers stopping to talk to someone they know or people trying to distract them by commenting on something seen through the window.
3 animals loose in cars

4 motoring at an unsafe speed for the road conditions, especially ice, snow, water and fog
5 driving too close to the car in front
6 overtaking when it is not safe to do so
7 turning right at a junction across the flow of traffic
8 unexpected faults which may develop with the car such as a puncture or tyre blowout, broken windscreen, faulty steering, brakes or accelerator.

Passengers, particularly children, and animals left in a poorly ventilated car for too long can become unconscious. Some people refuse to fasten their seat belts because they fear being trapped; children can quickly learn to slip their shoulders from a harness and even undo the buckles.

Reaching behind to see to small children's needs can be hazardous for both driver and front-seat passengers.

Whiplash injury of the neck can arise from emergency braking as well as chest, head and leg injuries from the impact of the steering wheel and crushed door panels.

Reducing hazards in the local environment

If you know there are poisonous plants in your neighbourhood, see if you can get them removed, but certainly warn any young children about the dangers from such plants. Try to use a playground well away from traffic hazards and with well-maintained equipment suitable for the child's age group. Watch out for hard surfaces such as concrete beneath play equipment – if children tumble off a swing for example, they may suffer severe head injuries or even death.

Crossing railway tracks or playing near railway lines should be forbidden to children and adults. Modern trains frequently travel at speeds in excess of 100 miles per hour. Most of Britain's rail system is now electrified and this can result in death if contact is made with the live rail. Another potential hazard is caused by children and teenagers throwing things onto railway lines, sometimes with disastrous results for the driver and passengers.

Canals are very dangerous places. Apart from the obvious risk of drowning if people fall in, there are other hazards such as rubbish, weeds which can entangle limbs, and dirty infected water. Canals usually have straight sides and can be very difficult to climb out of.

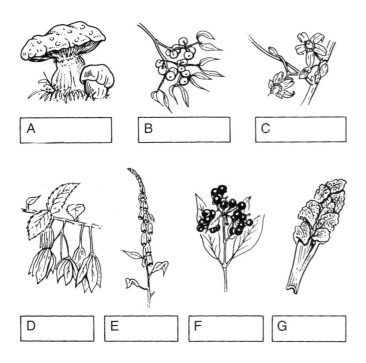

Figure 3.5 Can you identify these poisonous plants? The answers are on page 56.

Safety during recreation

We are more likely to be injured pursuing a leisure activity than when we are at work.

We are constantly being told of the benefits of exercise and sport, but it is essential to take safety precautions. The following safety points apply to most leisure activities:

1   Always wear the correct clothing and prepare for changes in the weather. Pay particular attention to footwear – nonslip soles, walking shoes or stout boots, etc.
2   Use well-maintained safe equipment and always have the special equipment for your particular activity, for example life jackets if sailing, survival bags if hill-walking, etc.
3   Always inform people where you are going, what you intend to do there and the time you intend to return.
4   If you are starting something new, begin slowly and build up strength, stamina or suppleness over a period of time.
5   Do not push yourself too hard, pay attention to any messages from your body, such as, pain, irritation or breathlessness, and take appropriate action. This might involve slowing down, resting, turning for home, etc.
6   If you have recently recovered from an illness, have an existing condition, are older or have not exercised for some time, then check with your doctor that it is safe to do so.
7   If you are travelling some distance or exercising strenuously in warm weather, make sure you have access to both fluids and high energy foods.
8   If you are undergoing strenuous activity, begin with a warm-up and finish with a cool-down.
9   Always follow printed rules, regulations and guidelines on display in recreational places, such as swimming pools, country parks, ski slopes and fell walks. You can only do this if first you find the notices, and second you read them!
10 Learn to swim and dive competently.
11 Avoid too much exposure to the sun – particularly at midday, wear a sun hat and appropriate clothing and use sun protection creams (of the correct factor for your skin).
12 Make sure children follow safety rules and are accompanied by adults. Encourage adults on walks, runs or climbs to go with someone else.
13 Watch your intake of alcohol – too much and your judgement may be affected. Lives may depend on your ability to make decisions, operate machinery or simply supervise others competently (see Figure 3.6).

Safety at work

This too is a huge topic with different safety rules depending on occupations. This section can only deal generally with safety at work and encourage

What happens when you drink?

Most of the alcohol you drink is rapidly absorbed into the bloodstream. Nearly all the alcohol has to be burnt up by the liver and the rest is disposed of either in sweat or urine. The concentration of alcohol in the body depends on how much you drink, whether your stomach is empty or not, your height, weight, age and sex. If you're smaller or lighter than average, or young and if you're not used to drinking, you're more easily affected by alcohol.

Drink can make some people lively and chatty, others silent and miserable. But it's worth remembering that alcohol isn't a stimulant, despite what many people believe. It's a depressant, in the sense that it depresses certain brain functions. That means it affects your judgement, self-control and co-ordination, so it will affect your ability to drive or operate a machine.

HOW QUICKLY DO THE EFFECTS WEAR OFF?

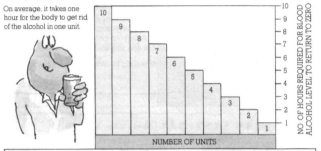

On average, it takes one hour for the body to get rid of the alcohol in one unit.

NO OF HOURS REQUIRED FOR BLOOD ALCOHOL LEVEL TO RETURN TO ZERO

NUMBER OF UNITS

Your blood alcohol level increases with every unit you drink. On the diagram, go up one step for each unit. For example, a man who has drunk 4 pints (8 units) will be on step 8.

It takes an hour to get back down each step, so it'll take him 8 hours to get his blood alcohol level back to zero.

Hangovers

Hangovers are caused by drinking too much alcohol. Dehydration is one of the problems. The alcohol which you drink tends to make the water move out of the body cells.

Different drinks affect people in different ways, so the only real way of avoiding a hangover is by being careful about how much you drink.

The long term effects

The liver is like a car with one gear – it can only work at one rate. The liver can only burn up one unit of alcohol in an hour. If it has to deal with too much alcohol over a number of years, it suffers damage.

Excessive drinking can cause ★ stomach disorders (gastritis, bleeding and ulcers) ★ depression and other psychiatric and emotional disorders ★ high blood pressure ★ vitamin deficiency ★ sexual difficulties ★ brain damage ★ muscle disease ★ problems with the nervous system (especially nerve pains in the legs and arms) ★ hepatitis (inflammation of the liver) and cirrhosis (permanent scarring of the liver). ★ cancer of the mouth, throat and gullet ★ more problems for people with diabetes.

Calories

Heavy drinkers can be overweight and still suffer from malnutrition. This is because they get their energy from alcohol instead of food and alcohol lacks essential nutrients and vitamins.

Alcohol is loaded with calories that go straight to the bloodstream. A pint of ordinary beer contains 180 calories. Add those on to your food intake and you can see how easy it is to become overweight.

How many calories in your drink?

The number of calories in different brands of drinks varies enormously. These figures give a rough idea only:

Beers, lager & cider	Calories
Half pint (284ml/10 fl oz) of:	
bitter	90
brown ale	80
light or mild ale	70
ordinary strength lager	85
low-alcohol lager	60
dry cider	95
sweet cider	110
Spirits	
1 pub measure (25ml/⅙ gill) of:	
brandy, whisky, gin, rum or vodka	50
Wine	
An average glass (113ml/4fl oz) of:	
dry, white or red	75
sweet white	100
rose	85
Sherry	
1 pub measure (50ml/⅓ gill) of:	
dry	55
medium	60
cream	70
Mixers, soft drinks	
ordinary tonic	35
low calorie tonic	0
can of coke	130
diet coke	0
glass of orange juice	80

Figure 3.6 Effects of alcohol

Health Education Authority, *That's the Limit: A Guide to Sensible Drinking*, 1989. Reproduced with permission.

individuals to seek as much information as they can from their employer or union representative.

The workplace is a dangerous environment. Serious injury, muscular strains, skeletal disorders, chemical inhalation, skin disorders, etc. – the list is nearly endless – all can result in an individual suffering hardship, pain, ill health or even death.

We all have a duty to ourselves, employers and work colleagues to minimise the dangers in our place of work. This is now the law as set out in the Health and Safety at Work Act, which states that employers and employees, the self-employed, suppliers and owners of premises have a duty to work together to uphold health and safety standards in the workplace. They must protect the general public against risks

from working activities and control the storage, use and discharge of harmful substances.

Here are some basic safety rules for employees:

1 Do not play practical jokes on people – they could have serious results.
2 Store tools or instruments properly.
3 Report any possibly dangerous events to your manager or supervisor together with any hazards or faulty equipment.
4 Always wear protective clothing and operate machinery with guards and safety devices.
5 Never mishandle or misuse anything provided for people's health, safety or welfare – even notices.
6 Follow all emergency procedures and take part in training whenever you can.

7 Only carry out work that you have the knowledge, skills and understanding to perform.

Ways to reduce risks of injury from hazards

In the home

Homes can be altered to improve their safety, but this is often expensive and unacceptable. Children should not be able to open windows, particularly upstairs windows, so they should be kept locked.

Doors on to the street should be kept locked and glass doors preferably replaced with less breakable material such as acrylic panels. Glass front doors leading onto the street and located at the foot of the stairs are very common and may be dangerous. Door locks and handles should be placed high up so young children cannot reach them.

Stairs should have hand rails fitted at both sides, particularly where there are older people and children in the house. Gates to stop children climbing upstairs or falling down should be fitted at the top and at the bottom. Banisters should not be so wide that children can squeeze through or get their heads caught.

It should be possible to have a good light in every room in the house, but halls, landings, stairs and any steps inside and outside the house, in particular, need to be well lit. Extra lights will be needed in cupboards and dark corners.

Heating systems are frequently responsible for burns and fires. A fire-guard should be placed in front of an open fire. Appliances should not be placed where they can be knocked over or fallen against. There should be adequate ventilation and a safe place for the storage of fuel.

If there are children in the household, then childproof catches or locks on certain items should be fitted.

Try it

Make a list of places in the home where dangerous items for young children (and often for older people as well) may be found and which should have security locks or catches on them.

When buying equipment check its safety features, as well as its ability to do the job. One way to ensure you have done this is to look for the kitemarks and symbols of organisations such as:

- the British Standards Institution
- the Design Council
- the Consumers Association
- Good Housekeeping Association.

British Standards Institution kitemark

You must always be sure to report anything dangerous in the things you buy. Be very careful when you buy second-hand items because safety tags have usually long gone or they may never have had them.

Try to see other people's view points when you think about safety – try to put yourself in their shoes, particularly if they are very young, old, blind, deaf or disabled.

Furniture must be stable, have no rough or sharp edges and open and close properly. Crockery should be easy to hold and preferably unbreakable if it is to be used by children or older infirm people. Saucepans should have handles which do not get hot and well-fitting lids. Handles must never be left overhanging the stove, and cooker guard rails provide extra safety with children around.

Cookers should be kept clean, and particular care needs to be taken with chip pans which are responsible for more kitchen fires than any other single item. Never leave a hot chip pan unattended; have it less than half full of fat, do not overfill it with food; and avoid putting in wet food, which will splutter.

Soft furnishings and night clothes should be made of flameproof materials. When you are working in the home, wear the right kind of clothing for the job.

Good housekeeping is one of the major ways of keeping the occupants of the house free from harm. Only use the essential materials for the job in hand,

keep them close together in a box or similar, and put them away safely when you have finished with them. Wipe up any spills immediately – cleaning greasy spots with detergents. Pick up anything left on the floor, in passageways, etc. Replace spent light bulbs straight away and always use sturdy stepladders for reaching heights. If you can, use longhandled brushes, etc. rather than climbing.

Assume all cleaning substances are poisonous and not suitable for being mixed. Replace the lid firmly and purchase bottles with childproof tops if these are available. *Never* put dangerous substances in containers normally used for food and drink, such as lemonade bottles. Try to keep labels clean and make sure they can be read. Attractively coloured liquids and containers or those which look like familiar, non-poisonous containers should be stored out of reach of children.

Electrical equipment must be regularly maintained. Flexes should not be frayed or plug wires loose. Correctly rated fuses must be used and equipment properly maintained. Sockets should not be overloaded and empty sockets should be guarded by dummy plugs. It is safer to have sockets higher on a wall and not at floor level. Appliances must be properly earthed and preferably double insulated. Never use a piece of equipment which you suspect is faulty. Always ask an electrician to check it first.

Smoke alarms should be fitted in appropriate places throughout the house, preferably one on each floor.

People who sew or repair things regularly must be very careful when using pins, needles, scissors and craft knives, which are all dangerous. Never hold pins in your mouth or stick them in upholstery; keep them in a special box or tin and pass a large magnet over the area afterwards to make sure they have all been picked up.

In the garden

Keeping the garden tidy is just as important as good housekeeping, for it should be free of dangerous rubbish. Garden tools, chemicals and fuels should be put away immediately after use and securely locked up. Children should be encouraged to put away all their play equipment so that it cannot cause falls. Grass that is cut short regularly is safer than long grass, which can hide sharp or dangerous objects. Children should not be around when appliances such as lawn mowers or hedge trimmers are in use – distractions can give rise to serious accidents.

Swimming pools and ponds must have safety covers and lifelines close by. Gardens should have secure gates to prevent young children leaving, without the knowledge of their carers.

On the road

Pedestrian road users should have been taught from their earliest childhood the basics of road safety. These are lessons which we should practise every day and in which we should set good examples to others. But unfortunately, this does not always happen – as we become familiar with patterns of traffic, we may grow careless and willing to take chances. Adults should be models for young children, always using

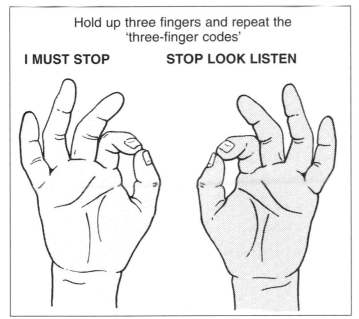

Hold up three fingers and repeat the 'three-finger codes'

I MUST STOP   **STOP LOOK LISTEN**

pedestrian crossings. Taking advantage of subways, islands, traffic lights and crossing patrols, which are all designed to keep us safe, should form the basis of

modern road safety procedure. Often, however, we feel we cannot afford the few minutes it takes to wait, especially if there is no traffic in sight; but it is important that we show children by our actions the right way to cross a road and explain every time what we do and why. Road safety experts suggest the use of the Green Cross Code for children around 7 years old, and for younger children the three-finger code, 'I must stop – stop, look, listen.

Toddlers should wear a harness to prevent them from suddenly running off, while older children should be held firmly by the hand.

If there is no footpath, always walk on the right-hand side of the road to face the oncoming traffic. At night wear light-coloured clothing or something reflective, or carry a torch so that you can be seen clearly by other road users. If there is a pavement, use it; if you are walking with an older person, walk on their road side to give added protection.

Many parents unwittingly tell their children that zebra crossings are magic paths that keep them safe from traffic. This is a dangerous thing to tell children, who should be told that everyone still has to be alert and practise road safety, even when they are using special crossings. Children should never be allowed to play in the road, run across in front of traffic or hang onto moving vehicles – even bicycles.

Children learning to cycle are safer practising in the garden or the park in the company of an adult. They should wear a safety helmet and sensible clothing. The cycle should not be too large and should be regularly maintained. The best training is from a road safety officer, who will arrange a basic proficiency test at the end of the course.

All cyclists should aim to see and be seen, by wearing fluorescent bibs or sashes and safety helmets. They should travel fairly close to the kerb in single file and return to that position as soon as possible if they have to pull out to overtake stationary vehicles. Although not obliged to take compulsory tests, cyclists should be familiar with the Highway Code, road signs and rules. By law, cyclists must have a reflector and lights when riding at night.

Drivers must obey the drinking and driving laws of the country and be aware it is safest not to drive at all after even one alcoholic drink. It is best to avoid driving when very tired, depressed, angry, upset, rushed or under the influence of drugs or medicines. Motorists should take extra care in wet, foggy, snowy or icy weather, and should always wear a seat belt. Many of the latest car models are fitted with airbags which protect the driver (and sometimes the

The good news

The good news is that, if you are a sensible drinker, you'll avoid making a fool of yourself, damaging your health, waking up with a headache, being involved in accidents, harming other people and hurting your pocket.

Here are some ideas you might like to try out if you want to change your drinking habits.

- Choose low-alcohol or non-alcoholic drinks instead of alcohol sometimes. You don't need a drink to enjoy yourself.
- Pace your drinking throughout the evening. If you manage to keep to your limits, give yourself a reward – a visit to the cinema, new clothes – something you'd not usually allow yourself. Enjoy a long lie-in rather than sleeping off a hangover.
- Are there some places where you always drink more heavily? One particular pub, perhaps? Or at home by yourself? Or with particular friends? Think about how you felt when you were drinking. Were you feeling angry, or tense, for example? Do you drink more at certain times of the day? Try rearranging your life a bit so that you avoid the times and places where you drink most heavily.
- If you drink with other people who regularly buy rounds for each other, it's easy to end up drinking more than you want. Try drinking more slowly so you can easily skip some rounds. Ask for a low or non-alcoholic drink now and then, or a smaller measure.
- If you feel you're likely to drink more than you really want to, create a deliberate delay. Go somewhere for five minutes, say to yourself, 'I'm in control of my own life'. You are. Often you'll be able to stick to your plan.
- Remember that getting drunk does not make you tall, rich, strong, attractive, smart, witty, sophisticated or sexy.

Source: Health Education Authority, *That's the Limit: A Guide to Sensible Drinking*, 1989

passenger) from impact in any emergency. Motor vehicle manufacturers spend a great deal of money on research and development of safety features, and many consumers now rank safety as a high priority when deciding which car to buy.

All drivers should be considerate towards other road users, think ahead and concentrate on their driving while being alert for hazards.

Children under 13 years, except those sitting in safety seats, must by law be in the back seat of a car and wear a seat belt, if fitted. Many safety experts now recommend that babies in safety seats are better protected in the event of accidents if they are facing the rear of the car. Children should not be allowed to play with door handles or locks and the car's childproof locks should be used if available. It is important for younger children to have something to occupy them so that they do not distract the driver.

Older people may be more badly hurt than younger people in a collision and may be better seated in the rear of a car if they are nervous passengers. As drivers, older people may have slower reactions, may not turn their heads so easily and may sometimes drive slowly. This could frustrate other road users and increase the risk of an accident.

In the local environment

In a playground young children must be supervised at all times by an adult ready to respond to an emergency. If there is climbing equipment check that the surface beneath it is designed to minimise injury in case of a fall. Avoid play areas with concrete surfaces. Make sure the playground is secure and children cannot run into the road after a ball, for example. Swings should be tied up when not in use, but this is seldom done so remember to teach young children to keep well clear of swings unless they are with a carer. Water and sand areas should be covered to prevent accidents and to keep them clean.

Children should be taught never to play near railway lines and canals. The dangers must be explained repeatedly and older children and adults should act as role models for younger children. Safety teaching should start as soon as babies learn to crawl.

Personal roles and responsibilities in health emergencies

When you suddenly meet an accident or are called to help someone who is ill, it is important that you do not just leap in and react without thinking. It only takes a few moments to consider your options carefully, and weigh up the possible results of what you might do.

Use the flow chart in Figure 3.7 to help you decide in what order to treat injuries.

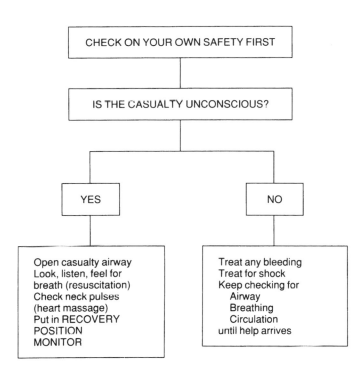

Figure 3.7 Chart to show priority action

Road accident	• Being run over especially in the dark or fog • Fire – petrol being set alight by cigarettes or sparks • Chemicals – fumes, fire, poisons
Drowning	• Currents – carried out too far • Cramp – too close to meals, and coldness • Being dragged under by casualty in panic • Hypothermia • Lack of experience in life-saving
Fire	• Burns • Fumes – difficulty in breathing • Becoming trapped in fire as well • Parts of building may collapse
Gas	• Risk of being in an explosion • Risk of fire • Suffocation • Poisoning
Electricity	• Electrocuting yourself • Risk of fire

Figure 3.8 Types of dangers which may be experienced by first-aider

Road traffic accidents can be very frightening. The blood, broken glass, bent and twisted metal and possibly fire all serve to increase the horror of the scene. One of the simplest things anyone can do in this case is turn off the car's ignition switch to reduce the fire risk. Leave any trapped casualties where they are, unless they need urgent resuscitation, because of the risk of neck and spinal injury. Even if you cannot move a trapped casualty you can still protect the airway *by lifting the head gently and pulling the chin forward and up.*

Approach carefully, look around and be sure that you will not put yourself in danger and increase the number of people ill or injured. Look at Figure 3.8 and work through the possible dangers you might come across in some situations.

Assess the situation carefully. Can you see all the people who are hurt? Sometimes people are thrown from moving vehicles over hedges, or are carried by a fast current downstream.

Do you need the emergency services? You certainly will need to call the fire brigade if there is any danger of fire or if anyone is trapped. This service has all the equipment for such jobs. The police will usually be informed in road traffic accidents, suspicious circumstances, and where there is injury or death. However, this is not your responsibility as a first-aider. Any problems associated with the sea and boats will involve the lifeboat service.

You will definitely need to call the ambulance service in cases of:

- unconsciousness
- absence of (or difficulties with) breathing
- absence of pulses
- haemorrhage (serious bleeding)
- suspected heart attack
- severe burns or scalds
- fractures of skull, back or legs (other fractures need hospital treatment but do not necessarily need an ambulance
- poisoning
- shock.

Sometimes it may be more appropriate to call the local doctor if you know he or she is much closer (such as in a small village). This is an occasion when you must include common sense in your 'first aid box'.

Having assessed the situation you should **act.** Who will you help first if several people have been injured? Give about 30 seconds to each one, while quickly assessing their condition. Go to the quiet ones first – if someone is screaming, groaning or crying you can be sure that they are breathing at least.

Now you will need to find out if there are other people around (bystanders) who can help you or who are more experienced than you – people *you* could assist? Try shouting for help as you work because there may be someone within hearing distance whom you cannot see.

But don't wait. The most serious cases cannot be left while you go to get help. You need to be there to keep the airway open, carry out resuscitation and external chest compression if required.

This poses a very difficult problem if the first-aider is on his or her own. In cases of serious heart attack, for example, the longer the delay in getting the person to hospital the smaller the chance of survival. However, you must not leave a patient in a condition which seems likely to change for the worse (an **unstable condition**). If the patient is conscious, breathing well, has controlled bleeding if any, is in the recovery position and appears unlikely to change, it may be possible to seek help. Otherwise, stay with the patient until help arrives.

Calling for an ambulance

If you are going to call for an ambulance, you must know what to do and say. If you are taking charge and sending someone else, you must be capable of telling *them* what to say. Make sure they can give the message and ask them to return to let you know how

> Dial 999 and ask for an ambulance.
> It is a free service.

long the ambulance is likely to be, and whether there are any special instructions to follow.

Find a place where you can use a telephone. Do not look only for public call-boxes; use common sense. Houses, shops and public houses usually have telephones.

This is what happens:

1 The operator asks you which service you require.
2 Ask for 'ambulance'.
3 The operator then asks for the phone number you are calling from. This can be found on the top of the phone or on a notice in the box.
4 The ambulance control officer will then come on to the line and ask for:
   ■ the location of the accident
   ■ the nature of the accident
   ■ how many people are hurt
   ■ what their condition is (for example, unconscious, bleeding)
   ■ what other risks there are (for example, fire, fumes).
   Give your answers as clearly as you can. If necessary, provide landmarks to help the ambulance crew. Put lights on and post lookouts if you have assistance.
5 Sometimes, first aid instructions are given by the ambulance controller. Listen carefully.

Try it

Contact the local ambulance depot to see whether a speaker can come to talk to your group. Alternatively, if you are carrying out self-supported study, make an appointment to talk to a controller.

Find out how many calls a day the service has, and the main reasons for the calls. Display the information in the form of a bar chart, and prepare this by using a statistics software package. Find out how much an ambulance costs to buy, to maintain and staff for 24 hours. Ask the ambulance officer what, in his or her opinion, is the most useful first-aid measure and what is the most harmful thing that people do, thinking they are helping.

Assessing an emergency

First, make sure your own emotions are under control, take a few deep breaths and stop to think. Are you in danger, is anybody else in danger and is there anyone present with more experience and knowledge than yourself? It is not brave to be careless about your own safety. You may increase the number of casualties and put more lives at risk.

If you do not know how to deal with the emergency, recognise this fact and use common sense to carry out tasks that you *can* do, such as making the area safe and sending for help. Other useful things to do are to talk to the casualty to make him or her feel safe and secure, or if a child is involved, talk to the parent or guardian first.

Explain any treatment that you might be going to carry out and answer questions as truthfully as you can. Do not leave the casualty except under the most serious of circumstances. Avoid asking irrelevant questions, try to obtain essential information from the casualty such as his or her name, address, who needs to be informed and so on. Hold the casualty's hands while you talk to him or her. Always act in a calm manner to give confidence, even if you are frightened.

You may need to give physical support to the casualty, for example, control bleeding, cushion or splint broken limbs or in more serious cases, resuscitate or place in the recovery position.

Conscious casualties do not like to be stared at, so try to make the area private by asking people to form a screen, for example by turning their backs to create a wall. Make sure victim's clothing is not awry so that they are caused embarrassment. Cover with a light blanket if available.

When the emergency services arrive, make sure they have accurate information, written down if possible. Tell them all you know about the emergency and the support you have given. If the casualty's condition has altered, make sure they know this. Give your name and address and encourage others who have witnessed the accident to do so.

The physiological basis of life-saving techniques

Opening and maintaining airways

An unconscious person is usually showing all of these three features:

- They are **not awake**.
- They are **not attentive**.
- They are **not aware**.

In addition, they may or may not be breathing and they may or may not have a pulse. In this case the person is at risk of dying because there is no oxygen, vital to the survival of living cells, being carried around the body.

Ordinary sleep can be said to be a lower or reduced form of the normal wakeful state (which is full consciousness). When you lift a sleeping person's arm, it feels loose and floppy, but it still has some firmness to the touch, because a few muscles are still contracting. In an *unconscious* person the limb is very soft and loose, like a rage doll's, because no muscles are contracting. This is very important to understand because it is the chief reason why, in unconscious people, the **tongue** tends to fall backwards and block off the air passages (see Figure 3.9). This obviously does not happen in ordinary sleep. Any unconscious person may need immediate first aid to unblock the air passage.

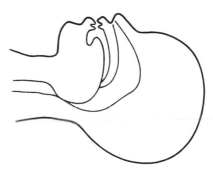

Figure 3.9 The tongue may block the airway

Reflexes are automatic muscular movements which occur as a result of some nerve stimulus (like a blink in response to a speck of dust in the eye). Reflexes are missing in unconsciousness, so any fluid or material in the throat cannot be cleared and may be breathed into the lungs, causing **asphyxiation** (suffocation). This serious effect is most often the result of bringing up the stomach contents (vomiting). When this happens the delicate linings of the lungs are intensely irritated. Watery fluids ooze out to fill the lungs, so stopping the oxygen in the air from reaching the bloodstream.

Remember:

Do not try to give an unconscious person anything to eat or drink.

Your first aim is therefore to **keep the person's airway open.**

To do this, first put one hand underneath the person's neck and the other on his or her forehead. Then *gently* tilt the forehead backwards so that the chin moves upwards. Moving your hand from the neck, gently lift the chin upwards and forwards – the mouth will stay slightly open and the nostrils should be directly upwards. This position will pull the tongue away from the back of the throat, and straighten out the air passages.

Think it over

If you can, obtain and carefully examine a model showing a section through the human head and neck, and trace the passage of air from the nose to the lungs, noting the position of the tongue. Now turn the model face-up and horizontal, and look at the relationship of the tongue and air passages.

Even if you suspect any injuries to the head, neck or spine **you must still clear the airway.**

Remember:

Many people die unnecessarily each year because they have been left face-up in an unconscious state.

Your next important job is to check **breathing and pulse.**

Is the person **breathing?** Put your ear close to the victim's mouth and nose for five seconds and:

Look for evidence of the chest and abdomen moving
Listen for sounds of breathing
Feel for the touch of breath on your cheek.

This sounds like the road safety drill you may have learned as a child. Perhaps you could learn it by repeating it over and over, just as you did with the road safety code.

If you find that the casualty is breathing, place the unconscious person in the **recovery position.** Stay with the person and regularly check the breathing until emergency medical help arrives.

If the casualty is *not* breathing, check and quickly remove any obvious blockage from the airway. 'Look, listen and feel' again and if there is still no breathing start **resuscitation** techniques immediately (see below).

The respiratory system

This body system consists of two lungs, their associated air passages and blood vessels (see Figure 3.10).

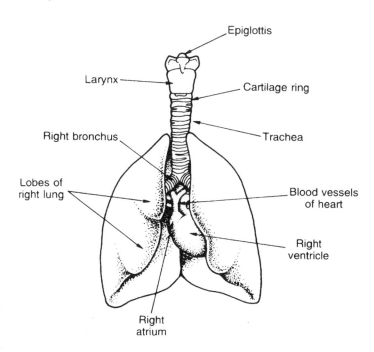

Figure 3.10 Diagram of lungs showing position of heart

Each lung is filled with tiny air pockets called **alveoli**, each of which is surrounded by capillaries from the pulmonary artery and vein. Alveoli are usually collected together in small clusters, each of which is served by an air passage or bronchiole. The bronchioles branch off much larger air passages called bronchi, one of which serves each lung (see Figure 3.12). The two bronchi join and the combined

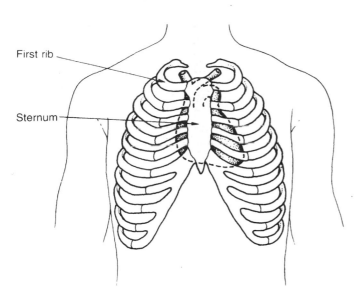

Figure 3.11 The position of the heart

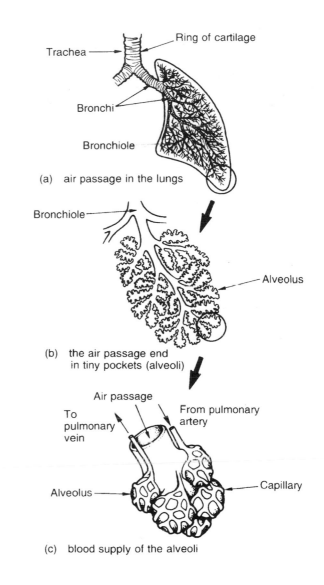

(a)   air passage in the lungs

(b)   the air passage end
        in tiny pockets (alveoli)

(c)   blood supply of the alveoli

Figure 3.12 Lung structure and alveoli

larger tube runs upwards to the back of the throat; this is the **trachea** (also commonly called the windpipe). The top of the trachea has a special adaptation for voice production, called the **larynx** (voice box).

The respiratory system so far described is enclosed in the airtight chest or **thorax.** This is bounded by the chest wall, composed of ribs and intercostal muscles, and a musculo-fibrous sheet below – the diaphragm. The diaphragm is dome-shaped and when it is relaxed it is high in the chest. On contraction the diaphragm moves downwards, expanding the volume of the thorax.

Ventilation

Ventilation is the movement of air in and out of the lungs to refresh the air deep inside them. In order to keep a high concentration of oxygen and to remove the accumulated carbon dioxide and some of the water vapour, this occurs at least 16 times every minute. During exercise this rate increases considerably – up to 30 times, depending on the severity of the activity.

Volume and pressure are inversely related. This means that when one increases the other decreases. On **inspiration** (taking air into the chest), the diaphragm contracts and moves downwards at the same time as the intercostal muscles contract – pulling the ribs upwards and outwards. The whole

effect increases the volume of the thorax, causing the pressure inside the lungs to drop below the atmospheric pressure of the air outside. As the thorax is an airtight cavity, the only way to equalise the pressure again is for air to rush in through the trachea. In this way the lungs become inflated with fresh air. **Expiration**, the expulsion of air, is the opposite. The diaphragm relaxes and becomes dome-shaped again, the ribs fall back to their original position and the lungs, being highly elastic structures, recoil to expel the air.

43

Gaseous exchange

This involves the exchange of dissolved gases between the alveoli and the blood in the capillaries of the pulmonary vessels. The exchange depends on a process called **diffusion**.

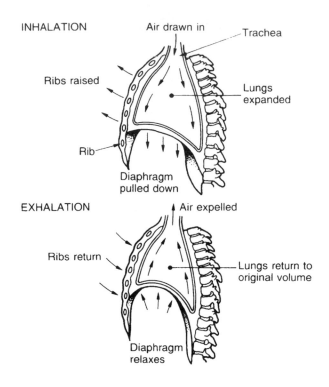

Figure 3.13 Inspiration and expiration

Diffusion is defined as the movement of molecules from a region of high concentration to one of low concentration. (In the respiratory system the important molecules are dissolved gases – oxygen and carbon dioxide.) In reality, this is sound common sense: if one starts with a lot of anything in one place and few in another, after a period of time and random movement the numbers should become more even! This is exactly what happens in the lungs. Air, with a high percentage of oxygen molecules, is inside the alveoli; while pulmonary artery blood in the capillaries surrounding the alveoli is low in oxygen molecules. Diffusion occurs because the two single cell layers of the alveolar and capillary walls allow the molecules to 'even up' and oxygen passes into the blood.

Exactly the same process happens with carbon dioxide (and water vapour) but in the reserve

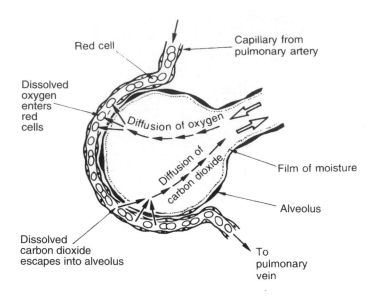

Figure 3.14 Gaseous exchange in the alveolus

direction, because the high concentration is in the capillary blood and the low concentration is in the air in the alveolus. Atmospheric air contains 0.04 per cent carbon dioxide, i.e. virtually none. This exchange means that air breathed out contains less oxygen and more carbon dioxide and water than air breathed in.

Content	Inhaled %	Exhaled %
Oxygen	21	16
Carbon dioxide	0.04	4
Water vapour	Variable	Saturated
Nitrogen	79	79

Artificial ventilation

When any casualty has stopped breathing and is turning bluish-grey you must get some oxygen from your own breath into their chest as soon as possible.

Approximately 20 per cent of the air around us is oxygen, and even when we have breathed this in and used some of the oxygen there is till 16 per cent left. This is enough to support another person and is the reason why **mouth-to-mouth resuscitation** works.

You cannot try this with another breathing person, so technology has provided us with dummies (more

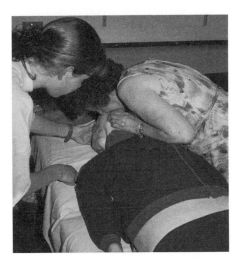

correctly called 'manikins') on which to practise. Manikins usually have inflatable chests and compressible hearts. They are quite expensive so you will probably have to join a first-aid class to gain access to one.

Procedure

1 With the casualty flat on his or her back, open the airway as described above, taking care to remove any obstruction by sweeping your finger around the casualty's mouth.

2 Close the casualty's nose by pinching the nostrils with the thumb and forefinger (see Figure 3.15).

3 Take a breath for yourself and seal your mouth around the casualty's mouth. Barrier devices such as face shields are available to help; in an emergency you could use a handkerchief or a piece of clothing to help you achieve a seal.

4 As you blow gently but firmly into the casualty's mouth, watch to see if the chest rises. Take your mouth away to breathe for yourself and watch the chest fall. Repeat the process 10 times to load up the casualty's lungs with oxygen. The rate should be approximately 10 breaths each minute; two seconds to inflate followed by four seconds of rest each time.

5 Check that the pulse is still there. If you can, call or telephone for help between series of 10 breaths, checking the pulse at these intervals as well.

6 If you are doing it properly you should begin to see a change in skin colour, particularly in the lips and tongue. If the colour does not improve, double-check your technique – especially the open airway and the pulse.

7 If the chest is failing to rise, check the airway position and your mouth seal. Is the nose blocked off and any obstruction cleared? Use your fingers

to hook out any obstruction you can see in the airway.

8 Continue until the casualty begins to breathe unaided. Then place him or her in the recovery position.

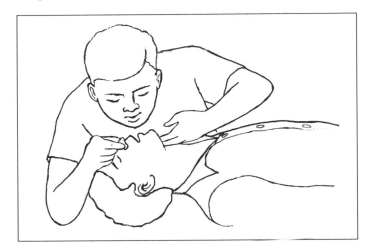

Figure 3.15 Mouth-to-mouth resuscitation

Mouth-to-nose ventilation

This is a variation which can be used if there is damage to the mouth or possible poisoning, or if the resuscitation is taking place in water.

Clearly, it is important to close the mouth with one hand. You are less likely to meet vomit or saliva using this method, but it is often more difficult to do.

Young children and babies

The procedure is slightly different for babies and children up to about 4 years.

Place the child on the floor or along your arm and seal your mouth around the child's mouth and nose. Give short, gentle breaths at about 20 per minute.

Blood circulation

If a person's heart stops pumping blood around the body, you will have to be an artificial pump until it restarts or until expert help arrives. The victim's blood has to carry oxygen around the body, and to the brain in particular.

The place to feel for a blood **pulse** is in the neck. Do not try to feel the wrist pulses, because the casualty's body systems are likely to have closed down the blood flow in the outlying blood vessels, to save the more important blood flow to the so-called vital centres – brain, heart and lungs.

There are two big arteries, one lying on each side of the windpipe (Figure 3.16) and it is here you should place two fingers and feel for the pulse for several seconds.

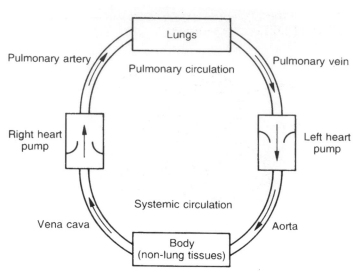

Figure 3.17 Blood flows round the body in a circle

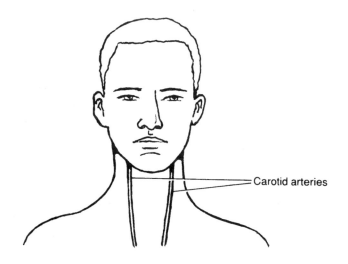

Figure 3.16 Front view of the head and neck showing carotid arteries

A person's heart may be pumping blood but they may have stopped breathing. In this case the heart will soon stop owing to lack of oxygen. The heart is like two pumps working side by side.

Each pump consists of two chambers; an upper chamber called the **antrium** (plural, atria) and a lower, the **ventricle.** Atria have veins supplying them with blood and ventricles have arteries taking blood away from them. The right pump receives blood from the body or non-lung tissues and sends it to the lungs. The left pump receives blood from the lungs and sends it to the body. In this way (see Figure 3.17) blood flows round the body in a circle.

Blood vessels taking and receiving blood from the lungs are said to form the **pulmonary circulation,** whilst those concerned with the non-lung tissues form the **systemic circulation.** Arteries carry blood away from the heart, so there is the **pulmonary**

artery serving the lungs and the aorta delivering blood to the rest of the body. Veins bring blood back to the heart, so again we have pulmonary veins from the lungs, but **vena cava** from the body. In fact, there are two venae cavae: the **superior** from the head and neck, and the **inferior** from the trunk and lower limbs.

The term **double circulation** is often used in human physiology because there are two circulations and the blood passes through the heart **twice** (through each half pump). The function of the pulmonary circulation is to allow the blood to release carbon dioxide and take up oxygen to supply the tissues. The systemic circulation acts in the opposite way; to release oxygen to the tissues and take up carbon dioxide to carry to the lungs. Following this through, the right side of the heart carries blood poor in oxygen, called **deoxygenated** blood, while the left side distributes oxygen-rich, or **oxygenated,** blood to the body or **somatic** tissues. The two pumps can now be imagined working side by side.

As blood flows in a circle, it must flow at the same rate comparatively through the blood vessels, whether they are large, near to the heart, or very small, supplying a group of cells. If the flow of blood was not at the same rate serious 'traffic jams' of blood could occur – causing a lack in other parts of the body. This might prove fatal if the part of the body concerned is a vital organ such as the heart itself, the brain or the kidneys.

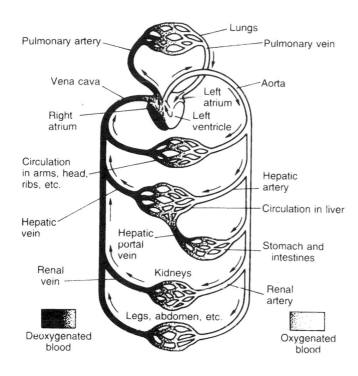

Figure 3.18 Human circulation

Chest compression (heart massage)

First check the **carotid pulse** (not the wrist pulse) in one of the two large arteries lying at the side of the windpipe in the neck (see Figure 3.16). Feel with two fingers pressed deep into the side of the neck.

Think it over

Take your own carotid pulse, by counting it for 15 seconds and multiplying the number by 4 to get the beats per minute. Now take a friend's or a relative's carotid pulse to get practice in feeling for it.

If the carotid pulse is absent you must call an ambulance then start chest compression immediately.

External chest compressions, if correctly performed, will artificially pump about one-third of the body's blood around the circulation, and if this blood contains oxygen it will keep the casualty alive for the time being.

The method squashes the heart between the vertebral column at the back and the rib cage/breastbone at the front. This action expels blood from the heart, towards the lungs and into the main artery (called the aorta). As you release the pressure, more blood is sucked into the heart from the big veins supplying it. You are therefore making the heart pump blood.

Method of chest compression

To be successful the pressure must be applied to the correct place.

1 Locate the base of the breastbone where the ribs meet in the centre at the bottom of the rib cage (see Figure 3.19). Establish a baseline two fingers' width up from that point.

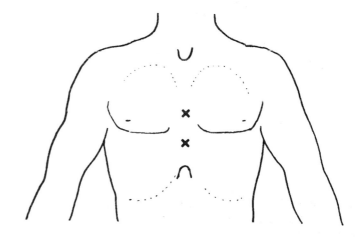

Figure 3.19 Finding where to apply compression

2 Kneeling beside the casualty at the level of your marked spot, place the heel of your hand on this point and the heel of your other hand on top, interlocking the fingers together.
3 Lean forwards over the casualty with straight arms. Push firmly down until the chest is compressed at least

Heel of your hand

4–5 centimetres and then release. Keep your fingers off the chest, using only the heel of the lowest hand. Do not move the hands in between compressions (see Figure 3.20).

4 You must aim for at least 80 pumps per minute. Experts agree that to help you keep to time, it is useful to say 'one and two and three and four...' up to 15, and then begin counting again.

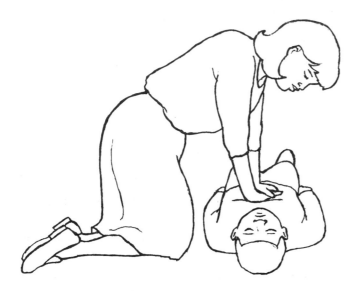

Figure 3.20 Applying compression

Cardio-pulmonary resuscitation (CPR)

CPR is exhausting and if you are on your own, you may not be able to continue for long. Therefore, before you start, shout or phone for some help.

While you are on your own carry out two breaths followed by fifteen chest compressions, followed by two breaths, fifteen compressions and so on. Do not stop to check pulses until you see some sign of blood circulation. If the heart restarts, check the breathing – if it is absent continue resuscitation. If there is breathing, place the casualty in the recovery position and re-check every ten minutes.

If you have a helper, one of you can be at the head doing mouth-to-mouth while one is doing chest compressions. In this case one breath is given after every five compressions of the chest. Monitor the casualty's response as above. Exchange tasks every few minutes so that you can both keep it up for longer.

Remember:

- *Do not practise on a living person!*
- Join a class so that you are properly trained in the techniques. The best way to learn is to practise.
- The ideas in this section will be easier to remember if you have tried them out in first-aid training.

An unconscious patient who is both breathing and circulating blood must now be placed in the recovery position.

If the person is semi-conscious (only half conscious) or worse, always put him or her in the recovery position and check **airway**, **breathing** and **circulation** (pulse). You should monitor these vital signs every ten minutes.

This is known to first-aiders as the **ABC rule**, and it provides you with the three important things to check for – and in the right order! Add to this – for an unconscious person – **monitoring** the levels of response, and you are well on the way to coping with serious emergencies.

The recovery position

Experts agree that if more people knew how to put an unconscious person in the correct position, many more lives would be saved.

There is really no substitute for a trained person demonstrating the technique to you, who then watches you practise several times. You should try to do this with all first-aid procedures, so if necessary join a local first-aid class. Your local library will be able to tell you where to find one.

The **recovery position** is a steady position which keeps the airway open, allowing fluid (particularly vomit) to drain out of the mouth so that it does not enter the lungs. It also prevents the tongue from falling back and blocking the back of the throat.

Putting a casualty in the recovery position.

The procedure is the same for a woman or a man:

1 Tilt the chin to open the airway.
2 Kneel alongside the casualty and straighten his or her legs.
3 Place the arm nearest to you at right angles to the casualty's body with the elbow bent and the palm facing skyward. (Some people like to tuck the nearest arm under the casualty's bottom.)

4 Lift the knee furthest from you and hold it. Take the furthest arm across the casualty's chest and tuck this hand palm downwards under his or her cheek to cushion the head. Cradle the head from this point on.

5 Draw the bent knee towards you and the casualty will roll onto his or her side with remarkably little effort.

6 Re-extend the airway of the casualty then make a ninety-degree angle of the bent knee.

7 Adjust the casualty's head to lie on the hand so that it remains tilted backwards and the other bent arm gives stability (if you tucked the arm under the bottom, pull behind now to stop him or her rolling backwards – the two positions of the lower arm are equally acceptable, but slightly different).

Figure 3.21 shows the final position.

Remember: it is best not to leave the casualty alone. If you have to go to get help, then return as soon as possible.

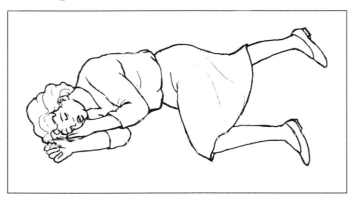

Figure 3.21 The casualty in the recovery position

You can now attempt a piece of work which will also count towards core skills.

Evidence collection point

Design an 'observation sheet' for recording the important observations you might make while dealing with a casualty at the site of an emergency. Decide how often you would make the observations and state exactly what and how you would be measuring/observing. What other information would it be sensible to include if you were making a thorough report, and what would you do with the information?

Keep your work on this task because it can count towards your core skills assessment.

Bleeding or haemorrhage

The body has efficient systems for closing off **wounds** and preventing **blood loss.** Unfortunately, when there is a massive bleed the systems do not get a good chance to work. Then help is required to stop the bleeding, prevent infection and the development of shock (which is dealt with in the next section). The first-aider must know what to do.

The sight of blood can make some people feel faint, and it can be quite frightening if a lot of blood is lost in a short time.

There are three types of bleeding, just as there are three types of **blood vessels:**

- **artery damage** leads to arterial bleeding
- **vein damage** leads to venous bleeding
- **capillary damage** leads to capillary bleeding.

Arterial bleeding spurts out at the same rate as the pulse. It is *bright red* in colour.

Venous bleeding flows out steadily. It is *dark red* in colour.

Capillary bleeding oozes out and clots readily. It is red in colour, neither bright or dark.

Care procedure for bleeding

There are *two* main things to remember to do:

1 *Raise* the bleeding part above the level of the casualty's heart. This simple procedure has saved many a person's life.

2 Apply direct *pressure* to the wound for long enough to allow the protective system to operate (about 10–15 minutes). If the wound is large it may be necessary to hold the wound edges together with both hands.

Occasionally, it may not be possible to press directly on the wound because of the injury. The indirect pressure is applied to the nearest point where an artery crosses a bone – called a **pressure point.** In an arm this is most likely to be in the upper arm on the inside surface. In a leg it will be halfway across the groin. Try feeling for these pulses on yourself.

After about 10 minutes release the pressure on the wound and note whether the bleeding has nearly or completely stopped. If it has, bind a pad of **sterile gauze** over the wound with a bandage. If you have no first-aid materials with you, tissues, handkerchief or similar will do, held in place with a tie, scarf, belt, tights, etc. *Do not tie too tightly* because you do not want to cut off the blood supply. If the blood continues to seep through, put more *on top* of the existing material. Do not attempt to remove your original dressing because you may disturb the clot and start the bleeding again.

If the blood loss is considerable, give the casualty first-aid treatment for shock.

With **internal bleeding** the symptoms of shock become apparent and you might see blood appearing from a body opening such as the mouth. Call immediately for an ambulance.

As usual, check and record **vital signs** – level of consciousness, breathing and pulse – and proceed as in Figure 3.22.

Breathing	Pulse	Conscious	Action
✓	✓	✓	Treat for shock
✓	✓	✗	Put in recovery position and monitor
✓	✗	✗	Cardiac compression
✗	✓	✗	Resuscitation
✗	✗	✗	CPR

Figure 3.22 An action checklist for bleeding

Nose bleeds

These are probably the most frequent bleeds apart from minor cuts and bruises. Sit the casualty with head forward and down, and get him or her to pinch the soft part of the nose for 10-minute intervals until the bleeding stops. The person should not cough, sniff, split or speak for fear of disturbing the clots. If the bleeding is excessive, take the person to a doctor or hospital.

Evidence collection point

Your evidence for Element 1.3 should be in two main sections.

Section A

1 Survey the hazards faced by the following individuals and explain the effect of the hazards on their health

  a Mrs Patel is a 75-year-old widow living in a small council flat on the third floor of a six-storey block. She has no garden and rarely goes out, except to shop at the corner shop in the next street. She does not need very much as she lives by herself. Whenever she goes out, she either walks or uses the local bus service.

  b Tracey Richards is 19 years old. She lives with her mother Mavis and younger brother Sam. She works as a machinist in a local clothing factory and is saving up to get married. Tracey and her boyfriend David like to go jogging mid-week and walking in the country at weekends. David has a motorcycle and Tracey rides pillion.

  c Mavis Richards is 45 years old. She lives in a small terraced house with a garden. Although not very interested in the garden, Mavis tries to keep it as tidy as she can because Sam (see below) likes to bring his friends to play there at weekends. There is a garden shed, which is used to store a lawn mower, gardening tools, weedkiller and pesticides, and bicycle. The garden contains a goldfish pond and a swing. The shed, pond and swing take up most of the space in the garden. Mavis's husband left her and the children three years ago. She has a part-time job as a check-out operator at a supermarket a few miles away. She owns a car.

  d Sam Richards is 7 years old and is a bit of a tearaway. He is not interested in school, but likes to play with his friends in the garden at weekends. He wants to be a railway engine driver and often goes to watch the trains pass by at the bottom of the garden, where there is a gate with a rusty lock – his mother never uses the gate. Sam and his friends have a den on the other side of the gate and often smoke cigarettes there. Sam's mother takes him to school in the car because she knows he does not want to go.

2 For each hazard mentioned describe what could be done to reduce the harmful effect.

Section B

Imagine one of the individuals mentioned above becomes involved in an emergency requiring cardio-pulmonary resuscitation and control of bleeding. You are passing by at the time and are requested to assist.

a   In a report describe what you would do in the correct order, and demonstrate the life-saving techniques on a manikin and a member of your group (recovery position and maintenance of airway only). Ask your teacher or tutor to provide assessment and feedback.

b   Explain the role of the respiratory system and cardiovascular system in your life-saving procedures.

 ## Fast Facts

AIDS   Acquired Immune Deficiency Syndrome – a condition caused by a virus, where the body's immune system breaks down and is unable to protect it from illness and disease.

Airway   The passageway which includes the mouth, nose, throat and windpipe (trachea).

Alcohol   A drug; a colourless, flammable liquid which causes the intoxicating effect of alcoholic drink.

Alveoli   The tiny spherical endings of the bronchioles which, because of their very thin walls, allow the exchange of gases to take place between the blood and the lungs.

Atherosclerosis   Hardening and narrowing of the arteries caused by the laying down of fatty deposits in them.

Atria   The upper chambers of the heart which receive blood from the veins.

Bronchi and bronchioles   The smaller tubes which are subdivisions of the trachea taking air to and from the lungs.

Bronchitis   An inflammation of the bronchiole – the small tube leading to the lungs – by mucus, which is then infected by bacteria.

Cancer   A condition where some body cells do not grow normally and result in a tumour.

Car driver   Someone who is at the wheel of a moving motor vehicle and is at risk from other traffic, faulty vehicles, not wearing a seatbelt and poor road conditions.

Carbohydrate   A nutrient in food which is particularly used for energy by the body.

Carbon dioxide   A gas present in small quantities in the air which has been exhaled from the lungs. It is a waste product of respiration.

Cardiac arrest   An emergency situation which arises when the heart has stopped beating.

Cardiopulmonary resuscitation (CPR)   Revival of both heart and lung function.

Carotid arteries   The major arteries which run up either side of the neck to serve the head and neck with oxygenated blood. In suspected cardiac arrest these pulses are felt for in preference to the smaller, more familiar pulse at the wrist.

Cirrhosis of the liver   A condition which can be caused by too much alcohol where the cells of the liver are killed, so preventing the liver from functioning as it should.

Constipation   A condition where waste products move too slowly through the body, causing the individual discomfort.

Coronary heart disease   A deadening of part of the heart muscle as a result of a blood clot blocking one of the arteries and preventing oxygenated blood from reaching it.

Cyclist   Person who travels around by bicycle. At risk from other traffic, faulty machines and poor road conditions.

Dependency   Relying on something or someone for physical or mental functioning.

Depressant   Something which lowers or reduces nervous activity or the ability to function normally.

Diet   The total amount of food and drink consumed by an individual.

Drug abuse   The socially unacceptable use of drugs.

Drug misuse   The improper use of socially acceptable drugs.

Emergency services   Police, fire and ambulance services who can respond to 999 calls. In coastal districts coastguards can be alerted as well.

Emphysema   Destruction of the bronchiole causing a shortness of breath.

Exercise   Physical exertion which works the muscles.

Exhalation   The releasing of air from the lungs back into the environment (expired air).

Fat   A nutrient in food which is used by the body primarily for energy, as it is the most concentrated form. It also protects vital organs and gives the body warmth.

Fibre Parts of food which are not fully broken down by the digestive process, and so aid the movement of food along the digestive tract (from mouth to anus).

Foetus The name given to the developing life within the mother's womb from 8 weeks to birth.

Gender Male or female social roles.

Genito-urinary Referring to both the genital organs and the urinary system.

Health and Safety at Work Act A legal obligation for employers and employees to safeguard each other's health, safety and welfare and those of the general public with whom they come into contact.

HIV Human Immunodeficiency Virus – the virus which causes AIDS.

Immune system The system which protects the body from illness and disease.

Infectious disease A disease which can be passed from one person to another.

Inhalation The taking in of air to ventilate the lungs (inspired air).

Lifestyle choice A choice made by individuals about the way in which they lead their lives.

Minerals Nutrients in food which are needed in minute amounts for the body to function correctly. There are a number of minerals including iron, calcium and phosphorus.

Nutrient Something that nourishes or feeds the body.

Obesity The state of being severely over the recommended weight for your height.

Oxygen A gas present in the air which is necessary to support life. Brain damage followed by death occurs when the body is deprived of oxygen for more than a few minutes.

Passenger Someone who travels in another person's vehicle. He or she is at risk from the driver, faulty vehicle, other traffic and not wearing a seatbelt.

Passive smoking Breathing in the smoke of others when you are not actually smoking yourself.

Pedestrian Person who walks to a destination and can be at risk when crossing roads, using a road without pavements and being pushed off the road by other groups, cyclists or prams.

Peer pressure Pressure placed on someone from his or her own age or friendship group.

Personal hygiene Keeping yourself clean, for example, through a washing routine and the use of deodorants.

Protein A nutrient found in food which is used by the body for growth and repair of cells in children and repair and maintenance of cells in adults. It can also be used for energy.

Recovery position A recommended stable position of the body which minimises the risk of inhalation of vomit and protects the airways.

Sebum The name used for secretions from the glands on to the skin.

Sexually transmitted A disease which is passed on through sexual contact.

Stamina The heart's ability to work under pressure.

Strength The physical power of the muscles and the whole body.

Suppleness The body's own ability to be flexible or bend without damage.

Trachea Another name for the windpipe, which is the tube taking air from the mouth and nose into the lungs and out again.

Unit The measurement used for alcohol. One unit equals one glass of wine or one half pint of beer.

Ventricles The lower muscular chambers of the heart which contract to drive blood into the lungs (right side) and around the body (left side).

Vitamins Nutrients found in food which are needed in small amounts for the body to function correctly. Vitamins are often listed by letters such as vitamin A, vitamin B and so on.

Self-assessment test

1 Which activity is best for developing all-round stamina, strength and suppleness?
   a Swimming.
   b Golf.
   c Dancing.
   d Walking.

2 Passive smoking is now recognised as a risk to health. The risk can be reduced by:
   a Not inhaling when smoking.
   b Providing more non-smoking areas.
   c Smoking low-tar cigarettes.
   d Smoking cigars.

3 Taking part in leisure activities can help improve health whatever a person's age. Which of the following would be appropriate for an active older person with raised blood pressure?

a Football.
b Step aerobics.
c Mountaineering.
d Golf.

4 Which method of contraception would best protect against infection from the HIV virus?
a IUD.
b Condom.
c Dutch cap.
d Spermicide cream.

5 The main cause of death by solvent misuse is:
a Accident.
b Respiratory disease.
c Pneumonia.
d Cancer.

6 Calcium and phosphorus are used in the body for:
a Cell repair.
b Red blood cells.
c Strong bones and teeth.
d Growth.

7 The body uses protein for:
a Growth and repair of body cells.
b Producing red blood cells.
c Its main source of energy.
d Preventing constipation.

8 Iron is used in the body to:
a Provide energy
b Maintain body cells.
c Enable the blood to carry oxygen.
d Produce a strong bone mass.

9 Which health risk for older people could be due to a reduced calcium intake?
a Arthritis.
b Hypertension.
c Senile dementia.
d Osteoporosis.

10 A client has constipation. How should his or her diet be adapted to overcome this?
a Increase the amount of fibre eaten.
b Increase the amount of protein.
c Eat small quantities of food.
d Increase sugar intake.

11 A group of teenagers are discussing their diet. Which change would help them lower their fat intake?
a Eat more fresh fruit instead of cakes.
b Eat more hamburgers.
c Change from white to brown bread.
d Eat regular meals.

12 Which of the following dietary changes is most appropriate for a pregnant woman?

a Increase fatty foods.
b Increase protein foods.
c Decrease calorie intake.
d Increase alcohol consumption.

13 Heart disease is one of the major killers in the UK. The risk of heart disease may be increased by which of the following in our diet?
a Sugar.
b Fat.
c Fibre.
d Protein.

14 A person's intake of dairy produce should be controlled because it contains large amounts of:
a Saturated fat.
b Polyunsaturated fat.
c Fibre.
d Vitamins.

15 Which of the following would help relieve constipation?
a Eat more butter.
b Eat more biscuits.
c Eat more fruit and vegetables.
d Eat more carbohydrates.

16 Regular drinking of excess alcohol can put an individual most at risk from:
a Bowel cancer.
b Liver disease.
c HIV
d Lung cancer.

17 The AIDS virus is called HIV and can be spread by:
a Kissing an infected person.
b Swimming in a public pool.
c Drinking from the same cup as an infected person.
d Sharing needles with an infected person.

18 An elderly person suffering from chest infections may be advised to:
a Stop smoking.
b Reduce alcohol consumption.
c Eat more fibre.
d Reduce salt in the diet.

19 Knowing and understanding the importance of good personal hygiene is important for people who work in care because:
a Carers meet clients' relatives.
b Poor personal hygiene can increase the risk of spreading disease .
c Carers need to smell of perfume.
d Only carers come into close contact with people in their jobs.

20 Which of the following changes would be most beneficial to dental health?
  a Reducing the frequency of consumption of sugary foods.
  b Increasing iron in the diet.
  c Reducing fat consumption.
  d Increasing fat consumption.

21 Before offering health promotion advice, a client's needs must be studied carefully. This is to ensure that:
  a Advice is relevant to interests, wishes and circumstances.
  b The programme can be timed.
  c Resources can be organised.
  d Facilities can be arranged.

22 Standard measures for assessing an individual's diet would be:
  a Recipe book
  b Department of Health food tables.
  c Weight machines.
  d Fitness tables.

23 An environmental health officer has to tackle the problem of smoky pubs. The best way to achieve success would be to:
  a Advise publicans to have smoke-free bars.
  b Send out leaflets on the dangers of smoking.
  c Distribute no-smoking signs in all pubs.
  d Change the law to ban smoking in pubs.

24 When planning a health promotion advice talk (with no written material), what would *not* be an essential consideration in the planning?

  a Concentration span.
  b Reading ability.
  c Understanding of vocabulary.
  d Visual aids.

25 A plan of health promotion advice on risks to health might include:
  a Road safety.
  b Operating industrial machinery.
  c Lifting clients.
  d Electrical hazards.

26 If you were planning advice for carers for older people, which is the most important consideration when preparing a presentation?
  a Costs must be low.
  b Appropriate style and format for audience.
  c A large screen for audio-visual equipment.
  d Comfortable chairs.

27 The government carries out a national campaign on the importance of vaccinations. For maximum effect this is aimed at:

  a Parents of 0–5-year-olds.
  b Adults of 60+.
  c Parents of 5–16-year-olds.
  d Adults in general.

28 The appropriateness of a video for use with a group of 8-year-olds would depend on the content. It should include:
  a A warning about what may happen if children do not follow the advice.
  b A lecture by a well-known person.
  c Lots of detailed facts.
  d Clear messages in a simple, pictorial form.

29 When designing a health promotion leaflet for non-English-speaking mothers, which is important?
  a Using appropriate medical terms.
  b Using an appropriate language.
  c Incorporating scientific facts.
  d Including clear pictures and diagrams.

30 Health leaflets can offer extra information at a health promotion session. Their main advantage is:
  a They are easy to obtain.
  b They are easy to distribute.
  c They promote products.
  d They can be referred to later.

31 To reduce the need for note-taking at a health promotion session, you could include:
  a Leaflets.
  b Posters.
  c Videos.
  d Films.

32 The most appropriate method to teach breast-feeding to a group of pregnant women would be:
  a Written instructions
  b Demonstration and practical advice.
  c Lecture.
  d Video.

33 Which would be the best way to explain a real-life situation?
  a Poster.
  b Written material.
  c Video.
  d Use of a textbook.

34 Which presentation aid might you use in a brainstorming or problem-solving discussion session on health advice?
  a Video recorder.
  b Textbook.
  c Leaflet.
  d Flip-chart.

35 When talking to clients about their health, feedback should be expert, constructive and non-judgmental.

In general, who is most likely to offer expert advice?
a Parents.
b Professional carers.
c Grandparents.
d Friends.

36 Which health promotion leaflet would best support an individual caring for someone with Alzheimer's Disease?
a Healthy eating leaflet.
b Drugs leaflet.
c *Who Cares?* (information for carers of people with dementia).
d Smoking leaflet.

37 Which method of delivery would be best used with an audience requiring expert detailed information on coronary heart disease?
a Formal lecture.
b Discussion.
c Role play.
d Brainstorming session.

38 Which part of a health promotion session would give the presenter feedback on the success of the programme?
a Questioning.
b Evaluation.
c Conclusion.
d Introduction.

39 When feedback from the audience is required, the method to use is:
a A discussion.
b A presenter-led talk.
c A poster campaign.
d A tick list of yes/no questions.

40 An evaluation is important because:
a It allows the presenter to establish what was successful and adjust his or her work in future.
b It tests the audience's knowledge.
c It is required by law.
d It is expected by the audience.

41 The percentage of oxygen in exhaled is:
a 20%.
b 16%.
c 4%.
d 0%

42 When there is no pavement, pedestrians should:
a Walk with the oncoming traffic behind them.
b Walk with the oncoming traffic facing them.
c Walk in the middle of the road.
d Walk on the side with the least traffic.

43 If you suspect someone's heart has stopped beating, where would you check the pulse to confirm?
a The wrist.
b The neck.
c The front of the elbow.
d The back of the knee.

44 The most suitable person to teach a young child road safety is:
a A school teacher.
b A road safety officer.
c The local police.
d A parent.

45 Which of the following is a poisonous plant?
a Foxglove.
b Dandelion.
c Nettle.
d Grass.

46 To find the correct place to compress for cardiac resuscitation you should:
a Halve the distance between the notch between the two collar bones and where the ribs meet at the bottom of the ribcage.
b Press where the ribs meet at the bottom of the ribcage.
c Find the point two fingers' width up from the base of the breastbone.
d Find the place just below where the two collar bones meet at the neck.

47 Mouth-to-mouth resuscitation works because:
a You are warming up the casualty.
b You are cooling down the casualty.
c You are giving carbon dioxide to the casualty.
d You are giving oxygen to the casualty.

48 In first aid it is important to know what the ABC rule stands for. Which words are represented by ABC?
a Any blood circulating.
b Any breathing or circulation.
c Airway, breathing, circulation.
d Air, breath, circulation.

49 On contacting the emergency services, the operator is likely to ask you:
a Which service do you require?
b Do you require an ambulance?
c Will you require police to attend?
d Is there a fire?

50 Which of the following will the 999 operator need to ask?
a What were the circumstances which caused the accident?
b How many first-aiders are present at the scene?

c What is the location of the accident?

d Have the police arrived?

51 In which room in a private home would it usually be best to fit a smoke alarm?
  a Main hallway.
  b Bedroom.
  c Bathroom.
  d Living room.

52 In which of the following would it be essential to send for an ambulance?
  a Faint.
  b Epileptic fit.
  c Unconsciousness.
  d Vomiting.

53 The three-finger code is a visual reminder of:
  a Electricity hazards.
  b Road-traffic hazards.
  c Danger in the garden.
  d Danger of drowning.

54 Dummy plugs should be inserted into empty electric sockets because:
  a Electricity may fall on to the floor.
  b Children may push things into the sockets.
  c Stops elderly people plugging too many items into the socket.
  d Stops sockets being overloaded.

55 Under a certain age children must sit in the back seat of a car and use a seatbelt. This age is:
  a 15.
  b 13.
  c 11.
  d 9.

56 During cardiopulmonary resuscitation, compression of the ventricles of the heart will force blood to:
  a The atria.
  b The lungs and the body.
  c The lungs only.
  d The body only.

57 The Health and Safety at Work Act protects:
  a Employees.
  b Employers.
  c General public.
  d All of the above.

58 When there are two emergency helpers carrying out cardiopulmonary resuscitation, the ratio of breaths to chest compressions should be:
  a 1:5.
  b 1:10.
  c 5:1.
  d 10:1.

59 Asking for the ambulance service in a case of suspected poisoning would cost:
  a £10.
  b £5.
  c Nothing.
  d £25.

60 Garden chemicals are:
  a Not usually poisonous.
  b Slightly poisonous.
  c Best treated as if they are all poisonous.
  d Not harmful.

Answers for Figure 3.5 Poisonous plants

A: Toadstools

B: Mistletoe

C: Deadly nightshade

D: Laburnum

E: Foxgloves

F: Common privet

G: Rhubarb leaves

Chapter 4

The development of individuals and how they manage change

Individual development

It is hard to imagine our long-term future, and our memory does not cover the whole of our past. Yet when we talk and think about another person, it is possible to imagine his or her life as a journey. This journey might be said to have signposts along the way. These might be labelled infancy, childhood, adolescence, adulthood, mid-life and old age or 'later life'. They are the names that are commonly used to describe sections of life's journey. **Infancy** usually means the first 18 months; **childhood** covers 18 months–13 years; **adolescence** describes the period 13–18 years. In the UK the right to vote gives **adult** status to all people over 18 years. **Mid-life** is the period between 35 years and the mid-60s. **Later life** might be a term applied to people over 65 or 70 years old. Many people in this age group will argue that they are not 'old', however!

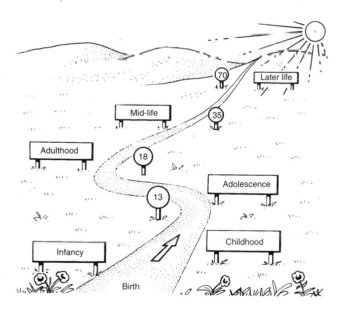

If we imagine life as a pathway or journey, we can ask questions about the journey: how does time affect people physically? Does age have an influence on intellectual, emotional and social behaviour? These categories are ways of dividing human experience into sections so that we can ask clearer questions and better understand development.

Every individual's personal experience will be different. Individuals have different life experiences depending on their carers, their culture, their social context and life chances. This chapter looks at some of the general characteristics of human development across a lifetime.

Physical development

Every individual has a unique pattern of growth and development. This is because there is such a large number of factors influencing our progress.

It would be logical to say that each one of us begins from the moment a sperm nucleus from the father joins with an egg nucleus from the mother, but the exact time of this process, known as fertilisation, is usually unknown. To obtain a more recognisable starting date, doctors ask a pregnant woman for the starting date of her last period and take off two weeks. The period when the egg is available for fertilising by the sperm is halfway between monthly periods (**menstruation**).

The fertilised egg is one of the largest cells in humans and just visible to the naked eye. Imagine the smallest dot you can make with a very sharp pencil and this is about the right size. After a short rest period, the fertilised egg begins to divide, first into two cells, then four, eight and so on. Very soon, the tiny structure becomes a ball of smaller cells. These cells begin to become organised into different areas. Some will be destined to form the new human being, but for a while the majority of the cells are preparing to become its coverings and developing placenta. It is important that these parts are ready to secure the food supply for the developing being as soon as it enters the womb or uterus of the mother. All the time so far has been spent in travelling down the tube leading from the ovary into the uterus.

At about one week old, the tiny structure, a hollow ball of cells, known as an embryo arrives in the uterus. The next few days are vital to the embryo – it must bury itself in the thickened lining of the mother's uterus (**implantation**) and secure a food supply before the mother's next period is due. If this does not happen, the embryo will be swept out of the mother's body with menstruation and will die. Once embedded in this way the embryo releases a hormone into the mother's blood which prevents the next menstruation.

Never again will growth be so rapid. By the third week after fertilisation (week five of the pregnancy calculation), the embryo has grown to be half a centimetre long and has started to develop brain, eyes, ears and limbs. There is even a tiny heart pumping blood to the newly formed placenta.

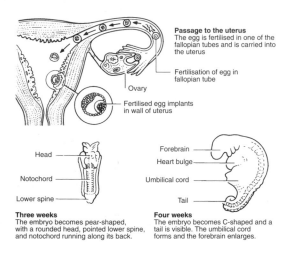

Passage to the uterus
The egg is fertilised in one of the fallopian tubes and is carried into the uterus

Fertilisation of egg in fallopian tube

Ovary

Fertilised egg implants in wall of uterus

Head
Notochord
Lower spine

Three weeks
The embryo becomes pear-shaped, with a rounded head, pointed lower spine, and notochord running along its back.

Forebrain
Heart bulge
Umbilical cord
Tail

Four weeks
The embryo becomes C-shaped and a tail is visible. The umbilical cord forms and the forebrain enlarges.

Internal organs at five weeks
All the internal organs have begun to form by the fifth week. During this critical stage of development, the embryo is vulnerable to harmful substances consumed by the mother (such as alcohol and drugs), which may cause defects.

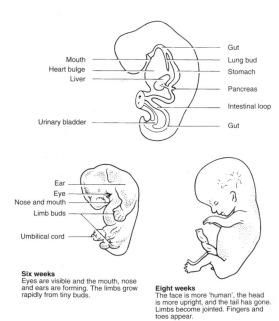

Mouth
Heart bulge
Liver
Urinary bladder

Gut
Lung bud
Stomach
Pancreas
Intestinal loop
Gut

Ear
Eye
Nose and mouth
Limb buds
Umbilical cord

Six weeks
Eyes are visible and the mouth, nose and ears are forming. The limbs grow rapidly from tiny buds.

Eight weeks
The face is more 'human', the head is more upright, and the tail has gone. Limbs become jointed. Fingers and toes appear.

Figure 4.1 Embryo development

The embryo continues to grow and develop at a rapid rate until at week eight all major organs have formed, there is a human-looking face with eyes, ears, nose and mouth, limbs have formed fingers and toes and the body length has increased to 3 cm. The name even changes – and from now until birth it is called a foetus.

The growth and development of internal organs continue and the next main stage is at 20 weeks. The mother will begin to feel movements of the foetus, weak at first, but getting stronger as the pregnancy progresses. The midwife looking after the mother can hear the foetus's heart beats through a special trumpet-shaped instrument called a foetal stethoscope. The heart beats are very fast and difficult to count without experience.

The foetus is clearly male or female because the external sex organs have developed and the total length is now around 25 cm. The weight of the foetus is close to half a kilogram already.

Try it

Look at Figure 4.2, which shows the length and weight of an embryo/foetus at intervals throughout pregnancy. You could draw two graphs to show the changes in length and weight up to birth. Find out the length and weight of a typical $6\frac{1}{2}$ month old foetus.

Time in months of pregnancy	Length in centimetres	Weight in kilograms
1	0.35	Almost none
2	3.5	0.05
3	8.5	0.1
4	15	0.2
5	23	0.4
6	30	0.75
7	38	1.5
8	45	2.0
9	51	3.5

Figure 4.2 Lengths and weights of a foetus during pregnancy

As you can see from your graph and from Fig. 4.2, at 9 months or 40 weeks the foetus is ready to be born.

It is about 50 cm long and weighs around 3.5 kg.

A newborn infant, often called a **neonate**, is a helpless individual and needs care and protection of parents or others to survive. The nervous system, which coordinates many bodily functions, is immature and needs time to develop. The digestive system is unable to take food that is not in an easily digestible form such as milk. Other body systems such as the circulatory and respiratory systems have undergone major changes as a result of birth, the change to air breathing and physical separation from the mother. A few weeks later, the baby's temperature regulating system is able to function properly and fat is deposited beneath the skin as an insulating layer.

For the first three months of a baby's life, movements are uncoordinated and many primitive reflexes are present. These gradually become replaced by learned responses.

Primitive reflexes

Rooting reflex

The baby turns its head in response to a touch on the cheek. This enables the baby to find the mother's breast and nipple. The sucking reflex occurs when the baby finds the nipple. A finger placed close to the corner of the mouth will cause this sort of response.

Grasp reflex

Any object put into the palm of the baby's hand will be grasped strongly. Often the grasp is so strong that the baby's weight can be supported.

Moro or startle reflex

When a baby is startled, its hands and arms are thrown outwards and the legs straightened. The baby often cries and then pulls the arms, hands and fingers inwards, as if trying to catch hold of something. This is one of the earliest reflexes to disappear.

Walking reflex

During the first two months, when a baby is held upright with feet touching the ground, the baby's legs make movements as if walking.

There are other reflexes, but these are the main ones. They are often examined by medical personnel to test the functioning of the baby's nervous system.

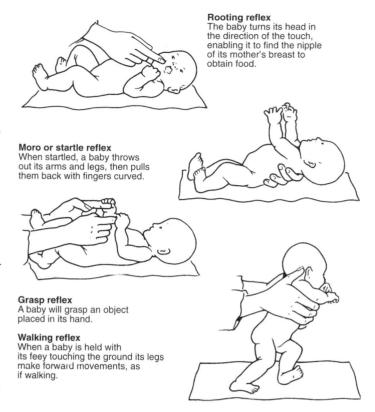

Rooting reflex
The baby turns its head in the direction of the touch, enabling it to find the nipple of its mother's breast to obtain food.

Moro or startle reflex
When startled, a baby throws out its arms and legs, then pulls them back with fingers curved.

Grasp reflex
A baby will grasp an object placed in its hand.

Walking reflex
When a baby is held with its feey touching the ground its legs make forward movements, as if walking.

Think it over

If you are able to visit a newborn baby, ask if a doctor or nurse can show you these reflexes.

Myelination

Nerve fibres attached to nerve cells gradually acquire a fatty sheath during the first years of life. This is known as myelination – nerve impulse travel a lot faster when they are insulated in this way. Many nerve cells have to 'connect up' with each other, and these two processes mean that both muscle and nerve coordination slowly increase.

Muscle coordination

Motor development is the term given to the development of muscle coordination. Its rate depends on the maturity of the nervous system. In Figure 4.3 average rates are given; many normal children will be slower or faster than these.

Age in months	Stage of motor development
Birth	Primitive reflexes only
1	Lifts up chin
2	Lifts chest up
3	Reaches for but does not grasp objects
4	Sits supported
5	Grasps objects
6	Sits on chair, reaches for and grasps objects
7	Stands with support
9	Stands alone but holding on
10	Crawls quickly
11	Walks holding one hand
12	Pulls up on furniture to stand
13	Crawls up stairs
14	Stands alone unsupported
15	Walks alone
24	Runs, picks things up without falling over
30	Stands on toes, jumps
36	Stands on one leg
48	Walks downstairs with one foot on each step

Figure 4.3 Average rates of motor development

Hand movements

Manipulation or hand movements can be picked out of a general motor development because they are easy to see and measure. Professional carers take notice of such fine movements in assessing development.

At six months children can reach for and grasp objects in their hands and transfer objects from one hand to another. Two months later, objects are held between fingers and the thumb, while around the first birthday, tiny objects can be picked up between the thumb and the first finger. A two-year-old child can hold a pencil like an adult and unscrew a top from a container.

Different growth rates

During childhood, different parts of the body grow at different rates.

Nervous system, sense organs and head grow very rapidly from birth to 6 years, reaching 90 per cent of the adult size. Six-year-old children can wear a parent's hat!

Reproductive organs grow very little until the onset of puberty (11–16 years) and then they grow rapidly to reach adult size.

General body growth is more steady than either of the above of parts, reaching adult size around 18–20 years, but with three 'spurts' at one year and 5–7 years and puberty. Girls generally start puberty earlier than boys – 11–13 years, with boys being two years later. The puberty spurt is caused by the secretion of sex hormones, oestrogen in girls and testosterone in boys. These hormones are responsible for the other changes which take place to turn the body of a child into that of an adult

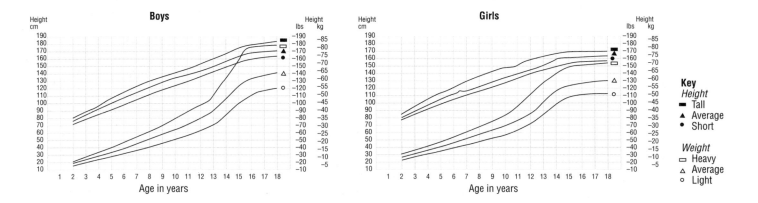

Figure 4.4 Growth charts of boys and girls, 1–18 years of age

male or female. These changes are known as the **secondary sexual characteristics**.

Male	Female
1 Enlargement of testes and penis	Enlargement of breasts and nipples
2 Pubic, facial, underarm hair growth	Pubic and underarm hair growth
3 Increased muscle and bone size leads to increased strength	Increased fat deposited under skin leads to increased curvy shape
4 Voice deepens (breaks)	Onset of menstruation

Figure 4.5 Secondary sexual characteristics

Development of teeth

A child's first set of teeth appears between six months and 3 years old. These are often known as the **milk teeth** or **deciduous teeth**. From about 6 years old, these teeth are gradually replaced by the permanent teeth. There are wide variations in dates when milk teeth come through and when permanent teeth replace them.

Factors influencing growth and development

Every individual has different patterns of growth and development because so many influences affect the rate of progress. A few of the influences on the speed of growth and development are:

- inherited characteristics
- health and disease of mother and child
- hormone balance which can influence growth
- environmental factors such as parents who smoke or drink alcohol
- type and quality of food eaten by the mother and child
- stimulation and activity, for example, a child will not hold a pencil correctly if he or she has never been given the opportunity to do so.

Adulthood

During adult life no major changes take place physically until females reach the end of their reproductive life. This is known as the **menopause** and takes place between 45 and 55 years of age. The ovaries have run out of eggs and as a result less of the female hormone oestrogen is produced. This produces physical changes, and some say

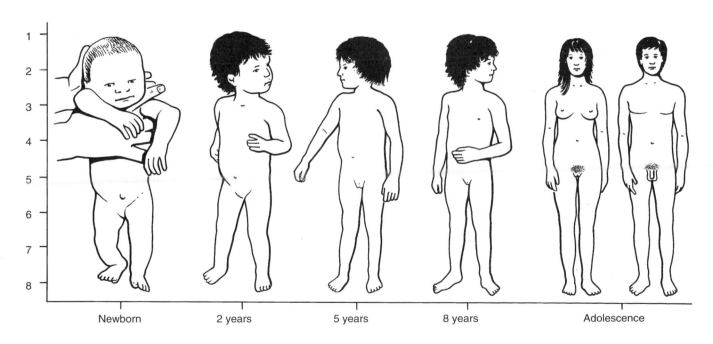

| | Newborn | 2 years | 5 years | 8 years | Adolescence |

Figure 4.6 Growth profiles from birth to adolescence

psychological changes occur as well, though this is less clear.

Menstruation stops and the reproductive organs shrink. Many women complain of hot flushes and night sweats, and body chemistry is altered. Bones become less dense and **osteoporosis** may develop later. (Osteoporosis causes bones to become more brittle and liable to fracture. It can occur in men who are ageing, but is much more common in women.) In recent years, hormone replacement therapy (HRT) (to reduce the effects of oestrogen deficiency in women) has become more widespread as a treatment. Males may continue to produce sperm until well into their 70s or later.

Loss of hair may affect both sexes in the middle years of life, but is much more common in men. Hair loss in men often starts from the temples, moving to the crown of the head, with a gradual widening of the bald area to the sides of the head.

Older people are usually less active than younger people but still continue to take in the same amount of food. This often results in a gradual thickening of the middle of the body, arms and legs, often called '**middle-age spread**'. Many people regard this as an inevitable stage in getting older, but it generally is a result of not matching food (and therefore energy) intake with energy output.

Older people

Physical and mental changes occur as time passes. Not many people live to be over 100 years old, although many can expect to live to 85 years of age.

Sexual activity does not necessarily decrease with age, although the rate of activity can decline due to illness, changes in social circumstances, personal beliefs and assumptions about later life. Elastic tissue, present in many organs, degenerates with age and this is most readily seen in wrinkled skin. Blood capillaries are more fragile, so bruising occurs from relatively little injury. Many people over the age of 65 experience a loss of visual ability and some hearing loss. Memory for recent events may also become less efficient than in younger people. Older people may have slower reaction times, compared with when they were young. Senses are less effective, particularly taste and smell.

Heart, breathing and circulation are all less efficient, causing difficulty when climbing stairs or hills or undertaking strenuous exercise.

Muscle tissues thins and weakens while joints become less mobile and total height decreases. Wound healing and resistance to infection decline with age. Functions of organs like the kidneys and the liver slowly decline.

There are positive aspects of growing older, however, despite the decline of physical systems – a combination of tolerance, wisdom and experience built up over the years often allows older people to avoid the mistakes made by younger, inexperienced people. Healthy older people may have greater emotional control and more developed understanding of their self-concept than younger people. Socially, older people may have time to appreciate people and the environment in which we all live.

Dementia

In the past, many people imagined that intellectual ability declined with age. There was a stereotyped image of older people becoming less mentally competent with every passing year until they eventually became demented. In the late 1940s and 1950s there were claims that people achieved a peak mental ability at 20 or 25 years of age. However, research over the past 40 years has revealed quite a different story. Many individuals who use their mental abilities and 'exercise their minds' seem to continue to increase their intellectual abilities. An increase in ability can continue into a person's 80s. Older people may slow down in terms of the speed at which they react, and they may experience increasing irritation because of poorer recent memory. But on average you can expect to keep the quality of your thinking at the level you achieve by adulthood. The key issue is to maintain your level of mental activity. There is evidence that people who do not do much mental reasoning tend to lose some of their mental skills as they age.

Dementia is not caused by any kind of wearing out and is not part of any general ageing process. Dementia is a pattern of symptoms probably caused by a variety of different influences. One type of dementia is caused by the breakdown of the blood supply to the brain. Another type (Alzheimer's-type dementia) involves a loss of brain tissue and the shrinkage of the brain, although the blood supply may be healthy.

Dementia can cause a range of disabilities. This includes a loss of ability to control emotion; difficulties in understanding other people; difficulties in communicating and expressing thoughts; serious loss of memory; disorientation in time and place; difficulties in recognising people and places; and difficulties in performing everyday living activities such as getting dressed.

People with severe dementia may lose the ability to swallow or even walk. Eventually, dementia may result in death.

Some types of dementia can develop in young adults and even adolescents. In general, dementing illness is uncommon before 65 years of age. Some studies suggest that 2–5 percent of people between 70 and 75 years of age may show signs of dementia. studies in the developed world suggest that 10–20 percent of people over the age of 85 years may experience symptoms associated with dementia.

It is important to note that 80–90 percent of over 85-year-olds do not show signs of dementing illness. Although older people may be more at risk of dementia than younger people, dementia is not a normal part of the lifecycle. As one expert has described it, 'dementia represents abnormal ageing'.

Figure 4.7 The majority of people over 85 years of age do not experience dementia

Intellectual development

As well as dividing life into physical stages, we can divide experience into areas such as intellectual, emotional and social. This helps us to focus on particular issues. We are unaware of life stages in our own experience – they are simply a way of classifying development. We experience life as a combination of physical, social, emotional and intellectual experience. Dividing life into categories just helps to explain things.

The category called intellectual development covers how we reason, think and understand our experience. Intellectual development covers our ways of remembering, use of language and how we make sense of things – our knowledge or 'cognition'.

Infancy

The first 18 months of life are a period when the infant cannot fully understand or use language. The word 'infancy' originally meant 'incapable of speech'. Although babies are born without language, they are born with a range of in-built responses.

Newborn babies will often make crawling motions if placed on their mother's body. The newborn baby will turn his or her head toward a finger touching the cheek, and attempt to suck it. It seems that babies are born with an in-built knowledge of how to suck and a desire to seek pleasurable sensations such as sweetness. Babies also seem to tune in to, or 'respond' to particular sounds and objects. They pay particular attention to human voices and faces. Some one-week-old babies can tell their mother's voice from other voices. By two weeks of age many babies can work out that their mother's voice and face go together. They get upset if they hear a different voice when they see their mother's face.

Think it over

Do babies find your face interesting?

The baby in the illustration is busy learning about people. Faces are particularly interesting to babies as they begin to learn about their world. Like all learning, it can be hard work. If the baby avoids looking at you, it may be because you are unfamiliar. Perhaps it is simply too much for the baby to cope with at present.

Babies seem to have an in-built ability to feed, to avoid pain and some other dangers. Most especially, babies have the ability to make relationships with their carers. These abilities are in-built. Babies are born ready to fit into their world and to begin learning about it.

Learning language

Infants can make crying sounds from birth. During the first two months of life, they will cry if they are in pain or are upset. In the third month or so of life, babies will begin to make 'cooing' sounds that mean the baby is happy. This develops into 'babbling' sounds, perhaps between four and seven months of age. It seems that babies experiment with ways of putting sounds together. Babbling involves making sounds like 'dadada' and 'mamamama', and later sounds like 'kagaga'. The child is building his or her ability to use sounds ready for later language. Research on hearing-impaired babies suggests that they 'babble' with sign language if they have been signed to from birth. This suggests that 'babbling' is not just learning to make sounds, but that it has something to do with organising our brains to use an in-built capacity for language.

It is probable that we have an in-built ability to learn languages. It is during the stage of infancy that children begin to adapt their biological readiness for language so that they will be able to speak one or more of the world's 4000 languages.

Adults seem to have a set reaction to talking to infants. This is called **baby talk**. Adults talk slowly in a high-pitched voice and use simplified facial expressions and sounds. Baby talk can be amusing when you see examples of it. Parents might say things like 'hello' in a high-pitched tone. 'He-ll-o, who's our little boy then?' may be said with a very

exaggerated smile and eyes focused on the baby's face. It may be that baby talk helps to make the baby interested. Very simple facial expressions and a high-pitched voice might help to keep the baby's attention, and to build a relationship between the baby and his or her carers. Baby talk is used by parents in many different cultures. Research suggests that babies respond to baby talk regardless of the language used.

Think it over

Do you or any of your friends have a pet? Do you or your friends use baby talk to it? It may be that humans have an in-built tendency to talk in a high-pitched voice and use simple expressions when they care for pets as well as babies. Do you think we see pets as baby-like?

Recent research suggests that infants listen to a wide range of sounds that might be used in language. One study found that infants tend to start to focus on particular sounds at eight months. This means that a child who is learning the Hindi language may focus on different sounds than a child who is learning the English language. Once infants have locked on to a language, they tend to lose their original awareness of the vast variety of sounds that could be used in different languages.

Towards the end of infancy, the child will begin to produce words. Usually, the child starts with name labels, such as 'mama', 'dada'. There is great variation in the age at which children first begin to speak. The social context of the child will influence when the child starts to use language and how it is used. It may be unwise to link the speed of the development of language to any theories of the child's ability.

Memory

Jerome Bruner suggests that there are three main ways in which people can learn and remember things. There are memories of actions that we have learned, memories of visual events or things we have seen, and memories of ideas we have learned through language.

Think it over

You can test how these types of memory work by trying some examples. You will know how to strike a match or tie a shoelace, but is this knowledge remembered as an action, as a set of mental images, or is it remembered using language? Try explaining how to strike a match or tie a shoelace to someone who deliberately only does exactly what you tell him or her. In other words, that person should carry out the action without using his or her own knowledge. You will probably have great difficulty in explaining exactly what to do. You may even get muddled. Most people's knowledge of things like striking a match and tying shoelaces are learned as actions. You instantly know how to do it – but you can't put it into words.

Try to describe the face of a close friend. If you are sighted (can see) then this memory will be remembered as a picture. Even if you can explain the picture in words, you will have to visualise your friend's face before you can explain it.

Now, finally, try to remember and explain what you know about human physical development. If you can remember ideas on physical development, you are probably using language. You may remember some diagrams using picture memory, but the rest of your knowledge will depend on concepts and language.

According to Bruner's idea, therefore, people can remember actions that they have learned. He called this **enactive memory** (memory for actions). He described picture memory as **iconic memory**, after the Greek word for picture, *icon*. Memories which are remembered in words are **symbolic**, because language is a set of symbols. Numbers are also symbols and we can remember a wide variety of symbolic ideas.

When we remember a friend's face, we are remembering a pattern. When we remember how to strike a match or tie a shoelace, we remember a pattern for the actions we have to perform. It may seem less obvious, but remembering details about physical development also involves recalling patterns of concepts and information. A psychological term for a pattern in our memory is a **schema**. When we talk about more than one pattern, we call them **schemata**.

When we learn and remember information, we don't record it as if our mind was a tape or video recorder. Our memories are almost never an exact copy of something we have heard or seen. When we remember a friend's face, we have to find the pattern – the schema – for that face and we have to re-invent the face in our imagination. When we remember details of physical development, they have to be 're-invented' in our imagination. Sometimes the details of our memory alter, so that information is lost and false information can become linked to the patterns in our memory. Remembering is a constant process of building and rebuilding patterns for actions, pictures, or language-based memories.

An infant's memory

Infants start to remember and learn from birth. Because they have no language, memory is linked to memory for actions and sensations like nice feelings, pain, warmth, smell, sound and vision. Two-week-old babies appear to be developing picture memories of their mother's face. They may know that a certain face pattern and voice pattern belong together in their mother. Babies also learn the smell of their mother while they are in skin-to-skin contact. As infants grow older, they will also begin to develop memories for actions.

Piaget's theory of development

Jean Piaget (1896–1980) was a famous psychologist who studied child development. To begin with, Piaget studied his own three children, by carefully watching how they developed and grew. He then went on to study children's **cognitive development** (how they understand the world) by observing children and asking them questions.

Children have to learn to adapt to the world they live in. To begin with, a baby will rely on in-built patterns for sucking, crawling and watching. But babies are active learners. Being able to suck is biologically necessary so that the baby can get milk from its mother's breast. The baby will adapt this behaviour in order to explore a wider range of objects. Babies explore by sucking toys, fingers, clothes and so on. They are able slowly to develop an understanding of objects, of their bodies and how to coordinate their muscles, to have an influence on the people and things around them.

According to Piaget, thinking is at first limited to memories of actions. The baby will remember grasping a toy. If given the toy, it may repeat the action. Piaget believed that the very young infant would not be able to remember objects that they could not see.

Suppose you were about to hand a toy rattle to a baby, but you dropped it and it rolled under the baby's cot.

If you use language (or symbolic) memory, you would think 'I've dropped it – it must have rolled somewhere – I'll find it'. If you used picture (or iconic) memory, you would still be able to picture the missing rattle and start searching for it. Piaget thought that young infants were unable to do either of these things. For example, if baby Jai drops his rattle and it goes out of his view, then according to Piaget, Jai would simply believe it had gone.

Because Jai has no picture memory for the rattle, he cannot look for it. It is a case of 'out of sight, out of mind'. Of course Jai might become upset and cry. Crying might make the rattle come back because Jai's father might come in and hand it back to him. Jai might develop a pattern memory or schema for crying, i.e. 'crying makes things better'.

A child has to learn that people and objects exist on their own. According to Piaget, Jai may even believe that when he closes his eyes, the world goes dark and ceases to exist. When he opens his eyes he makes it come back again.

The sensorimotor stage

Piaget called the first two years of a child's life the **sensorimotor stage**. At this time the child is learning to coordinate his or her senses and muscle (motor) behaviour. The sensorimotor stage ends when a child can picture objects and imagine that they exist even when they are not in view.

At the end of the sensorimotor period Jai will know that his father and mother still exist even if they are not with him. If he loses a toy, he will start to search for it, because he can picture it in his mind, and because he has learnt how objects work. If an object cannot be seen, it will have gone somewhere – it hasn't simply disappeared.

Recent research suggests that many eight-month-old infants begin to understand that objects exist on their own. Piaget may have underestimated how fast babies learn. A sensorimotor period lasting two years may be inaccurate. The way infants learn may turn out to be a complex story which may not fit into the simple idea of stages of development.

The development of language in childhood and adolescence

Young children are astonishingly good at learning words. Between 18 months and 6 years old, some children develop a 14 000-word vocabulary. According to the psychologist Philip Zimbardo, this works out at almost one word for each hour that the child is awake.

Figure 4.8 Intellect in Piaget's sensorimotor period

To begin with, children usually learn to use single words, often names of things. By naming things a child is able to divide his or her world into categories. Piaget explained that this would help the child to understand the world.

He believed that language developed because it helped the child to think more clearly. Other psychologists, such as Lev Vygotksy (1894–1934), thought that the main reason for language development was social. Once a child can label things, he or she can express needs and communicate more effectively with carers.

A single word like 'dadda' can be used to mean 'I want daddy to come here', 'I can see daddy', 'Where is daddy?', and so on. A carer can often tell what the child means because of the situation that the child is in and the way in which he or she says a word. Parents often repeat words back to the child. The use of baby talk helps to simplify language and encourages the child to learn. 'Daddy, there' might be a good reply to the infant who says 'dadda'.

Carers can help children to develop language skills by spending time talking with them, repeating what they say, then adding a little more. Children will often repeat words that carers use if they can understand them. Getting the right words for the right objects might be quite a struggle.

Children progress from one-word names to two-word sayings which tend to describe their social situation and thoughts. Phrases like 'Want drink', 'Cat goed', 'Daddy come' give a clear idea of what the child has seen or wants. At this stage, children seem to follow their own rules for language. 'Cat goed' means the cat went out. The child may only have the language for cat and go, so 'goed' makes sense to a child, even though he or she does not hear carers saying this. Although children learn a great deal of language by copying or imitating other people, it seems that they also follow their own rules and theories.

As language develops, children may pass through a 'naming stage'. This is where they are eager to learn the names for things, 'What that?', 'How called?', 'Why that?'. Constant talking with adults and learning their ways of speech help children to develop more grammatical speech. Even so, young children still over-use or over-extend their own ideas of how to use grammar. For example:

Carer: Where have you been?
Child: We went to feed the gooses.
Carer: What did you feed the geese with?
Child: Can't know.
Carer: Did you enjoy it?
Child: Yes, the geeses splashed.

Figure 4.9 Learning words such as cat, dog or daddy may be easy. The child may be able to picture the actual animal or person in his or her mind. It becomes difficult when the child tries to use these categories in a wider setting.

The way children speak, the way in which they organise their sayings (grammar) and the words they use will be greatly influenced by the people with whom they grow up. A child's culture, social class and day-to-day contact with adults will influence the speed of learning and style of language use.

A major influence on language development is the experience a child receives in the early days. Therefore, the emphasis put on language development by the family and/or the child's main carer is very important. Parents can help language development by reading stories and books, telling stories and having conversations. Children should be encouraged to use language by asking them questions which require more than a yes or no answer. Adults might repeat what a child says in order to correct and clarify a child's use of language.

Once children learn to read – around the age of 6+ – vocabulary will again increase. Before being able to read, new vocabulary consists only of words heard and memorised, but once children can read, they can add new words without having heard them in conversation. As they grow older they can actively extend their vocabulary by looking up the definition of new words.

After the age of 6 children may be able to adjust their speech according to whom they are talking to, i.e. the language they use with their friends is quite often different from that used to a teacher or parent. To a teacher, the child may describe an outing as being good, to a friend as 'class'.

The ability to read allows the child the potential to continue to increase his or her vocabulary throughout life. The use of language can hold the

key to future success. Adolescence is a period when many exams may be taken and a student's success in these can be affected by the command of language.

Language in adolescence continues to develop as an individual learns new concepts and ideas, but this growth is at a slower rate to that of a child. Adolescents also have their own 'code' which they use with their peers, and a different way of talking to adults. Through various means, such as reading books and the media, an adult may continue to develop linguistic skills.

After developing a style of speech based on that of their carer, children still have to learn the social skills and often unstated rules of conversation. A 6-year-old may well have clear language, but does not yet understand the social norms surrounding conversation. For example, on a busy bus he or she may ask questions like 'Why is that woman fat?', 'Why has that man got no hair?'. Sensible questions, but not acceptable things to ask publicly in terms of general British culture!

As well as learning norms of conversational behaviour, the older child and adolescent usually continues to develop non-verbal skills. The coordination of body language with spoken language continues into adulthood. Adults often have to improve their use of facial expression, voice tone and so on to communicate subtle messages (see Chapter 10). Constantly changing social and employment settings means that adults can never stop learning. Adults may need to review and develop their use of terminology and body language.

A final distinction that is sometimes made between children's language and adult language involves the skills of being able to understand another person's viewpoint. Listening to others and guessing what they feel and think is a specialist skill which many adults find useful in relationship building and employment settings. This skill is analysed in detail in Chapter 10.

Development of intellect in childhood and adolescence

Most 2-year-olds will have a memory pattern for their own body. They will understand that objects and other people have a separate existence from their own body. As children develop language, they have a new way of making sense of their world. They can remember actions, sensations and images, and how they can use words to classify thoughts and feelings. Objects, people, events and feelings can be remembered using language. Language provides a new type of thinking for the child.

While psychologists like Piaget and Vygotksy disagreed over why and how language developed, there is general agreement that language provides the child with a new way of thinking, learning and understanding.

> Piaget believed that there were four developmental stages. These are:
>
> - Sensorimotor stage (learning to use senses and muscles)
> - Pre-operational stage (pre-logical stage)
> - Concrete operational stage (limited logic stage)
> - Formal operational stage (formal logic/adult reasoning).

In Piaget's original theory, the sensorimotor stage lasted from birth to about 2 years. The majority of children were thought to go through the pre-operational stage between 2 and 7 years of age. The concrete operational stage lasted from 7 to 11 years. The formal operational stage was supposed to start at 11. Piaget believed that the stages of sensorimotor, pre-operational, concrete and formal logic were caused by an in-built pattern of development which all people went through. These ideas and the linking of the stages to age groups, are now the subject of argument. However some psychologists agree that Piaget's observations may describe an interesting pattern which can help us understand how thinking skills develop.

Pre-operational thinking

After the sensorimotor stage, language influences the child's thinking. Piaget observed that 2–4-year-olds often fail to understand concepts properly. A 2-year-old might use the word dog to mean any kind of animal he sees. It takes time for children to learn to use words in the same way that adults do. By the age of 4 and 5, children can use concepts, but to Piaget, they didn't seem to understand the sense behind their use of language.

For instance, Piaget laid out two rows of five counters (see Figure 4.10).

Children aged 4–7 agreed that there were the same number of counters in each line. Piaget then spaced the counters in one of the lines to make it longer.

Pre-operational children said that there were more counters in the long line, even though they had seen

Figure 4.10 When the counters are spaced differently, pre-operational stage children would say there were more counters in one line than the other

him rearrange the counters. The pre-operational child is not being logical.

In another famous experiment, Piaget filled two glass jars with water. Pre-operational children agreed that there was the same amount in each jar. Piaget then took one jar and poured the water into a taller, thinner jar. The children usually agreed that all the water had gone in, but when they were asked to judge if the amounts of water in the jars were the same, the children often said that there was more water in the taller jar! Some children said there was less in the taller jar because it was thinner. Again, this is not logical as the shape of the jar cannot make water increase or disappear. Yet 4–7-year-old children did not seem to understand this.

A third experiment involved asking a child to imagine the view from different sides of a model of some mountains. Pre-operational children thought that other people's views would be the same as their view from where they were sitting. Piaget claimed that this demonstrated that pre-operational children were **egocentric**. Egocentric means that the children could not imagine that other people would have different thoughts or experiences to their own. An egocentric child will believe that everyone will think and see what he or she thinks and sees.

Figure 4.11 Pre-operational children get confused by the way things look

A modern view of pre-operational thinking

The reasons why children get 'logical' tasks wrong may not be because they are completely illogical or egocentric. It might be that they did not fully understand the instructions they were given or that young children's memories are focused on the way things look, rather than the meaning of language.

Jerome Bruner reported a study which looked at the water and jars problem. This time the experiment used language and ideas which were familiar to the child. The adult in charge of the experiment started with two full jars and the children agreed that there was the same water in each.

The adult then floated a small plastic duck on the water in one of the jars, explaining that this was now the duck's water.

The adult then kept the child's interest by talking about the duck, explaining that the duck was going to move and take all its water with it.

Children could now cope with the change. They said that the two amounts of water were the same because the duck kept its water.

Children may be able to make logical judgements if the problems are simple and put in language that they can understand. Bruner believed that in Piaget's

Figure 4.12 Pre-operational children can be logical

jars experiment, young children were distracted by the way the jars looked. They might have understood that the water stayed the same, but became confused because picture (or iconic) memory suggested that the increased height of the jar should make it bigger.

Another researcher, James McGarrigle, repeated the counters experiment. This time a 'naughty teddy' (held by an adult) rearranged the two rows of counters into a long line.

Children aged 5–6 were now more able to understand that there were still the same number of counters. In a play-type setting, children may not be so fixed on the 'look' of a line.

Other research has shown that children can imagine views which are different from their own. Once again, it is important that children understand the language of the task and that they are interested in it.

It is clear that very young children take time to understand how to use concepts and that 4–7-year-olds can easily make illogical judgements. It is likely,

Figure 4.13 Children may give the right answer when the task is treated like a game

however, that children do develop an understanding of the logic in language between 4 and 7 years of age. Piaget may have underestimated children's thinking ability. If a child fails to solve a problem correctly, it does not necessarily mean that he or she has no understanding at all.

Concrete operations

Piaget observed that 7–11-year-olds rarely made illogical decisions so long as the problems set for them were practical. Children in the 'concrete' stage cannot cope with abstract problems. For example, if you ask a question like 'Ajit is taller than Corinne, but Ajit is smaller than Lesley, so who is the tallest?', an 8-year-old is unlikely to be able to answer this correctly. He or she may not be able to imagine the information in a way that will give the answer. If the child could see Ajit, Corinne and Lesley, then he or she would be able to point to the one who is tallest.

Children aged 8–11 may tend to concentrate on collecting information or facts about topics that interest them. Their real understanding may still be limited compared to older children and adolescents.

Formal operations

Piaget observed adolescents who had developed abstract reasoning. These individuals could engage in philosophical debate about truth, justice and the purpose of life. People with formal logic can engage in scientific problem solving. They can think things

through without having to handle or see practical examples.

Piaget originally believed that formal operations naturally developed in children soon after the age of 11.

However, there is now a great deal of evidence to suggest that many people never develop the use of formal logic or abstract reasoning. One study in the 1970s even found that many university students in the UK could not solve logical puzzles in the way Piaget's theory predicted. Cross-cultural studies suggest that formal logic only develops in people whose education and social context train them for it. It may be that formal operations does not represent a stage of development. Perhaps, instead, formal operations represent a particular area of skill which some people are able to develop.

Towards the end of his life, Piaget suggested that much of what we learn doesn't involve thinking in language. But learning to analyse actions using abstract concepts and theories can greatly improve our performance. For example, consider how we learn to ride a bicycle.

Learning to ride a bicycle

One of the first tasks is to learn how to keep your balance. It takes a lot of practice until you get the feel of this. What you learn is how to control your body so that you don't fall off. Talking or thinking about this is unlikely to help. You learn to control your balance by doing it.

Figure 4.14 At first, you 'just do it' – or fall over!

Next you have to learn to take corners at speed. This is a complicated action involving balance and turning the handlebars. Learning this is a matter of trial and error – not thinking in words.

Many people learn to ride a bicycle by watching someone else doing it and reacting to what happens while they are on the road. For some people that's all there is to it! You can ride or you can't – there is nothing to think about.

Piaget believed that being able to imagine practical actions, using concepts, would provide special advantages. Real understanding only comes about when you can think something through.

An instructor or a teacher will need not only to have been successful in practical skills, but will also need to be able to use concepts in order to understand and analyse how things happen. In Figure 4.15 Mesha is training for cycle races. Her coach uses concepts of angles and velocity to help her to improve her performance.

Figure 4.15 Concepts help us to understand and improve our skills

Intellectual developments in adolescence and adulthood may have a lot to do with learning to use concepts and theories in our imagination – these can improve our understanding of practical skills.

Learning to play snooker

You could learn the feel of the cue and use trial and error to hit balls. Young children can do this. Some,

however, do not understand what they are doing. They think that the balls bounce off the cushion like this:

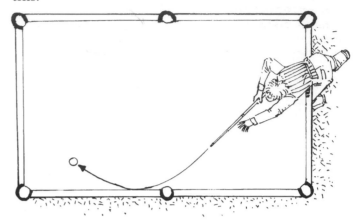

Some older children think that balls all bounce at right angles because it looks as if this is the case.

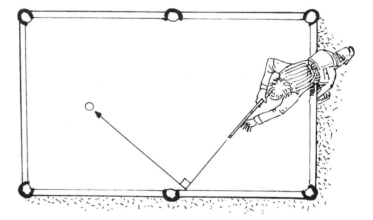

Real understanding and expert performance involve understanding how angles work, or that balls bounce off the cushion at the exact angle at which they come in.

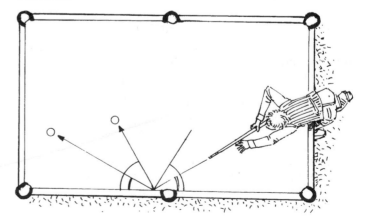

If you know this and can explain it, you can improve your performance and train others.

As a psychologist once said, 'There is nothing as practical as a good theory'. Learning during adolescence may need to focus on using concepts and ideas.

Intellectual development during adulthood and later life

Many adults need to continue to develop their mental skills. Adults who work in professional jobs may develop special mental skills where they control and monitor their own thought processes. Many adults specialise in particular styles or areas of mental reasoning.

Some American writers argue that adulthood involves learning to cope with continual uncertainties, inconsistencies and contradictions. Logic alone may not be sufficient to cope with life. As people grow older, happiness may depend on what many cultures call wisdom.

In general, mental abilities increase with age, provided they are used constantly. There is some evidence that mental ability can decline if it is not used. This may be particularly important in later life. Mental exercise may be as important as physical exercise for many older people.

Emotional and social development

Emotional and social development are often linked together because development in one is usually dependent on the other. For example, if a child is to make stable social relationships, a balanced emotional state is important. Social development looks at people's relationships and interactions with others; emotional development looks at feelings and how an individual copes with relationships and self-concept.

The foundations for emotional and social development are built as a child grows up. Effective social and emotional development leads to a positive self-concept and self-esteem. For self-esteem to develop, a child needs love, understanding and encouragement from those around him or her. This will enable the child to form meaningful relationships with others.

Emotional development

A very young infant may have no idea of the existence of his or her body. Young infants may know how to react to people – they may smile and 'coo' at human faces. Yet when infants close their eyes, they may feel that the world disappears. Babies may not be able to tell that the world is separate from themselves. Infants gradually learn to understand their own body as separate from the objects that they see and touch, and separate from other people such as their mother. This may be the beginning of a sense of self.

Infancy and the development of emotional bonds of love

Between the first six weeks and six months of life, babies may respond to other human faces and voices. Babies may not be able to recognise every face they see or be able to tell voices apart. Before six months of age, babies may not be emotionally attached to familiar people, although they may recognise the smell, voice and face of their mother.

Between six and nine months, babies seem to begin to make an attachment to their main care-givers. An infant's pattern of crying, smiling and babbling may indicate feelings of attachment or making emotional bonds with others.

John Bowlby's theory of bonding

John Bowlby studied mothers and babies in the mid-1940s, shortly after the end of the Second World War. Bowlby had noticed that some kinds of baby animals would make very fixed emotional bonds with their parents. For examples, baby ducklings would attach themselves to, and follow, whom ever they presumed to be their mother. Wild ducklings naturally attach themselves to the mother duck. Bowlby had studied research which showed that ducklings would attach themselves to people if only humans were present during a critical period when the duckling needed to bond. Bowlby's studies of infants led him to conclude that human babies were similar to some types of animals such as ducks. Bowlby believed that there was a biological need for mothers and babies to be together, and that there was a sensitive or critical period for mothers and babies to form this attachment which is known as **bonding**.

If the bond of love between a baby and his or her mother is broken through separation, then Bowlby believed that lasting psychological damage would be done to the child. If a mother left her infant to go to work every day or left to go into hospital, for example, there might be a risk of damage. Bowlby believed that children who suffered separation might grow up to be unable to love, or show affection. Separated children might not care about other people and might also fail to learn properly at school. They might even be more likely to turn to crime when they grew up.

Other researchers have questioned whether babies are really affected so seriously by separation. Michael Rutter found evidence which suggests that it is the quality of emotional attachment between a carer and the infant that matters. Not being able to make an attachment may damage a child emotionally. But it is the making of a bond of love between the baby and a carer that matters, not whether temporary separations occur.

There is also research which suggests that babies can and do make bonds with their father and with their brothers, sisters, or other carers! Carers can be men. In one study undertaken in the 1960s, almost one-third of 18-month-old infants had made their main attachment to their fathers.

It seems that babies give their love to the person(s) who give them the most quality affection and time.

Alan and Ann Clarke reviewed a wide range of research in the 1970s. They concluded that children can recover from almost any bad psychological experience provided that later experience makes up for it. It is whole life experience and not just the first 18 months of an infant's life that will decide whether a child grows up to care about other people, or takes to a life of crime. Even though people can recover from separation and poor relationships, it is very important that infants do have a chance to make a loving relationship or bond with a carer. The first part of a person's life may set the pattern for what will happen later. A lack of love in early life could be a very bad start for a child's emotional development. It would be unwise just to hope that some later improvement in quality of life could make up for it.

Think it over

The theory that mothers must always be with their babies or risk damaging them emotionally began in the 1940s when women had been running the country's factories during the war.

Would this be a popular idea with men returning from the war with little prospect of a job?

A psychological theory which pressurised women to stay at home and look after the family rather than going out to work, would be very useful to a country trying to readjust to the return of men from the Second World War. Gradually, the day nurseries which had been opened to care for children while their mothers worked for the war effort were closed and women were encouraged to become housewives once more.

The first emotional stage of a child's development may involve learning to attach to a carer or carers. In some cultures it will be the mother who provides most of the attention and physical contact with an infant, and so a boy or a girl's first emotional attachment will be with his or her mother. Where men provide the care, a baby's attachment could be with them.

The development of independence and self-confidence

During the first year of life, babies are dependent on their carers. They show distress at separation. The fear and unhappiness shown by a baby when a parent is about to leave, is an example of emotional behaviour. This is known as **separation anxiety**.

At the age of 2, this anxiety may diminish. Children who have been able to form firm attachments in the early months and have a secure home life may feel confident and able to explore the world around them. Children may begin to make relationships with other adults and children with whom they come into contact. They may have temporary difficulties with relationships when they start playgroup or nursery and they may try to cling to their parents, but this is usually just a temporary problem.

As children develop independence, they start to want to do everything for themselves. A child may refuse offers of help, even when it is really needed. A child will develop likes and dislikes and he or she will also have a very strong need to fulfil these desires, often immediately. The child's wishes may be different from those caring for him or her and this can lead to unhappiness as the child struggles between exerting his or her independence and his or her need to be loved by adults.

By the age of 3, a child may see himself or herself as an independent person, separate from his or her carer. The child may begin to attach to people and animals such as relatives and pets. A child may also show concern and worry for those around him or her.

Between 4 and 5 years, children are often self-confident and often boisterous. They do not like adults to interfere with a task they are doing, but may like to know adults are there for reassurance and help when required. A child of this age may frequently demand attention and praise, for example, saying 'Look at me' when doing something. Sometimes this is misunderstood as 'showing off', but it is an essential part of skill-building and the development of the child's self-confidence.

By the age of 5 or 6 years, increasing independence from the family is reflected in the importance of people outside the family in influencing the child. A child may enjoy the company of his or her peer group and same-gender friendships flourish. Friendships become increasingly important and complex. As children grow older, friendship groups may become smaller and children are more likely to have one 'best friend'. although children become increasingly independent from their immediate family, there is a need for close relationships with others for social and emotional reasons.

Adolescence is a period of life when individuals experience many changes including a greater need for 'freedom' and independence. During this stage, the peer group becomes increasingly important. It acts as a sounding board where adolescents can try out new identities, values and behaviours. Historically, adolescents have questioned adult authority and the standards that surround them in Western culture and the peer group may provide support during this period of uncertainty. Adolescents may need to develop independence and establish an independent self-concept. Adulthood often involves complete independence from parents. This is usually accompanied by moving out of the family home and taking on new, responsible roles. Most adults take on the responsibility of making decisions for themselves.

During adulthood, individuals may form close relationships with new partners. Responsibilities resulting from these may include living as part of a 'couple' or family. This means that adults may have to take account of others' opinions, wants or needs, and therefore will not be operating as isolated individuals.

Emotional development continues throughout life. The theorist Eric Erikson thought that people went through eight stages of self-development in a lifetime. These stages involved developing positive views of oneself. Not everyone manages to develop these positive qualities, though. The eight stages, based on Erikson's theory, are described in Figure 4.16.

Approximate age range	Self-development
0–1½ years	Infants need to develop a sense of trust and safety from their emotional experiences.
1½–3 years	Children need to develop self-control. They need to control the way their bodies work and develop a sense of willpower.
3½–7 years	Children need to develop a sense of initiative and a sense of purpose, confidence and self-worth.
Late childhood	Children need to understand themselves as being competent and not inferior to others in their social group.
Adolescence	Adolescents have to develop a secure self-concept and understanding of their social roles. This is called developing an identity.
Early adulthood	Adults need to be able to love and share their sense of themselves with partners or close friends. This is called intimacy.
Adulthood	Older adults need to remain emotionally involved with others rather than becoming inward-looking and selfish. This is called being generative.
Later life	Towards the end of life, adults need to feel that their life has had a meaning and been worthwhile. Older people need to achieve a state of 'wisdom'.

Figure 4.16 Emotional development based on Erikson's eight stages

There have been many other explanations of emotional development. Some writers argue that life doesn't really come in stages. People experience gradual changes and pressures to adapt. Erikson argued that his stages would be true in all cultures. Some writers think that the stages only really work in relation to European and North American culture though. Many people do accept that children need to develop a sense of **self-confidence**. This sense of self-confidence might first develop in relation to social activities at school with friends and with family. Erikson's stages of 'initiative' and 'competence' would describe the development of self-confidence in a child. There is widespread agreement that during adolescence in European culture, young men and women need to develop a sense of **independence**. This ability to become independent of parents and family depends on the development of a sense of **self-concept** or **identity**.

Adult self-confidence and independence

After adolescence, emotional development seems to be very varied. Not everyone develops a sense of self-respect and self-confidence. Some adults have difficulty forming loving relationships. Some adults experience long periods of conflict within their relationships with partners, friends and work colleagues. Although adults develop independence and self-confidence, it seems that this does not guarantee a happy life.

Figure 4.17 Independence and self-confidence may be necessary to enjoy life. Older adults may choose to enjoy independence and self-confidence in a different way from young people.

Some writers have suggested that adults have to learn to balance their self-confidence and independence with the demands of others before adult life can be satisfying. This means that adults often learn to be flexible in their feelings. They learn to understand that there are few simple answers to complex problems. Emotionally, adults have to accept that there are many different viewpoints – one person's opinion may be different from someone else's. Although each person is an individual, we all depend on other people to make our lives worthwhile and meaningful. Adult emotions may become increasingly complex as people learn to cope with the contradictions and paradoxes of life. Older adults sometimes develop a deep sense of independence and satisfaction with life, and yet they may not feel independent of the broad range of social relationships that they enjoy.

Social development

During infancy, babies learn to copy and imitate their carers. The attachments and language they learn lay the foundation for later social behaviour. From the age of 12 months infants might form attachments with older brothers or sisters and may imitate or copy their behaviour. Being brought up with older children or having lots of adult company might help with a child's social or intellectual development.

Social interaction plays a part in helping children discover who they are and what they can do. Social development is highlighted through children's reactions to and relationships with others. Linked closely with this is the development of cooperation skills. Figure 4.18 highlights this development through early childhood.

Age	Key feature
1–3 months	Babies respond to human contact by smiling, quietening when picked up and through body responses. Babies are fascinated by human faces.
3–6 months	Babies smile at most people but may begin to prefer main carer(s). Patterns of 'talking' reflect turn-taking.
6–9 months	Fear of strangers may start, and also distress if separated from carers.
9–12 months	Stranger fear may increase. Comfort objects may create security for the infant. Infants may demonstrate different emotions such as anger or frustration. Infants may look for attention.
1–2 years	Infants may need lots of reassurance. The infant may become more independent and assertive, or more defiant. Temper tantrums may start. Distraction may be used by an adult to avoid a tantrum when a child wants to do something a carer may feel is unsuitable or unsafe. Young children may like routines. They may be still wary of strangers but show some interest in them. The child may follow the carer around and be more social. Some feelings are expressed through play. The child may begin to be interested in other children but may not play with them. Play is solitary.
2–3 years	Children's emotions may become more balanced and stable, but mood swings still occur. This is the 'classic' age for temper tantrums. Behaviour can switch from clingy to independent or from rebellious to cooperative. Children may begin to gain confidence while away from carers. Children may need support to deal with new situations. They may show signs of jealousy of brothers and sisters. Children may play side by side with other children, and there may be more conversation as well as clashes of will. Given the choice, a child may prefer to play alone.
3–5 years	Children may become more secure emotionally and more independent but still need support to cope with new situations. Children may seek adult approval and enjoy helping adults. Children may begin to form social relationships. Friendships may start to occupy a good deal of a child's life. Children become more friendly and helpful to other children, but signs of jealousy may appear. Children may be interested in the actions and reactions of other children and this forms the basis of real play.
5–7 years	Children engage in cooperative play, i.e. playing with others and having shared goals. Children may also support each other. Initially they may be happy playing in pairs, but by the age of 6, groups have often become bigger. Sets of friends come and go and children may join formal groups such as brownies, beavers or cubs. Children become increasingly confident. They are more aware of right and wrong, and feel guilty when they are not behaving as expected.

Figure 4.18 Development of cooperation skills

Relationships in adolescence and adulthood

The peer group becomes increasingly important in adolescence. Friendships become more intense as they may seem to fill a hole left by changing relationships with parents.

Adolescents often socialise in large groups, which are formed essentially for social relations. Initially, friendships are predominantly with the same gender. However, as adolescence progresses, relationships with the opposite gender become more important.

Relationships with parents can become tense as the child grows into an adult – a time when communication between parent and child is extremely important.

Social relationships in adulthood are extremely variable and greatly influenced by the class and culture of individuals. Studies of people in the UK and North America suggest that, in general, people gain a lot of satisfaction from partnerships and friendships. Good relationships with partners and friends seem to help people to live more fulfilled and healthy lives.

Social relationships are explored further later in this chapter and also in Chapters 5 and 6.

Influences on self-concept

Self and concepts

Self-concept is a term used to describe the way a person sees himself or herself as a whole. It includes the way we would describe who we are and how much we value ourselves.

Infants develop a sense of their own body before they can use language. Our first sense of self is probably remembered as actions or picture memories for actions that we have learned to do. As children's understanding of language increases, they are able to describe themselves using words. If you ask an 8-year-old to describe herself, she might say, 'Well, I am a girl, I have dark hair and I like swimming, um, and I like my mum, and I live at 58 Uplands Road'.

Eight-year-olds can describe things about themselves, but they are unable to evaluate themselves. The 8-year-old described above can only think in terms of 'concrete' or factual descriptions of things, and also how much she likes them. Adolescents might be able to describe themselves using abstract concepts.

An adolescent might respond, 'Well, I'd say I was friendly. I get on well with people, a bit attractive – even if I say so myself [laugh]. I'm broke this week, I work hard, I am kind and I hate people who are cruel to animals. I'm honest…well, most of the time.'

This adolescent is using concepts to evaluate his sense of who he is. Piaget's theory describes how the ability to use concepts develops. Adolescents may be able to think using abstract concepts. Children are unlikely to be able to do this. An important factor which influences a person's self-concept is his or her level of intellectual development. The ability to use abstract concepts to evaluate yourself is likely to depend on the education you have received.

Try it

If you mix with children, you could ask them to explain who they are and what they enjoy. Compare their answers to the type of answers adults would give you. Exploring the way children explain their ideas of self may help you to write a report about intellectual development.

Self in childhood

A 2-year-old may have an awareness of his or her actions, but no self-concept as such. A deeper sense of self probably starts to develop as the child begins to mix with other children and develop socially. George Mead, a famous theorist in the 1930s, believed that children first began to understand an idea of self during their play and social activity with other people. Very young children are excellent imitators. They will copy the actions of older children and adults. Some children will even pretend to be a cat or other animal they have seen. By acting things out, children learn to remember and understand their world. 'Acting things out' soon moves on to acting out the roles that children see other people playing.

Children might act out the roles of a teacher and naughty children. One child pretends to be the teacher and the other children pretend to be naughty. Usually, the teacher is much stricter and the children much more obedient than in real life!

Children can only play-act in this way because they can imagine how adults act. They use their imagination to create characters. The child pretending to be the teacher will copy things he or she has seen on television, things the other children have acted out, and adult behaviours they have

experienced. Children's ability to imitate and imagine means that they can begin to use concepts to explain how people behave. The children are 'naughty'. The teacher might be 'strict' or 'kind' and so on.

Because children can create an imaginary world of other people, they can also begin to imagine themselves. A 5-year-old can begin to create an idea of 'me' using his or her imagination.

Think it over

Did you ever have an imaginary friend when you were 5 or 6 years old? Have you met any children who have imaginary pets, or talk to imaginary people? Sometimes, if you watch young children playing you may be able to see them inventing characters. One child might tell off his imaginary friend, another might take an imaginary dog for a walk. Watching young children may help you to understand how children develop their concepts of other people and themselves.

Children watch the way older children and adults act. They come to understand the roles that adults play. Children will copy the way they see their parents behave. They copy the way they see men and women behave. They copy shop assistants, bus drivers and various work roles. Children use their imagination to act out and understand how people work within their culture.

In the past, children would often play games like doctors and nurses. The girl acts out a caring and submissive role as the nurse. The boy pretends to be important, to make decisions and to have authority. By imitating what they think are adult characters, children learn about gender roles – if you are a girl, then you must be gentle and caring, but boys grow up to make the decisions and be important.

Children may learn about gender roles at an early age. These roles may become part of their self-concept during adolescence and later life. Of course, not every child lives in the same cultural situation. Britain is a multi-cultural society, and this means that there are many different beliefs and values about issues such as gender. Some children may grow up to believe that boys should be more important and powerful than girls. Other children will grow up having developed different beliefs. Some children may see girls as clever, resourceful and in control of social situations.

As children grow up, they will be part of a family or caring group. This is called **primary** (or first) **socialisation**. Children copy the ways of their carers during this period. The friends we mix with gradually become more important to our understanding of social behaviour. Learning from friendship groups is called **secondary** (or later) **socialisation**. Socialisation is the process of learning the belief systems of a social group, in order to become part of that group and in order to play roles within that group.

Socialisation will enable many children to develop a sense of self-confidence. They will feel that they belong within their family or care group. Children may feel that they are liked, loved and important. They may develop a sense of being competent and skilled at school, work and sport. The child's relationships within the groups of people they mix with will create this self-confidence. For other children, socialisation may not go so smoothly. Children also experience rejection, failure and a sense of not being good at school work, sport, etc. Some children may feel that they do not belong to a group. Failure to identify with other people, or failure to belong, may influence the sense of self and self-confidence that a child is developing.

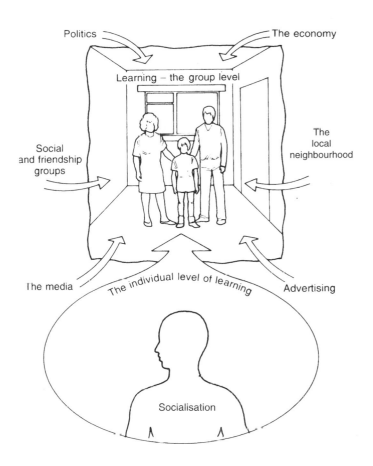

Figure 4.19 The individual learns about the beliefs of the social group – socialisation

good at the sport or people who were popular. Everyone would murmur, 'Oh good, we've got so and so'. The last people to be picked were the people who were poor at sport. The murmurs would change to, 'Oh no, we've got them – do we have to have so and so?' The last people do not belong – they are not wanted. Imagine how this feeling of rejection might influence the sense of self that a person is developing.

Self-concept in adolescence

Children develop a sense of self or a sense of 'me' because they can use their imagination to understand social behaviour. The process of socialisation, the friends or groups with which a person mixes, will influence how they understand this sense of self.

At some time during adolescence many people develop a level of physical, intellectual, social and

Think it over

At school, did you ever have to wait in line to be picked for a team? The team leaders would start by picking the people who were

Figure 4.20 It can be hard if you're the last one chosen

emotional maturity that leads to their sense of self becoming a developed self-concept or identity.

Physical influences

Sexual maturity causes adolescent males and females to become aware of their own sexual needs and desires. Erikson believed that the development of sexuality marked the end of childhood and childhood relationships with parents. Sexual needs would cause adolescents to seek independence from their carers. Sexually aware adolescents would need to develop a new sense of themselves. They would need a sense of identity or a working self-concept to develop sexual relationships.

Intellectual influences

Many adolescents may be able to think about themselves using abstract concepts. This new power of thought can enable a person to design his or her own self-concept! For instance, an 8-year-old might look in the mirror and think 'That's me'. That might be all she thinks! A 16-year-old is likely to look in the mirror and evaluate himself, 'So that's me – I'd like

to be more like my friend. Yes – shorter hair, earring, leather jacket – more muscles, how do I do it? OK, I buy the earring on Wednesday, have my hair cut next Tuesday, go to the gym Monday nights – I'll need to save money for the jacket'. Many adolescents can plan and evaluate how they want to look. They take control of their lives, using abstract powers of imagination.

Figure 4.21 An 8-year-old may not evaluate herself

Figure 4.22 Adults can change themselves, because they can evaluate themselves

Social influences

Appearance may identify you as a member of a particular kind of group. Your hairstyle, dress and behaviour can send messages about your gender, age group, wealth, social status, beliefs, culture. It is often important to present an image of ourselves when we meet people and seek to make relationships with them. Hairstyle and dress can be ways of expressing self-concept; ways of showing whom we identify with and what we want to be.

Friendship groups will influence style of dress and appearance during adolescence. It is important to be accepted by friends, but also to declare independence from adults who may have controlled our lives up to this point. Adolescents will often adopt clothing styles which are similar to one another, but very different from what their parents' generation would wear!

Appearance can make statements about age and culture of an individual. No one looks attractive to everyone. Your clothes and body shape will be seen differently by different groups (see Figure 4.23). Be careful to choose a self-presentation style to fit the groups/people you would like to mix with. Awareness of other people and their cultures may be necessary for self-awareness. Adolescents' self-concept will include an idea of whom each individual identifies with, whom they think they are like and whom they are not like. A person's self-concept will develop from an understanding of his or her social and cultural background.

Emotional maturity and self-concept

Emotional maturity will involve a sense of independence from parents and a clear, secure sense of who you are. A clear concept of self or self-concept should help a person to feel self-confidence in relationships with other people.

Developing a clear self-concept might lead a person to feel worthwhile, to have a sense of purpose, a feeling of being special and a sense of personal history. This understanding of self may give us the confidence to cope with changes in relationships and changes in our work.

Self-concept might motivate individuals to achieve. A strong sense of individual self might give a person the courage to cope with job interviews, exams and the stresses involved in achieving qualifications. A positive self-concept might be needed before a person can develop stable sexual relationships – at least in cultures that see the development of relationships as an individual task. A weak sense of self might leave an adult with emotional problems. Erikson thought that there was no feeling of being alive unless a person had this feeling of self. Happiness and coping with life might depend on your sense of self.

If understanding yourself – having a self-concept – is an important achievement for adults, then what about people who cannot explain their idea of a self?

During adolescence many people may be unsure of their own self-concept. Discussing self-concept may be difficult for some people. The only person's self-concept that you have a right to investigate is your own! Other people – other adults – may not feel safe talking about themselves.

Some people may not be able to explain their feeling of self in words. This does not mean that they do not have a concept of self. Not being able to explain something is different from not experiencing it. You may have experienced being in love, but you might not be able to explain it to others.

People who believe that they have no choices – no control over their lives – may fail to develop a clear

Figure 4.23 Appearance and how other people see you

self-concept. It seems that people who suffer discrimination and disadvantage sometimes believe that things just happen to them. They give up trying to influence what will happen and just accept that everything happens by chance. If you avoid thinking about life and just hope that more good things will happen than bad things, then you might not need to imagine a self. Imagining a self is only useful if you intend to control your life and make your own decisions.

If you let other people run your life, or if you are just part of a social group and the group decides everything, then again you won't need an individual self-concept. People without a concept of self may tend to dependent on other people, or they may tend to simply 'drift' though life.

Figure 4.24 If your life is controlled for you, you may feel as if you are on an escalator. Your life just goes by, you don't need to think, you don't need a self-concept!

Negative self-concepts

Some people are fortunate in that they have a positive view of themselves. They may see themselves as healthy, or as clever. Some people believe they are attractive, popular, good or skilled. It depends on how we have come to see ourselves in relation to what others say about us.

Other people believe that they are unhealthy, stupid, unattractive, unpopular, bad, or incompetent. These ideas come from the way they are treated by parents, by people at school, by society. Discrimination can have a serious effect on your self-concept (see Chapter 11).

If you have a negative self-concept, at least you know where you fit in with other people. Having a negative view of yourself may be better than having no self-concept at all!

Summary

Life stages:	Infancy, childhood, adolescence, adulthood, mid-life, later life.
Physical development	Embryo, infant reflexes, growth rates, sexual development, adult changes. Change in later life.
Intellectual development:	Piaget's stages (sensorimotor, pre-operational, concrete operations and formal operations). Modern view of these periods. Adult development.
Emotional development:	Bonding (Bowlby's theories and other views) Erikson's eight stages of development.
Social development:	Play, relationships with others.
Self-concept:	Our ability to understand ourselves. This develops with our intellectual growth and education. Self-concept is influenced by our understanding of social roles and socialisation. The way other people see us will influence how we think about ourselves. The changes in our sense of self might develop as shown in Figure 4.25.

Evidence collection point

Write a report which describes the main characteristics of human development and explains the factors that influence an individual's self-concept. Look at the summary above to help you.

The report will contribute to the evidence indicators for Element 2.1.

Coping with change

For most people it probably takes the first 14–20 years of life before they really develop an understanding of self that could be called a self-concept. But developing a self-concept isn't something that you can do once, and then it's finished! Our understanding of self changes with time. We have constantly to develop and change who we think we are.

If nothing changed in our lives, then things would become extremely boring. Change can be exciting and desirable. Just a change in the weather – the first snow of winter perhaps – can create a feeling of excitement. While some change makes life interesting, too much can create stress.

There are a range of major life events which can create excitement or be upsetting and stressful. Over a lifetime the list might include:

- coping with the arrival of a new brother or sister
- coping with changes in family structure – new step-parents for example
- starting at a new school
- changing friends
- starting work and changing jobs
- making relationships, breaking up and changing relationships
- leaving home
- entering a permanent partnership or marriage
- having children
- moving home
- coping with change at work
- retirement.

These changes are predictable in the sense that we expect that some of them will happen to us. We can often choose to leave home or marry. There may be a feeling that we can control these events by planning for them and preparing resources to help us cope. but not everyone is able to choose when and how some of these changes happen. Sometimes a

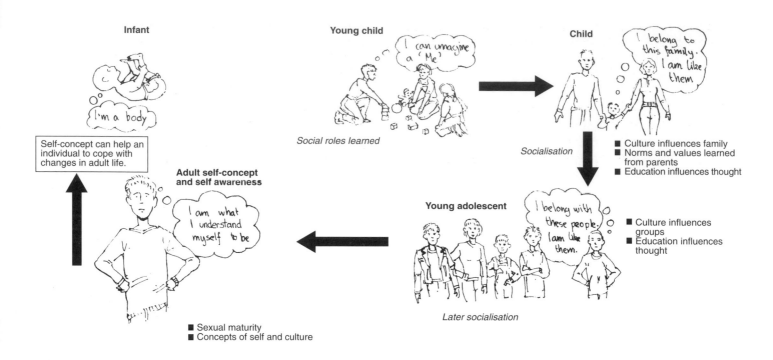

Figure 4.25 Some influences on self-concept

relationship will end when we don't want it to; changes at work happen whether we had planned for them or not. Some people have to leave home because their relationship with parents breaks down. We can predict that we will die, but not when or how. While death is predictable, it is often impossible to plan for it!

If major life events feel under our control then change may feel exciting. If we cannot plan for or control the events, then we may become distressed.

Certain unpredictable events such as redundancy, serious illness or disability, divorce and bereavement are always likely to cause stress and insecurity to individuals who experience them.

Michael Argyle researched a list of upsetting life events. The list shows how upset a sample of people were on average, using marks out of 20:

Death of child	19.5
Death of spouse	19.1
Sent to prison	17.8
Serious financial difficulties	17.6
Spouse unfaithful	17.3
Court appearance for serious offence	16.9
Divorce	16.3
Loss of job	15.9
Fail important exam or course	14.4
Demotion	14.3
Begin extra-marital affair	13.7
Child marries without approval	12.7
Retirement	10.1
Move to another town	8.6
Promotion	5.9
Marriage	5.4

Even promotion and marriage, which should be pleasant changes, create some tension in many people. Why does change cause upset and tension? Here are two explanations:

1 *Change creates uncertainty*. When you start a new school, you don't know what to expect. Will you get lost in the building? Will the staff be friendly? Will you know what to say? Most of all, will the other children like you? Will you get on well and make friends? There are so many questions, and you may not know how the future will work out. Uncertainty can create worry.

There is uncertainty if you decide to marry or live with a partner. You think you know your partner, but how can you be sure that he or she won't change? How can you be sure you will both stay in love? How can you be sure you won't fall out – many people do fall out. Many marriages end in divorce.

There is uncertainty in having children. Will you be a good parent? Will you be able to afford what you need for the children? Will you like your children? Will they like you? Will the children strain your relationship with your partner?

Almost every form of change raises questions about our future. When we don't know the answers, it can be scary.

2   *Major life events change your self-concept.* The way we see ourselves is partly due to the way our friends, relatives and other important people see us. When we change friends, relationships, jobs or school, then the people we mix with will change. New people might see us differently. New people might treat us differently. Our ideas of our skills, our social status, our importance, might have to change.

You may have been very good at a previous job, and seen yourself as clever. When you change jobs, your new colleagues might work in different ways. They might not see you as clever. Your concept of yourself might have to drop in value in your new job.

You may have thought of yourself as a really sociable and outgoing person. If you start a family you may have to stay in and care for the children. You may have to change the way you think about yourself. If you marry, you have to see yourself as part of a partnership – you cannot expect to take every decision and control every part of your life as you did as a single person. You will probably have to change your self-concept – your idea of yourself – if you are to have a successful partnership.

Redundancy, serious illness and bereavement may also wreck you self-concept. You may have seen yourself as important, fit, a partner in a loving relationship, only to find it has all been taken away. You can no longer be the person you used to be. You have to change your whole way of understanding yourself. Having to rebuild your idea of yourself can be a very painful process.

Major life events and the need for new learning

When you start at a new school, there is a vast amount to learn about the school and the people in it. New names, new places to find your way around, new customs, new teachers and so on. Starting a new job will be similar.

Having children involves a vast amount of learning: learning to care, as well as all the practical issues like feeding and bathing children. Moving home may mean learning about do-it-yourself, plumbing, decorating, finance and so on.

Redundancy, serious illness or bereavement might mean learning a whole new lifestyle.

Many people enjoy learning at their own pace in their own way. Major life changes may not allow you time or the chance to go at your own pace. You may become stressed because of the amount of learning and adapting that you have to do.

Major life events and a sense of loss

Changing schools might mean losing contact with old friends. Leaving home may mean you will not see parents, brothers and sisters as often. Having children may mean you have less time to spend with friends, and maybe less money to spend on yourself! Changing jobs means that you will lose daily contact with former work friends. Moving home means losing routines, people and views that you used to know.

Serious changes such as redundancy, sudden disability or bereavement can involve multiple losses. Bereaved people may have lost:

- the main person they talked to
- the main person who gave them advice
- their sexual partner
- the person who shared life tasks with them
- the person who made social life fun
- a person to go out with
- the main person who provided emotional support
- the focus of life at home
- the person who protected them
- a person who helped bring in money
- a person who did jobs around the home.

A person who loses both legs in a road accident may feel that he or she has lost the ability to get out easily. The individual may fear being labelled and stereotyped as a wheelchair user. He or she might feel like a burden and unattractive.

The individual may believe that he or she is of no use and that his or her partner might leave. If such a person ends up alone, he or she might have all the problems listed above for the bereaved person!

Major life events can create a serious sense of loss. A person might also feel threatened by what has

85

happened. It takes a great deal of mental work to recover and make up for serious losses in life.

Time, money and emotional resources

It takes time to learn a new job, to make new relationships, to look after children and so on. Time is a limited resource. Having children, moving home, leaving home or getting married may cost a lot of money. These events may also be emotionally draining. Going through planned life changes can be expensive in terms of time, money and emotional commitment.

Unplanned changes such as redundancy, serious illness, divorce and bereavement may also involve extra expenditure, additional work and more emotional involvement in order to sort out everything. This time, however, you are spending your time and money to sort out things that you never wanted to happen!

How do people cope with major life changes?

Individuals with a clear self-concept will use their own mental and intellectual abilities to help them cope with major life changes. It is obvious that anyone who chooses to get married or to change their job will think about planning for the change. Many people, if they are planning on starting a family, will sit down and check through (or evaluate) their time and financial resources.

People facing unexpected changes will sometimes go through a process of shock which prevents them from using planning and evaluation skills. Even so, many people will try to use their imagination, and their knowledge, planning and evaluation skills to cope with unexpected life changes. Few people have to struggle with major life changes entirely on their own. Most people will have family or friends to whom they can turn. As well as relatives, partners, people at work and other relationships, some people can turn to community figures, religious leaders and so on. Active Christians may be able to seek help from their church leaders or community. Muslims may receive support from their mosque and community. Hindu and Sikh communities will support their members. Some people live in areas where the neighbourhood creates a supportive community.

Where life changes involve legal, financial or medical issues, people may seek professional help. Individuals going through divorce might seek legal help with the sharing out of joint property. They might want medical advice for stress-related illnesses or financial advice to help plan their future.

Local organisations such as the Citizens Advice Bureau provide advice on a wide range of social and financial issues. The Relate marriage guidance agency provides help to people who are having difficulties in their relationships.

How do other people help us to manage change?

- *Talking helps some people.* We often think more clearly when we can talk through a problem with other people. There is an old saying: 'A problem shared is a problem halved.'

  Sometimes we feel much better for talking something over because our minds become clearer, and we understand more, when we hear ourselves talk. Another saying is: 'I know what I think, when I hear what I say.'

  Talking helps some people to make sense of the changes that they are going through – 'It's good to talk!'

  Carers can develop special conversational skills which can help people going through major changes or difficulties with relationships (see Chapter 10).

- *Relatives, friends and the community might provide practical help.* If you have to move home, you might need help to pack and unpack belongings. You could pay people to do this, but friends and relatives might give you their help for free. You will help them in return when they need 'a hand'. If you move home, you may know people who can assist you with decorating, with plumbing and so on. If you are starting a family, you may know people who will babysit for free – people you can trust in your community.

  Friends might give you advice if you are searching for work. Family might help you and visit if you are ill in hospital. Your family might give you a place to stay if your relationship with a partner breaks down. Family and friends provide company if you are left alone following divorce or bereavement. Family and friends might even protect you if you are in conflict with others.

Other people can provide advice

Some life changes can be planned for: marriage, changing jobs, moving house, for example. Sometimes family, friends or work colleagues can give you useful advice and information which will help with your plans. Colleagues might tell you about new routines at work, give advice on how to get on with a supervisor, explain how to fill in forms and so on. Friends could give advice on where to hold a wedding reception, or buy the things you need.

Other people can support us in feeling positive about ourselves

Being with and talking to other people can make us feel that we belong, that we matter, that we are 'worth something'. If people are interested in us and warm and friendly toward us, it is likely to boost our sense of self-worth. Conversation may be a very important kind of help for people who are struggling to cope with redundancy, disability or bereavement. Most of the time we need to feel valued and supported. This is why it is important to visit people when they are ill in hospital.

The opinions or views of other people can guide us when we have to change our concept of self. Change means that a bereaved person is no longer a partner in a joint relationship. Changing back to being a single person can be a hard and painful task. Other people's support may be very important to help come to terms with bereavement.

Watching other people can guide us

This may sound strange, but if we watch other people coping with marriage, having children, moving home, becoming ill and so on, we can learn from them. We watch their successes and their mistakes. When we come to face change, we can copy what others have done well. This can save us from feeling confused or frightened.

Professionals can provide specialist help

Doctors may be able to prescribe drugs that help with stress or illness. Solicitors may provide legal solutions to problems. The Citizens Advice Bureau may give advice on special services in the community, such as how we can obtain equipment to assist a person with a disability. Relate could provide guidance and counselling services.

Summary

Major life changes may cause:

- uncertainty

- change to self-concept
- a need for new learning
- a sense of loss

- pressure on time, financial and emotional resources.

Other people can help us to cope by:

- providing information and advice
- giving skilled support
- offering guidance from past experience
- providing company and conversation
- providing practical help.

Evidence collection point

Prepare three case studies: one based on yourself, one based on someone of a different gender and one based on someone of a different ethnic origin. Each of the case studies should describe:

- one major predictable (or 'expected') life event which affects people's lives
- one major unpredictable (or 'unexpected') life event which affects people's lives
- ways in which the person may manage the change caused by both types of event.

Your case studies will contribute to the evidence indicators for Element 2.1.

Four examples of case studies are given below and you may wish to present your material in a similar way. You may also be able to use broadcast or video material as a basis for your case studies.

Another option is to plan and undertake interviews. If you are interested in this method, then read the section on interviewing in Chapter 13. This section may help you to design your work to Merit or Distinction standard.

The impact of change

Starting school (predictable change): Samuel's story

Samuel is a black $4\frac{1}{2}$-year-old, who is starting nursery school. Until now he has always been at home with

his mother. He has played with other children many times in his home and also when his mother visited friends. Samuel is an only child. He has a close, loving relationship with his mother.

Samuel's first reaction to school was one of shock – there were so many other children and it was noisy. He had always looked to his mother for guidance, but she wasn't there and he was on his own. Samuel had been told all about school, but he couldn't really understand or imagine what it would be like. Another adult who looked very different from his mother was trying to get him to join in a game. Samuel felt frightened and lost. Samuel cried for his mother and told staff that he wanted her. A kind teacher who looked a little like his aunt spent time with him and he felt better.

Later in the day, Samuel enjoyed some food and joined in making music with the other children. When his mother came to collect him, he was relieved. He didn't really feel safe until she appeared. Now he felt tired, but important. He had been to school, he had learned about music, and his mother made him feel that everything was all right and safe again. This was a real adventure!

The next few days at school were easier for Samuel. He stopped worrying about not being with his mother and he started to like school.

Think it over

How does theory explain what happened to Samuel?

1 *Uncertainty.* Samuel didn't understand his first day at school, he didn't know what to expect, what to do, or how to cope.

2 *Sense of self.* Samuel's idea of himself had always included his mother being around. Now that she had gone, he felt unsafe.

3 *New learning.* there was so much to take in, Samuel couldn't understand it all. He felt frightened and overwhelmed.

4 *Loss.* Samuel had 'lost' his mother. He also felt that he was lost.

5 *Use of resources.* Samuel never thinks about time, and he doesn't understand about money yet. He became tired because he had been upset by the strangeness of everything. Samuel's emotional energy was 'used up' and this made him feel tired.

Samuel coped with going to school because at the end of the first day he felt that he had been successful. He had met a friendly adult with whom he could identify. Samuel had managed all the tasks and he had achieved something in making music with the other children. When Samuel's mother came, he felt important.

Now that Samuel has felt successful, the next few days will become an adventure.

The skills of the staff at the nursery school and the fact that they understood Samuel's needs helped him to cope. He felt more confident because there was someone with whom he felt safe.

Getting married (predictable change): Davinder Kaur's story

Davinder is 21 years old and is about to complete her studies for a university degree. Davinder is a Sikh. She has lived in a Sikh community in the UK all her life. Davinder has thought about marriage a lot during the past few years. Many times, she has discussed the possibilities and whom she might marry with her family. Davinder's family are very concerned that she should make a good marriage with someone of an equal educational status.

Davinder has met Sohan and thinks he is attractive and intelligent. Davinder's family know Sohan's family and have agreed that they would make a good couple. Sohan has visited Davinder's family and an 'engagement' ceremony has taken place at their local Gurdwara (or temple). Davinder has been given a gold ring by Sohan's mother.

Davinder is now looking forward to her wedding day. She is extremely happy and excited. She will be very important; she will go through a ceremony that will mark a major change in her life. After the ceremony she will live with her husband and not with her original family. Everything about this change is welcome. Davinder will wear red and gold, lucky colours. There have been many gifts exchanged between the families. Davinder feels a mixture of joy and anticipation. After the wedding she will be different, she will have her own house, and she will have a husband to care for, although she will not be with her own family. The change almost makes Davinder feel a bit 'giddy' when she thinks about it.

Think it over

How does theory explain Davinder's feelings?

1 *Uncertainty.* Davinder is very uncertain what the future would be like. She wants the change; she wants to be married. The uncertainty increases her excitement rather than causing worry.
2 *Sense of self.* Davinder is about to change into a married woman – this will completely alter her life and sense of who she is. This change is wanted, though, so Davinder feels excitement rather than fear.
3 *New learning.* Davinder will have a great deal of new learning to do in order to live with Sohan and be a good wife.
4 *Loss.* Davinder will lose her past lifestyle and daily contacts with her original family. Davinder may feel a little sorrow when she thinks of this, and she may even be tearful when the time comes to leave. But she wants the change, so Davinder will gradually come to cope with the loss.
5 *Use of resources.* Davinder will use a lot of time and mental energy coming to terms with her new role as a wife.

Davinder will cope with being married because she wants to be married. She has had a great deal of support from her family and feels that she has some idea of how to cope with her new role. Marriage is a major change that Davinder has looked forward to for a long time. She is sure that Sohan will be a good husband.

Coping with redundancy (unexpected change): Bob's story

Bob is white and 48 years old. He had a job in the sales force of a large manufacturing company. He had worked for the company for 23 years before he began to take time off as a result of a series of illnesses. Bob

was not suffering from any particular illness. While on holiday he twisted an ankle and had to take further time off work. On his return he was shocked to find out that his company had made him redundant. Bob's manager did not mention his health record; he claimed that Bob's area of work was being reorganised. Bob suddenly found himself in a very difficult situation. He was not old enough to be able to retire and claim his company pension, yet he couldn't see how he could find another job. Bob realised that he was likely to have serious financial problems, and yet he had always been careful with money and had expected to retire on a comfortable pension.

Bob searched for possible jobs at the job centre and in the local newspapers, but there was nothing that suited his skills. He began to feel that he was a failure, that life had been unfair to him and that there was little left to live for. All Bob's expectations about leading a comfortable life had been shattered. He began to wonder what the point of his life had been. Bob realised that he might have to sell his car and perhaps even sell his house.

Think it over

How does theory explain Bob's experience?

1 *Uncertainty.* Bob was not expecting to be made redundant. When he found himself unemployed it was a great shock. He didn't know how to cope with his new life.
2 *Sense of self.* Bob found that all his past ideas seemed to be wrong. He was no longer valuable or needed by his company; he no longer had work colleagues to talk to. Bob couldn't really make sense of life as an unemployed person.
3 *New learning.* Bob had to learn to look for work. He will have to learn to live on less money.
4 *Loss.* Bob has lost self-esteem and personal and financial security. Perhaps he has also lost the sense of who he is.
5 *Use of resources.* Bob will spend a lot of time and mental energy trying to come to terms with the change. He will worry about finance and about finding another job. He may become stressed and have difficulty in sleeping, and be more likely to become ill through worry. Although Bob does not work he may become tired and be unable to cope with life.

If Bob is to cope with redundancy, he will probably first experience a short stage of disbelief when he can not really accept what has happened. He may then experience anger and depression before he can start to come to terms with the change. Redundancy may involve the same pain as losing a relationship involves (see Chapter 5 on the breakdown of relationships).

Eventually, Bob may be able to rethink his life. He will need to change his lifestyle to cope with the loss of income. At first, this will be difficult. If Bob can change his lifestyle and perhaps if he could find another job, then he may begin to feel that life is all right after all. Bob may need support from friends or relatives to help him to do this.

Coping with bereavement (unexpected change): Mabel Kershaw's story

Mabel is white and 84-years-old. She had lived with her husband for 60 years before he died unexpectedly a year ago.

Mabel feels that she is now totally alone. Her children do not visit her very often and do not seem to need her. She feels that she is a burden, both to her children and to her neighbours who do her shopping for her. Mabel has a heart condition which means that she cannot get out easily. Because she cannot walk far she feels that she is unable to visit her friends, who live several streets away. When Mabel lost her husband she lost her main companion in life. She has no one to talk to now. Mabel also finds difficulty in paying bills and sorting out paperwork. Her husband used to do all this type of work.

Mabel felt frozen inside when her husband died. She couldn't eat for the first week. Ever since, Mabel has been desperately wishing that he was with her once again. Sometimes she hears noises in the house and thinks that her husband is back. Then she remembers the funeral. Mabel sometimes feels angry and depressed. She asks herself the question, 'What am I living for – what's the point?' Mabel often thinks that no one cares about her and that her only future is to be reunited with her husband in heaven.

Think it over

How does the theory explain Mabel's experience?

1 *Uncertainty.* Mabel is lost and alone. She has little effective social support now that her husband is gone. Mabel can only think of going to heaven where things will be all right again. Her world is very stressful and difficult to cope with at present. Apart from dying and going to heaven, Mabel doesn't know what to expect.
2 *Sense of self.* Mabel used to be one half of a couple, now she is not part of a couple any more. Mabel feels she has lost part of herself.
3 *New learning.* Mabel has to learn how to pay bills and do paperwork. She also has to learn how to cope with little conversation and with loneliness.
4 *Loss.* Mabel has lost her husband, her social life, her reason for living and the person who supported and protected her. Her heart problem means that she has also lost some of her independence.
5 *Use of resources.* Mabel will sit for long periods worrying and wishing her life was different. She will use time and mental energy grieving for her husband. She will often be tired because of her worries.

Recovering from grief often involves a long and painful process. At first, there may be a feeling of being frozen inside; then there may be a stage of longing for the person who has gone. People will often experience anger and depression. Finally, many people will gradually begin to make sense of what has happened and try to adjust their life so that they can cope. Experiencing the breakdown of a relationship and bereavement may be similar in some ways.

Mabel is alone. While she has little social support, she may have more difficulty in building a new life. It may be necessary for family, friends, community or social services to help Mabel if she is going to learn to live a worthwhile, independent life.

Chapter 5

Interpersonal relationships and their influence on health and well-being

Interpersonal means between people. Some psychologists, such as Steve Duck and Michael Argyle, suggest that relationships between people give life purpose and make life worth living. Many people say that relationships are the most important thing in life. Interpersonal relationships may be your main source of happiness or unhappiness.

Relationships are a fascinating topic to try to understand. Poets, writers, film-makers, song-writers, musicians and artists have studied relationships since people first began to write and to make music. The lyrics of many of today's songs describe the emotions of forming, enjoying, or breaking relationships.

Falling in love is the main type of relationship that almost everyone is interested in at some stage of their lives – or perhaps for most of their lives! Love is only one type of relationship, though. Studying the wide range of relationships that people have will help to make sense of life, and maybe of love as well.

What are interpersonal relationships?

Relationships involve recognising and knowing other people and having some feeling of belonging with those individuals. Very often relationships meet social and emotional needs. We will have feelings of being attracted, or liking or feeling relaxed with people we 'belong' with. Sometimes, however, we fall out with people who are in our family, friendship or work groups. Relationships do not always bring us happiness.

Think it over

Imagine you arrive early at a party. There are quite a few people there, but nobody knows you, and you have come by yourself. You might feel anxious. The other people are all in groups enjoying each other's company. You try to start a conversation, and other people are polite to you, but they want to talk to their friends – they don't know you. After about 10 minutes, you will probably start to feel awkward, and unwanted. You might feel lonely or embarrassed. It's very unpleasant not to feel wanted. Your concept of yourself might be attacked. Perhaps you had always seen yourself as friendly, but no one here seems to want you. You might even think: 'Right, I'm going, I don't like it here, I don't belong.' Suddenly three or four of your friends arrive. They greet you loudly, and make it clear that they are really pleased to see you. Suddenly, you are important, you belong, others recognise and know you – they want to talk to you. Your self-concept recovers, you are important, you feel confident, you belong with this group. You can now enjoy the party!

Belonging with other people seems to be necessary for most people to feel happy. Three broad types of group to which people often feel they belong, in the context of daily life are:

- the family group
- work groups – including colleagues at school or college, or in voluntary work or training for work
- other social groups, such as friends, community groups, religious worship groups.

Relationships in daily life

During almost all of our waking lives we are interacting with others and forming relationships.

Think it over

Try to fill in the circle below, starting in the middle with your closest relationships and working outwards with less close contacts towards the edge of the circle.

Your diagram probably looks like the one in Figure 5.1.

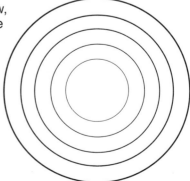

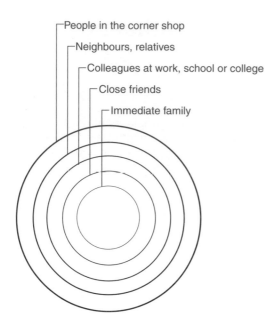

People in the corner shop
Neighbours, relatives
Colleagues at work, school or college
Close friends
Immediate family

Figure 5.1 Relationships

During the course of a lifetime a person develops contacts from the middle of the circle to the outer edges, but some relationships are more important than others.

It is well known that social contacts are essential for our emotional well-being. It is unusual for anyone to be deliberately deprived of human contact even in prison, because we know it is not good for people's health.

When babies are born their usual immediate experiences are with their close family – mother, father and maybe brothers or sisters. If the child experiences a home where he or she is cuddled and talked to, the child will feel secure. He or she can begin to make sense of the sights, sounds and smells around. He or she will feel confident enough to begin to experiment, to crawl, make noises to others and to start to learn.

The first relationship between an infant and his or her carers is the development of a bond of love. Bonding was discussed in Chapter 4. For many children their first relationship will be made with their mother. Research shows that this first bond can also be made with fathers or other members of the household. The important thing may be that every child has the opportunity to make a relationship and attach to a loving carer.

The quality of the relationship between children and their carers may influence children's emotional

development. The important thing is that the care-giver should be consistent and affectionate. Carers should respond to and encourage the child. It is far more helpful for a child's development to have two or three carers who play and talk with the child, and perhaps take the child out for walks, than to have one carer who sits by the television all the time and only takes notice of the child when he or she is in danger or needs feeding or changing.

Obviously, household chores have to be done, but the skilful carer will try to include the child as often as possible rather than make him or her feel that he or she is in the way.

Think it over

If you were going to the local supermarket with a 3-year-old, how would you try to involve the child? What would the child learn from this involvement?

You could ask the child to look in the food cupboards and the fridge at home to see if any items have run out. Even children who cannot read are able to recognise familiar products such as cans of baked beans and know the difference (from the pictures on the labels) between baked beans and other foods. The child could make his or her 'list' of items to find at the supermarket by sticking labels from packets or cans on a sheet of paper. Children are surprisingly able to select the correct brand when taken to the shelves where the type of item is stated. This is part of pre-reading learning and is very valuable experience.

Children can be involved in counting or pre-number activities in day-to-day shopping. For example, they can help to count fruit into bags or the number of eggs in a carton. Again this is valuable pre-number experience.

Think it over

Think about how you would involve a child in either baking or sorting washing.

Relationships formed in childhood

If you look back at Figure 5.1 you will realise that as a baby develops into a child, his or her social contacts grow wider. This is similar to the effect when a stone is thrown into a pond – it creates ripples which spread over a large area, but which are stronger in the middle and weaker around the edges.

Try it

Think back to when you first left home as a young child to go to school.

- Can you remember how you felt?
- Can you remember your first friend?
- If it is possible, ask you parents or carers how they felt.

Leaving home to begin school marks a transition during childhood. It is the beginning of independence from the first carers and a start in establishing wider contacts. Many children feel bemused by the fact that the adult in this situation, the teacher, has many other children to consider and cannot give attention to just one child.

You may have remembered from your childhood that you felt isolated or frightened by the noise of many other children. You may have felt different in some way, perhaps your clothes were different or oversized or hand-me-downs. Parents too have to adjust to not having a small child at home all day, and some mothers in particular will admit to a few secret tears after leaving a child in school for the first time! This is because parents know that their child will change. Until now, his or her experience has been bounded by what happens in the family home. From this point, the child will be influenced by other children and the new culture of school.

After the initial settling-period, it is essential that children develop friendships and learn to accept the teacher as a more formal carer than previous ones. Although teachers of small children will always comfort a crying child, they cannot encourage 'clingy' behaviour because they have to spread their time among all the children and cannot be monopolised by just one. In order to replace the close relationship they previously had with an adult, children begin to form friendships between each other. This is the beginning of independence, and if children have a positive start they develop the confidence to progress.

Children must learn to accept rules and authority. It is important for them to understand that certain behaviour is not acceptable and that although they may be reprimanded for misbehaviour they will still be loved. Children must be certain that it is their behaviour which is disliked and not themselves as people. Obviously, if children have been well disciplined at home and have been given reasons for not being allowed to do certain things it will be easier for them to adapt to the rules at school. On the other hand, if they have been used to running around all day at home picking up various activities and then moving on to the next – with no adult interaction to encourage them to complete an activity and achieve something – they might have difficulty settling down to concentrate at school.

Think it over

How can an adult encourage a 2–3-year-old toddler to learn to concentrate better?

If a child is building a tower of bricks, for example, he or she should be encouraged to see how many bricks can be piled up. While the child may do this alone it is more interesting for the child if an adult talks and encourages and is interested in the success or failure of the enterprise. An adult can extend a child's own ideas by making suggestions or asking questions. This does not mean adults should 'take over' the play, but they can try to make the child think further or introduce a new word. Even very small children can learn the meaning of quite complicated new words if they hear them in the context of their play. They will 'internalise' them, store them up, and when they are familiar with meanings, begin to use the words themselves. Of course, there is sometimes confusion, but it is important for the child to feel able to 'experiment' with words without fear of being embarrassed.

Until children settle down to the routine of the school day, they will not begin to learn. If children have a good vocabulary when they start school, they are more likely to make sense of the formal life of the classroom.

Think it over

Which children may experience difficulties socially?

Some children may experience difficulties if:

- they have a speech or hearing disability and are unable to communicate easily or follow verbal instructions
- their first language is not the language used in school
- they have not been used to learning activities or mixing with other children
- their behaviour or physical development is different from the other children
- their sight is impaired.

Relationships formed in adolescence

Beginning school marked the first widening out of a child's relationships and these continue to grow. When a child reaches adolescence there is a much wider gap between life in the family and life with friends or peers. At this age friends have a much greater influence than family. This is to help the young person prepare for leaving home and independent living.

In some cultures particular 'rites of passage' take place, after which the young person is deemed to be an adult member of that society. For example, young males of the Jewish religion celebrate their barmitzvah at the age of 13. This involves a ceremony in the synagogue at which the boy reads particular religious passages, and family and friends will be invited to a celebration of his new adult status. Other cultures have elaborate rituals in which young people spend a few days with older people of the same gender learning about their roles as adults. This is followed by a ceremony after which they are considered adults in society.

Nowadays young people have a much longer time to change from children to adults. It is necessary for them to demonstrate a difference from their parents' views and this is often the source of arguments within families.

Think it over

Think of behaviours adolescents use to prove they are breaking free from their parents and childhood.

You may have listed some of the following:

- different hairstyles, clothes
- going to bed very late; getting up very late
- experimenting with drugs, smoking or drinking
- experimenting with sex
- refusing to eat or to eat family meals; refusing certain foods
- using 'slang' expressions, the meanings of which are unknown to older adults.

There are many more!

Adolescence may be a difficult time both for the individual and parents. The long time-scale when adolescents are with their parents in European cultures gives young people the opportunity to develop new skills and practise independence from the safety of the home.

Adult life and work

During their time at school young people in the UK are trained to accept rules and to work regular hours under supervision.

Think it over

If you have a job or work placement how do you relate to the different people you work with?

There are several different levels of interaction with people at work:

- Sometimes people simply work with others to perform a task and there is little talk or friendship. If the contact is with someone of higher status it is likely that the type of language used will be more formal than that used with friends.
- People who meet together at breaks often play games and make jokes and have a laugh together, and this provides a welcome respite from work and cheers the day along. These people are thought of as part of a 'close-knit group' which is supportive in the workplace.
- People who work closely together and sometimes see each other socially are classified as 'friends at work'. One piece of research on this type of friendship found that only 27% of friends met outside work and most did not ask each other to their homes.

If you look back at the circle diagram you will see that by adulthood people are reaching the edges of the circle in their range of friendships and contacts. One way of thinking about relationships might be to look at the different contacts and think of them in terms of money, say with the central contacts being worth £1 and the ones on the outer edges only a few pence. We could rate our interactions in terms of money. We could imagine that everyone has a need to have a certain value in interaction, and the fewer contacts we have with the high-value inner circles, the more we need the contacts on the outer circles to satisfy us.

Young adults are likely to have a large number of contacts which they use as support as they become independent and establish themselves apart from their families. People often have to move to other parts of the country to get work or to go to college. This means that they are less able to rely on family for the support and friendship they need.

In other cultures, and until recently in the UK, people had a great deal of interaction with what was known as the **extended family**. This means grandparents, aunts, uncles and cousins. These days it is more likely that families will consist of just parents and perhaps brothers and sisters (siblings). Many children are brought up by just one parent because of divorce or separation.

This may mean that people have to have a greater number of contacts with people further from the centre of their circle in order to feel valued and to be supported both emotionally, socially and physically.

Try it

Using the chart below make a list of the contacts you have had over the last week. How much 'credit' or 'value' have they had for you?

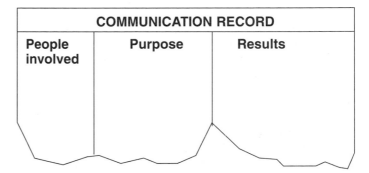

COMMUNICATION RECORD		
People involved	**Purpose**	**Results**

From your completion of the table you may see the pattern of your own interaction and may be able to decide how valuable your contacts are to you, and whether you are satisfied with them.

Evidence collection point

Using the same chart, talk with an older person, perhaps a client or someone you know. Chart their interactions for a week. This could help you to produce your report to meet the evidence indicators.

Some older people have limited opportunities for meeting with other people. If you look at their social circle, it often seems as if their circle is shrinking inwards. Of course, people's circumstances vary enormously. Just because people are old, it does not mean that they have no social life, but if they have mobility difficulties it often means they cannot get out to meet people as much as they would like. They may be dependent on social services transport or on family or friends.

When people retire from work, part of their circle of contacts is lost. Of course, people often keep in touch with friends they have made through work, but when a retired person no longer sees former colleagues on a daily basis, contacts often become less frequent or stop altogether. Sometimes this is because people become frail and unable to travel to meet each other.

Changes in relationships

Think it over

Do you have friends you no longer see? Why is this?

As we move through life, we often lose contact with people who were once friends. This may be because we move schools or jobs or areas, but it might also be because we change.

To understand that they have changed, older people only need to look through photograph albums to see pictures of themselves wearing clothes that they wouldn't dream of wearing now. Older people probably also remember using slang words which would seem silly if they used them today. These are small instances of how we change. However, not only do we change on the outside in a way that can be seen, we also change our thought and feelings. We change our views and ideas about life and what we want out of it.

Try it

Make a list of reasons that explain why people change. You may want to work with others to think through this topic.

You may come up with a very long list of reasons why people change! Some of them may be reasonably predictable and related to the life-cycle – as we grow older we tend to adopt what is known as **age-appropriate behaviour.** This means that there are certain expectations about how people of certain ages behave. Often these are unspoken and culturally based assumptions.

Behaviour	Description
Riding a powerful motorbike	Retired person
Sucking one's thumb	Business person
Using a mobile phone	Three-year-old
Sleeping in a deckchair at the seaside	Older adolescent

Try to match the behaviour/activity listed on the left with the description of the person on the right – you will probably have no difficulty!

Although to try to categorise people by age is to stereotype them to some extent, it is generally accepted that people are more likely to enjoy certain activities at certain ages. As we progress through life our tastes and attitudes are likely to change to some extent.

Think it over

How might changes in tastes and attitudes affect a couple who had married while still very young?

We should not assume that all people of the same age enjoy exactly the same things and think in the same way. This would be to stereotype people. It is likely that if a couple married very young, they may change as they age and have different wants and needs. It may be that one partner acquires extra qualifications and is exposed to new ideas and interests. If the other partner is not willing to share these new interests and disagrees with different ideas, the couple may find themselves drifting apart. More seriously, one partner may actively try to stop the other from developing. If this happens, the restricted person will be frustrated and the relationship damaged. It may be that when a couple married young, their energies were used in bringing up children. They will have had to adapt at this stage from being a couple whose attentions focused mainly on each other, to being a family where each parent used some emotional energy to interact with the children. When the children born to a very young couple are grown up, there are still many years left before the parents grow old. At this point, one or both of them may take stock of the situation and decide now is the time for them to do things they have always wanted to do.

Sometimes this involves an element of risk. For example, one partner may want to change jobs or go back to college. If the other partner is not willing to support this change, the couple will experience problems.

Apart from changes in life stages, most reasons for change in relationships can be classified as social or economic.

Try it

Choose one of the life changes below and describe how it would affect your life if you were in that situation:

- You or your parents becoming unemployed.
- Becoming disabled – a wheelchair user, impaired hearing or sight.
- Becoming a parent.

There are many other life events, both predictable and unforeseen, which would bring about major change, but the ones above would affect people both socially and economically. It is certain that all three would mean considering how you were going to manage financially.

Try it

Either by using a catalogue or looking in local shops, work out the cost of buying the following basic equipment for a baby:

- a pram
- a cot and bedding
- sterilising equipment and three bottles
- clothes – six sleepsuits, six vests and three cardigans.

If you cost only the most basic items needed for a new baby, you will see they amount to quite a lot of money. This does not include the expense of feeding and clothing the baby as he or she grows, nor the weekly expenditure on nappies. When considering the cost of having a baby, the possible loss of income of one of the parents must also be taken into account, or the cost of paying for childcare.

Couples have to think very carefully about how they are going to cover this and how they will manage their new responsibilities. This usually means that the relationship they had as a couple, only needing to think of each other, will change. They can no longer plan to spend all they earn on themselves, and one of them will have to take responsibility for the baby 24 hours a day, seven days a week.

Of course, in a supportive relationship, this responsibility is shared between the partners, but it means that neither of them can be as carefree as before. Spontaneous activities become out of the question. Leisure time has to be planned like a military campaign around the baby's feeding and sleeping times. The same is true of the couple's sex life. Spontaneity may be lost as it becomes difficult to find times when neither partner is working, exhausted, out, or looking after the baby.

For couples with a young child, it is easy to understand why one partner might see the attraction of relationships with new people. If the other person has a pleasing appearance and personality, there may be a temptation to 'opt out' of the pressures of home life to regain the type of carefree relationship experienced before parenthood. When someone is faced with a partner who has had little sleep because of spending the night caring for a sick child, or a partner who is short-tempered and badly in need of time for a shower and hairwash, it is easy to wonder where the person they settled down with has gone.

Not only has the relationship between the couple changed with the birth of a baby, but between them and their parents and friends. The couple's parents have become grandparents as opposed to just parents. Many people enjoy this role because it gives them the opportunity to enjoy the pleasures a child brings without all the work, expense and responsibility. Having grandparents to help may be very supportive for young parents and they may find their relationships with their own parents improve. They may come to realise why their parents took

Relationships and love

Some writers distinguish between passionate love, which is mainly focused on meeting sexual needs, and 'compassionate love' which is more focused on commitment and feelings of belonging. Steve Duck, in his study of human relationships, reports six different types of loving relationship. People's relationships will be more complex than just six types, but these descriptions may be useful in explaining what happens when some people 'fall in love'.

Romantic love

This love is based on physical attractiveness and passion. Relationships based on this type of love might develop from love-at-first-sight reactions. Romantic lovers value physical contact as central to their relationship. They often ignore abstract issues such as planning for the future, and might throw themselves into a commitment based on the enjoyment of each other's physical attractiveness.

Game-playing love

Some people see relationships as fun, but they may try to avoid commitment. Game-playing love involves flirting and going out with people that you are not really attracted to just for the fun of it. People who see relationships as just about pleasure, avoid commitment and aim for many different relationships with different people. Some individuals may even boast about the relationships they have had and how they have avoided commitments to partners.

Friendship love

This is love based on caring feelings for another person. People who fall in love this way become friends first and lovers second. People who believe in this kind of love may be very concerned that interests and beliefs are shared. The relationship is not based on excitement, but on shared lifestyles and a shared respect, concern for and commitment to each other.

Logical love

If you're going to commit yourself to another person, you might first want to check what kind of a deal

certain views. It is probably not until people become parents themselves that they realise how impossible it is not to worry about their children, and much of what they had thought of as 'nagging' from their parents was really caused by parents worried for their safety.

How active a part the grandparents are able to play, depends on whether they live near to the couple, how well they get on with the parents, how active they are themselves, if they are still in work and lastly, how inclined they are to get involved again in the exhausting business of child rearing!

The birth of a child will also have an effect on the couple's friendships and leisure activities. They will be less available for nights out with friends who do not have children, and they will have less money and leisure time. It is very good for parents to go out to meet friends and to carry on with hobbies, but these activities now take second place to caring and may become a 'luxury'. If couples are unable to find babysitters and decide instead to take separate nights out, there may be temptations to develop relationships outside the partnership. These are good reasons why people need to think very carefully before deciding to have a child. Having a child to try to 'rescue' a difficult relationship is very unlikely to succeed.

you will get. You might wish for a partner who will prove to be a good parent, a good earner, who will improve your own self-esteem or career chances, who will protect you, or fit with your own lifestyle and social activities. Logical love is about finding the 'right person' to fit your needs and desires before you commit yourself to them. Some people search for 'Ms or Mr Right'!

Possessive or dependent love

Some people are uncertain and anxious about the commitments they make to others. There may be a fear of rejection or losing control. Possessive lovers may become jealous and angry if the relationship is not working in the way that they wish it to work.

Selfless love

This involves a total commitment to the well-being of your partner, no matter what he or she does.

Steve Duck reports research which suggests that some lovers might start with romantic love, but that styles of loving relationship might change with time. The romance wears off but this type of love might be replaced by friendship or logical love. This means that while there might be less passion, the relationship can be just as binding. A person who is in logical love might feel that their life only makes sense if they are with their partner. A logical commitment may be as much of a commitment as a romantic one.

Breakdown in relationships

One cause of relationship breakdown is that two people may not change in the same way. Two people might fall in love with each other and enjoy months or even years of romantic love. If the feeling of physical attraction and attachment disappears, it might not be replaced by some other love style. If

this were to happen to you, you might think 'Whatever did I see in this person? He/she doesn't share my interests, and doesn't fit with my lifestyle or what I want in the future.' When you look at your relationship, suddenly there isn't any friendship or any logical reason for it. So when the romance is over, the relationship is over too!

A second cause is that lovers do not always know how their partner is experiencing the relationship. One person may experience romantic love, while his or her partner sees the relationship from a logical viewpoint, such as 'This person is a good bet'. If one partner stops being attracted and finds out that he or she is seen as a 'good bet,' that partner might decide to break up the relationship. Equally, if the logical partner changes his or her mind, the romantic partner might be left very unhappy.

In the 1970s, one piece of research found that less than half of romantic partnerships lasted more than five years. In Britain today, one out of every three marriages is expected to end in divorce. The theory of love relationships may help us to understand a little of the story behind the heartbreak of failed relationships.

Unemployment

These days very few people can say with certainty that they will never become unemployed and will stay in their jobs until they retire. Often people have no control over decisions made by their company to reduce the workforce or close down.

Think it over

Losing you job means more than losing you income. What else will you lose?

In our society people often think that their job defines their status. When people first meet socially, they will often ask each other what they do for a living. When people lose their job they may lose part of their self-concept. They are used to being known as a lorry driver, a teacher, a shopkeeper, etc. When they are no longer one of these things, they may feel that part of themselves has gone. Not only have they lost the income earned from the job, but they have also lost the respect which goes with the job. This will result in a loss of **self-esteem** (self esteem is the value we place on ourselves). Loss of self-esteem may particularly apply to women who have had a responsible job before having children. If they stop work, they are inclined to be thought of as 'just a housewife' or the wife of ... whomever their partner is.

Unemployment leads to yet another loss – the structure which having a job brings to life. People may no longer have their days divided into segments of time. An employed person gets up at a certain time, makes the journey to the workplace, works, has breaks, works and comes home at a certain time. Even shift workers have this structure, although it may take place at different times of the day or night. When people no longer have a reason to get up at a certain time, it may be difficult for them to structure their lives.

Unemployed people no longer meet former colleagues on a regular basis and so lose the stimulus of seeing a different set of people from those in their home circle. All these changes are likely to affect them both emotionally and financially. They may be depressed and bored. This means that they will need a lot of support from a partner, and to some extent, they may seem different from the person the partner settled down with.

Think it over

What opportunities does unemployment bring?

This may seem a strange question initially, when unemployment is generally something people dread happening to them. However, most things have plus and minus points and there may be advantages to becoming unemployed. Not having to keep to a rigid timetable to fit in work can be a relief. There are opportunities to go out during the working day and try new hobbies and interests. Parents will have more time to be with their children. Fathers may be able to experience taking children to school and have opportunities to visit school plays or festivals which would have taken place during work time. There will be time to play with babies and young children when parents are not tired at the end of the day, and their routine can be more relaxed with none of the pressures related to getting to work. People can retrain for new careers and perhaps discover talents they never knew they had.

However, it is undeniable that unemployment can bring pressure and if the relationship is not a strong

one, the partners may grow apart. The working partner may not be able to, or wish to, support the changed partner. Of course this is not always so, but unemployment, particularly long-term unemployment, will bring financial, emotional and social changes.

Much of the loss experienced by unemployed people may be similar to that of people retiring from work. Although retirement is often planned and does not involve the shock of losing a job, it can have many of the same consequences. Retired people may have to live on a pension which will be less than the wage they received; they no longer see their work colleagues every day; they do not have a timetable around which to work; and they no longer have a job title with which to identify. Retirement often means spending long periods with their partners at home and this can result in tensions. Women who have developed their own routines at home can feel that their husbands are 'under their feet' when they are home all day.

Disability

It is impossible to predict who may be affected by an unexpected disability. Disability can be caused by an illness during adult life such as Parkinson's disease, or be the result of a traffic or work accident.

When this sort of major event interrupts someone's life it will mean a lot of adjustment for him or her and for family and close friends. A person who has led an independent life with a responsible job may have to come to terms with being dependent on others for most of his or her needs. Disability may create a great deal of hard work for relatives in caring for a person.

Having to depend on others all the time can make people feel powerless. If they are used to organising their lives and jobs and possibly other people, then becoming dependent is a very difficult adjustment to make. Sometimes this can involve a reversal of roles with the child caring for the parent. Watching others doing jobs that the disabled person could do more efficiently before his or her circumstances changed can be very difficult. It will take a lot of patience and tact from everyone to adjust to the new situation.

Group influences

There are many other reasons why people's relationships change, most of which relate to social or economic change. People are influenced by those around them and if the 'culture' of our contacts changes, it is likely that we will too. If someone moves to a new job, he or she will be influenced by the culture of the workplace. For example, if extra-marital affairs are common among work colleagues, this can become acceptable behaviour within that group of people. If young people leave home to go to college, they are likely to adopt the student culture which may have different values from their family's. Sometimes people feel that they have 'grown apart' from their parents and families because although they still love them, their views and way of life have changed.

Some people function within two separate cultures. There may be certain standards of behaviour, language and dress within the home which are strictly kept.

However, the same person may behave quite differently when with friends or work colleagues. This can be quite stressful, because the person is having to adopt completely different codes of behaviour to be accepted by different groups.

Think it over

It is useful to think back to changes in your own life and try to see how you coped with them. Think of a list of changes you have made during your life. You may want to ask other people what you were like during these times. Ask yourself:

- What can I remember?
- How did I change?
- Did it cause a problem?
- Who or what helped?
- When did I resolve it?

Sometimes looking at old photographs can jog the memory of particular periods of life.

If you feel you are in a stage of transition now, you can ask yourself:

- What is changing in my life?
- How am I changing?
- Is this causing me difficulties?
- What or who might help?
- Will changing be to my advantage?

Why do people make relationships?

Emotional and biological reasons

Babies make attachments to their main care-givers. This is often the mother, but might be the father or other carers. There may be natural or biological reasons why love develops between parents and a baby, and the baby and his or her parents. A loving relationship will mean that the baby will be protected and cared for. This care will help the baby to survive, grow and become a healthy adult.

Infants may have in-built or biological tendencies to make relationships with their parents. This bonding relationship would also help to encourage parents to give good care.

Some psychologists believe that our early experience of love and loving relationships influences the way we form relationships in adolescence and adulthood. It may be that styles of conversation and emotional caring that you experienced early on may influence the way you relate to other people later in life. If you felt secure and safe within your family, it may be that you can feel relaxed and trusting in your relationships with other people later on. If there was a lot of conflict and aggression in your early relationships, then you may learn to act that way towards others as you grow older. People who didn't form relationships when young may have trouble developing relationships later in life. Some Freudian psychologists believe that we seek sexual partners who look like our fathers or mothers.

Other psychologists believe that relationships are strongly influenced by learning across a person's lifespan. It may be that people often explain their early experience in terms of how they think as adults. Some people might even alter their memories of their childhood to fit their current life experiences.

Whatever the importance of early love, it may be true that people have an in-built need to make relationships with other people.

Research has shown that people with a good range of support are happier and enjoy better physical and mental health than those who do not have good relationships. The relationships which have been shown to be the most important are the ones shown in Figure 5.1.

Partners

Studies show that people who are married or living with a partner and have a close relationship have the best support. Michael Argyle found that widowed or divorced people have more days off work ill and see the doctor more often than either married or single people. An analysis of a range of fatal illnesses showed that widowed and divorced people had higher rates of death – 1.5 to 2.5 times higher – than married people. Divorced and separated people are more likely to become mentally ill, commit suicide or become alcoholic than married people.

Try it

Look at Figure 5.2, which is based on a famous study which took place in California in the USA. The study looked at death rates among people who had different numbers of social connections.

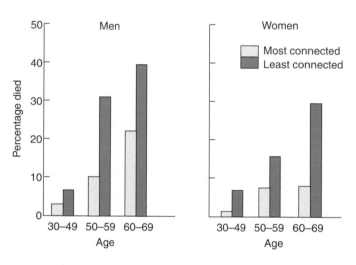

Figure 5.2 Age and sex specific mortality rates from all causes per 100

a Which group had the highest death rate?
b Which group had the lowest death rate?
c Did men or women survive better with few connections?

Stress can make us ill, but if we have an understanding partner or other forms of support the effects of stress will be less.

Family and relations

Family and relations are the next most important form of social support. Although children living at home can cause problems, particularly to the mother who is more likely to suffer from depression during this time, both parents will stay healthier if they often see their grown-up children. Brothers and sisters can be relied upon to provide help with serious problems, and research has shown that people with mental-health problems often lack family support, although they have friends.

Contacts with friends has been shown to be important particularly for the young and old. What is important is not the frequency of meeting but the quality of friendship.

Think it over

What do we mean by 'quality of friendship'?

Quality of friendship means how closely people relate to each other. Do they trust each other enough to discuss personal views and feelings? Can they rely on each other not to discuss with others what is confidential? Will they help each other if needed? Steve Duck found that close friends tend to think in the same way. They react in a similar way to emotional experiences. We like being with people who are interesting and make us feel accepted for what we are. Women tended to value conversation, discussing problems and giving and receiving support. Men tended to value friendships for fun and taking part in activities more. This may be why a man without a partner is more likely to become ill.

Some people with mental illness have been shown to receive support from others, but give nothing in return. For friendship to work, each person must be able to give and receive help. If one person cannot do this, the other person may feel less valued; his or her self-esteem may be reduced because he or she always seems to give and not to get anything in return.

Think it over

What do we get from work apart from money?

Research has shown that people who work are healthier and happier than those who don't. This is because, in spite of the stress work can bring, relationships with colleagues or supervisors can be supportive and satisfying. These contacts form another ring to the social circle. It can be a relief at times to leave the intimacy of the home and talk through problems with people who are not emotionally involved. It can sometimes be difficult for people suffering the same problem to give each other support. For example, if a couple has financial problems it is no good one partner complaining to the other. He or she is likely to be just as worried and unable to find a solution. On the other hand, discussing the matter with someone not emotionally involved may bring a new solution or approach. Even if the person cannot provide an answer, he or she can listen and sympathise. People often feel better just talking about a problem.

Neighbours and local organisations

These are the least intimate form of contacts, but can be valuable, particularly for some older people. If someone is confined to the house, neighbours are often the first to become aware of a person needing help. They can alert family or social workers and keep an eye on the older person on a daily basis.

Think it over

If you have visited a day centre, perhaps on a work placement, think of the types of support it offers to its users.

Sometimes older people go to local day centres where they are provided with a hot meal and some friendly company. The centre workers will also notice if their visitors' health seems to be failing, perhaps because they are not keeping themselves clean or properly fed. Centre workers can then alert social services. Churches or religious centres and day centres offer the opportunity to take part in regular social activities.

Research has shown that the most important part of social interaction is to have someone to share feelings or problems with and to have the opportunity of feeling valued. Without these our physical and mental health will suffer.

Try it

Find someone who is willing to talk with you about their relationships. This could be a friend or relative. Ask the following questions.

- Do you have other people to depend on in a crisis?
- Do you have someone with whom you can talk through problems?
- Have you got friends – people you feel close to?
- Do these people make you feel valued?
- Do you do things in return for these people?
- Can these people help you recognise your strengths and weaknesses?
- Is there anyone with whom you can share your good experiences?

When you have answers to the questions write notes about how strong the friendship system is.

Social reasons for relationships

Relationships protect us

Relationships protect us from the risks and stresses we would otherwise face in life. Young children are protected by their family or care network. Adults will teach them how to avoid dangers such as talking to strangers or crossing the road. Parents will look after the child's physical needs, provide food, shelter, clothing and so on. Parents will also seek to guide children in their social and intellectual development.

It seems that social relationships provide protection and support throughout life. Adult relationships with partners or friends help us to cope with life changes and with the daily stress of living.

Buffering from stress

The psychologist Michael Argyle describes the social value of relationships as **buffering**. A buffer is a kind of shock-absorbing barrier which gives protection. Buffers are used to protect trains at stations. Argyle's idea is that partners, family and friends act as shock-absorbers which protect us from the knocks that we take in life. If we change jobs, move home, get married, become ill, become unemployed and so on, our partners, friends or relatives might help us. Relationships with friends help us because they can take the shock out of these events.

Think it over

Imagine being unemployed and ill. Imagine being alone in a flat, with no friends or relatives around. You have no one to talk to, no one to help you, no one to go out and get your medicine, help you work out your bills, go shopping for you. Your life could be very difficult – without social services you may not even survive!

Think of what friends and relatives can do to help. Their conversation might make your life feel worthwhile. You may feel you matter to them. Friends can do shopping,

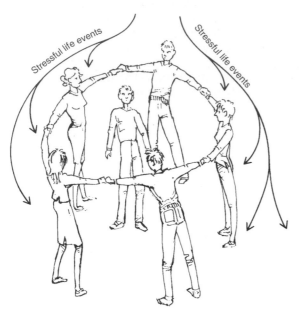

Figure 5.3 A circle of friends can protect you and buffer you from stress

arrange for doctors to come, sort out bills, etc. If you have family or friends, they can take the shock out of illness and unemployment.

Relationships can create happiness

Good relationships with partners, family and friends not only protect us from stress, but also help people to have happier lives and even to live longer and stay healthier. A number of studies in both the UK and the USA have found that people with good partnerships, marriages, family, friends and community links, are generally happier in their lives than people who do not have these relationships.

The need for conversational skills

Michael Argyle points out that some people say they have friends, but really they still feel lonely. Simply being with people isn't always what is needed. Only being able to talk with others about sport, cars or magazines can be boring.

Good relationships are ones where we can talk about our feelings. Being able to talk about our worries, share interests and talk confidentially about personal things may be the basis of real friendship. Argyle suggests that lonely people may feel lonely because they cannot talk about interesting and important personal issues. Good relationships may depend on people being good at conversation. The best friends may be people who are good listeners, people who are honest, concerned about you and understanding. You will also need friends who can keep a confidence, so that you can share what you really think and feel with them. If that is what you need in a friend, then your friends will expect you to behave in the same way. You should be a good listener, be honest, concerned and understanding, and be able to keep confidences. 'Friendship skills' are discussed in detail in Chapter 10.

Are women better at conversation than men?

Yes! In the 1980s research suggested that in general, both men and women believed that conversations with women were more worthwhile than with men. Women tended to discuss more personal and meaningful things than men. It may be that women learn to develop conversational skills in childhood and adolescence better than men do. Some men may have believed that conversation was not part of their role! Anyone can develop their skills and become a desirable friend (see Chapter 10).

Relationships can provide practical help and advice

Friends, partners, family and community groups might all be able to provide us with advice and information. Suppose you want to buy a second-hand car, but don't really know what to look for. You could work out what to do on your own – look in the paper, then go and look by yourself. But a better idea might be to get help from a friend or member of your family who knows more about cars than you do. Friends or family can support you when you go to look at a car; they can ask questions on your behalf.

An advantage of information and advice from friends and family is that it is given informally. Ideas come up while you are having a break from work or over a meal. You may feel that you are surrounded by a network of useful people. Simply having a chat with them can build up your knowledge and opinions. If you ever need professional advice, you may feel that you have to work out your questions in advance. If you forget a question, you may feel that it is more difficult to go back to ask for additional advice. Friends and family, on the other hand, may always be willing to chat.

As with everything in life, there are good and bad sides to advice from friends and family. One problem is that their information may not always be correct or up to date! There will be times when professional advice is best, even if it is a bit more formal.

Try it

You can probably think of many activities in your life where friends and family have given you practical help or useful advice and information. List a few of these ideas. This may help you to write your report on the reasons why people make relationships.

Relationships mean that we know where we belong

Ninety per cent of people in the UK share their living arrangements with at least one other person, while 42 per cent of people live within a **nuclear family**, i.e. a partnership or a married couple who live with their children but no other adults. Only 10 per cent of people live on their own, but of this percentage, many will still have friendship groups or community groups to which they belong.

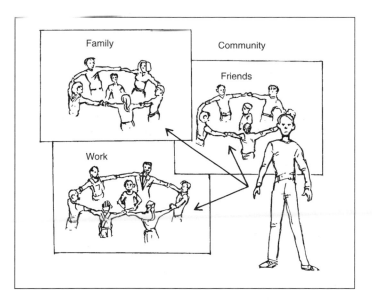

Figure 5.4 A person may have various groups where he or she belongs

Living with other people, having groups of friends, knowing colleagues at school, college or work, and knowing people in the local neighbourhood (or community) will give us a sense of roots – places and people where we belong. Our socialisation and self-concept will develop within the family and other groups to which we belong. Our idea of who we are will develop out of our relationships with family, friends, colleagues and significant people in our community.

Intellectual reasons

Relationships may stimulate our intellectual development – most of our learning takes place when we are playing, working or socialising with other people. We learn from play with other children. We learn from teachers at school. We copy what we see other people do. We are motivated to learn in order to be competent and meet other people's expectations. Our behaviour at work will be strongly affected by our relationships with colleagues and what they expect from us.

Our intellectual achievements will be influenced by other people's expectations of us and the roles we find ourselves playing. Many writers have explained how socialisation may affect achievement in school and college work. If your family and friends say that qualifications don't matter and school or college is a waste of time, you may agree with them. You may have developed many of your beliefs and ideas from listening to family and friends. If your friends are motivated to get qualifications, you may be motivated too. Relationships have a powerful influence on what we learn and how we learn.

Think it over

Thinking back to your school days, can you recall a teacher with whom you had a good relationship, a teacher whom you respected and whose lessons you enjoyed? How much did you learn from this teacher? Did you learn more or less than from teachers you didn't really know or didn't like?

When we think about our lives, we probably think a lot about the people we have known. Other people's views of us help us to form a self-concept. Our relationships with other people help us to think about, and understand ourselves. Our intellectual development of a self-concept will be strongly influenced by our relationships with family, friends and colleagues.

Other reasons for relationships – love and money

Relationships provide the setting for the fulfilment of sexual needs and for the experience of love. Networks of friends and acquaintances help some people to find work. Sometimes friends can help each other to advance their careers by sharing useful ideas and information. Networks of friends can help some people to save money, by sharing daily tasks between members of a group. You offer to babysit for someone and they repay you by helping you to repair your car! Relationships can have financial as well as emotional rewards!

Summary: why people form relationships

Emotional reasons

■ A biological need for parents to bond with their children and children with their parents. Adult relationships may also involve a type of bonding.
■ Relationships are necessary in order to experience love.

Social reasons

■ Relationships protect us – they 'buffer' us from stress.
■ Good conversation and relationships can create happiness.
■ People with good relationships may cope with illness and live longer than people with poor relationships.
■ Relationships can provide us with practical help and advice.
■ Relationships help us to experience a sense of belonging.
■ Relationships help some people to find work or develop their careers.

Intellectual reasons

■ Relationships may stimulate our intellectual development.
■ Relationships provide the setting for the development of our self-concept.

The role of the family

The family is where our first, and often our most important, relationships are formed. Relationships with parents and siblings (brothers and sisters) help us to understand how relationships are formed and managed. The relationships we make with partners, friends and colleagues in later life will be affected by those we make within our family in our early years.

The idea of 'the family' is so common to human societies that many social scientists have researched and studied it. In nearly all cultures, nowadays and throughout history, the family has existed as a basic unit of society. There are obvious biological reasons for this. As men and women get together to produce children they begin to form a unit. Reproduction and child-rearing are efficiently handled in the context of a family group. But there is far more to family life than the production of the next generation. For most of us our family has a variety of functions, and touches almost every aspect of our lives.

What is a family?

Practically everyone grows up within a family. There are a small minority of people who have been raised in institutions such as orphanages, and so never experienced family life; but most of us have been raised in a family of one form or another. Though the term 'the family' is used to describe this basic social grouping, the forms that families can take are very variable.

Families are sometimes described as being either nuclear or extended. The **nuclear family** is usually taken to mean a man and a woman and their children who live in the same residence and cooperate together economically and socially. The **extended family** includes other relatives, such as grandparents, aunts and uncles, and cousins.

The terms 'nuclear' and 'extended', however, do not take into account the variety of forms that the family can take, even if we are only looking at British society. For example, the term 'single-parent family' is used to describe a household with one parent and one or more children. This term acknowledges the fact that families often do not fit the nuclear and extended definitions. About one family in ten in the UK is a single-parent family, and the proportion is increasing. One out of eight single-parent families consists of a father and his children.

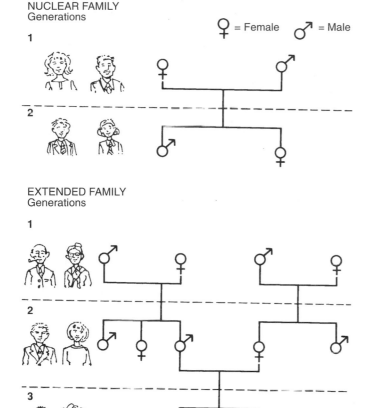

NUCLEAR FAMILY
Generations

♀ = Female   ♂ = Male

EXTENDED FAMILY
Generations

If we take the term 'family' to mean people living in the same residence, then the majority of families in the UK are of the nuclear type.

The functions of the family

One of the main features of family life is reproduction and child-rearing. Some social scientists have described this as a **function** of the family. A function is something that the family carries out as part of its role in society. Other social scientists have questioned the usefulness of looking at families in terms of function, but it does provide a way of examining family life.

The **reproductive function** is one of the most fundamental functions of families. Some people do not regard a couple as a family until children arrive. We speak of 'having a family' when children are born. Linked to this is the function of stable **satisfaction of sexual needs.** The belief that the sexual behaviour of adults needs to be regulated in

some way has supported the idea that the family provides a safe setting for sex to take place.

A third function is **maintenance** or looking after children. Parents are expected to maintain their children and care for them. This includes providing a home and making sure that there is enough money. Some families, particularly those with a lone parent, or with no employed members, may have difficulties fulfilling this function.

Another function is the **socialisation of children.** Socialisation includes the development of language and the passing on of ideas of right and wrong (known as values). Children learn the behaviour that is expected of them through the process of socialisation.

Placement is a further function of the family. Placement means working out an individual's place in society, and the status his or her family gives to this person. For some people the placement function is very important. An extreme example is the royal family, whose children are born into a very high social status. The education system has a great influence on placement and for many people family background is less important than educational achievement. Nevertheless, the family we are brought up in may have a major influence on our educational success, and this is discussed in Chapter 6

Family functions in modern society

All families fulfil the functions mentioned above to some extent. Some social scientists believe that in modern urbanised (town and city) societies the family has fewer functions to perform. They argue that the family's functions can be fulfilled outside it. Sexual and reproductive functions can take place outside the family group; nurseries and schools can fulfil the socialisation function; maintenance can be provided for by the state welfare system; and the education system provides for the placement function.

Other writers, such as Talcott Parsons in the USA and Ronald Fletcher in the UK, argue that the functions of the family have simply been changed. They believe that families have taken on new and more specialised functions in industrial societies. These authors believe that the family now has more functions rather than fewer. A key issue is the support that the family can provide for its members. An important aspect of this is **stability**, and this means that families are under some pressure to 'make themselves work' for the good of adults and children.

Families are expected to **protect**, **provide for**, and **support** their members. The family is seen as linked to wider society by the social and economic activities of its adult members. It is expected that the family will provide the setting for the management of the tensions and stresses generated outside the home. Families can offer support and emotional release to people returning from work.

Other writers, such as Steve Duck, have pointed out that this view of family life may not always be real. In fact most murders and violent attacks in Britain occur within the family setting! Stresses and tensions may be generated in the family that cannot be defused by the rest of society. Much of the work of social services departments is concerned with trying to deal with problems within the family. It is possible to speak of the **dysfunctions** (or failures) of the family as well as its functions. Despite this, the family has an important role in society and a fundamental place in the lives of everyone who lives in a family.

When relationships break down

Looking at all the positive reasons for relationships between people, it is easy to get the feeling that most people should be living lives full of happiness and joy. According to Michael Argyle, there is some evidence that more people were satisfied with their lives rather than dissatisfied with life in the 1970s and 1980s. So, perhaps, many people do enjoy good relationships with others for much of the time.

Figure 5.5 There are always risks in relationships

At some time or other, however, relationships cause everyone worry, pain and even heartbreak. Argyle's research suggests that people who feel the greatest joy with their lives may also experience the greatest sadness when things go wrong. If relationships make life seem worthwhile, life may not feel worth living when they break down.

Throughout life there are always risks in relationships – whether they will form successfully or whether they will break down. Some infants will not form a loving bond with their parents. In some cases, parents are too stressed or distressed to care for a demanding infant. In some situations, parents may not have learned how to care for their child. One theory called **the cycle of deprivation**, suggests that children who are not loved, and who may be deprived and abused, can grow up to be parents who fail to love their own children. Some children may show less of a bonding reaction to their parents than others. Being a good parent can be a difficult and demanding task.

Once a child has bonded there are always risks of upset and separation. A breakdown in marriage may mean that the child's biological mother and father will separate. Maintaining relationships with the child may become more difficult. Death and bereavement have always been risks that any relationship faces.

Relationships at school and work are threatened by changes as people grow older and move to new schools or jobs. People change – relationships in family and friendships alter as adolescents grow older and develop new ideas about their lifestyle and life goals. Adults change too – people fall in and out of love. For some people, life is a constant struggle with change! It can be hard to find relationships that are safe and stable.

Some theories on why friendship or love relationships break down

Understanding other people

One of the problems is that many people are not good at understanding other people. If you cannot imagine how your friend or partner thinks, then sooner or later you will probably upset him or her.

Communication skills

The way to become good at understanding another person is to be a good listener and become skilled at both verbal and non-verbal conversation. The problem is that many people are not good at these skills. If two people don't really understand each other and they cannot build their understanding through communication, then the relationship might be expected to go wrong eventually.

Specific problems causing breakdown

According to the psychologist, Steve Duck, relationships can also fail because of:

- **Cross-complaining** This is where an argument develops because one person 'picks fault' with a 'friend' and then the 'friend' replies by finding something wrong with the complainer. The argument then turns into a series of negative comments and complaints. The outcome is that nobody wins and both friends lose – they lose each other!
- **Breaking (unwritten) rules** Most people learn rules or norms during early life. When adults make friends or partnerships they often assume that the other person will live by the same rules that they have learned. But people sometimes learn different rules or norms. Sometimes, people simply do not live up to their partners' expectations.
- **Lying or deceiving** It is hard to be friends with someone you cannot trust. Relationships are usually built on trust.
- **Boredom** We often enjoy the company of friends and partners because they give us new ideas, they are exciting to be with or they lead us to new experiences. When a feeling of boredom develops, the relationship ceases to be rewarding.
- **Lack of communication** When people are unable to find time to meet or when they move away from friends, it can be difficult to keep a friendship going.

The consequences of breakdown in relationships

Sometimes the end of a relationship can lead to a sense of relief. If a relationship lacked satisfaction or was boring, or if your friend lied to you, you might feel that you are better off without him or her.

If it was you that wanted to end a love relationship, then you may feel a little sad, but you may also have a feeling of safety now that you have escaped from a commitment that wasn't right. You may feel free and happier to spend your time with old friends and family.

Some relationships end by mutual consent – both people agree that the friendship or partnership wasn't working. The break-up might please both people. They may both feel happier and relieved that they own no commitments to each other.

People and relationships constantly change and it may not be wise to believe that every friendship should last forever.

Even though we know that relationships can change, this can still create heartache and pain. When a relationship breaks down unexpectedly – a person may be bereaved or he or she may feel rejected – the person's life and feelings may be upset.

'Feeling gutted'

A common expression which sums up the pain of breakdown is to say 'I feel gutted'. This expression sums up the idea of loss – the person has lost things that really matter. The phrase may also suggest a loss of self-esteem, 'Part of me has been taken away, I don't feel so good about myself now'. People can actually experience an empty feeling in their stomach area, almost as if there was a hole there. This feeling may be to do with the stress response.

Figure 5.6 Emotional loss can create a feeling of emptiness

A breakdown in an important relationship can cause:

- a wide range of social, emotional and intellectual losses

- a loss of self-esteem and self-worth
- a feeling of being stressed.

Losses and loss of self-esteem

We grieve when we lose relationships that matter to us. Losing a very close friend or partner might mean that a person suffers any or even all of the following:

- There may be an emotional feeling that an attachment or bond of love has been broken.
- There may be a feeling of life being unsafe and threatening because the person's protector has gone. The most important person who 'buffered' or protected him or her from stress may have left.
- The person may feel that no one loves him or her now.
- The person may have lost the key person with whom to have good conversations.
- There may be a feeling of loneliness and unhappiness without the relationship. This could lead the grieving person to neglect himself or herself. He or she may not eat or exercise properly. Self-neglect can lead to poor health and risk of illness.
- The person may have lost someone who gave much practical help, information and advice. Life might be more difficult and complicated from now on.
- The person may feel that he or she does not belong anywhere. Perhaps the relationship created a sense of purpose and belonging. Now it is over, the grieving person may feel he or she has to lose a whole range of other relationships and social contacts.
- The person may have lost someone who kept him or her interested and excited. Life may be dull now that the relationship is over.
- The person may have lost someone who had become part of his or her self-concept. As a result, the grieving person may suffer loss of self-esteem, and feel of less value to other people. Sometimes a person might even say things like 'I don't know who I am now'. This is because that individual's self-concept is harder to explain.
- The person may be concerned about the loss of income now that he or she is alone.

All these losses might mean that a person feels sad and withdrawn. He or she may become less interested in, or feel worried about, joining in social activities. Serious losses might cause someone to feel emotions of shock, emptiness, anger, depression or sadness. An individual might feel that he or she can only think about personal worries and might become disinterested in work or daily life.

Zeph's story: part 1

Zeph is 18 years old. She met her boyfriend, Sean, at a party nearly a year ago. At first, it was an informal, social relationship. Zeph was attracted to Sean and knew that he liked her. Eventually, Zeph fell for Sean and believed that she had a formal relationship with him. Everywhere she went she explained that Sean was her boyfriend and that they were happy together. They did argue sometimes. For example, sometimes Sean would be late and Zeph would accuse him of not caring. This led to Sean accusing Zeph of not really being interested in him. Very often there would be bad feelings that would go on for days. Somehow they always managed to get over these arguments. Then one night Sean said he hoped they would always be friends, but that he was in love with someone else.

Zeph felt frozen inside. She felt that what she was hearing couldn't be true. Perhaps Sean was just testing her, perhaps he would come back to her. For the first week Zeph expected Sean to ring her and tell her it was all a mistake. She even tried to phone him, but he was never available when she rang.

Zeph's emotions began to change. She felt that she had trusted Sean and he had betrayed her. She also began to think that life was frightening and scary. How would she know if she could trust anyone? Zeph felt lonely and worthless. If Sean didn't want her, then maybe she was no good. At other times, Zeph felt very angry about Sean: how could he do this to her after she had been in love with him? Zeph thought of things she would like to say to Sean and his new girlfriend. Sometimes Zeph tried to think, 'It won't matter, I'll cope – I don't need him.' Usually, she felt depressed and sad. She had thoughts like, 'I don't have a future, what's the point of living, no one will love me – life will always be like this'.

During these times of feeling depressed, Zeph did not want to eat and she slept lightly, often waking and not being able to get back to sleep. Zeph lost her interest in going out and stayed at home in the evenings watching television. Zeph felt very stressed at this time.

What happened to Zeph?

Zeph experienced the loss of a 'bond' or an 'attachment' to her boyfriend. This loss made her feel that the world had become unsafe and threatening. How could she know if she could trust anyone?

Zeph's self-concept was upset – from time to time she felt she was not worth anything and her self-esteem was much lower than it had been. Zeph felt that life was empty and boring without Sean. She had lost the quality of life she used to enjoy. Zeph also experienced stress.

Stress

The breakdown of a close relationship can cause a person to become stressed. Stress can make people feel exhausted. This exhaustion can cause people to worry about aches and pains, and to have migraines, headaches, back pains, sleep disturbances and emotional tension. When stress continues for a long time, it can affect a person's health. Heart disease and strokes have been associated with stress in older adults. Other physical illnesses associated with stress include diabetes, stomach problems and skin problems including eczema and rashes. People who are stressed may be more likely to catch colds or flu, or other infections, than people who are not stressed.

People suffer all these physical reactions because of the way our **stress-response** works. We all have a biological reaction called the stress-response which helps us to jump, run or fight if we feel threatened. If you were crossing the road and suddenly realised there was a car coming towards you, you would feel scared. Because you are in danger your stress response would help you to escape. Your senses (eyesight, hearing, etc.) would become clearer, your muscles would enable you to jump or run. If you feel threatened, you can probably run or jump more quickly than normal.

If you escape from the car, you will feel 'wobbly' for a few minutes. You might breathe quickly and feel your heart pounding, but soon you will feel safe and your stress response will 'switch off'.

When a relationship breaks down we can feel threatened. Because we feel threatened our stress response is switched on. We want to escape, fight or run away, but there is nowhere to run and no way to escape. The threat is not physical, so we cannot escape it. Our stress response might keep going until we get exhausted and become ill.

Zeph's story: part 2

Most people have a few shocks and losses in their lives, but they find a way to recover. Zeph became exhausted with stress – she stayed at home and felt miserable. Gradually, Zeph began to believe that her

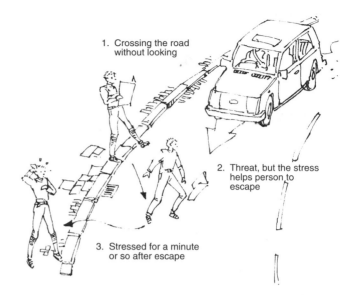

Figure 5.7 The stress response helps us to escape from threat

time with Sean was over, that it was part of her history. Zeph thought about her other friends. She had a close friend called Jody. She hadn't talked to Jody for a while because she had been going out with Sean. Zeph phoned Jody and spent time with her talking through her feelings. Jody was pleased to

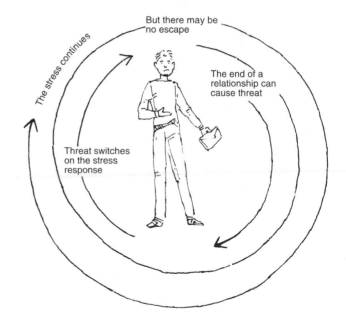

Figure 5.8 The end of a relationship may cause stress from which there is no escape

help by listening to her and talking over what had happened. Zeph felt better – at least she mattered to her real friend. After a while Zeph was able to start going out with Jody and a few of their friends. Zeph feels that she will never forget Sean, but now she thinks she understands that they would never have been really happy together. Zeph is now enjoying life with her old friends and hoping to meet a new boyfriend.

Emotional outcomes

The breakdown of a relationship can cause a major change in a person's life. At first, the person may want to deny it or pretend that everything is all right. This emotion may change to anger, withdrawal or depression, as the full realisation of what has happened becomes clear. With time and support from others, Zeph was able to accept her loss and start to build a new life. While Zeph will never forget the breakdown of her relationship, she will recover and have a positive view of herself. If she can feel positive about herself, she can make new relationships.

For some people, going through a major change in a relationship or the breakdown of a relationship may start a process of change. This process might start with disbelief and denial, go on to a stage of struggle, followed by coming to terms with the loss.

Summary: the consequences of breakdown in relationships

A breakdown can cause a wide range of social, emotional and intellectual losses including:

- loss of an emotional bond; loss of love
- loss of security and a sense of belonging
- loss of someone to talk to; loss of company
- loss of practical help and finance
- loss of excitement
- loss of self-esteem.

A breakdown in relationships might also cause an individual to become stressed.

Evidence collection point

1 Write a report describing relationships formed at different stages of life.
2 Prepare three case studies based on yourself, someone of a different gender and someone of a different ethnic origin. Each case study should:
   a identify causes of changes in relationships
   b describe reasons for participating in relationships
   c explain the role of the family in a person's development
   d identify the consequences of breakdown in relationships.
The report and the case studies will contribute to the evidence indicators for Element 2.2.

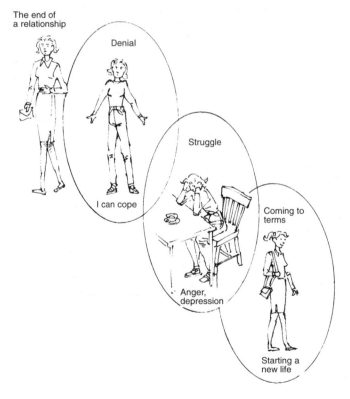

Figure 5.9 Working through the breakdown of a relationship

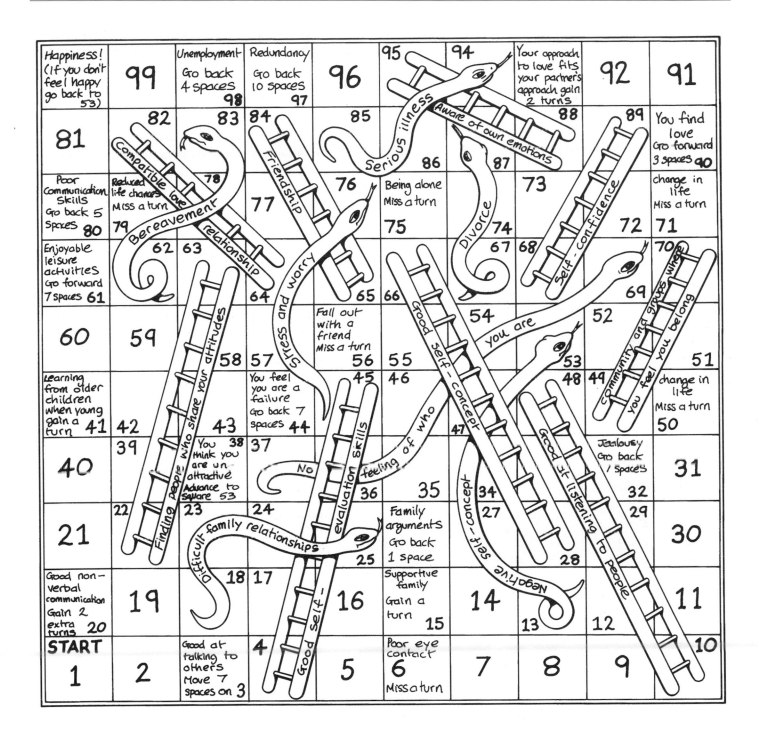

Figure 5.10 Play the Relationship Game and find out who's a winner!

Chapter 6

Social factors and their effects on health and well-being

Social factors

People in groups

We are all individuals with our own particular needs and desires, and yet at the same time we are not completely unlike everyone else. People with things in common often see themselves as members of the same **group**. Each of us belongs to a number of groups with which we feel ourselves to be linked, such as our family, our friends, our fellow students or people living in our neighbourhood.

There are also larger groups to which we belong, such as people living in Britain, or in Europe, and many other groups in between.

Some groups are quite **formal** and may be linked to a job or an organisation; for example the group of players that make up a professional football team, or the group of nurses working in a particular hospital ward.

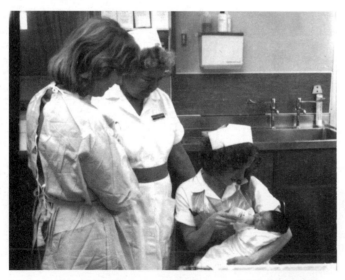

Many other groups are more loose and **informal**, such as our circle of friends or a popular personality's group of fans. Society can be seen as being made up of a multitude of groups which interrelate and overlap with each other, both in membership and in area of operation.

Everyone has their own range of group memberships, of which some are more familiar and more important than others. In small groups like our family and our close friends we are often aware of our membership, whereas our membership of larger groups may not be as important to us in our daily lives, and our links with other members are less strong.

Group settings

The types of groups we belong to can be classified by settings. Our **family** is usually our first, and our closest, group. It is here that we make our strongest bonds with other members, and that we are most consciously aware of our own membership.

Work is another setting for group membership. At work we group with our colleagues. Some people find that they are members of more than one group at work. For example, a nurse working on a hospital ward is a member of the team of staff in that ward. This group includes the other nurses, doctors and support staff who work together everyday. But the same nurse also belongs to the broader group of all nurses working in the hospital. This group may include members who seldom, if ever, meet each other. But all nurses see themselves as members of the hospital nursing staff group, with job conditions, pay levels and interests that are similar to other members.

Recreation is another setting for group membership. Groups joined for recreation are generally chosen by the individual. These are different from family and workplace groups, where membership is due to the circumstances people find themselves in.

This category includes organised recreational groups such as a football team or a choir. Here people 'join up' in a formal way. The group aim – playing football or singing – is often a more important reason for joining than a desire to mix with other group members. However, once a person has become settled in such a group, the relationships with other members may become the main reason for staying.

One of the most important groups in the lives of most people is their circle of close friends. This may be classed as a recreational group, but it is much more loose and informal than an organised sports team or a choir. The members may include people we met at work, people we grew up with or people we met through joining formal recreational groups. There are countless ways in which people meet each other and form friendship groups, and there are no rules for joining apart from acceptance by other members. Our close friends are usually very similar to us in age, background, outlook and interests. People with whom we have much in common are know as **peers**. For many people, the peer group is the most important group in their lives outside the family.

A fourth group setting is the **community**. We are a· member of a group of neighbours in our local area. This is an informal group and individuals will probably have different opinions on what 'the local neighbourhood' includes. There are also larger formal groups in the community which we may not often remember that we belong to. For example, people who are entitled to vote in elections belong to a group know as 'the electorate' or 'voters'. Also, all people who have an income above a certain level pay income tax, and so belong to a group known as 'taxpayers'. Of course, practically everything sold in Britain has tax added to its price so 'taxpayers' could include anyone who buys things, in other words, almost everybody!

Try It

Think about the groups that you belong to, and the group settings that they are in.

Write down the four group settings. **Family, Work, Recreation** and **Community** as column headings. Below each heading list the groups that you belong to in that setting. Some formal groups will be easy to name such as 'GNVQ Health and Social Care student group'. For other, less formal, groups you may need to think of a good description.

Keep your list for use further on in this section.

If you can make a 'map' of the groups a person belongs to, you will clearly see group membership. First, list all the groups a person belongs to, then draw a 'spider' chart like the one below in Figure 6.1.

The chart in Figure 6.1 is for an imaginary individual. A real chart can be larger, with more specific group names. There may be many overlaps and links between groups in a person's life, with groups having members in common. For example, a

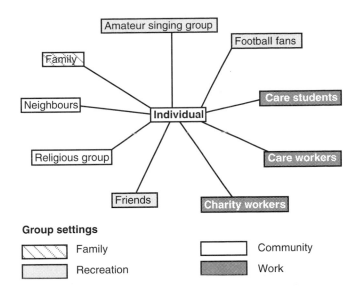

Group settings

- Family
- Recreation
- Community
- Work

Figure 6.1 Group membership chart

person may have several colleagues among the peer group with which he or she mixes socially. These links could be shown on a chart by lines joining groups together.

Try it

Now try drawing up a group membership chart for someone you know very well: yourself! Take the list of groups that you produced earlier. Draw a chart like the one above which maps your group memberships.

Roles

When you drew up your map of group memberships you had to think about the types of groups you belong to. You will have realised how different some groups are from others. These differences not only involve the groups themselves, but also your behaviour as a member.

Think it over

Choose two or three of the groups that you belong to. For each group think about how you behave when you are with other members. Write down a list of the things that you can do and those you cannot do in each of the groups.

For example, it is likely that you can relax, speak your mind, and even swear occasionally, when among your friendship group. When talking to your manager at work you probably use more respectable language, and mainly discuss work-related topics. With your friends you can break off a conversation when you choose: with your manager you may have to listen even though you do not want to!

Think about the individual members of each group. Do you have different ways of behaving towards different group members?

You will have seen that your behaviour changes, depending which group you are with. The behaviour that we adopt in a social situation is called our **role**, and we all have a number of roles that we are able to play. We play the role that is appropriate for the situation we are in, and the person with whom we are communicating.

At home you are a family member; at work you are a carer; and among your friends at a party you play another role.

People may well have more than one role within a particular group. For example, at work you may play one role towards fellow carers, another to your manager and a different one to clients. In the family the role we play towards our parents, as a son or daughter, is different from the role played towards brothers or sisters.

The roles that we play are not artificially adopted but are a part of ourselves that we display quite naturally when circumstances call for it. We simply find it appropriate to behave differently with our friends from the way we behave with our parents or employer.

We can map the roles played in each group using the method that we used for group membership.

For example, Figure 6.2 maps the roles played by an imaginary individual within her family.

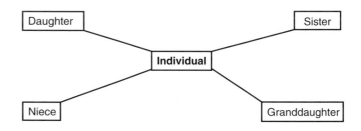

Figure 6.2 Roles played within a family

Now you can use role mapping to help build a picture of an individual as a group member.

Try it

Look again at your group membership map. Think about the roles you have in each group. Some are easy to name, like son or daughter, or fellow care worker. For others you will have to think how best to describe them. It may be advisable to indicate to whom you play the role if a description is difficult.

Draw up a role map for each group on your group membership map.

Now draw up a new version of your group map to include the results of your role mapping. List the roles under each group heading to produce a map of the roles you play in different parts of your life.

Figure 6.3 is an example of a group and role map for an imaginary person.

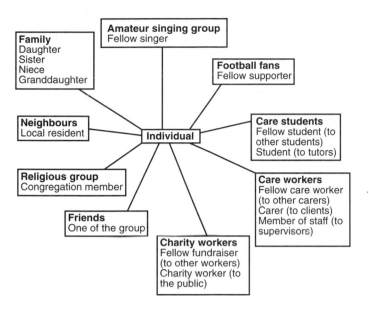

Figure 6.3 Group and role map

Now you can use role mapping methods to help you provide the evidence needed for Element 2.3.

Evidence collection point

Choose two individuals for whom you will produce a comparative case study of roles and group membership. Try to choose people who have different lifestyles, and remember that you will need to have their permission to use them as case study subjects in your work. Keeping to ethical standards requires that you tell subjects of your intentions; and you need willing volunteers to get good results.

You will need other information from your subjects to complete the case study. Details appear in the evidence assignments later in this chapter. If you will be unable to meet your subjects again later, it would be best to complete the reading of this chapter and then obtain all the information you need in one meeting.

Try to find out the range of groups of which your subjects are members. List the groups under the group setting headings of family, work, recreation and community.

Next find out the roles each individual plays in the groups to which he or she belongs. Draw up role maps for each of the groups.

Now draw up a combined group membership and role map for each individual.

This graphic view of the roles taken within groups will contribute to the evidence indicators for Element 2.3.

Belonging to a group

How do we learn our roles in a group, and how do we recognise ourselves and others as members?

For some more formal groups it is clear why we are a member and who are the other members. For example, when you began studying for a GNVQ you became a member of a group of health and caring students, and you may also be a member of a group of care staff. Often, though, group membership is not as straightforward as that.

Think it over

Think about your own family and decide whom you include as members. Then write down a list of who belongs to your family.

Look at your list and think why you consider them to be family members, and why you left out other relatives.

Think about another group that you belong to. Try to decide what makes you a member of the group and how you recognise other members.

You have probably realised how difficult it is to be precise about the rules of group membership where informal groupings such as friends and neighbours are concerned. How do people know that they belong to a community, or to a group? The answer is that all groups have their own form of organisation, and their own purpose for existence. Members have a knowledge of the rules operating in the group and can tell that they are included by the way other members behave towards them. These unwritten rules for membership and behaviour are called **norms**, and they vary widely from group to group. We are familiar with the norms of the groups to which we belong, but usually we never stop to consider what they are. We just 'know' what we are allowed to do and what is forbidden. Group norms are the conventions of behaviour that group members are expected to follow.

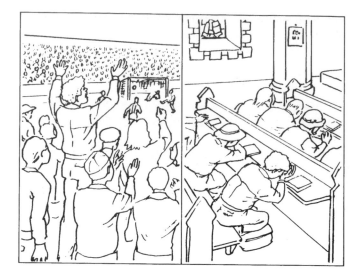

For example, it may be the norm for a football fan to wear the team colours and behave in a certain way when at a match alongside other supporters, but the norms of dress and behaviour to be followed as part of the congregation at a religious ceremony are very different. It is good supporter behaviour to cheer on your team at a football ground, but it is good behaviour to show quiet respect when part of a congregation in a place of worship.

There are great variations between groups in what is regarded as good or bad behaviour, and in concepts of right and wrong. Beliefs about what is good, important and worth striving for are known as **values**, and they are closely linked to norms of behaviour. Norms tell us how we should behave, and values help to explain why it is right to behave in this way.

Values are about what we believe to be good or bad. For example, it is a basic value of society that we believe it is wrong to hurt other people, and this is linked to the fact that it is the norm for us to try not to harm one another.

In most groups we find that our role is different from that of other group members. For example, in a family the role of parent is different from that of child. At work, an older and more experienced carer may play the role of 'wise old hand' in a group of younger, less experienced, colleagues. In all groups members tend to be ranked, whether this is spelled out in a formal way or not.

The term **status** is used to describe ranking of group members. High status members have greater power within the group and usually play a leadership role. Lower status members play a role in the group which

fits their status level, taking part in but not leading activities.

The behaviour of individuals within groups is also affected by rules and laws. Some laws affect everyone, such as laws on theft or assault. Other laws are aimed at certain groups, such as employers or motorists. Laws usually have an effect of the behaviour of the groups to which they apply. For example, when hiring staff employers may try to change the way they behave to comply with equal opportunities legislation. Sometimes, though, group norms of behaviour conflict with the law. All motorists are required by law to drive at the local speed limit. In fact, many motorists fail to obey this law at times. This is not because they are desperate lawbreakers, but because they copy the norms that they see other motorists following.

For some groups, challenging the law may be a reason for their behaviour. Young people who are part of a rough local gang may perform acts of vandalism, such as spraying graffiti on bus shelters, as part of their role as gang members.

In many more formal groups there are rules laid down to control relationships between members, and their behaviour. For example, the behaviour of care workers is partly set by the tasks they are expected to perform by their supervisors. The rules of the workplace, in relation to such subjects as smoking and health and safety, also help to define care workers' behaviour. In most formal groups there are rules affecting the roles of members. Rules define the status of the captain of a football team, or the soloist in a choir.

However, the way we learn the details of our role, our status in the group and the rules of the group is through relating to other members and learning from them. This is the process of **socialisation.**

Primary socialisation

Socialisation begins when we are born and continues to operate throughout our lives. However, we are far more responsive to influences when we are young, and our early socialisation within the family has more deeply rooted effects on us than experiences we have later. This period is so important that it is known as primary socialisation and is regarded as crucial in making us who we are.

During our early childhood we learn language and the norms of behaviour that our families expect of us. We learn the customs and values of society as a whole and are given indications of our own place within it. 'Primary' means first – as primary school is our first school – so primary socialisation is our first learning about norms. It is during the period of primary socialisation that we learn what is expected of us in the roles we will play later in life. For example, children build up a picture of what it is like to be a man or a woman, a parent or a child, and they act out their understanding of these roles in their play activities.

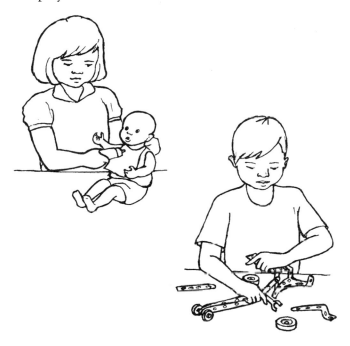

powerful influence than the toys they are given to play with.

 Try it

Find an opportunity to watch young children at play, perhaps at a placement or in some other setting.

Do the boys choose different toys from the girls, or do they play differently with the same toys?

In role-play games do girls take on different roles from boys?

See if you can spot the norms that the children have assumed about the roles they are carrying out.

This preparation for future roles is known as **anticipatory socialisation** and it can be very influential in people's lives/ It used to be generally believed that girls and boys ought to be raised differently, so that boys were prepared to lead and provide for a family and girls would be content as wives and mothers and homemakers.

Girls were encouraged to play at motherhood, and boys at work and competition. This anticipatory socialisation taught children to accept and perform these roles in later life. However, the roles for which boys were being prepared were once thought to have a higher status in society than those offered to girls. Ideas about sexual equality have spread during this century and nowadays some families attempt to give similar experiences to both boys and girls so that they are offered a more equal chance in life. However, children learn roles through imitation, and the behaviour of the adults around them is a more

Culture

During the period of primary socialisation, children are learning about the ways of their family group and of the wider society in which they live. They learn about other members of the group and about their own place within it.

The values and norms of a group and the status and roles of its members are all part of what is known as the group's **culture**. Culture is a very broad concept and it includes all aspects of the way of life associated with a group of people. The idea of a national culture is one that we are all familiar with, and when we speak of Japanese culture or British culture we have in our mind a picture of all the features of behaviour and attitude that we think of as being Japanese or British.

It is an impossible task to list all these features, as culture affects just about all aspects of our lives. Culture influences our dress, our diet, our speech, our religion and our ideas of right and wrong. Our cultural background is a fundamental part of our identity that remains with us throughout our lives.

The concept of culture can be applied to any group. For example we could say that a particular culture exists among fans of jazz music, or members of the police force. However, these groups are part of the wider society and are an aspect of what we think of as British culture as a whole. It is this wider view of the culture of a nation or ethnic group that has the deepest impact on our lives.

Our culture influences our beliefs and behaviour in every area of life and is fundamental to making us who we are. It is during the influential years of primary socialisation that we learn the norms and

values of the culture to which our family and ourselves belong. Britain is now a multi-cultural society, like many other countries across the world, and people from a variety of cultural backgrounds live here.

Children are raised within the social environment of their family and community and learn the ideas and behaviour that make them a part of their own cultural group. This primary socialisation will affect their lives in many different ways. It will affect the kind of food they eat, the style of clothes they wear, how they choose a sexual partner and how they raise their own children. In all our affairs, our culture shapes our thoughts and behaviour. It will also affect the way we are treated by the rest of society.

Peer groups

The process of socialisation is not limited to our early childhood years and it continues throughout our lives. School is another important socialising influence – here our earlier experiences are built on and we learn more about the culture of the wider society in which we live. We learn new norms and roles, and revise and extend our role set, shedding the role of infant for a more grown-up status. It is at school that we begin to learn more about the world in general, and find out about groups that exist both within the school and beyond it.

School is intended to provide children with an education and prepare them for adult life. There is a formal and organised side to the socialisation that takes place there. Teachers try to encourage behaviour that they believe will enable their pupils to get the most out of school, and the curriculum is intended to help with personal as well as academic development. School, like the rest of life, contains many different groups and it is there that we begin to form links with others who are in a similar position and whom we feel to be like us. In other words, we make friends. This circle of friends is our **peer group**, and is a major socialising influence in our lives.

The informal socialisation that takes place within our peer group may lead to conflicts with the socialisation that the school is trying to impose. This is because the norms of behaviour expected from members of the peer group may include behaviour that is forbidden by the norms of the school organisation. This is one reason why some people do not enjoy being at school. Of course, some children form peer groups whose norms fit well with those of the school, but many of us spend our school years balancing between the conflicting influences of peers and teachers.

We are part of a peer group throughout our lives, though we may change groups as we move from school to college, and as we go on to work. As our lives progress, we develop new roles and adapt old ones to fit changes in our group membership patterns. We have all experienced the process of socialisation into new groups.

Think it over

Think about some of the roles you have taken on within the past couple of years and try to decide in which period you began to develop them. For example, you could think back to period when you joined this course and began to develop the role of student. Can you remember how it felt to be a new student among many strangers in unfamiliar surroundings?

Think about the socialising influences upon you as you took on new roles. How did they operate to guide you into new patterns of thinking or behaviour?

Evidence collection point

To complete the work needed for your case study (begun on page 117), look again at the roles taken by your two individuals in the groups to which they belong.

You need to describe how laws, rules and group norms (or conventions) affect the roles each individual plays.

Try to find out how each person's behaviour differs between groups. How do formal rules, informal norms and the individual's status work together to affect the role played?

With each individual look through the groups one by one, checking and noting down the rules and norms that operate. Ask them both what is expected of them as a member of each group, and what they are not allowed to do. It may help your research if you encourage your subjects to make their own comparisons between the different roles they play. This may help them to understand what you are trying to find out and should improve your results.

Be sure to make good notes: you will need them to prepare your case study report.

So far this section has explained how individuals are socialised as members of groups, and how society is made of a multitude of formal and informal groupings. The idea of groupings can also be applied to society as a whole and used to divide the population into types or classes.

Social stratification

Class

Almost all societies see their population as split up into sections that are ranked in order of wealth and power. British society is often portrayed as being divided into **social classes**; with the upper at the top, the working class at the bottom and the middle class in between. You may have seen diagrams such as the one in Figure 6.4 to picture these divisions.

The pyramid shape is cut into three to indicate the numbers of people in each class and the classes are placed from top to bottom to show the ranking of wealth and power. The diagram divides society into layers, as rock is divided into layers – strata – and so the process of splitting society up into layers is called **social stratification.**

The pyramid diagram in Figure 6.4 is, of course, an over-simplified view of society; but the idea that classes exist in some form is a central feature of British culture. We all have an understanding of what classes there are and of the ways in which members are likely to differ from members of other classes. Our primary socialisation may have left us with an impression of what class our family, and we ourselves, belong to. These ideas are developed later through other socialising influences such as our peer group and our life at work.

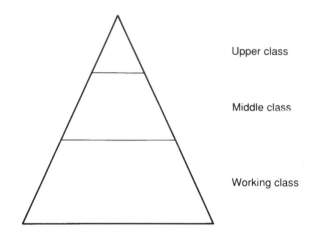

Figure 6.4 The traditional British class structure

For classes, as for other informal groups, the qualifications for membership and the norms of behaviour cannot simply be written down, and our personal view of what 'upper class' or 'middle class' means is unlikely to be the same as everyone else's.

Think it over

Try to define your own views on class in more detail.

Take a sheet of paper, divide it up into four columns and write the headings **Upper class, Middle class** and **Working class** at the top of the second, third and fourth columns.

Now think about the types of differences that might exist between the classes – in what areas do class differences show themselves? Your list could include education, lifestyle and income, and as many other categories as you wish.

Areas of difference	Upper class	Middle class	Working class
Education	Private	Some private Much encouragement	Low expectations Truancy

Head the first column **Areas of difference** and use it to list the areas in which you think classes differ. You can begin by writing the first of your areas of difference near the top of this column, for example, 'education'. Now write down what you think the differences are in this area under the class headings. Carry on doing this for each of the areas where you think differences between classes show themselves.

The exercise you have just completed should have helped you to define your ideas about class, and the characteristics and behaviours that you associate with members of different classes. The concept of culture can be applied to classes, and we may speak of working-class culture or middle-class culture when we refer to the values and norms of behaviour associated with members of these class groups. Your ideas about the differences in class culture might differ in their details from those of others, but there are certain areas where class differences are recognised by practically everybody. These areas include **income, wealth, occupation** and **lifestyle**, and they can be useful starting points if we want to try to divide the population up into classes and look at the consequences of class membership on the lives of individuals.

Class and income

Income means the cash received as wages, as interest on savings or as profits from business or some other activity. **Wealth** refers to the value of the things we own such as a car, house or country estate. Income and wealth are certainly important factors to be taken into account, but they do not tell us the whole story about a person's class. Some people such as successful performers or professional sporting personalities have very high incomes, but we would not describe them as upper or middle class simply because of this.

Wealth may be a better indicator of class than income as we tend to associate ownership of land and estates with the upper class, but wealth alone, or the lack of it, does not guarantee membership of a particular class. Someone from a working-class background who has become wealthy may never adopt the behaviour and lifestyle that we associate with middle-class people, and we would find it hard to describe a poor member of the aristocracy as working class.

Class and occupation

Occupation is often used as a main indicator of a person's class. It is useful because it carries with it ideas of the standing or status of a person, as well as pointing to their likely level of income. The Registrar-General is in charge of the government's statistical office, and the Registrar-General's social **classification** is based on occupation. It is widely used in government reports and other official documents (see Figure 6.5).

	Social class	Examples of occupation in each case
Middle class	*Class 1* Professional	Doctor, lawyer, accountant, architect
	Class 2 Managerial Technical	Manager, teacher, librarian, farmer, airline pilot
	Class 3A (*non-manual*) Clerical Minor supervisory	Clerk, sales representative, office worker, police officer
Working class	*Class 3B* (*manual*) Skilled manual	Electrician, tailor, cook, butcher, bricklayer
	Class 4 Semi-skilled manual	Farm worker, postal worker, packer, bus conductor
	Class 5 Unskilled manual	Porter, labourer, window cleaner, messenger, cleaner

Figure 6.5 The Registrar-General's social classification

The occupations given as examples for each class are chosen because they are linked to more than a level of income. They are ranked according to the general standing of the occupations within the community. This means that people in these occupations have a particular place or status in society, and the behaviour and lifestyle associated with it. This is illustrated by the way that Class 3 is divided into two, with non-manual placed above manual in the ranking of occupations. Though a skilled manual worker's income may be higher than a clerk's, he or she is still regarded as working class. Non-manual ('white-collar') workers are seen as tending towards the middle class and are expected to have many of the values and norms of behaviour associated with middle class culture.

Think it over

Think of ten occupations that do not appear as examples in the Registrar-General's classification in Figure 6.5.

Try to fit those occupations into the Registrar-General's classes using your own judgement of the standing of the occupation in society, and the income level and likely class culture of people who work in it.

This exercise should have started you thinking about the lives of people in different occupations and classes. What is it, apart from income level, that separates the life of a barrister or accountant from that of a cleaner or a labourer? We may think of differences in such things as taste in clothes and food, political views and preferred types of entertainment. People in the higher classes may be more likely to drive larger, newer cars, eat out and travel abroad, while people in lower classes are more likely to drive old cars or use public transport, eat at home, and holiday in Britain.

Of course, individuals do not possess all the characteristics of the class to which they belong, and fictitious images in the media of a 'typical' working-class or middle-class person are **stereotypes** (see page 212) rather than descriptions of real people. But the life of a barrister is different from the life of a labourer, and in more ways than income and style of work. Social class may seem to be difficult to define and hard to link to the different lives of real individuals. Nevertheless, it is used by government, business and other organisations as a way of representing differences between people in society.

Class and the lives of members

The reason that so much effort has been put into defining social classes as accurately as possible is that research has repeatedly shown that membership of a particular class has an effect on an individual's life chances. For example, the rate of infant mortality (the number of deaths of infants under one year old per thousand live births) is highest in Class 5, and gets progressively smaller as you move up the class ladder. The number of days taken off work through illness follows a similar pattern, and statistics on, for example, educational attainment and life expectancy show that membership of a higher class improves your chances in many areas of life. There is no doubt that inequalities between classes exist, and the reasons for this are both social and economic.

One reason for these inequalities is that class cultures operate to affect the lives of the individuals within them. Differences between classes in diet and leisure choices can result in less healthy lifestyles for people in lower groups. Middle-class people tend to take more exercise and eat a more varied diet, and are more aware of the importance of lifestyle in promoting good health.

The middle classes also make fuller use of the health and care services that are available to them, and the reasons for this are also linked to middle-class culture. Because of the type of work that they do middle-class people are usually accustomed to dealing with organisations, so they find it easy to communicate with health and care staff, whom they regard as their peers. Also, they are usually more assertive and demanding in pursuing their rights. In addition, people in higher social classes are more likely to be a member of private medical scheme. This is because they have a higher income and can afford to pay for it, and many work for organisations that provide free membership of private medical schemes to their employees. This means that people in higher classes are more likely to be able to avoid queues for treatment, whereas poorer people are dependant on the National Health Service and may have to wait.

Differences between classes in educational attainment are also partly due to the influence of class culture. Many working-class families may not expect their children to do well at school, and their children often receive less encouragement and help at home than children from middle-class homes. Working-class children may see formal education as useless to them, preferring to earn an income and get on with life as quickly as possible. Also, children from working class families may not be able to stay on at school because the family needs them to work and provide income. Middle-class children are more likely to see education as a way to get on in the long

run, and they are prepared to study in the expectation of greater rewards later in life.

Class culture has an influence on the life chances of individuals who grow up within it, but it is certainly not the only factor operating. Economic realities play a major part in the lives of people in class groups, and the Registrar-General's scale reflects income as well as lifestyle.

The difference in income and wealth between Classes 1 and 5 is very great indeed. At the top of Class 1 there are a few people earning more in one year than an average person in Class 5 earns during his or her lifetime. At the bottom of Class 5 are those on very low wages, and people dependant on state benefits, such as single-parent families and poor pensioners.

If we rank the whole working population on the basis of income and then divide it into five equal groups, we find that the top fifth receives just under two-fifths of the total wages paid nationally, and the bottom fifth receives just under a fifteenth.

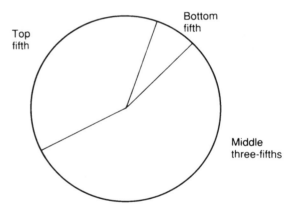

Figure 6.6 The wages cake

This means that the average wage for the best-paid fifth of the population is over five times greater than the average wage of the poorest fifth. These differences in income have a great effect on the lifestyles of individuals and families, and on the opportunities open to them. All families have to meet the basic needs of their members, but this can be hard to achieve on a low income.

The cost of providing food and shelter can absorb a large part of the income of a person on low pay, leaving little for improvements in lifestyle or environment. Poorer people live in cheaper and less well-maintained housing than the better off, and in more crowded conditions. This may have effects on the health of individuals, and can have a social impact also. For example, another reason why working-class children perform less well academically is that they often do not have the space at home to find a quiet place to study.

The diet of poorer people tends to be less varied, and less healthy and balanced than that of the better off. People on low incomes buy a higher proportion of cheap foods and have fewer facilities for the storage and preparation of food.

Try it

Families or households divide their income into different areas such as housing, food and transport. Try to think of other areas of spending that families have, and write your list, including the three above, as a column down the left side of a sheet of paper. Talk to your family and friends about your list and add any areas you may have missed.

Now imagine you are living on your own and are responsible for paying for the things you have listed. Try to estimate how much per week you would need to spend on each item and enter the amounts alongside your list. Total your estimates to see what level of income per week you would need to meet your needs.

Example of a personal budget

£

Rent
Transport
Food
etc.

Total per week

If you were budgeting for a family consisting of two parents and three children, what extra areas of spending would you need to add to your list?

Write down these extra areas, and then try to estimate how much this family would need to spend per week in all their areas of expenditure. Total your estimates and compare the result with your figure for a single person.

Many people on low incomes find that hire purchase, or some other form of credit, is the only way that they can buy expensive items such as furniture, a washing machine or a television. If financial commitments are taken on without careful planning even people in well-paid jobs can find that they have little money to spare. The cost of a large

mortgage, and perhaps other loans, can leave little money over for the other essentials of life. The pressure of finding the money to keep up payments can lead to social and physical problems such as strain on family relationships and stress-related illnesses. If circumstances suddenly change, perhaps through loss of income because of unemployment or the need to provide for extra dependents such as children or elderly relatives, it may become difficult or impossible for people to keep up their payments.

Those in this position risk losing their homes or possessions if they cannot adjust their budget to meet their financial commitments.

Evidence collection point

Complete a project, based on a standard classification system, which compares the characteristics of the lives of different socio-economic groups. These characteristics should include housing, environment, education, employment and financial status.

You could begin by listing the classes used in the Registrar-General's classification and noting the information you have on each class in terms of the characteristics listed above. You can use the notes to help you write a comparative report.

The project will contribute to the evidence indicators for Element 2.3.

Other evidence you need for this element includes a report on how these characteristics affect an individual's choices, and their health and well-being. The choices affected include use of health and care services; nutrition; alcohol consumption; smoking habits; personal hygiene; exercise; attitude to education; maintenance of housing; and use of available income. Your report should show how membership of different social classes affects attitudes to and access to the choices in this list.

Assessing classification systems

The Hall–Jones Classification

One of the criticisms of the Registrar-General's classification is that it has too few categories to take account of the variations in status, income and lifestyle within occupational groups. For example, a farmer in Class 2 may be a smallholder with a few acres of land, or the owner of a large farm with many acres of land and a number of employees. Clearly, the status and lifestyle of the two farmers would be very different.

An alternative scale of social classification was developed by J. Hall and D. Caradog Jones in 1950. Hall and Jones decided to research people's views on the status of different occupations. They asked a sample group of people to rank 30 occupations in order of their status. Hall and Jones found that people agreed with each other very closely in the status give to each occupation.

Once the occupations had been ranked, they divided their list into seven main occupational groups.

This became the Hall–Jones Scale of Occupational Prestige (see Figure 6.7).

Class	Title	Typical occupations
1	Professional and higher administrative	Company director, chartered account
2	Managerial and executive	Works manager, civil servant (executive branch)
3	Inspectional, supervisory and other non-manual, higher grade	School teacher, commercial traveller
4	Inspectional, supervisory and other non-manual, lower grade	Insurance agent, chef
5	Skilled manual and routine non-manual work	Fitter, carpenter, clerk
6	Semi-skilled manual	Factory worker
7	Unskilled manual	Bartender, docker, road sweeper

Figure 6.7 The Hall–Jones scale

Because it uses a greater number of categories the Hall–Jones scale may be thought to give more accurate results than the Registrar-General's classification. However, because it is still based on occupation the Hall–Jones scale shares with the Registrar-General's all the weaknesses described below. There are also other problems with the way the Hall–Jones scale was arrived at.

The sample of people used by Hall and Jones was not an accurate representation of the general population. They included too high a proportion of non-manual workers. Other research shows that when people are asked to rank the status of occupations they tend to upgrade their own and similar occupations. Another pair of researchers, Wilmott and Young, asked a sample of skilled manual workers to rank the same 30 occupations. They found that their sample agreed with Hall and Jones's sample about occupations at the top and bottom of the scale, but gave skilled manual workers a higher position in the middle. This means that the Hall–Jones scale suffers from inaccuracies in the ranking on non-manual occupations.

Because classes are defined by occupation, there are several groups in the population which are not included.

Evidence collection point

Think about the different groups in society who do not have an occupation. Make a list of these. Members of these groups will not be taken into account by the Registrar-General's classification. This list will contribute to the evidence indicators for Element 2.3, by helping you to assess a social classification system.

Failure to account for certain important groups is a major weakness of classification systems. For example, in recent years the number of unemployed people has risen considerably. This change in the size of an important group in society would not be recorded by the Registrar-General's classification system.

Another criticism of these classification systems is that they have too few categories. Market research organisations, which need to obtain meaningful results for marketing purposes, generally use much more detailed classification systems. They are concerned with factors such as culture, education, manner of speech and attitude. These factors are not taken into account by the Registrar-General's classification or by the Hall–Jones scale.

Even though these classification scales are widely applied, they use narrow classification criteria of occupation and status, leaving out some social groups. Since they use only a small number of categories, they are not precise in their measurement of differences between types of people. Important characteristics such as cultural background are ignored. Because of these omissions the Registrar-General's classification can fail to reflect important changes in society.

Evidence collection point

1 Assess how precise the classification system is in dividing up society into social and economic groups. Are there enough categories, and are they based on appropriate criteria?
2 Identify any omissions. Does the classification system cover all groups in society?
3 Assess whether the classification system is sensitive to changes in society. Are there weaknesses in the system which mean that some societal changes will be missed?

Your assessment will contribute to the evidence indicators for Element 2.3.

We have seen how the lives of individuals are influenced by both social and economic factors. Membership of a class or cultural group affects how we spend our time and our money, and who we choose to spend them with. Our level of income is likely to have a major effect on our lifestyle and spending patterns. As a carer, however it is important for you to remember that people are individuals and that you should always treat them as such. Treating people as if they are all the same because they belong to a particular group reduces them to stereotypes. It is nevertheless necessary to remember that people's membership of a class and culture, and their economic situation, will affect how they see themselves, the choices they make and how they are viewed and treated by others.

Fast Facts

Anticipatory socialisation The acting out of adult roles by children. Anticipatory socialisation helps children to learn, understand and prepare for the roles that they will take on in later life.

Appearance How we look. People use different clothes, hairstyles, cosmetics and adornments such as jewellery to express membership of particular age groups, class groups, cultural and friendship groups.

Babbling A stage infants go through before they can use language. The infant makes sounds which may later help him or her to use words.

Baby-talk Adults use a high-pitched voice and slow down their speech when talking to infants. Adults may also use exaggerated facial expressions. Baby talk may help to keep an infant's attention.

Belonging A feeling of identifying with a particular group of people. Feeling safe and supported by a particular group.

Bonding Making an emotional attachment to a person. Babies usually make an attachment to carers during the first year of life.

Buffering Partners, friends and family may protect a person from the full stress of life changes and conflicts. Michael Argyle called this protection buffering.

Change Life involves coping with a wide variety of change – some of which is welcome and some is not. Change can also be classified as predictable or unpredictable.

Class A group of people who share a common position in society. Class membership is linked to occupation, income, wealth, beliefs and lifestyle.

Cognition A term which covers the mental processes involved in understanding and knowing.

Concrete operations The third stage of intellectual development in Jean Piaget's theory. At this stage, individuals can solve logical problems provided they can see or sense the objects with which they are working. At this stage, people cannot cope with abstract problems.

Conventions The customs and practices that are expected to be followed by members of a group. Social scientists use the term **norms** to describe these group conventions.

Culture The collection of values and norms that are associated with a group, including the status and roles of individual members. Culture is intended to describe all the features of a group that make it different and distinct from other groups.

Dementia A term which covers a range of illnesses involving the degeneration (or wasting) of the brain. Dementia is not part of normal ageing. Most very old people show no sign of dementing illness.

Differential growth rates The nervous system grows rapidly in the first few years of life, the reproductive organs hardly grow until puberty, while general bodily growth occurs fairly steadily throughout childhood.

Egocentric A person who is egocentric thinks that everyone experiences things in exactly the same way that he or she does. Such a person is unable to imagine different points of view.

Embryo The developing child during the first eight weeks of life in the womb.

Emotional development A focus on the feelings that individuals may have in association with expected relationship patterns in their culture.

Emotional maturity The development of a stable self-concept, or identity, which enables an individual to become independent and take responsibility for his or her own actions.

Enactive memory Action memory – remembering how to do something, the practical knowledge for performing actions. A form of memory that does not use words or pictures.

Extended family A family which consists of parents and their children, and other relatives such as grandparents, uncles or aunts.

Fertilisation The point in time when a sperm nucleus from the father joins with an egg nucleus from the mother. This can begin the process which will lead to new life.

Foetus The name given to the developing life within the mother's womb from week 8 to week 40 (or birth).

Formal operations The fourth and final stage in Piaget's theory of intellectual development. People with formal logical operations can solve abstract problems.

Formal relationships Relationships based on fixed role expectations such as between a supervisor and a worker. Formal relationships may include roles influenced by contracts or job descriptions, or organisational roles in a voluntary or social group.

Functions of a family The things that a family carries out as part of its role in society.

Group A collection of individuals who are seen as being linked by common characteristics such as appearance, interests or behaviour.

Hall-Jones scale A method of stratifying the population along the lines of class. Occupational groups are used as the basis for deciding class membership, and there are seven class groups in the scale.

Iconic memory Picture memory - being able to recall or recognise how things looked. Being able to remember something because you can visualise it. Different from memory for actions or concepts.

Income Money received as wages, interest on savings or profits from business activities.

Independence Being able to function without being dependent on others. Adolescence is seen as a time of growing independence in Western culture.

Infancy A term used to cover the first 18 months of life.

Informal relationships Relationships that develop without a specified role, such as friendships between colleagues at work or friendships in a social club. Relationships which are not based on formal or pre-specified expectations.

Intellectual development The development of our ability to think, reason and understand. Here, the term covers use of language, remembering, thinking and the development of knowledge.

Later life A term used to cover the final stage of adulthood when people become elders. Used in preference to 'old age'.

Lifestyle choice A choice made by individuals about the way in which they lead their lives.

Love – relationship styles Loving relationships may involve different styles of emotional commitment: varying from commitments based on sexual fulfilment to selfless commitment to another's needs. Differing styles of emotional commitment may cause relationships to break down.

Maintenance Providing a home and income for a family. Maintenance is a function of families.

Maternal deprivation John Bowlby's theory that children would become emotionally damaged if separated from their mother during a critical period of their early life.

Menopause Cessation of menstruation, usually occurring naturally between the ages of 45 and 55.

Motor development How muscles coordinate and pull together to enable more and more complicated movements occur.

Norms The rules of behaviour which are followed by members of groups. Norms only apply to members of the group, and are usually different from the norms of other groups.

Nuclear family A family consisting of parents and children who share a residence and cooperate economically and socially.

Oestrogen A female sex hormone (actually a group of hormones) responsible for secondary sexual characteristics.

Peer pressure The influences on our behaviour which come from our close friends or others of our own age.

Peers People who are like us in terms of group membership and status. Peers are our equals, and our peer group is often our group of close friends.

Placement The determination of a person's place and status in society classified by the family in which they grew up.

Predictable life events Changes which upset people's normal life routes. Predictable life events can be welcome or unwanted. Emotional reactions may have more to do with the desirability of the change than with its predictability.

Pre-operational The second stage in Jean Piaget's theory of intellectual development. Pre-operational children are understood as being pre-logical. They cannot reason logically.

Primary socialisation The influential socialisation that takes place during our early childhood. This is when we are socialised into membership of our families and our culture.

Primitive reflexes Reflexes which are present in the newborn but disappear after a few months to be replaced by learned responses.

Puberty The period of change leading towards being capable of sexual reproduction.

Registrar-General's social classification A method of stratifying the population along the lines of class. Occupational groups are used as the basis for deciding class membership, and there are five class groups in the scale.

Reproduction The procreation of children. Reproduction is one of the main functions of the family.

Role The behaviour adopted by individuals when they are in social situations. Group norms, and an individual's status in the group, help to define a role.

Schema A mental pattern, or memory pattern, of knowledge. An organised area of memory for something, for example, the memory of how to tie your shoelaces.

Self-concept The way we use concepts to understand who we are. A clear understanding of self may be necessary for independent functioning in Western society.

Self-confidence An individual's confidence in his or her own ability to achieve something or cope with a situation. Self-confidence may influence and be influenced by self-esteem.

Self-esteem How well or badly a person feels about himself or herself. High self-esteem may help a person to feel happy and confident. Low self-esteem may lead to depression and unhappiness.

Sensorimotor The first stage in Jean Piaget's theory of intellectual development. Infants learn to coordinate their muscle movements in relation to things that they sense.

Sexual maturity A stage of physical development that results in the ability of males and females to reproduce.

Single-parent family A family consisting of one parent and children.

Socialisation The process of learning the norms and values of a group, and developing a role within it. Through socialisation people become part of a group or culture.

Social context A setting where social influences affect an individual's learning and development.

Social development A focus on the way groups may influence relationship patterns within a culture.

Social stratification The process of dividing the population into layers or strata. Society can be stratified on the basis of class, income, race, age, or any other characteristic by which people can be separated into groups.

Status A measure of the rank and prestige of a person or a group of people. Status helps to define how people are treated by others, and how they see themselves.

Social support The way in which partnerships, friends, family, colleagues and wider community and state systems may assist individuals to cope with life events.

Stress response A physical reaction that helps a person to fight or run away. The stress response may create problems when a person cannot fight or run or such a reaction is inappropriate. A person may become 'stressed' because he or she cannot escape from an emotional problem.

Symbolic memory Memory which uses symbols such as numbers and words. The memory for ideas uses concepts and language. Symbolic memory is different from the memory for actions or the picture memory.

Threat Something which is understood as a danger to physical, social or emotional well-being.

Unpredictable life events Changes which upset people's normal life routines and expectations. Unpredictable life events may be welcome or unwelcome. Unwelcome events may create a range of problems for an individual to cope with.

Values Beliefs about what is good and bad, right and wrong, and worthless or worth striving for. Group values help to explain and define group norms of behaviour.

Wealth The value of the property owned by a person. Wealth includes the value of houses, cars, savings and any other personal possessions.

Self-assessment test

1 All major organs of the embryo should have formed by:
   a 2 weeks.
   b 1 week.
   c 20 weeks.
   d 8 weeks.

2 A human from the eighth week of pregnancy until birth is called:
   a Neonate.
   b Embryo.
   c Foetus.
   d Baby.

3 The age range in years normally quoted for the onset of puberty in males is:
   a 7–9.
   b 8–10.
   c 12–14.
   d 16–18.

4 The stopping of monthly bleeding in females is known as:
   a Menarche.
   b Menopause.
   c Menstruation.
   d Menses.

5 The Moro reflex is demonstrated when a baby:
   a Grasps someone's finger strongly.
   b Throws arms and legs out when startled.
   c Turns head towards a touch on the cheek.
   d Makes stepping movements when held upright.

6 Myelination is the process by which:
   a Nerve cells acquire fatty sheaths.
   b Eyes begin to focus.
   c Muscle coordination develops.
   d Fat cells begin to form.

7 Wrinkling of the skin is due to:
   a Poor nutrition.
   b Osteoporosis.
   c Loss of weight.
   d Degeneration of elastic tissue.

8 The hormone responsible for the development of sexual changes during puberty in males is:
   a Oestrogen.
   b Testosterone.
   c Thyroxine.
   d Growth hormone.

9 Intellectual development covers:
   a Getting on with others.
   b Socialisation.
   c Knowledge, memory and language.
   d Listening to classical music.

10 Young babies pay particular attention to:
   a Television.
   b Human faces.
   c Cars.
   d Colours.

11 Piaget believed that a young infant in the sensorimotor stage who dropped an object would:
   a Not remember an object that was out of sight.
   b Look until he or she found it.
   c Wait for someone else to get it.
   d Always put something in the same place.

12 Egocentric means:
   a Children always want sweets.
   b Children always think everyone feels the same as they do.
   c Living in the centre of a town.
   d Developing logic.

13 Concrete operations means:
   a Children can often work things out if they can see the objects involved.
   b A very abstract way of thinking.
   c Dealing with a hard mass.
   d Having to go into hospital.

14 Bowlby's theory of bonding stated:
   a Children who did not bond would never get good jobs.
   b Children were capable of bonding to anyone.
   c A mother must never be separated from her child in case of emotional damage to the child.
   d Fathers were as important as mothers.

15 In order to develop self-confidence children need:
   a Plenty of pocket money.
   b Married parents.
   c To be good looking.
   d Supportive carers and friends.

16 By 'acting out' characters children learn:
   a Gender roles.
   b To speak.
   c How to do maths.
   d How to become actors or actresses.

17 Primary socialisation takes place:
   a At nursery school.
   b Within the caring or family group.
   c At the park.
   d On holiday.

18 Socialisation will enable children to:
   a Go to lots of parties.
   b Wear the best designer clothes.

    c Learn the norms or values of their family.
    d Grow strong and healthy.

19 Emotional maturity means:
    a Having a boyfriend or girlfriend.
    b Having sex often.
    c Independence from parents and a sense of self.
    d Wearing trendy clothes.

20 Negative self-concepts happen because:
    a The camera used for the photograph was faulty.
    b The person came from a poor family.
    c People are treated negatively by family, school, society.
    d A person's hair is the wrong colour.

21 Major life events include:
    a Disagreeing with your father.
    b Moving house.
    c Being late for an interview.
    d Hormones.

22 Managing change can be helped by:
    a Talking with someone.
    b Buying a new car.
    c Gender.
    d Giving up work.

23 Relate is:
    a A dating agency.
    b A late-night taxi service.
    c A guidance and counselling service.
    d A fertility clinic.

24 Bonding means:
    a Making friends.
    b Belonging to the same club as a friend.
    c Substance abuse.
    d Baby and carer forming a strong relationship.

25 A baby needs care from:
    a One person all the time.
    b Anyone as long as he or she is not left alone.
    c A few consistent and affectionate people.
    d A professionally trained nanny.

26 Children whose parents split up:
    a Always do badly at school.
    b Grow up feeling unloved.
    c Do not have successful relationships themselves.
    d May be perfectly well-adjusted and happy.

27 The best thing to do when caring for a young child who is playing alone is:
    a To be left in peace while the child is quiet.
    b To make sure the child does not miss its favourite TV programme.
    c To ensure the child will not get dirty.
    d To talk with the child.

28 Adolescence is:
    a A time of physically changing from a child to an adult.
    b Something which happens overnight.
    c When you can pass examinations.
    d Something which only happens to girls.

29 As people grow older they:
    a Only change on the outside.
    b Become nicer than when they were young.
    c Change both mentally and physically.
    d Stay the same.

30 Having a baby costs:
    a Hardly anything.
    b A lot of money for many years.
    c Not much because of grants.
    d Some money at first, but then the cost falls.

31 Having a child to sort out difficulties in a relationship:
    a Changes a couple's style of love relationship.
    b Is a good idea.
    c Will put the couple under more pressure.
    d Will 'cement' the relationship.

32 Unemployment usually affects a person:
    a Only financially.
    b Hardly at all.
    c By giving them a chance to rest.
    d Emotionally, socially, physically and intellectually.

33 Retirement means:
    a The person will not have any more worries.
    b Life will be much the same as before.
    c Adjusting to a new way of life.
    d Being in the house all of the time.

34 People going through change generally need:
    a Professional counselling.
    b Good relationships with others.
    c New clothes.
    d Advice from Relate.

35 To keep a friendship working it is important for friends to:
    a See each other every day.
    b Like the same clothes.
    c Trust each other or help each other.
    d Have the same hobbies.

36 Someone with lots of friends:
    a May be lonely.
    b Is never lonely.
    c Parties through life.
    d Is always with others.

37 A nuclear family is:
a A family that consists of a single parent and children.
b A family that consists of parents, children and grandparents.
c A family that consists of two parents and children.
d A family that shares a household with another family.

38 A household containing an extended family would consist of:
a Only one adult and children.
b Two adult partners with no children.
c Two adult partners and their children.
d Two adult partners with children together with other relatives.

39 The functions of a family are thought to have changed in modern industrial societies. This is because:
a Modern domestic appliances have made life easier.
b Some of the family's functions can now be fulfilled outside the family group.
c Society no longer needs these functions to be performed.
d Children born today are more intelligent than those born in the past.

40 Some social scientists believe that modern families have new functions to perform as part of the family's role. These functions include:
a Providing support for family members.
b Ensuring that children have access to television and other media.
c Making sure that they get on well with other families.
d Participating in local neighbourhood events.

41 People belong to both formal and informal groups. Which of the following is an example of a formal group?
a A family.
b A peer group.
c Students studying together on the same course.
d A group of football fans.

42 Peer groups are very important in the lives of most people. Peer group members are:
a Members of our family.
b Close friends who have many things in common.
c People who meet at work.
d People who study together at school or college.

43 People play different roles as members of groups. The process of learning roles is called:
a Socialisation.

b Familiarisation.
c Stratification.
d Normalisation.

44 People play several different roles in their lives. This is because:
a People belong to several different groups, and have their own place in each one.
b People need to have variety in their lives.
c It is hard to remember how to behave all the time.
d Playing the same role all the time can become boring.

45 Groups have their own rules for the behaviour of their members. Which of the following is the name given to these rules?
a Laws.
b Status.
c Roles.
d Norms.

46 Groups have beliefs about what is good and bad, and right and wrong. These beliefs are called:
a Religion.
b Values.
c Morals.
d Norms.

47 In groups different members are usually ranked in terms of power and prestige. Different group members are said to have different:
a Values.
b Norms.
c Beliefs.
d Status.

48 Primary socialisation may be described as:
a The things we learn in primary school.
b The process of learning our role at work.
c The process of learning language, norms and values during our early years.
d Learning to fit in with our group of close friends.

49 Young children often act out the behaviour that they see adults around them performing. Which of the following terms is used to describe this?
a Gender.
b Anticipatory socialisation.
c Imagination.
d Creative play.

50 The norms and values of a group, and the roles and status of its members, help to make it distinct from other groups. The term used for this collection of group features is:
a Socialisation.
b Role set.

c   Culture.
d   Class.

51 Social stratification means:
    a   Dividing the population into different groups.
    b   Treating all people equally.
    c   The process of learning to be a member of a group.
    d   Teaching children the values and norms of their culture.

52 Which of the following is used by the Registrar-General's scale as the basis of social class?
    a   Income.
    b   Occupation.
    c   Wealth.
    d   Lifestyle.

53 Which of the following is used by the Hall-Jones scale as the basis of social class?
    a   Occupation.
    b   Gender.
    c   Ethnic group.
    d   Age.

54 One reason for trying to divide the population into classes is:
    a   It helps employers to decide how much to pay employees.
    b   It shows how many people are unemployed.
    c   It helps us to see the differences in life chances between people in different classes.
    d   It helps us to see how many women go to work.

55 Which of the following statements is true of people in different social classes?
    a   People in Class 1 have lower life expectancy than people in Class 5.
    b   People in Class 5 have a higher income than people in Class 1.
    c   People in Class 1 have more days off work through illness than people in Class 5.
    d   There is a higher rate of infant mortality in Class 5 than in Class 1.

56 People in higher social classes often make fuller use of medical services than people in lower classes. One reason for this is:
    a   People in higher classes are more likely to be in a private medical scheme.
    b   People in lower classes usually live further away from hospitals.
    c   People in lower classes are more careful about their health.
    d   People in higher classes fall ill more often than people in lower classes.

57 People in higher classes are more likely to join a fitness club than people in lower classes. Which of the following is a reason for this?
    a   People in higher classes have more available money to spend on fitness club fees.
    b   People in lower classes are already very healthy.
    c   People in higher classes have a greater need to stay fit.
    d   People in lower classes have more facilities at home to help them stay fit.

58 People in lower classes eat a less varied and nutritious diet than people in higher classes. Which of the following is the main reason for this?
    a   People in lower classes enjoy eating only a small range of foods.
    b   People in higher classes need more nutrition because of the physical demands of their occupations.
    c   People in lower classes spend a higher proportion of their income on cheap, staple foods.
    d   People in higher classes have better shopping facilities available to them.

59 The Registrar-General's scale is often criticised for being imprecise. Which of the following most accurately describes the reason for this criticism?
    a   People may change their occupation.
    b   Occupation is an inadequate way of dividing people into classes.
    c   Having only five class groups means that very different types of people are put into the same class.
    d   The scale is based on inaccurate information about the members of occupational groups.

60 Both the Registrar-General's classification and the Hall-Jones scale are based on occupation. Which of the following is a major weakness of dividing the population in this way?
    a   Important groups in society may be left out of the classification.
    b   People may not enjoy their occupation.
    c   It is difficult to get information about people's occupation.
    d   Occupation is rarely linked to income and lifestyle.

The organisation of health and social care services

Many health and social care services are **statutory** – this means that they have been set up because Parliament has passed a law which requires these services to be provided. The two main providers of statutory services are the National Health Service (NHS) and social services departments.

Health and social care may also be provided by private and voluntary organisations. **Private organisations** provide care for individuals, or groups of people, on a profit-making basis and are run like a business, for example private hospitals or residential homes. Voluntary organisations are run on a not for profit basis such as many hospices or the Women's Royal Voluntary Service (WRVS).

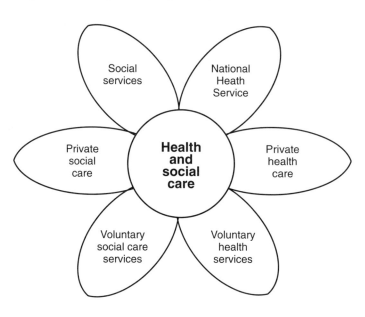

Figure 7.1 Providers of health and social care services

 Try it

Find out from your local *Phone Book* or from the library, social services department or local newspaper:

1 what *private* health care and social care organisations exist in your area
2 what *voluntary* health and social care organisations exist in your area.

The structure of the National Health Service

Central government

The Secretary of State for Health is responsible for the provision of services in both health and social care. The government department in charge of this is the Department of Health (DoH). It has responsibility for:

■ Making policy and issuing advice to Regional Health Authorities
■ Monitoring the performance of authorities
■ Allocating resources.

In recent years the NHS has been undergoing major reforms which have been more far reaching than any since it was set up in 1948. These reforms were set out in three government White Papers:

1 *Promoting Better Health* – 1987 – this dealt with the provision of primary health care.
2 *Working for Patients* – 1989 – this looked at the management of services and the way that services were funded.
3 *Caring for People* – 1989 – this covered care in the community.

Regional Health Authorities

There are eight Regional Health Authorities in England (see Figure 7.1), and three separate authorities for Wales, Scotland and Northern Ireland.

Each Regional Health Authority (RHA) is responsible for:

■ Planning services in its area within national guidelines

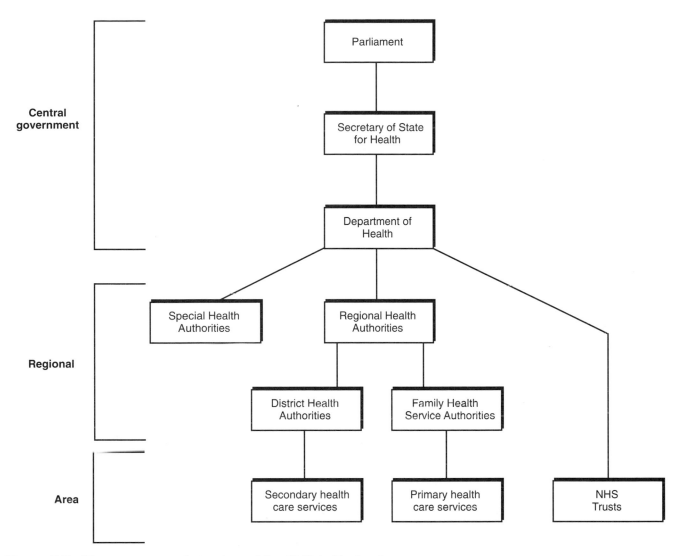

Figure 7.2 The management structure of the NHS in England

- Allocating finances to District Health Authorities, Family Health Service Authorities and fundholding GPs.
- Monitoring the services of the Regional Health Authorities and Family Health Service Authorities.
- Developing regional plans for specialist services, (for example, the treatment of severe burns).
- Building new hospitals.

The gradual reduction of the number of Regional Health Authorities in Britain (prior to 1994 there were 14 RHAs in England) might result in the eventual disappearance of RHAs.

Family Health Service Authorities

Family Health Service Authorities (FHSAs) are responsible for providing **primary care.** This includes:

- managing services provided by GPs, dentists, pharmacists and opticians
- assessing primary health care needs in their area
- planning the contracts for GPs
- managing GP development funds.

There are 90 FHSAs in England.

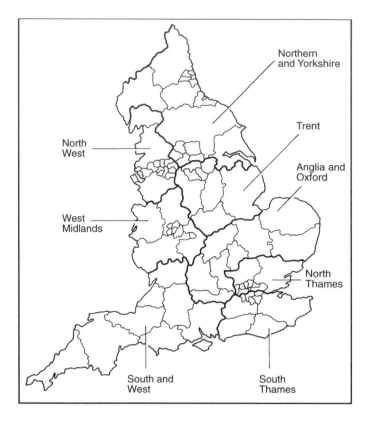

Figure 7.3 Regional Health Authorities in England

District Health Authorities

District Health Authorities (DHAs) assess the secondary health care needs of the population, which involves:

■ managing services under their control, such as directly managed hospitals.
■ purchasing services for residents
■ responsibility for public health.

There are 186 DHAs in England (see Figure 7.4).

Special Health Authorities

In addition to Regional Health Authorities, there are 16 Special Health Authorities (SHAs). They are directly responsible to the Department of Health. There are three types of SHAs:

1 **Non-hospital** SHAs provide support services, for example NHS Supplies Authority.
2 **Hospital** SHAs include specialist teaching and

District Health Authorities by region from 1 April 1994

Northern and Yorkshire
Northumberland, Newcastle, South Tyneside, North Durham, Hartlepool, South Tees, South Humberside, West Yorkshire, Leeds, East Cumbria, Gateshead, North Tyneside, Sunderland, South Durham, North Tees, North Humberside, North Yorkshire, Bradford, Wakefield, West Cumbria

Trent
North Derbyshire, Nottingham, North Lincolnshire, Leicestershire, Doncaster, Sheffield, Southern Derbyshire, North Nottinghamshire, Southern Lincolnshire, Barnsley, Rotherham

Anglia and Oxford
Cambridge, Suffolk, Kettering, Oxfordshire, North West Anglia, South Bedfordshire, Great Yarmouth & Waveney, Huntingdon, Norwich, Northampton, Berkshire, North Bedfordshire, Buckinghamshire

North Thames
Barnet, Brent & Harrow, North Essex, East & North Hertfordshire, South West Herefordshire, Ealing Hammersmith & Hounslow, East London & The City, Hillingdon, New River, South Essex, North West Herefordshire, Kensington & Chelsea & Westminster, Barking & Havering, Camden & Islington, Redbridge & Waltham Forest

South Thames
South East London, Greenwich, Canterbury & Thanet, Dartford & Gravesham, Medway, East Sussex, Worthing, North West Surrey, South West Surrey, Kingston & Richmond, Merton & Sutton, Bromley, Bexley, South East Kent, Maidstone, Tunbridge Wells, Chichester, Mid-Downs, Mid-Surrey, East Surrey, Wandsworth, Croydon

South and West
Southampton & South West Hampshire, Dorset, Basingstoke, Swindon, Isle of Wight, Gloucestershire, Plymouth & Torbay, Cornwall & Isles of Scilly, Portsmouth & North East Hampshire, Winchester, Salisbury, Bath, Bristol & District, Exeter & North Devon, Somerset

West Midlands
Coventry, East Birmingham, Mid-Staffordshire, Warwickshire, North Worcestershire, Shropshire, South East Staffordshire, Walsall, Wolverhampton, Dudley, Herefordshire, North Birmingham, North Staffordshire, Sandwell, South Birmingham, Solihull, West Birmingham, Worcester

North West
South & East Cheshire, North Cheshire, Chester, St Helens & Knowsley, Blackpool Wyre & Fylde, Blackburn Hyndburn & Ribble Valley, Chorley & South Ribble, Wigan, Bury, Oldham, Tameside & Glossop, Salford, Central Manchester, South Cumbria, Liverpool, Sefton, Wirral, Lancaster, Preston, Burnley Pendle & Rossendale, West Lancashire, Bolton, Rochdale, Stockport, Trafford, North Manchester, South Manchester

Figure 7.4 District Health Authorities

research hospitals, such as the National Heart and Chest Hospital.

3 **Specialist hospitals** like Rampton deal with the care of seriously disturbed offenders.

National Health trusts

National Health trusts are self-governing units within the health service. Trusts are run by a board of directors and are accountable to central government. Many major acute hospitals now have trust status, which means that they are no longer answerable to the District Health Authorities. Trusts can cover a wide range of services, for example hospitals and community services such as district nurses and ambulance services.

A trust is allowed to:

■ decide its management structure
■ employ staff under its own terms and conditions of service, including salary scales
■ buy, own and sell assets such as land or buildings
■ keep surplus money or borrow.

Think it over

Find out whether any hospital or community trusts operate in your local area. If there are any, what are they called and what services do they provide?

Scotland

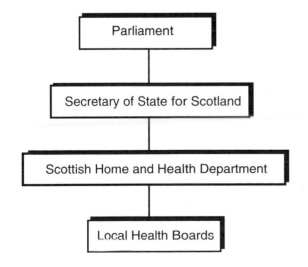

Figure 7.5 Health care structure in Scotland

The Secretary of State for Scotland is answerable to Parliament for health services in Scotland. The country's health services are run by the Scottish Home and Health Department. Local Health Boards are responsible for providing services at district level (see Figure 7.5).

Wales

Organisation of health services in Wales is similar to that in England, except that there are no Regional Health Authorities. There are nine District Health Authorities and the Secretary of State for Wales is accountable to Parliament for health services (see Figure 7.6).

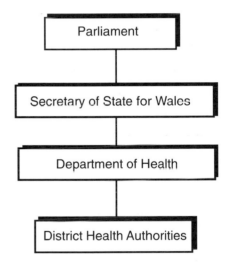

Figure 7.6 Health care structure in Wales

Northern Ireland

Northern Ireland's health services and social services are organised as a single agency. This is called a 'unified structure', and is outside local political control. Four Health Boards provide services at local level. The Department of Health allocates resources for the services to the four boards (see Figure 7.7).

Although the organisation of health services in Scotland, Wales and Northern Ireland may be different from that in England, the range and provision of services is much the same.

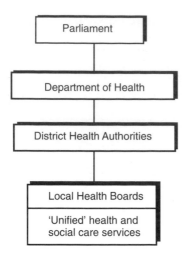

Figure 7.7 Northern Ireland's 'unified' services

The structure of social care

The Secretary of State for Health is responsible for the *provision* of social services. However, it is the local authorities that run them. Local authority social service departments have responsibility for the coordination of all forms of social care in the community (see Figure 7.8)

Figure 7.8 Structure of social care in England

Each local authority has a social services committee which looks after the social services within its area. It must appoint a Director of Social Services. The director is in charge of the department which runs the services. Social service departments are often organised into area offices from which the services for that area are operated.

Organisational structures within local authority social services departments have changed considerably in the past years to enable the departments to carry out their new roles, as required by current legislation and, in particular, the National Health Service and Community Care Act 1990.

Many social services departments now have inspection and monitoring sections which may also be responsible for dealing with complaints procedures. Planning and development sections have become more important as the authorities are now required to work more closely with health service planning colleagues, as well as with the private and voluntary sector. Additionally, some local authorities have sections which are specifically responsible for contracting with service providers. Many social services departments have also reorganised to reflect a clear division between staff responsible for those who provide the different service (see Figure 7.9).

County councils run local authority social services in England and Wales, as do metropolitan councils and the London boroughs.

Social services should not be confused with the Department of Society Security (DSS), which administers benefits and pays out money. Apart from an occasional small sum in an emergency, the social services do not hand out money. Their main function is to offer advice, to provide access to services and to supply a number of services themselves. They provide access to community and residential services for all client groups, such as children, people with mental health problems, people with mental or physical disabilities and older people.

Evidence collection point

Visit your local Social Services Department and find out the organisational structure. Make a diagram of the structure.

Figure 7.9 Example of a local authority social
Sservices department

Purchasing and providing in health and social care

At the centre of the reforms to health and social care
is the idea that there should be a clearer division
between the purchasing of services and the provision
of services. The Conservative government of the 1980s
and 1990s therefore acted to create a 'market-place
system' for the delivery of care. The marketplace
approach is based on the buying and selling of things,
in this case buy and selling health and social care
services. In health and social care the buyers are called
purchasers and the sellers are called **providers**.

In the health service it is the District Health
Authorities and fundholding GPs who are the
purchasers of care, and hospitals and other units,
such as NHS trusts, that are the providers of care.

In social service departments the purchasing and
providing roles have been split. Social workers within
social services departments are now responsible for
assessing the needs of their clients, agreeing care
plans to meet those needs and arranging for the
provision of suitable services.

The cost of care packages is often paid for out of
funds held by a purchasing officer. Providers within
social services departments include residential and
day-care units, as well as home-care services.
Increasingly, social services departments are not only
buying services from within their own organisation,
but are also purchasing services from the private
sector and from voluntary organisations. Some local
authorities, for example, purchase places in private
residential homes for older people.

Try it

Find out from the local social services
department what services are being bought
in.

The purchaser–provider theory

In a marketplace, traders – providers – set out their
stall, while customers – purchasers – work out what
they need to buy. Marketplaces often encourage
cheaper prices for things like fruit and vegetables.

There might be competition between providers – more than one stall selling fruit, for example. Providers have to work hard and try to provide good quality at the most competitive prices if they are to attract purchasers and stay in business.

Supporters of the market idea argue that it will lead to good quality care for patients. Patients will be treated more like customers; they will be seen as vital for the maintenance of staff jobs. Supporters of the market idea also argue that competition will lead to greater efficiency and that services will improve at no extra cost to the tax payer.

Not everyone supports the market idea for health care. Some people argue that a complex service like medicine will not adapt to the simple ideas which work when selling fruit and vegetables. Those against the market idea claim that certain individuals may be disadvantaged because 'their purchasers' are not in such a powerful position as other purchasers. Others believe that the market will eventually lead to a privatisation of all services. This would mean that certain types of care will only be available to individuals who can afford to pay privately. These issues are open to political debate.

Mixed economy of care

Many areas operate a **mixed economy of care.** This means that the major agencies work together to satisfy the needs of the individual.

The government has a policy of promoting care in the community, which means that people should be cared for in their own homes or an establishment in the community whenever this is possible. Under the NHS and Community Care Act, responsibility for services in the community lies with local authority social services departments. Each social services department appoints care managers who are responsible for purchasing services from the full range of statutory, voluntary and private providers.

In order to ensure the delivery of cost-effective health and care services of quality, the organisations responsible for the services need to work together. Community care, on one level, involves a partnership between the District Health Authority, social services department and Family Health Services Authority (representing GPs). On another level it involves the practitioners who provide the care – the social workers, community nurses, support workers and informal workers.

The partnership between the District Health Authority, social services department and Family Health Services Authority is at a senior (or strategic) level. These three organisations work together to produce a plan for the district they cover. Publication of a yearly **plan** is required by law under the NHS and Community Care Act. The 'strategic plan' provides a strategy or plan of action for the area. The three organisations look at the district's situation in relation to the health and care needs of people living the area and the services needed to meet those needs.

Funding

Funding the NHS

The financing of the health services is a major issue which is rarely out of the headlines in national and local newspapers. Expenditure in the UK increased from £444 million in 1949 to £29 billion in 1990. Allowing for inflation, expenditure has increased more than fourfold since the NHS was created in 1948.

Money for the NHS comes from three main sources:

1 central and local government tax revenues
2 National Insurance contributions
3 charges paid by users, and income generation.

Public services are funded by local and national taxes – income tax, value added tax (VAT) and National Insurance contributions by individuals and organisations. The main sources of income from 'charges' are from prescriptions issued by GPs and dentists, and for dental treatment and examinations.

The amount of money spent on the NHS each year is decided by the Department of Health and the Treasury. The Department of Health then allocates money to the Regional Health Authorities, according to the size, age and health of their resident population.

The Regional Health Authority then allocates money to the District Health Authorities in its area, which purchase services to meet the needs of residents.

The RHA also allocates funds to the Family Health Service Authorities so that they are able to purchase primary health care services.

A fundholding GP receives money directly from the Regional Health Authority in order to purchase

services for patients. GP fundholders are both providers of primary care and purchasers of secondary care. Some people argue that patients registered with fundholders who need secondary services are at an advantage compared to patients of non-fundholding GPs. The fundholder can buy services direct from a range of providers, but the ordinary GP has to place patients on a waiting list for District Health Authority funded services. Some critics claim that this creates a two-tier system; however, both fundholders and non-fundholders have to work within limited budgets.

Funding social services

Each district and local council has the responsibility for maintaining certain services, which include:

- social services
- education
- leisure and recreation
- housing – general funds
- highways and car parking
- refuse collection and waste disposal
- environmental health
- planning and economic development

In addition, local authorities pay towards police, fire, water and other services.

Funding for all these services comes from two main sources a yearly allocation of money from the government and from council taxes. The amount of money the government gives is based on a formula called the 'standard spending assessment'. The formula takes into account the number of older people living in the area, the percentage of rented accommodation, the number of single parent families, the percentage of people from ethnic minority backgrounds, the density of population, etc.

The local authority then allocates money to the various services. For many authorities their biggest expenditure is on education, with social services taking the next largest amount.

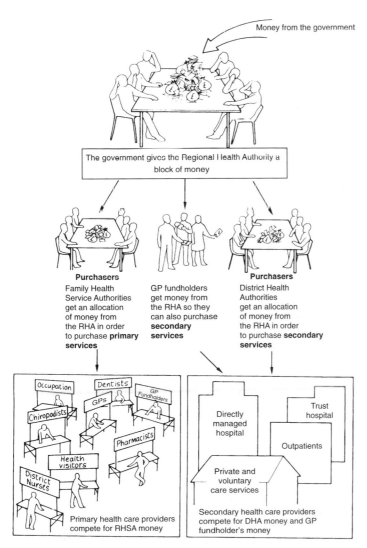

Figure 7.10 Funding the NHS

Try it

Find out from your local authority how much it spends on the various services each year. You will be able to do this either by looking at the information sent out with the council tax bill, which every household receives; or by looking at the authority's yearly expenditure plan, which it publishes at the beginning of the financial year.

The Director of Social Services is accountable for how the money allocated to the social services department is spent. Various amounts will be allocated to children's services, services for older people and services for people with various disabilities or mental health problems.

Some services provided by social services departments are free of charge; but others, such as meals-on-wheels, usually have to be paid for. People may be financially assessed and may be required to pay towards the cost of certain services such as residential care. Increasingly, users are having to pay towards the cost of services and in some areas, services which had been free of charge are no longer so, for example, home-care services, day care or transport to day-care centres.

Try it

Find out what social services in your area users have to pay towards. Which of these charges have been introduced in the past three years?

Funding voluntary organisations

Some voluntary organisations obtain funds from either their local authority via the social services departments or from District Health Authorities. However, it is very unlikely that they receive more than part of their total running costs from these bodies. For example, a local authority may give some funds to the local Age Concern group, which provides day-centre activities and luncheon clubs for older people in its area. A District Health Authority may have a contract with a local hospice to provide specialist care for people with a terminal illness, such as cancer or AIDS.

The remainder of voluntary organisations' funds are obtained through fundraising events, charitable donations from individuals or groups of people, and from grant-awarding bodies. Some large commercial organisations, such as the car manufacturer Ford, donate money to charities for specific purposes. Trust funds may also give donations (see Figure 7.11).

Think it over

How many charity shops are there in your area? Which charities do they support? Look in the local newspaper to identify any

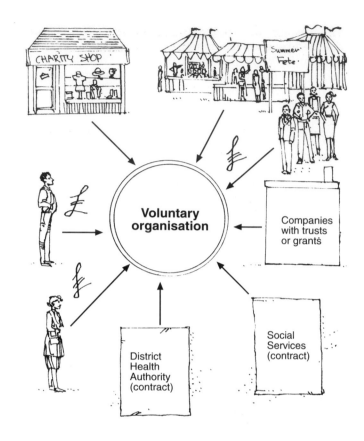

Figure 7.11 Financing voluntary organisations

social events that are being held in aid of charities. What type of events are they and for which charities?

Evidence collection point

Visit a voluntary organisation in your area and write a report on the source of its funds. Many voluntary agencies publish an annual report which gives details about their income and expenditure.

This will contribute to the Evidence Indicators for this section.

Financing private care services

Private organisations are run on business lines and are therefore self-financing. However, it is now possible for health and social service purchasers to contract with private sector providers. This gives private agencies, such as private nursing homes or home-care agencies, another source of financing.

National health services

The provision of health services can be divided into:

1 **primary services**, such as general practitioners (GPs)
2 **secondary care**, such as hospital care
3 **tertiary care**, i.e. long-term rehabilitation, such as physiotherapy
4 **community services**, such as district nurses.

Primary care is the first contact with health services and is delivered in the community. It is often preventative in nature and is offered by Family Health Services.

Secondary care usually follows referral from primary care. It is often curative in nature and is given in hospitals, day surgeries and out-patient clinics.

Some services may function as both primary and secondary care. A paramedic giving treatment at the scene of an accident is an example of primary care; whereas a paramedic in the ambulance service collecting a patient for treatment at a hospital is an example of secondary care.

Tertiary care may be provided by specialist units which are able to give longer term, rehabilitative treatment to patients – for example, a unit proving intensive physiotherapy following an accident where the patient suffered severe spinal injuries, resulting in paralysis of the lower limbs.

Community services provide care for individuals within the community, and where possible in the person's own home. These services include district nurses, health visitors, domiciliary midwife's, and some services offered by physiotherapist, chiropodists, occupational and speech therapists.

Primary health services

Primary health services are provided by professional people who are often the first line of call if there is a problem. GPs, dentists, opticians and pharmacists are the most obvious examples. This provision is overseen in an area by the Family Practitioners' Committee, which keeps a register of services and monitors the complaints of service users.

The GP's surgery is usually the first place to go if you feel unwell. The GP will, if necessary, refer you to the

other services you need. For this reason, the staff at the surgery are often known as the **primary health care team.** The 'team' consists of the GP, the district nurse, the health visitor, local practice nurse, midwife and the community psychiatric nurse. Sometimes a social worker is included. They are all based full-time or part-time at the local surgery.

Each member of the team has specific a role, and each one complements the others to provide overall care. Nowadays a GP's surgery offers a wide range of services, including 'well man' and 'well woman' clinics and possibly some minor surgical treatments. The primary health care team is interested in preventing illness as well as curing it.

Everyone can be registered with a particular GP to get treatment, although someone can register as a temporary patient if visiting another area.

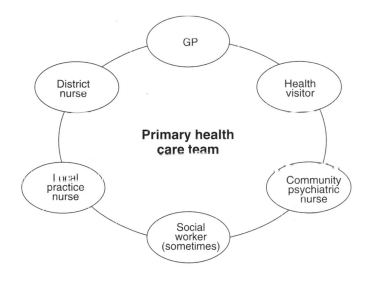

The GP contract

General practitioners are not directly employed by the National Health Service. They are independent contractors who have a contract with the local Family Health Services Authority to provide general medical services. GPs can advertise and employ their own staff to assist them.

The GPs' contract requires them to:

- publish a directory of services, an annual report on their facilities and give fuller details of themselves.
- specify minimum standards of care

- meet specified targets for various preventative measures like vaccination and screening
- be available 26 hours each week over five days and accept 24-hour responsibility for patients
- provide more services for the over-75s (including the offer of annual check-ups and home visits) and a more regular assessment of the development of young children.

'NHS Made Easy' (Department of Health)

Secondary care in the National Health Service

While primary care can meet around 90 per cent of the needs for health care, more intensive diagnosis and treatment is sometimes needed.

Hospitals

Hospitals are providers of secondary care. Access to them is made through a referral from primary care (except in the case of emergency or through direct referral to clinics such as those for sexually transmitted diseases).

In the past, hospitals have tended to be of two main types: those providing for short-term care (*acute care* – out-patients, accident and emergency, general surgery, etc) or long-term care (for the mentally-ill, older people and so on). In the future, hospitals may care almost entirely for the acutely ill on a short-term basis.

Hospitals might be grouped either as NHS trusts or Directly Managed Units (DMUs)

NHS trusts are self-governing units within the National Health Service. Each trust has a board of directors with complete responsibility for managing the trust's affairs. Each year it prepares a business plan, setting out proposals for service developments and capital investment. At the end of the year it prepares and publishes an annual report and accounts.

Directly managed units (DMUs) are controlled by District Health Authorities. Although not having the freedoms available to trusts, DMUs have a much greater responsibility for the management of their services than hospitals had previously.

Community services

Community nursing staff

Community nurses play a vital role in the delivery of community care. Under the NHS and Community Care Act, emphasis is placed on maintaining more dependent people in the community for longer periods; community nurses have a key role to play. These nurses assess nursing care needs. Both health visitors and district nurses have a knowledge of and contact with local community networks and so may play a valuable role in mobilising resources to meet individual needs.

Community therapy services

With more dependent people living in the community there is an increasing demand on therapy services such as occupational therapy, physiotherapy, speech therapy, psychology, chiropody and therapists for visual or hearing impairment. These community therapists have the skills to enable people to be more independent in the community.

The dental service

There are about 23 000 dentists practising in the UK – the majority (about 80 per cent) are contracted to carry out some work for the NHS. This is mainly care of children's teeth and care of patients who have been registered for some time. In many parts of the UK it is now quite difficult for new clients to register as NHS patients and often they must consult a dentist privately.

As with GPs, dentists have a contract. The dentist must not only leave the patient 'dentally fit', but is also required to offer care and treatment to secure and maintain the patient's oral health.

The contract between dentists and the Family Health Service Authority (FHSA) allows NHS patients the freedom to choose and change dentists as they wish. The dentist can also choose to accept or refuse any NHS patient.

Mental health services

In 'Health of the Nation', published by the Department of Health in 1992, one of the objectives was to develop comprehensive, locally based services. In January 1993 the Mental Health Task Force was set up to help ensure the transfer of services away from large hospitals to a balanced range of locally based services, including community-based beds.

The Department of Health has targeted three main areas in mental health:

1 elderly mentally ill people
2 child and adolescent mental health services
3 mentally disordered offenders.

In August 1993 the Secretary of State for Health announced a ten-point plan to reinforce community care for mentally ill people which involved a series of initiatives designed to improve their health and social opportunities. The proposals included the introduction of a new power of supervised discharge for the small number of mentally ill people who need special support when they leave hospital.

Think it over

Can you think of any services that have been developed in your area for people with mental health problems?

Child health services

These services were reviewed in 1993–94 by the Community and Acute Services Steering Group, which was set up to look at ways of moving services from acute settings to primary and community settings.

As part of this shift from acute care to primary and

community care, many District Health Authorities commissioned Home Care Paediatric Teams to work with the medical needs of children. District Health Authorities may also have Adolescent Health Clinics, often highlighting the needs of children and learning and physical disabilities, Child and Adolescent Mental Health Services and School Health Services.

Social care provision

Children

Child protection

Social services departments are required to keep an 'at risk' register of all children who they feel to be in danger from psychological, physical or sexual abuse. They monitor everyone on the list and must be ready to take action if necessary, such as obtaining a court order to remove the child from danger pending investigation.

Family support

Social services aims to support families as far as is possible. A range of help and support could be offered, with the aim of keeping a family together in their own home in the local area. Such help might include family aide – a person who offers practical help in the home while a parent is ill; or a family caseworker – to work with the family as a whole, trying to improve the quality of family life that a child is experiencing.

Some areas offer family centres where parents and children can go each week for support. Centre activities may include working with the parent and child to improve communication and understanding, or working just with the parents on the skills of parenting – while children are looked after by other qualified staff. There is a move away from traditional *nursery* provision, towards family centres. Nurseries generally only provide day care for children under school age and offer limited opportunities for working with parents or the family as a whole.

Fostering and adoption

This is now sometimes referred to as **family placements.** Sometimes children need to be looked after temporarily while they are away from their parents. There could be a number of reasons for this, such as illness, bereavement or being at risk. It is usually a short-term measure. The social services department takes on the role of organising a foster family which will suit the needs of the child. It also monitors the child in the placement.

Social workers have a crucial role to play in adoption. They assess the suitability of those who wish to adopt a child and match them with a suitable child. They may also prepare reports for the courts who make the adoption order.

Residential care

Children sometimes require accommodation in residential care homes. Reasons for this may include the illness or absence of parents or parents having difficulties in providing the necessary care or control of the child. Children's homes are usually run by social services staff; they aim to provide a stable background for the children, as close to home life as possible. Residential care also provides homes for children with special needs. Each child is usually offered a key worker who takes a special interest in him or her.

People with physical disabilities

Day care

Some day care for people with physical disabilities focuses purely on the personal development of the individual and programmes will focus on the needs of the individual. Many offer social activities and

some may be able to provide access to various kinds of therapy, including physiotherapy or occupational therapy.

Residential care

Short-term care may be available in specially adapted and staffed residential units. These can provide opportunities for people with disabilities to enhance their life skills, such as personal hygiene, cooking etc, as well as providing social events and contacts. It also means a rest for the carer. Long-term care may be offered in group homes rather than the more traditional hostel-type accommodation.

Home adaptations

Social services departments may be able to help with various adaptations to the home, such as putting in ramps, the installation of a shower unit or stair-lift, or widening doorways. This could enable the person to remain in his or her own home.

Equipment for daily living

Local authorities provide a range of equipment to assist people with physical disabilities to live and cope more easily within their own homes. Although local authorities may differ in what they offer, equipment for daily living might include hand rails in the bathroom, along passage ways or up stairways, and equipment to assist with washing, dressing, eating, getting in and out of bed and so on.

People with learning difficulties

People with learning difficulties may also have physical disabilities and so may require some of the services offered above.

Day centres

Day-care services can differ greatly from one local authority to another. Some are still termed 'adult training centres', although in more recent years many have been called 'social education centres'. Both these types of centre have tended to be large institutions which have offered clients employment in limited ways, as well as teaching life skills with the aim of encouraging independent living. However, more recently there has been a move away from these large, multi-functional buildings towards providing a range of innovative daytime activities in smaller units, or in community-based facilities such as adult education classes within colleges of further education. Other daytime activities may include such projects as drop-in centres or clubs for social activities, small business enterprises and community service ventures.

Residential accommodation

In the same way, there has been a move away from the provision of large hostel-type accommodation towards living together in small units in group homes. The amount of staffing for these homes varies, depending on the abilities of the residents. For example, in some homes there may be 24-hour staff cover, while in others a group home's officer may call in a few times each week or when there are particular problems.

Try it

Visit your local social services department to find out what services have been available to people with learning difficulties over the past 10 years. What services are being planned for the future, and how are they to be managed and funded.

People with mental health problems

In line with provision for other clients with special needs, such as those described above, day care and residential care provision for people with mental health problems is likely to be provided in much smaller units in the future. However, whereas the local authority has the lead role in provision of services for other client groups, it is the health service who now, under the NHS and Community Care Act 1990, will take the lead role in respect of services for people with mental illness.

Services for older people

Home care

Home care for older people has also changed radically in the past few years. The days of the domestic home help have passed and there is now a new type of home carer. The home carer's main role is focused on the personal care of the client, helping them to get up, wash, bathe, use the toilet, dress and undress, and get back to bed, as well as preparing meals. Social services departments may no longer provide a housework-only service; although helping people with domestic tasks may be provided as part of a care package

Many social services are also providing, either directly themselves or through the independent sector, specialists home-care services such as home-from-hospital teams, specialist bathing services or home carers specially trained to work with people with dementia, physical disabilities or learning difficulties. Other specialists services may include peripatetic light carers (*peripatetic* means moving from one place to another). These carers provide a drop-in service throughout the night to people who need assistance when using the toilet, or those who need help with turning in bed or who may, due to confusion, be prone to wander at night. Some authorities provide nightsitting schemes, although these tend to be rare. Many of these services may also be available to a wider range of client groups.

Meals on wheels

Some people are unable to prepare a meal for themselves and have no carer who is able to do so for them. In these situations the local authority may be able to arrange for the provision of meals. This can be done in a variety of ways. The meal may be prepared, cooked and then delivered hot to the client, in specially heated containers. Alternatively, frozen pre-cooked meals, which just need reheating at home, may be provided. These meals are normally delivered at regular intervals, i.e. twice weekly, once a week or even fortnightly. Meals services may be staffed by local authority employees or volunteers or may be provided by voluntary organisations or the independent sector.

Laundry service

This service is provided for older people with particular problems, such as incontinence, where bed linen needs frequent changing. In such cases, social services can sometimes arrange for a home carer to take care of personal laundry for the client.

Day care

Social services often provide day care for people with mobility difficulties which prevent them from getting out and meeting others. The centres may offer social activities and various therapeutic activities such as exercise classes to maintain or encourage mobility. They may also have reminiscence groups and exercises to help people who may be becoming disorientated.

The management of centres for older, more active people is increasingly being handed over to the voluntary sector, including organisations such as Age Concern, with local authority provision focusing on the needs of elderly frail people and people with dementia.

Sheltered housing

Sheltered housing is sometimes viewed as a mid-way solution between going into residential care and remaining at home. Sheltered housing consists of individual self-contained living units, either in bungalows or flats, with some communal facilities such as a lounge and laundry. The units are usually unfurnished so that the person can have some of their own things around them. The person is able to live independently but has the support of a warden.

Sheltered accommodation may be run by the social services department or the housing department of the local authority. However, there is an increasing number of sheltered housing schemes available in the private sector.

Figure 7.12 Sheltered accommodation enables a person to live independently but have the support of a warden.

Residential care

Residential accommodation provides 24-hour care for those people who have been assessed as requiring this level of support.

The introduction of 'Home Life Standards' has resulted in a move away from communal living in large, multi-bedded units, to 'unit living'. This aims to provide homely accommodation for small groups of people (5–10), who have their own lounge, dining, kitchen and bathroom facilities. Many more people are now able to have a single bedroom. However, where people do still share a bedroom, consideration must be given to how their privacy and dignity can be maintained.

Nursing homes

Nursing homes are similar in many ways to residential homes, but they also provide 24-hour nursing care for those people requiring it. Since April 1993 local authority social services departments have been responsible for the funding of nursing home placements for those people needing financial assistance. Social services is therefore responsible for assessing the need for nursing home care, although assessments are often undertaken with the help of, or by, health service staff.

The private and voluntary sectors

The work of voluntary and private organisations in health and social care has always been of great importance, but never more so than now. With the introduction of the National Health Service and Community Care Act 1990, the government expected local authorities to secure the delivery of services by developing a purchasing and contracting role, rather than simply act as providers of services themselves. Local authorities are now able to enter into contracts with the voluntary and private sectors in order to provide services.

Private sector provision

Most of us are familiar with some of the services provided by the private sector which include:

- private hospital treatment
- private dental treatment
- private nursing homes
- private residential homes
- private home-care nursing.

However, the range of services now being offered on a private basis is increasing. Some private agencies will undertake household tasks such as cleaning or ironing; others specialise in personal and/or nursing care. Private homes which at one time only offered residential care, may now take people on a day-care basis as well.

However, private hospitals and clinics may not be able to provide the same range of services as large acute hospitals. They may only be able to undertake minor operations, or may not have intensive care facilities for example. This could mean that if there are complications during a relatively minor operation, the patient may have to be transferred to a general hospital for special care.

Think it over

How many agencies in your area offer home nursing services? Use the *Phone Book*, local newspaper and information from your library or social services department to help you.

Try it

1 Using the information collected above, choose one agency and find out what services it offers.

2 Contact your nearest private hospital to find out the type of services it provides.

This will contribute to the Evidence Indicators for this section.

Voluntary organisations

There are many voluntary organisations concerned with the provision of health and social care. Most are registered charities, although not all are strictly charitable. Some are non-profit making. Many employ staff as well as having volunteers working for them.

Every year the number of volunteer and self-help groups increase. A few of these are described below.

These include two that provide social care services for children, two that provide for older people or for other adults, and two that provide primarily health care.

To find out about other groups, consult directories of voluntary organisations, such as *The Voluntary Agencies Directory*, published by the National Council for Voluntary Agencies, which should be available in your local or college library.

Services for children

National Society for the Prevention of Cruelty to Children

The National Society for the Prevention of Cruelty to Children (NSPCC) was set up to protect children from abuse. The organisation receives approximately

88 per cent of its running costs from public donations. It operates throughout the UK and its workers are organised into area teams. These child protection teams assess and help abused children and their families. The work is carried out either in the family's home or in NSPCC centres. The teams also offer a 24-hour advice service, and local education, training, consultation and advice for other professional and voluntary organisations. The library at the NSPCC's headquarters in London is open to professionals and the general public.

Barnardo's

This is a Christian-based child care agency which has 167 local projects across the UK. Barnardo's helps around 18 000 young people and their families each year. It helps young people with special needs who face emotional and social stress or whose parents need support. Barnardo's is committed to caring for, supporting and helping young people to reach their full potential, and works with people of every culture, ethnic background and religion.

Services for older people

Age Concern

Age Concern is a registered charity which depends largely on public support for the financing of its activities. Although Age Concern provides services throughout the UK, it is divided into four regions: England, Scotland, Ireland and Wales. There is a network of over 1400 local groups, with the support of around 250 000 volunteers plus some paid staff. The aim of Age Concern is to improve the quality of life for older people and to develop services appropriate to local needs. These services may include advice and information, day care, visiting services, transport schemes, clubs and specialist facilities for older people who have physical disabilities or who are mentally frail.

Age Concern England is also involved in training and information giving. It publishes leaflets offering practical advice and guides to welfare rights and benefits, for example. It also campaigns for retired people and those who work with them.

Abbeyfield Society

Abbeyfield is a national society which houses over 8000 elderly people who are unable to live alone. The society manages around 1000 family-style houses, and each house has 8–10 residents. Residents have their own bedsitting room, which they furnish themselves, but a housekeeper provides two main meals a day and looks after the welfare of the residents. The society also manages 40 extra-care houses, which provides 24-hour care for frail older people.

Services for adults

John Groomes Association for the Disabled

This charitable organisation was set up in 1866. It provides residential accommodation for people with severe disabilities; sheltered work and specialised housing throughout England and Wales. The association also provides holiday and short breaks for people with disabilities, their families and friends. It runs an information service about the problems and needs of people with disabilities.

Women's Royal Voluntary Service (WRVS)

The WRVS undertakes a variety of health-related and social care work, as well as having volunteers who can help in national and local emergencies. It undertakes, for example, non-medical work in hospitals such as running shops, canteens and trolley shops. In the community its volunteers run library services, collect and distribute clothing, provide social and luncheon clubs, organise meals-on-wheels and books-on-wheels, support families including parent and toddler groups, play groups and toy libraries. They also work in prisons and courts.

Health-related voluntary organisations

The British Red Cross

The British Red Cross has about 100 000 volunteers, including a youth division. Teams of Red Cross workers provide emergency services throughout the UK. Volunteers also raise funds to support the international work of the British Red Cross. The International Red Cross is the world's largest voluntary organisation, and there is a Red Cross Society in nearly every country of the world.

Cancer Relief Macmillan Fund

This voluntary organisation is a national charity founded in 1911, devoted to improving the care available to people with cancer and their families. There are now over 1200 Macmillan nurses nationwide. The majority work with GPs and district nurses, giving support to people in their own homes. Some nurses work in hospitals, in specialist units that treat adults or children who have cancer. The organisation also builds its own Macmillan Cancer Care Units, which provide in-patient and day-care facilities for people with cancer. These units are also used to train doctors and nurses in the skills of pain relief.

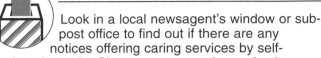

Evidence collection point

Find out from your local library which voluntary organisations have a group in your area. Phone or visit two of these to identify the services that they provide locally.

Self-employed helpers

Apart from those people who are employed in statutory agencies, or those who staff voluntary organisations, some services may be provided by people who are self-employed. Examples of self-employed people include childminders, who provide care for children during the daytime; home helps who undertake domestic tasks in people's homes; and providers of other services such as ironing or gardening.

Childminders have to be registered with their local authority. The authority checks that the house where the child is to be looked after is safe. It also decides how many children and of what ages, the childminder may supervise and it provides help and support for the childminder.

Similarly, in some areas the local authority has a register of self-employed home helps. The local authority makes sure that home helps are properly insured and provides them with support and some training. It also tries to ensure that the person wanting the service has a suitable home help. However, the working contract is between the home help and the person needing the service.

Other people provide services totally on a private contractual basis. The person offering the service may advertise in the local newspaper, or a local newsagent's window. It is then up to the person wanting the service and the one providing the service to agree the terms and conditions and the payment to be made.

Evidence collection point

Look in a local newsagent's window or sub-post office to find out if there are any notices offering caring services by self-employed people. Choose two examples and write down what services are being offered.

Informal carers

In recent years the term **carer** has been used to describe anyone, other than a paid worker, who is looking after someone who is ill or disabled. The carer may be an adult person looking after an ageing parent, a husband or wife looking after a sick partner, a parent looking after a child with a physical or mental disability, or even a child who is helping to look after a sick or disabled parent. A friend, or neighbour, may also fulfil this informal caring role.

Some people do not like the term 'carer', but it does usefully acknowledge that the carer is doing a 'job' of work, and one which can be very difficult and demanding.

Informal carers may:

- help people to get up from bed and return to bed
- help them to wash and dress
- help them to bathe or shower
- prepare refreshments and meals
- monitor and dispense medicines
- provide transport for social and medical purposes.

Evidence collection point

1 In what other ways might an informal carer help?

2 Make a list of the sort of help that the following might need:

a a child who has a broken leg

b a teenager with a mental disability

c an older person who has had a stroke.

Informal carers may also be people who belong to a local group, such as a church or religious body, or a group set up to help advise and support carers. There are many organisations that offer information and advice for people with particular illnesses or disabilities.

Help offered	By whom	Contact
Adaptations to the home		
Advice on adapting or extending the home	Occupational therapist	Social service department
Adaptions to the home	Local authority	Social services department
Assistive equipment		
Advice on the type of special equipment available	District nurse	GP
Aids to help with dressing, eating toileting	Occupational therapist	Social services department
Pads, pants and other incontinence aids	District nurse	GP
Equipment for the bedroom, e.g. special beds, hoists	District Health Authority	District nurse/GP
Equipment for the toilet, bathroom, e.g raised toilet seat, hand rails	District Health Authority or local authority	Social services department
Walking sticks, walking frames, wheel chairs	District Health Authority	District nurse/GP
Medical/Nursing help		
Nursing care at home	District nurse	GP Agency
	Private agencies	
Help with speech problems	Speech therapist	GP
Help with incontinence problems	Continence adviser or district nurse	GP
Foot care/chiropody	Chiropodist	GP
Practical help		
Gardening	Voluntary groups, e.g. Age Concern, church groups	Individual group
	Self-employed person	Individual person
Housework	Local authority	Social services deparrment
	Private agency	Individual person
	Self-employed person	
Ironing	Private agency	Agency
	Self-employed person	Individual person
Laundry	District Health Authority	District nurse /GP
	Local authority	Social services department
Meals	Local authority	Social services department
		Voluntary agency, e.g. WRVS
Personal care	Local authority	Social services department
	District Health Authority	GP
	Private home care agency	Agency
Shopping	Local authority	Social services department
	Private home care agency	Agency
Washing and bathing	District Health Authority	District nurse/ GP
	Local authority	Social services department
	Private home care or nursing agency	Agency

Figure 7.13 Help in the home

Try it

Write to the National Carer's Association, First Floor, 21–23 New Road, Chatham, Kent, ME4 4QJ – to ask if there is a branch in your area. Find out what type of support your local branch is able to provide.

Help in the home

There are many services that can be provided to enable people to stay in their own homes, even though they may not be able to do many domestic or personal care tasks themselves. Figure 7.13 shows the type of help that people may need, who provides that help and the contact.

Needs of clients

'Needs' can be defined as those things that are essential to our well-being. We all need food and shelter, for example. So needs are the things that individuals require to be able to grow, function or live life as fully as possible. Needs are different from 'wants' because a want is not essential for life. For example, a young person *needs* a balanced diet providing all the essential nutrients. They may get their nutrients from a daily diet of three meals but they may also *want* snacks between meals, such as chocolate and crisps.

Think it over

How far are our needs and wants a reflection of the society in which we live? Would a young person in a Third World country have the same needs and wants as a young person in Britain?

Every individual has needs, whatever his or her gender, job, family circumstances or wealth.

The needs of the individual are complex. Some of these needs are shared by others such as the need for food and warmth. Some needs are special to a particular age, stage of life or section of a family. Others are special to individuals. Often these special needs are a result of personal circumstances. For example, an older person living in his or her own home may have the same common needs as an older person living in residential care of similar age and physical health, but each will also have individual specific needs.

Needs change according to a person's age and stage of life and individual circumstances. Therefore, the services to meet those needs have to be flexible.

What are needs?

Needs are often classified into:
- physical
- intellectual
- emotional
- social.

Physical needs include food, shelter, oxygen and warmth, for example. They are basic human needs and as such are a requirement for life. However, the term 'physical needs' can also be applied to physical conditions:

1 **Chronic condition** – a condition, disorder or set of symptoms which have gone on for a long time is called 'chronic'. Symptoms might develop slowly. An example of a chronic illness can be diabetes, a condition where a pancreas does not produce enough insulin for the absorption of glucose from the blood stream. Once diagnosed, diabetics have to adapt their lifestyles to cope with diets and insulin injections. Other chronic conditions include asthma, coeliac disease, and various disabilities. Medical treatment may help or alleviate some of the symptoms, but a chronic condition is usually long term.

2 **Acute conditions** – a condition, disorder or set of symptoms which have developed suddenly and are severe are called 'acute'. The symptoms are likely to last only a short time, such as a common cold. The term 'acute' also covers broken limbs. Acute problems often respond to medical treatment.

Think it over

Can you think of other examples of acute and chronic conditions/illnesses which you have come across or may come across when working with different client groups?

Emotional needs are concerned with feelings. Emotions include joy, sorrow, fear and happiness. People often need extra emotional support after a major life event such as the death of a close relative or divorce. Support helps individuals to come to terms with the intense feelings they have and enables them to return to 'normal' life.

Emotional needs can be chronic or acute. For example, postnatal depression can be considered an acute condition: the mother will need support while she is depressed and until she feels able to cope.

Social needs cover the need for company and the preference of human beings to live in a group rather than alone. People may need help in forming and/or maintaining relationships with others. This may involve looking at self-awareness and self-concept.

Intellectual needs refer to our needs for mental stimulation. Humans have an ability for understanding, thinking and reasoning, and most people enjoy mental activity, which includes watching a television programme or reading a book. These activities require people to use their minds to follow a story or to understand words. Even social conversation provides mental stimulation. Mental stimulation may help older people to remain alert and is often an important part of social care work.

Physical, intellectual, emotional and social needs change as an individual grows and develops. Growth and development is discussed in Chapter 4.

Maslow identified physical, intellectual, social and emotional needs when he developed his hierarchy of human needs.

He suggested that each 'layer of needs' in the pyramid has to be met before the next can be achieved. Therefore, physical needs have to be met before emotional needs can be. It is difficult to concentrate on other things if your stomach is telling you that you are hungry. The higher up the pyramid you go, the more satisfaction with life is linked to social and intellectual rather than physical needs.

Needs of different client groups

People who use services are know as **clients** or **service users**. Clients may therefore mean babies, children, adults, young people, older people or families.

All individuals are different in the needs that they have. Maslow's theory suggests that we can think of some client groups as having similar needs, even if each individual may have special and personal needs.

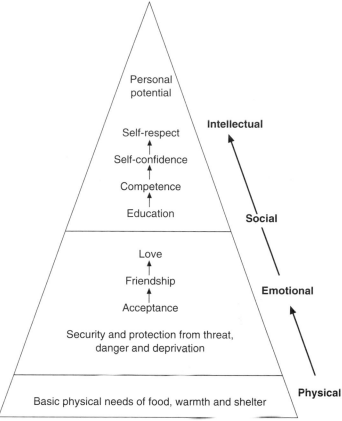

Figure 8.1 Human needs pyramid based on Maslow's ideas

Evidence collection point

Using the chart below, try to identify examples of common needs in each classification for different client groups. Do not just make assumptions. Base your lists on evidence gained through interviewing appropriate people or using questionnaires.

Client groups	Physical needs	Social needs	Emotional needs	Intellectual needs
Babies				
Children				
Young people				
Adults				
Elderly people				
Families				

Each of the common needs you identified may reflect the services required. Chapter 7 explained the difference services available to client groups. Services are designed to meet physical, intellectual, social and emotional needs.

An example of services to meet needs might be services for babies:

1 *Physical needs* – these are usually met by the primary carer of the child (the mother or father). Advice is often given by the health visitor attached to the GP's surgery. Regular visits to a clinic mean that parents can get advice. Clinics are free. Parents are told about clinics as part of the antenatal care they receive. This care includes a health monitoring service for the child to check his or her development and provide preventative medicine such as a vaccination programme.

2 *Social needs* – these may be met by interaction with others, including the baby's parents and family and sometimes a childminder. Babies may mix with other children through parent and toddler groups and some nursery schools, which may accept babies. Social groups may be provided by local voluntary groups, private providers or the local authority.

3 *Emotional needs* – the need for love and support will be provided by the parents and the wider family or community.

4 *Intellectual needs* – these are provided by the child's carers through play. Intellectual development would be supported by the parent and toddler nursery groups.

Evidence collection point

Once you have identified the needs of various client groups, copy and complete the chart opposite.

For each client group, try to identify the services which will meet the needs you have identified. Link your work with the explanation of the different services in Chapter 7.

As you can see from your chart, one service may meet a need that occurs across a number of client groups. For example, a library can provide intellectual stimulation for all ages. Equally, services may have to be flexible to deal with specific circumstances of individuals; for example the Red Cross has a range of equipment available for different conditions which can be adapted or have different sizes to fit individuals.

Client group	Services to meet physical needs	Services to meet social needs	Services to meet emotional needs	Services to meet intellectual needs
Babies				
Children				
Young people				
Adults				
Elderly people				
Families				

Meeting specific needs

As we saw above, all individuals within each client group have specific needs depending on their circumstances. These needs may be met by a range of services.

For example a parent of a 6-month-old baby may seek the advice of a health visitor at the child health clinic about weaning from a diet of milk to solid feeds. However, a baby showing signs of weight loss once on solid food, may be examined for coeliac disease (a condition which damages the villi in the small intestine so that nutrients are not absorbed). If the child was found to have the disease, a dietician and peadiatrician would become involved as well as the health visitor. This example can be repeated across a range of client groups and circumstances.

Think it over

1 Choose one client group, look at each need and think about the special circumstances that could affect the services they may require.

2 Compare this to another client group. Are the services needed by different groups the same? Different client groups may sometimes need similar services.

Services provided

The services provided to support and meet needs can be classified according to the costs involved.

1 Some services are free to all clients. For example, everyone is entitled to be registered with a GP and to gain access to him or her. There is no direct charge for this service. Access to a social worker is also free, as are advice services such as the Citizens Advice Bureau.

2 A basic fee is charged for some services such as prescriptions and dental and eyesight check-ups. Apart from a few exceptions, for example people on low incomes and children, everyone is expected to pay the set fee, regardless of income.

3 A number of services are means tested. In some cases, the amount an individual has to pay for a service depends on his or her income and savings. Those with more savings or income pay more for the same service compared with those who are less well off. An example of this is entry to a care or nursing home where the local authority decides if, and how much, the person will pay towards the charges of the home. If the person's income or savings are above a certain amount, then he or she will have to pay all or part of the costs. Services in an older person's own home where means testing applies include home-care workers or home helps and meals on wheels.

4 Some services are run by charities or voluntary groups. When carers work on a voluntary basis this can keep costs low, so that services may be supplied to users at a reduced rate or may even be free. Meals-on-wheels, a service often run by, the WRVS, is one example. Costs are calculated according to a person's ability to pay. Some towns have a free community bus run by a local charity or voluntary group to serve the needs of older people. Charities and voluntary groups also offer advice and help if required.

5 There are a number of services which individuals have to pay for in full, regardless of income. Private services sometimes complement those available through statutory provision. These may be services which are not available through bodies such as the NHS or social services.

The ability to pay may also reduce the waiting time for appointments, for example to see a specialist.

The provision of private services has been extended since the NHS and Community Care Act 1990, which implemented the policy of keeping individuals who require care in the community rather than in large institutions. Private agencies provide services which can be bought either by large purchasers, such as the NHS or social services, or private individuals.

Try it

Janet Fleming, 82, is a widow living in her own home. She manages to look after herself, but needs regular support from a home-care worker. She also attends a day centre twice a week and has an emergency lifeline connected to her home. She attends the GP's surgery for regular check-ups and to obtain repeat prescriptions for high blood pressure.

1 List the services that Janet receives and briefly explain each one.
2 Identify any other services that might benefit Janet.
3 Indicate how each of the services is paid for.

Mixed economy of care

In many areas, services operate a **mixed economy of care**. This means that the main agencies work together to satisfy the needs of clients. An individual's care plan may involve support from services in the statutory, private and voluntary fields and may also be a combination of free services, those for which a basic fee is charged and services for which the client has to pay the total cost.

Supporters of mixed economy of care believe that competition between providers creates a service which is responsive to the needs of clients and is cost effective.

Methods of referral

Individuals can access services in the following ways:

1 **Self-referral**, individuals decide to make contact themselves. For example, a person living with an ageing parent may find out directly from social services whether support is available.

Think it over

What other services can you refer yourself to?

2 **Professional referral**, where an individual first seeks help or advice from a professional such as a GP. The GP may then refer him or her to a specialist, for example, a consultant at the local hospital.

Once the referral takes place, the individual may not be able to obtain an immediate appointment to see the specialist, with a further delay possible if treatment involves an operation for which there is a waiting list. The length of waiting lists varies from area to area and with the particular branch of medicine involved – gynaecology may have a shorter waiting list than ears, nose and throat for example. The specialist will also assess whether the individual's condition is an emergency which requires urgent treatment.

3 **Referral by others,** where, for example, a person may be concerned about the way a child is being treated and contacts the social services. A social worker may then refer the family for other help.
4 **Referral by the emergency services**, following a road accident, for example. Being taken to hospital in an ambulance can be classed as a way of referral to that service. On arrival, hospital staff will decide whether to admit the patient.

Think it over

Find out about the range of services provided by your local authority. Explain how an individual may access these services. Are they free or is payment required?

Support for individuals

Some clients need extra support when using services. This support may include the provision of more detailed information or involve physical help such as a translator.

Clients' rights when using services are often set out in a charter such as the Patients' Charter. A charter outlines the services clients can expect, often with details of maximum waiting times etc. The charter may also explain how to complain.

Other services can help explain clients' rights if the charters are not clear. These include personnel at health centres and Citizens Advice Bureaux, videos, where these are available; and leaflets written in a range of languages, which can be obtained from the local Health Promotion Unit, health clinics and GPs' surgeries where there is a high proportion of clients for whom English is not their first language, for example, people who speak Gujarati, or Polish.

In addition some people may need a translator to interpret services as well as to express their wishes. An advocate, someone who speaks on behalf of the client, may also be needed.

Many of the Department of Health's information leaflets and posters are available in the following languages:

- Bengali
- Chinese
- Greek
- Gujarati
- Hindi
- Punjabi
- Turkish
- Urdu.

Evidence collection point

Identify three clients from different client groups who have used services to meet needs. One must have used the NHS and one must have used a service outside the NHS.

1 Identify the service each used and explain the referral process to that service.
2 Outline any additional support which was given to help the client make the best use of the service. Explain how it helped.

Chapter 9

Jobs in health and social care

There are many jobs in the field of health and social care, far too many to be able to give full details of them. However, this chapter looks at some of the main jobs in the direct provision of health and social care, and some of the jobs that are necessary to support those involved in direct provision, for example, portering in hospitals, and administration in social services departments.

The description of some of the main jobs is given in some detail, while others are presented only briefly.

Should you wish to find out more about other jobs not detailed here, you will be able to obtain more information in careers and occupational guides. Copies of these can be found in your college or local library, or at your local careers office.

Qualifications for entry into professional training have been described in terms of GCSEs and GCE A levels. GNVQ and BTEC qualifications are often accepted as the equivalent of GCSEs, and A levels, but sometimes the detailed regulations about GNVQ and BTEC qualifications vary between different colleges, schools of nursing and universities. For this reason only GCSE and GCE requirements have been used here, but this should not be taken to imply that these are the only qualifications that will be accepted. The term 'equivalent qualifications' is used throughout the text to make this point.

Think it over

How many jobs can you think of that are related to providing health and social care? Make a mental list of all these jobs.

Jobs in health care

The National Health Service (NHS) is the biggest employer in Europe. There are many different types of job that are carried out to provide comprehensive health care. Some jobs require a basic training, such as nursing; while others require more specialised training in addition to the basic training, such as midwifery.

This chapter looks in some detail at jobs concerned with the direct provision of health care:

- general practitioner (GP)
- hospital doctor
- hospital nurse
- nursing auxiliary.

Brief accounts are provided of the following:

- district nurses, health visitor, occupational health nurse, community psychiatric nurse
- dentist, optician, pharmacist
- physiotherapist, occupational therapist, speech therapist.

In the support services, detailed descriptions are given of the role of:

- medical technical officer
- ambulance person
- medical records clerk

and brief accounts of:

- health service manager
- catering staff (cook)
- hospital porter.

General practitioner

The GP, or family doctor, is very important in the provision of primary health care. The GP is often the first person to be consulted when someone feels unwell. It is the job of the GP to listen to patients, make any necessary examinations and, where possible, to make a diagnosis of the problem or illness and prescribe appropriate medicines. GPs will also advise people how to manage an illness, disability or problem. Increasingly, GPs are performing minor surgery. Where appropriate, GPs refer patients to hospitals or clinics which provide more specialised services. They can also refer patients to social worker psychiatric services or for other forms of therapy such as physiotherapy or speech therapy.

After surgery, GPs may visit patients in their home but they will also have to write referral letters, mak phone calls on behalf of patients and write up thei patients' records. They may also need to write out certificates for various purposes.

Most GPs work as part of a team. The size of the team depends on the size of the practice. However, much of their time is spent on a one-to-one basis with patients. Increasingly, GPs work in modern, purpose-built health centres.

Entry requirements and training

In the UK a qualified doctor must have a degree in medicine. Medical students should have at least three A level subjects in order to gain entry to a medical degree course. The degree course lasts five years for students who studied science subjects at A level, and six years for those who did not.

Following a medical degree, all doctors undertake another year's training in a hospital. GPs then undertake a further specialist three-year training before they can be registered as a GP.

The upper age limit to begin training as a doctor is generally considered to be 30 years of age, although some medical schools are reluctant to take people beyond the age of 25.

Pay and conditions

Seeing patients either at the surgery, or in their homes, usually takes up at least 26 hours per week. In practice, most GPs work a 50-hour week, including administration, reading, etc. Approximately two and a half hours are spent seeing patients in the morning and afternoons or evenings. A Saturday morning surgery is often needed. All GPs are 'on-call' at night and at the weekends, but the frequency of this depends on the size of the practice.

GPs can earn around £40 000 per year, but this will depend on the area and number of services offered by the GP.

Prospects

There are about 34 000 GPS in the UK. There are few prospects for moving to other jobs, other than working as an adviser to a company, or as a police surgeon.

Hospital doctor

Hospital doctors work through four grades of training:

- house officer
- senior house officer
- registrar
- senior registrar.

House officers and senior house officers examine patients as they arrive at the hospital, take notes and organise initial investigations and treatment. They may also prescribe drugs for minor symptoms. They keep relatives informed of the patient's progress. House officers can be called upon by the nursing staff at any time of the day or night and often work long hours without proper sleep. They regularly work one weekend in three. Registrars supervise the work

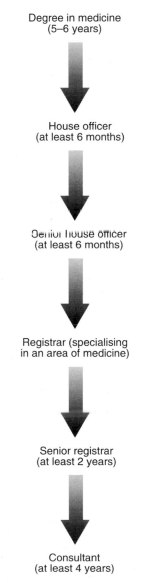

Degree in medicine
(5–6 years)

House officer
(at least 6 months)

Senior house officer
(at least 6 months)

Registrar (specialising
in an area of medicine)

Senior registrar
(at least 2 years)

Consultant
(at least 4 years)

Figure 9.1 Career routes for a hospital doctor

of the house officers. They can also examine and treat patients with diseases in which they have specialised.

Consultants

This is the only grade of hospital doctor considered to be fully trained. They are responsible for the treatments that they prescribe; they supervise the work and training of all senior registrars, registrars, senior house officers and house officers who work under them.

Hospital doctors specialise in various areas of medicine. There are over 40 types of speciality, but the main four are:

- medicine
- surgery
- pathology
- psychiatry.

Hospital doctors work as part of a team with other doctors, nurses, radiographers, physiotherapists, occupational and speech therapists, plus other administrative and support staff. They deal with patients and their families on a daily basis. Most work in hospital departments and wards, although pathologists work in laboratories.

Entry requirements and training

This is the same as for GPs; however, once a doctor becomes a registrar, he or she may choose to specialise in general practice, hospital medicine, community medicine or other specialities. Training for consultants takes at least eight years following registration.

Pay and conditions

In 1995 annual salaries for hospital doctors within the NHS were as follows:

House officer – £13 000
Senior house officer – £18 000
Registrar – £21 000
Senior registrar – £24 000
Consultant – £38 000 – £49 000

Most hospital doctors work two types of shifts – full and partial, as well as an on-call rota system. By law they must not work more than 83 hours per week, but the hours are long and irregular.

Prospects

There are about 43 700 doctors in the NHS. There are often fewer openings the further up the training/career ladder a doctor goes. Doctors may therefore have to wait several years before going to the next grade. There are even fewer consultant posts.

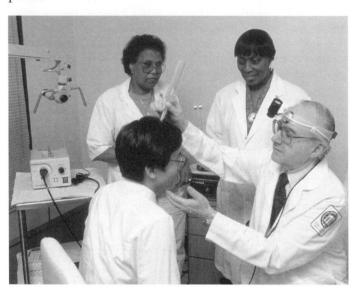

Try it

There are many television programmes that portray the working life of doctors, for example, *Casualty*. What can you find out about the working pattern of doctors from watching one of these programmes?

Hospital nurse

Hospital nurses are responsible for the nursing care of patients in hospitals. Nursing care involves tasks such as taking the temperature, blood pressure and respiration rates of patients; giving patients injections; administering medications; cleaning and dressing wounds; bandaging and splinting; administering blood transfusions and drips; as well as routine tasks like bedmaking and ensuring patients are comfortable.

Nurses must familiarise themselves with the patient's medical history and circumstances; keep careful records of the treatment that is given; and record the patient's progress. They must also take into account the emotional and social needs of the patient, thus providing a 'holistic' approach to patient care.

Nurses work as part of a team of nurses on the wards, or in other units within the hospital, such as in the accident and emergency unit or out-patient clinics. They also work as part of a multi-disciplinary team, including doctors, occupational therapists, physiotherapists and social workers, all of whom work together to ensure that patients gains as much independence as possible and have sufficient help and support once they return to the community.

There are many different types of ward and units which nurses may work on including medical, surgical, orthopaedic and children's wards; or out-patient clinics, operating theatres, maternity units and intensive care units. There are other types of specialist work as well, for example, working with people with neurological problems (such as people who have epileptic fits), or people receiving treatment because they have cancer.

Think it over

Can you think of other types of specialist units where a hospital nurse might work?

The types of hospital where a nurse might work vary. Some hospitals are very large and have a number of specialised wards and departments, out-patient clinics, accident and emergency unit and operating theatres. Other hospitals may be much smaller and may specialise in certain areas of health care such as care of the elderly, people with learning disabilities or people with mental health problems.

Nurses may choose to specialise in one form of nursing from the start of their training. The four major branches of nursing are:

■ adult and general nursing: Registered General Nurse (RGN)
■ children: Registered Sick Children's Nurse (RSCN)
■ mental health: Registered Mental Nurse (RMN)
■ mental handicap (learning disabilities): Registered Nurse – Mental Handicap (RNMH)

Nurses undertaking adult and general nursing training will spend time on many different wards during their training, but may specialise in special aspects of nursing later.

Although most of a hospital nurse's work will be based in one particular ward or unit at a time, he or she may be required to escort patients to other departments within the hospital, such as the X-ray department or operating theatre.

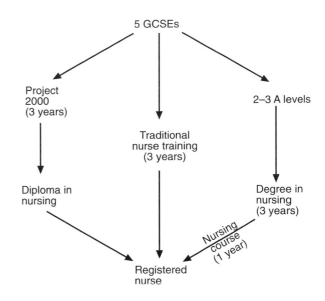

Figure 9.2 Career routes for a hospital nurse

Entry requirements and training

The minimum entry requirements for training as a registered nurse are five GCSEs (A–C grades), or the equivalent. However, some colleges of nursing ask for higher than the minimum qualifications. Some may ask for specific subjects such as English and/or a science subject.

It is also possible to take a degree course in some areas of nurse training, in which case two or three A levels are needed in addition to GCSEs. Science subjects are usually required, plus English and maths, at least at GCSE level.

The minimum age of entry to nurses' training is $17\frac{1}{2}$ years. (The minimum age of application for training is $16\frac{1}{2}$ years.)

Nurses' training is currently undergoing a period of change. A new form of nurse education – Project 2000 – is being introduced. Under Project 2000, trainee nurses will have full student status and will not be treated as staff during their training. The nursing course will cover a three-year period and will lead to qualification as a registered nurse and to an academic qualification at diploma level.

While Project 2000 is being introduced, students may still enter training through the traditional system. Trainee nurses using this pathway will receive a salary, but Project 2000 entrants will receive non-means-tested grant.

Pay and conditions

Salaries for registered nurses range from approximately £10 000 to £15 000 per annum, depending on the amount of responsibility the nurse has and his or her experience. Sisters and charge nurses may earn around £14 000 to £20 000 per annum. However, nurses may receive extra allowances for working in specialised areas such as psychiatry. The NHS also provides free uniforms and subsidised meals.

Standard working hours in the NHS are 75 hours over a two-week period. Nurses are required to work in shifts which include weekends, bank holidays and sometimes nights, although a separate night shift is often in operation. During the day-time, a three-shift system is usually used.

Prospects

The NHS employs more nurses than any other organisation. In 1995 about 400 000 nurses were employed by the NHS, with another 7000 employed in private hospitals and nursing homes. Other opportunities include working within the armed forces, working in prisons or young offender institutions or working abroad.

Try it

Find a copy of *Nursing Times*, *Midwifery* or the *Health Visitor* journals (available in larger newsagents), and note what sort of nursing posts are being advertised, what salaries are being offered for the different posts, and how many and what types of posts are being advertised for jobs abroad.

Nursing auxiliary/health care assistant

The post of health care assistant was created as a result of the introduction of Project 2000. Nursing auxiliaries, or health care assistants, undertake some of the work which used to be the responsibility of student nurses. People in these posts can now obtain NVQs/SVQs which give recognition to their skills and allow them to progress to more complex duties. Nursing auxiliaries/health care assistants may work in hospitals, residential or nursing homes, or in the community. They support the work of professional trained staff including nurses, midwives, district nurses, occupational therapists, physiotherapists, chiropodists, etc. They often work as part of a team.

The duties of a nursing auxiliary/health care assistant can be very varied and depend upon the setting in which they are employed. For example, on a hospital ward they may:

- help patients to dress and undress
- assist patients to walk
- help patients to feed themselves
- make snacks and hot drinks
- give out and empty bedpans
- help patients to use the toilet
- change incontinence pads, etc.
- give bedbaths and assist patients in the bathroom
- take and record patients temperature and pulse
- weigh patients
- put on simple dressings
- accompany patients to the theatre.

They may also be involved in helping to comfort anxious or frightened patients, play with children and help patients use recreational facilities. In addition, they may be required to help with the laying out of a patient who has died and in completing the related paperwork and administration.

In specialist hospitals, such as psychiatric hospitals, nursing auxiliaries may concentrate on helping the patient to gain confidence and independence.

In the community, nursing auxiliaries/health care assists may help patients in their own homes with tasks such as giving baths, renewing simple dressings, etc. or they may provide social and personal care for people who would otherwise have to remain in hospital.

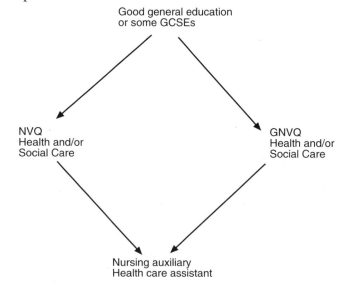

Figure 9.3 Career routes for a nursing auxiliary/health care assistant

Entry requirements/training

No formal entry requirements are needed, but applicants must be literate and numerate. Some authorities may ask for GCSEs. Many people who are interested in this kind of work undertake a NVQ or GNVQ course in health and/or social care prior to application.

Many different approaches are being used to training, which may be at work, or a combination of part-work and part-time in a school of nursing or at college.

To find out about opportunities for training, contact the personnel departments of an NHS or private hospital or colleges of further education and job centres.

Pay and conditions

Nursing auxiliaries may earn £7000–£9500 per annum depending upon experience and how much supervision they have while carrying out their tasks.

Most nursing auxiliaries/health care assistants work approximately 37 hours per week usually on a three-shift system. However, many hospital have flexible working hours and some part-time posts may be available.

Prospects

There are many related types of jobs, for example, care assistants, home helps, ward clerks and special needs teaching auxiliaries.

District nurse

District nurses visit people in their home or in residential care homes. The people that they look after might include those who have returned home from hospital following an operation, those with long-term illnesses or disabilities who require some nursing care, or people who are close to death but wish to remain at home. District nurses provide practical nursing care, but they also provide emotional support for patients and their carers.

Although much of their work is on a one-to-one basis with their patients, district nurses work as part of a team, which is usually based at a GP's surgery or in a health centre. They also liaise closely with other agencies who may be involved in the care of their patients, such as social workers. District nurses have both a general nursing qualification and a District Nursing Certificate. Salaries for district nurses are £16 000–£19 000 per annum.

Hours vary from area to area, but most district nurses work a rota system, 9am–6pm, seven days a week, including weekends and bank holidays. Some district nurses may also be on a rota system for on-call duties during the night.

Health visitor

The role of health visitors is to promote health and to help prevent illness. They do this by teaching people about healthy lifestyles and how to maintain health. Their work includes giving advice on health matters such as diet, hygiene, exercise, drug abuse, infection control, etc. Health visitors may work in clinics or visit people in their homes, and although they liaise closely with other professionals, such as GPs, district nurses and social workers, they are responsible for organising their own work and work much more independently than other nurses.

Health visitors must be registered nurses (most have a general nursing qualification) and have some experience of nursing before they undertake the special training required to become a qualified health visitor. Salaries for health visitors are £15 000–£18 000 per annum.

Health visitors usually work office hours, Monday to Friday, although occasional evening and weekend working may be required.

Occupational health nurse

The work of the occupational health nurse is divided into three main areas:

- identifying potential health hazards in the work place
- promotion and maintenance of good health and prevention of ill-health
- organising emergency treatment for people who are injured at work, and the treatment of minor illnesses and injuries.

The majority of occupational health nurse posts are in industry, although some hospitals and other organisations provide this service for their staff.

Occupational health work is open to registered and enrolled nurses with at least two years' experience following qualification. There are also special Occupational Health Nursing Certificate and Diploma courses.

Salaries start about £13 000–15 000, but a senior occupational nurse may earn in excess of £25 000 per annum. Working patterns vary a great deal, with some occupational health nurses working office hours and others working in shifts to provide 24-hour cover. Some work alone and others work in teams which may include doctors, as well as other nurses and other professionals, for example, physiotherapists.

Community psychiatric nurse

The role of the community psychiatric nurse is to enable people who have a mental illness to remain within the community, or to return to the community following a period in hospital. The community psychiatric nurse works between the hospital and the community, visiting people in their homes, seeing them at a clinic or in hospital. At a practical level they administer drugs by injection, oversee the patient's self-administration of tablets, etc. However, they also provide emotional support for patients and their carers, counselling them and exploring ways of helping them overcome or come to terms with illness.

Entry requirements are the same as for general hospital nursing, but nurses must have specialised in mental health as part of their training. Salaries for psychiatric nurses are £11 000–£ 14 000 per annum. Senior nurses may earn up to £24 000.

Community psychiatric nurses (CPNs) usually work office hours, but may operate an on-call rota system at nights or at weekends in some areas. They spend much of their time on a one-to-one basis with their patients, but belong to a team of CPNs. They also liaise closely with other health and social care professionals.

Dentist

The role of the dentist is concerned with promoting dental health and hygiene as well as identifying and treating diseases and disorders of the teeth and gums. Dentists are employed in private practice and/or by the NHS. They work in dental practices or hospitals. Dentists in general practice may work on their own or as part of a group of professionals such as dentists, dental nurses, hygienists, dental technicians, etc.

Dental schools normally require dental students to have A Levels at high grades including chemistry and two other science subjects. Training usually lasts five to six years.

Dentists in general practice can expect an average income of about £36 000 per annum.

They can arrange their own working hours. Most dentists start work at about 8.30 am and finish at about 5.30 pm. Some may work evenings and Saturday mornings, and this may be on a rota basis.

Try it

When you next visit the dentist make a note of the people working in the practice. Observe what they do and write this down. Also note what times the practice is open.

Optician

Most opticians work in private practice, taking fee-paying and NHS patients. Their role is to examine eyes and to prescribe and dispense glasses and contact lenses. Opticians also treat vision defects and abnormal eye movements.

Opticians tend to work mostly on their own, on a one-to-one basis with their patients, although many have receptionists working for them. Some opticians work in group practices, clinics or hospitals, where there may be a team of different professionals working together.

To become an optician it is necessary to have a degree in ophthalmic optics and a year's work under supervision. The minimum requirement for the

WELLFORD HOSPITAL NHS TRUST
Trauma Directorate
TRAINED NURSE
Grade E

Hours: 37 $\frac{1}{2}$ hours per week internal Rotation to Night Duty

Salary: £12,950–£15,000 pa

Job requirements: 1st level registration with Orthopaedic qualifications or recent experience in Orthopaedics. Outline of duties: to lead a team of nurses. Responsible for assessment, planning and implementation of a high standard of care for patients admitted for elective Orthopaedic surgery and Rheumatology conditions.

For an informal discussion or to arrange a visit, please contact: Human Resources Manager. Please quote Job Ref: DV 3105.

For an application form and job description please contact Human Resources Department.

The closing date is April 7

(T...

Welford Community Mental Health Services
COMMUNITY PSYCHIATRIC NURSE
Grade F/G
(Depending on qualifications and experience)
(£17,464 - £22,726 pro-rata)
18 $\frac{3}{4}$ hours per week

We require an enthusiastic and experienced RMN to join our service. You will be responsible for a defined caseload and carrying 24-hour Nursing responsibility for your work. There is regular supervision from senior team members and individual development is encouraged through the IPR procedure.

You will join a multi-disciplinary team offering care to clients with severe and enduring mental health problems in Wellshire. The service has recently been reorganised to offer an Urgent Assessment, Walk-in and Out-patient service, from our new Community Mental Health Resource Centre. The post offers the opportunity for a wide range of Mental Health Nursing experience.

Informal discussions are welcome.

For ...
... form and job description, please contact the ...
... st

(HM40 2)

WELLFORD HOSPITAL NHS TRUST
Medical/Elderly Unit
WARD MANAGER – LECTURER/ PRACTITIONER
Trust Grade A
Full-Time
Ref: WM 206

An innovative person is required to work as a Ward Manager Lecturer Practitioner within the Medical/Elderly Care Unit, Wellford General Hospital, and the School of Health Care Study, Wellshire University

The post holder should be able to demonstrate clinical expertise and have proven management skills, and will be required.

- To manage a specified ward area.
- To take a lead in clinical/educational development.
- To participate within the Senior Nurse Team of the Unit
- To make a major contribution to the development of teaching modules within the Nursing/Midwifery programme.
- To contribute to activities within the School of Health Studies.

Applicants should also have the following skills:
- RGN qualifications.
- A Degree in Nursing or relevant studies.
- Teaching qualification or experience.
- Minimum of two years experience within a senio...
- Good communication skills.
- Proven management skills.

**Application forms are available by telephonin...
answerphone) or by writing to The Personne...**

Closing date: April 27th
Interviews: End of May

DIRECTORATE OF CHILD HEALTH
FULL & PART TIME STAFF NURSES

RSCN's/RN Child Branch
£12,950–£15,000 p.a. pro rata
£11,320–£12,950 p.a. pro rata

Due to promotion, maternity leave and the future developments within the Child Health Directorate, posts for all four clinical areas have become available.

The four wards are in Wellford.

The specialities covered are trauma/orthopedics, general paediatrics, oncology, haematology, surgery, opthalmolc dermatology and infectious diseases.

This is a very exciting time to join the Child Health Directorate as we enter into a period of extensive development resulting from a major building program on the Wellford site.

Application forms and job descriptions are available the Employee Services Section.

Closing date for completed applications: 14th April

WORKING TOWARDS EQUAL OPPORTUNITIES

CARING FOR ONE AND ALL

Occupational Health Nurse

Fire Brigade Headquarters, Wellford
£16,248–18,894

You will be responsible for the provision of Health Screening and a quality pro-active health care service to over 800 full and part-time employees.

You must be a Registered General Nurse having Part 1 of the Register. Occupational Health experience is desirable. A current driving licence will be required owing to the geography of the Brigade and a flexible approach to working hours is considered to be essential. Experience of computerised systems, sickness audits and report writing would be advantageous.

Serving England's Most Beautiful County

167

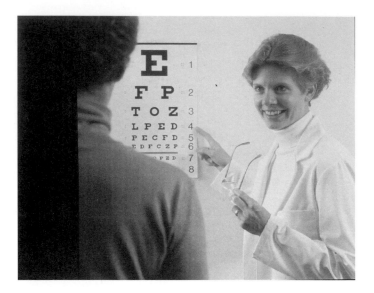

degree course is two A Levels (either maths, biology or physics) and five GCSEs (A–C grades). Other qualifications are considered when equivalent to entry requirements.

Newly registered opticians in private practice may earn £12 000–£15 000 per annum, but this could increase to approximately £30 000 with experience.

Most opticians work a 35-hour week, which normally includes Saturdays.

Pharmacist

Pharmacy is concerned with the development, preparation and dispensing of drugs. Pharmacists work in one of three main settings:

- community (or retail) pharmacy
- hospital pharmacy
- industrial pharmacy.

The main duties of a pharmacist in the community are to prepare and dispense drugs prescribed by GPs for patients. However, the pharmacist may also give customers advice regarding prescribed and non-prescribed drugs, and how they should be used. A community pharmacist is also likely to be a business manager and run a chemist shop. The work therefore includes financial management, merchandising and staff management.

Pharmacists hold a degree in pharmacy, and the entry requirements are two A Levels plus three GCSEs (A–C grades). Following their degree course, trainee pharmacists must work in a supervised position for a year, before they can become registered.

Prior to registration a pharmacist may expect a starting salary of about £7 500. Employed pharmacists usually can get £16 000–£22 000 per annum.

Community pharmacists usually work shop hours, i.e. 9 am – 5.30 pm, five or six days per week. Some shops are open for late-evening, all-night, or Sunday dispensing.

Physiotherapist

Physiotherapy is concerned with the rehabilitation of people who have suffered an injury, who have a physical disability or who need help to restore or maintain their mobility, which may have been limited through illness.

Treatments that are used by the physiotherapist are mainly based on movement and manipulation, although other methods include electro-therapy, ultrasound and heat treatments. The work can be very strenuous – moving limbs, helping patients to move and providing support.

Many physiotherapists work in hospitals, although others may visit people in their homes. Although mainly working in a one-to-one situation with their patients, physiotherapists may also work very closely with other professionals such as doctors, occupational therapists and social workers.

The minimum qualifications for a degree in physiotherapy are two A Levels plus three GCSEs (A–C grades).

NHS pay scales range from £22 500 for newly qualified people to £27 000 for district physiotherapists. Working hours vary from normal office hours in some settings, such as hospitals, to evening and weekend working in the sport and leisure sector.

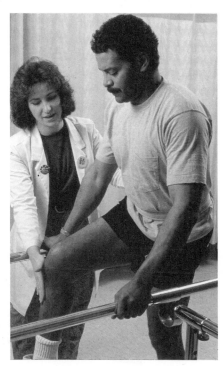

Occupational therapist

Occupational therapists help people to build up confidence and independence after an injury, illness or disability, and to adjust to everyday living. They give individual treatment to people and run groups. They see people in hospital, clinics or in their homes. Occupational therapists are also able to advise and provide equipment to assist people with daily living such as specially adapted cutlery for those unable to use normal cutlery, walking frames for people unsteady on their feet and special mattresses for those people who have to spend much of their time in bed.

Like physiotherapists, occupational therapists spend a lot of their time with patients, but also work closely with other health and social care professionals.

Occupational therapists must be state registered and have a degree in occupational therapy. The minimum qualification to gain entry to a degree course is two A Levels plus three GCSEs (A–C grades), which should include English and a science subject.

Starting salaries are around £11 000 per annum, increasing to £18 000. Senior posts have salaries of about £27 000.

NHS occupational therapists normally work a 36-hour week, Monday to Friday.

Speech therapist

Speech therapists treat speech, voice and language defects and are responsible for the assessment, diagnosis and treatment of patients. They deal with all sorts of communication problems, but mainly treat disorders of fluency, articulation, voice and language, which may have been caused by deformities since birth (for example, deafness) or may have occurred through injury or illness such as a stroke.

Much of the work is directly with the patient. However, speech therapists liaise with other specialists such as doctors, teachers, social workers and psychologists.

Candidates must have a degree such as English or Biology and the minimum requirements for a degree are two A levels plus three GCSEs (A–C grades) including English. Salaries range from £11 000 to £28 500 per annum. Speech therapists working in the NHS usually work 9 am to 5 pm, Monday to Friday.

Support services in health care

In order for people who provide care directly to patients to be able to work effectively, they often require the help of support services. In hospitals, clinics and social services departments the support of all sorts of administration staff is needed. In residential and day-care facilities, whether they are run by health or social care agencies, catering services and possibly laundry services are required. As new technology is being used for diagnosing health problems and there is more sophisticated equipment for treating people as well as information technology for recording service users' records, staff with many different kinds of technical knowledge are required.

Medical technical officer

Medical technical officers are responsible for operating and/or maintaining equipment used in diagnosing and treating illnesses and in monitoring the results of treatment. Medical technical officers specialise either in medical physics or physiological measurement.

Medical physics technicians may be concerned with radiotherapy, which is one of the main treatments for cancer; radiation protection – ensuring the safety of staff and patients from radiation; ultrasound, which uses sound waves to monitor functions and identify abnormalities within the body; renal dialysis – involving an artificial kidney machine; and various other forms of technology, including the use of lasers.

Physiological measurement technicians work closely with patients, measuring the capacity of various parts of the body in order to help medical staff diagnose and treat diseases. These technicians may specialise in **audiology** – measurement and evaluation of people's hearing capacity; **cardiology** – working with people who have, or are suspected of having diseases of the heart; **neurology** – which involves measuring the electrical activity of the brain; or **respiratory physiology** – which is concerned with the way people breathe.

Entry requirements and training

Entry requirements are not always defined but applicants must be able to undertake an appropriate course in a medical science or technical or engineering subject. Usually, this means four GCSEs (A–C grades), in English, maths and two science subjects. Trainee technicians undertake an in-service training course, which may include attending a day-release or block-release course at a college of further education.

Pay and conditions

Within the NHS there is one trainee grade and five other grades of technician. A trainee's salary starts at about £5 500 per annum rising to £7 000. The annual salary of a qualified medical technical officer (MTO) is £7 500 – £25 500. Most MTOs work a 37-hour, five-day week. This may include some weekend or on-call duties.

Ambulance person

In the UK there are about 67 ambulance services providing transport to hospitals. The majority of calls on the ambulance service are for non-urgent situations. Only a small part of ambulance service work is concerned with emergencies.

Ambulance personnel usually work in pairs, with one person driving the ambulance and the other attending to the needs of the patient. Ambulance personnel mostly work with people – patients, hospital staff or other professionals.

There are three levels of personnel:

- ambulance care assistants, who mainly transport people to and from hospital for out-patient clinics
- ambulance technicians, who are involved in a full range of accident and emergency duties
- ambulance paramedics, who are technicians but with additional training, and are qualified to use more advanced forms of life-support equipment. Ambulance personnel spend most of their time in their vehicles, returning to the control room only at the beginning and end of a shift and for meal breaks.

Entry requirements and training

The minimum age to become an ambulance crew member is 18 years, although some areas have cadet schemes for 16- and 17-year-olds. Applicants must have a clean, current driving licence. Also, employers are likely to require four GCSEs (A–C grades) including English, maths and a science subject.

Ambulance care assistants undertake an in-house course which usually last 2–4 weeks. Technicians

must first complete the care assistants course, gain some experience and then undertake further training. This training is often in the form of an eight-week residential course, followed by twelve months' experience in the full range of accident and emergency work. To become a paramedic, the person must have completed at least twelve months working as a technician and be accepted for training through a selection interview. Successful applicants then take an eight-week course.

Pay and conditions

Ambulance care assistants, which is the grade at which most entrants start, earn an annual salary of about £9 000. Ambulance technicians earn about £13 500 and paramedics, £13 500.

Ambulance personnel work a 39-hour week. Ambulance care assistants mostly work Monday to Friday. Technicians and paramedics tend to work rotating shift systems, including nights and weekends.

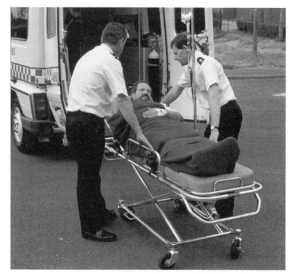

Medical records clerk

The role of the medical records clerk is to provide administrative support within hospitals. Medical records clerks undertake reception duties, provide clerical support concerned with the treatment and care of patients and maintain links between hospital personnel such as consultants and community personnel, for example GPs.

Out-patient receptionists, admissions and ward clerks are all in contact with patients and their families, either face-to-face or by telephone. Out-patient receptionists work in out-patient departments. They take details of the patient for the consultant, arrange follow-up appointments and deal with letters to and from GPs. Admissions and ward clerks keep records of all patients admitted to and discharged from the hospital. Ward clerks assist the nursing staff, carrying out clerical duties and answering telephone calls.

Medical records clerks also work in other areas of the hospital, undertaking filing and general administration, as well as collecting statistical information. Most jobs now involve the use of computers.

Entry requirements and training

There are no minimum educational entry requirements, but keyboard skills are an advantage for most posts.

Training varies from hospital to hospital and is mainly on-the job.

Pay and conditions

Basic annual pay starts at about £5000 at 16 years of age. At 18 and over the basic salary ranges from £7000 to £8500. For those taking on a supervisory role, the salary scale is £8500–£14500 per annum.

Full-time staff usually work 37 hours per week, Monday to Friday, although some units such as accident and emergency departments may operate a shift system including evenings and weekends.

Health service manager

Health service managers work within all levels of the health service including Regional Health Authorities, District Health Authorities and NHS Trusts, etc. They may be involved in either the purchasing of services, or the providing of services.

The work of health service managers varies according to the setting, including for example financial managements, personnel matters, purchasing of supplies, planning and development of services, information management, etc. Applicants for general management training schemes need to be over 21 years old and hold two A levels. Salaries range from £8000 for juniors to £33000 for the most senior posts. Hours of work are 37 a week, Monday to Friday.

Catering staff (cook)

The National Health Service runs a trainee cook scheme. The training takes place at selected hospitals and includes a day-release certificate course over a two-year period. The most usual course is the City and Guilds 7060 – Cookery for the catering industry. No formal qualifications are normally required for entry to the training course for employment, but a good general education is needed.

The work involves planning, preparing and cooking meals for patients and staff. It also involves purchasing the necessary food and equipment, budgeting, record keeping, stock control and accounting. Cooks must also be aware of health and hygiene regulations, as well as health and safety laws. Assistant cooks earn from £7000–£13000 per annum, but rates of pay vary according to qualifications and experience. Within a hospital setting, a shift system is likely to be operated, including evenings and weekends.

Hospital porter

The role of the porter is very important in the smooth running of a hospital. Porters ensure that people, equipment and supplies are in the right place at the right time.

Hospital porters undertaken three main areas of work.

- light portering services
- general portering
- reception and enquiry work.

Light portering involves delivering laundry, mail, meals and flowers to patients. It may also include operating lifts or car park duties.

General portering includes delivering stores, collecting rubbish, moving furniture, collecting and delivering equipment. Porters also transport patients between wards and other units in the hospital, such as X-ray departments and operating theatres. Night duties may involve fire and security checks and refuse disposal.

Reception and enquiry duties involve directing patients and their relatives about the building doing simple clerical tasks, and cleaning and preparing specialist equipment, for example, oxygen cylinders.

Applicants must be over 18 years of age, but no formal academic qualifications are required.

Salaries range from £115 to £122 per week. Shift allowances and overtime may be paid.

Porters work a 40-hour week on a shift system.

Jobs in social care

People working in social care may be found in public, private or voluntary organisations. They may undertake residential work, day care or 'fieldwork'. **Fieldwork** means that the worker operates from an office base, but often goes out to meet people, sometimes in their homes.

As in health care, apart from those people whose job it is to provide care directly to people, there are many other people employed in jobs that support the direct provision of services, such as clerks and catering staff.

Much social care is provided by care assistants and social workers. The majority of care assistants and social workers are employed by local authority social

services departments, although others may work in voluntary organisations, such as the National Society for Prevention of Cruelty to Children (NSPCC). Many care assistants are also employed in the private sector, for example in privately owned residential homes, day centres, day nurseries or in home-care agencies.

In this section the jobs covered in some detail are those of:

- field social worker
- nursery nurse
- administrative assistant.

There are also brief accounts of the following:

- youth and community worker
- care assistant
- psychologist
- local authority manager.

Field social worker

Social workers, who are usually organised in teams, aim to assess the needs of individuals and families and to set up and co-ordinate the services required to meet those needs. For example, a young adult who has had a road traffic accident, which results in him or her having to use a wheelchair, may need someone to help with personal care (getting up, washed and dressed) someone to help with household tasks (cleaning, shopping, laundry) and need special transport in order to get about.

Most social workers work in teams that specialise in assessing the needs of a particular group of clients, for example children and families, older people, people with physical disabilities, people with learning disabilities or people with mental health

Figure 9.4 Career routes for a social worker

problems. The team they work in may also include other professionals such as occupational therapists, home care assistants and clerks. The team will be supervised by a senior social worker (team leader).

Social workers meet their clients and families when appropriate, to assess clients' needs and to determine the short and long-term courses of action. Sometimes this can be done quickly and easily, but in other instances careful assessment and planning over a long period of time may be required. Social workers need to build up a relationship of trust with clients, in order to help them explore the options that are open to them and to make informed choices about how their needs can be met.

Although social workers spend much of their time with clients, they also undertake routine organisation, planning and arranging for services to be made available to clients. This may involve consulting with other professional people or agencies. Social workers may also help clients to help themselves – in setting up support groups or self-help groups, for example.

Many social workers work in the community. Some may work in hospitals, health centres or GPs' surgeries. Social workers, especially those involved in child care, may also be required to attend juvenile courts.

Entry requirements and training

Until recently, there were two professional qualifications in social work: the Certificate in Social Service (CSS) and the Certificate of Qualification in Social Work (CQSW). These, while still recognised, have been replaced by a new qualification – the Diploma in Social Work (DipSW).

Applicants for this qualification must usually be over 21 years of age because the qualification cannot be awarded before 22 years of age. The Central Council for Education and Training in Social Work (CCETSW) does not specify any specific qualification requirements for applicants over 21. However, many colleges do, as the diploma involves higher education study.

Pay and conditions

There are over 26 000 field social workers employed by local authorities in England and Wales. The nationally agreed pay scale ranges from £12 000 to £18 000 approximately, depending on qualifications, experience and the level of responsibility.

Most social workers are contracted to work a 37-hour week. However, social work is not a 9–5 job, as many clients need to be seen outside these times. Some social workers are required to work weekend and night-time duty rotas.

Prospects

Within local authorities there is a well-defined career structure, with opportunities to progress from the basic social worker grade to senior social worker, and eventually to team leader. It is also possible to progress to managerial levels within the social services department.

Think it over

Think about working as a social worker in a children and families team. How might this be different from working in a team which deals with the needs of older people? Think about the difference under the following headings:

a usual working hours
b the types of need which clients may have
c the services that they might require to meet these needs
d other professionals who might be involved.

Nursery nurse

Nursery nurses work in many different child-care settings such as local authority and private nurseries, workplace creches, college creches, children's wards in hospitals or with individual families. However, the work, wherever it is carried out, involves taking care of young children, and taking into account their emotional, social and physical needs.

Most nursery nurses are responsible for the routine care of young children, i.e. feeding, washing, dressing, taking them to the toilet, and supervising their play. Those working with older children help to organise the routine of the child's day, and supervise their play and other activities. In some settings the nursery nurse may also help with early reading and number work, or other simple learning tasks. Nursery nurses also monitor the health and general development of the child. They may be required to observe the children, make detailed reports of their progress and identify and resolve any problems. This may involve liaising with other professionals. Additionally, nursery nurses need to be able to give first-aid and comfort when required.

Social Workers

Children & Families

£15,126–£19,308 pro-rata per annum

Wellford Social Work Centre

Ref No: 414E

Full and part-time qualified Social Workers (CCETSW approved qualification) required to join a Team specialising in work with children and their families, serving a landward area of the Region. Excellent accommodation and working conditions, good Team spirit and challenging work in the field of Child Protection, together with pro-active work with young people in difficulty at home, at school and in the community. Informal enquiries to Practice Team Manager on 0123 314137

Closing Date: Friday, 31 March

QUALIFIED SOCIAL WORKER

Mental Health/Learning Disabilities

£15,159–£20,886 p.a. inc.

An exciting new post has arisen in the Wellford Social Work Team with both adults who have a learning disability, and adults who have long term mental health problems, linked to a Community Mental Health Team. The successful applicant will have had experience of both client groups and will need to be ASW qualified or eligible for ASW training in September 1996. You will receive regular supervision and opportunities for training and personal development. Car driver essential.

…iscussion contact Personnel Manager

…s from Social Services Centre, Wellford

…: SW27

Interview date: 12. April

SOCIAL SERVICES DEPARTMENT

NORTH EAST ADULTS TEAM

Qualified Social Worker Jobshare – 18.5 hours

Salary £14,647 – £19,830 Review at £16,791

pro-rata to hours worked.

The team provides a service under the Community Care Act to adults living in North West Quarter of the town. Workers aim to ensure sympathetic needs led assessment and informed provision of service with full user participation.

Applicants must have a commitment to anti-oppressive practice and must either hold the Diploma in Social Work or expect to obtain it this summer.

The 18.5 hours are normally worked during Wednesday, Thursday and Friday.

Application forms from Director of Social Services Wellford.

Closing date: 30 March

- Job Sharers welcome.
- Generous relocation package available, worth up to £6,000 including subsistence allowances.
- This Council has a No Smoking policy and Smoking restrictions apply.

Social Worker

OLDER PEOPLE & HOSPITALS …

£13,737–£19,803 (PRO-RATA FOR PA…

You should be committed to the pro… of high quality and innovative services in line with the requirements of the NHS and Community Care Act 1990.

You must be qualified (DSW, CQSW, CSS or equivalent) ideally with a knowledge of care management and a positive approach to its implementation in the current climate of change.

A current driving licence is essential. Job share applicants are welcome.

Informal enquiries to Team Leader. Application forms are available from the Director of Social Services, Wellford.

Closing date: 31st March

An equal opportunity employer.

…ychiatric Social Worker

£20,811–£22,509 inc.

Temporary Post

…citing opportunity has arisen within the Child Guidance Service for a qualified and experienced Social Worker to join the off-site education provision of our Unified Support Service. You will provide consultation and training to teaching and support staff to enhance their skills in working with pupils who have emotional and behavioural difficulties. You will also offer counselling to some pupils and set up support networks for parents.

The post is a temporary appointment, from June 1996 to end March 1997.

For an informal discussion please contact Human Resources Manager.

For an application pack please send a sae to The Central Team, Personnel Section, Child Guidance Service, Wellford.

Closing date: 30 March Interviews: 26 April

Nursery nurses work indoors and outside with the children.

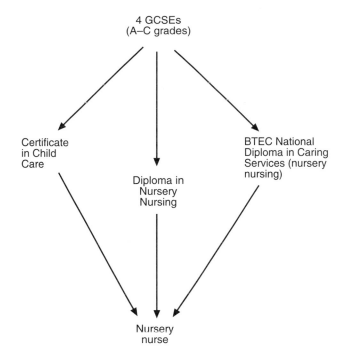

Figure 9.5 Career routes for a nursery nurse

Entry requirements

There are two basic qualifications in nursery nursing: the Certificate in Children's Care and Education and the Diploma in Nursery Nursing, both awarded by the Council for Awards in Children's Care and Education (CACHE). Many colleges ask for four GSCEs (A–C grades), for entry to the Diploma. Colleges of further education have a minimum entry age of 16, although many private colleges have a minimum starting age of 18 years.

It is also possible to study for a BTEC National Diploma in Caring Services (Nursery Nursing). This is usually a two-year, full-time course.

Pay and conditions

These vary greatly from setting to setting. In the public sector, such as local authorities, nursery nurses are paid £5 000–£10 000 per annum. An officer-in-charge can earn £11 000–£18 000. In a day nursery or creche, many nursery nurses work a shift system, as the nursery or creche could be open from 7 am–8 pm. However, most nursery nurses work a 36–40 hour week.

Nursery nurses working for a private family negotiate their own salaries and working conditions. An average wage would seem to be around £60 per week, but some earn more. Live-in nursery nurses (nannies) are usually provided with at least bed-sit accommodation, and this is reflected in the salary.

Prospects

Qualified nursery nurses have little difficulty in finding work once they are qualified. However, promotion opportunities are limited.

Youth and community workers

Youth and community work is concerned with education in its broadest sense, and involves encouraging people to participate in community affairs, enabling individuals and groups of people to make significant changes in their lives, with support from professionals.

For example, community workers may work with tenants' groups, working to improve facilities on housing estates or encourage parents to set up play groups or toy libraries. Community workers may also help people from all walks of life to be able to take part in social, community and political activities.

Youth workers are mostly concerned with the educational and emotional development of young people aged 11–25 years. Many youth workers run clubs and drop-centres. The club or centre may provide activities, informal and formal discussion groups, as well as individual counselling.

Applicants for training in youth and community work usually require five GCSEs (A–C grades), although this may be waived for mature and experienced candidates. At any age, experience in working with people is also necessary. A number of applicants have degrees in related subjects.

Salaries range from £10 000 to £20 000 per annum.

Hours vary, but usually cover a 35–7 hour week, which may include specified evening and weekend working.

Care assistants

The role of the care assistant is to assist people who need help with various everyday tasks such as getting up, washing, dressing, shopping and housework. The tasks will vary according to the needs of the individuals with whom they are working. Care assistants may work with all types of client groups, for example, children and young people, people with disabilities or older people.

Care assistants may be required to help with the physical needs of individuals, whatever their age, including helping them to get up, wash, dress, bathe and to use the toilet. They may also undertake domestics duties such as washing up, making beds, ironing, preparing meals and shopping. In some instances, care assistants may also help people to learn new skills, including budgeting or cooking. They may also help set up activities for their clients, as well as providing friendly support and a listening ear.

Care assistants can work in a wide variety of settings – nursing homes, residential homes, day centres, hostels, group homes or in an individual's home (as home carers/helps).

Care assistants may be employed in public, private or voluntary organisations.

No academic qualifications are needed for entry into this work. However, there are courses that will help prepare candidates.

There is often in-service training for care assistants, leading to NVQs/SVQs in Care.

Pay varies according to employer, type of work, location and experience, but is about £7 000–£9 000 per annum.

Day-care assistants often work regular hours, Monday to Friday.

Those working as home care assistants may be required to work at weekends and bank holidays. Care assistants in hostels and residential homes often work shifts. Some assistants may be required to live-in, while others may be employed to live with clients in their homes.

Try it

There are many different work patterns for care assistants. These depend on the setting in which they work. Find out from the local social services department the normal hours of working for care assistants in the following settings:

a home care
b day care for people with physical disabilities
c a hostel or group home for people with learning disabilities
d a residential home for older people.

Psychologist

Psychologists observe and interpret human behaviour. They specialise in various types of issues. Clinical psychologists work with clients who have mental health problems. Educational psychologists deal with the problems of children from birth to 19 years of age, liaising with teachers, social workers and other professionals. Occupational psychologists are employed in places of work and may advise companies on improving training, job satisfaction and productivity, as well as providing a counselling service for staff. Other psychologists may specialise in criminology, or work in special hospitals, prisons or youth custody centres; they may also help and advise police in their investigations.

A degree in psychology is essential and normally requires the candidate to have at least two A Levels and five GCSEs (A–C grades).

Salaries depend on specialism, seniority and levels of responsibility. An NHS basic grade clinical psychologist's pay could start around £9 000 per annum rising to £31 000 for top posts. A qualified educational psychologist's salary will start at approximately £18 000 and can rise to about £36 000.

Many psychologists work normal office hours, Monday to Friday.

Support services in social care

Support services play an essential part in enabling any organisation and agency to run efficiently and smoothly. The management of any service is especially important to ensure that resources are used effectively and that the person receiving the service has a constant and good quality service. Management and administration of the service is therefore very important.

Administrative assistant

Administrative assistants and officers in any of the caring agencies, whether in health or social care, may perform a wide range of tasks.

The work of an administrative assistant may include keeping records, either manually or on a computer, sorting and filing papers, simple figure work, writing basic letters and answering enquiries.

Administrative officers have more responsibility than assistants. Their work may include handling incoming correspondence, writing and drafting letters, checking accounts, maintaining records and assisting the public. Usually, administrative staff work in an office, sometimes with other administrative staff, but sometimes alongside the people who provide the services, for example within a team of social workers.

Entry requirements

Many organisations do not require any specific academic qualifications, other than a good general education. Other organisations require GCSEs (A–C grades) in two subjects, which would normally include English. Keyboard skills would also be an advantage, especially with the increasing use of computers in the workplace.

In-house training, or on-the-job training is often available. Courses may also be available on a full-time or part-time basis, including NVQ courses.

Pay and conditions

Administrative assistants and clerical officers normally work a 37-hour week during normal office hours, Monday to Friday. Flexitime is often available (i.e. core hours of 9.30 am–4.00 pm must be worked each day, but the remainder of the 37 hours may be worked in any combination either side of these hours. For example, one person may work 8.00 am –4.00 pm; another may choose to work 9.30 am–5.30 pm).

Salaries vary a great deal depending on experience, location, responsibilities of the job and qualifications. However, the average starting salary is about £5 000 per annum, rising to £10 000. Staff taking on supervisory roles may be able to earn up to £18 000 per annum.

Local authority manager

Local authorities employ over 3 000 000 staff throughout the UK. They range from gardeners, refuse collectors and clerks to professionally qualified staff such as accountants, architects and social workers.

Local authority managers plan and organise the work of the various departments which supply services to individuals and communities. They work within policy guidelines and the financial limits set by the planning and finance committees of the local authority.

For direct entry into management grades, most authorities require at least one A level plus five GCSEs (A–C grades), although many require a degree. Some authorities offer day or block-release training for people already employed by them to enable them to progress to management level posts. NVQ, BTEC and certificate and diploma courses are available in management studies.

Most managers are contracted to work a 37-hour week. Monday to Friday, although attendance at meetings outside these hours may be required.

Salaries depend on the level of responsibility, experience and nature of the job, but range from £10 000 to £50 000 per annum for those at director level.

Stereotypes

People often have a fixed idea about the sort of person who will undertake a certain type of job. They may also have fixed ideas about what a job actually entails.

These stereotyped views are sometimes reinforced by television programmes, although other programmes try to present more realistic images which challenge these stereotypes.

For example, a GP is often portrayed as an elderly, white male, wearing spectacles and sitting behind a large, old-fashioned desk, on which stands a black medicine bag. Of course, there are now many female GPs, as well as GPs from a wide variety of ethnic and cultural backgrounds.

Two standard stereotypes of social workers also come to mind. One is of a small, thin male with a beard and wearing 'hippy'-type clothes and sandals; the other is of a rather large, middle-aged lady, wearing a twin-set and pearls. The 'lady-bountiful' image is reminiscent of the 'lady of the manor', who would distribute food and possibly clothes to 'needy' tenants of the manor and to local villagers. The 'hippy' image may have arisen from the 1970s when social services were undergoing great changes and many people were being recruited as social workers.

A popular image of a midwife is of a middle-aged female, riding a bicycle at great speed, in order to attend the delivery of a baby. Although midwives do supervise the delivery of babies, they also play a considerable role in monitoring the health of the mother and the development of the foetus before the birth. This involves making various physical and medical checks. Midwives also have an advisory and caring role and are concerned with the post-natal care of the mother and baby. Increasingly, there are male nurses undertaking midwifery courses.

Traditionally, nursery nurses are depicted as being young females. Even today, this type of work does not seem to attract many male candidates; the reasons for this are quite complex, but may partly be due to the limited prospects and also because caring for children is still primarily regarded as being the role of women. However, this may be changing slowly.

Think it over

What would be the advantages for children in having male and female nursery nurses? Are there any arguments against men taking on the role of nursery nurse?

Try it

Undertake a survey among your relatives and friends. Ask them to describe what they think the following people would typically look like, and what their jobs entail:

a a GP
b an occupational therapist
c a social worker
d a member of an ambulance crew
d a home care assistant
e an administrative assistant in a social services department.

Evidence collection point

Make a list of the main jobs in health and social care under the headings 'Provision of Care' and 'Support Services'.

Choose three of these and write a profile of the work of the jobholders, including one person who provides health and medical care, one person who provides social care, and one person who provides a support service.

The profile should include:

a a description of their day-to-day work
b a description of their career route to date
c a comparison of their actual role with a stereotype of their role.

These profiles will contribute to the evidence indicators for Element 3.3.

Fast Facts

Access Means by which an individual becomes a client of a particular service.

Acute A condition which starts quickly and lasts for a short time, for example a common cold.

Advocate Someone who speaks on behalf of another person.

BTEC Business and Technology Education Council. An awarding body that awards national qualifications.

Career routes The pathway which an individual takes in order to qualify and then move to more senior roles in a certain job or profession.

Charter A document which sets out the standards of service a client can expect.

Chronic   A condition which develops over time and is long lasting.

City and Guilds   An awarding body that awards national qualifications.

Community health care   Care provided for individuals in the community and where possible in their own homes.

Contracts   Formal legal agreements to ensure the delivery of services.

CQSW   Certificate of Qualification in Social Work.

CSS   Certificate in Social Services.

Department of Health   A central government body which administers health and social care.

DipSW (DSW)   Diploma in Social Work.

District Health Authorities   Purchasers of health care.

Emotional needs   Needs which cover an individual's feelings.

Family Health Services Authorities   Employers of GPs, dentists, opticians and pharmacists. They share the same geographical boundaries as District Health Authorities.

Intellectual needs   The need for mental stimulation.

Local authority social services   These departments are responsible for the provision of social care to meet the needs of the people in the community.

Means testing   An individual's income and savings are taken into account when deciding on the cost of a service to the client or whether he or she is eligible to receive the service.

Mixed economy of care   A system where all the care services work together to deliver the most cost-effective, efficient service.

National Health Service (NHS)   In England the Secretary of State for Health has overall responsibility for the NHS. The organisation of the NHS in England includes the Department of Health and Health Authorities.

National Health Service and Community Care Act 1990   An Act of Parliament which aims to allow vulnerable people to live as independently as possible, within their own homes or in a homely setting in the community.

National Health Trusts   Self-governing units within the NHS, such as hospitals and community services, which provide services to patients. They are directly responsible to the Secretary of State, without intervention from District or Regional Health Authorities.

Need   A need is an essential requirement which must be met in order to ensure that an individual reaches a state of health and social well-being.

Primary health care   Care, which is often preventative, delivered in the community, for example GP services.

Private services   These provide an alternative form of care for which there is a charge. Private organisations are run as businesses and are profit-making.

Provider   An organisation that sells services to a purchaser.

Purchaser   An organisation that buys in necessary services.

Referral   Methods by which a client is referred or passed to a service.

Regional Health Authorities   A department within the NHS that allocates resources to District Health Authorities, Family Health Services Authorities and GP fund-holders.

Secondary health care   Health care, often curative, provided in hospital situations.

Social needs   Needs which include the individual's need for relationships with others and the need to belong within a group.

Special Health Authorities   Organisations providing specialist health care needs, with regional or national catchment areas.

Statutory organisations   Health and social care organisations that provide services which must be set up by law (statute). The NHS and local authority social services departments form the two main providers of statutory health and social care.

Stereotype   A fixed opinion or view of people – the way they look and/or the way they act; the abilities they have and what they do.

Support services   Services which support professionals to enable them to deliver a service effectively and efficiently.

Tertiary care   Care provided through long-term rehabilitation.

Therapist   A person who carries out treatment that will enhance another person's well-being.

Translator   An individual who interprets one language into another.

Voluntary organisations   These provide a vast network of services to bridge gaps in statutory provision. Their services are often provided free of charge. They are non-profit-making organisations.

Wants   Something an individual wants to have but which is not essential for health, social well-being or survival. Different from needs, which are necessary for health and social well-being.

Work patterns   How, where and when people work in particular jobs.

Self-assessment test

1 Social services are responsible to:
a Department of Health.
b District Health Authorities.
c Local authority.
d Family Health Services Authority.

2 Pharmacists are responsible to:
a District Health Authority.
b Local authority.
c GP surgeries.
d Family Health Services Authority.

3 Which service have National Health Trusts been set up to organise?
a Dentists.
b Health centres.
c Hospitals.
d Opticians.

4 GPs, district nurses, health visitors, practice nurses and community psychiatric nurses work together in a team known as:
a Regional health care team.
b Secondary health care team.
c Primary health care team.
d Local health care team.

5 The primary health care team is usually based at:
a Hospitals.
b Social services departments.
c GP's surgery.
d District Health Authority.

6 One function of the District Health Authority is to:
a Employ social workers.
b Allocate home care workers.
c Allocate grants to individuals who choose to live at home.
d Purchase health services.

7 The main role of a nursery nurse is to:
a Run playgroups.
b Visit people with children.
c Care for young children.
d Teach in schools.

8 The best way to describe a voluntary organisation is:
a One which makes a profit for its organisers.
b One which improves all services in an area.
c One which provides work experience for students.
d One which supports existing care services in an area.

9 A list of registered childminders can be found at a:
a Library.
b Social services department.
c Health clinic.
d GP's surgery.

10 The main role of the Citizens Advice Bureau is to:
a Offer contraceptive advice.
b Allocate benefits.
c Offer impartial advice.
d Offer counselling.

11 A foster parent would be classified as:
a A private provider.
b A voluntary provider.
c A self-employed provider.
d A statutory provider.

12 A service funded by charity would be a:
a Statutory service.
b Voluntary service.
c Private service.
d Discretionary service.

13 An example of an informal carer is the client's:
a Social worker.
b GP.
c Daughter.
d Bank manager.

14 Informal carers are:
a Always paid.
b Usually professionals.
c Often relatives or friends.
d Qualified in care skills.

15 A local support group for informal carers would:
a Provide payments.
b Set salary levels.
c Provide support and advice.
d Offer loans.

16 Government grants and donations are used to fund the work of:
a Social services departments.
b National Health Service
c National Society for the Prevention of Cruelty to Children.
d Accident and emergency departments.

17 A donation is:
    a   A payment for a service.
    b   Something given for free.
    c   A grant given by the government.
    d   An insurance payment.

18 A client could find detailed information on benefits to help with daily living at a:
    a   Social services office.
    b   Library.
    c   Post office.
    d   Social security office.

19 Which key service is provided free for all?
    a   Cosmetic dental treatment.
    b   Prescriptions.
    c   GP's appointment.
    d   Eye test.

20 Providing benefits is the responsibility of:
    a   Department of Social Security.
    b   Social services department.
    c   Department of Health.
    d   Department for Education.

21 Saffron was involved in a car accident and is paralysed from the waist down. You invite Saffron to your next youth club meeting. Which need would this satisfy?
    a   Social.
    b   Emotional.
    c   Physical.
    d   Intellectual.

22 Providing nourishing food and drink for an adolescent would satisfy:
    a   Physical needs.
    b   Emotional needs.
    c   Social needs.
    d   Intellectual needs.

23 Cold weather payments are make to some pensioners in winter when the temperature falls below a certain level. This satisfies:
    a   Emotional need.
    b   Physical need.
    c   Social need.
    d   Intellectual need.

24 A carer brings a jigsaw and books for a sick child. This satisfies a:
    a   Physical need.
    b   Intellectual need.
    c   Social need.
    d   Emotional need.

25 Assessment of clients occurs in a number of ways. Which is an assessment of physical needs?
    a   Observation by a play worker.

    b   Medical examination by a GP.
    c   IQ test.
    d   Chat with a child's teacher.

26 Which need would you link with a child whose parents are going through divorce?
    a   Physical.
    b   Social.
    c   Emotional.
    d   Intellectual.

27 Providing Kosher food for a Jewish client would be meeting his or her:
    a   Cultural needs.
    b   Social needs.
    c   Intellectual needs.
    d   Physical needs.

28 Who might help a client with long-term mental health difficulties to learn to cope with daily living skills?
    a   GP.
    b   Occupational therapist.
    c   Social worker.
    d   Home care worker.

29 A day-care centre would like to attract more clients from ethnic minority groups. To do this, it should:
    a   Newly furnish the centre.
    b   Meet different dietary and religious needs.
    c   Open longer hours.
    d   Increase the fees for using the centre.

30 A client injured in a car accident and now in a wheelchair wants to gain employment. Who could best help him or her with this?
    a   Physiotherapist.
    b   Disability employment adviser.
    c   Occupational therapist.
    d   Social worker.

31 A doctor refers a child to a hearing specialist. This is:
    a   Self-referral.
    b   Referral by a friend.
    c   Referral by a professional.
    d   Referral by a therapist.

32 An individual accesses a service for himself or herself. This is known as:
    a   Self-referral.
    b   Referral by a friend.
    c   Referral by a therapist.
    d   Referral by a professional.

33 Under the Children Act, a child can ask social services to take him or her into care. This is known as:
    a   Referral by a third party.

b Referral by a professional.
c Self-referral.
d Referral by proxy.

34 A person makes an appointment to see a GP. This is:
a Referral by a third party.
b Referral by a professionals.
c Referral by a relative.
d Self-referral.

35 Some services cannot be accessed by individuals. An example of this would be:
a Specialist consultant.
b Citizens Advice Bureau.
c GP.
d Dentist.

36 A social worker receives a call from a WRVS volunteer about an elderly man who has not answered his door. This is an example of:
a Referral by a professional.
b Self-referral.
c Referral by a third party.
d Referral by a relative.

37 A client wants information on respite care for a disabled child. The Citizens Advice Bureau should refer him or her to:
a Health visitor.
b GP.
c Social services.
d Department of Health.

38 Information on free prescriptions is available from:
a Bank.
b Solicitor.
c Pharmacist.
d Dentist.

39 Someone who speaks on behalf of a child is called:
a An advocate.
b A translator.
c A linguist.
d An adviser.

40 A client for whom English is a second language could be entitled to help when accessing a service. The most appropriate help would be:
a A translator.
b A dictionary.
c An early appointment.
d A longer appointment.

41 A health visitor:
a Delivers babies.
b Advises on child care.
c Examines clients in hospitals.
d Carries out immunisation programmes.

42 A support service in a hospital would be:
a Catering.
b Operations.
c Nursing care.
d Doctors' rounds.

43 A client is discharged from a psychiatric hospital. Who of the following would be responsible for monitoring his or her progress in the community?
a Psychologist.
b Social worker.
c Community psychiatric nurse.
d Counsellor.

44 Who is most likely regularly to change dressings of older people living in their own home?
a GP.
b Home care assistant.
c Social worker.
d Community nurse.

45 A home care worker:
a Carries out domestic tasks in hospitals.
b Works at a day centre.
c Works at a GP's surgery.
d Visits people in their own homes.

46 Who treats foot disorders?
a Chiropodist.
b Childminder.
c Physiotherapist.
d Occupational therapist.

47 A social worker might assess a client as part of his or her job to:
a Monitor the client's health.
b Find out information about a client's private life.
c Establish the needs of the client and arrange services.
d Get to know the client better.

48 Who is most likely to prescribe medication?
a Nurse.
b Midwife.
c GP.
d Health visitor.

49 A characteristic of a childminder's job is that:
a He or she often works alone all day.
b He or she always drives.
c He or she must be qualified in child care.
d He or she must live in detached housing.

50 An example of a qualification which a care worker could be assessed for in the workplace is:
a SRN.
b NVQ in Care.
c GNVQ in Health and Social Care.
d Post-graduate degree.

51 Stereotyping means:
    a To use fixed opinions and ideas to classify all people who carry out a certain job.
    b To treat everyone the same.
    c To offer equal access to all.
    d To offer some people higher pay for the same jobs.

52 Which of the following is an example of stereotyping in a job?
    a All social workers wear open-toed sandals and support extreme left-wing politics.
    b All social workers have different training.
    c Social workers have different thoughts on topics.
    d Social workers work with a range of client groups.

53 GPs usually work:
    a A 36-hour week, during normal office hours.
    b A 40-hour week, including weekends and bank holidays.
    c A 40-hour week, including mornings, evenings and some weekends.
    d A 50-hour week, including mornings, evenings, some Saturdays and an on-call rota at nights and some weekends.

54 Project 2000 is a new form of nurse education. It is different from traditional training in that:
    a Student nurses will have full student status and will receive a salary during training.
    b Student nurses will have full student status, will not receive a salary, but will be eligible to apply for an educational grant.
    c Student nurses will continue to be regarded as members of staff, but attend college more often.
    d Student nurses will spend more of their time on the wards and will continue to be regarded as members of staff.

55 As a result of the introduction of Project 2000, the role of health care assistant is to be established. Health care assistants will work:
    a Alone.
    b As part of a team of health care assistants.
    c As part of a team with student nurses.
    d As part of a team with student nurses, trained nurses and other professionals.

56 The role of the community psychiatric nurse is:
    a To administer drugs to people with a mental illness.
    b To provide counselling for people with mental health problems.
    c To administer drugs to patients and provide emotional support to both patients and their carers.
    d To provide emotional support to patients and their carers.

57 Social workers work:
    a A 40-hour week during normal office hours.
    b A 37-hour week including some evenings.
    c A 40-hour week including weekends.
    d A 37-hour week including some evenings and possibly a night-time and weekend rota.

58 The role of a midwife includes:
    a Looking after women during the birth of their children.
    b Delivering babies and looking after them following their birth.
    c Monitoring the welfare of the baby before, during and after the birth.
    d Advising and caring for the mother and baby before, during and after the birth.

59 The role of the health visitor is to:
    a Monitor the health of people in the community.
    b Promote health by teaching people how to maintain a healthy life style.
    c Help diagnose and treat illnesses.
    d Administer drugs to people who are ill.

60 Ambulance crews, consisting of ambulance technicians and paramedics, usually work:
    a A 39-hour week, Monday to Friday.
    b A 45-hour week including evenings.
    c A 39-hour week with rotating shift system.
    d A 45-hour week including evenings and weekends.

Develop communication skills

The importance of communication

Think it over

When you hear the word 'communication', what do you think of?

You might suggest:

- talking to people
- passing on information
- telling people things
- explaining how to do things
- spreading news.

Communication often focuses our minds on giving information to others, speaking to others and explaining things using words. When viewed socially, however, communication involves much more than simply passing spoken or written messages to other people.

Think of other types of communication

We also communicate our feelings and our thoughts through our actions, through the way we use our eyes to look at people, and through the way we use facial expression and posture. We send messages with our appearance – the way we dress. Even the way we wear jewellery or our hairstyle can send a message about our self-concept. Every time we mix with other people we are communicating with them.

Communication between people is important for:

- making relationships and maintaining social relationships with others
- creating social settings and social groups
- understanding our self-image – our self-concept and social and emotional development
- happiness – in our relationships with others
- intellectual development
- working effectively as a carer.

Relationships

Babies take a keen interest in human faces and begin to imitate the sounds that they hear around them. From birth babies communicate with their carers, and parents talk to them using 'baby talk'. A child's intellectual, social and emotional development depends on the relationship that he or she develop with people. Relationships depend on communication.

To have relationships with people, you have to remember what they are like and be able to learn about and understand them. Watching people and listening to what they say will help you to learn about them. The more you learn, the stronger the relationship will be. Good communication skills help people to understand each other and to build relationships.

Figure 10.1 These people are communicating: they are sending a message to others whether they intend to or not

If you are good at listening and understanding other people's feelings and thoughts, then you are likely to attract friends. Poor listeners and those that lack understanding of other people may find it more difficult to make lasting friendships. Couples who communicate and understand each other are more likely to have a fulfilling, enjoyable and stable life together. Parents who communicate with and understand their children may enjoy family life more than parents who do not listen to their children.

Developing good listening skills and learning to understand other people's body language may help us in our relationships. Some people seem to develop listening and observation skills naturally. But we could all improve our listening and observation skills by studying this area.

Creating social settings and social groups through communication.

If we want to avoid people, we try not to look at them or to use encouraging body language. Conversation, if necessary, is kept brief and formal. So when we want to develop relationships, we do the opposite – plenty of eye contact, smiles and talking.

Groups develop a feeling of belonging together because people communicate with each other. For example, a family might create a sense of belonging

Figure 10.2 Communication is a necessary part of belonging to a group

by sitting down together at mealtimes and talking. Friendship groups also develop because people communicate with one another. Friends meet to do things, to go out or maybe even share a meal. To do so, they need to communicate with each other. Communication is necessary for groups to form and develop

Social and emotional development and self-concept

We build an idea of who we are as we develop through childhood, adolescence and adulthood. The messages that other people communicate to us influence our ideas. The way people react to us, what they say, the way we compare ourselves with others, all affect our concept of self. Our communication with others affects our self-confidence and self-esteem. Therefore, communication influences how we develop emotionally and socially.

Communication influences happiness

Our communication skills – particularly our ability to listen to and understand other people's thoughts and feelings – will affect the quality of our relationships. Relationships, self-confidence and self-esteem are important to general happiness in life. Happiness may depend on much more than our ability to listen to and understand others or other people's ability to understand us. Even so, good listening and understanding skills may help us gain social satisfaction.

Intellectual development

We communicate using language. The concepts we learn help us to build our intellectual ability. Concepts help us to understand our experiences and to know how to act. A concept such as 'social role' can help us to work out what to do when working in a care setting. A person in a care-worker role has one type of relationship with clients and another kind with friends. A person's role influences the way he or she acts. Concepts help us to understand our lives. Even practical concepts about movement can help us to ride a bicycle.

In the same way, using concepts about listening, body language, verbal and non-verbal communication helps us to develop insights into the way social relationships work.

Working effectively as a carer

Carers are required to use effective communication skills in order to support clients in care. Good communication skills, the ability to listen to and learn about others, are necessary in order to understand each clients' beliefs and preferences. Effective listening skills are essential in order to understand another person's cultural background, political and religious beliefs, or expression of sexuality.

Effective caring skills

Think it over

What makes a person a good carer? Are certain people natural carers of others, or is this something anyone can learn to do?

There are various answers to this puzzle. Sometimes people say that experiences of caring for others early on in life are important. Other people say you have to have a calm nature or a good sense of humour. One thing is definite – good carers have to be interested in others and good at building a 'sense of liking' between people.

For example, imagine you are talking to a friend on the way to work in the morning. He tells you that he feels sad because his pet cat died last night, and then becomes quiet. How can you help?

In such a situation most people would start with an expression of sympathy; 'Oh, I'm very sorry to hear that – how did it happen?' A skilled carer will do more. The carer will ask about the details, not because of a need to know, but so that the other person has a chance to talk. Skilled carers will show that they are listening and that they understand the feelings of the other person. A skilled carer will try to make the person feel glad that he talked about his sadness. If this is successful, the other person will feel that he matters to the carer.

Listening to someone who is unhappy is a very important caring skill. There is an old saying: 'A problem shared is a problem halved'. Listening to someone and showing that you care gives that person a chance to think through his or her worries. Knowing that someone cares might make them feel better.

Many people find it difficult to listen to others. What happens is that they feel embarrassed – lost for words. So, unskilled people hearing about a lost pet may say:

1 'Oh that's bad, but I suppose you can always get another cat – I saw some kittens for sale in the paper'.
2 'Oh that's a bit of bad luck … still, these things happen. Oh! About that piece of work, can I talk to you later about it?'
3 'Tough, still, could have been worse; never mind, we all lose pets don't we. Lots of people have worse trouble than that.'

These statements are not examples of providing emotional support.

Statement 1 ignores the feelings of the person who is sad. Saying 'you can get another cat' makes it sound like losing a glove – 'Oh, can't find it, well get another one'. The cat really mattered, it cannot simply be replaced. The person who said this did not care enough to listen and to find this out, but jumped in with some bad advice.

Statement 2 also ignores the feelings of the sad person. This is even worse though, because the person who said it did not want to listen to the other person at all. Perhaps hearing about sadness upsets him, so he changed the subject.

The person who used statement 3 not only wanted to avoid listening, he or she wanted to lecture the other person about life. Some people might find this the most uncaring response of all. Hearing that others have even worse trouble than yourself is only comforting if you are in competition with everyone else. This statement is likely to make the sad person angry or perhaps depressed.

Caring is not just common sense – it requires a range of special skills. Perhaps the most important skill is to be able to listen to others.

Listening

It is useful to separate the idea of listening to what people say from the idea of hearing the noise that people make when they talk!

Here, *listening* means hearing another person's words, thinking about what they mean and planning what to say back to the other person. *Hearing* the other person means picking up the sounds they make.

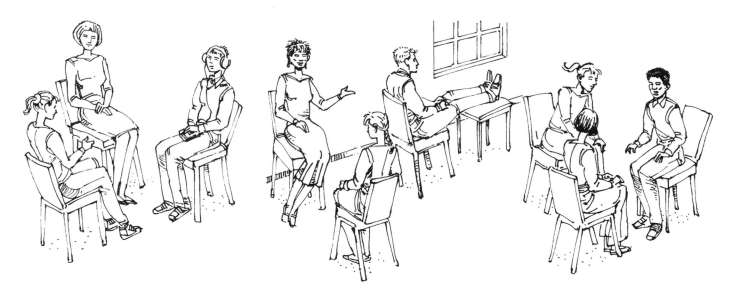

Figure 10.3 Listening skills

Look at Figure 10.3. The person with the personal stereo cannot hear or listen to the others. The person with legs up, looking out the window, is behaving as if he is not listening. The person might hear what the other two are saying, though. In the third picture the people are listening to each other because each person can explain what the last speaker said. They have heard the message, remembered what was said, and planned their own comments, before replying.

Listening is a skill. It is far more than just being around when something is said. Listening involves **hearing** and then **remembering** what has been said. If we are going to remember what someone else has said, we have to **understand** it first.

Some psychologists believe that we usually only remember about one out of every 2000 things that we hear in a day! Most of the sounds that come to our ears are not important enough to bother about remembering.

Think it over

Last night you may have watched TV or talked to family or friends. Just how much can you recall of what you heard?

If you cannot remember much about what you watched on TV, perhaps it does not matter; the important thing may be that you enjoyed it. But it is different when you work with people. Listening skills are needed here.

To understand another person you need to know something of his or her background, lifestyle and personal situation. As well as knowing about these, you have to be able to make sense of them to feel that you understand and have some idea of what to expect. This understanding develops from *experience* of listening to people. Perhaps we gradually get better at it.

Sometimes, getting ready to listen involves switching into your store of knowledge and understanding. For some people this is a conscious switching-on process. You want to help the person who has just lost his pet. You will need to say and do the right things, but what are the right things?

Each person is different. Everyone has his or her own way of thinking. If you know the person who had the pet, you can 'switch on' to your own memories. What used he to say about the cat? What do you know about his feelings: how much did the cat mean to him, and can we guess how he feels?

Listening can feel like really hard mental work. Instead of just living in our own private world planning to say whatever we think, we have to think about the other person. So, if someone is saying that he or she is sad about losing a pet, we have to *first* hear their words and *then* imagine how the other

187

person feels. We have to make sense of what is said, perhaps imagining how we would feel if it happened to us. Having thought through what we have been told, we have to think again before we speak.

Listening *is* hard mental work – it takes time. Because real listening takes thinking time, sometimes people do not bother to listen.

Listening can often be difficult. If you are going to listen, then the other person has to keep talking. Some clients do not find it easy to keep talking, so how can a carer encourage a client to talk? Here are some ideas:

- Use skilled non-verbal messages.
- Use reflective listening skills and silence.
- Use questions in an appropriate way.
- Always try to show that you respect and value others' sense of self.

These ideas are explained in detail in this chapter.

Non-verbal communication

Verbal means 'using words', so verbal communication occurs when people speak with words. Non-verbal, on the other hand, means 'without words'. Non-verbal communication means that you can send messages to other people, which they can understand, without using words.

The important thing about non-verbal communication is that we are always sending messages to clients by the way we use our face, eyes, voice tone, movement, muscle tension, hand signals, touch and body posture. We cannot help but communicate something all the time! And clients send messages to us all the time too!

Observing non-verbal messages.

Think it over

In a residential care situation an older person comes up to you and mumbles sounds that you cannot understand, but non-verbally she looks at the window, points, looks upset, worried and afraid – her eyes send the message: 'Please help me'. How do you make sense of this? Can you help?

The person has communicated that she is anxious; perhaps she has a desire to be outside or back home. Perhaps she is confused as to where she is. Whatever the message, you could help by being calm, trying to explain that all is well – offering to stay with the person, offering to walk outside with her. You could respond to the 'please help' if you listen to the message.

Being able to make sense of non-verbal language from a client grows with thinking about our experience with people, and it grows with knowledge of the background, culture and personality of individual clients.

In many social situations the non-verbal communication is more important than what is actually said.

Think it over

Think of yourself at a social gathering with friends. Perhaps you can think of one in the last week or so. You maybe sat talking. How much can you remember of what the other people said?

'The real messages may have been: 'We all like each other – we are all friends'. These messages will have been sent non-verbally. What people actually talk about may not always be important.

Using our senses

All non-verbal messages are associated with what we learn from our senses. We use our senses in the following way.

The sense of touch

This can send messages for:

- guiding others' movements

- greeting people
- affection
- expressing power and dominating others (aggression).

The sense of sight

A long gaze is used when we feel comfortable and know someone well. Sometimes a long gaze may be used in an attempt to be threatening towards someone.

A short gaze, of a couple of seconds say, is used to:

- catch someone's attention
- check how we are being received
- end/withdraw from conversation
- signal that we wish to bring someone into the conversation
- a signal that we wish to exclude someone.

The tone of voice

The tone, the speed, the pitch and the rhythm of speech are all important. Have you ever heard people speaking in a foreign language and been able to tell they were angry purely by hearing the speed and tone of what they were saying?

The sense of smell

This is probably the sense used least by adult humans for communication. We try to cover up natural smells by using deodorants, perfumes, etc. It is, however, extensively used by animals and by particular groups of human beings. For example, you may know that babies can recognise their mother by her smell.

Think it over

Can you think which other people might rely on a sense of smell more than others?

People who do not see well rely more than others on the sense of smell. As well as relating smells to people, they use this sense to help them remember their way around new surroundings. For example, a blind child newly arrived at a boarding school will remember the distinct smells of the dining room, classroom and bathroom, to build a 'mind map' of the way around the building.

When we know people very well we can recognise their non-verbal clues very easily, but with people we know less well, it is necessary to watch carefully to be aware of all the clues given out.

Remember, too, if a client has a disability such as reduced sight or movement, it is necessary to face him or her to allow maximum view of your own non-verbal language. Be aware that communicating is harder for people if they only get the verbal signals. Someone with a hearing impairment will rely heavily on the non-verbal signals you send.

Using the body to send messages

Understanding people involves understanding their non-verbal communication as well as what they say. The feelings we have about other people are often based on the non-verbal messages they send to us. We use our body to send non-verbal messages, so non-verbal communication is sometimes called **body language.**

Body language is always there and we are not always conscious of the messages we give out. We are usually very careful in what we say and we can usually explain why we have said it. Body language or non-verbal communication is different – most people do not think about it, they just experience it. *Skilled carers need to be able to understand their own and others' body language and be consciously aware of it.*

Some of the most important body areas to use, and to watch others use, are:

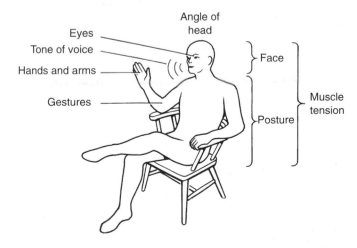

Figure 10.4 Body language that sends messages

- the eyes
- the face
- voice tone
- body movement
- posture (how we sit or stand) and head angles when looking at others
- muscle tension (how tense or relaxed we are)
- gestures (use of arms and hands).

Important special messages are sometimes sent by:

- touch
- how close people get to each other
- mirroring of body postures and movements.

The eyes

Our eyes can send a vast range of messages and may often be the most important part of our body when sending non-verbal messages. One poet called the eyes 'the window of the soul', meaning that sometimes we can see the feelings and thoughts of another person by looking at their eyes. Looking at the eyes might be like looking through a window into the other person's feelings!

You may feel that this is too romantic, but your eyes will usually send messages as to how you feel emotionally. Skilled actors learn to control their eyes by remembering an emotional feeling and then trying to send that feeling with their eye movements. Most people do not learn to act to that level of skill, but their eyes still send messages.

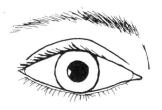 

Our eyes widen when we are excited or interested in someone. If we feel attracted to a person we will probably send him or her this message just with the look in our eyes. Equally, if we are angry, the eyes quickly send this message.

The way our eyes widen and narrow may not be as important as the way we use our eyes to make contact with others. People who think you are interesting or attractive, will want to look at you. If your eyes meet someone else's there is often a momentary widening (excitement) in the other person's eyes, this is followed by quickly looking

away, followed by looking back (perhaps to see if you are still looking). A person who is not interested and just happened to be looking your way may move his or her eyes more slowly – there will be less jumpiness in the way the eyes move.

Anger and hostility are often communicated by staring. A person who is angry with you might fix a gaze on you. When your eyes meet, the other will not look way – eyes can become locked in battle!

As well as sending messages about emotion, we send all sorts of social messages with our eyes. For instance, many people can say 'It's your turn to talk now' just by using their eyes and the tone of their voice.

This works because when people talk they do not just stare at each other. Usually, the person talking will spend a lot of time looking away, not making **eye-contact** with the listener. This looking away is useful because it helps the speaker to organise what he or she is going to say. The speaker will look back at the other person to see how things are going: 'How am I affecting your feelings . . . .Are you understanding me?' These looks are often just *glances,* short and quick moments when the eyes meet.

A good listener might choose to keep his or her eyes on the face of the speaker so as to be able to give eye-contact when the speaker looks for it. This says 'Yes, I'm listening, I'm interested, keep going'. As the speaker runs out of things to say, he or she looks back at the eyes of the listener for longer than normal, and drops the voice slightly and slows down just a little. This sends the non-verbal message 'I am getting ready to stop – it is your turn next, you get ready to speak'.

The next thing the speaker does is to look away – perhaps look at the floor, stop the sentence and look directly into the eyes of the person listening. This says 'Go on, I've finished'. The listener sends the message or signal 'OK, here goes', by breaking eye-contact and looking away. Sometimes the listener may emphasise this with an intake of breath and head movements.

Try it

People are carrying out this kind of non-verbal communication with their eyes every day when they talk to you. Have you ever analysed it before? Watch a video of people interviewing each other, and use the pause button to pick up the exact eye contact between listener and speaker.

Facial expression

Eye movements are mostly unconscious actions. However, we often *think about* what expression we want our faces to have. In other words, facial expressions are often 'acted' or put on *deliberately* to send a message. Most people can smile when they are not really happy, or can act happy, puzzled or pained just to impress others. Many people can control their faces and can avoid sending out messages from their faces about feelings that they do not want other people to know about.

Carers do need to think about the messages they send. It is possible to feel tired and hungry and have a depressed and bored looking face. If you suddenly meet someone and do not change your expression, you send him or her the message 'Oh, not you – you make me feel bored and depressed'. Sometimes, carers try to overcome this by smiling all the time. But this simply makes them look unreal, because no one is happy all the time. The best thing to do is to smile always when meeting people and then vary your expression to fit what is happening. Changing your expressions when listening to clients is one way of showing that you are listening and that you *do* care about what is being said to you.

Facial expressions are quite easy to 'read' or interpret. Even simple diagrams can usually be interpreted as having a meaning – see Figure 10.5.

Voice tone

Words are verbal, but *the way we say them* is described as non-verbal. The tone of voice sometimes

Figure 10.5 Facial expressions that send messages

communicates more than actual words might. Some researchers say that people often pay attention more to the tone of voice of a speaker than they do to the message.

For example, a person may be told: 'I'm sorry, but your work is not good enough. Unless it improves you will have to leave'. If the sentence is said in a calm, slow, gentle way with a low but varying tone, the person might get the message: 'Well, things aren't as good as they could be, but there is nothing much to worry about'. If the same sentence is said loudly and quickly in a high-pitched voice, the listener may find it aggressive and become shocked and angry.

It is sometimes difficult to adjust our voices to just the right level to communicate exactly what we want!

In care work, *voice tone is very important because clients may be happy or distressed.* If carers speak with an appropriate but calm and varied voice, they can sometimes use their voices to relax clients and make them feel safe. Quite often, the real skill is not in what is said to clients but in the way it is said.

Body movements

Very few people keep still when they communicate with others. They move their arms, their hands, their feet, their eyes, head, facial expressions and so on. The speed and type of movement can send many messages. People can signal how interested they are by the way they move. They send messages of affection and attraction by the way they tense and relax their body. The way people walk, turn their head, sit down, etc. sends messages about whether they are tired, happy, sad, bored and so on.

Many people use 'head-nods' to signal 'I am listening to your' and 'I agree', or 'I understand what you are saying'.

Try it

Spend some time studying the movements of other people. Much of the time you can guess how they feel from the way they move and the other non-verbal messages they send. Try a group exercise: Get everyone to talk without moving a body muscle. This will be very difficult, but if people can do it, it might be a shock to realise how hard it is not to use non-verbal communication.

Posture

The way we sit or stand is often interpreted by others. Standing or sitting stiffly upright may be seen as formal and dominant. Standing or sitting with crossed arms can be seen as being closed to ideas: 'I hear what you say, but I'm not taking any notice'.

Leaning at an angle when sitting or standing can send the message: 'I'm tired, bored, or very relaxed'. It can send the message: 'I'm too relaxed to be taking anything in from what you are saying – I'm not listening'.

Leaning forward towards the speaker often communicates: 'Wow, Tell me more, this is astonishing.' Overdoing this posture can send too strong a message of interest.

There is no single *correct* posture to show interest and attention, but most people keep a balance between being too tense and too relaxed. Sometimes, the easiest thing to do is to copy the type of posture of

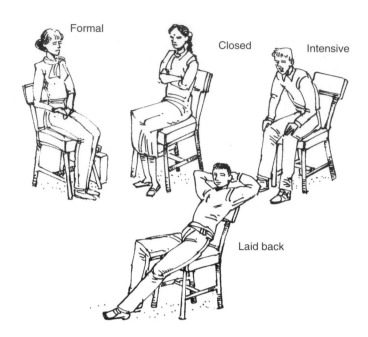

Figure 10.6 Body postures that send messages

the person you are talking to. This sometimes sends a message of liking the other person: 'Look, I'm like you'. Sometimes it is not a good idea to send this message – especially when you are *not* like the other person.

Face-to-face encounters

Is it a good idea to face another person 'eye-to-eye'? This body posture can send *many different meanings,* and most of them have strong emotions attached. 'Eye-to-eye' or 'square-on postures might mean: intimacy, attachment or love, confrontation, hostility or aggression, honesty or openness in commercial dealing.

Sitting face-to-face can indicate formality or a confrontational conversation. However, in *informal* settings it can imply the opposite – closeness, intimacy or love.

Standing at a slight angle can indicate informality and being relaxed. It can send non-verbal messages of: 'I'm calm' or even 'I'm cool!' Sitting at angles can also send message of 'This is informal', and 'We can be relaxed' (see Figure 10.7).

As well as keeping a body angle to the other person, if you want to communicate a relaxed, calm message it may be important to adopt a very slight angle to

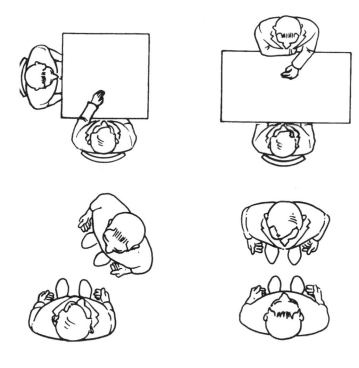

Figure 10.7 Face-to-face encounters

your head (see Figure 10.8). Some people feel that this communicates interest and involvement.

Your Country needs You!

Figure 10.8 Calm....or intense?

On the other hand, a face-to-face position is intensive. The famous First World War poster 'Your Country needs You!' was intended to influence men to join the armed forces. Is this the kind of intensity you want in your work with your clients and day-to-day conversation? A more relaxed (but not over-relaxed) posture may be more appropriate.

Muscle tension (tense or relaxed)

Feet, hands and fingers can give signs of being relaxed or tense. When people are tense they sometimes clench their hands or press their fingers together. Continuous moving of feet or changes of body posture can indicate tension.

When someone gets very tense, their shoulders stiffen, their face muscles tighten and they sit or stand more rigidly. When the face becomes tense, the mouth will be closed and the lips and jaw tightened. With a lot of stress, people develop wrinkled lines where the face is always tensed – this may show in the person's forehead.

Tense people always breath more quickly, and you can often notice that their heart is working faster. As a carer, *these signs of tension are important to spot in others*. If a person becomes tense during a conversation, maybe something is wrong. Perhaps the person is becoming tense because of emotional feelings like grief. The best thing here might be to stay with the person while he or she cries. There may be nothing to say, but emotional support might be provided through body language.

Gestures

Gestures are hand and arm movements that add meaning to things people say or carry a particular message on their own. Some common gestures are shown in Figure 10.9.

'I don't know'

'stop, don't do that'

'success – everything's going well'

'perfection' or 'perfect'

Figure 10.9 Some gestures common in Britain

As well as these signs, people move their arms and hands to indicate emotion while they speak, or to place emphasis on what they are saying. Together with other body language, gestures can be important to watch when trying to understand them.

Culture and interpreting body language

Body language is just that – it's a language. There are many languages in the world and they do not all have the same concepts and sounds. Body language is not the same everywhere.

For example, in Britain the gesture shown in Figure 10.9 with palm up and facing forward, means 'Stop, don't do that.' In Greece it can mean 'You are dirt' and is a very rude gesture.

Why do the same physical movements have different meanings? The answer lies in culture.

Culture means the history, the customs and ways that people learn as they grow up. One explanation for the hand signs say that the British version of the palm-and-fingers gesture means 'I arrest you, you must not do it', whereas the Greek interpretation goes back to medieval times when criminals had dirt rubbed in their faces to show how much people despised them.

Without looking at history and culture, it is confusing to understand why gestures mean what they do. No one knows all the history and all the cultural possibilities of body language and non-verbal communication. What is vitally important is that carers should always remember that people have different cultural backgrounds. The carer's system of non-verbal communication may not carry the same meanings to everyone. We can easily misinterpret another person's non-verbal messages.

Remember

- Non-verbal messages do not have fixed meanings.
- They are linked to culture.
- There is no dictionary of non-verbal messages.

Sometimes cultural differences are very marked. White British people are often seen as 'unusual' or odd when they go outside Europe because they keep a large personal space around them. Other people are not allowed to come too near when they speak, or to touch them. In many other cultures, standing close is normal and good manners – touching an arm or shoulder is just usual behaviour. Some British people feel threatened by such non-verbal behaviour because it is not what they have grown up with. For some British people, strangers who come too close or who touch are trying to dominate or have power over them. They become afraid or defensive. However, things often work out because this need for space and distance is understood and allowed for by people from other cultures.

From a caring viewpoint, respect for other people's culture is the right attitude. People learn different ways of behaving, and good carers will try to understand the different ways in which people use non-verbal messages. For instance, research in the USA suggests that white and black Americans may use different non-verbal signals when they listen. According to this research, black Americans tend not to look much at the speaker. This can be interpreted as a mark of respect – by looking away it demonstrates that you are really thinking hard about the message. Unfortunately, not all white people understand that this is a cultural difference in non-verbal communication. Some individuals misunderstand and assume that this non-verbal behaviour means exactly what it would mean if they did it. That is, it would mean they were not listening.

Learning the cultural differences

There is an almost infinite variety of meanings that can be given to any type of eye contact, facial expression, posture or gesture. Every culture develops its own special system of meanings. As a carer, you have to understand and show respect and value for all these different systems of sending messages. But how can you ever learn them all?

In fact, you cannot learn every possible system of non-verbal messages – but you can learn about the ones people you are with are using! You can do this by first noticing and remembering what others do – what non-verbal messages they are sending. The next step is to make an intelligent guess as to what messages the person is trying to give you. Finally, check your understanding (your guesses) with the person: ask polite questions as well as watching the kind of reactions you get.

So, at the heart of skilled communication is the ability to watch other people, remember what they do, guess what actions might mean and then check out your guesses with the person.

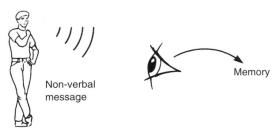

Non-verbal
message

The person gives you more verbal information

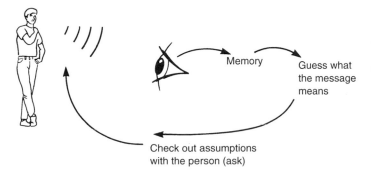

Figure 10.10 The process of understanding another person's body language

---

Remember:

■ Never rely on your own guesses, because often these turn into assumptions
■ If you don't check out assumptions with people, you may end up misunderstanding them.
■ Misunderstandings can lead to discrimination.

Think it over

You are working with an older person. Whenever you start to speak to her she always look at the floor and never makes eye-contact. Why is this?

Your first thought is that she might be sad or that you make her sad. If you must make this assumption, you might not want to work with this person – she is too depressing and you do not seem to get on. You might even decide that you do not like her. But you could ask: 'How do you feel today; would you like me to get you anything?' By checking out what she feel, you could test your own understanding. She might say she feels well and is quite happy, and suggest something you could do for her – she cannot be depressed, then!

Why else would someone look at the floor rather than at you?

1 It could be a cultural value. She may feel it is not proper to look at you.
2 She may not be able to see you clearly, so she prefers not to try to look at you.
3 She may just choose not to conform to your expectations. Looking at the floor may be important to some other emotional feeling that she has.

So it would be unfair to assume that she was difficult or depressed just because she did not look at you when you talked to her.

Remember

Good caring is the art of getting to understand people – not acting on unchecked assumptions.

We can never rely on non-verbal messages, we always have to check them. Non-verbal messages can mean different things depending on the circumstances of the people sending them. But all messages are like this. Words can be looked up in a dictionary, and yet words do not always carry exactly the same meaning.

Think it over

Think about the statement: 'I really do care about you'. All the words have a dictionary definition, but what does the statement 'really' mean?

It could mean lots of things!

■ If there was stress on 'really', i.e. 'I *really* do care about you', it would mean 'No, honestly, I really, really care – please believe me!'
■ If there was stress on 'do care', i.e. 'I really *do care* about you', it might mean 'I am concerned about what happens to you, I am worried, I don't want bad things to happen to you, etc.'
■ If there was stress on 'I' and 'you', i.e. '*I* really do care about *you*', it might mean, 'I love you, 'I'm always thinking about you!'

The same words with a slightly different tone of voice can give quite different meanings. If we could not quite hear the tone of voice, we could guess the meaning from the circumstances or the surroundings in which things were said.

For instance, suppose the speaker looked anxious and tired, and said 'I wish you could see my point of view, I really do care about you', we could easily guess the words mean I *really* do care.

If the speaker had an arm round a partner, looked into her eyes and said 'I really do care about you', it would mean 'I love you'. Messages only make sense when we look at the whole picture. It is important to be aware of voice tone, body movements, body posture, eye contact and words all together. When we see the whole picture, we are better prepared to check out meanings.

As well as looking at the whole picture of people's words, their non-verbal messages and where they are, we also need to understand their culture, their individuality and how they see their social situation. This is why caring is such a skilled area of work. People can improve their skills constantly through experience, and through linking new ideas to their experience. The main thing is always to check out your assumptions. It is important to remember that we often misunderstand others. By checking out ideas we can cut down the risks of being uncaring or discriminatory.

Responding skills

As a carer, it is important for you to be good at starting conversations to gain information. Our non-verbal behaviour may be as important as what we say.

Before starting a conversation, a person is likely to:

- make eye contact
- smile
- nod
- have the appropriate facial expression
- change position (e.g. stand up, sit down)
- use a gesture.

All these things are likely to happen before any words are spoken and will give indications of what type of conversation is likely to take place. If the exchange is not a friendly one, the facial expression, position and gestures will easily be seen as being threatening.

Responding to conversation

Depending on how well the people know each other, some form of greeting will be used – for example, 'Hi', probably followed by a remark such as 'How are things?' In a friendly and warm encounter, general remarks might continue with topics such as the weather, etc. In contrast, if the encounter is an interview with a boss who is not pleased with you, it is likely that the subject of the meeting will be introduced straight away.

If a conversation is to be satisfactory to both or all the people taking part in it, it is necessary to take turns to speak and for one person not to dominate the conversation. Have you ever looked at a young baby 'talking' with an adult? Think about what happened, how the adult behaved and how the baby responded.

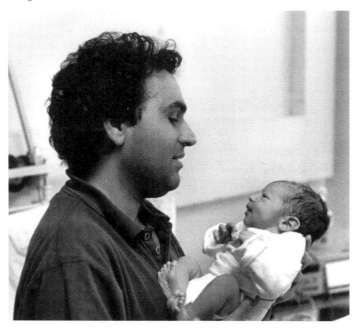

We learn turn-taking rules before we can even speak. The young baby will babble and then stop and wait for the other person to speak. When the person stops, the baby will babble again. The baby will babble for a similar length of time to the person he or she is 'talking' with. If the person 'talking' were to speak angrily or scowl and look fierce, the baby would become upset and probably cry.

The amazing part about this is that all this takes place without the baby understanding the words used. It tells us a lot about the power of non-verbal communication. Remember, you are giving people messages all the time without saying anything at all.

There are a number of ways by which we judge when it is our turn to speak. You can try this out by closing your eyes during a conversation and trying to judge when it is your turn to come in. Think carefully about what clues you are getting.

Think it over

You should notice:

- There is a tendency for the last part of the speech to be drawled or slower.
- There is a drop in pitch (a change in voice tone)
- The statement is completed.

With your eyes closed you do, however, miss some of the clues that are available – those of non-verbal or body language. When a person has finished his part of the conversation, he may use a hand gesture or relax his body position.

Questioning

Being a skilful questioner is a useful social skill. It means that you are able to keep a conversation going. One thing many people enjoy is talking about themselves, so if you are a skilful questioner you can easily become a good conversationalist. Also, as a care worker, you may need to get information from clients to help you understand how to respond to their needs.

Think it over

Sometimes the answers we get to questions do not tell us what the person really thinks. Can you think of reasons why someone might not say what he or she really thinks?

A client may be worried about upsetting staff, being thought of as a trouble-maker, if he or she complains. The client may therefore say what he or she thinks you want to hear rather than what he or she really wants to say. Can you remember ever doing this? You may have done so when a teacher or parent asked you why you were acting in a certain way. Often when we do not know how to start telling someone how we really feel, we say 'Nothing' when asked what is bothering us.

In other circumstances a person may want to look good, so will agree with the person speaking even when he or she really disagrees. Have you ever tried to impress someone in this way?

At other times a person may make up an answer to a question rather than admit ignorance of the true answer, to avoid looking silly.

Obviously, then, while asking questions can be a useful way of getting a conversation going, it can also seem threatening to the person being

questioned. Most of the reasons above for not giving true answers were based on the fact that the people being questioned did not feel confident, or needed to protect themselves in some way. It is important not to make others feel they are on trial or being harassed! *It is all about watching carefully to see how the person you are talking to is responding and knowing how far to go and when to stop.*

Closed and open questions

Some questions are known as **closed** questions. This is because it is possible to answer them simply without widening the conversation.

Imagine asking children if they have been to school today. What might a typical answer be? Many children would simply say 'yes' or 'no', which does not extend the conversation very much. If, however, you used an open question – such as 'What did you do at school today?' – you have a better chance of them giving an answer that you can use to carry on the conversation. Of course, the answer may still be 'nothing', but at least you will have built in the chance of getting more information!

Open questions keep the conversation going, but sometimes you may want to structure the conversation to focus on a specific subject. For example, you may want to plan some leisure activities for an older client group. If you were to ask them what they wanted to do, they might all say they do not know. If you were to use a questioning technique called **funnelling** you could get more information.

Funnelling means starting with an open question and then narrowing down to concentrate on something definite. This is an example of a funnelling conversation:

Care worker: What sort of things did you used to do in the evenings before television came along?
Client: Oh, all sorts really. We used to have some fun though.
Care worker: I suppose you had to make your own entertainment?

Think it over

Try to think of more questions and answers following on the above conversation.

It is possible that you could develop the above conversation to see whether the client group would enjoy having some recordings of old singers or inviting someone in to play the piano/accordion for a sing-song, or perhaps getting some crafts going such as rug-making, or comparing old photographs. This technique is based on the idea of knowing where you want to steer the conversation, while allowing the other people time to collect their thoughts and develop them in their own way.

Another technique that is useful with all client groups, but particularly with older people who may not have a great many exciting events currently happening to them, is to use recall questions such as 'Where did you live when you were a child?' However, you will always have to think carefully about what you are asking, because some areas of their lives may have been painful. Think carefully then about using questions such as: 'Do you feel embarrassed when talking about …'.

Think it over

Try to remember a time when you were talking with someone about an experience that was painful to him or her. Make a note of what you needed to do as well as listen.

You would have needed to be very aware of non-verbal signals, such as:

- facial expression
- whether the person leaned forward or pulled back
- how near he or she was positioned to you
- how much eye-contact was used
- the tone of voice
- the speed at which he or she spoke
- the rhythm of the speech (smooth or jerky).

Remember always: the person is 'saying' more than just words.

Reflective listening

It is very important to understand the people we work with. To understand people, we have to listen to them. But listening is not always easy. Some people will talk easily, some people talk too much. But sometimes, people do not find it easy to talk, then special conversation techniques are needed.

Think it over

Imagine that you are caring for an older man and start talking to him. He is very miserable and perhaps angry about things that have not gone right. Suddenly he turns to you and says: 'Nobody cares about me. Do you know what my son said to me last time he came to see me? He said: "Well, you won't live much longer, you'll be dead soon and then I won't have to bother visiting you".' He then goes quiet and looks at the floor. You're the carer – what do you do now?

First, you cannot just walk away because that would look as if you did not care either.

You might be able to ask a question – but can you think of a sensible one? You can't say: 'Ah, so do you think your son does not like you then?' The man has made the situation clear – you could insult him if you get the question wrong.

You could go silent too. Silence can be a good technique (see below) – but not here. Going silent might look like not knowing what to do.

If you feel a bit shocked, if you feel 'that's awful', and if you are lost for words, 'what is left to say?' You could just repeat the words 'He said you'll be dead soon and I won't have to visit you'. If the client's words are repeated with the right tone of voice – a tone that gives the message 'that's awful' – then you have proved that you were listening to the client, and that you have taken him seriously. The simple act of repeating the statement also invites him to keep on talking: you have proved you were listening, and that you are concerned, so is there anything he can add to what he has said?

Simply repeating the client's message can keep the conversation going, but you should not do this too often. If you keep repeating what the client says, you will sound like a parrot. The client will think you are making fun of him. However, repeating the client's words once can get you out of a jam. It can keep the conversation going a bit longer. It is now the client's turn to speak again. Perhaps you will be told some details about his life, perhaps you will learn more about his needs and understand more.

Repeating the client's words in this way is the simplest kind of reflection, but a better kind of reflection is to put what the client said into your own words. You might say something like: 'Your son does not want to visit you and does not care whether you are alive or dead.' When you use your own words, it almost becomes a new question – you are testing your understanding of the client's message. This type of reflection is also called **paraphrasing**.

Paraphrasing

When you sum up what another person has said, it is called **summarising**. Both paraphrasing and summarising are types of reflective listening.

Putting the client's statement into your own words is usually better than just repeating what he said.

1 It shows that you thought about what he said.
2 Your statement is not mechanical – you speak in your own usual way.
3 The other person has to do more thinking to check that what you said is what he meant. He is more likely to keep talking, after this extra thinking.
4 Because using your own words often sounds more caring and sociable, you can use this reflective technique more often.

So, repeating what another person said is a useful way of keeping a conversation going. However, it can be more than that. If you use the right non-verbal messages and your words do make sense to the other person, then repeating the other person's statement is like holding a mirror for them. He can see his thoughts and feelings in the mirror that your words have created (see Figure 10.11).

A person may say 'no one likes me, nobody talks to me here', and you can hold a mirror up to this: 'No one cares at all?' The person will probably want to say more: 'Well, you do, you listen – but nobody else does.'

Because of the holding up of a mirror, the person has now thought things through a little further. It is not that 'no ones cares' – she thinks you provide emotional support, so 'you care'. This can be very important. *By learning the technique of reflective listening you can help people to sort out their thoughts.* If you are seen as caring, that is so much better than believing that no one cares.

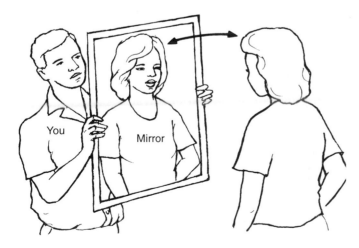

Figure 10.11 Helping another person to 'see' her thoughts and feelings

Reflecting back what someone has just said is a very powerful caring technique. To make it work properly, you should not do it too often in a conversation and you need to be careful not to twist and change what other people might mean when they speak.

If a person said 'No one likes me, nobody talks to me here', and the carer said 'Perhaps no one likes you because you are always sitting here', would this be a reflection? It can only be reflection if it acts as a mirror – if it bounces back *just* what the person says. This example twists things. The carer talks about where the client sits, and that's not reflection.

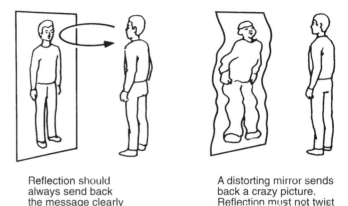

Reflection should always send back the message clearly

A distorting mirror sends back a crazy picture. Reflection must not twist what is said

Figure 10.12 Ensure accurate reflection!

Reflective listening can lead to **reflective learning.** Reflective listening is when the carer bounces the client's message back like a mirror. Clients can hear their own message and think about it – is it exactly what they were thinking, can they improve on it, make the meaning clearer, add more detail? The idea behind reflective listening is that it makes both the speaker and the listener think more. This thinking sometimes becomes a kind of reflecting inside your head. Thinking things through in our head is an important kind of learning – reflective learning.

Try it

Try it out in practice. Find someone who is studying this unit and get a tape recorder. Sit down with him or her and explain everything you know about reflective listening. Describe what it is, how you do it, when it could be useful, what would help make it work, what would stop it from working. Ask your colleague to listen to you, and to use some reflective listening if possible, with just an odd question, probe or prompt. Tape record what you say.

There is a Chinese saying: 'I know what I think when I hear what I say'. Listen to what you said!

By trying reflective listening in practice and by thinking the idea through, you can probably learn more than if you read this chapter many times! You will be doing thinking work. If your colleague reflects what you say effectively, you will be able to sort your ideas out by talking them through. Reflective listening may lead to reflective learning.

Remember:

- Reflective listening may help people to think things out.
- Thinking things out helps people to learn.
- Thinking things out may help some people to feel better.

Silence

If you are having a conversation with someone and cannot think what to say, it may feel embarrassing. A long silence seems to mean 'I can't think properly', or 'I do not understand', or 'I wasn't listening'. A pause puts pressure on the conversation, and you may feel that you have to invent something to say to avoid a silence.

One definition of friends is people who can sit together and feel comfortable in silence. Silence can mean different things depending on the situation. If we have only just met someone and we are trying to get to know them, a silence may look like incompetent questioning. If we do know the person, then silence might be all right. Silence might mean 'take your time', 'think about things', 'reflect in your own mind'.

When people need time to collect their thoughts, they might signal non-verbally that they are thinking. We can show respect by just communicating non-verbally, and not speaking.

Imagine, for example, that a doctor or nurse has to tell a patient some bad news. If he or she says it and immediately continues with details of the next thing to do – what hospital the patient will have to go to and so on – the patient may not be able to take it all in, may be shocked and unable to think of questions to ask.

A more caring way might be to tell the patient the bad news and wait. The doctor or nurse could ask if the person had any questions, and could communicate a caring attitude non-verbally. Leaving a silence would give the patient time to think. The silence would be caring.

Sometimes, too, it can be better to stay silent when a person has told you something. You can communicate your feelings non-verbally. You can often communicate 'I'd like you to say more about it' using head-nods, eye-contact and facial expressions. This use of silence can encourage the other person to reflect and to keep talking. Silence is sometimes a good alternative to repeating the verbal message. Silence can be another reflective technique.

Remember:

- Silence can link with reflective listening.
- Silence can give people a space to think
- Silence can be a skill in caring communication.

Social context

People are influenced by where a conversation takes place as well as to whom they are talking. As long ago as the 1930s, researchers found that children would say different things depending where they were when they were asked a question. In the school playground, a child might say that if he found some money then he would keep it – 'finders keepers'. In a religious setting children might say that they would give the money to an adult, because it belongs to someone else.

Context means the setting or the surroundings in which a conversation takes place. A social context is the people and the place that might influence the conversation. A conversation between two friends will follow a different pattern from a conversation between two strangers, for example.

A conversation between colleagues at work might be rather formal. There might be strict rules for turn-taking. You might have to choose your words very carefully and prepare what you are going to say. Anything you say might be quoted back later. A conversation with friends at a party could be very different – why bother with turn-taking! Your friends will let you off if you say something silly, you can relax and just say whatever you like. If you say whatever comes into your head in a formal work meeting you may find that you break the unwritten rules or values of the work group.

Status

Status is a term used to describe someone's social position or social importance. If a person has more power than you in a particular social situation, we might say that he or she has a 'higher status'. People can have more or less power for a variety of reasons. If you are employed, your manager will have the power to require you to do certain things as part of your job. At work, managers might be said to have a higher status than carers. This is because they have the power to require carers to work in particular ways. Some people have more knowledge than others. An experienced member of staff might have more status at work than a new member because he or she understands more about the work. A teacher or tutor might be seen as having a higher status than a student when teaching.

Communication tends to be influenced by status. People with a higher status may receive more attention during group discussion. The things 'high status people' say may be treated more seriously than other people's statements. People with a high status may be expected to organise a group discussion and be seen as leaders of the group.

Communication in groups

In everyday language 'group' can mean a collection or set of things, so people will say any collection of people is a group. For example, we might talk about a group of people who are waiting to cross the road.

These people have not spoken to each other, they may not have communicated non-verbally – they are simply together in the same place and time. They are a group in the everyday sense of the word, but not in the special sense of 'group' that is often used in health and social care work.

In caring, working with a group of people implies that the people belong together and would identify themselves as belonging to a group. Groups have a sense of belonging which gives the members a 'group feeling'. Sometimes this might be described as **group identity.**

Usually, a group will have some task or some common purpose or social role which acts as a focus for meeting. A group of people studying for a GNVQ might meet to try out practical ideas together. They would be a group in the care sense if they feel that they belong together. The learning tasks might contribute towards making the group feel that they belong together in the first place.

How groups get started

Usually, a collection of people will come together because they have a **common goal.** If the group is going to get started, its members will need to have good communication skills and may need a 'leader'. The individual skills associated with providing emotional support will be a good foundation for assisting in group development, or in becoming a leader in the group.

To get a group going, people have to feel that they will belong to the group. To start with, the group will need a clear task or purpose in which all the members feel they want to join. A playgroup for children will need to be organised around particular games. A reminiscence group for older people will need to be organised around photos or objects from the past. The organisation for these groups needs to be planned in advance. A discussion group (perhaps to discuss GNVQ skills) would need to be planned. Who would introduce the topic, what material would be needed, and would the discussion be recorded on video.

Use of space

An important aspect of a discussion group is how the group sits. When working with a discussion group it is very important that everyone can see and hear one another. Non-verbal communication will be important, and if people cannot see everybody's faces, this will not be possible. Usually, chairs are placed in a circle when planning a discussion group. In a circle everyone can get non-verbal messages from everyone else.

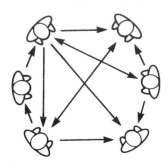

Organising a group to sit in a circle sometimes suggests that everyone is equal, that everyone is expected to communicate with everyone else. This freedom to communicate is also linked with creating a feeling of belonging: 'We can all share together – this is our group!'

Other patterns of seating send different messages. Teachers might sit in the middle of a half-circle. This sends the message 'We are all equal and we can all communicate with each other, but the teacher is going to do most of the communicating!'

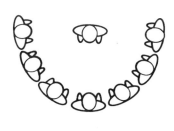

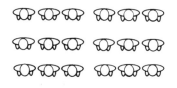

At a formal lecture, people sit in rows. This sends the message 'The lecturer will talk to you. You can ask questions but you should not talk to one another!'

Some less formal seating arrangements are chosen to create blocks. Sometimes a table acts as a block. Perhaps the two people behind it were too tired to move it, but they might be sending the message 'We are not sure we want to be with this group.' The table can make them feel separate 'We'll join in only if we feel like it.'

Sometimes space is used to create a gulf. In this next arrangement, person A cannot see person C properly

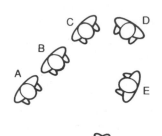

– so the two of them are unable to exchange non-verbal messages. Person A sits 'square on' to person F. Perhaps A does not want to talk to C. Perhaps F and A do not trust each other. The layout of seats makes it look like there could be tension or reluctance in this group.

Space can also signal social distance. A and B are keeping their distance from the rest of the group. There could be many reasons, but perhaps they are sending the message 'We do not really belong with you four!'

How tight or spaced out a group of people is should also be considered. Below, group A are huddled together, whereas group B are more spaced apart. Why do people get closer or further apart in groups? Some answers include: being close can signal that it's noisy – the group has to get close to hear. It can

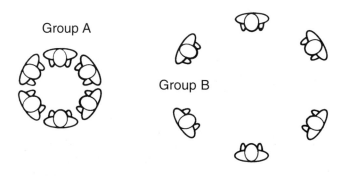

Group A

Group B

signal that the members like each other and are very interested in the discussion topic. It might signal that group members feel unsafe, and that being together gives more confidence that everyone will be supportive.

Whenever you meet a discussion group, study how people sit and where they sit. You may be able to guess a lot just by watching how people choose to arrange the seats.

Think it over

At Lincoln jail in the nineteenth century the authorities built a chapel so that the prisoners were each shut in a cubicle and could see the person giving the sermon but not each other! Why do you think this was done? The theory was that they could be controlled more strictly if they could not be in a group. They could not form a group because the partitions blocked them off from one another.

Turn-taking

Working in a group can be more difficult than holding an individual conversation. If a group is going to be worth belonging to, people must take turns in listening and speaking. Once everyone is speaking, no one is listening! Turn-taking between individuals is easy; even young children are quite good at it. Turn-taking in groups is not easy. Sometimes people think of something that comes into their minds and then just drop it on the group. Usually no one really listens, but people imagine that they are making a point.

Turn-taking involves complicated non-verbal behaviour. When a speaker is finishing he or she usually signals this by lowering and slowing the voice and looking around. Who gets to go next depends on eye-contact around the group – not just with the speaker. Group members have to watch the faces and eyes of everyone else in order that just one person takes over and speaks in turn. If people get excited or tense, then they usually add gestures to their other non-verbal messages to signal forcefully that they want to speak next. Sometimes people will put their hand out or nod their head to say (non-verbally): 'Look, it's my turn next!'

Eventually turn-taking goes wrong, and two or more people start talking at once. This is called a failure to 'mesh'. **Meshing** means that conversation flows easily around the group, between people. People interlink together in conversation, like interlinking in 'wire mesh'. When two people talk at the same time, one person has to give way. The two should take it in turns.

A **group leader** can act as a 'conductor' to check that turns are taken. If there is no leader, then individuals in the group have to sort the order out. Supportive behaviour in groups requires that people do not speak until others are ready to listen. Meshing or turn-taking is an important feature of a group that is working well.

Try it

In a group of five or six people, take four matchsticks each and agree on a topic for group discussion. Next, agree the following rules for the discussion. Only one person may speak at a time. Whenever that person speaks he or she must place a matchstick on the floor. When people run out of matchsticks they cannot say anything. No one may say anything unless others have finished. Non-verbal communication is allowed. People should not speak for more than one minute.

This exercise should emphasise the importance of turn-taking and the non-verbal messages that might help it. It should also be fun to do.

Reflecting before speaking to the group

When you try the matchstick game above you will find that conversation becomes difficult. Sometimes people discover that they have forgotten what they wanted to say by the time they have put down their matchstick. This is because we often join in with the conversation in a group whenever we feel like it. We respond to what other people have said, but we have not thought out our own ideas to the point of being able to say them clearly. If the group goes quiet and people look at us, we forget what we were going to say!

It is important to be able to say what you think, when you have others' attention. One of the best ideas to help with this is to think out your ideas before speaking. You need to check what you are going to say before you come out with it. This might sound easy or simple, but it can often be a very difficult thing to do.

People sometimes just say anything that they feel. You have probably been in groups where a person will speak and another person will say something like 'That's rubbish'. This kind of behaviour does not show respect and it can disrupt the group. Instead of just dumping such feelings on the group, the person should have reflected 'Why do I feel that they are talking rubbish, what can I do to challenge this in a supportive way which shows respect for the other person?' The answer might have been to ask a question, rather than make a judgement. The person could have said 'Did you just say ....? Why do you believe that?', or 'What evidence do you have for what you just said?' These questions can lead to a discussion of the issues without causing the group to break up in an argument. Follow the rule 'Think *before speaking'*. In care work, you need to think to yourself 'How well does the other person understand what I am saying?' Ask yourself questions if you are not sure what to say.

Observing own and others' behaviour

Part of good care skills is to be able to listen to others and understand what they really mean. We have to be careful not to make assumptions about other people. To improve our listening skills in a group we need to be able to reflect on what others have said and ask questions to clarify things. Skilled group discussion needs a lot of mental work. This mental work involves our own and others' behaviour.

Evidence collection point

Learning to observe might start with sitting outside a group and watching its members discuss something. Alternatively it might start by watching a video-tape of a discussion and monitoring the behaviour. If you can work with a group of people, use the 'fish-bowl' method of observation.

Figure 10.13 The fish-bowl method

The people in the middle are being watched – they probably feel like goldfish in a bowl! They will need to trust you if the observation is going to work. They discuss something important while you sit on the outside

and listen and watch. What will you monitor? A wide range of things can be monitored, but to start with you might like to watch:

1 non-verbal messages – how do people organise the turn-taking? How does eye-contact work?
2 questions – how good are people at asking other people for their ideas?
3 giving opinions – do people ask one another for their views and share ideas?
4 the pace of conversation – how do people speak? Are there any silences?

After five minutes or so of listening and watching, the group should stop and people should share what happened. Did the people in the group remember what the people outside saw and heard? After discussing the monitoring, it is your turn in the fish-bowl, to give the others a chance to do some uninterrupted monitoring.

Although learning to observe group behaviour can be started by watching groups at work, the importance of the skill is to use it *to check your own behaviour when working in a group*. Carers have to think about the effect their words and non-verbal behaviour will have on others. Keeping records of observation of others might help you to be aware of your own performance.

Think it over

Sometimes people behave very differently when they are part of a group. Can you think of a time when you have said or done something as part of a group which you would not have done if you had been alone?

You may remember speaking in a certain way in a situation with others which was different from what you would have said if you had been alone. You may have dressed differently when with a certain group of people than you would have done otherwise. Your social context will influence how you behave.

Group power

There are many possible ways in which being with a group may affect the way we behave. A group of people together can become very powerful. Group power is sometimes used to achieve undesirable ends, which the individuals within the group would have rejected as part of their normal behaviour. For example, a crowd at a football match may become over-excited or violent. The people as individuals may not normally behave violently towards others, but in this situation they have stopped acting as themselves and have gone along with the combined fervour of the group.

It is as well to realise, then, that when you are part of a group you may find yourself behaving differently, uncharacteristically. It is important to keep a check on what you say and do. Ask yourself if what is being said or done is really what you feel should be happening, or if group power has taken over and people are not thinking as individuals.

Speaking out and raising your worries can be important if a group is to keep going. You do have to be careful, though, how you raise your concerns. If you think someone else is dominating the conversation you could speak up by first acknowledging his or her point of view, but then firmly saying that you have a view to put to the group such as 'You are saying that we do not have to do this work, OK, but I would like to put my view now'. If the person starts talking again, you could be even firmer with 'I have not finished my point yet, are you listening to me?' You should never say 'Shut up, you have had your say, it's my turn now!' This is too aggressive.

Think it over

You can sometimes tell people to 'shut-up' in care work! You can tell them that they have said too much! You can only do this when you have a special relationship and you know that you are actually showing respect and value by using such language.

You might also be able to tell a friend to 'shut-up'. This is acceptable because you know you both respect one another anyway. Being rude or aggressive is a chance to break the rules when you know that no one is going to get hurt. The important thing is not the words that you say, but the way the message will be understood. Saying 'shut-up' to a client may make them angry or upset, whereas you can say a lot worse to friends and they will only laugh.

Individuals and groups

If a group is going to develop a 'feeling of belonging' then the individuals who make up the group will need to feel that they 'belong'. To achieve this feeling you will have to learn about others, remember what you have learned and use the

learning to convey warmth and interest, exactly as with individual conversations.

When starting to work with a group of people, you will need to be interested in each group member's 'sense of self'. You must check that you do not make false assumptions – be careful to ask others for their thoughts and feelings. Never live in your own private world and just put your thoughts on the group.

If you know little about the others in the group, conversation skills and listening skills will help. Over time, the important thing is to build up a memory of knowledge about the individuals and use this knowledge to make members of the group welcome.

Figure 10.14 Switching on to the individuals in the group

You can convey a sense of respect and value by remembering important things about group members' interests and lifestyles, and asking about them. Groups often need to chat at the beginning before getting going. This is a good time to ask questions 'How did you get on last night? Where did you go? Did anyone else go there?' Such questions pick up on what you know about the individual.

Values

When a collection of people first get together there is usually no sense of 'belonging'. To begin with, people just talk about general things or else they introduce themselves and begin to learn about one another.

After people have settled in there is often an uneasy stage when people are tense. Having to be in a group can be a threat – the sense of self and self-esteem can be threatened. People sometimes compete with one another for leadership. Sometimes people try to dominate the group or control the group to protect their own sense of self-importance.

At this stage the group may become either difficult or unpleasant to be in. It may, on the other hand, develop a sense of unwritten rules for working together. Then everyone can trust the others to work together in a particular way. This sense of trust might come about because the members of the group share a sense of **values**. Once a group has shared values, there is a sense of belonging and the group is a worthwhile thing to belong to.

Think it over

Can you recall the start of a group, where you felt uncertain of what to expect? Can you, for example, remember starting a programme of study at college? How did the group settle in? What values did the group come to share?

Are you in a safe working place?

Groups can form around all sorts of purposes and values. Some people just want to belong to something and will go along with anything. Some groups create a sense of belonging by breaking social rules (taking drugs and so on). Other groups unite around values, like opposing fox hunting – they share a common value in being opposed to something.

In care work it is important that groups respect and value individual group members. Valuing individual people is part of the unwritten rules for working together. The Care Sector Consortium which designed the professional standards for NVQ qualifications have written down the values needed for care work.

Demonstrating respect and value for others is not just skill, it also provides the value base for creating the sense of 'belonging' among individuals in a discussion group.

In care work all individual conversations and group work have to demonstrate these values:

- Support individuals through effective communication.
- Acknowledge individuals' personal beliefs and identities.
- Promote individual rights and choices.
- Maintain confidentiality.
- Promote anti-discriminatory practice.

Getting groups to work

Most care groups have a purpose or task to work on. Children get together to play games, adults may get together in recreational groups. Groups often need a focus – a game to play, an activity to join in or a topic to discuss.

1 If individuals are going to join in a group meeting, then someone will need to introduce the activity – start the conversation. From time to time when the conversation wanders, someone will need to steer it back to the main topic.
2 Occasionally, group members will need to clarify, or make sense of, what is being said.
3 Throughout the group meeting people will need to exchange ideas on the activity or topic being discussed.
4 Towards the end of a meeting, group members will need to agree on what has happened (who won in some types of game) or what the group has decided. The group will come to some kind of conclusions.

As well as performing their tasks, groups have to be 'maintained'. Group maintenance involves encouraging a sense of belonging and keeping the whole meeting enjoyable. The following are some behaviours to maintain group discussion:

1 Allow a bit of laughter to relieve tension and create a warm, friendly feeling that everyone can join in.
2 Show interest in the people in the group – learn about the 'individuality' of group members.
3 Be 'warm' and show respect and value when listening to people who are different from yourself or who have had different life experiences. This behaviour makes it safe to be in the group.
4 Express feelings honestly and with sincerity. This will help others to understand *your* individuality. Help others to understand you as well as trying to understand others.
5 Take responsibility for everyone having a chance to speak and take part. Some people may need to be encouraged or invited to speak, some people may need organising, so that turn-taking works.
6 If necessary ask people to explain what they have said, and to talk through disagreements. Group members need to feel that their shared values will make it possible to arrive at solutions when people disagree.

A group leader must keep reflecting on what is happening in the group. Does the group need to come back to the task? Is this the right time for a funny story? Should I make it clear that I am listening and that I value what is being said by this person? Every other group member who really wants the group to work will also monitor how the group is getting on with its task.

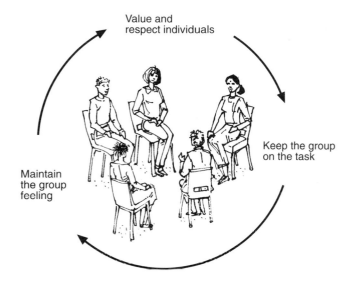

Value and respect individuals

Keep the group on the task

Maintain the group feeling

Figure 10.15 The dynamics of a caring group

To summarise: groups need to provide a task, create a sense of belonging and make sure each individual is supported and valued.

Communicating respect for others

As we grow up, we gradually start to become aware of a sense of who we are – a thinking and feeling of self. We need to be 'someone' and to have a feeling of being something we can call 'I' or 'myself'. This sense of being someone motivates us to do the things we do, choose the clothes we wear, make friends with the people we do and so on.

Being able to study depends on choosing to be a person who is keen to study. Going to school, college or work depends on our sense of who we are – it is often nicer to stay in bed, but we make ourselves do other things because of this sense of being a special individual, or perhaps we have an idea of what we would wish to be like.

Think it over

What are your earliest memories of choosing things to buy? How did what you bought influence your sense of independence and 'self'? What are your earliest memories of being told you were good at something? How did this influence how you understood yourself – your sense of individuality?

Our sense of our own 'individuality' or 'self' develops and changes during our lifetime. Our sense of self is influenced by our physical body and feelings, and our family or care relationships. As we grow our individuality is influenced by the community, culture, friendships and group situations that we experience. Many adults believe that our sense of self is something that we consciously choose to develop. Words like 'self-development' and 'personal growth' are used to describe this process.

'I am me; I am unique'

Three things which many people include in their sense of self are:

1 **A need to feel special.** We are different from everyone else. There is no one else exactly like us.
2 **A need to feel that we have 'roots'.** We have a personal history. While we do change, we never stop being the person we were born to be.
3 **A need to like the person we think we are.** This is called self-esteem. There may be things we would like to alter in our life, but we like our own personality.

Think it over

Think about these three ingredients of the sense of self. Do you choose clothes or jewellery that make you feel special? Do you ever think about your past and how your life has

207

changed? Does this give you a sense of having 'roots'? Are you glad to be alive? Do you enjoy life in general? How is your sense of self-esteem?

If a person has problems with feeling special, or with feeling a sense of life-long development, or with self-esteem, then this may lead to personal unhappiness. Sometimes people become depressed if they lose their sense of self.

Understanding other people

All people have their own special view of themselves. For many people this might involve thoughts and feelings which could be listed under headings like 'culture', 'religion', 'gender', 'age', 'physical appearance', 'physical and mental abilities', 'sexuality'.

If you care about individuals, you will want to make them feel special. To do this you will need to find out about them and make it clear that you respect and value their individuality. Learning about other people's sense of self involves looking at how they present themselves – what clothes they choose, what jewellery they wear, what non-verbal messages they send. People will often display something of their individual sense of culture, religion, gender and age, just in their clothes and non-verbal behaviour. If you talk to people, you can learn so much more.

Communicating **respect** involves learning about other people, remembering what you have learned and reflecting it back. For instance, first you must learn the names of the people you are working with – the name that the client prefers to be called by. Next you must remember things you have been told, and use them later when you meet the client again 'Hello Mrs Andrews, how did your son get on at that job interview you told me about?'

Communicating respect involves getting into conversations with others and showing that you listen to them. You need to show that you value what they have told you enough to remember it. You switch on your memory when you next meet. Naturally, the way you make people feel special will involve sending non-verbal messages of interest and

respect as well. So you could greet Mrs Andrews with a smile and make eye-contact (both are messages which say 'I'm interested in talking to you'). If Mrs Andrews wishes, use hand movements to signal interest and then say 'How did your son get on at that job interview you told me about?' You are sending the message 'I'm interested in you and I remember what you told me. I respect and value you as an individual.'

Not everyone does this. Sometimes people don't even bother to learn the clients' names 'There are too many of them so I call all the male old people "pop" and all the women "dear"!' This kind of behaviour sends the message 'You are not special. I don't care about you as an individual.'

Not only this, but words like 'dear' can send a message 'I am more important than you', 'I have power over you', 'I have more status than you'. These messages can be dangerous. They can mean that the client will dislike the carer, and the carer may come to dislike the client.

Another important issue is to make sure that you do not label people. Because each person is an individual, you have to be careful not to make **wrong assumptions.**

Imagine two people are having a conversation. One is a Muslim and the other person is not, but the second person has tried to learn about the Islamic faith. Perhaps the non-Muslim has heard of Ramadan, a time of fasting during daytime. The non-Muslim might say 'Oh, it's Ramadan so I did not get you a drink.' What this person has done shows that he or she was trying to learn about religion – but forgot about individuality. Each individual will keep his or her own religious observances, so the speaker should have checked what the other person thought, before jumping to conclusions. Many Muslims do not drink during the days of Ramadan, but is that the code this individual actually follows? You need to understand culture and religion on an individual level when you work with individuals. Failure to do this may cause you to stereotype others.

When trying to communicate with others it is also important that you show respect for **individual self-esteem needs.** You should always be careful to offer people choices so that they can express their individuality. You should always ask their opinion, rather than guessing what is needed. The idea is this: if people make their own choices and are asked for their views and opinions, then they are *in control*.

People express their sense of self by making choices and having opinions. You can be sensitive to this and thus increase a sense of self-worth in others.

Remember:

Being sensitive to others involves listening and memory. You build up an understanding which helps you to say the right things, and to send the right non-verbal messages.

You also need to express **warmth.** Warmth involves not being critical about other people, but being accepting of differences between yourself and others.

Think it over

Think of a person you have met who is totally different from you – someone with different interests, habits, lifestyle, culture, etc. Do you think first about what is wrong with the other person – for example the things you would disagree with, what you would argue against? Or do you think first about what is exciting and interesting in this other person?

'Warmth' describes the feelings of excitement and interest when we meet different people. Judging others in a critical way is uncaring and unsupportive.

When we begin to think about other people and their life situations, we are bound to notice the difference between their ways of thinking and ours. Where differences exist, one response is to argue about them, to challenge the other view as 'wrong'. In other words, when people lead different lives or have different problems from our own, there can be a tendency to assume that we have a better way of thinking, a better lifestyle, etc., and that we do not really need to know about theirs!

Remember:

To show 'warmth' is to have the ability not to sit in judgement on someone – not to compare yourself with others. It is the ability to listen, understand and not criticise other people's individuality. You accept that they have the right to be the way they are; you are secure enough in your understanding of your own self that you are not threatened when thinking about alternative lifestyles.

Finding the right behaviours to communicate 'warmth' will also help you to avoid working in a **discriminatory** way with clients.

Finally, practical work in showing respect for others requires you to be sincere. When learning anything new there is a tendency to model yourself on other people. Sometimes we act out what we think are skills in the hope of achieving a better performance. *The problem is that respect needs to be real or genuine. It needs to be an expression of your own self.*

In trying to listen, understand and be warm, you still have to 'be yourself'. Attempts to use stock phrases, or to copy a performance you have seen others do, destroys the safety and trust that can develop if people are to believe they are understood and accepted. They must also understand a little about you in order to trust you. So there must be an **openness** in the way you communicate understanding and acceptance for it to mean anything.

Obstacles to effective communication

There is a range of problems that prevent people from listening to each other.

If people cannot hear one another because of background noise, or if they cannot see one another properly because of poor lighting, then they will not be able to understand non-verbal messages. Furniture can act as a block. For example, if desks or tables are arranged badly, then people may not be able to see or hear one another easily.

Less obvious problems include those that arise when people do not attempt to respect one another or to respect the self-esteem needs of the people they are talking to. Both conversations and relationships break down when people do not attempt to communicate respect. Respect involves trying to understand the language and terminology that other people use. Sometimes people talk in their own 'slang' language or in jargon (technical talk that is hard to understand). If people really wish to communicate, they will alter their way of speaking to meet the needs of others. There are several other reasons why people do not listen to one another.

1 Listening takes up too much mental energy – we might be tired.
2 People say they have too little time and too much work to do. Sometimes this might be true, sometimes it might be an excuse.
3 It seems like we have heard it all before and there is nothing we can do to help – it feels easier to switch off.

4 Some clients in care are seen as unimportant and their worries are not considered worth listening to – so they are not treated with the respect they deserve.

5 Sometimes we do not understand the backgrounds and lifestyles of other people. It becomes easier not to have to learn about people different from ourselves – not listening saves us from having to adjust our views and beliefs.

6 Sometimes clients can make us worry. They might talk about pain, suffering and grief. Some people are afraid to talk about such things, so not listening means that they do not have to.

7 Some people like to control clients. It is quicker and easier just to get on with practical day-to-day tasks – asking the client's opinion gets in the way.

8 Most important of all, some people imagine that they should always be able to offer simple advice to anyone with a worry or a problem. They feel that they have to have an answer for everything. This belief stops them from listening.

Obstacles to communication in groups

Certain behaviours have to be avoided in groups because they can destroy the ability of people to communicate. Some behaviours can destroy the sense of belonging that people need if group conversation is to work. It is important to check that you do not display the following behaviours when you want to get a group to work.

Dominating the talking

People who talk too often or for too long may think that they are powerful. Very often they simply stop the group from working. They are not leading the group because they fail to listen to the views of other people. Other people do not follow their lead, they just 'switch off' instead.

Putting other people down

Sometimes group members can be sarcastic or aggressive to others. When this happens it can destroy any sense of belonging. The aggressive person might be putting themselves 'above' other people in the group – saying that they have a right to criticise or judge.

Excluding others

Groups may break into smaller groups, with some people talking only to their friends. Sometimes a particular person might be excluded from discussion. The sense of 'belonging' in the group will be lost.

Talking only to the leader

A group that has a real sense of belonging will involve everyone. Members of a group that is not working so well may talk mainly to one person – the recognised leader, or another whom they trust.

Where people talk mainly to one individual or leader they will probably not get the same satisfaction from being in the group as when everyone can communicate.

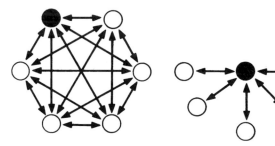

An ideal communication pattern   Communication only with the leader

Figure 10.16 Two extremes of communication in groups

The best way to learn about communication is to evaluate your own individual and group work.

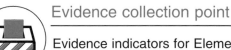

Evidence collection point

Evidence indicators for Element 4.1 require that you make records of interactions carried out in two settings, one of which is one-to-one, and the other involving a group. One context should also involve at least one person who is of a different status to yourself.

Your records of communication work have to be evaluated or 'appraised' by both yourself and an assessor. You have to evaluate the quality of your communication work, and how you could make improvements in the future.

Summary

Ideas about quality of communication presented in this chapter included the following:

One-to-one

- How did you start the conversation?
- Evaluate the quality of the listening skills you used.
- What verbal and non-verbal behaviour did you use to keep the other person talking and to show interest?
- How did you use reflective listening skills?
- How did you ask questions? How well thought out were the questions?
- Did you make use of silence?
- How did you communicate respect?
- What obstacles to communication did you find? How did you deal with them?

Group communication

- What was the context and purpose of the group?
- How did the group use space?
- How did you use the idea of turn-taking?
- Did you 'reflect' before speaking to the group?
- How effective was your verbal and non-verbal communication with the group?
- How did you observe others' verbal and non-verbal behaviour? What do you understand about the way other group members behaved?
- If you communicated with a real group that had existed for a while, what were the values of the groups?
- Did you attempt to lead the group? If so, how did you manage?
- How did you communicate respect?
- What obstacles to communication did you find? How did you deal with them?

Chapter 11

The effects of discriminatory behaviour on interpersonal relationships

Equality and diversity

One of the basic principles on which the health and care services operate is equality of provision for all, and this principle applies to access, quality of care and all other aspects of service delivery. Equality is a value in the culture of the health and caring professions. The right of individuals to equal treatment is stated in the policies of all health and caring services and in the government's Patients' Charter.

Statements about equality made by managers and good intentions on the part of staff do not guarantee that all patients and clients receive the same level of care and attention. Many people find that they are treated differently from others and are discriminated against in their dealings with the caring services. If you work as a carer you will need to understand why discrimination happens, how it can affect the lives of the victims and how you can work to identify and prevent discrimination in your own behaviour.

Labelling and stereotypes

Discrimination begins when someone is seen as being in some way different from other people. Of course we are all different from one another as individuals, but we are also members of groups and we share characteristics with other group members. Personal characteristics of physical appearance and behaviour

are the things we first see when we meet another person, and we are quick to notice the differences and similarities between themselves and us. This is a natural part of the process of communication and is a skill which can help us to understand the needs of an individual more fully. Our perception of a person (i.e. the way that we see them) helps us to decide how best to meet their needs.

However, these features of appearance and behaviour may be used to label an individual as a member of a particular group. People have no control over the ways others choose to label them, and they can even find themselves being seen as a member of a group to which they do not feel they belong. Once a person has been labelled as a member of a group, he or she is no longer being seen as an individual. They are assumed to have the characteristics that members of the group are believed to share, and are expected to behave and think in a certain way. People may be expected to conform to a **stereotype** of an image of how members of the group should be.

Stereotypes are not descriptions of real people. They are a collection of ideas about things such as habits, dress, behaviour and attitudes that are put together and used to create a picture of a 'typical' group member. A stereotype is a sort of social collage that is pinned on to an individual when they are labelled, and then taken to be a true likeness of them.

Think it over

On page 122 you were asked to link personal characteristics to particular social classes. Look back at this task and try to decide why you linked these collections of characteristics to particular social classes. Where do you see these stereotypes used?

Why do you think certain characteristics are associated with certain social classes?

People who have been labelled with a particular stereotype can begin to find themselves discriminated against in different ways. Behaviour towards them will adapt to what is regarded as the 'right way' to deal with people from that group, and the process of discrimination begins.

'I wanted you to feel at home, so I made a curry'

Who is discriminated against?

For some people, being labelled as a member of a group causes few problems. For example, being labelled as upper class, or as a film star, may affect how a person is treated, but it is unlikely to have serious negative effects on his or her life. In fact, in these cases positive discrimination can take place, and special attention may be given to people who are seen as members of groups with a high status.

For most people though, the experience of being labelled as a member of a particular group is a negative one. Some groups are given a lower status and have less power, and people labelled by their

race or ethnic group, their gender, their age, their religion, their sexuality or their disability are particularly vulnerable to discrimination by others.

Race

One of the ways in which people are labelled is by their race. But what exactly is a race of people? Human beings all belong to the same biological species whose members vary physically from each other in a wide variety of ways. We inherit our physical characteristics from our parents and some of these are more visible than others. Social stratification systems have been invented that are based on the idea that members of racial groups possess certain physical features in common, such as a particular skin colour or facial shape.

For example, the apartheid system which existed in South Africa used a complicated system of stratification based on race to define the political, social and economic status of members of the population. Since people's appearances are infinitely varied it is impossible to draw a neat line so that everybody falls into one group or another, yet the South African government put much time and effort into classifying people.

This was an important decision for the individual because at that time in South African society different racial groups were legally forced to live apart. People classed as being 'white' had considerably better conditions than were available to other racial groups. They had better housing and health care, and access to the better-paid occupations. Also, importantly, they had the right to vote and hold political office.

Quite apart from the moral questions raised by the apartheid system, it met enormous difficulties when trying to draw clear lines between racial groups. Skin colour and facial features can vary infinitely, and trying to decide whether someone is African, Asian or white can be so difficult that we begin to see how pointless it is even to try.

Biologically, the genetic makeup of individuals is basically the same, and the variations which give us the appearance we associate with different racial groups are minute. Differences in hair and eye colour are inherited in exactly the same way as skin colour, and make just as much sense as a basis for social stratification. Differences in blood groups have far more biological importance than physical appearance and can be accurately measured so that people are clearly separated into different groups, yet this is not

'Please madam – let me open the door for you'

used as a basis of social stratification and discrimination.

This all points to the fact that the idea of race is a concept that has been developed socially and has little to do with the biology of human beings.

Ethnicity and religion

Racial divisions based on biological differences may allow some individuals to be singled out easily for discriminatory treatment, but they take no account of differences in background, attitudes and behaviour. A person's culture or ethnicity may form the basis of discriminatory behaviour by others, whether they appear different in racial terms or not. The cultural or ethnic background of an individual may be indicated by his or her appearance: but clothes, accent and mannerisms are more likely to indicate ethnic background than skin colour and facial shape. Ethnic groups have their own culture, and members following the norms of their culture can be identified.

Religion is often linked to ethnicity and may be a strong unifying feature in some ethnic groups. For example, the Jewish religion is a fundamental feature of Jewish culture. Observance of their religious practices has linked Jewish communities across the world for centuries. It has also meant that Jews have been identified as different, stereotyped and viciously discriminated against.

Social stratification based on ethnic background is the basis of discrimination against many groups. Sometimes racism is directed at people who look black, but sometimes it is aimed at people's culture. Gypsies, Irish and Jewish people have a similar physical appearance to the majority of British people, but they are often discriminated against.

Try it

Make a list of all the ethnic groups you can think of that live in Britain. Talk to other students and try to make your list as complete as you can.

Now think about how these different ethnic groups are treated by the rest of society. Rewrite your list ranking the groups according to how much you think they may be at risk of discrimination. Put the group that is at most risk at the top and the rest in order below, finishing with the group that has the lowest risk in your view.

Look at this list and think about those groups and the top and bottom. How do you think the life experience of individuals in each of these groups compares? Why do you think race and ethnic group influences the way these individuals are treated?

Gender

Gender is also used as the basis of discrimination. Though women are not a minority group, comprising half the population, they are usually given a lower status in society than men, and are discriminated against in both social and economic areas. Stereotypes of women abound in the media and they help to define the roles that are available to women, and how they are treated by men.

Women are discriminated against in education and in the labour market. Though the basic abilities of boys and girls are equal, traditionally fewer girls study to a high level in subjects such as science, maths and engineering, which have been seen as boys' subjects. At work women make up 40 per cent of the labour force and yet there are very few women in senior positions, and the average wage for women is only 75 per cent of the average for men.

Assumptions about a woman's role as a wife and mother are instilled into children of both sexes during primary socialisation, and are reinforced by media images and the influence of society at large. Many women become socialised into accepting traditional roles and never expect to compete with men at work. Women who do take on non-traditional roles and work in occupations that are male dominated may be regarded as eccentric (or

odd) by members of both sexes. There are very few female engineers or builders, for example.

Women may be stereotyped as less serious contenders for jobs than men, who are generally regarded as the main breadwinners. Also, women may be expected to leave a job after a short while to have a family, and child-bearing may be presumed to signal the end of a woman's career.

Women who do try to develop a professional career may find that their chances of promotion are far worse than those of their male colleagues, even in jobs where there is a high proportion of women. For example, around 90 per cent of primary school teachers are women, yet over 50 per cent of primary school heads are men.

These statistics indicate the extent to which discrimination on the grounds of gender occurs. The low-status roles that are generally available to women enable this discrimination to continue.

Try it

Make a list of all the occupations you can think of. Talk to other students to make your list as large as possible.

Now go through your list marking occupations that you believe are stereotyped as women's work with a W, and those you think are stereotyped as men's work with an M.

Are there equal numbers of professions associated with men and women?

Try fitting 'women's' occupations into the Registrar-General's scale of class (see page 123). Do women's occupations have the same status as those of men?

Age

Another way in which society is stratified is on the basis of age. People are identified as belonging to a particular age group and treated differently from those seen as belonging to younger or older age groups. The processes of labelling and stereotyping cause the needs of the individual to be ignored and discrimination begins to take place.

Discrimination based on age especially affects people who are seen to be particularly old or young, whose status and power in society are lower than that of people in their middle years.

Though discrimination based on youth may seem unjust, we do grow older. Adolescents may feel that they are being treated like children, but adjustment to the role of adult takes time, both for the individuals and for those around them.

The rules and restrictions we place on younger children and even teenagers are not seen as discrimination, but are regarded as essential for their safety and development. But people labelled as 'elderly' are often stereotyped as dependent and helpless like small children.

Older people are likely to be less physically fit than others, and some will make increasing demands on family and the health and care services when the illnesses of old age occur. Many cultures have great respect for age, and if they stereotype older people it is as wise and learned members of society. But in British culture the elderly are often stereotyped as overgrown children whose opinions and feelings are not to be taken too seriously. This becomes the basis for discrimination in a variety of ways that the victims are powerless to prevent. Even though many older people are fit and able, they are liable to be discriminated against by people who see them as belonging to a different group. In this case, the discrimination comes from a younger generation.

Illness and disability in old age increase people's vulnerability to being stereotyped, but disability can become the basis of discrimination against a person at any age.

Disability

People with disabilities come from all areas of society; from different classes, age groups and ethnic backgrounds. Despite this diversity, it is often a person's disability that is seen as the most important thing about him or her. Some disabilities are easier to see than others and this makes stereotyping more likely. People who are wheelchair-bound are usually regarded as disabled, whereas people with severe dyslexia or asthma are very unlikely to be seen in the same way.

The stereotype of a disabled person is of someone who is dependent and helpless, and there may also be assumptions made about their intellectual ability. People with physical disabilities frequently report that they are assumed to have a learning disability as well. Physical disability has no biological relationship with learning disabilities, but the stereotype of disability links them together and can be the basis of discrimination in education and in other areas of life.

Don't assume we're at the same intellectual level

Try it

Think about different types of disability that people may have and make a list.

For each entry indicate whether or not you think it is likely to be noticed by others. Indicate those likely to be noticed with an asterisk.

Some people make assumptions about disabled people. What sort of assumptions do you think are most likely to be made about people with the disabilities you have listed?

For each entry on your list write down these stereotypical assumptions.

Look again at your work and at the particular assumptions made about the more visible disabilities. Write a paragraph outlining which groups are most likely to suffer from discrimination and explain why you think this is so.

Sexuality

Discrimination on the basis of a person's sexuality is very common in society. In law, the age of consent for homosexual people is higher than that for heterosexuals. Recent court cases involving the armed forces have brought their rules against homosexuality into the spotlight.

Discrimination on the basis of sexuality happens in many ways.

Gay men may be subject to physical attacks, and they may be socially shunned. With the growing public awareness of HIV and AIDS, discrimination against gays has sometimes focused on fears about these diseases. Assumptions about infection may lead some people to avoid physical contact such as shaking hands with gay men, even though HIV cannot be transmitted in this way, and gay individuals are very unlikely to be infected.

Forms of discrimination

We saw above how individuals are sometimes labelled as members of groups, and how stereotypes about group members are applied to real people, resulting in discrimination against them. The word **discrimination** means to treat differently, and it can be used to refer to any situation where a person is treated less well than others. People who find themselves linked to one of the groups we have looked at may experience many forms of discrimination at different times of their lives. It may range from being talked down to, or patronised, to being subjected to a violent attack. But some types of discrimination are more likely to be experienced by particular groups, and if we look at the types of things that happen to them we will be better equipped to identify discrimination and prevent it.

Physical and verbal abuse

One of the most extreme and brutal forms of discrimination is physical or verbal abuse. Members of some ethnic groups are particularly liable to suffer this sort of treatment, and some people have been killed simply because they were regarded as a member of a particular group.

Many cases of physical abuse are the result of organised attacks by racist groups, and this has included attacks on businesses and property and the firebombing of family homes, as well as personal assaults on individuals. Other physical abuse is not planned, but is the result of people being regarded as 'fair game' because they have been labelled as belonging to a different and 'inferior' race. Fear of assault by other groups in society is one of the reasons why members of some ethnic groups live close to each other.

Verbal abuse is also suffered by members of ethnic groups, and the words often show that stereotyping has taken place. The same insult may be used towards people who have no connection with each other except in the minds of the aggressors.

Verbal and physical abuse are also suffered by members of other groups who are commonly discriminated against. Attacks on women are not usually motivated by dislike of them as a group, but are more likely to be linked to the role and status of women in society. Women are often in a subordinate position in the family and have a lower status and power than males. Some suffer physical attacks from husbands, partners or male relatives who feel that their superior roles allow them to do this. Women are often unable to defend themselves either physically or socially from these attacks.

Stereotyped sexual images of women may also be linked to verbal and physical abuse. Sometimes people have sought to excuse sexual attacks on the grounds that the woman victim was provocatively dressed, or behaved in a provocative manner. These arguments have been used to plead for light sentencing in rape cases. This shows how the consequences of stereotyping can sometimes be blamed on the victim, who has no power to prevent it happening.

Physical and verbal abuse towards older people or disabled people also occur. As with women, violence is not likely to stem from hatred of the group, but is linked to the low status and power of elderly or disabled people. They may be stereotyped as less than full adults, and some are disciplined physically for behaviour that is regarded as bad, such as incontinence. People who are dependent upon others for their care may also suffer physical abuse through neglect of their needs.

Exclusion

Verbal and physical abuse are usually easy to identify, but other forms of discrimination, although more common, are less obvious. One of these is the deliberate exclusion of members of some groups from access to jobs, services and other facilities. This is a form of indirect discrimination.

It is against the law to discriminate on the basis of ethnic background or gender in these areas, but discrimination can be very subtle and hard to detect. Job advertisements must be worded to allow everyone an equal chance to apply, but in practice the personal bias of members of the interview panel can exclude some applicants from the chance of appointment. We saw above how women may be excluded from access to better-paid jobs, and a similar situation occurs for people who are labelled ethnically. Many people have found that they are turned down for jobs for which they are well qualified because of their ethnic background or skin colour.

People from ethnic groups may also be excluded from access to other resources. Another reason why members of ethnic groups live close to each other is that they may be prevented from buying property in other, better areas. Again this is very difficult to prove in individual cases, but easy to see when statistics are examined. Health and care services can also be denied to members of ethnic groups, or made more difficult to obtain. This could be through giving inadequate or incorrect information, or by ignoring any difficulties with the English language that some people may have.

In their contacts with the health and caring services, some people may be excluded from access to the help they need by being treated less well than other clients. The behaviour and attitude of a member of the caring staff may differ from client to client according to the personal bias of the carer. Feelings of hostility can be projected in conversations with clients, which can put them off seeking the help they need, and exclude them from care. Inadequate and misleading information may also be given so that access to care is made more difficult for some people than for others.

Discrimination may also take the form of rules or working practices which make services less accessible for particular groups. For example, in a nursery the range of food provided for the children may not include items required by the religion and culture of some members of the community. Children from these families would not find their needs being met, and the nursery would in effect be excluding some children from access.

Another way that indirect discrimination happens is through tone of voice and body language. The personal manner of an individual also conveys messages about how he or she sees the other person. These communications, both verbal and non-verbal, can transmit hostility and have the effect of putting off further discussion. People from minority ethnic groups may be deterred from seeking the help they need because of the way they are dealt with when they apply for it.

Elderly and disabled people can also suffer from exclusion and avoidance of contact. Older people are generally excluded from the job market even though they may be fit, healthy and willing to work. Disabled people often have useful skills and

knowledge which would easily allow them to work effectively despite their disability. Nevertheless, the stereotype of the disabled person as useless and dependent may be in the mind of the interviewer, so that the applicant is regarded as a potential liability rather than an asset. There is a legal requirement for larger businesses to employ a proportion of disabled people, but in practice many firms fail to fulfil it. They are exempted from doing so if too few disabled people apply for a job. Firms also cite the unsuitability of the facilities and environment for people with some disabilities as a reason for not employing disabled people.

Exclusion because of environment is suffered regularly by some disabled people. This is a subtle form of indirect discrimination which includes, for example, lack of wheelchair access to shops and other public places, and the lack of easily accessible toilets. Transport is a particular problem for some disabled people who cannot use public transport or taxis very easily. This is a form of discrimination by neglect, in that the needs of a disabled people are often forgotten in the design and planning of public places and facilities.

Try it

Think about ways in which disabled people can be helped to gain access to facilities. Examples could include wheelchair ramps at entrances and designs to include wider corridors.

Write down a list of the features you think could be provided in public facilities to help disabled people to make full use of them.

Visit a local public facility such as a shopping centre, or sporting complex. using your list as a guide, assess the design and the facilities in terms of access and convenience for disabled people.

Note where features on your list have been provided and where they have not.

Write a short report on your findings, including the changes you would like to make to allow disabled people full access.

Devaluing

The forms of discrimination that we saw above have obvious social and physical repercussions for the victims, but there are other forms of indirect discrimination that have effects which are less easy to see. Individuals who belong to certain groups may find that their beliefs and opinions are regarded as worthless by some people. though they are not subjected to physical abuse, or exclusion or avoidance, they find that they are held in low esteem and their views are not taken seriously. The norms of their culture may be criticised or ridiculed, and their beliefs devalued or denied.

Think it over

You are part of a group of students sitting at a table in a school or college cantoon. You notice that one student keeps on devaluing the views of the only black student present, and behaving as though his opinions are irrelevant. Eventually, the others leave and you are left alone at the table with the aggressive student.

What type of discriminatory behaviour took place and what effects could it have on the victim?

This process works to undermine the confidence and self-esteem of the victim, which can have serious personal consequences for them. People treated in this way may come to accept the view projected onto them and begin to regard themselves as having less worth than others. Children growing up in an environment where they are constantly devalued can suffer serious setbacks in their personal development. They may see academic failure as inevitable for them and fail to develop their potential in other areas of life.

This form of discrimination is applied to all the groups we have looked at, and it is one of the ways in which the low status of members is reinforced.

Women's opinions on most subjects are often regarded as less important than men's, and the tasks they are credited with being good at are generally ones given low prestige, such as child-rearing and running a home. Many women are socialised into low self-esteem by this process and build up a picture of themselves which fits the subservient role they adopt in life.

Elderly and disabled people also find that their opinions and beliefs are not taken seriously by other people, and that their power and status are lowered in the process. People whose self-esteem is damaged and who have come to believe that their opinions are irrelevant generally have difficulty expressing their needs. They are reluctant to comment in case of ridicule, or because it seems pointless.

Stereotypes and self-worth

Though people may believe themselves to be free of prejudice, practically everybody has some knowledge of the features included in the stereotypes of different groups. Jokes involving ethnic groups, or gender roles like mother-in-law, rely on the listener having the same stereotype as the comedian for them to be understood. In fact, such jokes are a form of direct discrimination.

Stereotypes are common in society, and many people use them to discuss other people and form judgements about them. Presumptions about a person's behaviour based on his or her appearance may well be incorrect. If we expect a person to behave or think in a certain way because we see him or her as belonging to a particular group, we are making assumptions based on a stereotype. This is very common throughout society and can work to influence the self-development of people who see themselves as part of the groups being stereotyped. People can develop a concept of themselves which includes features of the stereotype, and begin to behave in ways which fit this self-concept.

Legislation for equality of opportunity

There are legal safeguards against discrimination which are designed to protect vulnerable groups from abuse. Parliament has passed laws that seek to prevent discrimination on the basis of race, gender and disability. Organisations such as the Equal

Opportunities Commission (EOC) and the Commission for Racial Equality (CRE) have been set up to help make the law effective.

Equal Pay Act 1970

The Equal Pay Act passed in 1970 attempted to improve the position of the rising number of women in the workforce. It made it unlawful to discriminate between men and women in their pay and conditions at work. Later amendments to the act made it possible to claim equal pay for work that was of 'equal value' to that done by the opposite sex.

Sex Discrimination Act 1975 and the Equal Opportunities Commission

The 1975 Sex Discrimination Act went further to ensure that women were not discriminated against in education or employment because of their gender or marital status. The act applies to men too, but women are far more likely to be discriminated against in these areas. The act identified two forms of discrimination:

- Direct discrimination occurs when a woman is refused a job or service on the basis of her gender. It is unlawful to advertise a job as being for men only, or to turn down a woman because she is married and may have children.
- Indirect discrimination occurs when conditions are applied which favour one sex over the other. Unless the conditions can be justified as essential for doing the job, the employer is acting illegally.

The Equal Opportunities Commission was set up as the Sex Discrimination Act was passed. Its job is to monitor, advise and offer information about the act. The Commission offers help and advice to people who feel that they have a case to be answered under the act.

Race Relations Act 1976 and the Commission for Racial Equality

The Race Relations Act was passed in 1976 to strengthen the law on racial discrimination. It makes it illegal to discriminate against any individual on the grounds of race in employment, access to goods and services, education and in many other situations. The act was modelled on the Sex Discrimination Act. It deals with discrimination on racial grounds, i.e. on the grounds of a person's colour, nationality or

ethnic origin. It defines three ways in which discrimination can take place and prohibits them.

- Direct discrimination, which means treating a person *less favourably* than other people would be treated in the same circumstances. This includes refusing employment, or care, to a person because of skin colour or ethnic background. It also includes deliberately giving a lower standard of care to certain people because of their race.
- Indirect discrimination involves attaching conditions to applications for jobs and services which exclude certain groups of people and cannot be justified on non-racial grounds. For example, to require a high standard of English from a labourer may break the law if it excluded people from a racial group who had limited English, but who could do the job perfectly well.
- The victimisation of people who have made or supported complaints of discrimination. This part of the act is intended to protect those who make complaints under the act, and people who undertake to be witnesses for them. It is also unlawful to victimise or discriminate against people who are thought to be about to make a complaint.

The Race Relations Act is intended to prevent discrimination on the grounds of race or ethnicity, and to help people to report instances where it occurs. The Commission for Racial Equality was set up to ensure that the act works. It offers advice and support to people who wish to report a complaint of discrimination on racial grounds, and has offices in several major cities.

Think it over

The Race Relations Act is intended to prevent discrimination on racial grounds and promote equality of opportunity. Think about the ways in which discrimination can take place. List these on a sheet of paper.

Now think about the way that the act tackles discrimination. For each item on your list try to decide how the act would deal with it. What do you think would be the biggest barrier to the act being effective in preventing discrimination in each case?

Disabled Persons Act 1986

The Disabled Persons Act of 1986 followed earlier acts designed to prevent discrimination against disabled people. All companies employing 20 or more people should ensure that at least 3 per cent of their workforce is registered disabled. There are ways in which employers can avoid carrying out the terms of the act, for example, if the work is unsuitable for people with disabilities, or if they can show that too few disabled people apply. The act also tries to ensure that disabled people have access to public buildings and spaces, and to the workplace.

 Evidence collection point

Write a report on discrimination. It should:

a convey the meaning of the term 'discrimination' by giving examples of four different bases of discrimination, such as race or gender
b describe behaviour which indicates discrimination, how different groups can be stereotyped and the possible long-term and short-term effects of discrimination on the victim
c identify the equality of opportunity rights which individuals have under current legislation.

The report will contribute to the evidence indicators for Element 4.2.

Summary

The following topics covered in this chapter may help you to prepare you report:

- Discrimination as unequal treatment
- The role of labelling and stereotyping
- Groups who are discriminated against
- Bases of discrimination:
  - Race
  - Religion
  - Gender
  - Age
  - Disability
  - Sexuality
- Forms of discrimination:
  - Physical and verbal abuse
  - Exclusion
  - Devaluing
- Stereotypes and self-worth
- Legislation for equality of opportunity:
  - Equal Pay Act 1970
  - Sex Discrimination Act 1975
  - Race Relations Act 1976
  - Disabled Persons Act 1986

Chapter 12

Working with clients in health and social care

Caring relationships

Most people make relationships throughout their lives. Babies bond with their parents. Brothers and sisters make attachments to one another. Couples make emotional commitments to love and support each other. Friendship and family groups involve honest, open sharing of time, mutual help and enjoyment of one another's company. Because we are so used to living with other people and so used to our relationships with them, it is easy to think of paid care work as being the same as friendship or family relationships.

Think it over

Think about the differences between professional care work and being with a group of friends or family. Some of the differences are shown in Figure 12.1, but you may be able to add to the list.

It is clear from Figure 12.1 that professional or paid caring relationships are not the same as family or friendship relationships. When people fail to realise the differences, there may be various dangers for clients and carers.

Dangers of confusing friendship and family with caring relationships

Treating clients like children

Some people are used to caring for infants. It is good to do everything for infants, to protect them and to use baby-talk when you speak to them.

Sometimes clients are treated as if they are in need of infant care – even if they are 84 years old! Carers may speak in a high-pitched voice, talk slowly and say things like 'Come along now, pops. Shall we put our little slippers on?' This kind of talk does not show respect for clients. Many clients think that they are being patronised or that their dignity is being insulted.

In care	Family or friends
You may work with different adults or children each day.	Always the same people - you will know them well.
You might work with 30 or 40 people in a home, or even up to 300 people on different days in day care.	Most people have a small number of family and friends that they meet regularly.
The clients can change – if you work with young children, they grow up and leave. Older people move to other services. Older clients may die.	Friends and relatives can stay constant for long periods of your life.
You have to work with the clients during a shift – you may have to talk with them.	You don't have to meet with friends – you can even decide not to talk to your family.
You can't pick who you want to help.	When making friends, you can choose who you want to have a relationship with.
You are required to listen to others and give them your help, even if you do not enjoy their conversation and behaviour.	You listen to your friends because they will listen to you. You may help friends because they may also help you, or because you enjoy being with them.
You must be able to work in an anti-discriminatory way. This means you must be able to work with people who are different from you, and have different opinions.	Your friends and family can be people like you. All your friends may share your opinions and views on life.
Young children may be vulnerable because they don't understand life. Older people might be vulnerable because they are in pain, or are grieving, or are ill, or are not in control of their lives. You may have some power over the quality of clients' lives. The way you act will affect them.	Your friends and family may be no more vulnerable than you. You may feel that you and your friends are all equal in status and power.
Your clients may not necessarily be attracted to you or like you.	Your friends like you and want you to be with them.
You need constantly to develop communication skills.	Your family and friends probably accept you even if you are not skilled at communicating.
You must work within a professional set of values (see below)	Your friends and family will have their own rules (or norms) about how you behave together.

Figure 12.1 The differences between relationships

Carers sometimes treat clients as if they were children because that is the only kind of relationship that they know. In other words, carers have helped young children using baby-talk and then they think that this is the way to help everyone who needs help.

Figure 12.2 Baby-talk encourages infants to talk. When used to communicate with older people, it may encourage them to say things you would rather not hear!

Losing an emotional attachment or bond with clients

We become attached to family and friends and would be upset if anything bad happened to them. Many people feel as if their family and friends are part of them. When carers first build a professional relationship with clients, they may start to attach in the same way. But clients grow up, they move to other services, they fall ill and some even die. Carers who make close emotional attachments to the people they work for, may experience a great deal of stress – those working in a nursing home could regularly suffer bereavements, for example. Therefore emotional commitment has to be limited.

Clients becoming over-demanding

We expect to meet the needs of our family and friends. A commitment to a sexual partner might be without limit. Without limit means we would do anything, give our time, spend our money, take risks, in order to help our partners if they were in difficulty. If we behaved in the same way with

clients, we might soon become 'drained' of our energy and resources. For example, suppose you gave your phone number to several lonely clients in the community. They might ring you at all hours to tell you about their worries. You would not be able to live your own life because of all the demands they might make on you. Caring relationships have to have limits to them.

Figure 12.3 Be careful who you give your phone number to!

Clients becoming dependent

If you try to make everything right for some clients they can be very grateful, but they might also become dependent on you. You might change jobs, or go on holiday, and when this happens your clients may not be able to cope without you. It is important that clients continue to be as independent and in control of their lives as possible. Doing everything for people might create problems for them in the long run.

Careworkers discriminating against some clients

In a friendship, you choose how and when you help people. If care work seems like mixing with friends, carers might stop providing quality care. Instead, carers might decide to discriminate between clients and give a better service to the people they feel most friendly with. It is very easy to feel more attracted to some people than others. If this attraction influences the service care workers deliver, then they will discriminate against some clients.

Figure 12.4 Treating clients as friends may result in discrimination

---

Careworkers not seeing clients as people

Normal friendships are pleasant and rewarding. We enjoy being with our friends. Some clients have needs which mean that they are not always exciting or pleasant to work with. Some children are badly behaved, some adults can be demanding and difficult. If carers expect a kind of friendship, they may be disappointed. When carers find people unrewarding, stressful and difficult, it is easy to stop seeing them as human beings.

In the 1970s people with Alzheimer's disease were labelled as 'dements' (they had dementia). If they walked about a lot, there was even a label called 'a wandering dement'. Meeting a 'wandering dement' sounds like something that would happen in a game of dungeons and dragons – not in a hospital or nursing home with real people. Other people were labelled according to their illness, for example, 'Oh, he's a heart attack'. This type of labelling dehumanises people.

Some carers try to cope with not having friendship-type relationships with clients by forgetting that people are beings with feelings. If you don't work

with real people, you don't need to think about your relationships with them.

What is different about a caring relationship?

If we make emotional attachments to clients, it puts us at risk emotionally. But if we see clients as not being real people, we will put them at risk. There has to be a better way of coping with the carer-client relationship. Part of the answer is to understand caring as involving a caring role.

Caring roles

Roles are the characters played by actors when they are on stage. A role is everything that a character is supposed to do and say during a play. As soon as actors are out of the audience's view, they stop playing their parts and return to their normal ways of behaving. As long as actors can be seen by the audience, they must only do and say things that the audience would expect from the characters that they are acting.

Being a carer is not the same as acting out a play. But the idea of role means that there are fixed

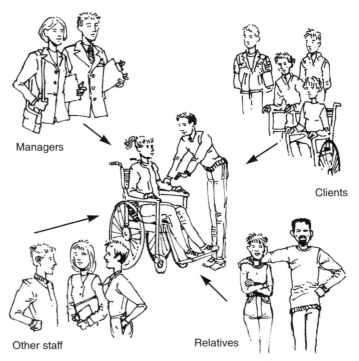

Managers

Clients

Other staff

Relatives

Figure 12.5 Other people have expectations of how you should behave in care work. Their expectations create your role

expectations of things that you must do and things that you cannot do. You will have a **role-set** of people who have expectations of you. For most carers this role-set will mean that managers, other care workers, clients and relatives of clients will expect them to behave in certain ways, i.e. to act out a carer role, not to act in the same way as a friend or relative would act.

Each care job may involve differences in the detail of what managers, other staff and clients expect from you. Learning your role is something you might need to do on every placement or new job. There are some general expectations of care roles, though. Carers must try to provide practical care, making sure that they:

■ do not discriminate between clients because they are more attracted to some than to others
■ maintain confidentiality
■ encourage clients to control their own lives and make choices
■ show respect for clients and value their individuality
■ display good communication techniques which help clients to maintain their self-esteem
■ understand the boundaries of their role.

Role boundaries and knowing what to do

Knowing that there are limits to the caring role may make caring easier. Some professions make the idea

of role straightforward by providing a uniform. A district nurse is in a nursing role when he or she wears the uniform. If the nurse is in ordinary clothes, then he or she is not in the caring role at that time.

However, in some care situations uniforms may create too formal a statement about role. Being in a care role might be like mentally putting on a 'uniform', however once you are at work, you have to meet other people's expectations.

Boundaries

A boundary is like a fence – it marks where your role ends. You can think of a boundary as the line between your role and ordinary relationships.

> A boundary is a line which you go up to – but should not cross over.

Boundaries of the care worker role clarify what you should not do. Deciding on the boundaries of your role means that you need to decide the limits of what you can do and what you should refuse to do. If you are at work, or on a placement, then understanding the boundaries of your care role may be an important task. Setting boundaries may help you to feel safe and comfortable with the pressures that the careworker role might place on you.

Figure 12.6 With friends we say what we think

In the care worker role we have to meet other people's expectations

Try it

If you are at work or on a placement, discuss the boundaries of your care role with your supervisor. Try to check out the limits of your responsibility.

Whether you work with children, people with learning disability, or other adults, there are some general boundary areas. You need to decide:

- how much time it is right for you to give clients
- how far you should become emotionally involved with clients' needs
- how far you should tell your clients about your own life history, lifestyle and feelings
- how much practical support you should provide for certain individuals.

Checking care plans may help you to clarify some of these issues.

How clients respond to care

Dependence

A caring relationship often means that one person feels a certain responsibility for the other and one person has a dependence upon the other.

A baby is totally dependent upon others for everything he or she needs. As children grow older they are expected to become less dependent. This is a long process, as every parent will know. Children take very little control over their lives. For example, if children are getting ready to go to school it is likely an adult will have to remind them several times to 'brush your teeth', 'remember your homework' and so on. If such reminders are not given, the children are likely to become 'side tracked'. This is because they are not old enough to take responsibility for themselves.

As we grow older we have to control our lives more. While people will often help out in an emergency, we have to think about our needs and make sure we can provide for them ourselves.

Think it over

What do you have to remember before setting off for school, college or work?

You probably have to think about how you are going to travel, how much money for bus/train fares, the time you will need to set off, etc. You will have to think about where you will eat during the day. Will you take a packed lunch and if so, have you the ingredients and time to make it, or will you buy something, and have you enough money?

These are the sort of everyday decisions adults make automatically. We take it for granted that we are independent and so have responsibility for ourselves, and that with responsibility goes choice.

Think it over

Is it possible, even as adults, to choose to do exactly what we want?

It is not usual for most people to be able to do exactly what they want. We normally have to consider other people's needs and wants. This is because although we may be responsible adults, we all live alongside others and how we behave affects other people. We give to others and receive from them. We accept that they have a right to their own views and we to ours. This is known as **interdependence** – depending on each other.

Interdependence is a state of cooperation and consideration of other people's views. Each person has an equal amount of power in the relationship.

It is important that carers and those receiving care balance their relationship so that each has individual rights and a share of power in making decisions. In a caring relationship the client and the carer both have needs and rights. A psychologist called Maslow listed the basic needs which we all have:

- enough suitable food and drink
- to be able to get rid of waste products from the body (eliminate)
- to be able to breathe
- to live at a comfortable temperature
- rest and sleep
- to be clean and healthy
- to have suitable clothes
- to feel safe
- to be free from pain
- to communicate with other people.

These are needs which carers may have to help their clients to achieve. Each person will vary in how he or she wants to be cared for, so it is important that carers ask clients how they like things to be done.

Most people will like to do as much as they can for themselves. It is valuable to encourage people to be independent, even though it may take longer for the client to do a task than for someone to do it for them.

Try it

You will need a toothbrush, face cloth, soap and toothpaste for this activity. Working with another person from your group, take it in turns to wash each other's hands and face and clean the other person's teeth. If this is not possible, imagine how it would feel to do this exercise.

Make the following notes:

a Did the 'carer' talk to the 'client', asking such questions as 'Do you use soap for your face?', 'Is the water warm enough?'

b Did the 'carer' tell the 'client' what he or she was about to do, for example, 'I am just going to clean your teeth, is that all right?'

c Did the 'carer' do things differently to how you do it yourself?

d How did it feel, or might it feel, to have someone doing such personal tasks for you?

For most adults it is a very strange experience to have someone perform personal services such as washing them or cleaning their teeth. It is useful to remember how this feels when meeting a new client. Everyone will approach things differently and it is important for clients to have such things done in the way they prefer. It is likely that some tasks will be very intimate, such as taking clients to the toilet or bathing them. If you felt slightly embarrassed about someone washing your face, imagine how you would feel, for example, if you had a disfigurement and someone new came to help you. Carers must never criticise a client's disability and must always consider the dignity of clients and respect their privacy. You can do this by encouraging them to do as much as they can for themselves and making sure the rooms in which they bathe, wash and use the toilet are private. This means that no-one is likely to come in without first knocking and waiting for an answer, and that conversation from inside the room cannot be heard outside.

A carer is someone who looks after other people and this may be as a job or because the person needing care is a relative or friend. In either situation both sides of the relationship must be considered. If the carer is looking after a relative or friend he or she is likely also to have an emotional involvement.

Think it over

Why might a parent caring for a child with spina bifida have more difficulties than a care worker?

There are several reasons why a parent caring for a disabled child may have more difficulties than a care worker. Very often parents are carers for 24 hours a day, seven days a week. People working as carers only do so during their working hours, then they have time off from that particular client/client group.

It is also likely that parents caring for their own child will have emotional responses. They may feel guilty that they have 'made' a child who has a disability. They will probably worry about the future when the child grows up and they are old. Who will care for the child when they are no longer able to do so? They are likely to compare their child with other children of the same age and feel hurt that their child cannot do the same things or have the same opportunities.

These emotional pressures will make caring for the child more difficult and tiring for the parents than for a care worker.

Try it

Read the following case study and comment on Elizabeth's emotional involvement:

Elizabeth is married with two children in their late teens. She has always lived close to her parents and seen them several times a week. Her parents helped out when her children were young and always took their holidays with Elizabeth, her husband and children.

Her mother, who had always run the household, died two years ago and Jack, Elizabeth's father lived alone until he had a stroke. After an initial period in hospital, the doctors say he no longer needs medical care and will be discharged although he is unable to walk, is incontinent of urine and diagnosed as having dementia.

Elizabeth's husband does not feel he wants his severely disabled father-in-law living with them. Elizabeth refuses to allow her father to go into a residential home and moves into his home to look after him. Her two brothers and sister who all work full time relieve her by taking turns to stay with their father on Friday night and over the weekend.

How might Elizabeth's emotional state complicate her work of looking after her father?

Elizabeth is likely to feel torn between her desire to look after her father rather than have him go into care and her distress at having to leave her husband and children. Although her children are old enough to look after themselves and she understands her husband's reluctance to have her father living with them, it is still a situation where she feels torn.

She is also distressed to see her father deteriorating and becoming very frail. She must now carry out very intimate tasks such as putting on his catheter attachments. Her father has always been very dignified and scrupulously clean and it is distressing for her to have to change him when he is wet and dirty. Because he is demented, he does not seem to mind his incontinence.

Think it over

How can Elizabeth be helped to cope with the situation?

Before someone is discharged from hospital the services available should be discussed and a care package designed. This package should take note of the client's racial, cultural and religious background. Whenever possible the clients themselves should be involved in the planning. The carer should be given information about benefits and how to cope with the condition of the client. All carers are individuals in their own right and it is important to remember they have needs of their own. People who are caring for others must have time for a break, to do what they want away from the person they care for. This may mean a regular time each week or a longer spell which would allow them to go away for a holiday.

It is important for the carer to have someone to talk to about his or her emotional needs both during the care, before it begins and when it is finished. Talking things over will help the carer to feel someone is sharing the difficulties, even if the person is not doing anything physical, it will help the carer not to feel 'trapped'. It is very important for the carer not to become isolated, to maintain their own interests to try to keep fit and have time to relax.

Practical help is also important. Perhaps welfare assistants may be able to come to help get the client ready for bed or to bath him or her. If no lifting equipment is available, adult clients will need two people to be lifted safely. Services such as incontinence laundry collections and home helps are invaluable.

Finally, carers need to feel that they are appreciated and doing a good job. They must not set themselves impossible tasks. Sometimes caring can last a long time, so it may be wise to undertake less rather than trying to do everything and finding it impossible to do so.

Responses to care

As we saw above everyone begins life being totally dependent on others for survival and as we grow up, we gradually take on more responsibility for ourselves. Sometimes this is a chore. It would always be easier to walk into a warm home and have a tasty meal put in front of us at the end of a hard day's work. However, as adults, most people have to do much of their own domestic work.

This has two sides to it. Chores may be boring and can be hard work, but the person who does the shopping and cooking can decide what to eat. Someone living alone in a flat can choose when to clear up, when to do the washing and the cleaning. It is this element of independence – choice – that we value.

When we are fit and able-bodied, we are able to control our lives and choose how we live. However, if we are not, we may have to rely on others. When this happens, either because of an accident or illness or because we are ageing, the inability to take control for ourselves can be very frightening.

Figure 12.7 While we are fit and able-bodied we can control our lives

These feelings of being out of personal control can also grow out of proportion and cause great fear and anxiety to the client.

Think it over

If you were involved in a car accident which left you permanently unable to walk, how would this change your current lifestyle? Try to list the changes, and how you might feel.

The changes it would bring would depend on your present living and working circumstances, but undoubtedly it would mean major adaptations to your lifestyle and a great dependence on others.

You might feel:

- confused
- frightened
- threatened
- trapped
- hopeless
- suicidal
- lacking in energy, motivation
- hostile
- craving for alcohol or drugs
- powerless.

Think it over

We all have ways of coping with stress. Some strategies are short term, others are long term. The box below lists some short-term strategies – try to add to them.

- crying
- withdrawing

Other short-term strategies you might use are:

- sleeping
- denial
- diversional activity – i.e. doing something else in the hope that the problem will go away
- anger
- aggression
- abuse of alcohol, cigarettes, drugs
- eating/not eating
- spending money
- humour.

These are called short-term strategies because if they continue for too long they will cause problems for the user. We all know the feeling of being fed up and deciding to treat ourselves to a new compact disc or pair of jeans, but if this went on for long we would soon run out of money. Similarly a night out and a few drinks may temporarily cheer some people up, but if they continue depending on alcohol, they may have long-term health and social problems. Even using humour to laugh about our problems does not necessarily help us to face them and solve them. Many of the people you may care for will have feelings of anger or despair. It is the carer's job to help people feel more positive about their lives and to enable them to develop long-term coping strategies.

Clients can be helped to think through possible courses of action, outcomes, risks and priorities. This can lead them to make decisions. Decisions should always be made by the client, not the carer. The carer's role is to spend time talking situations through with clients which will allow them to reach conclusions and make decisions.

Giving clients the opportunity to talk things through will also help them to come to terms with loss, to express their feelings and to think through emotional relationships with others. They will be able to choose a way to cope within their capability, using what skills they have.

If people are able to think through a situation and find ways to manage it, they will be able to accept the situation cannot be altered but that they are in control again. This means their self-esteem will be enhanced – they will value themselves and feel more able to deal with similar situations.

Long-term strategies include:

- seeking information
- talking to others
- exploring alternatives
- making plans
- setting goals
- learning new skills
- attempting to change the situation/ re-evaluating
- going for help.

Of course, some people going into care may do so with relief. If they have been living alone, unable to get out of the house and on a very low income, they may be relieved to know they will be warm and cared for and need not worry about bills or their safety.

If people have a high self-esteem, they will view receiving care in a balanced way. If they have had a successful life and rewarding relationships, while they will regret the change in their circumstances, they will be confident and assertive enough to deal with it.

People going into care may have a sense of relief at no longer having to take full responsibility for their lives. Even so, they may experience a sense of loss. They may feel that by giving up their home they will lose independence and self-esteem.

Think it over

If you had to leave your home and move into a residential setting, what would you choose to take with you?

Most good care homes invite people to bring some of their possessions, but obviously these are limited to the space available. It helps people to feel in control of their lives if they are able to take small items of furniture, special ornaments and most importantly, photographs. The way new residents are treated by the carers they first meet will make much difference to how they settle down.

Photographs can be a very good way for carers to start a relationship with a new resident. It will help them understand the person's past life and to know what he or she is likely to want from the new one. It is particularly important to recognise people's varying cultural needs, and if carers are unsure, they should ask and not treat everyone in the same way. Take time to listen to what the client wishes to say, or use silence if he or she needs to think through emotions.

For people to feel accepted in a new situation they may need to form relationships and eventually companionship with groups of people.

Try it

If you work or are on placement in a residential situation you may be able to ask a resident to tell you how he or she felt on first arrival. What or who helped them to settle in?

Types of support

The type of support that is available to people with disabilities will depend upon the area in which they live. Generally, towns are more likely to have a range of resources than villages.

The type of support someone may need will depend on the nature of their disability. When a person has a disability or becomes disabled his or her **p**hysical, **i**ntellectual, **s**ocial, **c**ultural, **e**motional and **s**exual needs (PISCES) must be taken into account when planning care.

Try it

Read the case studies and try work out what support each person is going to need. Remember that the disability does not just affect the person concerned, it may affect the whole family.

Rose

Rose is a 67-year-old widow living alone. She has had a stoke which has affected movement in her left arm and leg. She also has some difficulty eating and speaking. The village where she lives has no shops, and there is only one bus a day, which stops at the village at 7.30am to take people to a nearby factory.

Malik

Malik is 4 years old. He has spina bifida and some learning difficulties. He cannot yet walk and does not sleep well. During the night he wakes several times, which means his parents get less sleep than they need. He has a younger brother aged 2 and his mother is expecting a baby in three months. His mother takes him to a hospital school in the morning and brings him home in the afternoon.

Andrew

Andrew is 20 years old. He is paralysed from the waist down following a motor-cycle accident six months ago. He is now ready to be discharged from hospital to live at home with his parents. His father suffers badly from arthritis and his mother has a slipped disc.

Suneeta

Suneeta is 22. Since leaving school at 19 she has been unable to find work because of her learning difficulties. Apart from a slight coordination problem, she is physically fit, but bored with being at home all day. This is causing her to become frustrated and aggressive. Her father works; her mother does not speak English and seldom leaves the house.

Each of these people may need the following types of support:

- information – on social activities, financial help available
- financial – money to pay for care, transport, special equipment and other services
- physical – help with bathing, going to the toilet, feeding, etc
- social – group support and social activities
- emotional – the development of relationships with others
- intellectual – how they can learn and develop new skills.

Malik, for example, has his physical and emotional needs met by his family and school. However, his parents have another young child to care for and are expecting a baby. If too much of their time is taking up caring for Malik, the other two children may suffer. Their parents will not have the time or energy to play with them or help them with their learning. The parents may be short tempered due to lack of sleep and 'take it out' on the other children. Eventually, these problems may put their marriage under stress. As well as time with the other children, the parents need time together for their own recreation.

It might help the family if Malik could sometimes be cared for by others. This may be in a respite care unit or by specially trained foster carers. This would give his parents a rest and time to spend with their other children.

Because Malik is not yet able to walk his mother has to carry him. This is a difficult burden for someone who is six months pregnant. If the local authority's Education Department were asked, it might be able to arrange for him to be taken to and from school.

As he grows older Malik's parents will be able to claim an allowance for caring for him. This can be used to pay for extra help with housework or for sitters while his parents spend some time away from the family. They may also be able to claim mobility allowances and allowances for adapting their home to meet Malik's needs.

If Malik's family receives these types of help, his parents are more likely to be able to continue looking after him at home giving him the love and care he needs. If they are put under too much stress by not having financial, physical and emotional support the family may break down.

Effective interaction

Interaction means everything that happens between clients and carers. It includes communication and physical care. Good quality care depends on carers understanding and working within the *value base* for care. Values guide carers as to what is important in their work. Values help carers to decide what to do when they are not sure how to do their job or perform their role.

Values are particularly important in care work. People often receive health or social care services because they are vulnerable. Clients may often be afraid, in pain, unhappy, or just simply young and easy to influence. Care workers have to ensure that they follow five major principles or values when they work with clients. These values have been defined by the Care Sector Consortium and form the value base of National Vocational Qualifications in Caring.

The five areas of the value base are:

- to work in an anti-discriminatory way
- to support clients through effective communication
- to understand and acknowledge clients' personal beliefs and identity
- to support clients' rights and choices
- to maintain confidentiality.

These principles of caring should guide communication between carers and clients so that it is the client and not the carer who is important.

When we have conversation with friends, our thoughts and feelings are as important as theirs. In care work, the needs of the child, adolescent or adult with whom we are working are the most important. Children need to be encouraged to tell us what they feel and think. Older people might want to tell us about their lives. People who are sad or worried might wish to talk about their worries. The role of a carer is to listen, rather than to tell clients what they should do.

The five principles in the value base are intended to show how important the client is and to guide carers to put the needs of clients first. Carers should not take power over their clients and try to control them. Rather, carers should try to make clients feel important and valued. Clients should be empowered to control conversation and information as much as possible. **Empowerment** means that clients should be in control of their daily lives and activities rather than being dependent on a carer who controls them.

As well as being the principles of care, the five care values might be seen as steps which enable clients to become empowered during interactions with their carers.

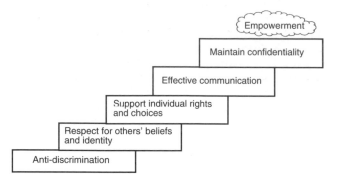

Figure 12.8 Five steps towards empowering clients

What the Patients' Charter says

The First National Standard in the Patients' Charter is:

'Respect for privacy, dignity and religious and cultural beliefs. The Charter Standard is that all health services should make provision so that proper personal consideration is shown to you, for example by ensuring that your privacy, dignity and religious and cultural beliefs are respected. Practical arrangements should include meals to suit all dietary requirements, and private rooms for confidential discussions with relatives.'

Source: NHS Patients' Charter

Anti-discriminatory interaction

Discrimination happens when a client receives poor service because of his or her race, class, religion, gender, age or sexuality.

Research has shown that we tend to be attracted to people who are similar to ourselves. We like people who are like us. It is all too easy for carers to be attracted to some clients and to discriminate against others. Some clients may be made to feel welcome, are given attention or good quality conversation, and other 'less attractive' or 'less similar' clients may get less time and attention because they are discriminated against.

Very often, carers discriminate without fully realising what they are doing. We can give body language (or non-verbal) messages that we feel nervous or that we do not want to be with someone. We may not realise that we spend less time talking to some people than others. We may not realise that the quality of our conversation is different when we talk to different people.

Working in an anti-discriminatory way is an advanced skill which involves becoming aware of and monitoring (or checking) our caring behaviour. A good way to do this is to discuss day-today care work with a supervisor or colleagues. The discussion could focus on the quality of interaction and practical work, and whether we were communicating with different clients in an effective and non-discriminatory way.

You can also avoid discriminating against clients by:

- avoiding the mistake of treating everyone the same
- watching out for stereotyped thinking.

Treating everyone the same

One common misunderstanding is the idea that if you treat everyone the same, then you are being fair. At first, this sounds like a good policy, but in practice it does not work because people are all different. They have different cultures, beliefs, religions, identities or self-concept. If everyone receives the same treatment, some people might be pleased and satisfied, while others might be angry or upset.

Think it over

Imagine that you are working in a day centre for older adults. Your clients include people of the Hindu, Buddhist, Muslim, Christian and other beliefs. It is lunch time and you are going to serve everyone a hot meal. If you treat all the day centre members the same, they will all be given the same identical type of meal. If, however, the meal consists of meat and two vegetables, it might be offensive to Hindu and Buddhist members and should the meat be pork, it would be offensive to the Muslims. Situations such as this have really happened and carers have said 'Well, if you don't want the meat, then don't eat it'. This is discriminatory because the beliefs of some people are being ignored, and they will not feel welcome.

It is important that carers should learn about the culture, beliefs and ability of the individuals they work with and that they should alter the way they behave to meet individual client needs.

Stereotypes

A stereotype is a fixed set of assumptions by which we classify things or people. We stereotype other people when we decide that we know enough about them to guess what they are like and how they will act. Sometimes a stereotype can become so powerful that it blocks our ability to understand and make relationships with others.

People who are vulnerable often become stereotyped. Homeless people may be stereotyped as untrustworthy. Older people are stereotyped as being stupid and childish. People with physical disabilities become stereotyped as having learning disabilities. People who have a learning disability are stereotyped as not having emotional attachments or needs. Stereotypes of race, gender, and religion also confuse carers.

Figure 12.9 People with physical disabilities may be stereotyped – stereotypes can lead to disempowering care.

Carers can check the common stereotypes that exist for the groups of people that they work with. Awareness of common stereotypes might help to ensure that carers do not allow stereotyped thoughts to affect their relationships with clients.

Effective communication

Carers often spend more time listening to clients than talking themselves. In friendship it is often 50 per cent listening and 50 per cent talking. In caring, the client's thoughts matter most.

Carers will try to learn important details about clients so that these can be used in future conversations. This shows that carers are trying to understand their clients. In friendship, this learning happens naturally. In caring, carers might have to make an effort to remember. Carers try to alter the things they say to show value for the culture and background of the client they are talking to. With some clients you might have to be formal to show that you respect them. With other clients you might be quite informal. For example, a formal approach would be 'Good morning Mr Nikolaus. Is there anything I can get you this morning?'; on the other hand, an informal approach might 'How are you doing, Liz? Do you want anything?'. Carers have to learn to vary their style of behaviour to show respect and dignity for each individual. Formal speech might sound 'snobbish' to Liz; she might think that you are trying to show that you are better than her. Yet Mr Nikolaus might be offended by informal speech – he might feel you had no respect for him.

As carers, we cannot behave just as we feel. We have to act out a role to meet the needs, including the emotional and social needs, of others.

The conversational skills needed for developing and understanding another person's identity, culture and beliefs are explained in Chapter 10. The important

point here is that carers use their skills to learn about the people that they are working with so that each person can be treated as. an individual. The act of listening to and valuing other people will help them to have the confidence to make their own choices in care. Conversational skill, along with an understanding of discrimination, may provide the first steps towards establishing a quality care relationship.

Using conversation to build self-esteem

It is important that carers become skilful in helping their clients to feel emotionally secure. This security comes from having a high level of self-esteem. You need to be able to observe people carefully to see what messages they are sending out, and to be able to respond to these messages. Since the messages will often be unspoken, the skill is in understanding non-verbal signs as well as verbal or spoken ones.

The best way to get an understanding of what other people are feeling is to attempt to see things from their point of view, to 'step into their shoes'. Before this is possible, however, it is a good idea to try to get a picture of how you feel you communicate at present, so you can begin to work on the areas that need improving.

Think it over

Opposite is a list of skills which people use every day in order to get along with people and feel good about themselves; in short, to have a good level of self-esteem. Read each skill carefully and give yourself a score.

- Score 1 if you are NEVER good at it.
- Score 2 if you are SELDOM good at it.
- Score 3 if you are SOMETIMES good at it.
- Score 4 if you are OFTEN good at it.
- Score 5 if you are ALWAYS good at it.

There are no right or wrong answers. It is only important that you identify your present level of skills and see where you can improve.

If you have a high score in points 1 to 3 you are well on the way to being able to demonstrate observational and conversational techniques to identify others' self-esteem needs.

Points 4 to 6 are skills that you will need when listening and using questioning to make information clearer.

Points 7 to 9 examine how you respect and value other people's individuality. It is important to realise that people may have different views and have a right to think differently. You may dislike their views, but you should still value them as people.

Your scores for points 10 to 13 will tell you how good you are at adapting conversations to meet others' self-esteem needs.

1 **Starting a conversation:** Talking to someone you do not know well about general matters (for example, the weather), and then moving on to more serious points.

2 **Carrying on a conversation:** Starting a conversation, carrying it on and responding to the reactions of the other person.

3 **Responding to contradictory messages:** Recognising and dealing with confusion when a person tells you one thing but says or does something which indicates something else (for example, if a child is jumping around obviously needing to go to the toilet, but says he does not need to).

4 **Listening:** Paying attention to what someone is saying, trying to understand and letting it be known you are trying.

5 **Asking for help:** Requesting help from someone who is qualified to help you handle a difficult situation that you cannot handle yourself.

6 **Being open to others' views:** Carefully considering others' opinions and views with your own, and taking a course of action that you feel is the right one.

7 **Expressing appreciation:** Letting another person know you are grateful for something he or she has done for you.

8 **Responding to anger:** Trying to understand why another person is angry and letting it be known you are trying to see his or her point of view.

9 **Negotiation:** Being able to reach an agreement with someone who has taken a different position to your own.

10 **Finishing a conversation:** Letting the other person know you have listened to what has been said and then skilfully and appropriately ending the conversation.

11 **Giving a compliment:** Letting someone know you like something about him or her.

12 **Expressing affection:** Letting someone know you care about him or her.

13 **Responding to others' feelings:** Trying to understand how another person feels and letting it be known you are trying.

Now that you have a good idea of how you relate to people at present, you can work on any areas that are not perfect!

Techniques for identifying others' self-esteem needs

When you are trying to build self-esteem in others it helps to ask yourself how you would feel in certain situations.

There are two ways in which you can tell how people are feeling. Most obviously, you can listen to what they tell you about how they feel. Second, you can learn to 'read' the non-verbal clues which people give you – their body language. Whenever and wherever you are with other people, you can practise 'reading' how they are feeling (beware, this can become a fascinating hobby!)

Building self-esteem and self-confidence

Carers who work within the value base for care are likely to meet the self-esteem needs of their clients. If clients are empowered to make their own choices, if their confidentiality is guaranteed, if they are shown respect and not discriminated against, then their feelings of self-esteem should be protected.

Maintaining self-esteem in conversation involves the techniques of listening to others, building an understanding of their needs, being non-judgmental, warm and accepting in your attitudes and being honest and sincere. These techniques were described in Chapter 10.

Both self-esteem and self-confidence can be built by clients if the carer empowers them to do this. A careworker cannot build someone else's sense of him or herself. Careworkers may, however, be able to influence the way others feel. Empowering care may help a client to build self-esteem and self-confidence.

Think it over

Leyla is a refugee. When she came to Britain she found it very hard to learn to write English. At first, she was excited about learning new skills and she thought that she would learn everything quickly. After about four weeks of study Leyla found that she still had a great deal to learn – she could

not write clear sentences and she began to think 'This is hopeless; I'll never learn to write English. It will take me years. Perhaps I'm no good at learning'. As soon as she became downhearted, she lost her self-confidence. Because Leyla was not confident in her own abilities it affected her sense of self. She compared herself to other people who had good written skills. Leyla's evaluation of herself was that she was a poor learner. She wasn't good at writing and this made her feel less valuable, a bit of a failure (a person with low self-esteem).

The Leyla met a teacher who understood her feelings. The teacher explained that she had also spent a long time learning English. The teacher listened to Leyla and explained that most people need a great amount of time and practice, and that it might be important to take one step at a time. Leyla started to do some simple written work, and she found that she could do it easily. Then she began to rethink her self-evaluation. 'Perhaps I can do the work if I follow this study plan. I might be good at learning after all. I was expecting it to be easy and that was the mistake'.

Leyla found that her written work improved. She enjoyed working with the teacher and she even started to help a younger boy who was having trouble learning to write. Because Leyla was skilled enough to help others, she began to think 'I'm good at learning – I'm a success'. Leyla began to feel self-confident and started to develop a sense of self-esteem.

People are strongly influenced by the successes or failures that they experience in life. Very often people label themselves as good or bad at certain skills. Self-labelling and self-evaluation can make us feel confident or unconfident. Leyla started to lose her self-confidence because things were not as easy as she thought they would be.

The teacher could not give Leyla self-confidence, only Leyla could do that. However, the teacher was able to help her to plan and study in a more effective way. By listening to Leyla the teacher understood that her pupil's expectations were unrealistic and was able to help her to lower them to an achievable level. The teacher helped Leyla to be successful. There is a saying, 'Nothing succeeds like success'. Once Leyla felt successful, she was motivated to try to achieve once again.

When Leyla started to help others, her self-esteem and self confidence was boosted and she was empowered to become very successful.

Effective interactions that build self-confidence usually require good listening and communication skills. Often they may also require special skills to help others to be successful. If you work with children or with people with learning disability you may be able to observe some of the skills that teachers and instructors use.

Respect for clients' beliefs and identity

Our identity is how we understand ourselves and make sense of our life in relation to other people and society. Each client may have a personal identity or concept of himself or herself. This personal identity or self-concept will be strongly influenced by the social experiences that the individual has had.

Support for individual rights and choices

Clients' rights include freedom from discrimination. Freedom from discrimination is a basic right in care situations, as it is elsewhere in life. Clients also have a right to dignity. This means that they are treated as being worthy of respect, and that their feelings are considered in the care they receive.

Some people are particularly vulnerable to loss of dignity because of the level of help they need from others. Infirm elders or disabled people may need assistance with many personal aspects of their care. It is important that the dignity of the client is respected when providing this care. Clients who feel that they are treated as though their feelings do not matter may find that their self-esteem is affected by their experience of care. Maintaining the dignity of clients in situations where they are dependent on others is a skill that carers need to develop, and it is a right of clients to have their dignity respected.

Choice

Being able to choose what we wear, how we look, what we eat, where we go, who our friends are – these are the ways that we express our self-concept or identity. When we were very young our parents may have made all the choices for us. If we felt attached to our parents, this may have felt all right. Our self-concept may have included our relationship with our parents. As we grow up, freedom to make our own choices becomes more and more important.

Think it over

Being able to choose your own lifestyle is very important when you become an adult. By 16 or 17 years of age most people want to control their own lives through their choice of clothes, food, music, etc. Parents sometimes have difficulty adjusting to this move towards independence. They still may wish to influence their children's decisions or control their choices. This can cause tension and stress.

Suppose you had become independent, lived your own life, but had become disabled. Imagine how it would feel if you had carers who wanted to make all your decisions for you; tell you what you could watch on TV, tell you what to eat and when to eat it. You might lose any sense of self-esteem that you had. You might lose your dignity and independence. Not being able to make choices might mean that you even lost your sense of who you were.

Children learn to become independent through learning how to make decisions. Adults need to be able to make choices about their lifestyle in order to preserve dignity and independence.

Carers need to empower clients to make their own choices and to control their own lives. Not to have choices is to be controlled by others. Being controlled by others is to be disempowered. Empowering care tries to help clients to make decisions and choices about their lifestyle.

Confidentiality

If clients feel vulnerable, if they are ill, or do not understand what is happening around them, they will need someone that they can trust to help them. How do clients know whether they can trust a careworker? The answer lies in a guarantee of confidentiality.

Individuals must be sure that they can talk freely and openly to a carer and that anything they say will not be repeated to others.

Figure 12.10 Without a guarantee of confidentiality the client may be guarded in what he or she says to the carer

Figure 12.11 You may never know who is listening – confidentiality is necessary to protect clients

Another reason why confidentiality is so important is to maintain the safety and security of clients.

I think it over

Imagine you are working in a nursing home and the doctor tells you that a client has a terminal illness, which he has not yet discussed with her. Because the information is not kept confidential, other staff and residents learn about the client's illness before the doctor has an opportunity to talk to her. She finds out about it from another resident. How do you think she will feel about receiving such information this way?

Confidentiality is part of the professional care role because it is needed to protect the emotional and social well-being of clients.

Confidentiality is also important if clients are to be free to choose their lifestyle and control their lives. It is hard to be independent if everything you do is monitored and checked by others. Clients have a right to see what information is kept about them and to privacy and independence.

Freedom from discrimination, effective communication, respect for others' beliefs and identity, maintaining individual rights and choice,

Figure 12.12 Clients have a right to privacy

and confidentiality – all contribute to empowering clients in care. Empowerment means giving control to clients, making them feel valued and worthwhile. Empowering care gives clients a sense of dignity and self-esteem. Clients who are empowered will be able to enjoy the company of their carers, make independent choices about daily living activities, and trust care staff with confidential, personal details.

Disempowering care

Try it

How many of the five care values are ignored in the following interaction, which takes place at 7.30 am in a resident's bedroom in a rest home?

Carer: Morning, Mabel, let's have you up then, come on.

Resident: What time is it?

Carer: It's 7.30 – time you were up and dressed for breakfast.

Resident: I want to stay in bed.

Carer: Now come on, don't give me a hard time. I have to get you up, just like everyone else. They'll say I'm not doing me job if you stay here, and I'm not having that. (*Lifts resident to side of the bed*). Right now, what dress shall we have today? The blue one, that would look nice – let's help you into this.

Resident: What's for breakfast?

Carer: Bacon and egg, same as always – something nice eh, I wish someone would wait on me and get my breakfast.

Resident: I don't eat bacon!

Carer: Well, you ought to be grateful – you don't have to eat it you know. Here, you're not one of those nutty ones who don't eat meat, are you? I hate all those moaners, never pleased whatever you do for 'em, meat's too good for 'em, that's what I say.

Resident: Nurr......

Carer: Right now, I'll wash your face and hands, it will be quicker, I haven't got all day you know. After that, I'll put you on the loo while I help Rose downstairs. (*Shouts down the corridor*) I'm just putting this one on the loo, I won't be a minute, Rose.

This is not a pleasant way to wake-up! The client has no power, the carer does everything and decides everything. The client is disempowered. Did you spot the ways in which the client is disempowered?

1 **Discrimination:** The client may not like bacon because of her ethnic customs, religious or moral beliefs. People who do not like meat are labelled 'nutty ones' by the carer. The carer is discriminating against people who do not think the way she or he does. The carer is also being very oppressive by forcing opinions on a powerless client.

2 **Effective communication:** The communication consists of orders from the carer and self-opinionated comments. It fails to value the client and ignores what she thinks or wants. In the end, the client is reduced to groaning 'Nurr.....'

3 **Respect for others' beliefs and identity:** There is no evidence of respect. The client is accused of being 'nutty'. She is not allowed to stay in bed; although part of her past identity may have involved getting up late. The client's routine is not respected.

Finally, the client gets put on the toilet while the carer helps Rose. This must be a shock to personal identity and dignity. The client is treated like an object rather than a person.

4 **Rights and choice:** The client's rights are not respected, and they have no choice. She has no dignity, and is ignored, for example, by being pulled out of bed against her wishes. The client is not given any independence and has to follow the carer's routine. The client has no choice of what to wear or to eat for breakfast. Everyone gets bacon and egg.

5 **Confidentiality:** The client has no right to privacy. The carer shouts down the corridor that 'this one' is being put on the toilet. Going to the toilet is now a public event – the client is denied any privacy or confidentiality for her personal body functions.

All five care values were disregarded in only a few minutes of interaction. If this were to go on through the day, the client would have a very poor quality of life. Some people might suggest that she would have little to live for.

Care using the five value areas:

Carer: Good morning, Mabel. How are you feeling this morning?

Resident: What time is it?

Carer: It's half-past seven. Do you feel like getting up for breakfast yet?

Resident: No, I want to stay in bed a bit longer.

Carer: That's all right. Shall I come back in half an hour?

Resident:	Mummmm.....
Carer:	See you later. [*Later*] Good morning, Mabel. It's 8 o'clock. Are you ready to get up now?
Resident:	All right.
Carer:	What would you like to wear? There's the blue dress or the white one – the yellow top and skirt – what do you think?
Resident:	Don't know.
Carer:	Well, would the blue dress be good? It matches the colour of your eyes, you know.
Resident:	(*Laughs*) Come on then...... What's for breakfast?
Carer:	Well, there is bacon and egg.
Resident:	I don't eat bacon.
Carer:	Oh, I'm sorry, I forgot you don't eat bacon, there's lots of things you can have – toast or cereal, or fruit, coffee, bread and marmalade. What would you like?
Resident:	Don't know.
Carer:	Well, we'll go through the list when we get downstairs.
Resident:	Toast.
Carer:	OK, toast. I'll make sure you get some toast. Would you like to wash now or later? Would you like me to help you? Do you use a flannel? Let me see if I can find it for you.

In this interaction the carer has time for the client. Her needs are understood and she is not discriminated against. Communication is effective, the client's beliefs and identity are respected. Because the client is respected, she makes her own choices. There is no breaking of confidentiality.

The empowering interaction shows how care work can help clients to keep and build their self-esteem. The disempowering interaction showed how clients can have their self-esteem and self-confidence taken away from them.

Empowerment – putting the client first – is an important goal of all care work

Try it

Watch a video of care practice or keep a logbook on daily practice in your placement or work setting. Try to record examples of good practice, i.e. carers checking that they are not discriminating against some clients, effective communication; respect for others' beliefs and identity; and offering personal choice.

Describe a piece of work which shows effective empowering interaction.

Ways to protect clients' confidentiality

There are various practical steps which carers can take in order to protect clients' confidentiality.

Record-keeping

Clients have a right to see any records that you write about them as a careworker. The law tries to protect privacy and dignity by preventing organisations from keeping records on individuals without their knowledge. The Data Protection Act 1984, The Access to Personal Files Act 1987 and the Access to Medical Reports Act 1988 require that people have access to (are allowed to see) records kept about them.

It is essential that anything written about clients or recorded on computer databases or disks is factual and unbiased. Clients have a right to know what is recorded about them. If you are keeping records, you should check your recording skills with your supervisor. It is important for carers to develop good communication skills when writing notes so these might be used by other staff and can be seen, if requested, by clients.

Try it

Find out about developing good communication skills in Chapter 10. Read about confidentiality in assignment work in the Introduction.

Passing information to other people

The Care Sector value base (or '0' unit) states that the confidentiality of records and information should be discussed with clients wherever possible. Some clients may not wish their relatives and friends to know about their finances or their medical details, or even to know about day-to-day life details. Wherever possible, careworkers should discuss how records are kept and what they can and cannot pass on to other people as far as clients are concerned. Sometimes a resident in care or a patient in hospital might want to talk to their relatives directly rather than have a care worker or nurse talk to them.

Figure 12.13 Residents and patients may prefer to talk for themselves

However, it is important to know a client's wishes and not simply to answer any question that is put to you.

Information should only be given to people who have a 'need to know'. Your colleagues, supervisors and managers may need to know what has happened with individual clients. Otherwise, you should maintain a client's confidentiality when talking to other people such as neighbours, unless the client has given you permission to speak to them. Carers have to be careful what they say and who they say it to.

Security and passing on information

As a care worker, you may have to answer phone calls or meet strangers who ask you for information. If you are unsure who someone is, never pass on confidential details such as a client's address. If pressed, explain that it is your policy (or the organisation's policy) not to give confidential information.

On the other hand, you might receive a phone call from a social worker requesting information. If you

do not know the social worker, you should always say that you will phone him or her back at the office with the information. That way you can check the caller is genuine. You cannot be sure of identification over the phone. Your caller could be lying.

Equally, if a visitor came into the building and made enquiries about a client, it would be vital that you had proof of his or her identity and that you were sure the person had a right and need to know before you disclosed anything about your client. If in doubt, you could ask the visitor to meet the client or to speak to your manager.

Written and computer-based records should also be kept in a secure place where they cannot be read by unauthorised people. This usually means in a locked office or locked cupboard, or an IT system protected by a password.

If clients know that their wishes are respected and their security needs are respected, they are more likely to trust you and to feel empowered.

Boundaries to confidentiality

Client's security, their right to choose who knows about their details, their dignity and their trust in you all depend on your ability to keep confidential the things that they tell you. Confidentiality is part of the care-worker's role, just as giving clients choices is part of the role. But these values of confidentiality and choice are not absolute rules that should govern everything we do!

Think it over

Imagine an older client decides that you should not go home at the end of your work shift, but give up your free time to stay and talk to him or her. Do you have to do what the client wants, because you have to respect his or her choice?

Obviously not! You would never have a worthwhile life if you spent every day trying to fulfil the wishes of others. Care workers have to empower their clients, but not at the expense of making their own lives miserable.

There have to be boundaries to the care worker role. Care workers have to respect the beliefs of their clients, but they have a right to their own beliefs and identity. Care workers do not have to share the beliefs of their clients. This would be outside the boundaries of the care worker role. Care workers have to try to meet the choices and provide choices for clients, but they do not have to do anything a client wishes – that would also be outside the boundaries of the caring role. The same is true for confidentiality. Confidentiality has boundaries – limits – in care work.

Values and ethics

Values explain what is valuable. The five care values which lead to empowering care explain what is important when we work out how to provide a service to clients. In real life the care worker role can be very complicated. Each person we work with has different needs. Different age groups have different needs. People have varying emotional and cultural needs. Every work setting is different. It is almost impossible to meet individual needs simply by following rules or by obeying orders from someone in authority. Each day carers may have to make individual decisions as to how they should speak and what they should say to each client. The values guide our decisions, but they do not always explain exactly the action that we should take. For example, when we are not sure of the boundaries to choice or confidentiality, we have to work out what we should do – this is called **ethical decision-making**.

Ethics are about working out what is right and how we should live and work. Although we know that we should give clients choices and keep information confidential, we may still face problems when we actually start to work with clients.

Working out the boundaries of confidentiality

Think it over

You are working with older people in a rest home. You have built an empowering relationship with one of the residents who likes and trusts you. One evening he says, 'I can trust you can't I? If I tell you a secret, you will keep it confidential, won't you? Only I've been saving all my tablets – I've got these pains and I don't want to go on. When the time is right, I'm going to take all of the tablets and kill myself. I wanted you to know why I'm going to do it.'

Would you follow the empowering value of confidentiality unquestioningly and keep the resident's secret? Would you let him commit suicide, or would you decide it was right – ethically right – to break confidentiality?

Ethical questions are not always easy to answer. In this case, the answer is that you should break confidentiality and tell the manager of the home about the tablets. The reason is that confidentiality has a limit or a boundary to it. If you are told that someone may do harm to themselves or to others, then this information lies outside of the boundary of confidentiality. The carer's role means that you must report the danger.

Ethically, the carer's role requires you to protect the health and well-being of clients. This responsibility can conflict with the need to keep things confidential, but the duty to protect the client's life is more important than the general principle of maintaining confidentiality.

> The caring role requires that you should report information about risk of harm to a client or to others despite the need to maintain confidentiality.

There is one other reason for breaking confidentiality. This reason is that carers have rights too. How would you feel if a resident put you in the situation where you knew he or she intended to commit suicide, but then tried to make you powerless to do anything? Is this fair on you? You might also be at risk professionally – you might lose your job, or fail to get a good reference if you do not protect the health and safety of clients. You have a right to protect yourself, and this right has to be considered when making ethical decisions with respect to the boundaries of confidentiality.

Your right not to know

Sometimes a client might start to tell you about a particular worry, for example, that he or she gets picked on or about a serious family problem. You realise that you may have to pass on the information. Rather than listening to the details and then worrying about confidentiality, you might decide to raise the issue with the client: 'Well, look, this sounds as if your social worker should know about it. I think you should tell him, but if you tell me all about it, I may not be able to keep it all confidential. Are you sure you want to tell me the details?' In a situation like this, the client can decide to tell you everything knowing that it may not be kept confidential. Or he or she may prefer that the situation should be kept confidential, and therefore stop the conversation.

Ethical decisions

Think it over

1 Suppose you work with an older person who tells you 'My son in-law takes my pension every week, but don't tell anyone. He might stop my daughter from visiting me and I couldn't bear that.'
You need to ask yourself whether there is a risk of harm to the older person or to others. You might decide that the older person is at risk – she is being financially abused. The older person is vulnerable to her son-in-law's behaviour and the situation would need careful handling. You would have to be very careful who you spoke to about this problem. Your manager might be the only person you could share the information with.

2 Suppose a young child tells you that his adult brother may have stolen some money.
Is there a risk of harm to the child or to others? There does not seem to be a risk for the child or any obvious risk of future harm to others. The information you have been given may not even be correct. Unless you have more information, it may be best not to repeat stories that you hear from clients.

3 Suppose an adult tells you that she is seriously worried about her marriage and thinks she may have to get a divorce.
Is there a risk of harm to the adult or to others? Again, there is no risk – the adult may become very upset later, but the information should be kept confidential.

4 Suppose a patient in hospital tells you that he is in severe pain, but that he wants you not to let anyone know.
Is there a risk of harm to the patient or to others? There might be. The pain could be a sign that some serious problem is developing, or it might just be in the client's mind. This is a difficult situation.

What to do in difficult situations

We can usually work out what to do when issues are straightforward. Very often, however, real-life problems are not simple or straightforward. Even the examples above become less clear cut if more detail is added to them:

1 The older person lives with her son-in-law and her allegation cannot be proved.
2 The police have just interviewed you about thefts in the area.
3 The adult tells you that she feels suicidal.

When situations are not straightforward, it may be important to explore them with tutors, supervisors or managers. In order to avoid breaking confidentiality, you might be able to describe a situation without actually identifying a client.

Ethical decision-making can be very complex – the important thing to understand is that the care role has boundaries and that not all information can be kept confidential.

Evidence collection point

Write a report describing caring relationships and how a caring relationship differs from other forms of relationships. The report should describe the ways in which clients respond to care and the role of effective interaction in caring relationships.

You should also explain the importance of confidentiality in health and social care settings and the ethical issues which can arise when dealing with clients.

You might find it easier to write this report if you have had placement or work experience. You may be able to use log book evidence to explain the issues in relation to your own practical experience.

The report will contribute to the evidence indicators for Element 4.3.

Summary

The following topics covered in this chapter may help you to prepare your report:

■ a list of differences between care-worker relationships and relationships with family or friends
■ some dangers of confusing care and friendship relationships
■ the idea of care roles and role boundaries
■ dependence in clients
■ independence and responses to care
■ types of support
■ the value base for care – effective interaction and empowerment:
  – anti-discriminatory interaction

- effective communication
- building self-esteem and self-confidence
- respect for clients' beliefs and identity
- supporting individual rights and choices
- confidentiality – reasons for it
■ disempowering care versus empowering care
■ confidentiality, record-keeping, passing information to others
■ boundaries to confidentiality
■ values and ethics
■ the boundaries of confidentiality and ethical decision-making.

Fast Facts

Anti-discrimination Practical work which aims to stop members of particular age, class, cultural or other groups from receiving a lower standard of service than others.

Appearance How we look. People use different clothes, hairstyles, cosmetics and adornments to express their membership of particular age groups, class groups, cultural and friendship groups.

Assumptions These are ideas which we assume to be correct but which we haven't checked. In care work it is very important that we do check our ideas about other people and their needs. Wrong assumptions can lead to the breakdown of conversations and to the breaking up of groups. They can also be discriminatory.

Baby talk Adults use a high-pitched voice and slow down their words when talking to infants. Adults may also use exaggerated facial expressions – baby talk may help to keep an infant's attention.

Body language This is the language of non-verbal communication, messages we send with the body. It consists of signs that other people can read in the way our body looks, or the way it moves. Non-verbal communication has a slightly wider meaning than body language. 'Non-verbal' covers everything which is not actual words (for example, tone of voice). Body language focuses on the way the body, face, eyes, hands etc. look and move.

Body movements The speed and type of people's movements can send a vast range of messages. We can interpret tension, anger, attraction, happiness and many other emotions by watching how people move their hands, eyes, head and body.

Boundaries A boundary may represent a line that you may go up to, but must not cross. Boundaries divide areas into different sections. In practical care work, boundaries define the limits of a carer's role.

Caring This describes being concerned about, interested in, and giving attention to others. The *caring professions* all require respect for the individuality, the rights and dignity of others. The ability to use conversation to 'value' other people is a central caring skill.

Confidentiality A care value and part of the NVQ value base. Confidentiality means keeping information that you have about others to yourself; only sharing it with individuals who have a 'need to know'.

Culture The customs and ways of thinking that people learn define their culture. It is the social learning that influences how people understand themselves, and so has a very important influence on how people explain their own individuality. Differences in culture lead to non-verbal messages being interpreted in different ways.

Dependence Having to rely on others in order to maintain physical, social or emotional well-being. People can also become dependent on drugs as aids to daily living.

Devaluing Stereotyping the views and beliefs of others as worthless or ridiculous. Devaluing a person's culture and beliefs can undermine his or her personal development.

Disability A physical or intellectual impairment which has an impact on the life of the person suffering from it. A person who is described as disabled may be prevented from doing only a few things by reason of the disability itself, but prevented from doing many more because of social factors.

Discrimination Treating a person or group in a different way from others. Discrimination can be either negative or positive; but when used on its own, the word usually refers to negative discrimination, which is to treat certain people less well than others.

Distance Distance is one of the things to look for when trying to interpret other people's non-verbal messages. Distance has no fixed meaning, but in some cultures, standing or sitting close can mean affection or love, anger or aggression, fear, or difficulty in hearing one another! Standing or sitting back might mean feeling comfortable or feeling separate. The cultural setting and other communications help us to work out the best interpretation.

Emotional support A general term, used to include listening and conversational work to support other people's individuality and self-esteem.

Empowerment Giving power to others. Using your situation to enable other people to make their own decisions and to control their own lives.

Ethics   Moral principles and moral theories which aim to guide decision making in complicated and difficult social situations.

Ethnic group   A group whose members share a common culture which is broad enough to influence all areas of individual and family life.

Exclusion   A form of discrimination which operates to prevent certain people from gaining access to resources and services.

Eye contact   This happens when people's eyes 'contact' each other and send non-verbal messages. Eye contact is important in both individual and group communication. Turn-taking in conversation often relies on eye contact. Messages of interest, attraction, affection, hostility and many other emotions can be sent by eye contact alone.

Facial expression   The face is an important area of the body for sending non-verbal messages. Even line diagrams can convey instant meaning to people. Facial expression is often easier to control than our eyes. Much non-verbal communication using the face is conscious if not always deliberate. People think about their faces and control them.

Funnelling   This involves planning questions so that they narrow or 'funnel down' to the central question you really wanted to ask. Funnelling is an advanced interviewing skill which is useful to develop. Funnelling is very useful when planning questionnaires because it enables the questioner to get the other person to think carefully before coming round to the really important questions.

Gender   The role associated with people of a particular sex. Sex is defined biologically as male or female, whereas gender is defined socially by the behaviour of individuals.

Gestures   These are non-verbal messages sent (mainly) with the arms, hands and fingers. Gestures are especially sensitive to cultural interpretation. A hand-signal can mean 'everything is fine' in one culture, and can be a serious insult in another.

Groups   In social care a 'group of people' means people who feel that they belong together. They will share some common purpose, common culture, or common values.

Group formation   Groups take time to build a sense of belonging. A collection of people will probably be very cautious at first. There is often tension until people feel that they belong – that they share common values. Once people feel that they all belong together, the group may work well.

Group values   These are shared beliefs which everyone agrees with or supports. Respect and value for other people's individuality, using supportive communication, preventing discrimination and encouraging choice and control in others are caring values.

Independence   Freedom from dependence on others. The right to choose and control one's own lifestyle.

Individuality   This is a general term covering the sense of self that people develop from culture, religion, gender, age, race, social circumstances and their own physical and intellectual nature. Individuality is everything that makes the individual special. Recognising individuality is a necessary starting point for creating equality or a feeling of being equal. Recognising individuality involves not making assumptions about people.

Interest   Communicating interest is a step on the way to building an understanding of other people during conversations.

Labelling   Identifying individuals as members of a particular group, whether or not they see themselves as members. Labelling is linked to stereotyping, and people are expected to conform to the behaviour associated with the stereotype with which they have been labelled.

Listening skills   The ability to build an understanding of another person's views when expressed verbally. Listening skills may include reflective listening, questioning skills, ability to understand non-verbal behaviour, ability to show respect for others, use of silence and self-monitoring skills.

Meshing   When the contributions to a conversation link in a smooth and effective way, they are said to mesh. They fit together like links in a 'wire mesh' fence!

Minimal prompts   Prompts are used to keep people talking by offering an answer to a question such as 'Well, did you enjoy it?'. A minimal prompt will be a short 'nudge' or 'idea' to try and help someone answer a question, such as 'OK', or 'What now?'. Non-verbal signals may also be used as minimal prompts, to try to keep the person talking.

Mirroring   Not to be confused with reflecting! Mirroring is when a person copies another person's non-verbal messages. A person who is attracted to someone may copy their way of sitting or standing when talking to them. For example, a person may cross his or her legs if the other person has crossed legs. Successful mirroring sends the message: 'I'm like you', or perhaps 'I like you'.

Monitoring own behaviour   This is a really important

skill for developing caring abilities. Monitoring involves reflecting on your own behaviour and on the reactions of other people. It involves thinking about what is happening within group or individual communication.

Muscle tension   This is one type of non-verbal message. Tension can communicate messages about the other person's emotions, especially when linked with body posture. It is something else to look for when trying to understand other people.

Observational skills   Observation of others will involve trying to understand their appearance, verbal and non-verbal communication. Observational skills may imply the ability to monitor own and others' behaviour.

Obstacles   Things that get in the way. Obstacles to communication include physical difficulties, failure to understand the context or background to the message, or emotional reasons for failing to understand.

Pace of communication   The speed of a person's conversation. Speech that is too fast or too slow can be hard to understand. Some people may require you to speak slower than normal so that they can understand your everyday speech.

Paraphrasing   Putting another person's words into your own words. Part of reflective listening.

Personal space   This is an area of space out of which an individual tries to keep other people. It can be seen as the distance between people when they communicate with one another. Like many non-verbal messages, distance is used in different ways by different cultures. How close people stand will depend on their culture, their feelings for one another and the physical and social situation.

Pisces   Needs can be described as physical, intellectual, social, culture, emotional and sexual. Together the initials of these words spell PISCES.

Pitch   The degree of high or low tone in someone's voice. A high-pitched voice is used in baby talk.

Posture   This is the way a person positions his or her body. Posture usually sends messages about the individual's degree of tension or relaxation. It can also send all sorts of social messages, such as: 'I'm really interested', 'I'm bored', 'I don't want to be here', and so on.

Probes and prompts   A probe is a very short question like: 'Can you tell me more?' which follows an answer to a previous question. Probes try to dig deeper into the person's answer, they probe or investigate what the person just said. A prompt is where you suggest a possible answer, 'Was it good?', 'Did you enjoy it?' Prompts try to keep the other person talking and get him

or her to add to previous answers. Probes and prompts are both useful ways to improve skill in asking questions.

Questioning   This is an important skill for keeping a conversation going. Questions can be open or closed. A closed question is where the kind of answer required is simple and fixed. 'How old are you?' is a closed question because the answer has to be a number – once you've said it there is little else to say. 'How do you feel about your age?' is open because the other person could say almost anything – how long they speak for is 'open'. Giving a short quick number is a 'closed' reply. Closed questions are of limited use in working with people. Open questions are often much more valuable for building an understanding.

Race   The idea of a group based on biological differences between people. In practice, a person is often assigned to a particular race on the subjective impressions of others, not on the basis of easily measured biological differences.

Race Relations Act 1976   An Act of Parliament which made discrimination on the grounds of race illegal.

Reflective listening   This is a care skill which involves either using your own words to repeat what another person said, or repeating the words exactly, or using non-verbal messages with silence. The idea of reflection is to use conversation like a mirror, so that the other person can see his or her own thoughts reflected. They can then be altered more easily.

Responding skills   Use of verbal and non-verbal communication to respond to others. Responses may use reflective listening, questioning and skills focused on understanding the other person.

Role boundaries   Boundaries to the commitment or duties involved in a 'caring relationship'.

Self-confidence   An individual's confidence in his or her own ability to achieve something or to cope with a situation. Self-confidence may influence and be influenced by self-esteem.

Self-esteem   How well or badly a person feels about himself or herself. High self-esteem may help a person to feel happy and confident. Low self-esteem may lead to depression and unhappiness.

Self-disclosure   This happens when we tell other people about our own experiences, thoughts and feelings. Some self-disclosure can be useful when trying to understand others. It can create a sense of trust .

Sensory contact   Touch, smell, vision, hearing or other sensations which give us information about other people.

Sex Discrimination Act 1975 An Act of Parliament which was designed to prevent discrimination on the grounds of gender.

Sexuality An expression of a person's sexual preferences. Heterosexual people prefer relations with people of the opposite sex. Homosexual people prefer relations with people of the same sex as themselves.

Silence Silence is a useful part of some conversations. Sometimes silence is better than just talking to fill a gap. It can provide an opportunity for feelings to be expressed non-verbally.

Sincerity This involves being real and honest in what we say to others. Without sincerity, warmth and understanding usually break down or 'go wrong'. Honesty with clients is an important part of relationship and supportive work.

Social context A setting where social influences affect an individual's learning and development.

Status A measure of the power or prestige of a person. Status helps to define how people are treated by others and how they see themselves.

Stereotyping Judging an individual to be a certain type of person by his or her appearance or behaviour. A stereotype is not a description of a real person. It is a collection of characteristics which members of a particular group are expected to possess. People who have been stereotyped are expected to behave as 'typical' members of the group to which they have been assigned.

Stress A physical condition. Symptoms may include tiredness, irritability, lack of clear thinking, difficulties in sleeping and physical illness.

Tone of voice Voice tone is the sound of the voice, rather than the words that are spoken. The tone of someone's voice can send messages about attraction, anger, sympathy and other emotions. Because voice tone is separate from spoken words, it is classed as 'non-verbal'. The sound of our voice is separate from the word messages we send.

Touch This is another way of sending non-verbal messages. Touch can be a very important way of saying 'I care', or 'I am with you'. Touch can be interpreted in various ways. It can send messages of power and dominance, and can be sexual as well as caring. The important thing is how a person understands touch, not what you intend.

Understanding An important goal of caring is to learn about other people's individuality. It is necessary to build

some understanding so that you correctly communicate respect and value.

Values Beliefs about what is valuable. Values provide the context or setting for further ethical decisions about what should be considered right or wrong.

Value base A system of values to guide the care profession. The NVQ value base is defined in the NVQ '0' Unit. This covers the promotion of anti-discriminatory practice, the maintenance of confidentiality, the promotion of individual rights and choice, the acknowledgement of individuals' personal beliefs and identity, and the support of individuals through effective communication.

Verbal communication Spoken messages – messages which use words – are 'verbal'. The opposite is non-verbal communication, which means messages sent without words. Non-verbal language is often harder to understand than verbal language.

Warmth This expresses the feeling that exists when people respect and value each other.

Self-assessment test

1 How could you best show that you are listening to someone else?
   a By asking them closed questions.
   b By telling them all about your own thoughts.
   c By having good eye contact and reflecting back things they had said to you.
   d By asking them to evaluate your conversational skills.

2 Which of the following questions is an open question?
   a Do you like salads?
   b What do you think about today's menu?
   c How much did that lunch cost you?
   d What days do you eat here?

3 You are asking questions about a menu. Which of the following statements is a prompt?
   a Do you think the food is fairly priced here or not?
   b What made you decide to eat here today?
   c Can you tell me more?
   d Is the food expensive?

4 Someone who is angry with you is likely to use:
   a Eye contact, involving looking away from you, and slow speech.
   b Fixed eye contact and fast, loud speech.

c Varied eye contact and quiet speech.
d Slow speech and eyes focused on the floor.

5 When talking to a baby many adults use:
   a A high-pitched voice and slower speech with exaggerated facial expressions.
   b Fixed eye contact and quiet speech.
   c Fixed body postures and minimal prompts.
   d Open questions and reflective listening.

6 Which of the following behaviours best sends a message of being interested in another person when sitting down and facing him or her?
   a Staring at him or her.
   b Leaning forward a little, head at a very slight angle, varied eye contact.
   c Sitting with arms crossed, legs together and head back.
   d Sitting at an angle, only looking at the person while he or she is speaking.

7 Which of the following shows respect and value for the other person?
   a Remembering details of a person's chosen interests, achievements and lifestyle, and using them in a conversation with the person.
   b Asking a person what his or her self-esteem needs are.
   c Reflecting back details about having a difficult journey to work.
   d Using prompts and probes

8 A person is supposed to be joining in a group discussion, but he is sitting behind a large desk that he could have moved and is some distance away from the others. What message does this send?
   a He is an active member of the group.
   b He is of very high status.
   c He does not want to join in with the group.
   d He will be able to use verbal communication more effectively.

9 Deciding that a person belongs to a particular group because of his or her appearance or behaviour is known as:
   a Discrimination.
   b Stereotyping.
   c Exclusion.
   d Labelling.

10 The stereotyping of individuals can lead to discrimination against them. Which of the following best describes stereotyping?
   a Expecting a person to behave as a typical member of the group to which he or she appears to belong.
   b Refusing to give information to a person because of his or her colour.

c Ridiculing a person's beliefs.
d Treating a person's opinions as worthless.

11 Discrimination means:
   a Giving someone misleading information.
   b Treating a person less well than others.
   c Assuming that someone belongs to a particular group.
   d Taking care to treat people according to their needs.

12 A health-centre receptionist behaves in a hostile way towards a black client, and discourages her from seeking an appointment. This is an example of:
   a Labelling.
   b Stereotyping.
   c Indirect discrimination.
   d Direct discrimination.

13 A care worker always speaks loudly and uses simple language when addressing older clients. Which of the following best describes the care worker's behaviour?
   a The care worker is being sensitive to her clients' needs.
   b The care worker is making stereotypical assumptions about her elder clients.
   c The care worker is treating her clients as individuals.
   d The care worker is trying to help her older clients to come to terms with their situation.

14 People in some groups often find that their opinions are regarded as unimportant or worthless by members of more powerful groups. Which of the following best describes this sort of behaviour?
   a Stereotyping.
   b Exclusion.
   c Direct discrimination.
   d Devaluing.

15 There is legislation to prevent discrimination in the job market. However, discrimination in employment is not illegal on the basis of:
   a Gender.
   b Age.
   c Race.
   d Ethnic origin.

16 The Equal Opportunities Commission was set up to help prevent discrimination on the basis of:
   a Disability.
   b Race.
   c Gender.
   d Sexual orientation.

17 Paid caring relationships may be different from friendship relationships because:

 a Friends never get upset or criticise you.

 b Clients are always difficult to talk to.

 c You have to work within a care role and meet client needs; with friends you can choose how to behave.

 d Clients make demands on you whereas friends never ask for help and support.

18 An older person in respite care might respond positively to the services offered. Which of the following represents a positive response?

 a Sleeping most of the time.

 b Screaming and swearing at staff.

 c Arguing with other residents and complaining about them.

 d Saying how relieved he or she is to be with the staff.

19 Which of the following represents empowering behaviour from staff?

 a Helping a person into a wheelchair because it is quicker to get them to the dining room that way.

 b Helping someone to get dressed because otherwise they take too long.

 c Choosing food for someone who can never remember what he or she wants.

 d Asking a client if he or she would like help when getting up in the morning.

20 It is most important to preserve confidentiality because:

 a Otherwise clients may complain.

 b Confidentiality is necessary to preserve trust and protect clients.

 c Because you should never pass on information about a client to anyone else.

 d Professionals always keep everything confidential.

Communication

If you want to work with other people, you will need good communication skills. Communication is a core skill needed for many careers. Most people have to be able to express their ideas in words and images, and understand other people's ideas if they are going to be successful at work.

> **Communication** is about getting your ideas across to other people and about understanding other people's ideas.

Understanding other people and exchanging ideas with other people is a central skill in all care work. You will be using communication skills all the time if you work in a health or social care setting.

Communication involves talking and listening to individuals and talking and listening within group discussions. Communication skills include being able to write so that your meaning is clear. Communication can involve the use of diagrams and sketches, photographs, tables and other images which can help explain your ideas.

Carers need to be able to produce clear and accurate reports and records, so it is essential that you have good reading and writing skills. Carers must also be able to understand and make sense of other workers' reports.

Communication is the sending and receiving of information and messages, a two-way process.

Face-to-face communication

Listening and talking skills are so important in care work that Unit 4 explores the specialist skills which paid carers may often need. Professional carers do not simply send and receive information when they talk to other people. A skilled carer uses a whole range of techniques to understand another person.

For example, suppose you saw a nurse 'chatting' to a patient. Most people probably think 'Oh, he's just having a chat, nothing to it – anyone can do that'. If the nurse is a skilled communicator, however, there is probably a whole range of skills being used.

To start with, the nurse will need to remember who the patient is and his or her situation. The nurse will need to remember any previous conversation he or she has had. The feeling of remembering all this detail might be like 'switching on' to the patient. The nurse might click on to his or her memories for this person.

Next, the nurse will need to understand the other person's body language and eye contact. This is a skilled job also. Details of non-verbal communication can be found in Chapter 10, but in summary it includes the following:

- eye contact
- body posture
- facial expression
- body movements
- muscle tension
- gestures
- tone and speed of verbal communication
- touch.

Figure 13.1 Communication is a two-way process (Winged Fellowship Trust Images of Caring Competition by Ian Ferrie)

The nurse will need to understand all of these types of unspoken communication in relation to the situation and remember what he or she knows about the person and his or her culture.

Next, the nurse will need to monitor or check that his or her own behaviour is communicating respect and value to the other person – this is part of the **value base** for care. The nurse will have to keep adjusting his or her non-verbal and spoken communication until he or she is sure that this respect is coming across to the other person.

When the nurse asks questions, he or she will have to start with friendly 'safe' questions like 'How are you feeling today?', 'Do you have any pain?', 'How did you sleep last night?'. Skilled use of questions will help to get the conversation going. Even more importantly, the nurse may need to use skilled reflective listening, and the occasional silence, if the patient is going to trust him or her.

As the conversation develops, the nurse may be able to pick up on things the patient says such as, 'So your family hasn't visited for three days now'. The nurse might be able to use summaries of things that the patient has said. Summarising what people say and reflecting it back to them, will help a carer to check his or her understanding.

Within three or four minutes the nurse may be able to communicate respect and value to the patient and to learn that the patient is upset because he or she has not seen a particularly close relative recently. The nurse cannot put this right, but he or she can help the other person to decide what to do – perhaps the patient might want to phone the relative. By spending time with the patient, the nurse is able to make him or her feel better.

The nurse makes the patient feel better because of skilled communication. Some people never think about communication skills and are never successful

Figure 13.2 Examples of skilled and unskilled discussion

in developing them. Their conversations may not always be interesting or worthwhile.

You may have watched people when they visit others in hospital. How many people cannot manage to listen to others or keep the conversation going?

Evidence collection point

If you have studied Chapters 10 and 12 you may be able to provide evidence for discussion work in relation to the tasks suggested there. Another idea is to use work involving interviewing skills. Interviewing skills are explained further on pages 270–280. If you develop good interviewing skills, you will be able to demonstrate one-to-one discussion skills at level 3.

Group discussion

Taking part in a group discussion involves many of the skills needed for individual conversation. You need to be a good listener and be able to remember what people have said. Understanding non-verbal communication is as important in group situations as it is in one-to-one discussion. Being able to summarise and reflect things that others have said is also important. If you are talking to a friendly group of people, you will not always need to think about questions. Even so, understanding how open and closed questions may influence a conversation can be useful.

Group discussion is different from one-to-one conversation because you will often have more time to think about what you want to say and how you are going to speak. So group discussion is easier in this way. On the other hand, many people are less confident when speaking to a group.

Reasons why people find group discussion difficult

- You can watch the non-verbal communication of one person – it's hard to understand what a group of people might be thinking. You often worry that they might not understand or like what you are saying.
- It is not always easy to get a turn to speak – you don't always know when to talk.
- Arguing with one other person is easy; disagreeing

with a number of people can be frightening. Some people worry that they may be ignored or emotionally 'put down' in group discussion. Group pressure can hurt our sense of self-esteem and self-confidence.

So group discussion can be more difficult than one-to-one discussion:

> It is harder to understand the non-verbal communication of a group of people and there can be a fear of not being accepted or not getting on with the group.

Figure 13.3 Groups do not always help you to be confident

How to cope if you don't feel confident

Learning any new skill always involves some worry. Many people say that they are nervous before taking their first driving lesson. Learning to join in or even lead group discussions can be a scary experience at first. Like any new skill, you should find simple, safe ways to begin to learn it and choose a supportive instructor who can help you. If you try to learn in an easy setting, you may soon get the idea and feel confident. If you try to learn group discussion skills just in your everyday life, you may be lucky and you may become confident, but many people fail to develop confidence because day-to-day life does not always provide the right opportunities.

So, here are some ideas to help you to learn group discussion skills.

1 Practise group discussion with a group of friends or with a group of supportive people.

   It is important that you work with a group that has a caring value system. You need to feel that you will not be put down or criticised by the group.

2 Make sure you know about the topic that a group will discuss. You cannot join in effectively if you do not understand what people are saying.

3 Take time to listen to what other people are saying in a group before rushing in with your ideas. Try to link your ideas to what others have said, 'Well, like you were saying, I think we should do...'.

4 Watch what other members of the group are doing non-verbally; become skilled at understanding non-verbal communication.

5 If you have to give a talk to a group, plan your talk in advance. Try to think of an image (perhaps a photo or a diagram) that you could use to help you remember what you are going to say and to focus your talk.

6 If you are giving a talk, first explain your ideas to a supportive member of the group. This will help in two ways. First, it will enable you to remember what to say because you have said it once before. Second, he or she can give you advice and guidance on your talk. This may help to boost your confidence.

Think it over

Two group exercises which may help you to develop your skills are the matchstick game, to study conversation pace and turn-taking, and the fishbowl exercise, which looks at group conversation patterns. Both are discussed in Chapter 10. If you cannot remember these ideas, it may be worth looking back at them.

Giving a talk in practice

Anya has to give a short talk to her colleagues, which will be observed by her tutor. The talk has to focus on her placement work with younger children.

Anya decides to say something about her project on reading stories to the children.

At first Anya is worried; what can she say about the work? In order to feel confident Anya decides that she will need to plan the talk.

Planning

Anya looks at her log book and the notes she has made about the story-telling. She decides to take in the books from which she has read stories – just to show to the group. Anya thinks about the children. There is a photograph of the class at the school where she was working. Anya decides to ask permission to borrow the photograph so that she can use it as an 'image' when talking to her colleagues.

Anya then decides to share how she prepared the stories and to talk about how the children reacted to the stories.

Monitoring

Before the group discussion, Anya talks to one of her teachers. Anya explains what she will say and how the story-telling sessions went. The teacher says it sounds interesting and asks Anya a few questions. These questions help Anya to think about the talk in more detail. She decides that she will talk about the children and about two children who did not pay attention to the story. Anya also thinks of two questions she can ask the group about her work:

1 Have you tried reading stories to large groups of children and if you have, did all the children listen?'
2 Why do you think children don't always listen?

Anya's talk

Anya felt nervous at first and she slowly explained where she worked. She described how she came to be invited to read to the class, how the teacher discussed possible stories with her and helped her to practise reading aloud before doing it in front of the children. Anya showed two books to the group to make the session more interesting. She then showed the class photograph and explained how it felt to be reading to the class. (Anya was careful not to talk about the needs of individuals so as to maintain confidentiality.)

At this point, several members of the group became interested and started to explain how they felt when they worked with children. Anya began to feel that it was her talk and she became confident enough to summarise what some of her colleagues had said: 'So you all felt nervous at first', 'So you went quiet when you tried to talk and the teacher asked you to speak up.'

Anya then decided to ask her questions. The group agreed that it is hard to keep children's attention. They became involved in discussing reasons why children do not listen; perhaps the stories do not relate to the children's background or culture; perhaps there were other interesting things going on.

At the end of the talk Anya's tutor went over the standards for Communication Element 2.2 with her. They both agreed that she had produced evidence for discussion skills. Anya had made relevant contributions, to meet the first performance criterion. She had made contributions in a way that suited the audience and situation. She had summarised what other people had said in order to confirm that she had understood their contributions, and she had taken the discussion forward with her ideas.

Anya's teacher said that there was evidence toward level 3, discussion skills, and evidence toward Element 2.3, Use of images.

Anya felt pleased and confident. She decided to write notes about how the talk went, to link with her planning notes. She evaluated how her work met the standards. Anya then had evidence for the grading criteria as well.

Telephone conversations

Another area of communication which people sometimes find difficult is using the telephone.

Most people are familiar with using the telephone as a convenient means of keeping in touch with friends and family. When you know someone well it is easy to chat without being able to see him or her. You are familiar enough with the way the person speaks to be able to tell when he or she has finished talking and you can begin.

If you are talking on the telephone with someone you do not know, however, you do not have the advantage of non-verbal language to tell you when it is your turn to speak. When you are speaking face-to-face with people you can see their facial expression, you have eye contact, you can see if their bodies are tense or relaxed and you will each be positioned in relation to the other. On the telephone you will have to make do with hearing the speed and tone of the person's voice to give you extra clues as to his or her meaning.

Making a call

Many people are afraid of making business telephone calls. One of the reasons they are worried is that they fear they may forget what they intended to say. If you feel like this, it will help if you make a list of what you need to say before you dial the number. Then, if your mind goes blank with panic you can refer to your list.

When you make a business call, the person at the other end will not recognise your voice as a friend would, *so you need first to say who you are and then who you would like to speak to.* You should have your list of what you want to say, and it is a good idea to make quick notes of the replies. Always have a pencil and paper with you beside the telephone.

Try it

Here is an exercise on planning telephone calls. Write down some notes of the points you would need answers for.

You are a care worker working with young adults with physical disabilities. All these people use wheelchairs. There is a rock concert in a local sports stadium and a group of residents wants to go. Before a decision is made, it is necessary to find out if there will be access difficulties. Your officer-in-charge does not want to agree to the outing only to find the group cannot be accommodated and so risk disappointing them. You are asked to ring the stadium to see if a visit by your clients would be possible. Don't forget to ask about toilet and refreshment facilities and any fire regulations. Make notes of what you would say.

Sample conversation

1 Ask to speak to the concert organiser.
2 Say where you are from, i.e. where you work and your name.
3 Say you are ringing about the possibility of a group of people who use wheelchairs attending the rock concert.
4 Ask if there is wheelchair access to:
   a the stadium
   b the toilets
   c the refreshment areas.
5 Ask if there are any fire restrictions regarding wheelchair usage.
6 Ask if there is a maximum number of wheelchairs that can be accommodated.
7 Thank the person for the information. Remember to stay polite if the answers were not what you would want them to be. The person you speak to will probably not be responsible for making the rules, just for telling you what they are.

You can award yourself extra points if you asked if there was a group discount!

It is a great deal easier to make telephone calls which need answers to several questions if you make a note of what you need to ask in advance and the answers as you get them.

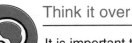

Think it over

It is important to reflect before making telephone calls in the same way as reflecting before speaking to a group.

Putting theory into practice

Helping clients make the most of their leisure time is a very important part of a carer's job. Because clients are likely to need many kinds of help it is often not possible to make plans on the spot. Often things have to be thought through in advance so that difficulties can be anticipated to enable outings to go smoothly.

It is important that clients are given as wide a choice as possible for holidays and activities. Carers can help by providing information and guiding towards suitable possibilities.

Think it over

What sort of restrictions might a group of physically disabled children come up against when planning a holiday.

The first consideration, whether someone is disabled or not, is the cost. We would all like to visit faraway places, but can it be afforded?

Other considerations will be access, distances, support available and the support needed.

Try it

You might like to do this test in a group. Visit your local travel agent and choose a variety of brochures showing different types of holiday.

Select a range of holidays and make some visual aids giving details and showing pictures. Some of the children may have difficulty seeing or reading, so you may have to change the wording in the brochures to suitable language which can be easily understood.

Using your information technology (IT) skills design a voting slip listing the range of holidays.

Make a presentation of the different choices to your group. Listen to their views and discuss ideas with them. After everyone has been given a chance to say what they think, ask them to use the slip you designed to vote for three holidays, in order of preference.

Now that you have the votes for preferences, you could use your IT skills to make a graph showing the choices.

Using the discussion from a group meeting, you could work out how to write a letter to a local agency asking for financial support for the children's holiday. Use the graphs, but remember to use a form of language suitable for a business letter.

Answering the telephone

Taking notes of what someone tells you when you are answering the telephone is vital. If you are busy, or a nervous phone user, it is easy to forget exactly what the message was.

When you answer the telephone at work you should immediately say either the telephone number or the name of the establishment. You should then say '.... speaking', using your own name.

The person calling will usually then say who he or she is. If not, you need to ask who is calling in order to give an accurate message about the call. An example might be:

> 'Good morning, "The Grange", Mary Knight speaking.'

> 'Good morning. This is Andrea Ahmed from Area Social Services. Could I speak to the officer-in-charge please?'

Below is a conversation between a care worker and a relative of a resident. The relative is in a pay phone-box and in a rush to leave a message.

Carer: Hello. 'The Grange', Mary Knight speaking.

Relative: Hello. It's Emma Brown's daughter. I can't stay on long, I'm on a pay phone. Tell her we'll have to cancel the hairdresser. I'm on the A27, broken down, think it's the fan-belt. Does she want to go tomorrow? I'm on afternoons so it would be after two and I'm going to the dentist at 4.30. It's up to her. Please ask her to make the arrangements and to telephone me at home tonight. My money's running out, I'll have to go. Bye.

In this situation your message could be something like this:

- Message for Emma Brown from her daughter.
- Daughter will not be coming this afternoon – her car has broken down.
- The appointment at the hairdresser needs cancelling.
- Does Mrs Brown want to go to the hairdresser tomorrow between 2 and 4.30?
- If she does, a new appointment will have to be made.
- Mrs Brown should telephone her daughter at home this evening to let her know if she wants to go to the hairdresser tomorrow and if an appointment has been made.

Try it

Compose a sample message you would write before making each of the two telephone calls outlined below.

1 You need to call the meals-on-wheels supervisor. Sam Kent has to go into hospital for two weeks (give the dates) and will not be needing his meals delivered. Give his address and say when he would like them restarted. He is having an operation for the removal of his gall-bladder and will need a special diet for a month after he leaves hospital. He would like meals on alternate days of the week beginning on Mondays. His family will provide the others and weekend meals.

2 Kim Havel has been waiting for a shower with ramp and rails for six months. Until it is installed the district nurse is having to call every day to bathe her. This is a waste of resources because she does not need medical care every day. You are her social work assistant and will need an exact date and time from the Area Housing Office so that the home help can be on hand to help move household effects for the builders to do the alterations.

Producing written material

Punctuation

Why do we bother to use punctuation? The answer is that we use **punctuation marks** – such as commas, full stops, apostrophes – to make what we write easy for others to understand.

A **sentence** will tell you something about someone or something. To be complete it must make sense. A sentence is a group of words which begins with a capital letter and ends with a full stop. It must have a subject and a verb.

Grammar

Some of the main parts of grammar are listed on page 256.

Try it

Which of the following is correct?

1 The film were good.
2 My present was exciting.
3 The puppies was hungry.
4 The kitten was sleeping.

- **Sentence.** This is words put together to make complete sense. A sentence must have a verb and a subject.
- **Verb.** A verb is simply a word which describes an action. For example, 'We *danced* all night' or 'I *wore* my uniform'.
- **Subject.** This is the name given to the noun or pronoun (see below) about which a statement is being made. In the examples above, 'We' were the people who went dancing and 'I' was the person wearing the uniform. 'We' and 'I' were the subjects of the sentence.
- **Noun.** This is the name of an object or person or place: cup, Indira, Australia. If the noun is a **proper noun** – i.e. the name of a town, country or person – it begins with a capital letter.
- **Pronoun.** A pronoun is a word used instead of a name such as him, her, or it. We often use pronouns when we are writing so as not to keep repeating the same word: 'It was Lee Ping's birthday. We gave *her* a present.' If we were to write a few sentences about the same person or object it would be boring to keep saying the noun, so we use pronouns sometimes.
- **Adjective.** This is a word which tells us something more about a noun we have used. For example, 'The old lady was *frail*', 'The weather was *bad*'.
- **Subject-verb agreement.** The subject of a sentence must agree with the verb. For example, 'We was all happy' should be 'We were all happy' because 'we' is more than one person – it is plural – so the verb 'was' should also be plural, i.e. 'were'.

The passage below has no capital letters or full stops. In fact it has no punctuation at all. Try reading it.

what is the difference between a playgroup and a school nursery they are both for young children they both prepare children for school by getting them used to mixing with other children whether children attend a playgroup or nursery they will have to get used to leaving their homes and parents for short periods the difference is that a nursery school will build definite educational aims into the activities the activities may appear to be unstructured and the children given choice but in the nursery the teacher will have developed activities to teach specific skills in the playgroup the children will be offered a range of similar activities but there will be more or less free choice and the outcome of the learning will not be formally defined children in a nursery school

attached to a primary school will also have the opportunity see the older children and get used to the idea of going to school full time when they are old enough they will become familiar with the building and the move from home to school will be easier.

The same passage is repeated below with the capital letters and punctuation inserted. It should be easier to understand.

What is the difference between a playgroup and a school nursery? They are both for young children. They both prepare children for school by getting them used to mixing with other children. Whether children attend a playgroup or nursery, they will have to get used to leaving their homes and parents for short periods. The difference is that a nursery school will build definite educational aims into the activities. The activities may appear to be unstructured and the children given choice, but in the nursery the teacher will have developed activities to teach specific skills. In the playgroup the children will be offered a range of similar activities, but there will be more-or-less free choice and the outcome of the learning will not be formally defined. Children in a nursery school attached to a primary school will also have the opportunity see the older children and get used to the idea of going to school full time when they are old enough. They will become familiar with the building, and the move from home to school will be easier.

As you can see, it is much easier to understand when it is written in sentences, and with the help of a few commas and question marks.

A **comma** is used to show a pause and to separate items in a list. It is also used to separate different parts or descriptions within a sentence – for example, 'The bride's wedding gown, which was a family heirloom, was made from silk and antique lace'. The sentence would still have made sense without the 'which was a family heirloom'. This part was giving more information within the sentence, but putting it between commas made the sentence easier to understand.

A **question mark** is used *instead* of a full stop when a question has been asked. It only comes at the end of a sentence, in place of the full stop, not in the middle.

Remember

Punctuation is to make writing easier to understand.

When we are speaking to others we do not need to be as grammatically correct, because we use other ways of showing our meaning. For example, we use our facial expressions, actions, body language and tone of voice. On the other hand, when we are writing something, the reader can only tell what you mean from the marks on the page, and so you have to be much more careful about making meanings clear. Do not risk being misunderstood!

The apostrophe

Another device which we use to give clues about our meaning is the **apostrophe.** This little mark ' is used in two *different* ways.

First, the apostrophe shows that a letter or letters have been **missed out** of a word. When we use the apostrophe in this way we put it where the missing letters would have been. For example, we sometimes shorten 'is not' to 'isn't', and in this case the apostrophe in 'isn't' goes where the 'o' would be in 'is not' if the full words had been written. In the same way, the apostrophe in 'I'm' goes where the 'a' in 'am' would be. Sometimes people put the apostrophe in the wrong place (or omit it all together) because they have not learnt this rule. Have you ever seen 'is'nt' or 'Im'?

The second use of the apostrophe is to show that something **belongs** to something else. For example, 'The care worker's wages have not been paid'. In this example the apostrophe is there to show that the wages belong to the care worker.

Note that if we were referring to the wages of more than one care worker, the apostrophe would be in a different place: 'The care workers' wages have not been paid.' The wages still belong to the care workers, but putting the apostrophe after the 's' shows that there is more than one care worker owed wages.

Think it over

Can you see that if this was written in a message from the Wages Department it would be important to the care workers to get the apostrophe in the right place?

Try it

Write out the two passages below, putting in possessive apostrophes.

1 Ten minutes walk from the towns centre, on ones way to the technical college, is Park Nursery. The Education Departments plan for this, the towns main nursery, is that it should be privatised and used for both visitors and students children. The fee charged would be according to the parents income.

2 'Hes lucky he could go to bed. Ive spent the night on the front room sofa and the last four or five hours trying to get in the bathroom. By the time I do manage to get in there Im feeling a bit sour at having all these people barging about the place, and forget to shoot the bolt behind me. It doesnt improve my temper when young Dorothy and Angela catch me without pants. This amuses them no end and I wonder if I cant arrange to fall downstairs and break a leg and give them a real laugh. A couple of proper horrors, Dorothy and Angela, twins, belonging to Auntie Agnes, one of my mothers sisters. I know the Old Lady cant abide them and she only had Chris ask them to be bridesmaids because she didnt want to get across Auntie Agnes whos one of them sensitive types who go through life looking for any offence left lying about for the taking.' – Stan Barstow, *A Kind of Loving.*

Remember

- Apostrophes show possession or omission.
- If in doubt, leave them out – you should never use them simply because you think an 's' looks lonely!

Relative clauses – or 'link words': who, whom, which, that

People often use the words 'who', 'whom', 'that' and 'which' to link two sentences such as in the following examples: 'There is the boy. He was hurt.' 'There is the boy who was hurt.' 'We have a dog. It chases cats.' 'We have a dog which chases cats.' 'I saw the women and their shopping. They filled the bus.' 'I saw the women and their shopping which filled the bus.' 'I met a girl. I knew her.' 'I met a girl whom I knew.'

Use 'who' and 'whom' for people. Use 'which' for things. Use 'that' for people or things. For example:

- **Who** – Was it Ann *who* won the prize?
- **Which** – The guinea pig *which* escaped from its cage, was in danger from foxes.
- **That** – It was the highest mountain *that* they had seen.
- **Whom** – The person by *whom* you were sitting is my husband.

- I like the curtains. They are in my room.
- Tom recognised the singer. He had sung on television.
- We saw the travellers and their luggage. They filled the train.

Writing letters and memos

You will often need to write letters as part of your work. A business letter needs to be written in a more formal way than a letter to a friend. If a business letter is not set out correctly, it may be delayed in getting to the correct person, or the reply you expect may be delayed. Figure 13.4 shows a sample layout.

23 Ramsey Street
Erinsburgh
Cheshire 1CV 6SJ

Your Ref: AS/md324
23 April 199–
Social Services Department
Town Hall
Summerbay
Cheshire 1FF 3AG

Dear Sir/Madam

Application for Ramp

Main part of letter . . .

Yours faithfully

[signature]

M Green

Figure 13.4 A typical layout of a formal letter

Practise letter writing by writing a sample letter to your local social services department. Write on behalf of an elderly gentleman saying you are his son or daughter. You have been asking the social services department to arrange for a wheelchair ramp to be put outside your father's front door. Until this work is done, getting his chair in and out is impossible without someone to lift it. Ask for a definite appointment for someone to come and assess what is needed. Quote the reference on the letter in Figure 13.4.

Sometimes messages within a department or company are written in the form of a **memo** (which is short for memorandum). This is a written message, like a letter, but because it is internal to the department or company it does not need to have addresses. Figure 13.5 shows an example.

MEMORANDUM

To: T Burnley

From: S Dontineni

Date: 3 April 9–

Subject: Wheelchair access

I attach a copy of a letter regarding arranging a ramp for this client. Please make an appointment to visit within the next week.

SD

Figure 13.5 Sample memorandum

Evidence collection point

Practise writing memos by writing one back to T Burnley from yourself saying you are on leave next week but have made an appointment for.... (state the date). You can use both the letter and the memo as evidence of correspondence.

Filling in forms

From the very minute we are born details about us need to be recorded. Whether a baby is born at home with a midwife in attendance, or in hospital, details of his or her weight, length, head circumference and family name are recorded immediately. Within a few days details of the time and place of birth and the parents' names are recorded on a birth certificate. This makes the child a citizen of the country in which he or she was born.

Think it over

You have probably filled in forms such as an application for a provisional driving licence, a family allowance form or maybe the back of a doctor's prescription to get your medication. Think for a moment about whether you had problems doing this.

Care workers will often be called upon to help clients fill in forms. For example, when someone goes into care the establishment needs to record that person's details in an organised way on an admission form (Figure 13.6). Below are details of a lady talking with a care worker. See if you can work out from what she says what details would need to go on the admission form.

ADMISSION FORM

Surname: Date of birth:

Forenames: Religion:

Home address:

Next of kin: Relationship:

Address of kin:

Telephone number:

General practitioner:

GP's address:

GP's telephone number:

Medication:

Diet preferences:

Wears dentures: yes/no

Wears spectacles: yes/no/for reading only

Aids used:

Figure 13.6 How an admission form might look

I came into the world on 19 June 1919. I was the youngest of six. I had two brothers and three sisters. Emma Webster I was born and Emma Webster I have stayed. I never had any children; I was always too busy helping with my nieces and nephews.

There's only me and our Alice now. My two brothers were killed in a mining accident and our Marjorie went to Australia to be with her son. We phone each other every day, me and our Alice – Alice Dixon as she is now. I had her number on my telephone memory button, Horbury 270509. Funny, I can remember things that happened years ago but I can't always remember things now, so I put her number on my phone memory just in case.

I had a lovely flat you know, in Water Lane, Horbury, number 10 it was. It had views of the river and everything, but it got that I couldn't manage the stairs with my Zimmer frame and the lift didn't work always. Our Alice lives just round the corner on The Wharf, 37, but she has a ground floor flat.

Dr Smith, lovely man, you know, Grove Surgery in Horbury, wanted me to have a hip replacement, but I said no, not at my age. I've never had anything, you know, except my teeth out. Apart from that it's only been visits to the optician. Funny, I can see things far away, but I can't see to read the paper or do my knitting. I have to have them when I go to church too, or I can't see the hymn book. I go to St Austin's Catholic you know.

We couldn't afford the doctor when I was young. We had to keep ourselves healthy eating the right food. We had none of this fast food. There wasn't much meat, but we had plenty of veg that we grew on the allotments. I don't believe in them laxatives or tablets, make you dopey half the time. No, I keep my system healthy eating the right food. The only tablets I take are those for my arthritis and I only have one of these before bed so I'm not kept awake with the pain.

Evidence collection point

Now you have read Emma's account, try to put the details on the admission form. You can use it as evidence for completing a preset form.

Writing your curriculum vitae (CV)

One document which you will almost certainly need to prepare is a **curriculum vitae.** This is a Latin name for a document which people send to potential employers when applying for a job. It gives all their personal details and information about their qualifications and experience. Figure 13.7 shows an example of how a curriculum vitae may be set out.

Evidence collection point

Prepare your own CV using a word-processor. You can use it as evidence both for completing outline forms and your word-processing skills (IT).

CURRICULUM VITAE

Surname: Singh

Forename: Parvees

Address: 69 Cumbrian Way, Summerbay

Date of birth: 4.3.78

Education:
1989–1994: Summerbay High School
1994 to date: Summerbay College

Qualifications:

GCSE	Grade
English	C
Combined Science	C
Mathematics	D
Childcare	D
French	E

Work experience:
I have worked for one year on a toffee stall in the market. I have to control stock, serve customers and handle cash. I am entirely responsible for the stall. I also babysit once a week for a child of three.

Interests:
I am taking the Silver Stage of the Duke of Edinburgh Award Scheme. I have undertaken an expedition which meant a group of us had to live for three days and two nights in the countryside. We had to cook our own food and walk each day. This taught me to cooperate and take responsibility for both myself and others.

For the Community part of the Award, I have been helping a family with a child who has learning difficulties. I have found it very rewarding to see the progress he has made. When I first began he could not speak, but now he will point to pictures and say small words.

I also enjoy swimming and playing badminton.

Figure 13.7 Example of a curriculum vitae

Introduction to reports

If you have been on a placement you will know that care staff have to keep notes, and sometimes write reports on their clients. You may not have to do this in order to achieve communication core skills at level 2, but it is worth looking at the structure and style of reports.

Most notes that you are likely to write have to be open for clients and their relatives to read. This means that carers have to be very careful to write accurate and factual statements that do not stereotype or label clients.

Before open access laws were introduced, notes could be kept secret. This meant that care workers could write whatever they wanted. Nowadays, carers have to check that they are not making assumptions and not labelling other people. The value base for care requires carers to show respect for other people's beliefs and identity. The value base also requires anti-discriminatory working and effective communication to support clients. Effective written communication must also show respect for clients (see Chapter 12).

If carers wrote anything they felt like, they might produce a report like this:

> 'Rose is confused and difficult to work with. She makes constant demands on staff in the day centre and is never satisfied. Rose is often rude and abusive to other members at the centre. She appears to have dementia and never concentrates long enough to take part in activities.'

This report stereotypes and labels the client as confused and demented, rude and abusive. Rose is said to be 'never satisfied', but there is no factual evidence to support any of these statements. Rose is said never to concentrate – but again that is only opinion; there is no factual evidence for the statements made.

Carers need to report in a style which:

■ keeps to the facts
■ doesn't stereotype, label or discriminate against clients
■ provides details and evidence of events.

An acceptable report

'During the past week Rose has complained three times that staff are trying to poison her. On two occasions she has claimed that she had no dinner, shortly after eating this meal.

Rose has had three arguments with other members of the centre this week. Two of the arguments were about eye glasses. Rose claimed that other people had stolen her's. On three afternoons staff have tried to involve Rose in activities, but Rose has refused to join in. Rose often looks worried, stressed or upset.'

This second report gives straightforward details of the events of the past week. The only interpretation and opinion is that Rose often looks 'worried, stressed or upset'. This interpretation is based on Rose's non-verbal behaviour. Words like 'worried' do not label people in the same way as 'demented' or 'confused'. Everyone has worries from time to time. Dementia implies a diagnosed illness, which puts Rose in a fixed category.

This second report provides information; the first report only provides opinions.

Think it over

When you report on events, are you able to report on facts and avoid stereotypes and labels?

Structure and style

When you write assignments, reports or design your own CV, it is important that you help your reader to understand your ideas. You will need to think about the way your work looks.

- Paragraphs will help to break up your points and help the reader to find ideas.
- Headings and sub-headings will help the reader to be clear about the content of your work.
- You might highlight words to emphasise their importance.
- You might use boxes around text to put emphasis on a point.
- You might want to use images to help the reader's memory. There is an old saying that a picture can be worth a thousand words.

Using images

A care worker often has to help people who have difficulty understanding spoken words. Their difficulties can be caused by many factors. They may not hear well, they may have a learning difficulty and not understand the meaning of some words, they may have had damage to the part of their brain which deals with language, following a stroke or an accident.

Whatever the cause of their difficulty, you can help by using as many means, besides words, as possible to get meanings across. This is called total communication.

Think it over

Make a list of as many different ways of communicating as you can think of.

You have probably thought of hand-signing, body language, sketches, diagrams, still photographs, graphs and perhaps more ways of communicating. It would be a good exercise to spend some time in a group of people not speaking and see if you can make yourself understood.

We often see diagrams, such as the ones on page 262, in public places. They are designed to convey information quickly and reinforce the written or spoken word. Before written language as we know it now was invented, people used to leave messages for each other by drawing what they had to say. Some of these are still in existence today. This is a very useful way of extending meaning where there is a difficulty in understanding or where people speak different languages. Diagrams are also often used nowadays to keep people's attention – for example, during a presentation where charts to illustrate what the speaker is saying are often used.

Evidence collection point

If you had to teach a skill to someone with little English, or who had a hearing impairment, you could do so by illustrations. Figure 13.8 shows an example of beginning to teach someone how to make buns using illustrations. If you choose a task, and produce a series of illustrations to teach it, you may be able to use it as evidence for your portfolio.

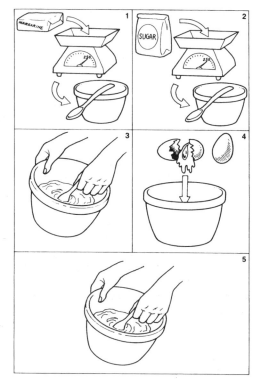

Figure 13.8 Using illustrations for making buns

Try it

Below is an explanation, written for teenagers with learning difficulties, to let them know what a key worker is and how they can be helped by their key worker. The first two examples have a small drawing beside them to help the person understand and remember what the written part said. Read through the information and draw symbols to show how you would illustrate the six sentences which are shown without a drawing.

 While you are at school your key worker will help you: in your learning both in class and in the group.

to make friends and learn to be a member of a group

... to keep in contact with your family and friends at home
... by listening to what you say and knowing how you feel
... by helping you to decide what you need for your life
... to arrange special times in your life like birthdays, holidays, and your free time
... to look after yourself and your clothes
... to look after your money and possessions.

These are the kinds of diagrams you might have produced:

  to keep in contact with your family and friends at home. (The telephone and envelope show the person that these are means of 'talking' with family and friends when they are living far away.)

 by listening to what you say and knowing how you feel. (The picture of an ear tells the client that the key worker is always – within reason – ready to listen to and try to understand his or her feelings.)

 by helping you to decide what you need for your life. (The picture of a figure apparently 'balancing' with its hands is meant to indicate choices, decisions which the key worker would help the client to talk through.)

to arrange special times in your life like birthdays, holidays, and free time. (This diagram reminds the client that on special occasions we don't always follow the same routine and the key worker will help to plan for different times.)

 to look after yourself and your clothes. (A picture of neat clothes reminds the client he or she will need to take responsibility for some aspects of care and the key worker will help with the necessary skills.)

 to look after your money and possessions. (A picture of money and a person keeping something close to the body reminds the client not to leave valuables around.)

Evidence collection point

Below is an explanation of a group meeting. Make a small drawing for each statement to help someone who has difficulty reading and remembering to understand the meaning of what is written.

- We have a meeting in each cottage every week.
- Everyone living or working in the cottage can attend the meeting if they wish.
- We have meetings so that everyone is able to share in making decisions about the cottage.
- As a member of the group, you will be able to put your ideas to the people at the meeting. You will be helped to put these ideas on a list called an 'agenda' by your key worker.
- Each week a different member is encouraged to lead the meeting. Someone will also take notes so that we can remember what has been agreed. The notes will be pinned upon the noticeboard and you will be given help to read them if you need it.
- We make a cassette of our meetings so if you would rather listen than read, you can borrow the cassette.
- If you feel that your ideas have not been fairly heard, you can complain to your key worker who will help you deal with your claim.
- We look forward to seeing you at our next cottage meeting.

When you have made your drawings to illustrate this information, you could use them as evidence in your portfolio of sketches produced to meet a specific need.

There are times when it is helpful for people to have something to refer to in the form of a sketch or diagram to remind them of what they need to do. Can you remember asking someone how to get to somewhere, and being given verbal instructions?

When we give people verbal instructions on how to get somewhere we are 'reading' a mind map, which is in our heads but not theirs. It seems perfectly simple to the person giving the instructions because he or she is familiar with the place, but to someone who isn't familiar it is very hard to follow if nothing is written, either in words or, better still, in the form of a diagram.

Evidence collection point

Below is a conversation between Sharon, a student on a placement at a community health centre, and a mother, new to the area, asking where the local hospital was so that she could take her child to an appointment.

Read through Sharon's directions and draw a map to direct the mother to hospital. You can use this map for your portfolio as evidence of drawing diagrams to illustrate points.

It's easy to get to the hospital. You just go down Drake Street, to the corner shop – what's its name – the dress shop? Lynn, what's that dress shop called? You know the one where you got that yellow dress in the sale last summer. Cor, did it? I bet you felt embarrassed. Did you take it back? Well I would have. I mean, sale or no sale you don't expect it to split first time on do you? Well, what's it called, then? Oh, yes, 'Inspirations'. Yes, that's it. Well you turn right at 'Inspirations' and then left again into another road. That's Green Street. I mean the road you get into after you turn left is. You turn left again in Green Street you see. The hospital is right at the end on the left. It's a big new building. Well, that's the front of it. You won't be allowed in there. That's only for emergencies. Out-patients have to go through the side entrance. That's in Green Street. Come to think of it, Greek Street comes out on to Drake Street further down just past Boots. You'd do better really to go down Drake Street to Boots and turn right just past it. Oh, you don't know Drake Street? I thought you'd have known that well, you know where the No. 3 buses go down? Oh, you don't know how to get there from here? Well you go out through the front door and turn right outside. Well, not exactly right because that goes into the swimming baths, but sort of crooked way right. Past the Bingo, well, when you come on to the road there's two roads come together opposite you. You take the right-hand one – right hand if you've got your back to the Bingo I mean, of course, and follow it down to Drake Street. You'll recognise Drake Street because of the traffic lights. You turn left in Drake Street and that dress shop I was telling you about is about a hundred yards down on the right and the hospital is just past it.

It's good thing it wasn't an emergency hospital visit. One of the main reasons people don't give clear directions is that they assume others know what they know. This is often not the case. If it were, the person asking would not need directions!

Using tables and charts

Sometimes information is displayed in columns arranged in a certain order. These columns (or tables) of information are useful for making comparisons. The information is easier to understand than it would be if it were all written out in sentences.

A care worker may use tables in many ways. An example might be of comparing how nutritious different foods are, or how to make up a bottle for a baby of a certain weight.

Evidence collection point

1 While Sharon Lee was on placement at the community centre she often had to help people read tables and charts. Below is part of a table on the back of a packet of dried baby milk.

FEEDING TABLE				
Approx. age	1–3 weeks	6 weeks	3 months	4 months
Approx. weight kg	3.5	4.5	5.5	6.5
lb	8	10	12	14
Number of feeds per 24 hours	5	5	5	5
Number of scoops per feed	4	5	6	7
Water per feed oz	4	5	6	7
ml	115	140	170	200

a How much milk should Sharon advise a mother to give a baby who weighed 4.5kg or 10lb?
b How many feeds a day would the baby need?

2 Another client, Mr Nicholaus, has been referred to the clinic by his doctor who has told him he is overweight. He is 1.75 metres tall and 40 years old. How much would Mr Nicholaus be advised he should weigh according to the table shown here?

WEIGHT CHART FOR MEN (in stones and pounds				
Height without shoes (m)	25 yrs+	23–24 yrs	21–22 yrs	19–20 yrs
1.52	9.12–8.3	9.11–8.2	9.9–8.0	9.7–7.12
1.55	10.1–8.6	10.0–8.5	9.12–8.3	9.10–8.1
1.57	10.4–8.9	10.2–8.8	10.0–8.6	9.13–8.4
1.60	10.8–8.12	10.7–8.11	10.5–8.9	10.3–8.7
1.63	10.12–9.1	10.11–9.0	10.9–8.12	10.7–8.10
1.65	11.2–9.4	11.1–9.3	10.13–9.1	10.11–8.13
1.68	11.7–9.8	11.6–9.7	11.4–9.5	11.2–9.3
1.70	11.12–9.12	11.11–9.10	11.9–9.8	11.7–9.7
1.73	12.2–10.2	12.1–10.0	11.13–9.12	11.11–9.10
1.75	12.6–10.6	12.5–10.4	12.3–10.2	12.1–10.1
1.78	12.11–10.10	12.10–10.8	12.7–10.6	12.5–10.4
1.80	13.2–11.0	13.1–10.12	12.13–10.10	12.11–10.8
1.83	13.7–11.4	13.6–11.2	13.4–11.0·	13.2–10.12

3 Convert a sample of these measures to kilograms as part of your Application of Number evidence.
4 In order to lose weight, Mr Nicholaus will need to be aware of how many calories he is eating in different foods. He has been told to cut down on fat but is not clear about what energy value different foods have. He likes cakes and biscuits. He needs to know how much he can eat of different foods to keep him at the correct calorie intake.

Below is a list of different foods and their calorie values. Make a simple chart of different food types and their calories for Mr Nicholaus, so he will know when he is being naughty. You can use this as evidence of 'Responding to written material' .

Caramel wafer, 54 each
Baked beans per oz, 26
Tomato soup per oz, 10.8
Toast and butter, 119
Mars bar, 284
Mayonnaise per oz, 105
Sausage roll, 112
Frozen peas per oz, 18.5
Medium pork sausages, 72 each
Choc ice, 145 each

Weetabix per oz, 100
Prawns per oz, 29.5
Orange, 10
Cheddar cheese per oz, 120
Melon per oz, 6
Cola per oz, 12
Brown ale per 10 oz, 80
Steak and kidney pie per oz, 87
Ovaltine per oz, 109
Pork chop (grilled) per oz, 129

White bread per oz, 69
Apple, 46 each
Packet of peanuts (small) 160
Crumpet per oz, 54
Banana, 119
Cod in batter, 210 per portion
Raspberries per oz, 22

Butter per oz, 226
Clear mints per oz, 100
Corn flakes per oz, 102
Whisky per pub measure, 60
Fish fingers per oz, 54
Chips per oz, 68

5 Convert ounces to grams as evidence for gathering and processing (Application of Number core skill).

Using photographs

Another way of communicating with images is to use photographs. Photographs can record images with almost total accuracy. When used over a lifetime they can become a personal pictorial history.

It is very important to particular client groups to have photographs of themselves to help them form a clearer picture of where they came from, what their experiences have been and who they are now.

Figure 13.9 A photograph is a valuable visual reminder of people, events and places past

Photographs can be used to help older people to remember their lives. Photographs can help people with learning difficulties to remember what they did and where they went. They can be especially useful to help people come to terms with loss. If a person no longer has a loved one, or if a child is no longer living with both parents, having a photograph is very valuable. A photograph is a permanent visual reminder of people, events and places past.

Think it over

If you are on work placement you may notice clients' pictures around, and they may like to talk to you about them.

Reading and responding to written material

Understanding information

Read the following short story. On a separate piece of paper write the numbers 1 to 12 down the left-hand side. When you have read the story read the statements below. Write 'True', 'False' or 'Don't know' in answer to the questions against the numbers on your sheet of paper.

An officer-in-charge had just turned off the lights in a community home when a man appeared and demanded drugs and hypodermic needles. The owner opened the drugs cupboard. The contents of the drugs cupboard were snatched up and the man dashed off. The people were informed of what had happened.

Statements

1 The man appeared after the owner had turned off the lights at the community home.
2 The robber was a man.
3 The man who appeared did not demand drugs.
4 The man who opened the drugs cupboard was the owner.
5 The home's owner snatched the contents of the drug cupboard and ran away.
6 Someone opened a drugs cupboard.
7 The robber demanded drugs of the owner.

9   The robber did not take the drugs with him.

10   The robber did not demand drugs of the owner.

11   The owner opened a drugs cupboard.

12   Taking the contents of the drugs cupboard with him, the man ran out of the community home.

The full story ... The authorities in a particular area were worried about the use of low-quality drugs and sharing of dirty needles among addicts. They therefore offered drug users an amnesty. If they took their drugs and dirty needles to the local community home they would be entered on a list of registered addicts. This would mean they could get prescribed drugs. The home would be the centre for a needle exchange, where addicts could be supplied with fresh hypodermics in an effort to prevent the spread of AIDS. The drugs were collected from the home and the police were involved in the routine collection of drugs for destruction.

Answers

1   *Don't know.* We don't know because we are only told the officer-in-charge had turned the lights off. We don't know if this was in fact the owner or another person.

2   *Don't know.* We have nothing to prove the man who demanded drugs and hypodermic needles was a robber.

3   *False.* The man who appeared did demand drugs.

4   *Don't know.* We know the owner opened the drugs cupboard, but we don't know if the owner was a man.

5   *Don't know.* We are not told who snatched the contents of the drugs cupboard.

6   *True.* We know someone opened the drugs cupboard.

7   *Don't know.* We don't know if the officer-in-charge and the owner were the same person.

8   *Don't know.* We don't know if the owner was the robber or if it was a different person.

9   *Don't know.* We can't tell who snatched the drugs.

10   *Don't know.* Again we don't know if the officer-in-charge was the owner, or if in fact the owner was the robber.

11   *True.*

12   *Don't know.* We don't know if the person who snatched the drugs was the robber or the owner or the officer-in-charge.

Comments

If you feel confused it is not surprising. When you first read the story it probably seemed quite straightforward. You almost certainly thought that a man had held up the owner of a community home and stolen the store of drugs. The point of the exercise was to show that in order to come to that conclusion *a lot of assumptions have to be made.* We often think we know the whole story, but what we see and hear is often very superficial. We jump to conclusions without understanding the whole story.

It is particularly important to remember this when dealing with people. You are only seeing what is happening to them now. Before you met them they had many experiences of which you are not aware. These experiences have made them what they are now, and this is nearly always more complex than can be seen from the surface. It is therefore very important to ask the right kind of questions and to think around many possibilities before even trying to come to a conclusion.

The second point of the above exercise was to show how unwilling most people are to say they don't know something. Most of the correct answers to the questions were 'Don't know', but people often feel they *should* know, so they try to avoid admitting they don't.

When you were doing the exercise you probably found you had to check back constantly on the first simple story to see if you had understood the points made. As a care worker you will need to make sure you check your understanding often, both when reading and when speaking with colleagues and clients. The 'drug robbery' story shows how easy it is to assume you are thinking what someone else is thinking when in fact you aren't.

Every day, in both our working and personal lives, we take in a great deal of information. We cannot possibly remember word for word all of what is said to us or all we read. What happens is that we listen to what is said or read and *pick out the important points*. This is sometimes called summarising. Can you remember the last time you did this?

It is almost impossible not to summarise sometimes. You have probably told a friend about what happened in a television programme that you saw and he or she missed. You could not repeat all that was said, but what you could do was to pick out the important parts of the storyline and update the other person. If you have been out for an evening you can tell a friend about the conversations you had without going through them word for word.

Once you realise that you are already very skilled at summarising, it is easy to summarise written words too.

Try it

Read the sentences below, which are rather long-winded, and write out shortened versions that quickly get to the point.

'I am extremely pessimistic, at the moment, about the possibility of our team gaining victory.'

'Anyone who owns, or has ever owned, a dog will know that a dog prefers a bone to any other form of nourishment.'

'To discover in detail what the life of man or woman on earth was like a hundred, a thousand, ten thousand years ago is a tremendous achievement – just as great an achievement, in fact, as to make ships sail under the sea or through the air.'

Try it

When you have practised shortening sentences, read the passage below. It is taken from *Who Cares?*, a report published annually by the Stepney Children's Fund which supports disadvantaged and abused boys and girls from London's East End. Befriending young people is an important means of helping them to stay out of trouble with the police and encouraging them to try for a better future.

When you have read the report, try to reduce it to one-third of its original length. Remember the principles:

- Look for the important point in each sentence or group of sentences.
- Try to find a single word or phrase which will replace a group of words or a longer phrase.
- Find a general term instead of listing examples.
- It is often better completely to rephrase something rather than try to chop out words and end up with a 'jerky' sentence.

Towers Hamlets Safeline Befriending Scheme

The Befriending Scheme has formally been in operation for two years. During that time, 42 mainly teenagers (11-16 years) have been referred to the scheme by the Borough's Multi-Agency Panel. Those referred are local youngsters who have been cautioned by the police on several occasions for a variety of offences including theft, shoplifting, motor-vehicle crimes, criminal damage, burglary, handling etc. Their referral to the scheme acts as an alternative to prosecution and allows them that last chance to see the error of their ways. Most leap at the opportunity. Others don't.

Each family has a home-visit from the Coordinator to establish the referred youngster's interest in the scheme, which of course is completely voluntary. One 15-year-old who joined us six weeks ago did so because 'I'm bored. Nothing to do around here. No money anyway'. Since then, he has gone on weekly outings with his befriender, taken part in a First Aid course, gone on activity days with local primary schools as a young leader with the Outreach Project, been a photographer with a disposable camera supplied by the scheme and has developed seamanship skills as a junior crew member on board a sail-training ketch. Nothing to do? He doesn't know what's hit him.

On joining the scheme, each youngster is matched with a fully trained volunteer adult-befriender and they see each other weekly for about three hours, equivalent to an evening or weekend afternoon. The young person is offered six months on the scheme and a good number have completed all of it, successfully.

Some, however, do not attend for all the six months for various reasons, one of which may be peer-pressure on the estates in which they live. Peer-pressure is very strong and some youngsters are unable to break free from it, for example, explanations for failing to keep an appointment with us such as, 'Sorry, went out with my mates', says it all. It may only amount to a knock on the door, with a group outside suggesting you join them, but to refuse can mean a youngster becomes isolated locally, and on some council estates in the inner city, that vulnerability in itself can be a dire problem for a teenager.

It wouldn't bother him the same if he was from a secure, supportive family, was doing well at school, was good at sports, had sensible friends and various developed interests, but if he has NONE of those, he may be unable to say no. We have learned from experience it is better for a befriender to pick up his young person from home!

The basic aim of the scheme is to keep our youngsters out of further trouble or to substantially reduce their involvement in crime. It's a tall order, but we are showing adequate signs of success although I must emphasise, we do not win them all. Some are even non-starters!

What can the scheme offer young people vulnerable to crime and offending? Sometimes, their needs are basic, like a space in which to talk quietly to their befriender over a cup of coffee, to enjoy a game of pool at our Drop-In Centre, where it is comfortable safe and non-threatening, to talk through new interests they can develop together.

We also aim for our young people to develop a sense of responsibility towards themselves and the community in which they live. One befriender took her 15-year-old tree-planting for a whole day. Another has organised for hers to do voluntary work in a local primary school with reading support. He's a bright one and has earned a Duke of Edinburgh's Award for his work there.

Motivating some of our teenagers who have had little, if any, success in education, have low prospects of future employment, no money, lots of domestic aggravation and no self-worth is a daunting task. However, having said that, there are a number of successes.

K wrote: Pete (befriender) and Helen (Coordinator) have helped me to build up confidence in myself. I have gained another chance to get further education and to start afresh. I hope I will do well and not let them down.'

C wrote that his befriender had made him think about 'What the consequences are' and she 'tort me to be on time'.

Like many others, W didn't want to leave the scheme at the end of six months. 'How can I be expected to keep out of trouble if I haven't got a befriender?' he asked.

A parent said to her son's befriender on their last meeting at the end of six months. 'If he gets into trouble again, it's your fault, because you're walking out on him and he still needs you.'

For many of our youngsters, Mum is the only parent and she is only too willing to admit she has lost control yet it is so uplifting for a parent to learn of a son/daughter's achievement on the scheme. A number of youngsters have been awarded certificates; some have received Duke of Edinburgh's Awards for recreation. 'I'd never played squash before in my life 'til my befriender started taking me'.

Our volunteers have been excellent, although there is a high turnover. Some, who are university students in their last year, identify with the youngsters. 'I know how they feel. I had a rough time when I was young' said one. Another felt that because of her privileged background, she wanted to 'give something back'. Other volunteers are youth workers, home/school support workers, a teacher, a community worker etc.

The scheme has benefited in countless ways from being part of Stepney Children's Fund through the sharing of contacts in the form of people, agencies and other organisations. The Inter-Agency Steering Committee chaired by Lord Northbourne has during the year

supported our efforts by trying to keep our young people out of trouble and given much consideration to future funding of the scheme which is now desperately needed.

Source: Helen Craig, Who Cares?

Evidence collection point

When you have read and shortened the report, you will have a good idea of the reasons for such a scheme and how it works. You could collect extra evidence by finding out if such a scheme runs in your area. Collect any information which is available and make a booklet of information for users. You could also present this information to your group.

Don't forget that many people could benefit from a befriender scheme. It doesn't have to be young people from disadvantaged backgrounds. It could be older or housebound people or young people with learning difficulties being befriended by people of their own age group.

Evidence collection point

Earlier in the chapter there was an exercise about checking to see if people using wheelchairs could be accommodated at a stadium for a rock concert. If the access at the concert had been all right the next step for a care worker would be to plan the actual outing.

The outline map shown on page 269 is of the city where the rock concert would take place. You need to plan for a group of five wheelchair users and five helpers to spend the day in the city before going to the concert.

Like most groups, this one has people who want to do different things. Some people want to look at museums, some at churches, some at shops and some want to take a trip on the river.

Look at the map to see where the museums, churches, river and shops are. Look to see where the mini-van you will travel in could be parked. You will have time for two activities in the morning and two in the afternoon. You will also need to go to a café for something to eat before going to the concert, and will need to identify where the toilets are for use during your tour.

Write out a plan showing:

1 where you will park for each activity
2 where you will visit in the morning and in the afternoon
3 where you will have a meal
4 where you will have opportunities to use toilets.

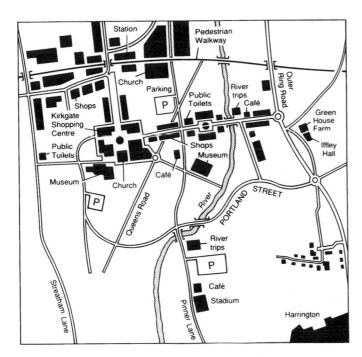

Remember that the wheelchair pushers will not be supermen/women, so take distances into account.

You can use this as evidence of using diagrams produced to meet a specific need. If you discuss and tape-record the reasons for your decisions with another person, you could use the tape as evidence of taking part in discussions.

Meeting evidence requirements using interview skills

Elements 2.1 and 2.2 of Intermediate Health and Social Care ask you to understand how life changes affect people and how relationships change. Guidance notes suggest that one way of gathering evidence for this would be to do some practical interview work. Element 4.1 asks for evidence of one-to-one interaction, and Communication core skills requires evidence of one-to-one discussion work. Interviews are also one possible way in which information on the needs of client groups and career opportunities might be gathered to meet the evidence requirements of Elements 3.2 and 3.3.

You are not required to use interviews to achieve your GNVQ Intermediate award. But using interviews could be a skill that is worth developing, for all the following reasons.

■ Much of practical caring work depends on good interpersonal skills. Interviewing may provide useful practice in developing your caring skills.
■ Interview skills will provide a useful foundation for future research work on the Advanced GNVQ programme.
■ Interview skills may make studying for your Intermediate GNVQ more real and more practical than just using 'other people's' case studies.
■ Developing your own practical interview work is one way you can collect evidence for Merit or Distinction grades. Students have to demonstrate initiative and independence in order to get good grades.
■ Using interviews might help you to provide evidence for the additional core skills of 'Improve own learning and performance' and 'Working with others'.

This section is designed to offer some guidance on planning to gather evidence using interview techniques. It is also designed to offer some ideas on planning work to meet the grading criteria.

Interview skills in a health and social care context may be developed from the conversation skills described in Chapter 10.

What is meant by interviewing?

The interview is a technique used in social science research and a technique used by clinical experts. On a much simpler level an interview may be described as 'a conversation with a purpose'.

This section does not explore the research or clinical applications of interview technique. The ideas suggested here are ideas for leading a conversation in order to collect evidence or information.

The style of interview explained in this section is sometimes called an **informant interview.** The assumption is that the person who gives you information (your informant) is willing, helpful and perhaps even pleased to share the ideas with you. An informal conversation can be used to gather information, rather than a more formally structured research approach. Because planning is critical to all 'conversations with a purpose', some readers may regard this section as offering advice on a semi-structured interview approach; rather than on the range of interview approaches described in the GNVQ Advanced book.

Who should you plan to interview for GNVQ information?

If you are practising a new skill for the first time, it is important that you practise it in a safe situation where you will have help and support from others. People learning to drive, for example, will have an instructor to help them. If you wanted to learn to rock climb, you would start with an easy situation and be given plenty of advice and support. You might not live long if you tried to learn rock-climbing by experimenting on your own on a lonely mountainside!

Interviewing is a special conversational skill. It is possible to upset and embarrass yourself and others if you do not understand what you are doing. A good piece of advice is to start with simple conversations with people who will assist you. Friends, family, colleagues, supervisors, tutors or teachers will be prepared to help you practise and develop your skills.

Figure 13.10 Learning any new skill is best done with support and guidance and in easy, safe situations

Think it over

If you are studying Units 2, 3 or 4, think of a list of people who might be able to help you by answering your questions and by assisting you with your interview style.

People you should not interview

You should not interview anyone who is 'vulnerable'. This means that you should not interview anyone who is at risk of being emotionally upset by your questions. In practice, it will also mean that you should not interview clients on placement. Some clients may be able to answer your questions, but you need to be confident that you can interview skilfully and within the value base for health and social care (see Chapter 12). You will be practising interview skills and it may be inappropriate to practise with clients.

Confidentiality

You must always ask other people for their permission before you try to interview them, even if they are friends or relatives. You will be asking them to help you with your studies and part of this request should include a guarantee of confidentiality. This guarantee means that you will not use a person's name or address, or explain any personal details that

could identify him or her. You might say that you talked with a friend, a relative, tutor or teacher. You should not identify who you interviewed in any of your written work.

This guarantee of confidentiality is necessary to create trust, provide security and to ensure that other people's rights are respected (see the section on confidentiality in Chapter 12).

Even if you feel that relatives or tutors do not need to be protected, it is still good practice to maintain confidentiality in your written reports.

Reasons interviews go wrong

Turning the interview into a quiz

Everyone knows that interviews are about asking people questions. Some people suppose that this means you can just write a list of questions and then ask them. This is the first major problem with interviews. Interviews should not be a series of questions and answers, like the television programme 'Mastermind'. The kind of interview you will need for GNVQ should feel more like a conversation than a quiz.

An interview will turn into a quiz if you use too many closed questions. A **closed question** is a question which asks for a fixed reply. For example, to the question 'How long have you worked here?', the reply is a certain number of months or years; or to the question 'Do you like it here?', the answer is either yes or no. Some people string a whole range of closed questions together when interviewing. This gives a very unsatisfactory and jerky feeling to the conversation.

Interviewer: How long have you worked here?

Informant: 12 years.

Interviewer: Do you like it here?

Informant: Yes.

Interviewer: If you had the chance would you like to work with children?

Informant: Yes.

Interviewer: Do you get paid well?

Informant: No.

Interviewer: Do you think it's a good job?

Informant: Not really.

Interviewer: Anything else you would like to say?

Informant: No!

The interview above is boring and fails to produce information from the informant. If you simply ask a list of closed questions, you will probably find out very little.

Going too fast

Another reason why interviews fail is that interviewers forget how difficult it is to answer some questions. If you ask a question such as 'How did you

feel when you were made redundant five years ago?', the other person has to think back five years. This will take time and not everyone can give a clear answer until they have talked around the question for a while.

Think it over

Think about the last five years of your life. What were you doing this month five years ago? Can you remember? If not, think about the year. What can you remember happening in that year, five years ago? Now if you can remember things that happened in the year, can you remember anything that happened in the month?

By thinking for a while it may be that your memory will come back to you.

Very often an interviewer has to keep the other person talking until he or she can remember clearly. People take time to sort out their thoughts – they can't find information as if they were a computer.

Imagine someone asked you a difficult question, such as 'Please would you explain your self-concept?'. Very few people could answer it. Yet if you really stop and think, you probably can start to describe how you think about yourself. You could explain your social relationships, your history; you could describe what you enjoy and what you would like your life to be like in the future. You might be able to describe things that you are proud of, or things that make you feel special. Yet, you weren't

asked to do those things. A question like 'Tell me about your self-concept' is too complex for people to be able to give a straight answer. People can't find the answers unless they can slowly find their memories and collect their thoughts together.

Most people cannot always instantly recall what they know – it takes time and lots of talking before they can collect their thoughts to answer difficult questions.

Confusing people with biased and leading questions

The way a question is asked will often influence a person's thoughts. It is possible to ask your questions in such a way that you bias or lead the way another person thinks. Look at the difference between these two conversations. The first interviewer is biasing the interview by focusing on bad things.

Biased interview

Interviewer:	So was it terrible when you were made redundant?
Informant:	Well, in a way I suppose it was.
Interviewer:	What was the worst thing about it?
Informant:	Well, it was the shock – one minute everything was going OK and the next minute – I'd lost my job.
Interviewer:	Did you feel sad and angry about that?
Informant:	Yes, I suppose I did at the time.
Interviewer:	So were you treated unfairly?
Informant:	Yes, that's right, I did feel it was unfair.

Balanced interview

Interviewer:	So how did you feel when you were made redundant?
Informant:	Well, I was shocked at first. It was unexpected, but then I thought, well, when one door shuts, another one opens.
Interviewer:	Could you explain about the doors – I didn't really understand.
Informant:	Yes, I was upset, but then I thought well, I've just got to find another job – there must be something.
Interviewer:	So what did you do then?
Informant:	Well, I went to the job centre and all that, but then a friend said that there was this job going at the home where she worked and she wondered whether I could do that kind of job.
Interviewer:	So how do you feel now?
Informant:	Oh well, now I've found this work I'm really happy. I look back on the redundancy and I think – best thing that ever happened to me.

These interviews have been kept short, but you can see that the first interviewer has been told about unfairness, while the second interviewer talking to the same person has been told how positive his or her experience was.

> What people tell you depends on what you ask them, and the way you ask questions.

The first interviewer asked questions which invited the informant to talk about 'how terrible' redundancy was, the 'worst thing' about it, how 'sad and angry' he or she was, and whether it was 'unfair'. If you are made to think about sadness and

Conversation	Interview
Both people talk a lot and share their ideas.	The interviewer keeps the other person talking. The interviewer talks a lot less than the informant and does not share his or her personal views with the informant.
Both people ask questions.	The interviewer asks most of the questions.
People don't monitor and are usually unaware of their non-verbal behaviour.	The interviewer may be conscious of non-verbal messages. He or she will use non-verbal messages to keep the conversation going.
People often forget what the other person has said quite quickly.	The interviewer will remember the answers. He or she may write them down or even ask to tape-record the interview.
The conversation is unplanned.	The interviewer plans question areas in advance.
Both people can end up talking about anything that interests them.	The interviewer tries to control the conversation so that it covers the issues that have been planned.
The conversation just happens.	The conversation has been formally arranged.
The conversation is not usually confidential.	Confidentiality is discussed.

Figure 13.11 Differences between ordinary conversation and an interview

anger, you are likely to agree with your interviewer that it was unfair. These questions are leading because they encourage the informant to agree with the interviewer that redundancy was bad and unfair. Without leading questions, the informant described it as a positive experience!

Forgetting that you are interviewing

Interviews for GNVQ evidence should be relaxed and informal. The danger with this is that some people may end up having a conversation where they have forgotten their purpose. The interview can become a chat, and the interviewer can forget what he or she was going to ask.

Figure 13.11 lists some differences between an ordinary conversation and an interview.

Preparing to interview

The key to a successful interview will be in preparing for the conversation. All interviews have to be planned.

Planning

First you will need to consider the area of GNVQ you are dealing with. Perhaps you are exploring redundancy for Element 2.1, or maybe you are interested in career opportunities for Element 3.3.

You will need to think of appropriate people whom you could interview about these issues.

When you have worked out your area of interest, you should make an appointment to interview your informant. In order to arrange this you need to explain to your potential informant why you wish to interview him or her, how it will help you on your programme, and say how you intend to use the information. You should also mention that you will keep names and personal details confidential. You will also need to agree with your informant how long the interview will last.

The next step is to try to imagine the way your conversation might go and what questions you will need to ask. In other words working out the question areas and what general questions, probes and prompts you need to prepare to help you with the conversation. At this stage you might need to identify your information needs.

Identifying information needs and using sources

Before you decide on which questions to ask, you might need to re-read some theory on the area. You might get ideas about redundancy from Chapter 4, for example. Chapter 9 might provide ideas on job opportunities. Other library textbooks might also remind you of concepts about which you would like to ask.

Figure 13.12 Keep a record of how you identified information needs and used sources of information

Do you feel clear about the theory of open questions, of keeping a conversation going, of communicating respect? You could look at Chapter 10 for guidance. Have you checked the evidence indicators and are you clear about how you can use your interview work?

Part of the planning process for interviewing will involve checking and perhaps sorting out priorities among your information needs. Keep a written record of your thoughts and any sources to which you have referred. This will give you evidence of working within the GNVQ grading criteria.

Checking your ideas

If possible, it is always a good idea to discuss your questions with a colleague or friend. If you try to explain your interview style, you may realise that there are still areas which need extra work. You are not discussing your questions in order to copy other people's ideas; you are using the chance of talking to sort out your ideas.

Finally, before you meet your informant, check your plans and question design with a teacher or tutor. This check is to help you succeed and to ensure that your ideas are appropriate and ethical.

The interview

Make sure you have a quiet, private room or space to talk in. If you are working with a friend, you may want to agree to take the interview seriously, so as to avoid it turning into an ordinary conversation. If you are going to take notes or even tape-record the interview, then you would first need to agree this with your informant.

Before you start to ask questions you might wish to explain the purpose of the interview once again. Explain how it might help your studies and how you will use the information. You will also need to explain the details on confidentiality and respect any other wishes that your informant has. You might want to agree to show any written conclusions to your informant for checking before handing it in. Then you can start your conversation work, using the ideas on communication skills in Chapter 10.

As soon as the interview is over, you should make notes on what happened. Even if you tape the interview, you might need to make some notes on your own feelings or the skills you used. This might lead on to your evaluation.

Evaluation

What did you learn? Where you able to ask the questions you wanted to ask? Did you enjoy the interview? Was your informant helpful? How good was your non-verbal communication for keeping the conversation going? How good were your questioning skills? Did you use probes and prompts effectively?

By evaluating your practice, you have covered the process needed to meet the GNVQ grading criteria. If your final write-up demonstrates an effective command of language and synthesis (combination) of ideas, then you have evidence toward a Merit or Distinction grade.

How it may feel to interview

Keith's interview for information on career pathways

Keith has a placement working with older people in a nursing home. He decides it would be useful to speak to a senior care worker at the home in order to obtain evidence for Element 3.3 Investigate jobs in health and social care. By interviewing a senior care worker he can create one of the three profiles he needs for this element.

Keith talks to the carer and explains that he has to explore work roles in social care as part of his GNVQ. The senior care worker says she will be pleased to

Plan the interview (planning stage)

Do the interview (practical stage)

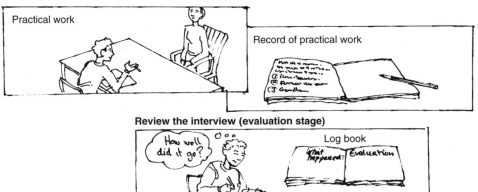

Figure 13.13 Developing interview skills to cover the grading criteria

talk to Keith and explain her job. They agree to an interview. Now Keith has to work out what to ask.

Identifying information needs

Keith looks through the standards as the first source of information that he needs to help him. His profile has to cover:

- a description of the senior care worker's day-to-day work
- a description of the senior care worker's career route to date
- a comparison of the senior care worker's actual role with stereotypes of her role.

Keith feels confident about day-to-day work and the concept of stereotypes, but decides to look up career routes to see if he can get any extra ideas on what to ask.

Keith almost forgets, but remembers in time, to make notes on an action planning form. He notes the date and that he has fixed an interview for a week's time. He also records how he has identified what he needs to know and that he has used a textbook to check the idea of career routes.

Next, Keith works out his questions. He realises he will need to thank the senior care worker and explain the purpose of the interview again. He then plans the following questions:

- **Career routes**
  - Could you tell me how long you have worked as a senior care worker?
  - What work did you do before this?
  - Why did you decide to work in social care in the first place?
  - Would you like promotion? What other jobs could you go on to?

- **Day-to-day work**
  - What hours do you normally have to work?
  - What does your work with clients involve?
  - Please could you describe how you work with other staff, for example, do you work as a team, with people of the same or other disciplines?

- **Stereotypes of role**
  - Do you think there is a stereotype of people who work with older people? (If there is, could you tell me about it?)

Keith then thinks about probes and prompts. He decides he can ask standard probes like 'Please can you tell me more?', 'Could you say a little more

about that?'. Keith could explore questions like 'What other jobs could you go on to?' with prompts like 'Could you become a manager? Would you want to become a manager?', or 'Do you have time to talk to clients?'.

Keith has thought about probes and prompts, but not really organised his questions in a structured way.

He is happy about his preparation, but following a class discussion, he decides to change round the order of the career route and day-to-day work sections. Keith's tutor says this will be all right and confirms that it will be satisfactory to ask the questions that Keith has planned.

What actually happens

Interviews have to be planned, but they never go exactly as they were planned. It is hard to guess exactly what the informant will say. Keith has decided on three areas that he wishes to explore and has prepared some questions, but he is ready to try to use his conversational skills to follow up any interesting ideas put forward by the senior care worker.

After explaining the reasons for the interview and confirming confidentiality, Keith starts with his first question on day-to-day work.

Keith:	Could you tell me what hours you have to work?
Carer:	Yes, a 39-hour week.
Keith:	Oh, I see – but what about shifts?
Carer:	Oh, you want to know about times of the day. Well, they change from week to week. I do early mornings through to 2 pm some weeks and then afternoons and later on other weeks. Shall I show you the rota?
Keith:	Oh, that's OK, I really just wanted to learn about the kind of work that you do – what does your work with clients involve?
Carer:	Well, physical care, emotional care, everything really.
Keith:	Could you tell me about a typical day at work?
Carer:	Yes – take yesterday... [*The senior carer gives a full description of yesterday's work events.*]
Keith:	Thanks, that was really helpful. I can understand what the job involves now.

Could you tell me about working with other staff?

Carer: Yes – do you mean how do I get on with them?

Keith: Well, what work do you have to do?

Carer: Ah well, I'll show you my job description. I'll get you a copy of it. Basically, I do everything. I have to hold the home when the manager and assistant manager aren't here. I have to know all the residents and I'm responsible for the care-plan records.

Keith: What does 'hold the home' mean?

Carer: That I'm in charge. I have to take over and make decisions until the manager returns.

Keith: That sounds like a lot of work.

Carer: It is! I feel exhausted at the end of the day. I really wonder if it's all worth it sometimes.

[*Keith hasn't looked at his notes and can't remember what to ask next so he quickly thinks of something.*]

Keith: Why did you come into care work, I mean, why did you choose it in the first place?

Carer: Now that's a difficult one! Let's see, well, I suppose I'd always enjoyed looking after people. I used to look after my gran you know, and when a job as a care assistant came up I went for it.

Keith: So you worked as a care assistant first?

Carer: Yes, for eight years, then I did an in-service course at college one day a week. After that I became a senior care worker. I've worked for four years as a senior care worker.

Keith: What's an in-service course?

Carer: Oh, it's a certificate for a one-year part-time course. It's not run any longer. We did three assignments and a couple of residential courses in a hotel. You have to achieve an 80 per cent attendance rate. It was great fun, I enjoyed it.

[*Keith forgets what he was going to ask and can't check with his notes in time; but he keeps the conversation going.*]

Keith: Umm, do you think there are stereotypes of people who work with older people?

Carer: Well, I expect so, what do you really want to know?

Keith: Well, I just thought that the work you do

might not be how relatives and the public imagine it.

Carer: Right, that's absolutely right. A lot of people imagine it's all serving tea to nice old ladies and sitting around having chats. Well, you've seen what it's like – you never sit down, or if you do you can't stand up again; and that's just the easy bit. All the paperwork, the phone calls, it never used to be so bad.

Keith: Why has it become more difficult?

Carer: Well, more regulations, more work – like care plans – but fewer staff to do the work and the clients are much more demanding. When I started, only six or seven residents had dementia, now most of them do.

Keith: I guess I'm running out of time, but could I just ask about career routes? Would you like promotion? What jobs could you go on to?

Carer: Oh, I don't think I'd want to be a manager – no, life's hard enough, but some people go on to management. It helps if you can get the right qualifications – there are Diplomas in Management Studies, HNCs, a City and Guilds Management qualification.

Keith clarifies some of the final details and thanks the senior care worker for her time. The senior care worker says she thought it was a good interview and that she will be pleased to help Keith sort out any details.

Think it over

Did Keith do this interview effectively? How would you evaluate his performance?

Points to think about

- Keith had worked out some notes to help him, but he discovered that he either couldn't remember them or could not look at them throughout the interview.
- Keith discovered that he could not keep the conversation going and follow the order of his notes at the same time.
- Keith did not manage to ask every question on his prepared list.
- Keith managed to keep the conversation going. There were no embarrassing gaps; when he forgot something, he always coped by asking something else.

- Keith covered most of the issues needed for the evidence requirements.
- Keith coped with unexpected replies because he had understood the issues he wanted to learn about. He was not simply reading from a fixed set of questions. When Keith did not get good answers, he was able to ask questions that helped him find out what he really wanted to know, like 'Could you tell me about a typical day at work?'.
- Keith was able to reflect on what he was told with statements like 'That sounds like a lot of work'. This meant that the senior care worker enjoyed the conversation. She felt respected and valued.

Keith wonders about the interview – did it go well? The senior care worker said it did. Did he cover his questions? Well yes, he covered nearly everything. He found out about working patterns when the senior care worker explained a typical day's work. During the interview he was able to keep the conversation going; he used effective verbal and non-verbal skills.

Before completing his evaluation, Keith looks back over Chapter 10 of this book to see if he can find any ideas for improving his approach. He looks at the idea of funnelling and realises that he could have tried to organise his questions so that they gently led on from one another. What he actually did was a bit jerky. When Keith asked about stereotypes, the senior care worker wasn't really sure what he was trying to ask and she was slightly surprised by the question. Keith decides that he can evaluate his interview as effective and well done, but that he could have improved it by organising his questions and his notes a little more clearly.

Verdict

Keith's interview was fairly successful, but it might not have worked if he had been less skilled at conversation. Keith had planned his questions, but he was not sure what would happen in the interview. Because he did not know what the senior care worker would say, he could not really keep to his question order. Keith used his basic conversation skills to keep the interview going and used his questions as a prompt sheet to remind him what to ask when he had an opportunity. Although Keith lost the structure of his questions, he succeeded in getting his evidence.

Michelle's interview on coping with predictable and unforeseen events

Michelle has agreed with Karen, who is on the same GNVQ programme, to interview her about a house move four years ago (a predictable life event) and a

road accident in which Karen was involved last year (an unforeseen event that led to temporary disability). This will provide evidence for Element 2.1.

Michelle has planned her questions and checked her knowledge in relation to change and how people

---

The questions Michelle has prepared for Karen

So how long ago did you move house?

I know you had to move with your parents, but why did they move?

Can you remember when you first knew you were going to move?
[Prompts: one month, six months before the move?]

How did you feel about having to move at that time?
[Prompts: excited, unhappy, worried?]

Did you lose touch with any friends because of the move?

How did the move affect your life?
[Probe: did you make new friends, was the new house better, was there anything you missed?]

Looking back, how do you feel about it now?
[Prompts: angry, it's OK, sad, worried?]

Well, thanks very much. Can we talk about the accident now?

How long ago did the accident happen?

Could you just explain briefly what happened?

After you realised what had happened to you, what were your first feelings?
[Prompts: were you upset, angry, worried?]

When you came out of hospital and you couldn't walk, how did people treat you?
[Prompts: just the same, ignored you, felt sorry for you?]

How did you feel after you came out of hospital?

Looking back at the accident how do you feel now?
[Prompts: angry, it's OK, sad, worried?]

manage it. She has recorded her planning and information needs ready to provide evidence for the grading criteria.

Michelle has prepared the question sequence on page 279 to guide her through the interview:

Michelle: Thank you for coming to talk to me about the house move. As we agreed, I'll take a few notes as you speak if that's still OK.

Michelle already knows a little about Karen's accident and house move, so she is able to plan a series of questions which lead into each other. These questions are cleverly designed to allow Karen time to think and collect her thoughts about what might have happened. The questions are not leading and even the use of prompts is balanced. Although the first question is a closed one, this is just to introduce the topic. The questions then become open and funnel down to the difficult ones, 'How did you feel about having to move?', 'How did people treat you?'.

When Michelle asks these questions, she will be able to stay with the question order, because Karen is likely to be able to explain each issue as the questions are asked. If Karen does start to explain unexpected ideas, Michelle will be able to listen and record the information. Michelle should then be able to bring the conversation back to the sequence of questions she was using.

Michelle's interview is likely to be very successful in getting the evidence that she needs. She will write up her planning for identification of sources and evaluation work to meet the grading criteria.

The key to Michelle's questions is that she already understands a little of Karen's experience and she understands some of the likely emotions involved with major life events.

Well-structured interviews may not always be easy to plan, particularly when you do not know much about the area you are investigating. If you are exploring an issue which you know little about, you may have to rely on your general conversational skills and some general preparation.

Like learning to drive a car, practical experience is the best basis for learning to interview. Concepts about conversational and interview skills will make more sense when you have begun to experiment with the ideas in practice.

Fast Facts

Adjective A word which says something about a noun.

Agenda A list of items for discussion at a meeting.

Apostrophe A punctuation mark used either (a) to show something belongs, or (b) that something has been omitted. If the person or thing to which the object belongs is plural, the apostrophe goes after the 's'. When a letter or letters are missing, the apostrophe is put where they would have been.

Assumptions These are ideas which we assume to be correct but which we haven't checked. In care work it is very important that we do check our ideas about other people and their needs. Wrong assumptions can lead to the breakdown of conversations and to the breaking up of groups. They can also be discriminatory.

Capital letter This is used at the beginning of a sentence, and for names of people and places.

Comma This is used to separate items in a list, or different parts within a sentence.

Communication An activity that can be verbal or non-verbal (or both). It can involve using sketches, diagrams, photographs, tables or graphs to make meanings clearer.

Curriculum vitae (CV) A form used when applying for a job. It gives all the necessary details about the applicant, such as name, address, date of birth, qualifications and experience.

Key worker A care worker who has special responsibility for certain clients. A key worker helps the client with all aspects of daily life, gets to know him or her well and helps to plan things. Key workers will help plan leisure activities, holidays, birthdays and help the client keep in touch with friends and family.

Memorandum (memo) A message between workers of the same organisation. It will not have an address in the heading.

Non-verbal communication Using the face, body or voice tone to convey meaning.

Noun The name of a person, place or object.

Pronoun A word used instead of a noun such as him, her, it.

Sentence A group of words put together to make complete sense. It must have a subject and a verb.

Structure and style Your way of laying out written material to make it easy to use.

Subject The name given to the noun or pronoun about which a statement is being made.

Summary Picking out the important points from information in order to make a shorter version.

Total communication Using words, body language and signs, often together, to help get meaning across.

Verb A 'doing' word (for example, 'I *walked* to college').

Application of number

This chapter is designed to help you to achieve your core skills in the application of number. It explains how number skills are used in everyday life and in the field of health and social care to work things out. Examples include working out how much to increase the quantities in a recipe that serves four so that it can serve 20 in a residential setting; and calculating how many staff are needed for effective care of a particular number of clients.

Number skills are also used to collect **data**, to put it into a suitable form for **analysis**, and then to draw **conclusions** from the results. This can help to show patterns that might, for example, be used for forward planning of services.

Collecting and recording data

When you need to carry out a task to do with quantities, amounts, volumes, angles and all the other items you can think of to do with numbers, it may be rather bewildering at first. Most of us are used to a teacher providing us with a set format for calculations and we can either do them or not. It is more difficult to set the calculations yourself and then perform them to achieve answers to practical problems. There needs to be a logical process. Ask yourself the following questions:

1 What am I trying to find out?
2 Is there more than one thing that I am trying to find out?
3 If so, what is the order of the things I am trying to find out? Take particular care to note whether the solution to one problem is necessary before you can complete another. If the problems are not dependent on one another, tackle easier ones first to give yourself practice and gain confidence. Take each problem one at a time.
4 What do I already know about the problem?
5 What data have I got?
6 What data do I need?
7 How will I collect the extra data?
8 Do I need measuring instruments?
9 Once collected, how will I record the data?
10 What will I do with the recorded data to find out the answer to my problem?
11 What is the next problem to solve?

Carry on until you have found out everything you need to know.

You are really doing the following:

Complete in the order A, B, C.

Where am I now?	What do I have to do?	Where do I want to get to?
A	B	C

An example

Due to the opening of a social services day nursery nearby, Sandcastles a privately owned nursery, has found that the number of vacant places is increasing by three each year. The nursery can take 25 children on a full-time basis and charges £70 per 5-day week, including meals. This year, the nursery has 19 children and has already reduced the number of its staff to five full-time nursery nurses. The salary bill is £31 200 per year, catering is £12 350 per year, and rental and maintenance of the premises is £250 per month. The owner, Anne Gregory, says that she has to make a 15 per cent profit in order to cover her living expenses; otherwise Sandcastles will have to close. Total profit which includes Ann's share is taxed at 25 per cent. Anne knows she can only increase fees by the rate of inflation or the parents will go elsewhere. Find out the following.

1 How long can Anne continue to run the nursery if, overall, she loses three children a year to school or the rival nursery? (She will lose more than this but some new children will enrol so the net loss will only amount to three). You should assume a ratio of one member of staff to four children. Catering costs £12.50 per week per child; staff supply their own meals.
2 The staff agree to a 10 per cent cut in salary. Will this enable the nursery to stay open for a further year?
3 If fees were increased by 3 per cent (the current rate of inflation), will this enable the nursery to remain open for a further year?

4 Construct a bar chart showing Anne's profit share for four years if the nursery stays open.

Anne wishes to give her staff sufficient time to find other jobs, so she has to work out these figures in advance and have them checked by the nursery supervisor. If you were the supervisor, could you work this out?

Answers

1 Income
This year = 19 × £70 × 52 = £69 160
Year 2   = 16 × £70 × 52 = £58 240
Year 3   =13 × £70 × 52 = £47 320
Year 4   =10 × £70 × 52 = £36 400

Outgoings (£)

	This year	Year 2	Year 3	Year 4
No. of children	19	16	13	10
Premises	3 000	3 000	3 000	3 000
Staffing	31 200	24 960	24 960	18 720
Catering	12 350	10 400	8 450	6 500
Owner's 15%	10 374	8 736	7 098	5 460
Total	56 924	47 096	43 508	33 680

Profit = income – expenditure

Therefore profit:

This year = £1316
Year 2   =   £224
Year 3   = –£7108 (a loss!)

Tax to be paid on profit and owner's share:
This year = £1316 + £10 374 = £2922.50

Anne needs to consider closing down immediately as she will not be able to pay her tax bill and take her 15 per cent profit.

2 If staff take a 10 per cent cut in salary this year, the nursery could be run for this as the saving of £3120 would cover the tax bill. Next year's tax bill would be:

£224 + £8960 × 25 per cent = £2240

Profit after Anne's share is £224 plus a saving of £2496, equal to £2720 which would cover the tax bill, so the nursery would survive next year (Year 2) with the cuts in salaries.

3 Year 3 looks impossible because of the huge loss, but let's see what happens if fees are raised to help as well. An increase of fees at 3 per cent will increase the income to £48 739.60, an increase of £1419.60 but not enough to pay the tax bill on Anne's share, 25 per cent of £7098 equals £1774.50.

4

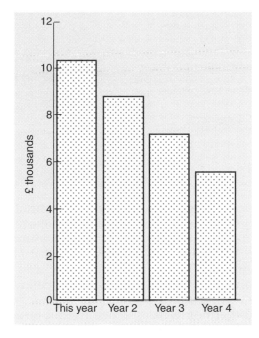

Figure 14.1 Value of the owner's profit share

Conclusion

If the staff are prepared to accept a salary cut of 10 per cent the nursery can survive for the remainder of this year and one further year. The nursery will definitely have to close after that: Anne's share is decreasing significantly each year and she cannot afford to take less than 15 per cent profit.

Data collection

Measuring instruments

Thermometer

There are many different types of thermometer, but the most common are those containing mercury (silver) or alcohol (coloured; frequently red). Both types either have a scale running alongside the column of liquid or a scale engraved on the glass or plastic wall of the container.

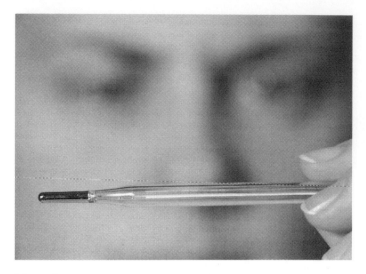

Nowadays, temperature is usually measured in degrees Celsius (°C), but some older thermometers, particularly in people's homes may measure in degrees Fahrenheit (°F), a measurement no longer in common use. Thermometers normally read from 0°C (the point where ice forms) or a few degrees below, to 100°C (the boiling point of water) unless they are clinical thermometers designed to read body temperature, where it is only necessary to measure a few degrees either side of normal body temperature. Thermometer scales are usually divided into intervals of 10°C by long marks and 1°C intervals by much shorter marks.

Clinical thermometers have scales in one-degree intervals, with one-tenth of a degree shown by shorter marks. You can read off a body temperature of 36.9°C. There would be no point in having smaller

markings, say of one-hundredth of a degree, as the eye would not be able to distinguish between 36.91°C and 36.92°C with any accuracy.

The bulb of a thermometer contains the reservoir of liquid used in the construction of the thermometer, and should not be handled. To measure the temperature of a substance the bulb should be carefully lowered into it. Care must be taken that the substance has an even temperature throughout or inaccuracies will result. For example, taking the temperature of water being heated in a beaker with the thermometer resting on the base of the beaker will result in a higher temperature being recorded than if the thermometer was held or clamped off the base.

With a clinical thermometer, you must make sure that it has been shaken after use. This is necessary to ensure that the mercury thread links directly with the mercury in the ball and that the thread is well below the expected reading. The thermometer is usually placed in the client's armpit, or less commonly these days, under the tongue. Allow sufficient time for the thermometer to register the highest temperature – 2 minutes. Shake and clean the thermometer after use.

Weighing scales

Just as there are many types of thermometer, there are even more types of weighing scales. Digital reading scales are simple to use as long as the scales are given sufficient time to come to a steady state. You can then read off the quantity direct. Other types may involve moving weights along a balance

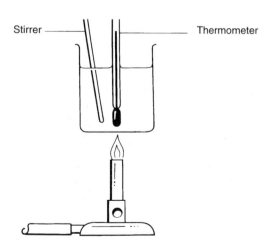

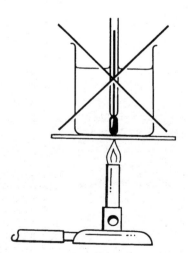

Figure 14.2 The correct and incorrect way to measure temperature

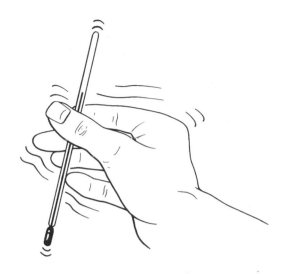

Figure 14.3 Always shake the thermometer before and after use

arm until the arm is neither up nor down but balancing freely in between, or reading off a scale at a point reached by the marker when the item is on the scale pan.

In the metric system, weight is measured in micrograms (μg), milligrams (mg), grams (g),

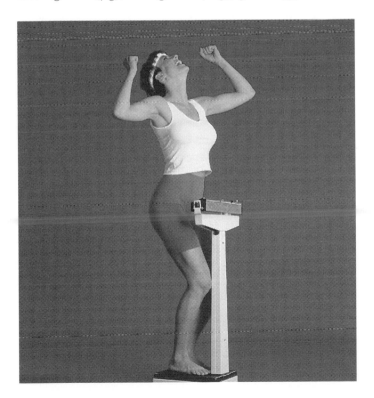

kilograms (kg) or tonnes (t) (the largest of this series). Each unit is 1000 times smaller than the following one and 1000 times larger than the previous one. In the imperial system weight is measured in ounces (oz), pounds (lb), stones (st), hundredweight (cwt) and (tons). Some firms in the UK still sell goods in imperial units despite a national changeover in 1971. If you are not familiar with these units, the following should help you:

    16 oz = 1 lb
    14 lb = 1 st
    112 lb or 8 st = 1 cwt
    160 st or 20 cwt = 1 ton.

In the UK people frequently still give their body weight in stones and pounds, ask for pints of beer, and often yards of cloth.

The choice of which weighing scales to use depends very much on what you are weighing. For example, it is no good weighing 4 oz of jelly babies on a weighing machine meant for commercial lorries full of gravel – the machine would not register as the quantity is too small.

Similarly, you would need a scale for use in a school laboratory which might measure to 0.1 g but not to μg, as you would be unlikely to deal with anything quite so small.

Scale rule

Measurement of length by the metric system once again uses the factor of 1000, which makes it simpler to understand than the imperial system. The two systems are shown below:

Imperial system
12 inches = 1 foot
3 feet = 1 yard
1760 yards = 1 mile

Metric system
1000 millimetres = 1 metre
1000 metres = 1 kilometre

As 1 millimetre (mm) is very short and 1 metre (m) quite long, an additional unit is used to make measuring more practical. This unit is the centimetre (cm) and as its name suggests, there are 100 of them in a metre. Therefore, 10 mm make 1 cm.

Some engineering industries do not use the centimetre, while in other contexts it is a very useful measure indeed.

School rulers tend to display both systems, so as to be as useful as possible. One side can be marked in inches, 6 or 12 altogether depending on the ruler length, with each inch being subdivided into tenths or sixteenths by smaller marks. Half inches are shown by intermediately sized marks. If you look carefully at your ruler, it will usually tell you what the subdivisions are. The other side of the ruler is marked in centimetres, 30 or 15, with millimetres shown in smaller divisions. A ruler is a very useful instrument and you should not be without one when studying.

In a laboratory, wooden metre and half-metre rules are available for measuring. Unlike school rulers, there is no unmarked end section; if the end of a metre rule is damaged or worn, the measurement might be inaccurate. To avoid this, it is often better to start measuring a length at the 10 cm mark and then take 10 cm off the final measurement.

Protractor

This is familiar to most of us as a semi-circle of plastic marked with graduations around the edge and lines coming to the midpoint of the straight base. It is used for measuring angles. Do not use a scratched or faded protractor; it will lead to inaccurate results.

An angle is formed where two lines meet. To measure an angle already drawn or to draw one, you must begin by placing the line running parallel to the straight base of the protractor over a drawn line on the paper. Then read off where the other line meets the scale around the edge of the protractor. The answer will be in degrees. There are 360 degrees in one full circle, 180 in a semi-circle and 95 in a quarter circle.

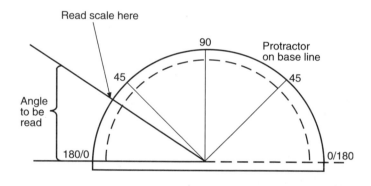

Measuring jug

Volume or capacity measured by the imperial system is in pints and gallons; the metric system measures in millilitres (ml) and litres (l).

Imperial system
20 fluid ounces (fl oz) = 1 pint
8 pints = 1 gallon

Metric system
1000 millilitres = 1 litre

A measuring jug has a scale printed or etched into the glass with either imperial or metric units. The interval between marks will depend on the size of the jug. For example, a small jug might measure individual millilitres, but a large one might only record in 100, 250 or 500 millilitre intervals.

Money

In the UK since decimal currency was introduced in 1971, money has consisted of pounds and pence (100 pence = £1).

Before decimalisation, 12 pence (d) equalled 1 shilling and 20 shillings made £1. Although we rarely discuss shillings in today's financial transactions, many older people still look on the 5 pence coin as a shilling, and the 10 pence coin as two shillings.

Time

Everyday language to do with time tends to revolve around the 12-hour clock, to which we add am or pm to explain whether we mean day or night time. The separating times are called 12 noon or 12 midnight.

Timetables, public services, the armed services and other organisations use a 24-hour clock. This does not add am or pm, as the numbers after midday continue with 13 until midnight (24), when the clock starts again at 00.00. You will notice that there are two figures each for minutes and hours, for example, 7 pm on the 12-hour system is 19.00 (hours) on the 24-hour clock.

On both clocks each hour is divided into 60 minutes, and each minute is divided into 60 seconds. A second is a very short space of time, about as long as it takes to count out loud in double figures – saying 'twenty-one, twenty-two, twenty-three' takes about three seconds.

Conversation of data into required units of measurement

When you are carrying out numerical tasks such as comparing, multiplying, adding, dividing, etc. you must always make sure that your units are from the same numerical system and of the same size. If they are not, then you must convert them into the chosen size by multiplication, division, scales or tables. For example, if you are comparing the birth weights of babies born to smoking and non-smoking mothers, it would be pointless if some weights were in kilograms and others were in pounds and ounces.

If on a children's outing, you are trying to find out how many ice-creams you could buy for £3.00, assuming each ice-cream costs 45 pence, you would need either to convert your money to pence or the ice-cream costs to parts of a pound (this is a harder calculation and you would be very unlikely to do the sum this way).

£3.00 = 300 pence

Number of ice-creams = 300 ÷ 45 = 6 with 30 pence change.

Conversion tables

It is useful to have conversion tables (or scales) to help you transfer measurements from one system to another. It is often necessary where different sets of scales are regularly used (for example, metric and imperial in weights and heights, miles and kilometres for distance). Figures 14.4–14.6 show some examples. You should note that these tables give *approximate* conversations for convenience.

To use the tables, find the figure on the reading you have taken and read directly across the adjacent figure. That is the equivalent in the other scale.

You can also convert by doing simple calculations. To convert *to* metric *multiply* by the figure shown. To convert *from* metric *divide* by the figure shown.

miles/kilometres	1.61	pounds/kilograms	0.45
feet/metres	0.30	ounces/grams	28.34
inches/centimetres	2.54	stones/kilograms	6.35
pints/litres	0.56		

imperial (fl oz)	metric (ml)	imperial (fl oz)		metric (ml)
1	30	8		230
2	60	9		260
3	85	10	($\frac{1}{2}$ pint)	280
4	110	15	($\frac{3}{4}$ pint)	425
5 ($\frac{1}{4}$ pint)	140	20	(1 pint)	570
6	170	40	(1 quart)	1140
7	200	160	(1 gallon)	4500

Figure 14.4 Approximate imperial to metric conversion table for volumes

metric (g)	imperial (oz)	metric (g)	imperial (oz)
10	$\frac{1}{3}$	100	3
20	$\frac{2}{3}$	120	4
30	1	150	5
40	$1\frac{1}{2}$	200	7
50	$1\frac{3}{4}$	250	9
60	2	300	$10\frac{1}{2}$
70	$2\frac{1}{2}$	400	14
80	3	450	16
90	3	500	$17\frac{1}{2}$

Figure 14.5 Approximate imperial to metric conversion table for weight

For example, to convert 12 stones to kilograms:

$$12 \times 6.35 = 76.2 \text{ kg}$$

To convert 400 grams to ounces:

$$400 \div 28.34 = 14.1 \text{ oz}$$

For convenience, these figures are sometimes rounded to the nearest whole number – so 400 grams would be 14 ounces. You can use these conversation figures to make *estimates* of the approximate answer before you complete the calculation. This will help you to judge if your final answer is likely to be correct.

For example, if converting 4 inches into centimetres, a rough estimate of the result would be $4 \times 2.5 = 10$ cm (2.5 is used because it is close to the actual figure and easy to multiply).

Remember

- You can check your result by converting the answer back to the original figure (for example, 10cm ÷ 2.5 = 4 inches).
- You can use estimates and checks like this for many kinds of calculations.

Gas Regulo	Centigrade	Fahrenheit		Gas Regulo	Celsius	Fahrenheit
	°C	°F			°C	°F
	70	150		4	180	350 (normal hot frying)
	80	175		5	190	375 (upper limit for frying)
	100	212	(boiling point of water)	6	200	400
$\frac{1}{4}$	120	225		7	220	425 ('hot' oven)
$\frac{1}{2}$	130	250		8	230	450
1	140	275		9	240	475 ('very hot' oven)
2	150	300		10	250	500
	160	310	(normal gentle frying)		270	525
3	170	325			290	550

Figure 14.6 Cooking temperatures

Estimation

This means an **approximate judgement.** You certainly want to get your number applications correct, so it is very useful to have a rough idea of what your answer should be so that you know when you have made a mistake. Many people do not use estimation and common sense in their arithmetic, and then they complain about the number of sums they get wrong.

For instance, many people do not realise that when two fractions are multiplied together the answer is *smaller*. Take two simple fractions you are familiar with, $\frac{1}{2}$ and $\frac{1}{2}$. Multiply them together and you get $\frac{1}{4}$. This may seem puzzling because you are used to thinking that $\frac{1}{2} + \frac{1}{2} = 1$, and indeed it does. But when multiplying these fractions together you are in fact saying a half *of* a half and when you reflect on that, the answer *is* a quarter.

Another estimating tip useful with both fractions and decimals is to look at the whole-number parts. For example, if adding together 16.956 and 2.305 look at the whole numbers 16 and 2 (added together = 18). Next look at the decimals – the first shows 9 in the tenths position and the second shows 3, so when added together these are going to make at least another whole one. Hence your answer is going to be 19 point 'something not very big'.

Also try to get into the habit of 'rounding' in your estimates. Take for example 3.75 × 5.02. This sum is 'nearly 4' multiplied by 'just over 5', so your answer must be in the region of 4 × 5, which is 20.

Remember

Practise estimation in your work – it only takes a few seconds, but pays off in accuracy.

Another useful tip is to get used to the mental images of lengths, areas, volumes, weights, etc. so you have a better understanding of them. For instance:

- The average weight of an adult man is 70 kg, but it is not unknown for a care worker to write someone's weight as 7000 kg. Clearly, the unit has no real meaning for such a person.
- A litre is approximately $1\frac{3}{4}$ pints – we are all familiar with a pint milk bottle, so a pint is roughly $\frac{1}{2}$ a litre (just over in fact).
- Most people know the feel and size of a 2-pound bag of sugar, but many have not noticed that sugar comes now in 1 kilogram bags (= 2.2 pounds). They did not notice that it had changed because the weight is so similar. So, try to remember that a pound is roughly $\frac{1}{2}$ a kilogram, or 500 grams (just under in fact).
- Fabric used to be measured by the yard, and a popular way of 'measuring' in the UK was to hold the length of fabric between your nose and fingers of an outstretched arm – this was approximately a yard. Now, a metre is only about 3 inches longer than a yard, and this is about the length of a nose – so if the head is turned away from the outstretched fingers, one can still use the old-fashioned way to measure a metre!

- An excellent way of estimating some lengths or heights is to use your own body. Get to know your own height in metres and in centimetres (or millimetres). The average height for a woman is 1.60 metres, and her fully stretched handspan (from little finger tip to thumb tip) is about 20 centimetres. Measure yours to check.
- Measure your biggest stride and you will always be able to pace out a distance.

When you get a feel for measurements, estimating will be that much easier for you.

Data handling

Questionnaires

Questionnaires are a cheap, effective way to find out about people's activities, thoughts and opinions on various topics. They can be used to collect information about why people choose to do things. They can be short or long, but to get effective results questionnaires have to be well thought out and planned. There are several things you need to do before you start to write questions for a questionnaire:

- Research and read around the topic area. This will give you some ideas about the questions to ask.
- Decide on the aim/focus of the questionnaire. This helps to keep the questions relevant. For

example, in a questionnaire on people's attitude to smoke-free areas it would not be relevant to ask how much a packet of cigarettes costs.

■ Decide who you intend to ask. Is it focused on one group (such as adolescents) or should there be a cross-section of ages?

■ Plan what type of question and how many questions you are going to ask. It is often useful to trial these on a small number of people first, to ensure they are clear and draw out the information you want.

■ Think about how you are going to record your results. This can be affected by the type of question you ask.

You should also consider the people whom you hope are going to answer your questionnaire. The style and size of the questionnaire can encourage a person to complete or not complete it. Bear the following points in mind:

1 *The length of the questionnaire.* Don't make it too long as this puts people off. Don't make it so short that it is ineffective.

2 *Format of the questions.* People are less likely to answer a questionnaire if they have to do a lot of writing. Use a mixture of questions where they can tick boxes and write short answers.

3 *Who you give the questionnaire to.* If the person knows you, they are more likely to reply.

4 *An introductory letter.* This is useful if you are not giving out the questionnaire personally. The letter would explain the purpose and importance of the questionnaire and encourage people to fill it in.

If you wish people to return the questionnaire, a stamped-addressed envelope provided by you will get a better response.

To obtain the most unbiased, honest answers, a questionnaire that the respondent can complete alone is sometimes best. If you ask the respondent to complete it in front of you, you may be likely to get the accepted 'norm' of attitudes and feelings. If you suggest that respondents answer the questionnaire alone, you may also get more thoughtful and detailed answers – they have more time to think and consider their replies.

Types of questions

Once you have planned the approach to the questionnaire, you need to write the questions. The type of question used is the key to obtaining relevant data. There are two types of question: those which seek **facts** and those which record **attitudes and opinions**.

Factual questions gain **objective** information – that which is not so open to individual interpretation. For example:

Tick the annual income bracket you fall into:	
Up to £5000	☐
£5001 – £10 000	☐
£10 001 – £15 000	☐

Other areas often covered by factual questions include sex, age, marital status, number of children, level of education, etc.

Attitude or opinion questions aim to collect **subjective** information – that which is the thoughts or opinions of the individual. For example:

Do you think young people today are brought up:
☐   too strictly?
☐   not strictly enough?

Questions to gain thought or opinions can be open or closed. Open questions allow the respondent to answer more fully than 'yes' or 'no'. An example would be:

'What do you feel makes a caring environment?'

Closed questions limit the replies the respondents can give. They can require just a 'yes/no' answer (for example, 'Do you feel a carpet is necessary for a caring environment?'). Alternatively they can allow a number of restricted choices. The following is an example of the latter type:

A carpet is essential in a caring environment.	
Strongly agree	☐
Agree	☐
Neither agree nor disagree	☐
Disagree	☐
Strongly disagree	☐
Please tick the box which most closely reflects your thoughts.	

You should avoid asking questions which cover more than one aspect. The question 'Do you think that old people should be encouraged to live in residential care and to be as independent as possible?' asks two separate things – the risk is that you will only get one answer!

Trialling the questionnaire

Once you have written your questionnaire, you should trial it on at least five people to check that the questions are clear and are gaining the information you need. Adjustments may need to be made before you use the questionnaire with larger numbers of people.

Questionnaire sampling

When collecting data, it is important to get a balanced view of the group you have chosen to study. For example, if you were doing research into people's thoughts on banning smoking in public places, you would not get a fair picture if you asked only smokers. You need to select your respondents at random (for example, every sixth passerby). This would give you fairer results. However, if you were trying to find out smokers' views on this, then using only smokers is appropriate.

Observation

Another way to find out how people behave is to **observe** them. You could do this by **participant observation**, where you become part of the situation you are observing. For example, in watching children play you could play with them as you observe – this makes you less obvious as a researcher and you can get fairer results as those being observed do not start 'acting'. However, it can be difficult to be involved and also get detailed observations.

Alternatively, you could use **non-participant observation**, where you are more likely to sit back and observe from a distance. You are likely to see a lot of detail using this method, but sometimes those being observed feel uncomfortable and do not act naturally.

With the observation method you do not always know *why* people are behaving the way they do.

If you wish to use observation as a way of collecting data, you should do the following:

- Decide what you want to observe (for example, discussion at a mealtime at a residential home).
- Compile an **observation sheet** using headings to cover what you want to observe (situation, people involved, seating arrangements, topics of conversation, etc). This will help you to focus your observations and help you note relevant points. However, as observation is active, it is impossible to predict all that will happen and a sheet should not stop you noting the unexpected or unusual.

Surveys

A survey is another way to collect data. To carry out a survey you may talk to people to gain opinions or you may just record what you see. A survey is sometimes shorter than a questionnaire and may have less detail than an observation sheet. It can be a quick way to gain information. Before you carry out a survey, you need to be clear about:

- what you wish to survey
- where you are going to carry out the survey
- if you need to sample the participants in any way (for example, talk to every sixth person).

You also need to construct your recording sheet *before* going to do your survey.

The recording sheet needs to reflect the possible answers/results you may get. It should allow the results to be recorded easily. For example, if you were going to survey the age ranges of the people who visited care workers at the local health centre on a particular morning, the sheet might look like Figure 14.7. Ticks are inserted for each consultation. This would give you a view of both age range and who visitors were seeing. A variety of conclusions could then be drawn from the data.

Age range	Nurse	Doctor	Health visitor	Other
5 yrs	✓	✓✓	✓✓	✓
5–10 yrs	✓	✓	✓	
11–19 yrs	✓✓✓	✓✓✓✓	✓	✓
20–30 yrs	✓✓	✓✓✓✓		
31–50 yrs		✓✓✓✓	✓✓	
51–70 yrs	✓✓	✓✓✓✓	✓✓	
70 yrs		✓	✓✓	✓✓

Figure 14.7 A simple survey recording sheet

Extraction of data from sources

It is often necessary to find data from a mass of information at source.

Example 1

Figure 14.8 shows the blood sugar of a healthy person before and after lunch.

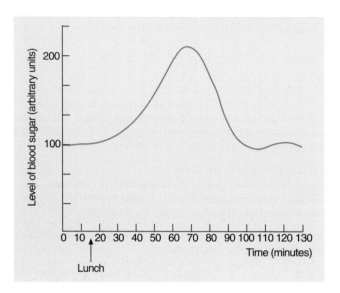

Figure 14.8 Blood sugar level of a healthy person, over a period of time, before and after a meal

a Find the blood sugar level 45 minutes after eating lunch.
b At what time did the blood sugar reach its highest level after the meal?

How to set about this:

a Lunch was eaten at 15 minutes on the graph, so 45 minutes after was 15 + 45 = 60 minutes on the graph. Find 60 minutes on the time axis and extend vertically until the graph line is crossed. At this point draw a horizontal line to meet the vertical axis and read off where it crosses the scale. This is the answer to **a**.
b Find the highest point on the graph and extend a vertical line from that point to meet the time axis. Where this line meets the axis read the scale figure. This is the answer to **b**.

Example 2

Examine the table for converting imperial volumes into metric volumes (Figure 14.4). Find out how many millilitres 14 fluid ounces would equal.

You will need to look up for 10 fl oz and then 4 fl oz and add them together to make 390 ml. You have extracted data from a table!

Recording to specified levels of accuracy

Calculators are important tools in today's society. They shorten the tedious business of long and complicated calculations and of repeating the same type of sum over and over again. Yes, of course, you should use a calculator in your GNVQ work, but a word of warning: *they cannot get the sum correct for you if you do not enter the correct data or use the right method.* It is therefore sensible to make sure you know what you are doing with the figures first.

People sometimes use a calculator to perform a long division sum and quote their answer to 6 or 7 decimal figures. They may be surprised or upset if tutors cross out all but the first decimal place or two. The fact is that those last figures are nonsense, because the data entered into the calculator may only have been gathered to an accuracy of one decimal place.

If you take a ruler and measure the page width of this book, you will need good eyesight to be accurate in measuring to half a millimetre, and you certainly could not be accurate to 1000th of a millimetre. So it is usually nonsense to quote an anwer to that degree of accuracy in health and care situations. A calculator has not got common sense and will go on dividing as long as it has spaces to do so.

Decimals

A decimal number is one that includes a decimal point (for example, 0.681, 12.833, 143.99). The figures to the *left* of the decimal point count as a whole number. The place values of figures on the right of the decimal point are tenths, hundredths, thousandths, tens of thousandths, etc. For example, in the number 6.983 there are 6 whole numbers, 9 tenths, 8 hundredths and 3 thousandths.

Think it over

If you get the places and decimal points in numbers muddled, for practice make a table like the one shown here and insert the following numbers into the table:

100.5		0.35	.	40.69	
14.008		0.99		1.10	
0.1		10.95		10.10	

Hundreds	Tens	Units	●	Tenths	Hundredths	Thousandths
		6		9	8	3

The number 6.983 is said to have three decimal places. So has 0.003, but 142.89 only has two decimal places. The **number of decimal places** is simply the number of figures on the right of the decimal point.

Calculations

Addition

The symbol for addition is +, which means 'plus' or 'add'. It is placed between two numbers that are to be added together. Numbers can be added together in rows or in columns, although columns are always used if there are a lot of numbers to be added or if they are large.

First the units are added. If the units add up to more than ten, the right-hand part (the unit) is put down and the left-hand part is carried to the next column to the left. This 'carry over' can be written in tiny figures below the total lines. There may be no 'carry over'.

Next the tens column is added up, not forgetting any carried over from the units column. Once again, if double figures are reached, the left is carried over to the next column, and the right is written down in the total. Carry on with this same procedure until all the columns of figures are dealt with. An example is shown below. *Always remember to line up the columns correctly!*

Example

Add together 72, 578 and 2319.

$$
\begin{array}{r}
72 \\
578 \\
+ \ 2319 \\
\hline
2969 \\
\end{array}
$$

_{1 1}   ← Numbers carried over

Try it

1 Nurses working on Tuesday for a care home earned £102, £134, £99 and £117. How much was the 'nurse bill' for the home on that Tuesday?

2 A health visitor had four calls to make on Friday. The distances she recorded were 6 km, 11 km, 4 km and 6 km. How far did she travel that day?

Check your answers:

(1) £452, (2) 27 km.

Subtraction

The symbol for subtraction is –, which means 'minus' or 'less'. It is placed between two numbers when the second is to be taken away from the first. As with addition, we may do the sum in rows or in columns but must be careful to line up the units under one another, then the tens and so on.

When we take the second number away from the first, which is bigger, that poses no problem (for example 9 – 7 = 2). However, if the first number in the units column is smaller, we will have to 'borrow' from the tens column of the first number. You have to be careful to note that the figure in the tens column of the first number is now one less.

Example

In a mixed school of 1836 pupils, 789 are girls. How many pupils are boys?

$$
\begin{array}{r}
{}^{7\ 12\ 1} \\
18\!\!\!\not3\!\!\!6 \\
-\quad 789 \\
\hline
1047 \\
\hline
\end{array}
$$

Try it

1 Nurse Troy wanted to represent her colleagues in the union at the hospital where she worked. Two other candidates' names were also put forward, so there was an election. Nurse Troy received 234 votes, and a theatre porter got 179 votes. She know that altogether there were 534 workers in that union who voted. Calculate how many votes the third candidate received, and therefore who became the hospital union representative.

2 A hospital ward held 25 patient beds, but the day-room had only 18 chairs. If every person on the ward went to the day-room, how many more chairs would they have to find from other areas?

Check your answers: (1) Third candidate received 121 votes, and so Nurse Troy became the elected representative. (2) Seven chairs.

Multiplication

The symbol for multiplication is ×, which means 'times'.

Imagine that 8 hospital patients each needed 3 units of blood to be transfused. How much blood would have been used in total? To find this we could add:

$$8 + 8 + 8 = 24$$

or $3 + 3 + 3 + 3 + 3 + 3 + 3 + 3 = 24$

but it is easier to say:

$$8 \times 3 = 24$$

If calculations are done without using a calculator, multiplication tables can be memorised. This can shorten the time taken to do calculations by hand.

When multiplying involves double or more figures a simple technique solves the problem.

Example

A hospital has 350 beds and the manager has allowed for 3 sheets per bed each week. It costs 58 pence to launder each sheet. Calculate the weekly cost of laundry.

$$
\begin{array}{rl}
350 & \text{beds} \\
\times \quad 3 & \text{sheets} \\
\hline
1050 & \text{sheets} \\
\hline
\end{array}
$$

$$
\begin{array}{rl}
1\,050 & \text{sheets} \\
\times \quad 58 & \text{pence} \\
\hline
8\,400 & \\
+ \quad 52\,500 & \\
\hline
60\,900 & \text{pence} \\
\hline
\end{array}
$$

In the second calculation, multiply first by the 8, then by the 5. You only have to multiply by 5 (instead of 50, which it really is) because putting a 0 under the left-hand figure converts multiplying by 5 into multiplying by 50. This works in exactly the same way if you are multiplying by 253 or by 1937 – merely add an extra 0 every time you move to the next left figure.

Remember

You must make sure the columns line up under one another.

Example

In the section on addition, the health visitor had travelled 27 km. Now calculate her expenses claim if the health authority paid 44 pence per kilometre.

$$
\begin{array}{rl}
27 & \text{kilometre} \\
\times \quad 44 & \text{pence} \\
\hline
108 & \\
1080 & \\
\hline
1188 & \text{pence } (=\pounds 11.88) \\
\hline
\end{array}
$$

Try it

1 A candidate had an assignment to do for her GNVQ qualification and her tutor said 2500 words would be acceptable. She decided to word-process her work and found that she could get on average 12 words to a line. The candidate had written 8 sides of A4 paper, which had 24 lines to each page. Did she write too much, too little or was it approximately correct? You could try this calculation 'by hand' and check your answer using a calculator.

2 At his work placement, a candidate found that one of the elderly residents was going to have a 100th birthday party in three weeks' time. The officer-in-charge was trying to fit in the organisation of the party with a busy schedule, and asked the candidate for some help. The cook thought that each guest would eat 4 small sandwiches and 2 cakes. From 2 slices of bread, they would make 4 sandwiches and each loaf contained 22 slices, including crusts (which they were not using). The officer-in-charge estimated that 50 guests from outside, 24 other residents and 10 staff would be present. How many loaves and cakes did the candidate have to order?

Check your answers: (1) The candidate had probably written 2304 words, so this was approximately correct. (2) A loaf of 20 slices of bread (excluding crusts) makes 40 sandwiches, which feeds 10 people. There were 84 people like to come. He needs to order 9 loaves and 172 small cakes.

Division

The symbol for division is either ÷ or a line —, both of which mean 'divided by'.

Division is a process involving sharing. The first number is to be shared between the second number of groups. For example, $15 \div 5 = 3$ means that 15 is to be divided into 5 groups, and there will be 3 in each group.

There are two methods of dividing without using a calculator. These two methods depend on the size of the figure you are dividing by (sometimes called the **divisor**).

The first method uses figures less than 12. This is because many people know their multiplication tables up to $\times$ 12. It is called **short division**.

Example

Divide 8896 by 4.

$$4\overline{)8896}^{2224}$$

The thought processes in carrying out this division could be as follows:

- 4 into 8 goes 2, none left over. Write down 2.
- 4 into 8 goes 2, none left over. Write down 2.
- 4 into 9 goes 2, but 1 left over. Write down 2 and carry 1 to the next column to the right.
- 4 into 16 goes 4, none left over. Write down 4 and the sum is finished.

If the sum does not divide exactly as in the example, you will have some left over.

Example

Divide 397 by 5.

$$5\overline{)397}^{79} \leftarrow \text{with 2 left over}$$

In this case there are 2 left over. Sometimes it would be fitting to say *79 remainder 2*, but modern techniques are more likely to ask you to put this as a fraction or a decimal. There will be more to say of this later.

The second method of dividing is known as **long division** and is used mainly when the sharing figure is over 12 (for the reason already given).

Example

Divide 7395 by 35.

$$
\begin{array}{r}
211 \\
35\,\overline{)7395} \\
-70 \\
\hline
39 \\
-35 \\
\hline
45 \\
-35 \\
\hline
10 \quad \leftarrow \text{ remainder}
\end{array}
$$

Now the thought process is like this:

- 35 into 7, won't go.
- 35 into *73* goes 2. Write down 2 immediately above the 3 (not above the 7). Now do a multiplication (35 times 2 = 70) and put 70 below the 73. Subtract it, leaving 3.
- Bring down the next figure to the side of this 3. In this sum, *39*. Now 35 will go into 39 once, so write 1 next to the 2 on the top row, carry out a multiplication (1 × 35 = 35) and subtract 35 from 39. This leaves 4.
- Bring down the next and last figure, which is 5, to give *45*. Again 35 will go once into 45, so write the 1 up at the top and do a multiplication (1 × 35 = 35). Subtract 35 from 45.
- This leaves 10 as a remainder.

This is the type of whole-number arithmetic many people have forgotten or never learned, because it is much easier to use a calculator. To explore how the arithmetic works, however, try working out these sums. Cover the workings on the right – they are there so that you can check your answers.

a Divide 240 by 15.

$$
\begin{array}{r}
16 \\
15\,\overline{)240} \\
15 \\
\hline
90 \\
90 \\
\hline
00
\end{array}
$$

b Divide 268 006 by 33.

$$
\begin{array}{r}
8121 \\
33\,\overline{)268006} \\
264 \\
\hline
40 \\
33 \\
\hline
70 \\
66 \\
\hline
46 \\
33 \\
\hline
\text{remainder} \rightarrow \quad 13
\end{array}
$$

Try it

1 You have been asked to organise seating for a lecture on NVQ training at your workplace. The supervisor tells you that about 270 people are expected to attend. When you investigate the lecture hall you find it is already laid out in rows with 29 seats in a row. You do not want some people in the front rows nor others right at the back, so you decide to limit the number of rows to be used and mark the rest: 'Not to be occupied'. Work out how many rows you need. If there are 50 rows in total, how many need to be closed off? If the outside chairs of each row only will carry the closed notice, how many notices do you need to make? How many people could be seated in the hall if necessary?

2 A health visitor finds that she has almost no fuel left in her car's petrol tank. She is going on holiday by train tomorrow and she reckons on travelling by car to see four clients today. They are 16 km, 12 km, 8 km and 13 km apart. The health visitor is anxious not leave excess fuel in her car while she is away. She estimates that her car can travel 19 km on 1 litre of petrol. She certainly cannot risk running out of petrol because her area is mostly rural, there are very few petrol stations around and her clients are expecting her to turn up. Work out how many litres of petrol will enable the health visitor to see all her clients.

Check your answers: (1) 10 rows used, so 40 rows blocked off. Therefore 80 notices needed. Total capacity of hall is 1450. (2) 3 litres of petrol needed.

I wish I had learned to do divisions properly

A word about brackets

Brackets are used with more than one number, when those numbers are to be treated as a single number. For example:

$$4 \times (6 - 2) = 4 \times 4 = 16.$$

The sums inside the brackets are always worked out first, as in the above. When more than one pair of brackets appears in a sum, the *innermost* ones are always worked out first, and then the next, and so on. For example:

$$20 - (4 \times (6 - 3)) = 20 - (4 \times 3) = 20 - 12 = 8$$

Ready reckoners

Ready reckoners are charts or tables designed so that people do not have to be good at multiplication or addition to get things right; they only have to read the correct answer from a chart.

Figure 14.9 shows the amount to which £1 will grow at various rates of interest for the number of years stated.

Use of mathematical procedures in the correct order

It is important when carrying out calculations that a certain order is followed. The word BODMAS was coined by a mathematician to describe this order. It stands for the following items:

B Brackets
O Of
D Division
M Multiplication
A Addition
S Subtraction

Interest rate	Number of years									
	1	2	3	4	5	6	7	8	9	10
9%	1.090	1.1881	1.2950	1.4116	1.5386	1.6771	1.8280	1.9926	2.1719	2.3674
9½%	1.095	1.1990	1.3129	1.4377	1.5742	1.7238	1.8876	2.0669	2.2632	2.4782
10%	1.100	1.2100	1.3310	1.4641	1.6105	1.7716	1.9487	2.1436	2.3579	2.5937
10½%	1.105	1.2210	1.3492	1.4909	1.6474	1.8204	2.0116	2.2228	2.4562	2.7141
11%	1.110	1.2321	1.3676	1.5181	1.6851	1.8704	2.0762	2.3045	2.5580	2.8394
11½%	1.115	1.2432	1.3862	1.5456	1.7234	1.9215	2.1425	2.3890	2.6636	2.9699
12%	1.120	1.2544	1.4049	1.5735	1.7623	1.9738	2.2107	2.4760	2.7701	3.1058
12½%	1.125	1.2656	1.4238	1.6018	1.8020	2.0273	2.2807	2.5658	2.8865	3.2473
13%	1.130	1.2769	1.4429	1.6305	1.8424	2.0820	2.3526	2.6584	3.0040	3.3946
13½%	1.135	1.2882	1.4621	1.6595	1.8836	2.1378	2.4264	2.7540	3.1258	3.5478
14%	1.140	1.2996	1.4815	1.6890	1.9254	2.1950	2.5023	2.8526	3.2519	3.7072
14½%	1.145	1.3110	1.5011	1.7188	1.9680	2.2543	2.5801	2.9542	3.3826	3.8731
15%	1.150	1.3225	1.5209	1.7490	2.0114	2.3131	2.6600	3.0590	3.5179	4.0456

Figure 14.9 Ready reckoner table

BODMAS will help you to recall the correct order when tackling problems.

Percentages, ratios and proportion

Percentages

Percentage means exactly what the name tells us. 'Per' stands for 'for each' and 'cent' stands for 'one hundred'. So 'per cent' means 'for each hundred'. We can use the symbol % to represent a percentage. Percentages are really fractions which always have the denominator of 100%. Fractions and percentages are therefore easily interchanged.

To convert a fraction into a percentage, simply multiply the fraction by 100%. For example:

$$\frac{6}{20} \times 100\% = 30\%$$

Example

Out of 396 people surveyed, 132 still smoked. Express this as a percentage.

$$\frac{132}{396} \times 100\% = 33\frac{1}{3}\%$$

To convert a percentage into a fraction, divide the percentage by 100 and simplify the fraction if possible. For example:

$$55\% = \frac{55}{100} = \frac{11}{20}$$

Example

In a nursing home with 40 residents, 15% of the patients had suffered a stroke in the last twelve months. How many patients did not have a stroke in that period?

Check your answer: Either (i) work out 15% of 40 and subtract the figure from 40, or (ii) work out (100 − 15)% of 40:

(i) $\qquad 40 \times \frac{15}{100} = 6$, and $40 - 6 = 34$

(ii) $\qquad 40 \times \frac{85}{100} = 34$

Ratios

A ratio is a comparison of two figures. We can either write the two figures like a fraction, or more commonly with the symbol : in between. For example, if one care worker earns £10 per hour and another earns £5, their earnings are in the ratio of 10:5, which is the same as 2:1. Note that in ratios the units for the quantities *must* be the same. You can multiply ratios up or down to simplify the figures as long *as you do the same to both sides* (as we did above). It is better to get one of the sides down to 1 as this gives you an idea of the relationship very quickly.

Example

Mr and Mrs Winston have discussed with the elder Mrs Winston whether it is the right time for her to stop living on her own and get expert care in a nursing home close by. They all decide to look further into the costs. There are two nursing homes nearby. The first costs £110 per week and the second costs £100 per 4-week month. Find out the ratio of the cost of the first home to that of the second.

First the costs must all be expressed in the same units, so it is important to bring the second home's costs to a weekly figure (or the first's to a 4-week month figure). So divide £500 by 4 to make £125 per week. Then:

$$\frac{\text{cost of first home}}{\text{cost of second home}} = \frac{110}{125} = \frac{22}{25}$$

The ratio is 22:25 in lowest terms.

Example

Nurse Osborne works 37 hours each week on ward 33. Find the ratio of his working hours to non-working hours.

Time working = 37 hours
Time in week = 24 × 7 = 168 hours
Time not working = 168 − 37 = 131 hours

$$\text{Ratio} = \frac{37}{131} \text{ or } 37{:}131$$

Try it

1 Mr Biggs received a very pretty card signed by all the residents of the nursing home to celebrate his 100th birthday. He is so attached to the card that everyone decides to pay a share so that the card can be framed. You decide it would be much better to enlarge the card at the colour copy centre in the next street and frame it so that Mr Biggs still has the original to look at and touch. The card measures 12 cm × 8 cm with a border 3 cm wide. It is increased so that the length becomes 27 cm.

a What does its width become (it is increased in the same ratio)?

b Find the ratio by which the area has increased.

2 The costs of three similar drugs for treating migraine are £3, £2.50 and £2 for 100 tablets, and the numbers of pharmacists who buy these drugs are in the ratios of 3:4:5.

a Find the number of drugs bought in a locality if the total amount spent is £1914.

b What fraction of pharmacists buy the cheapest drugs?

Check your answers: (1) (a) 18 cm. (b) Original area = 12 × 8 = 96 cm^2 and new area = 27 × 18 = 486 cm^2. So ratio of increase 96:486, which is the same as 1:6.

(2) (a) 79 200 tables. (b) $\frac{5}{12}$.

Proportion

If the ratio between two dimensions is always the same then the two dimensions are always in **proportion**. For example, if x is always in the same ratio to y, then if x halves so must y and if x doubles so must y.

Other signs and symbols

Squares and square roots

When a number is multiplied once by *itself*, the result is known as the **square** of that number. It is represented by a small number 2 after and to the top of that number:

$$4^2 \text{ is the same as } 4 \times 4$$
$$25^2 \text{ is the same as } 25 \times 25$$

The **square root** is shown by a $\sqrt{\ }$. This symbol means that a number can be made from the multiplication of another number times itself (squared). For

example, $4 \times 4 = 16$, so the square root of 16 is 4. The square root of 625 is 25, because 25×25 makes 625. These can be written:

$$\sqrt{16} = 4 \text{ and } \sqrt{625} = 25$$

Cubes and cube-roots

Cubs are similar to squares, but this time the number is multiplied by itself twice. For example e.g. the cube of two is

$$2 \times 2 \times 2 = 8$$

This can be written 2^3. Similarly, 2 is the cube root of 8.

Statistical averages

When you have collected a mass of data it will not be in a suitable form for analysis until it is arranged in a chart or graph format.

Another way of making data easier to understand is to try to find one value to represent several values in your data. This single value is called an **average**.

There are three kinds of average known as:

- The (arithmetic) **mean** which is equal to the total of all the values divided by the number of values.
- The **median** is the value which lies half-way along your values arranged in ascending or descending order of size. If there is an even number of values, take the mean of the two values.
- The **mode** of a set of values is the one which occurs most often. Should everything occur the same number of times there may be no mode, or conversely, more than one mode may occur.

Range

When considering data, you may wish to refer to the range. This is the spread of the values from the highest to the lowest.

For example, a hospital administrator was examining figures which counted the number of nights 14 patients stayed in a particular ward. They were as follows:

1, 4, 12, 3, 6, 11, 10, 7, 3, 5, 13, 12, 2, 4.

The report he prepared included the statement: 14

patients stayed in ward 32 overnight and the number of nights stayed ranged from 1 to 13.

Two-dimensional and three-dimensional shapes

Plane shapes

A **plane shape** is one that is flat (i.e. not curved or round).

Rectangles and squares

A **rectangle** (or *oblong* as it is sometimes known) is a plane shape that has opposite sides equal in length and parallel to each other. If all the sides of the rectangle are equal, we call it a **square**, so that is also a plane shape.

To calculate the **area** of a square or a rectangle is a simple matter of multiplying together the lengths of two adjacent sides, provided they are already in the same units. The answer is then expressed in 'square' units and may be written with a small 2 raised after the unit name.

For example, the area of a rectangle with sides of 6 cm and 4 cm is:

$$6 \times 4 = 24 \text{ cm}^2$$

and the area of a square with sides of 1 metre is:

$$1 \times 1 = 1 \text{ m}^2$$

We can construct a simple formula for calculating area:

$$\text{Area} = \text{Length} \times \text{Width}$$

The **perimeter** of a rectangle is the distance around the edge. It will therefore be twice the length and twice the width added together. For the rectangle mentioned above this is $6 + 4 + 6 + 4 = 20$ cm. (Note that as we are simply adding up lengths there is no 'square-ing' involved.) The square mentioned above has a perimeter of 4 metres. We can construct a simple formula for working out perimeters:

$$\text{Perimeter} = 2 \times (\text{Length} + \text{Width})$$

The two formulae above represent word equations to which you may wish to refer to produce core skills evidence.

Triangles

To calculate the area of a **triangle** you need to multiply the base by the height and divide by 2.

Think it over

Can you say why you have to divide by 2? Think of a rectangle cut in half diagonally.

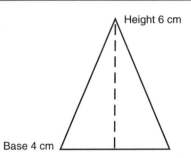

To find the area of the triangle shown here, multiply 4 cm by 6 cm and divide by 2. Note that we are 'square-ing' again, so the answer will be in 'square' units. It is:

$$\tfrac{1}{2} \times (6 \times 4) = 12 \text{ cm}^2$$

Complex plane shapes

Many shapes are *combinations* of rectangles, squares and triangles, and appropriate dividing lines can be drawn if the areas or perimeter needs to be calculated.

Try it

A group of students held a fund-raising activity to carpet a newly opened day-centre for older people in their neighbourhood. They chose a carpet priced at £25 per square metre and decided to make a plan of the area to find out how much money they needed. Their plan is given below. Work out how much money they needed to raise.

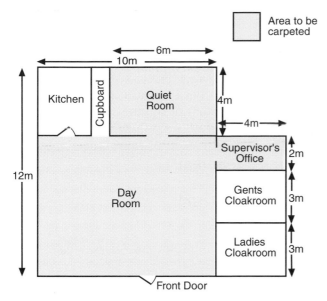

Area to be carpeted

Check your answer: Area of day room = (12 – 4) × 10 = 80 m². Area of quiet room = 6 × 4 = 24 m². Area of supervisor's office = 4 × 2 = 8 m². Total area to be carpeted = 80 + 24 + 8 = 112 m². Cost of carpet = 25 × 112 = £2800.

Irregular shapes

Occasionally you may be required to measure the area of something which cannot be divided into rectangles and triangles and where you want more accuracy than rough estimation. An example might be the hand!

A reasonably accurate method is to draw around the shape on to a piece of squared paper such as graph paper. With larger objects you might need to make your own squared paper in bigger units. Having done that, count the *number of squares* the shape occupies.

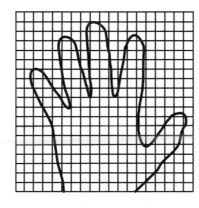

Have a system for counting parts of squares. For example, if half or more than half a certain square is included in the shape outline then count it as a whole one, but if less than half ignore it. Finally, multiply the number of squares you have counted by the area of a single square. A surface calculation for the hand would be doubled as there are two surfaces,

the palm and the back of the hand. Remember that your answer is in 'square' units (for area).

Volume of a simple solid

The **volume** of something is the amount of space it occupies. For a symmetrical shape it can be worked out by multiplying the length, width and height together. Note that this time we are dealing with three dimensions, so the answer is in 'cubed' units. This is shown by a small raised 3 after the units.

For regular shapes such as cubes or rectangular blocks, the lengths of the sides are multiplied together. For example, the volume of a block with sides measuring 5 cm, 3 cm and 4 cm is:

$$5 \times 3 \times 4 = 60 \text{ cm}^3$$

We can construct another formula for this:

Volume of solid = Length × Width × Height

Different units may be used depending on the shape of the object, but always remember to make all the units the same before multiplying (for example, all in millimetres, or all in inches).

Volume of a cylinder

The volume of a cylinder is found by multiplying the area of its cross-section (a circle) by the length.

You now need to know that the area of a circle is

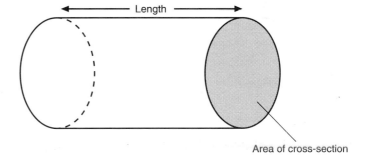

Length

Area of cross-section

calculated from πr^2.

The *r* represents the **radius** of a circle, which is the measurement from its centre to its outside. π represents the **ratio** between the **circumference** of a circle and its **diameter** (which is twice the radius, or 2*r*). It is a Greek letter pronounced 'pie'. It always has the same value – as a decimal it is about 3.142. As a fraction it is $\frac{22}{7}$.

The units for the area of a circle will again be 'square'

as *all* areas are measured in such units. When the area of the circle is multiplied by the length of the cylinder, the units become 'cubed'.

For example, a cylinder with a radius of 2.5 cm and length 10 cm has a volume of:

$$3.142 \, (\pi) \times 2.5 \times 2.5 \times 10$$

$$= 196 \text{ cm}^3$$

Try it

A baby's feeding bottle has a diameter of 6 cm and it is 15 cm long. What is its capacity when full? Give your answer in cubic centimetres. Also try converting the capacity to fluid ounces (fl oz) and pints, making use of the table in Figure 14.4. One millimetre (ml) is the same as 1 cm³.

Check your answer: Volume = 424 cm³. Did you remember to take half the diameter to get the radius before doing your calculation?

A parallelogram

This is a four-sided shape with its opposite sides parallel to each other. None of the angles is a right-angle (90°).

A trapezium

This is best described as a four-sided shape with only one pair of opposite sides parallel.

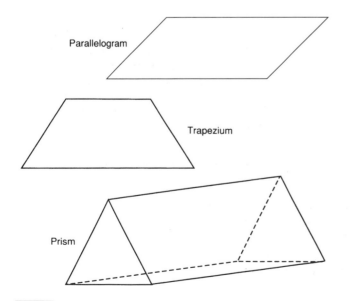

A prism

Any solid object with a *uniform* (i.e. unchanging) cross-section can be called a prism. It can have any shape for the cross-section. The most common cross-sections are triangles (like some well-known triangular chocolate bars) or squares. If the section is a circle or an oval, the solid is known as a cylinder.

Pythagoras's theorem

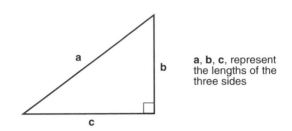

a, **b**, **c**, represent the lengths of the three sides

Figure 14.10 Pythagoras's theorem

Pythagoras's theorem states that the square on the hypotenuse (side **a**) of a right-angled triangle is equal to the sum of the squares on the other two sides (**b** and **c**).

In other words, using letters to represent the lengths of the sides as in Figure 14.10:

$$a^2 = b^2 + c^2$$

This can be used to work out the distance between opposite corners or ladders from walls, etc.

Techniques for presenting data

There is a range of different ways to present data you have collected. Graphs are often used to show *changes* in data over a certain period of time. Graphs, bar charts, pie charts and tables can be used to illustrate text, and doing this will help you gain core skills in Communication.

When collecting data, however you choose to do it, *always be well prepared*. Make sure your notes are clear and legible, so that when you come back to use them at a later date you can still understand them.

Whatever method you choose to present your data, you should *always* label the presentation clearly. The work should be neat (and coloured if appropriate).

If using figures to work out an answer, *always* show your workings. Core skills credit the methods used and the process followed, as well as the right answer!

Bar charts

One common type of data presentation is a bar chart. An example is shown in Figure 14.11.

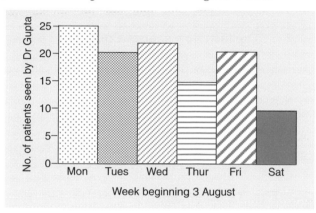

Figure 14.11 Bar chart

Line graphs

A line graph can be used to show clearly how values

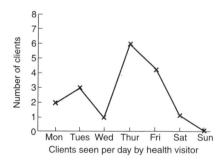

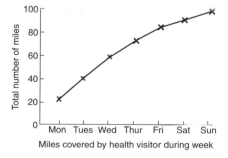

Figure 14.12 Line graphs

have changed over a period. It can also show cumulative information. An example of each is shown in Figure 14.12.

Pie charts

If a circle is divided into 1 degree segments, there will be 360 segments in total. Segments of varying size in a circle are often used as a clear way of showing shares of a whole.

Example

Using the case study on Sandcastles nursery which appeared earlier in the chapter, we can immediately see the different amounts spent on keeping the nursery going (Figure 14.13).

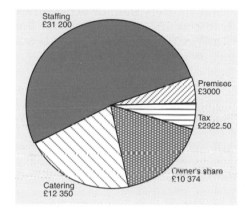

Figure 14.13 Sandcastles nursery expenditure for this year

As with almost all other care establishments, staffing Sandcastles accounts for most of the outgoings, it is approximately half the outgoings. The owner's share and the catering are almost identical, as are the premises and the tax. The pie chart allowed us to evaluate the data quickly and easily. Now you can see how useful pie charts are.

Constructing a pie chart

Seaview, a day-centre for people with learning difficulties, found that it spent its money in the following way:

Salaries £60 000
Premises £15,000

Catering £9000
Maintenance £3000
Other items £3000

Construct a pie chart to illustrate this so that some clients and relatives might understand where the income goes.

First, find the total of the expenditure or outgoings, so add all the figures together

= £90 000

This must be equal to 360 degrees. Therefore, to find out how many pounds each degree is worth divide £90 000 by 360.

$$\frac{90\ 000}{360} = 250$$

So, each degree of the circle represents £250. We know the value of every item of expenditure, so if we divide each one by 250, we will find out how many degrees of the circle individual segments need to be. For example, premises cost £15 000 so:

$$\frac{15\ 000}{250} = 60 \text{ degrees}$$

Place your protractor on a faint pencil line through the centre of the circle to get a start and measure 60 degrees – label this segment, 'Premises'. (See page 286 for information on using a protractor if you are unsure.)

Work through the other costs in the same way and you should have a pie chart like the one in Figure 14.14:

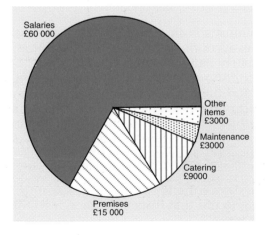

Figure 14.14 Expenditure of Seaview day-centre, 1995

Tables

A table can be used to present a range of information in a neat way. It is particularly useful if you want to compare data.

For example, Figure 14.15 shows the formal qualification of staff in a nursery at two different times since it opened.

Qualification changes of staff				
	1985	%	1991	%
NNEB	2	20	5	50
BTEC Nursery Nursing	0	0	2	20
Teaching	1	10	1	10
PPA	3	30	2	20
None	4	40	0	0
Total	10	100	10	100

Figure 14.15 Tabulated data

Pictograms

These are bar charts made up of pictures rather than bars.

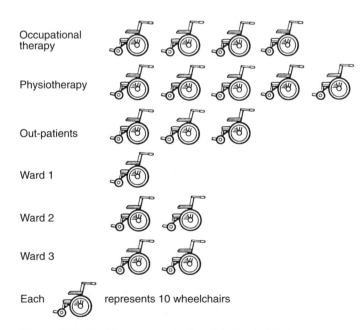

Figure 14.16 Numbers of wheelchairs in Turley Hospital departments

Graphical representation

Graphs show data clearly so that they may be understood quickly. Two lines called **axes**, at right angles to one another, are drawn horizontally and vertically on the page. Each axis should be clearly labelled with the data logged on that axis and the units in which it is measured. When interpreting graphs it may be that the overall fluctuations of the graph are important and the units in which it is measured are not. In such a case, the constructor of the graph may label the axis **arbitrary units**, in which case these may be treated as any figures. Some graph axes may have arrow heads alongside or the axis may end in an arrow to represent a continuing increase. All graphs should be titled so the interpreter knows what values are being plotted, for example, 'Graph to show how ... varies with ... '.

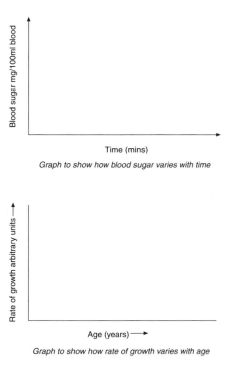

Graph to show how blood sugar varies with time

Graph to show how rate of growth varies with age

Figure 14.17 Examples of graphs

When you are constructing a graph you will need to know which set of data to put on the horizontal axis – often called the *x* **axis** – and which to put on the vertical axis – *y* **axis**. The data you have control over or have set the intervals for should go on the *x* axis (horizontally along the bottom). Conversely, the data over which you have no control are on the *y* axis (vertical, going up).

Example

Let us take a simple example, a temperature chart for a client with a fever.

Body temperature is going to be measured every 4 hours or every 2 hours or every hour – you set the interval. However, you do not know what the temperature is going to be (that is why you are measuring it); you only know the extremes between which it will be. Therefore, the chosen time interval will be on the *x* axis and the temperature on the *y* axis. Very often in graph construction, you will find an aspect of time forms the *x* axis, but do not take this for granted – it is not always so.

The place where the axes meet usually represents zero on both scales, but again this does not have to be so.

One of the most confusing things in drawing graphs seems to be choosing a suitable scale. You will have your lists or charts of data, so find the smallest and the largest values. For example, in the graph to show how rate of growth varies with age (Figure 14.17), age runs from 0 to 25 years. The graph paper to be used has 28 cm squares vertically and 19 horizontally. Would it matter if the graph was drawn in landscape format?

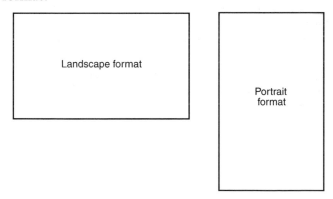

In this case, the answer is no, so the paper is turned around: 25 intervals will fit well into 28 spaces at 1 cm per year interval. What about the other scale? Rate of growth will range from 0 cm/month to about 10 cm/month, i.e. 10 intervals, and that will also fit well at the same scale on the vertical axis. Sometimes, however, it is not possible to turn the paper to suit the graph, particularly if there is text before and following the graph such as you might find in an assignment.

In portrait format, 25 intervals have to fit on to paper 19 cm wide; clearly, the same scale of 1 cm per year cannot be used. Could 1 cm represent 2 years? Yes,

305

but that would leave nearly one-third of the paper blank, so try 0.75 cm per year for 25 years, which equals 18.75 cm, about the right size for the paper.

Now is the time for individual choice. If you are not very experienced at plotting points, you may choose the first easier scale, but the graph will not look quite so well on the paper. If you are experienced and can plot 0.75 cm accurately, then the second scale would be preferable. You should now be able to follow the same procedure to work out the scale for the y axis.

Plotting points

You will generally have two sets of data, usually in a table. To make sure that you find the right value on the correct scale, move the two lines inwards (a ruler is useful as a guide) until they intersect (cross) and mark with a dot. Take away the ruler and look at the point – is it in the correct place? When you are satisfied with the position, mark the dot more definitely as described below.

When all the points are plotted, the next task is to join them together by a line. The line may be straight, curved or jagged. If it is clearly straight or curved, but one or two points do not quite fit, then make a straight line or curve using the line which best fits most of the points – do not worry if one or two points lie outside the line. It would be quite unusual to have everything matching perfectly!

To ensure that the graph shows data to the best advantage:

■ use graph paper whenever possible to present your information

■ use the paper to the best advantage – do not squash the graph into a corner and leave the rest of the paper blank

■ draw the graph axes in pencil, but with label lines and titles in ink

■ plot the points carefully, using either a cross (the centre of which coincides with your desired point) or a dot surrounded by a circle. Use a sharp pencil so that errors can easily be corrected

■ if there is more than one line on the same graph, try to avoid using colour – use the different ways of plotting points as described above

■ label each line neatly

■ make sure that the interval between scale marks is the same along your axis – pay particular attention to decimal intervals, which are often confusing.

Probability

If a coin is tossed it has an equal chance of coming down heads or tails. In this case we often say there is a 50/50 chance (or an even chance) that it will show heads (or tails). In number work we give a value to the likelihood of a particular outcome.

For instance, the likelihood of heads turning up with a tossed coin is 1 out of 2 (= $\frac{1}{2}$ or 0.5). The probability of a particular score on a die (singular of dice) is 1 out of 6 (= $\frac{1}{6}$), as there are 6 possible numbers. Similarly, the probability of producing the queen of hearts from a pack of cards is 1 out of 52.

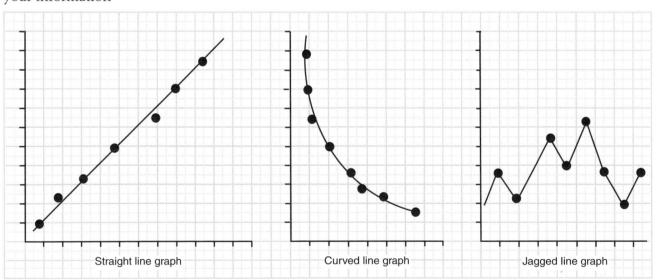

Straight line graph   Curved line graph   Jagged line graph

Example

Suppose now we have two dice, one with numbers and one with colours. What is the probability of a red and a 6 turning up? What is the probability of blue and an odd number being thrown together?

The following table will help us to work this out.

Colours	Numbers					
	1	2	3	4	5	6
Yellow	×	×	×	×	×	×
Green	×	×	×	×	×	×
Blue	✗	×	✗	×	✗	×
Brown	×	×	×	×	×	×
Red	×	×	×	×	×	✗
Black	×	×	×	×	×	×

All the equally likely outcomes are shown with a cross, and we can see that there are 36 possibilities (= 6 × 6). The favourable ones we are seeking are shown in bolder type. From this we can see that 'red + 6' can only happen in one way, so that the probability of this happening is 1 out of 36, or $\frac{1}{36}$ (= 0.028). On the other hand, 'blue + any odd number' can happen in three ways, so the probability of this happening is 3 out of 36, or $\frac{3}{36}$ (=0.083).

Try it

1 Find a client group that you can access in a group setting.
2 Choose an aspect of their physical development which can be measured and recorded accurately (e.g. height, age, mass, shoe size).
3 Collect the appropriate data from the clients, and collate it in a pictorial form.
4 Calculate the mean from your sample (show your workings). See page 299.
5 Draw conclusions from your findings and justify why you have drawn those conclusions.

Try it

Study the chart opposite and answer the questions, showing your workings.

1 What trend can you identify from the data?
2 What reasons can you give for this trend?
3 What was the increase in places between 1970 and 1990?

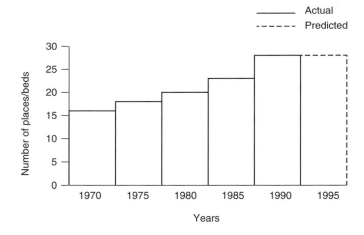

4 The ratio of nursing staff to clients is 1:4. How many nurses were needed in 1970, 1980 and 1990?
5 If a nurse was paid £120 for a 30-hour week in 1990, what would the salary bill have been for one week in the ward?
6 There is also one sister who works on the ward who is paid £200 per week. What ratio is this to the nurse's pay?
7 A pay rise of £6 per week is awarded for 1991 for the nurses. What percentage of their salary is this?
8 The sister was given the same percentage rise. How much increase in salary per week will she receive?
9 How much extra pay per week would the hospital need to find in total for this ward following the pay rise?
10 If the ward was asked to make a 5% cut in its staffing budget, how much would this be? How many nurses' hours would it have cut to cover this cost?

Checking procedures

Many errors are made if simple checks are not carried out on calculations. For example, if 15 467 – 956 = 14 511, then to check this simply add 956 to the answer, i.e.

$$14\ 511 + 956 = 15\ 467$$

so you know the answer is correct.

Similarly, with division or multiplication:

$$18.75 \div 3 = 6.25$$

check:

$$6.25 \times 3 = 18.75$$

Also check by rounding up:

$$4.85 \times 3.5 = 16.975$$

We know that 4.85 is nearly 5, so $3 \times 5 = 15$ and add on half of 5 = 17.5. Since the approximate answer must be slightly less than 17.5, our actual answer is likely to be correct.

Rounding up to 10 or 100 is another way of checking whether your answer is likely to be accurate.

$$9.85 \times 19 = 187.15$$

This can be checked by approximation $10 \times 19 = 190$, so the answer will be slightly less than this.

Predictions

This is a forecast of what is to come, usually based on a few results when many are expected. Predictions can turn out to be fairly accurate or wildly inaccurate. If you have ever watched television on general election day, you will see predictions: a multitude of different graphical displays show how Parliament will be made up and which will be the party of government. As the night wears on and more and more results are announced, the predictions become more accurate. So with a few results, questionnaires, surveys, etc. a prediction can be made, but its accuracy is questionable. As more results become available, the accuracy of the prediction increases.

Fast Facts

Area   The space covered by a shape. It can be a regular shape (for example square) or irregular.

Area of a circle   Pie (π) multiplied by the radius squared.

Area of a rectangle   Length multiplied by the width.

Area of a triangle   Half the base length times the height.

Axes   The lines containing the scales which form the framework of a graph. They usually meet in the left-hand corner of the page. The horizontal line is called the *x* axis and the vertical line is the *y* axis.

Calculator   A device for calculating quickly. Beware of quoting answers to large numbers of decimal places – rounding to two is usually enough (for example, 6.3486 would be 6.35).

Circumference of a circle   Pie (π) times the diameter.

Closed questions   Questions with closed types of answers (e.g. yes/no).

Conversion   Changing one unit into another (for example pounds to ounces or ounces to grams). If you are using any of the **four rules of number,** *always* check that all figures are in the same unit.

Decimal number   A number which includes a decimal point. Remember during calculation, moving the point to the left makes the figure smaller; moving the point to the right makes the figure larger.

Estimation   Making a close guess or approximate judgement as to the value of your answer. This helps to check that no serious mistakes have been made.

Four rules of number   Plus, minus, divide and multiply. (Remember always to line your units under one another if not using a calculator.)

Fractions   Expressing a part in relation to the whole. The upper number is the numerator, the lower figure is the denominator. Remember when using the **four rules of number** with fractions, you must work out a common denominator.

Generalisation   Picking out the pattern or trend shown by a set of figures or chart.

Justification   Reasons or proof used to back up statements made.

Landscape format   Paper turned so that the greatest length goes horizontally, like a landscape painting in an art gallery.

Mean   The average of a set of values. The total amount of a set of values divided by the number of values. For example,

1, 3, 3, 3, 4, 6, 9, 15, 19 mean = $63 \div 9 = 7$

Median   The half-way value of a series of values. For example,

1, 3, 3, 3, 4, 6, 9, 15, 19 median = 4

Mode   The most common value in a set of values. For example,

1, 3, 3, 3, 4, 6, 9, 15, 19 mode = 3

Observation   Collecting data by watching a set of activities for a certain period.

Open questions   Questions with no fixed answer.

Percentage   Rate or proportion per hundred (per cent). A fraction can be converted to a percentage by multiplying by 100. The symbol is %.

Perimeter   The distance around the outside of any shape. The perimeter of a circle is the same as its circumference.

Pictogram An eye-catching method of presenting data which is quick and easy to understand.

Portrait format Paper turned so that the greatest length goes vertically, like a portrait painting.

Precision This is the same as accuracy. Measurements made with precision are therefore accurate rather than estimates.

Prediction Using figures or data to guess what might happen in the future.

Probability The likelihood of an event happening

Protractor A device shaped as a semi-circle marked in degrees of a circle. The instrument is used for measuring angles.

Questionnaire A written set of questions used to obtain data about a particular topic.

Range The spread of values from the highest number to the lowest number.

Ratios Ratios are a way of comparing two or more quantities.

Recording The noting down of information.

Respondents People who answer questions put to them.

Sample A name given to a group of your choosing to represent the whole set.

Scale An item marked in such a way that the distance between two marks measures a quantity.

Sequence Doing a calculation in the correct order for example, BODMAS – this gives you the correct order for calculating – Brackets Of (usually means multiplying) Division Multiplication Addition Subtraction.

Survey A collection and examination of information on an area – perhaps to draw conclusions.

Three-dimensional object One with depth as well as area. Everything in the world is really 3-dimensional. A piece of paper is 3-dimensional because it does have some depth (its thickness).

Trialling Using a new questionnaire with a sample of respondents before applying it to the whole set of a chosen group of people.

Two-dimensional object A shape that is flat on the page and which is therefore reckoned to have an area but not a volume.

Volume The volume of a container is the same as its capacity. It is the amount of space inside the shape.

Volume of a rectangular block Length times width times height.

Volume of a cylinder Pie (π) times radius squared times length (i.e. πr^2). The radius is half the diameter.

Information technology

Information technology (IT) has an increasingly important place in the modern world. Most bills that come through your door have been generated and printed using a computer. Magazines and newspapers are produced using IT methods. Shops and businesses use computers to keep track of their sales and stocks of products. In fact, many of the products themselves, from cars to coffee jars, are made with the help of computers. Nowadays, whatever career you follow, IT has a central role in the workplace.

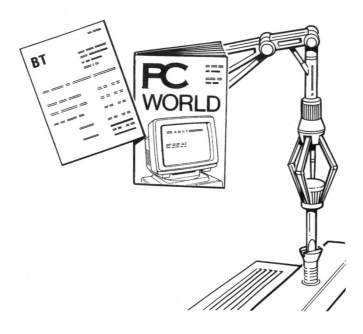

Figure 15.1 IT is central to the world of work

GNVQ students need to learn about IT, and find out how to use a computer for themselves. IT is a GNVQ core skill, together with Communication and Application of Number, because it is so widely used.

You will find that most of the evidence you need to pass the IT unit will be among the work you do in the course of your health and care studies. This chapter will help you to use IT effectively by showing you how it can be applied to things you will be doing as a health and care student. It will also help you to identify work which may count as evidence

towards the IT unit. The computer screen icon appears occasionally to emphasise important points.

Important information will appear here.

Whether you are an experienced user or a beginner, you should find this chapter useful. If you have never used IT before, the best thing is to read the chapter carefully, and try all the suggested tasks. You should find that everything starts to make sense once you begin to put IT into action. If you *have* used IT before, you will still find this chapter useful, as it shows you how to apply IT skills to the work you do on a GNVQ health and caring course. You may come across some techniques and ideas that you haven't met before!

The most important thing to do is to use the equipment that is available to you. You need to become familiar with the machines you will be using, and with the tutors who can help you to use them. This chapter will indicate what you need to do, but it is up to you to put IT into action for yourself.

IT basics

What do we mean by information technology? Obviously, this refers to the use of new technologies to deal with information, but there are a number of terms used where the meaning is not so obvious. So let's start with some basic explanations.

Hardware

Hardware simply means the physical equipment used in IT. This includes the computer itself (sometimes referred to as the base unit), the monitor screen, the keyboard and the mouse. Hardware is also the term for other equipment such as the printer, and the cables that connect all the machines together.

There are other useful devices that fall under the heading of hardware, and you may have access to some of them. For example, scanners can be used to enter a picture (or graphic) into the computer from a paper-based copy. The key point to remember is that hardware means the physical equipment that is used in IT.

Software

Software is the term used for the set of instructions which the computer follows when performing a task. You may have heard this referred to as a **program**, or as an **application**. This can seem confusing, but remember that they are basically just different words for the same type of thing.

There are many different types of software, each designed to perform different types of task. One important type that is needed by all computers is known as the **operating system**. The operating system is used to get the computer up and running, and to control its activities. Operating systems manage the entry, flow and display of information between different parts of the computer. The operating system must be running before you can

> **Software is the name for the set of instructions that the computer follows.**

run other types of software. In fact, this is an automatic process. When you switch on the computer the operating system begins to run, and sets up the machine ready for use.

Other types of software are designed so that you can do different things such as write letters, perform calculations, create graphics or even play games. You will be using software applications like these in your GNVQ studies. You will find that they are designed to be easy to use. You don't need to know anything about programming a computer to use IT effectively, any more than you have to understand mechanics in order to drive a car.

Types of software

You will be using some of the most useful and popular types of software during your GNVQ studies.

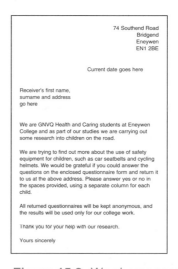

Figure 15.2 Word-processed documents

Word-processors are used to handle text (i.e. words and numbers) and produce letters, reports and other documents. Word-processing is one of the most common uses of IT. You will discover how easy it is to create, edit and print professional-looking documents.

Database software is used to work with information in the form of lists. Your address book is a form of database. You could think of a database as an electronic file card index, such as you may have seen in libraries or offices. However, they are much easier to use, and can do much more than simply store information. Databases are an ideal way of dealing with any repetitive information, such as names and addresses, or types and prices of products.

NAME	ADDRESS	TEL NO.
BLOGGS	10 LONG LANE	0181 906 3342
SMITH	2 SHORT STREET	0181 983 3711
JONES	2 RED ROAD	0171 943 2222

Figure 15.3 Example of a database

Spreadsheets are designed to handle numerical information. With a spreadsheet you can enter numbers, perform calculations and present your

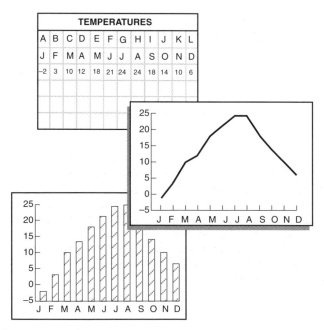

Figure 15.4 Spreadsheet and charts

results neatly as a chart or graph. For work in science, business, or any task where calculations need to be performed, a spreadsheet is a flexible and powerful tool.

Graphics applications are used to create and edit drawings, illustrations and other types of graphics. There are two main types of graphics software: drawing applications and painting applications. If you want to create an illustration with lines drawn in precise positions, and a 'clean' look to the result, use a drawing application.

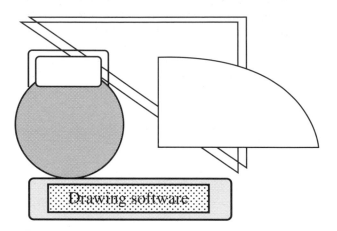

Painting software produces a freer result with brush and spray effects.

All of these applications – word-processing, databases, spreadsheets and graphics – are powerful tools, and each has a wide range of uses which fall beyond the scope of this chapter. They can be even

Painting software

more powerful when used together. A graph of results from a spreadsheet, or a graphic from a drawing application, can be put into a word-processed report. A word-processed letter can be blended with a list of names and addresses in a database to send a mass mail shot. This ability to share information between applications opens up many possibilities, and we will be looking at some of them later in the chapter.

There are other types of software that may be available to you. These include specialised accounts applications, which are designed to make business management and accounting easier, and **desk-top publishing** (DTP) applications. DTP software is a cross between a word-processor and a graphics application. If you want to mix graphics and text together, for example to produce a magazine or a poster, then use DTP software to produce good results easily.

Compatibility

The term compatibility refers to the ability of computers and software to work with other computers and software. Several different types of computer have been developed over the past 25 years. Many of these were designed to work in their own particular way and run software specially designed for them. This meant that work done on one type of computer could not be transferred to a different type. Nowadays, this is no longer a problem since only a couple of computer types dominate the market; and good quality software is often able to convert work from other formats.

You should find that the machines and software available to you during your GNVQ studies are compatible with others. However, this is not guaranteed to be the case, so it is a good idea to find out more about the machines you will be using.

Try it

1 Talk to your IT tutor about the equipment you will be using during your studies.
2 Find out which machines and software applications are compatible with each other.
3 Find out when you can get access to a computer, and the days and times that there is someone there to help you.

Memory and storage

The computer's memory is know as **RAM** which stands for **random access memory.** The RAM holds the information and instructions that are being used by the computer during your work sessions. But RAM is not a permanent storage place for your work as everything is deleted from it when you turn off the computer. We will look at how you can save your work below.

Computer memory is measured in **bytes.** A byte is a single piece of information, and any single keypress such as a letter, a number or a space is one byte of information. You are more likely to hear memory size described in terms of **kilobytes** and **megabytes.** One kilobyte (K) equals 1024 bytes and one megabyte (Mb) equals 1024 kilobytes (or 1 048 546 bytes).

The computer's memory is measured in bytes. One keypress is one byte of information.

Saving your work

As we have seen, the work that you do on the computer is temporarily stored in the memory, and when the computer is switched off the work is lost unless you save it first. Where do you save your work? The answer partly depends on the equipment you are using, but it will be some form of electronic storage disk. There are two types of disks that you are likely to encounter: hard disks and floppy disks.

Hard disks

Most computers that you use will have a hard disk installed in them. The hard disk is permanently fixed inside the computer's case and cannot be removed from it.

The hard disk cannot be removed from the computer.

It can be used to store large amounts of information and can be heard clicking away to itself when you switch the computer on (known as 'booting up'), and when you use some software applications. You may save your work on the hard disk, but it is unwise to rely on it, and could be against the local IT users' rules. It is unwise because any work saved on the hard disk can be called up later by other people using that computer, which could result in tampering or even accidental but complete erasure of your work! This dreadful prospect can be avoided easily by saving your work on your own floppy disk.

Floppy disks

Floppy disks are a compact, cheap and secure way to save your work. You can buy a disk for less than £1 and most will store the equivalent of over 200 pages of text, which is very good value for money! Nowadays, most computers use $3\frac{1}{2}$-inch disks.

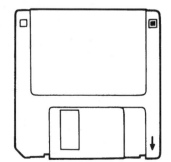

Figure 15.5 A $3\frac{1}{2}$-inch floppy disk

Floppy disks are the best way of keeping your work secure. You can insert you own personal disk into the computer and save your work on to it. When you correctly shut down the application, the only copy of your work that remains is on your floppy disk. Remove the disk and you will have all your work safely in you own possession, which is the safest way to keep it.

Formatting a floppy disk

Before you can save work on a new floppy disk, you will need to prepare it for use by a process called **formatting**. Floppy disks work rather like a cassette tape in that you can 'record' and 'playback' information on them, but the way they store your work may seem more like a CD or LP record as the surface of the floppy disk is divided into tracks and sectors. These invisible storage blocks are created by the computer when the disk is formatted.

It is very easy to format a disk: simply put it into the disk slot and tell the computer to format it. Beware when reformatting a used disk though, because formatting permanently removes any work that was previously stored on it and you could lose something you didn't mean to! You can avoid accidental erasure by closing the read/write gate on your floppy disk. When the tab (gate) is closed, you can still read the information on the disk but it cannot be altered or deleted. This is a very secure way of saving but of course it prevents you saving any new files on the disk or reformatting it.

Disk capacity

The storage capacity of a floppy disk is measured in bytes, like the computer's memory size. This becomes important when you need to buy and format a $3\frac{1}{2}$-inch floppy disk because they come in two common sizes, 720K and 1.4Mb. The difference between them is that a 1.4Mb disk can hold twice as much information. You can use either type to store your work, but you need to format your disk according to its storage capacity.

Now you need to find out the details of how to format a disk on your local equipment.

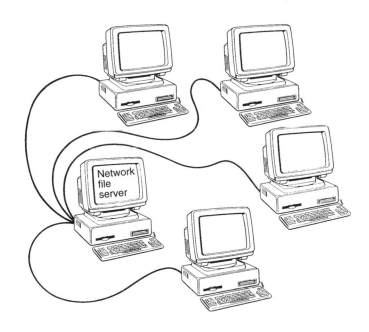

Try it

1 Buy a floppy disk. Check with your IT adviser for a local supplier.
2 Find out how to format disks correctly using the local equipment, and format your floppy disk.

When you have completed this task you should have your own floppy disk, formatted and ready to receive your work.

Stand-alone computers and networks

The computers we have discussed so far are complete machines in themselves. They can keep applications software on their internal hard disk, and save work there. They need to be connected to a printer to get paper copies, but they are not connected to other computers. Machines like this are known as **stand-alone computers**.

Nowadays, many organisations, including businesses and educational institutions, are linking computers together to form computer **networks.** It may well be that you will be using a machine on a network during your studies. All the machines in a network are linked to a piece of hardware called a network **server** – an extremely large hard-disk drive which can hold a vast amount of data. Each separate computer, or **workstation**, loads software from the server, and can usually save work on it. A workstation computer doesn't even need to have its own hard-disk drive, as the network server can act as a hard disk for all the machines on the network.

Networks have several advantages over stand-alone computers:

- The network file server can hold a much greater range of software than an individual computer's hard disk, and this range is available to users at each workstation.
- Specialised hardware can be connected to the server and so made available to all users. For example a CD-ROM (compact disc-read only memory) device can allow encyclopedias and other reference works to be used at each workstation without the need to install expensive hardware in every machine.
- In most situations, information can be shared between different computers in the network.

Figure 15.6 A computer network

Businesses use networks to help information flow between different parts of the organisation.

In the case of students' work, it is usually more important to keep work secure than to share it electronically with others. If you use a local hard disk, or a network server, to save work you should always keep copies on a floppy disk which you can keep securely. This is called **backing up** your work.

Always back up your work on a floppy disk.

Directory systems – keeping track of your work

Files

Each separate piece of work that you create and save on the computer is known as a **file.** Files are linked to the applications that they were created in, so that a word-processed letter is saved as a word-processor file and a database listing books you have read is saved as a database file. The computer will ask you to give your files a name as you save them, and it will add its own code at the end to remind you what application the file belongs to. The problem is that you are restricted to a maximum name length of only eight characters when you save, and as you add files to your floppy disk it can soon contain a confusing list of meaningless initials, unless you take care to organise it.

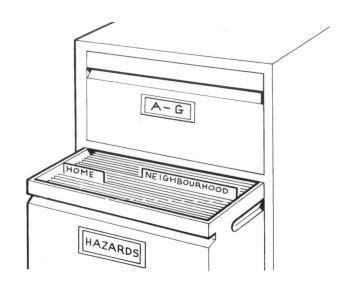

Directories

There is an easy way to avoid having to deal with a bewildering list of file names and that is to organise your files into groups. The computer can set up a storage system on a disk so that files that you want to keep together are stored in the same place – in a **directory.** It may be helpful to think of the files you save as though they were paper files and were to be stored in a filing cabinet. You would probably want to put all the work you were doing for a particular assignment together in the same drawer, but you may want to divide that up further so that you can easily find work intended for a particular part of the assignment.

Suppose you were preparing a project on the hazards to health faced by children in their local environment and in the home. You may want to split your work into two parts: an investigation into the hazards faced in the local neighbourhood and an investigation into the hazards faced in the home.

Your filing cabinet drawer could be divided up into two sections. You could label the drawer HAZARDS, and label the sections inside HOME and NEIGHBOURHOOD.

As a GNVQ student you could have used IT to make the 'Hazards' task easier and well organised.

For the first part of your investigation you might use the word-processor to create an interview form asking local parents about hazards faced in the neighbourhood. You might then use a database to produce a list of different hazards faced by children in their neighbourhood.

For the second part of the investigation, you could word-process a questionnaire form to find out parents' views on hazards faced by children in the home. Later on you would need to deal with the results of your survey, and present them. This could be done using a spreadsheet.

The computer can create a similar arrangement to the filing cabinet example to help you to keep track of your work.

You can tell the computer to create a directory called HAZARDS to hold all the work that you do. The directory can be used to save any type of file, so you can save a word-processed letter together with a spreadsheet in the same directory.

In our example, you are intending to split the work into two parts, and keep each part separate within the HAZARDS directory. You can create further divisions within your directory, known as **sub-directories.** Your sub-directories need names of eight characters or less, so you could use NGHBRHD (to stand for 'neighbourhood') and HOME.

For your 'neighbourhood' work you created a word-processed interview form, and a hazard database. You can save both your form as INTERVEW, and your database as HAZBASE in the NGHBRHD sub-directory.

For your 'home' work you created a word-processed questionnaire and a results spreadsheet. These could be named QUESTNRE and RESULTS, and saved in the HOME sub-directory.

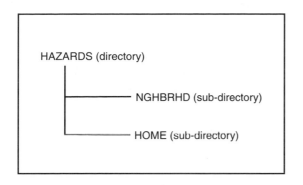

Figure 15.7 Example of a directory with sub-directories

Now there is a **path** to each file. For example, your interview form is in the NGHBRHD sub-directory of the HAZARDS directory. The path to your interview form would be written as HAZARDS\NGHBRHD\INTERVEW, showing the route to be taken to the location of your file on disk.

This path provides a unique 'address' for your files which you use to reload it for editing or printing.

You can keep track of your work by thoughtful use of directories and sub-directories. The computer can quickly show you the layout and contents of your floppy disk so there is no need to remember the paths to all your files.

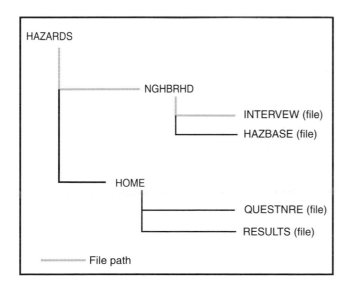

Figure 15.8 Files within sub-directories

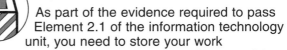

Evidence collection point

As part of the evidence required to pass Element 2.1 of the information technology unit, you need to store your work systematically. This means giving your files sensible names which indicate their contents. It also means creating and using directories to group together related files. Use the methods explained above to keep track of your work, and you will have the evidence needed for this element.

Also, you should save, or back up, your work regularly as you create it to avoid any losses. Backing up your work regularly is another requirement of this element, and is wise in case a problem occurs while you are working. Backed-up work can be reloaded and continued with. Work that is not backed up is lost forever if an error causes the computer to shut down!

Using computers safely

Protecting yourself and others

The equipment that you are using has been designed to be as safe to use as possible. The computer itself and peripheral equipment such as printers are powered from the mains electricity supply, like other domestic electrical appliances. They are insulated and earthed to protect users from electrical hazard, but they must be treated with care to prevent accidents.

Figure 15.9 How many hazards can you identify?

Cables connecting items of equipment to the electrical supply, or to each other, must be arranged so that they do not endanger health and safety. Cables must be protected from damage, and must not be allowed to work around work areas so that they form a hazard in themselves.

If you connect items of equipment like printers, be sure to arrange the cables safely.

The arrangement of your work surface is also important. The computer keyboard is light and mobile. This means that you can arrange its position to suit your own preferred way of working, but it also means that you can clutter you work surface with paper notes, pens and other equipment. Try to avoid doing this as a crowded work surface increases the chance of accidents, and is not likely to make your work any more efficient!

Never eat or drink around IT equipment! Liquids are particularly dangerous. A spilled drink can cause a serious electrical hazard, as well as damaging the equipment. Make sure that this rule is enforced, both for your own safety and that of others.

Setting up equipment for your needs

Computer equipment is designed to be adjustable so that it can be set to the individual requirements of the user and the environment. The keyboard has small pull-out feet at the back edge to increase its angle of incline, which some people prefer, and it is easily moved into the most comfortable position for typing. The monitor may be swivelled left and right, and tilted up and down. This allows you to orientate the screen to a position where it is facing you directly, so that you are not forced to sit in an awkward or uncomfortable position to see it clearly.

The screen is also adjustable for brightness and contrast and you need to set these so that you can see your work clearly. It is also important, however, not to work with the screen turned up too brightly. Prolonged use of a bright screen at close quarters can strain eyes and should be avoided.

The lighting conditions in the room can affect the visibility of monitor screens. The screen will need to be turned up much more brightly to be seen in a well-lit room, particularly if lights are reflected directly on to it. Sunlight creates the same problem and a screen facing a sunny window is very difficult to see indeed. Try to make sure that you adjust the lighting conditions so that you do not need to have your screen excessively bright to be able to work.

Another important feature of the environment is the seating used with the computer equipment. Most organisations provide adjustable typists' chairs for IT users. They are designed to be adjusted to a variety of positions to suit the height and build of the user and it is important to set your chair to meet your requirements. Set the seat height so that your feet are comfortably on the floor, and the back rest so that your back is adequately supported. Working at a keyboard in a badly adjusted chair can lead to backaches and discomfort in a short time, so always take the trouble to adjust the chair to your needs.

Protecting your work

Apart from protecting yourself and the computer hardware from damage, it is also important to look after your stored data. Though floppy disks are really quite hard, and durable enough when used and stored correctly, they must be protected from physical damage. Keep them in a dry secure place as you would a CD or cassette tape. Remember that information is stored electrically on floppy disks and that this can be damaged or erased if the disk is exposed to strong magnetic or electrical fields. Many domestic appliances produce electrical fields, so the best rule is to keep disks away from electrical apparatus. It is important to keep back-up copies, and to keep them safely. Remember that work you save on hard disk drives can be loaded and altered, or deleted, by other users.

Evidence collection point

As part of the evidence needed for Element 2.4 of the information technology unit, you need to explain the importance of working safely, and in line with good working practices.

You could use a word-processor to produce a checklist of Do's and Don'ts to be observed when using IT equipment. Your checklist should include recommendations for the safety of users, for the protection of equipment, and for the protection of information from loss, corruption or unauthorised use.

Errors and faults

Generally, using IT should make work easier and be trouble free. Occasionally, problems do occur though. These problems could be due to errors made by the user (you!), or to faults with the equipment itself.

User errors

However carefully you try, you are likely to make some errors when you are learning to use a computer. Everybody makes the odd mistake, and even experienced users expect to make occasional errors when learning to use new software. Most errors are easy to spot as you go. For example, pressing the wrong key generally shows instantly on the screen and can be corrected immediately. Other user errors may be less easy to detect. Do not worry though – as you become familiar with the software you are using, the errors you are likely to make become familiar to you as well. You will soon be able to work out what has caused the problem, and know how to rectify it.

Equipment faults

Sometimes you may find that the problems you are having are not caused by mistakes you have made, but are the result of faults in the equipment. While IT equipment is usually reliable, occasionally things do go wrong.

One simple cause of many problems is poorly, or even incorrectly, connected cables. For example, the reason that the printer is not responding to your request for a paper copy may be that your computer is not connected to it. Similarly, the cable connecting the base unit to the monitor may be loose, causing your monitor to have no picture. Usually, cable faults are easy to check and correct.

Potentially more serious problems are caused by equipment failures. If the computer suddenly stops working, it could be due to the machine being accidentally turned off. More rarely, it could be that the equipment has broken down. The biggest problem for you in this situation is that your work will be lost. If you have made regular back-ups though, this will not be so serious. Remember that switching off machines when software is running can damage information stored on the hard disk. Always take care to close down properly, following the steps shown you by your IT tutor.

You should be able to deal with simple equipment problems yourself, but always check with your IT tutor that you have diagnosed the problem correctly, and that you have chosen the correct solution.

Evidence collection point

As part of the evidence required for Element 2.4 of the information technology unit, you need to keep a record of the errors and faults that occur during your use of IT resources.

Whenever you use IT, keep a log of the errors that you make, and record their effects on your work. Similarly, record equipment faults, and your solutions if appropriate. Again make comments on the effects of equipment faults on your work.

As part of the evidence required for Element 2.1 you need to make sure that a GNVQ assessor has seen you correct errors that you make, and seen you put right simple equipment faults.

It might be a good idea to use an exercise book as a 'faults log book' in which you can keep records of errors and faults. Your assessor can indicate that your corrections and repairs have been observed.

The mouse

Most computers are equipped with a mouse. The mouse, like the keyboard, is an **input device.** That means it is a way of giving the computer instructions and information.

The mouse controls the movement of an on-screen pointer. You can use the pointer to perform tasks within software applications. You also use the mouse and pointer to start up software.

When you switch on the computer, you will see a number of small graphic pictures, known as **icons.**

Each icon represents a different piece of software. You simply position the pointer over the icon for the software you need and double-click the mouse button. The software then starts up.

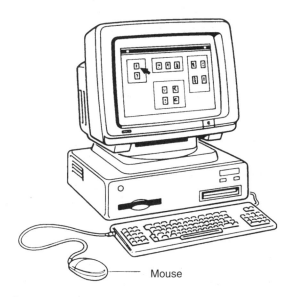

Mouse

The mouse makes using some software features very easy, though there are usually ways of using the keyboard to do the same job. One exception is with graphics software. The mouse is an essential tool when using a drawing or painting application.

Try it

It is a good idea to familiarise yourself with using the mouse when you begin to use IT. Many computers come with a short training

guide in the use of the mouse. Ask your IT tutor to show you how to run the 'Using a mouse' guide.

Word-processors

Word-processors are one of the most commonly used types of application. They are used to work with text, which means words and numbers, and they have many features designed to make it easy to produce high-quality, written documents.

With a word-processor you can:

- enter any text that you wish
- make corrections, revisions, and even major changes easily and without a lot of retyping
- create special styles for headings and important points
- alter the layout to suit your requirements
- add headings and page numbers
- import information from other applications such as a spreadsheet or database, and incorporate it into your document
- print your work when you are satisfied with it
- save your file so that you can reload it later and make further changes, and copies, if you wish.

Using a word-processor

To begin with you need to switch on the computer and start up the word-processing application. In this, as with other functions of IT described here, your local equipment will have particular ways of doing things and you need to find out the details from

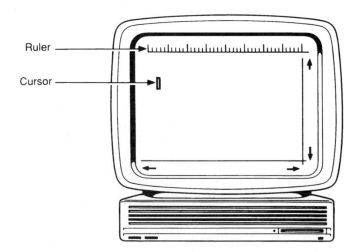

Ruler

Cursor

Figure 15.10 What the screen looks like initially

your IT tutor. The next step in creating your document is to open a new word-processor file and you will then see the screen in which you will be working.

Towards the top left of the screen is a flashing line, known as the cursor or the insertion point, which indicates where your typing will appear. Above this there is usually a ruler.

There are marks near each end of the ruler to show the margins set for your text, and your cursor should be just below the left-hand margin mark, ready for you to begin typing.

Entering text

As you type, the cursor moves to the right ahead of the text. As you approach the right-hand margin, continue typing: the word-processor automatically starts a new line without breaking up a word. This is known as **word-wrap.** If you want to start a new line – for example, a new paragraph – you use the enter (return) key. This is the key labelled ⏎

> **New lines are started automatically. Don't press enter unless you need to start a new line.**

In fact, it is unwise to use the enter key unless you want to start a new line. This is because the word-processor remembers every key push as a character, including enter and space. Unnecessary use of the enter key can produce some odd results if you change the layout of your document later.

You type in (enter) text using the letter, number and punctuation keys. Press the enter key twice to create a blank line between paragraphs. If you make a mistake, you can press the backspace key and the cursor moves to the left, deleting the incorrect text.

You can also delete spaces and enters just like other text.

When your lines of text increase so that the whole document cannot be displayed at once, you will see that the document slips up the screen so that the insertion point is always visible. This is called **scrolling.**

Figure 15.11 Imagine scrolling like this

If you want to look at the earlier part of a document that has scrolled partly out of view, you can do this by moving the cursor using the direction arrow keys on your keyboard. These keys move the cursor left and right, and up and down. As you move the cursor up your document the earlier parts scroll back into view (remember, though, that you cannot move the cursor down below the end of a document).

You can also use the mouse to move around your document. You will see a bar running up the right-hand edge of the screen. The bar has arrows at the top and bottom, and is called a **scroll bar.** If you position the mouse pointer on the top arrow and press the button your document will scroll upwards. Using the bottom arrow scrolls it the other way.

You can use the mouse to place the cursor by putting the pointer where you wish and clicking the mouse button. As with the arrow keys, you cannot put the cursor outside the text area, or past the end of the document.

Being able to position the cursor anywhere in the document is an extremely useful facility. You can move the cursor to a particular point and type in new text. You can also delete unwanted text using the backspace key. When you type new text within a document, you will find that all the text below moves along to make room for it. This is called **insert mode**, and you can change it if you wish so that your typing overwrites the original text (**overtype mode**).

Evidence collection point

With this basic knowledge of how to enter text and make corrections you can begin to use your own word-processor.

First, you need to pick a piece of written work that you would like to word-process. Try to choose something fairly simple, i.e. a piece of text that does not need a complicated layout involving tables or columns of figures. You can always return to it later and make improvements as your IT skills develop.

Now use the word-processor to produce a document based on your piece of work.

You need to:

- boot up the computer and run the word-processor
- start a new file
- type in your text, making minor alterations as you go
- check your work carefully and correct any mistakes using the methods discussed above
- save your work on a floppy disk using an appropriate file name
- print out a copy of the document.

You could talk to your IT tutor about starting new files on the word-processor, and saving your work on a floppy disk.

As part of the evidence needed for Element 2.1 of the information technology unit, you must show evidence of your use of software. Here you could keep the source materials you have used, and a printout of the result. You may eventually decide not to include this example as good evidence towards Element 2.1 but it is still a good idea to get into the habit of keeping source material and printouts as records of your IT work.

Using IT in your work

To get the most from the resources available, you need to plan the use of IT in your work. We can illustrate this by looking at the work of a group of GNVQ Health and Social Care Intermediate students. They are looking at mandatory Element 1.3 and are interested in hazards to health faced by children and young people on the road. The students decide to draw up a simple questionnaire to find out how

---

> Children on the road
> Questionnaire
> 1   Does your child wear a safety helmet when riding his/her bicycle?
> 2   Does your child wear a rear seatbelt?
> 3   Does your child travel in the family car?
> 4   Does your child travel in a specially designed child seat?
> 5   Does your child ride a bicycle on public roads?
> 6   What do you think could be done to improve safety for children on the roads?

many local children wear helmets when riding bicycles, and how may wear rear seatbelts in cars. They plan to use a word-processor to produce the questionnaire form, and to use other software to help with the survey and its results.

For the questionnaire, the students decide to use 'closed' questions, i.e. ones that require only a 'yes' or 'no' answer. This will make the results far easier to deal with. They agree on a set of questions and enter them as a new document on a word-processor.

The print-out of their document looks like the one opposite.

Having looked at their first version, the students decide to make some changes. They feel that question 6 should be left out as it is an 'open' question which could lead to long answers that are difficult to assess numerically.

They think that the question order could be improved and decide to begin with question 5, followed by question 1, with questions 3 and 4 next and question 2 at the end.

In addition, they want to allow space for parents to answer if they have more than one child, and create more space overall. So they decide to put space between the questions, and to add columns for answers so that results for up to four children can be recorded.

The students also decide to add a question to find out the age group of the child, and they decide to put this at the beginning.

Finally, they believe that the look of the questionnaire could be improved with better headings and with the question numbers hanging out to the left of the question text.

This sounds like a lot of work, but in fact it can all be done in a few minutes. Let's see how the students can use the word-processor to make the above changes to their document.

Editing text

You have already met text editing in the form of the use of the backspace key to delete text you have just typed. As you now know how to move the cursor to any part of the document, you can delete and insert text wherever you wish. But suppose that you want to move a large piece of text to another part of the document. The method above would involve the slow, character by character, deletion of the existing text and the even slower process of typing it back in at another location. And what if you then changed your mind?

There is an easier way to manipulate text, whether you want to move, copy or delete it, and it is made possible by the ability of the word-processor to 'select' text. You can select a character, a word, a line, a sentence, a paragraph, even an entire document. Text can be selected using either the keyboard or the mouse. Once you have selected the text, it is easy to move, copy or delete. In fact, the backspace key can be used to delete selected text and this is a much quicker method than working backwards character by character if you need to delete more than a few words.

The process of selecting and moving or copying text is also known as **cut and paste**, and this describes quite well what you do. First, you select the text you want to move or copy. Then you tell the word-processor to 'cut' if you want to move the text, or 'copy' if you want to leave the original text unaltered. You then move the cursor to the place where you want to insert the text and tell the word-processor to paste. Your text will then appear, and of course the text below moves down to make space for it. Now that you know how easy it is to rearrange

text to your satisfaction, let's see how to improve headings and layout.

Formatting characters

Changing the way your document looks is called **formatting**, and formatting characters refers to the effects that can be added to your text to alter its appearance. You can use **bold**, or *italic* or <u>underline</u>, or CAPITAL LETTERS, or even ***<u>ALL FOUR</u>*** to make parts of your text stand out. The method of first selecting text and then changing it can be used to format headings with these highlights, which can be used in any combination.

As well as applying these effects, you can also make changes to the size and shape of your chosen text. The text that is printed out by the computer has a consistent shape and style, whether it includes letters or numbers, and the term for a full set of characters in a particular style is a character set or font. Most typewriters use a font called Courier `which looks like this,` and this book is set in a **font** called Stone Informal. Text size is measured in **points.** Normal text is usually formatted at 10 point or 12 point – 6 point is getting too small to read and 24 point is too large for most uses.

This is 6 point

This is 10 point

This is 12 point

This is 24 point

You can change the font and size of selected text and greatly alter its appearance. Careful selection of fonts and sizes can much improve the look of the whole document, as any available fonts can be applied to any part of the text. You can add even greater emphasis to headings, and can create good-looking title pages, but beware! It is all too easy to ruin a perfectly good-looking document by using too many fonts and effects. The golden rule is to keep your character formatting simple and neat for the best presentation. You will be limited in the range of fonts and sizes available to you by the equipment you are using, but some word-processors and printers can produce a large number for you to choose from.

Remember that all the different character formats mentioned above can either be applied to text you have already entered by selecting it, or chosen before you begin so that everything you type comes out in the style you require.

Keep your formatting simple to avoid a messy presentation.

Formatting paragraphs

Formatting can also be applied to paragraph layout, and you are able to control the alignment of the paragraph and the line spacing.

Printed text is aligned between the margins of the page in one of four ways:

> Left-aligned text is arranged so that lines are even on the left-hand side but the right-hand side is ragged.
>
> Right-aligned text is similar to the above except that it is lined up on the right.
>
> Justified text is adjusted by the computer so that the lines are of an even length, though it can lead to a lot of extra spaces being added. Newspapers are printed in justified text.
>
> Centred text is centred across the line.

Line spacing can also be adjusted if you wish. The standard spacing is one line, but you can increase this in half-space steps. You can choose a format and spacing before you type or select and change as with other editing features we have looked at.

Alignment of paragraphs takes place between the margins, as was mentioned above, and you can change the position of these margins for particular paragraphs or for the whole document.

One of the changes that the students in our example want to make is to have the question numbers hanging out to the left of the text. This can be achieved by selecting the question paragraphs, and then setting the left margin in a short way, but setting the first line of each paragraph back over to the left. This produces a **hanging indent**, and although it may sound complicated it is a common procedure, so your word-processor will be designed to make it easy for you to do.

> This is an example of a hanging indent. The beginning of the first line protrudes on the left.

The students have been using some of these methods on their questionnaire form.

They began by selecting and deleting question 6, then rearranged the order of the remaining questions by selecting and moving the text. Lastly, they renumbered them.

Next, they inserted a blank line between each question by moving the cursor to the question numbers and pressing the enter key.

Using the tab key they moved the cursor a short way over to the right along the blank line below each question and inserted a few dots. This was repeated four times to provide answer columns. Using the tab key helps to line up the answer spaces correctly and it is easier and quicker to use than the spacebar.

The students then selected the question paragraphs and set a left margin with a hanging indent so that the numbers stand out to the left.

It had been decided to ask the age of the children, and the students wanted to put this before the other questions. They used the tab key again to space the check boxes along the line.

Finally they tackled the headings. Both headings were centred and **emboldened** with 'questionnaire'

Children on the road

QUESTIONNAIRE

Please fill in a column for each child in your household

		1	2	3	4
Age group of child	0-4				
	5-8				
	8-12				

1   Does your child ride a bicycle on public roads?

2   Does your child wear a safety helmet when riding his/her bicycle?

3   Does your child travel in the family car?

4   Does your child travel in a specially designed child seat?

5   Does your child wear a rear seatbelt?

THANK YOU FOR YOUR HELP

Figure 15.12 The students' revised questionnaire

in capital letters. They decided to leave the size and font as they are, and add a 'thank you for your help' at the end for reasons of politeness.

When they have completed these changes they saved and printed the file. The revised questionnaire is shown in Figure 15.12.

The new document is much clearer to read than the original draft, and the students' questionnaire form now looks like a well-presented document.

Evidence collection point

As part of the evidence required to pass Element 2.2 of the information technology unit, you need to show that you have made editing changes to word-processed documents.

You should make and keep printouts of your work before, during and at the end of the editing process. The copies you submit for assessment towards the IT unit need to be annotated so that the effects of changes you have made are indicated. Remember to keep copies of early versions of your work whenever you decide to make changes.

Where can I use the word-processor?

You can use the word-processor to produce all sorts of documents during your studies. Your notes, letters, case studies and reports will all look better, and be easy to improve.

Try using the word-processor to produce a range of documents, and using editing facilities to improve them. Make sure that you keep your source material, and keep printouts of your work at different stages to show how improvements were planned and carried out.

Using manuals and on-line help

Even though you may have been shown how to perform a particular task with your software, it is often difficult to remember everything at first. You can ask your tutor, but it may be easier and quicker to get help using the computer itself.

Most software that you will use comes with built-in help. You can remind yourself of how to do something by calling up the help facility available for that particular area. Sometimes the help facility is 'situation sensitive' and you can press just one key to get help on the job you are currently trying to do.

You can also use the help facility to find out new things about the software, and what it can do. This can be fun, and 'help browsing' can extend your knowledge of the software's capabilities.

Help and information can also be found in the printed manual that comes with the software. The manual may contain more information than the on-screen help facility, and some people may find it easier to use a manual at first. Check with your IT tutor whether manuals are available for the software you use.

Evidence collection point

As part of the evidence needed to pass Element 2.1 of the information technology unit, you should make use of manuals and on-line help facilities, as well as asking tutors when necessary.

Make sure that you know how to call up the help available with the software you are using, and can find your way around it.

Database software

Now that they have finished their questionnaire form, the students need a list of people to send it to. They have decided to use their local contacts, such as family and neighbours, to compile a list of families with children in their area. They know that their list is unlikely to be complete, but try to include as many families as possible.

The students intend to use database software to store their contact list so that they can use the information in a variety of ways later. We will now have a look at some of the features of database applications.

What is a database?

A database is a list of information. We have already given the example of an address book. A recipe book is another example.

Figure 15.13 A recipe book and card-file index are types of databases

Computers are very good at handling lists and the software application that is used for this is called a **database manager**, though it is usually referred to simply as a database.

The sorts of things you can do with a computerised database include:

- locate particular information instantly
- add extra information
- update and alter information
- rearrange the order of the list
- make smaller sub-lists from your information
- share information with other software applications.

Setting up a database

To begin setting up a database, you first need to decide what information you want to record. Suppose that you want to keep track of the books that you have read or referred to during an assignment. For each book you would want to note the title, author (first name and surname), publisher and date of publication. Each of these categories of information is known as is a **field**, and you can enter data into these fields for each of the books you wish to list. The information held for a particular book is called a **record**, and in our example each record will contain the title, author, publisher and date fields.

To set up a new database you must tell the computer what fields you need. The information you are storing will be of different types, some will be numbers and some will be words (or perhaps words and numbers together). Data made up of numbers, such as a price or a quantity, is known as **numeric data,** and data made up of text, or a combination of text and numbers, is called **alphanumeric data.** Names, titles of books and telephone numbers are all examples of alphanumeric data. Telephone numbers are not used to do calculations with, so it is easier to treat them as alphanumeric data. You need to decide what type of fields you need to create for your data, and in our example we would need only alphanumeric fields as no numbers are being stored.

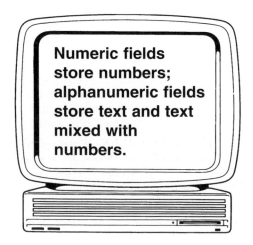

Numeric fields store numbers; alphanumeric fields store text and text mixed with numbers.

You also need to decide on the length of your fields which is specified by a number of characters. Let us allow 80 characters for the title, 20 characters for the author's surname, 20 characters for the author's first name, 25 characters for the publisher, 4 characters for the publication date.

When you have set up your fields you will have a blank record looking something like this:

Title:

Author's surname:

Author's first name:

Publisher:

Publication date:

All you need to do now is enter the details of the first book into the fields. When you have finished you move to the next record and fill in the data for the next book, and you continue creating new records until all the data are stored.

When you have finished this process you have created a database.

The students have created a database of local parents and have included the following fields for each record:

Title:

Surname:

First_name:

House_number:

Address_1:

Address_2:

Address_3:

Postcode:

They are now able to look at the entries they have made in a variety of ways. Looking at records is known as *browsing* and you have a lot of control over how you arrange them.

When you browse records they are displayed in rows with the field names written as column titles at the top, like this:

Title	Surname	First_name	House_number
Mrs	Collins	Susan	25
Mrs	Fellows	Maureen	58
Mrs	Siddiqui	Naeem	12
Mrs	Spencer	Brenda	109
Mr	Wilcocks	Andrew	8

Not all the field columns can be displayed on the screen at once. They have not disappeared, but simply cannot be fitted on to the screen. You can think of the screen as a window that can only show part of the scene at any one time. You can move the window around to view other areas using the cursor keys. Just as you can scroll down a document with the word-processor, so you can move across the database to view the contents of the other fields.

In the example of the students the records have been displayed alphabetically using the surname field as the index. The records could be displayed sorted by the First_name, or by the Address_1 field (which is used for street name, or the name of a block of flats), or by using any of the fields.

Records can be sorted by using any field as the index.

The students have found out that Mrs Brenda Spencer and family have moved out of 109 Laurel Crescent, but that another family with young children have moved in. They do not know the new occupants' names, though. The students decide to edit the record.

You can ask the computer to search for a particular record, or group of records, in a database and edit the data they contain. You need to specify the text or numbers that you are looking for and all the records that contain it will be displayed. In this case the students search for the word Spencer in the Surname field and the following record is displayed:

```
Title:  Mrs
Surname: Spencer
First_name: Brenda
House_number: 109
Address_1: Laurel Crescent
Address_2: Bridgend
Address_3: Eneywen
Postcode: EN1 2BE
```

The students amend the record by moving the cursor to the data they want to change and entering the new information. The record now looks like this:

```
Title: Sir/Madam
Surname:
First_name:
House number:_109
Address_1:  Laurel Crescent
Address_2:  Bridgend
Address_3:  Eneywen
Postcode:   EN1 2BE
```

They have left the Surname and First_name fields blank, but have included the words 'Sir/Madam' in the Title field. The reason for this will become clear later when we look at merging database information with a word-processed standard letter.

The students have been told that the family at 42 Station Road has moved, but none of the group can remember the family's name. This time they know that they are looking for a family at 42 Station Road,

so they decide to search the database. To make the search they need to specify which fields they are interested in and the data that they are looking for in these fields. So they specify the data entry '42' in the House_number field, and the data entry 'Station Road' in the Address_1 field. As there is only one family at 42 Station Road, the following record is displayed:

```
Title:  Mrs
Surname:    Mutyaba
First_name: Ramlah
House_number:42
Address_1:  Station Road
Address_2:  Railton
Address_3:  Eneywen
Postcode:   EN2 4EX
```

The students then delete the entire record from the database.

Searching the database for a particular record is very useful, but what if you want to look at a group of records that have something in common? The students want to check how many families from the Railton area they have included in their database, so they decide to query the database. A query is made by specifying the fields to be queried, and the information to be searched for. The records which fit the requirements are displayed as a list and you can work on this list using all the database management tools that we have described.

Query the database to list records with similar contents in certain fields.

The students want to see all the records with Railton in the Address_2 field. Their query displays the following list of records:

Title	Surname	First_name	House_number	Address_1
Mrs	Cooper	Jean	48	Shunters Hill
Mrs	Fardoongi	Surina	191	Beeching Close
Mrs	Harris	Emily	27	Station Road
Mr	Spiers	Roger	5	Beeching Close
Mrs	Watkins	Alice	22	Marples Ave

Remember that these records have not been taken away from the main database, but that they have simply been chosen for display, leaving the other records hidden. The students are satisfied that they have included enough families from the Railton area and save their complete database file on floppy disk.

Where can I use a database?

You can use a database to manage any information in list form. One example would be to keep a record of books and other source material that you use during your studies. This makes it easy to find material again and to print out a bibliography, and it provides evidence of your reading on the course.

You may want to use a database to record the names and addresses of contacts you make during your studies, together with their areas of interest and expertise.

Another possible use of a database is to create a glossary of technical terms that you come across. This can prove useful for revision and project writing.

As part of your work for Unit 1, Promoting health and well-being, you could produce a database of drugs, listing their uses, effects and dangers.

In all of these examples careful choice of fields is the key to making your database useful. For example, a 'Work_I_used_it_for' field in your books database allows you to create a bibliography for any piece of work you have done.

Evidence collection point

Work that you do using a database can produce evidence towards Elements 2.1, 2.2 and 2.3 of the information technology unit.

First, you need to decide what information to store in your database. Remember that you can store any information that is in the form of a list. You then need to decide on the field titles and lengths that you will require.

When you have decided on your data you need to find out how to:

- set up a new database with the fields that you want on your local equipment
- search the database for particular records
- add, delete and edit records
- query the database for a list of records containing certain information in common.

Talk to your IT tutor to find out how to perform these tasks on your equipment.

Practise using the database management tools described above, and when you are satisfied save your file on a floppy disk.

Remember to keep a printout of your work, and your original source material. This may be needed as evidence towards the IT unit.

Combining information from different sources

The next stage in our students' work involves sending letters and questionnaires to all the addresses on their database. They intend to use the word-processor to create a letter and to link it with their database of names and addresses. We will now see how this is done.

Form letters

The document that you create on the word-processor for a **mail-merge** is known as a **form letter.** Form letters are typed in like an ordinary letter, except that you indicate the places where information from the database is to appear. The students want to send the same letter to each of the people on their list, but will need to have a different name and address on each copy of their letter.

One student has agreed to use his home as the sender's address, so he will be sent all the responses. The group plan the letter leaving spaces where information from the database will be included. Figure 15.14 shows the text of their letter, with boxes to indicate where they want to put database information:

74 Southend Road
Bridgend
Eneywen
EN1 2BE

Current date goes here

Receiver's first name, surname and address go here

Dear Receiver's title and surname go here

We are GNVQ Health and Caring students at Eneywen College and as part of our studies we are carrying out some research into children on the road.

We are trying to find out more about the use of safety equipment for children, such as car seatbelts and cycling helmets. We would be grateful if you could answer the questions on the enclosed questionnaire form and return it to us at the above address. Please answer yes or no in the spaces provided, using a separate column for each child.

All returned questionnaires will be kept anonymous, and the results will be used only for our college work.

Thank you for your help with our research.

Yours sincerely

Figure 15.14 The first draft of the students' letter

The students now need to create their form letter. They need to indicate where database information is to be included so that the right information appears in the right places. This is done by typing the name of a database field into the letter, positioned where they want the data contained in that field to appear. It has to be made clear to the computer that they have typed a field name and not just another word, and the

word-processor they are using will have a way of indicating this. These specially marked field names are called **merge fields** and act as an instruction to the computer to bring information from a database file into a word-processor file when it is printed.

Merge fields in a form letter show which data fields the information will be imported from.

It is important to realise that merging only takes place when the document is printed, so that you do not see the details of particular records displayed on the screen in the letter – only the field names of the database in which the records are stored.

The students have created a form letter on the word-processor, and have included merge fields where they want database information to appear. They have also included a special field for the current date to be inserted when the letters are printed. They have been careful to type the field names exactly as they are written in their database file so that the computer can recognise them, and have enclosed them in angled brackets, which their particular word-processor uses to define a merge field. Fig. 15.15 shows their letter as it appears on the computer monitor screen.

The merge fields have been carefully placed so that the printed letters will have database information in the right places.

The receiver's title, surname and first name appear in the right order, and the address is laid out neatly beneath.

You may remember that the students did not know the name of the new residents of 109 Laurel Crescent, Bridgend. For this record the students left the Surname and First_name fields empty, and typed Sir/Madam in the Title field. This means that the letter to 109 Laurel Crescent will begin Dear Sir/Madam.

74 Southend Road
Bridgend
Eneywen
EN1 2BE
<DATE>

<First_name><Surname>
<House_number><Address_1>
<Address_2>
<Address_3>
<Postcode>

Dear <Title><Surname>

We are GNVQ Health and Caring students at Eneywen College and as part of our studies we are carrying out some research into children on the road.

We are trying to find out more about the use of safety equipment for children, such as car seatbelts and cycling helmets. We would be grateful if you could answer the questions on the enclosed questionnaire form and return it to us at the above address. Please answer yes or no in the spaces provided, using a separate column for each child.

All returned questionnaires will be kept anonymous, and the results will be used only for our college work.

Thank you for your help with our research.

Yours sincerely

Figure 15.15 The students' letter with field names included

Printing a merge document

The students are now ready to print their letters. To begin with they run the word-processor and load the file containing their merge letter. They then tell the computer to perform a **print merge**, which is one of the print options available. The students take care to specify the path to their database file, and its name, so that the computer can find it.

Finally, they tell it to print and the computer produces a personalised letter for each record on the database.

The students now need to print labels for the envelopes, which they will do from the database. They run the database programme and load their mailing list file. Their database has address labels

included in its printing options. They simply specify the fields to print and the position they are to appear on the label. When they instruct the computer to print, it produces a label for each record in the database.

Mailing labels can be printed from a database.

There may be occasions when it is only necessary to print a letter for a few records on a database, and this can be done when printing the merge document through the word-processor. As well as specifying the name of the database, you can identify particular records that you want to print by using a method similar to querying the database. The students could have used this method to print letters to all the people in Railton on their list. With their merge letter loaded into the word-processor they would need to select print merge and then specify not only the database name and path, but the particular field contents to look for. In this case they would specify the entry Railton in the Address_2 field. The computer would then produce letters to all the Railton residents on the database.

Where can I use mail-merge?

Merging a list from a database with a word-processed document is one of the ways that information can be combined from different sources.

You might use this method to send out letters for information you need, or to carry out an investigation, during your studies. Any time that you need to send similar information to each member of a group mail-merge will be useful.

As part of the evidence required for Elements 2.2 and 2.3 of the information technology unit, you need to combine information from different sources, and ensure that the result appears in a consistent format.

You could use a mail-merge exercise as evidence of combining information. If you use mail-merge methods, make sure that the information from the database appears in the same format as the letter it appears in. Make sure that font style and size are the same, for example. Keep printouts of your work at all stages, and of the final result.

	A	B	C	D	E	F
1						
2						
3						
4						
5						
6						
7						
8						

Figure 15.16 A typical spreadsheet display

Spreadsheets

The students in our example have sent out their letters and questionnaires, and are now receiving replies. They have decided to use spreadsheet software to help them handle the results. We will now look at the sorts of things a spreadsheet can do.

What can spreadsheets do?

Spreadsheets are designed to work with numerical information.

With a spreadsheet you can:

- enter numerical information in well-organised rows and columns
- give the rows and columns any titles you choose
- make changes to the numbers and titles in your spreadsheet whenever you wish
- perform calculations on the numbers in your spreadsheet
- make a graph or chart from numbers in your spreadsheet
- export results and other data from your spreadsheet to another application such as the word-processor
- save and print your spreadsheet, and charts made from it.

What does a spreadsheet look like?

The information in a spreadsheet is organised into columns and rows, and you can see this arrangement on the screen when running the spreadsheet. Figure 15.16 shows part of a typical spreadsheet screen.

As you can see, the spreadsheet is composed of **cells** which make up the columns and rows. Each row and column is labelled, and in this spreadsheet example letters are used to label the columns and numbers are used to label the rows, which is the system found on most spreadsheets.

This labelling system means that each cell has a unique address, known as the **cell reference**, which is written using the column letter and the row number. the cell in the top left corner of Figure 15.16 is highlighted and its cell reference is A1 – it is in the column labelled A and in the row labelled 1. You can move the highlight from cell to cell, using the cursor arrow keys or the mouse, and highlight any cell in the spreadsheet. The highlighted cell is called the active cell. Information that you type in is entered into the active cell, and to enter information in a particular cell you first need to highlight it as the active cell.

Information is entered into the active cell of a spreadsheet.

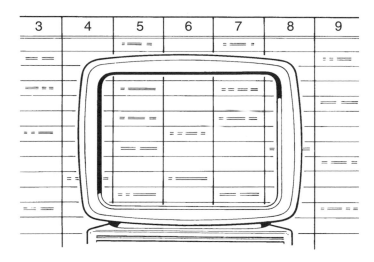

Figure 15.17 You can only see part of a spreadsheet at once

	A	B	C	D	E	F
1		Jan	Feb	March	April	May
2	Food	80	74	82	76	85
3	Clothes	20	35	12	18	20
4	Entertain	70	75	50	67	54
5	Books	50	12	35	50	22
6	Savings	29	30	41	24	32
7						
8						

Figure 15.18 Monthly expenditure of a student using a spreadsheet

The computer screen can only display a part of the spreadsheet at any one time, as happens with the other software applications that we have looked at. You actually have a large number of rows and columns available to you. As you move the active cell highlight across, or up and down your spreadsheet, other parts will come into view.

You can enter text or numbers into the cells of a spreadsheet. Text is used to label columns and rows, and to create spreadsheet titles. The job of a spreadsheet is to work with numbers though, and there are a range of facilities with which to do this.

How are spreadsheets set up?

With a spreadsheet you can perform calculations easily. To illustrate this, Figure 15.18 shows a spreadsheet that has been set up to record the monthly expenditure of a GNVQ Health and Caring student.

The student has entered the months as text in cells B1 to F1 to provide column headings, and has entered spending categories as row headings in cells A2 to A6. The amounts spent per month have then been entered into the appropriate cells. The computer recognises which cell entries are text and aligns them over to the left, whereas numbers are aligned to the right.

Each entry has been made by positioning the active cell highlight to the required position and typing.

The entry appears in the active cell, and also in a special part of the screen outside the main spreadsheet area. You can edit the entry until you are satisfied and then you press the enter key to confirm it.

The look of a spreadsheet can be improved by changing the size of rows and columns, and by formatting the text and number entries to suit your requirements.

The word 'Entertainment' will not fit in the space provided, but this can be solved by increasing the width of the A column to provide enough room. Also, the numbers entered are amounts of money, so a £ sign would help. These adjustments will leave the spreadsheet looking like the one in Figure 15.19.

	A	B	C	D	E	F
1		Jan	Feb	March	April	May
2	Food	£80	£74	£82	£76	£85
3	Clothes	£20	£35	£12	£18	£20
4	Entertainment	£70	£75	£50	£67	£54
5	Books	£50	£12	£35	£50	£22
6	Savings	£29	£30	£41	£24	£32
7						
8						

Figure 15.19 Formatting improves the appearance of a spreadsheet

Where can I use a spreadsheet?

You can create your own spreadsheet to deal with any number-based information you are working with.

You can use a spreadsheet to record information on diet, fitness, or on physical measures such as height/weight ratios. The results of scientific experiments, or social research, can also be displayed using a spreadsheet. Any numerical information that is likely to result in the production of a graph or chart can be saved and worked on with a spreadsheet.

One of the most popular uses of spreadsheets is in financial management and budgeting. If you are doing any work where costs need to be considered, then a spreadsheet is the ideal tool.

Evidence collection point

As part of the evidence needed for Elements 2.1, 2.2, and 2.3 of the information technology unit, you need to show that you have used IT resources to work on numerical information.

You need to enter numerical data, edit it and perform calculations, and present the data or results.

Decide on a piece of work that would be appropriate for use with a spreadsheet. You must decide on the information you want to store and what column and row labels you will need. When you have decided what information to store in your spreadsheet you will need to find out:

- how to set up a new spreadsheet and enter text and numbers in the cells you wish to use
- how to change the appearance of your spreadsheet by varying column width and altering the format in which text and numbers are displayed.

Remember to keep copies of your source materials, printouts of your work in progress and your final result, so that the editing changes and calculations you make are well documented for evidence purposes.

Formulae

As we have seen, the spreadsheet is a very neat way to display numbers, but its real power lies in its ability to use formulae to perform calculations on the numerical contents of cells.

Formulae use mathematical and other symbols to operate on the contents of different cells in the spreadsheet. A formula is entered into the active cell and operates on the contents of other cells in the spreadsheet. The result is calculated and displayed in the active cell.

The symbols used for basic arithmetic calculations are: + for add, − for subtract, * for multiply, / for divide, which are all available on the keyboard. Maths symbols like these which are used in formulae are called **mathematical operators.** Formulae can include a range of mathematical, statistical and scientific symbols, and your equipment will have a set of such symbols that it will recognise and use. You can also use parentheses, or brackets, in formulae as you would in mathematical calculations.

Writing formulae

Suppose that you want to add the contents of cell A1 to the contents of cell B1 and display the result in cell C1. First, you use the arrow keys to make C1 the active cell. You then need to tell the computer that you are entering a formula. Your machine will recognise a particular symbol as indicating a formula and it is essential that you enter it correctly, otherwise your formula will be treated as a text cell entry. Now type the first cell reference, followed by the operator, then the final cell reference. The formula in cell C1 would look like this:

$$[=A1+B1]$$

(*Note*: In this example the equals sign (=) is used to signify a formula.)

Like other cell entries the formula appears both in the active cell and outside the spreadsheet area until you press enter to confirm your entry. When you press enter the formula is no longer displayed in the cell but the result of the calculation appears there instead. The formula remains visible in the other part of the screen so that you can recognise that the spreadsheet is displaying the result of a calculation.

This is the spreadsheet before the formula is confirmed as the contents of cell C1:

=A1+B1

	A	B	C	D	E	F
1	8	12	=A1+B1			
2						
3						
4						

When you press enter, the computer will add the number 8 in cell A1 to the number 12 in cell B1 and the result (20) is displayed in cell C1:

=A1+B1

	A	B	C	D	E	F
1	8	12	20			
2						
3						
4						

Using formulae means that results are automatically recalculated when changes are made to the contents of a cell that has been referred to in a formula. For example, if we change the contents of cell A1 from 8 to 10, the result displayed in cell C1 automatically changes to 22.

In the GNVQ Health and Caring student's expenditure spreadsheet (Figure 15.19), it would be useful to find out what the total spending was in each month. This can be done by entering formulae into the cells where you want the results to appear. So to display the total spending for January at the bottom of the 'Jan' column, we need to enter a formula in cell B7 that adds together the contents of cells B2, B3, B4, B5 and B6. We could simple enter B2+B3+B4+B5+B6, which would do the job, but spreadsheets will accept certain shortcut commands that make formulae easier to write. We can use the command SUM to add together the contents of a number of cells along a row or down a column. First, highlight cell B7 as the active cell, then enter the formula SUM (B2:B6), remembering to indicate that this is a formula and not ordinary text. The symbol ':' has been used here to tell the computer to include all the cells from B2 to B6 in the calculation: your machine may use a different symbol. When enter is

pressed, the result is calculated and displayed in cell B7 as shown in Figure 15.20.

Now we need to enter formulae in the other cells of Row 7 to calculate the total spending for the remaining months. You could do this column by column, changing the cell references in each formula so that it adds the contents of the cells above, but there is a much better way to repeat similar formulae along a row or down a column.

Copying formulae

You are able to copy cell contents to other cells in a spreadsheet, whether the cell contains text, numbers or a formula. There may well be occasions when you want to copy text or numbers, but the ability to copy formulae to other cells is especially useful. This is because the cell references in the formula adjust to the new location so that the formula now refers to a different range of cells.

For example, if the contents of cell B7, which is the formula SUM(B2:B6), is copied to cell C7 it changes to the formula SUM(C2:C6) so that the result displayed in cell C7 is the total of the contents of cells C2 to C6. Cell references in formulae which are able to change in this way are called **relative cell references**, and the formulae we have seen so far have contained only relative cell reference. This is because we have not indicated otherwise to the computer.

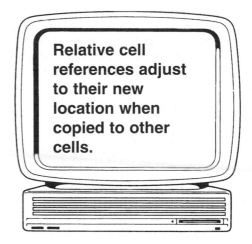

Relative cell references adjust to their new location when copied to other cells.

If we wanted to fix a cell in a formula, so that it does not change when the formula is copied to a different cell, we can indicate this using a symbol that the computer recognises. Cell references in formulae

=SUM(B2:B6)

	A	B	C	D	E	F
1		Jan	Feb	March	April	May
2	Food	£80	£74	£82	£76	£85
3	Clothes	£20	£35	£12	£18	£20
4	Entertainment	£70	£75	£50	£67	£54
5	Books	£50	£12	£35	£50	£22
6	Savings	£29	£30	£41	£24	£32
7		£249				
8						

Figure 15.20 Using a formula to obtain a column total

which have been fixed in this way are called **absolute cell references.**

Copying the formula in cell B7 to cells C7, D7 and so on can be made even easier by using the spreadsheet's ability to copy the contents of one cell to a number of other cells. First, you select a group of cells along a row or down a column, beginning with the one containing the formula you wish to copy, and then fill the formula into the selected cells, either across or down as appropriate. All the relative cell references in the formula will adjust to suit their new location and the results of their calculations will be displayed.

To copy the formula into all the cells from cell B7 to cell F7 we first select cells B7 to F7 (Figure 15.21).

=SUM(B2:B6)

	A	B	C	D	E	F
1		Jan	Feb	March	April	May
2	Food	£80	£74	£82	£76	£85
3	Clothes	£20	£35	£12	£18	£20
4	Entertainment	£70	£75	£50	£67	£54
5	Books	£50	£12	£35	£50	£22
6	Savings	£29	£30	£41	£24	£32
7		£249				
8						

Figure 15.21   Copying a formula across cells

Then the computer is instructed to fill the selected cells with the formula. When enter is pressed, the formula is copied and the results are displayed as shown in Figure 15.22.

=SUM(B2:B6)

	A	B	C	D	E	F
1		Jan	Feb	March	April	May
2	Food	£80	£74	£82	£76	£85
3	Clothes	£20	£35	£12	£18	£20
4	Entertainment	£70	£75	£50	£67	£54
5	Books	£50	£12	£35	£50	£22
6	Savings	£29	£30	£41	£24	£32
7		£249	£226	£220	£235	£213
8						

Figure 15.22   The completed spreadsheet

Now that we have seen some of the features of spreadsheets, we will look at how students have used a spreadsheet to record their results.

Spreadsheets in action

You may remember that the students in our example produced a questionnaire that asked five questions:

- Does your child ride a bicycle on public roads?
- Docs your child wear a safety helmet when riding his/her bicycle?
- Does your child travel in the family car?
- Does your child travel in a specially designed child seat?
- Does your child wear a rear seatbelt?

They intend to find out the proportion of cyclists wearing helmets, and the proportion using car seatbelt protection in each of the three age bands.

Figure 15.23 shows the spreadsheet that they have created to display their results before any formulae are inserted.

	A	B	C	D	E	F
1		Children and road safety – Results				
2	Age range	Rides bike	Helmet	Car travel	Sp. seat	Rear belt
3	0 to 4	15	10	16	14	0
4	5 to 8	24	14	22	13	4
5	9 to 12	18	8	17	0	12
6	Totals					
7						
8						
9						
10						
11						
12						
13						
14						

Figure 15.23   The data entered

They have used row 1 to provide a title for their spreadsheet and have entered the question topics as column headings in cells A2 to F2. Cells A3, A4 and A5 contain the row labels for the age groups of the children. Cell A6 has been given the row label 'Totals'. The results have been recorded in the appropriate cells so that the number of children using bike helmets and specially designed car seats or rear belts are shown.

They now need to calculate the totals in cells B6 to F6 and are going to use formulae for this. They make B6 the active cell and enter the formula SUM(B3:B5) which will calculate the total number of bicycle riders and display the result in cell B6 as they require. To total the remaining columns they copy the formula across as far as cell F6, using the methods described above. As the formula uses relative cell references, their copies adapt to their new locations and calculate the correct totals. Figure 15.24 shows the revised spreadsheet.

	A	B	C	D	E	F
1		Children and road safety – Results				
2	Age range	Rides bike	Helmet	Car travel	Sp. seat	Rear belt
3	0 to 4	15	10	16	14	0
4	5 to 8	24	14	22	13	4
5	9 to 12	18	8	17	0	12
6	Totals	57	32	55	27	16
7						
8						
9						
10						
11						
12						
13						
14						

Figure 15.24 Calculating the totals using the formula SUM (B3:B5)

The students want to show their results as percentages of children in each age group using cycle helmets and safe car seats. They enter row labels in cells A9 and A10, and column labels for the age groups in cells D8, E8 and F8. Their spreadsheet now looks like the one shown in Figure 15.25.

To calculate the percentages of children travelling safely they need to use a formula like this in the cells where they want the result to appear:

$$\frac{\text{Number of children wearing helmets}}{\text{Number of children riding bikes}} \times 100$$

For example, to calculate the percentage of 0–4-year-olds wearing cycle helmets, they need to divide the number of 0–4-year-olds wearing helmets by the total number of 0–4-year-old cyclists, and multiply the result

	A	B	C	D	E	F
1		Children and road safety – Results				
2	Age range	Rides bike	Helmet	Car travel	Sp. seat	Rear belt
3	0 to 4	15	10	16	14	0
4	5 to 8	24	14	22	13	4
5	9 to 12	18	8	17	0	12
6	Totals	57	32	55	27	16
7						
8				0 to 4	5 to 8	9 to 12
9	% wearing cycle helments					
10	% using sp. seat or rear belts					
11						
12						
13						
14						

Figure 15.25 Preparing to calculate percentages

by 100. They have earmarked cell D9 as the place to display the result so they make D9 the active cell and enter the formula C3/B3*100. When they press return the answer appears in cell D9 – see Figure 15.26.

	A	B	C	D	E	F
1		Children and road safety – Results				
2	Age range	Rides bike	Helmet	Car travel	Sp. seat	Rear belt
3	0 to 4	15	10	16	14	0
4	5 to 8	24	14	22	13	4
5	9 to 12	18	8	17	0	12
6	Totals	57	32	55	27	16
7						
8				0 to 4	5 to 8	9 to 12
9	% wearing cycle helments			66.6		
10	% using sp. seat or rear belts					
11						
12						
13						
14						

Figure 15.26 Calculating the percentage of children wearing cycle helmets in the 0–4 age group

The students then enter formulae into cells E9 and F9 to calculate the percentage of helmet wearers in the other age groups. They enter formulae to calculate the percentages using 'safe' car seats in cells D10, E10 and F10. Their final spreadsheet appears in Figure 15.27.

	A	B	C	D	E	F
1		Children and road safety – Results				
2	Age range	Rides bike	Helmet	Car travel	Sp. seat	Rear belt
3	0 to 4	15	10	16	14	0
4	5 to 8	24	14	22	13	4
5	9 to 12	18	8	17	0	12
6	Totals	57	32	55	27	16
7						
8				0 to 4	5 to 8	9 to 12
9	% wearing cycle helments			66.6	58.3	44.4
10	% using sp. seat or rear belts			87.5	77.3	70.6
11						
12						
13						
14						

Figure 15.27 The final spreadsheet showing the students' results

Evidence collection point

As part of the evidence needed for Element 2.2 of the information technology unit, you must use IT resources to perform calculations on numerical data. This means using formulae in a spreadsheet. Decide what calculations you need to make and try writing them down using spreadsheet cell references in your formulae.

To enter formulae into your spreadsheet you will need to find out:

- what symbol to use on your equipment to indicate that a formula is being entered
- what range of mathematical and statistical and other operators your spreadsheet is able to use in formulae.

To copy formulae along rows and down columns you need to find out how to:

- select a range of cells along rows and down columns
- copy a formula along a row and down a column.

Your equipment may well have sophisticated presentation features to make your spreadsheet look better when printed, so try experimenting with these. As with other uses of IT remember to keep your source material and printouts of early versions of your work. Also, you will need to save your spreadsheet file in an appropriate directory on a floppy disk.

Graphs and charts

The spreadsheet does an excellent job of recording and performing calculations on numerical data, but often we want to display the results in a form that emphasises the point we wish to make. A good way to do this is by the creation of a chart or graph from part of the spreadsheet.

Charts and graphs can be presented in a variety of forms such as a pie chart or a bar chart as in the following examples.

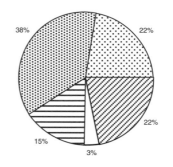

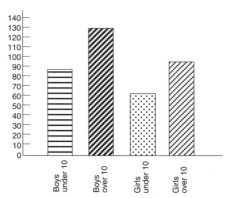

The students want to create charts from the results of their 'Child safety on the road' research. First, they need to decide which cell contents they want to display in their charts. They choose the percentage results for helmet wearing and 'safe' car seat use. Next they decide which type of chart will best display the results. They agree that a bar chart will show up the differences that they wish to highlight in the final report.

Figure 15.28 shows the chart that the students created using their 'cycle helmet' results:

The students create a similar chart for the percentages of children using specially designed car seats or rear seatbelts. They save their charts as files

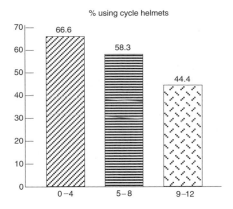

% using cycle helmets

Figure 15.28 The students' bar chart

in a suitable directory on a floppy disk, ready to incorporate them into their report.

Evidence collection point

As part of the evidence needed for Element 2.3 of the information technology unit, you could present the results from spreadsheet calculations as a graph or chart.

Nearly all spreadsheets have a chart-making facility. You need to:

- find out how to make a graph or chart from selected parts of your spreadsheet
- experiment with different types of chart and graph and make a printout of your experiments (you need to show that you have tried out different ways of presenting information for Element 2.3).
- save your chart for incorporating later into another document (you also need evidence of combining information for Element 2.3).

Graphics software

If you want to produce a diagram, illustration or any other sort of graphic, then there are several computer-based methods you could use. There are two basic types of graphics software: drawing programs and painting programs. As you saw earlier, each type produces work in its own style. Both, though, share the advantages of using computer-based methods.

With graphics software you can:

- create diagrams and illustrations easily
- use powerful software features to develop and adapt your work

- save your work, and reload it later to make improvements and new versions
- export your graphic to another application, such as a desk-top publisher or word-processor, and incorporate it in another document.

You may well have access to both types of graphics application so we will look at what each of them can do.

Drawing software

Drawing software, as the name suggests, is designed to allow you to make precise and clear illustrations and diagrams. Some drawing software is intended to be used for technical drawing and computer-aided design (CAD). These specialised uses need the precision offered by drawing software. Other drawing packages are intended for more general use, and there is less emphasis on the exact position of every line and object. These too, though, are capable of producing very accurate work.

The drawing screen consists of a main drawing area in the middle, where your drawing is created, and a number of small graphic 'buttons' around the side. These buttons represent the different drawing facilities, or **tools** available within the software.

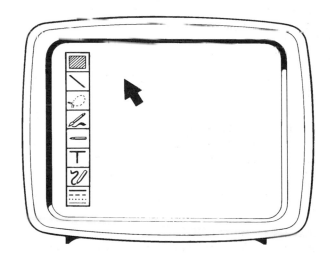

Figure 15.29 Examples of a graphics toolbar

You will see that tools are available for creating standard geometric shapes, such as circles, ovals, squares and rectangles. Other tools allow you to draw smooth curved lines, do freehand drawing, or create polygons with as many sides as you wish. There will also be a text tool which lets you add text in whatever font and sizes your machine has available.

The mouse is an essential tool when using graphics software. You use the mouse pointer to select a drawing tool, and to draw on the screen with it. It can be quite difficult to draw with the mouse at first, and practice is the best way to improve. Try out the features of your drawing application so that you become familiar with them, and with using a mouse to draw.

Drawing basic geometrical shapes

To draw circles, ovals, squares and rectangles you first need to select the tool that produces the shape you want. Select the circle tool and move the mouse pointer to the part of the screen where you want the circle to appear. To draw a circle simply hold down the mouse button and drag the pointer to a new position. The circle appears drawn between the point where you pressed the mouse button and the pointer's new location. Do not release the mouse button, but keep moving the pointer around the screen. You will see that your circle changes shape and direction as you move the pointer. This allows you to control the look of your shape before you fix it by releasing and clicking the mouse button. The circle tool thus produces ovals as well, and the square tool produces rectangles by the same method.

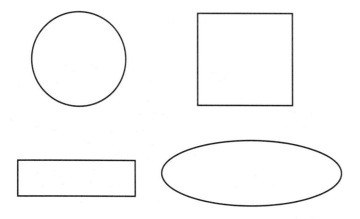

When you first release the mouse button you will see that your shape is surrounded by several small squares. These disappear when you click again to fix the shape. These small squares indicate that the shape is selected for editing, and you can now make further changes if you are not satisfied with it. You can use the pointer to change the size and shape of a selected object, or to move it to a new position. You can also delete it. There are other editing features that you can perform on selected objects, and these are discussed below.

The shapes that you draw can be either filled or unfilled, and you can choose this before you draw or change to it during later editing. The fill may be displayed in colour or as a hatched tone of grey. You can select the colour and shade you need. Remember, though, that you will only get coloured printout with a colour printer. Monochrome (black and white) printers are much cheaper to run and are more common. If you draw in colour and print in monochrome you will not be able to judge how the final result will look. It is best to do your drawings in monochrome, unless you know it will always be displayed and printed in colour.

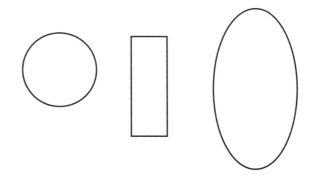

Figure 15.30 Filled shapes

You can draw straight lines, curved lines and in freehand, by clicking and dragging the mouse pointer. You can adjust these shapes before fixing as well, using the methods described above.

Another feature that you can adjust is the weight, or thickness, of the lines you draw with. This applies to the borders of shapes as well as to free-standing lines.

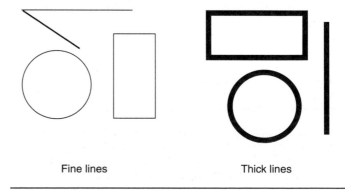

Fine lines   Thick lines

'Bring to front' and 'send to back'

As you experiment with drawing software, you will notice that new shapes sit on top of existing ones, and cover up all or part of them. The new shapes are in

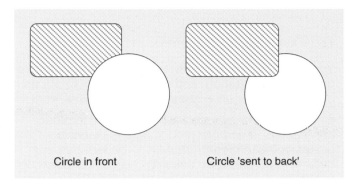

front of the old ones. This creates nice effects, and you can control which object is displayed in front and which behind. All you need to do is select the object you are interested in and send it to the back or front. It will then be on top, or hidden, as required.

This is a very useful feature, and can create impressive multi-layered effects. When used with text you can produce bordered titles, as in Figure 15.3.

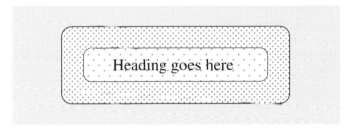

Figure 15.31 Example of a bordered title

Working with objects

As you saw above each shape and line you create with a drawing application can be edited and worked with on its own. Each separate piece of a drawing can be individually selected and edited. In a way it exists in its own right, and so it is referred to as an object. You can make alterations to an object leaving other parts of the drawing unaffected, except perhaps for being covered over by the edited object.

Sometimes, though, you may want objects to stay together so that you can make editing changes without affecting the arrangement of the group. You can do this by **grouping** any set of objects. You just select the objects required and define them as a group. Grouped objects behave as though they were a single object, and you can move and adjust them all together. When you have finished editing, you can ungroup the objects, and select individual parts for further editing if necessary.

There are many different editing facilities available which can be used on individual objects or on groups.

Selected objects can be copied, moved, and even reversed, or flipped. Figure 15.32 shows several of these techniques.

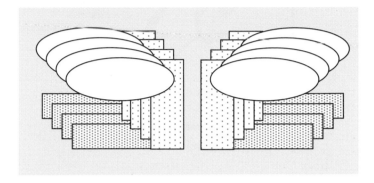

Figure 15.32 Grouped objects after copying and flipping

The features of drawing software described above open up a huge variety of possibilities for creative work. With a little experience you can produce any type of graphic. As with other software practice is the best way to improve your skills.

Painting software

Painting software is also used to create graphics and illustrations. Like drawing software, the painting area is displayed in the middle of the screen and buttons to select the painting tools are shown. Many features of painting software seem similar to those used in drawing. You can create circles, squares and other geometrical shapes. You can draw straight, curved or freehand lines, and you can add text. Paintings made using these facilities may not seem much different from those you could produce with drawing software.

Painting software has other facilities which make it very different to use. You can apply colours, or grey tones, with a variety of effects. The shape and size of the brush can be altered, and you can use a spray effect to produce artistic-looking shading. Another useful facility is the 'fill' effect. This fills an area with any colour or tone you select. Beware, though, as your fill will continue until it reaches paint already applied, or the edges of the drawing. If you try to fill a shape that is not fully bounded, it will spill out and fill your background too!

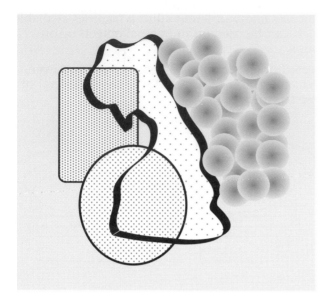

Figure 15.33 Using fill and spray effects

Figure 15.33 shows some of the features mentioned above.

Painting software enables you to obtain a more 'painted' look than you can achieve through drawing software, but the big difference becomes obvious when you need to edit your work. Things that you create in drawing software can be treated as separate objects, and individually selected for editing. Things you paint using painting software become part of the overall picture and cannot be separated from it later. A painted circle is not an object, but behaves as though you had actually painted it. You can go over bits of your painting with another colour to make changes. For example, you could tidy up your painting by going over rough edges with the background colour. It is best to think of painting software as though it really did use paint. You can touch up as you wish, but cannot just select all the paint of a particular colour, or all that is in a particular shape.

Editing paintings is made easier by using the **zoom-in facility.** This lets you zoom in to a particular area and work in fine detail. When you zoom out again your editing returns to the normal scale.

Painting software gives different effects to drawing software. You need to use the application that suits the work that you want to do. Once you have experimented with both types, you will be able to decide which one to use to get the best result.

Where can I use graphics software?

You can use graphics software whenever you need a diagram or illustration, and when you want to put an interesting cover on a report or other piece of work.

Graphics can be blended with work done in other applications. If you are producing a leaflet or a poster, you can create graphics to be included in a document prepared on a word-processor or desk-top publisher.

Evidence collection point

As part of the evidence needed for the information technology unit, you must show that you have used software to handle graphics. Creating your own graphics with painting and drawing software is one way of achieving this.

Try to incorporate graphics in your work, where appropriate. Use the facilities available to you to improve title pages of reports and generally improve the look of your work.

Remember to keep any source materials you have used, and printouts of your work at different stages of development. Always save your files on a floppy disk so that evidence of your work is available for assessment.

Combining information from different sources

When you have completed a research project like the one that the students in our example have been working on, the best tool to help you compile your final report is a word-processor. We have already seen some of the word-processor's capabilities, and the creation of a longer and more detailed document introduces other features.

Importing data

The students have created a word-processor file to use for their 'Children and road safety project'. They want to put the charts that they have created into the report, and to attach a sample questionnaire form and letter. They also decide to incorporate graphics into their work to produce a well-designed cover and to bring out important points in the text.

The software applications they are using are able to share data between them, and the students use this facility to import their charts into the report file. They run the word-processor and load their report file. The cursor is moved to the part of the document where the first chart is to appear and the import procedure is begun. The computer must be given the path and file name of the chart file, and the disk containing it must be put into the computer's floppy disk drive. The chart is copied into the word-processor file at the insertion point and the original chart file on the floppy disk is unaffected.

The students decide to import copies of their letter and questionnaire form into the report file rather than print separate copies from the original files. This is because they intend using the computer to insert page numbers on the report and want these documents to be included in the numbering. The procedure is similar to that used for the charts except that this time they are importing another word-processor file, and of course the path and file names are different.

When importing data you must specify the file name and path correctly.

All that remains now is to arrange the document for printing.

Formatting long documents

The pages of a word-processed document can be formatted in several ways before printing. The word-processor prints text between four margins on each page, the left, right, top and bottom.

As explained earlier, the text wraps on to the next line automatically when you reach the right margin, and in a similar way a new page is begun when you

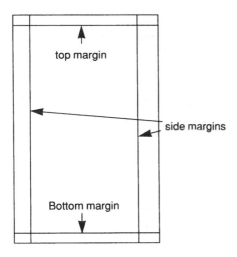

Figure 15.34 Each page has four margins

reach the bottom margin. The page margins can be altered so that text gets closer to or further from the page edges. This can be used to alter the look of a document and to vary the number of pages by fitting more or less text on to each sheet.

There may be an occasion when you want to keep part of the text on its own page, without the possibility of it being spread into a second page if you later add text to an earlier part of the document. This can be done by inserting **page breaks**. A page break is an instruction to the computer to begin a new page regardless of how far down the current page you have reached. Insert a page break before the section you are concerned with and it will begin on a new page. Insert one after and it will be printed on a page of its own.

Another option in page design is which way round the paper is printed on. Paper printed on this way round is in portrait layout:

This is portrait layout.

and paper printed on this way round is in landscape layout:

This is landscape layout.

Work is still confined within the margins you have selected whichever layout is used.

It is also possible to add page numbers automatically throughout the document. The page number can be omitted from the first page so that it can be used as a title page, and numbering will then begin on the second sheet.

These are just a few of the ways a word-processor can help you to deal with longer documents. Your equipment will have its own range of additional facilities.

Evidence collection point

As part of the evidence needed for Element 2.3 of the information technology unit, you have to combine information from different sources. Bringing information together to create a report is a good way of achieving this evidence.

It is important that the information you import is in a format consistent with the master document. This means that items such as font style and size should be harmonised, and that page numbering runs smoothly.

If you follow the recommendations in this chapter, you should be able to provide good evidence for this, and for other elements of the IT unit.

Fast Facts

Absolute cell reference In a spreadsheet formula an absolute cell reference remains unaltered when the formula is copied to other cells. A special symbol is used to indicate an absolute cell reference.

Application A word used for the set of instructions that the computer carries out. The word application refers to software that has been designed to be applied to a particular task such as word-processing or spread sheeting. See also **software** and **program.**

Byte A single piece of information: one key press is one byte. Bytes are used as a measure of computer memory size. See also **kilobyte** and **megabyte.**

Cell In a spreadsheet a cell is the area where an item of data or a formula is stored. Spreadsheets are made up of a large grid of cells.

Cell reference The unique address of a cell in a spreadsheet. The cell reference is given by the row and column headings which apply to the cell.

Compatibility The ability of hardware and software to work together. Software packages that are compatible

can share information. Hardware needs to be connected to other hardware that is compatible with it.

Cursor A blinking line or dash on the screen which indicates where your typing will appear, or your editing take place. Sometimes this is referred to as the insertion point.

Cut and paste A term used for the process of selecting and moving text. Text is cut from one place and pasted down in another.

Database A database manager (usually referred to simply as a database) is a software application used to deal with information in the form of lists. Strictly speaking, a database is any listed information – a telephone directory or your address book are databases, for example.

Directories Electronically created compartments on a disk which are used to group files that you wish to keep together. Directories help you to keep track of your files.

Drawing application A graphics application that is used to edit and produce diagrams, plans and many other types of graphic. Drawing applications give a clean, well-designed look to graphic work.

Field A category of information contained in a database. Records contain data entered into fields.

File A piece of work that has been created and saved on the computer. Each file has a name, which is followed by a few characters indicating the type of file it is, and the software that it can be loaded into, for example, RESULTS.DOC.

Floppy disk A portable piece of hardware used to store data. Floppy disks are small, lightweight and durable. You can store a large amount of information on a cheap floppy disk.

Form letter A word-processed letter containing merge fields linked to a database. Form letters are used to create mass mail-shots.

Formatting floppy disks The process of electronically dividing a floppy disk into tracks and sectors. Disks must be formatted before files can be saved on them.

Formatting text This refers to alterations made to the way text looks, either by changing character size and type, or by varying the arrangement of paragraphs.

Graphics application A software application designed to deal with graphical information. There are two types of graphics application, drawing software and painting software. Graphics applications are used to produce plans and artwork of all types.

Grouping In drawing applications, separate objects can

be joined together as a group. The objects can then be edited as a single unit.

Hard disk A piece of hardware used to store information. The hard disk is permanently fixed inside the computer's case and cannot be removed from it.

Hardware The physical equipment used in information technology. This includes the computer, the monitor, the keyboard, the mouse, cables and other devices such as printers.

Information technology The term is used to refer to modern, scientific ways of handling information. It is applied to the computer, video and telecommunications sectors and the rapidly developing links between them.

Kilobyte A measure of amount of information. One kilobyte (K) equals 1024 bytes. See **byte.**

Landscape layout Work printed with the long edge of the paper horizontal. The picture on a monitor or television is in landscape since the top and bottom edges are longer than the sides.

Margins The boundaries within which your work is printed. There are margins at the top and bottom of the page, as well as on either side.

Megabyte A measure of amount of information. One megabyte (Mb) equals 1024 kilobytes (or 1 048 546 bytes). See **byte.**

Merge fields Specially marked parts of a form letter with contain the titles of fields in a database. Merge fields allows information in a database list to be merged with a word-processed document.

Mouse A piece of hardware used to communicate instructions and information to the computer. The mouse, and its on-screen pointer, are basic equipment these days, and are essential when using graphics software.

Network When several computers are linked together so that information is shared they form a network. Networks allow a large range of software, and other facilities, to be used by many people at once.

Operating system Software which starts the computer running and controls its activities. The operating system must be running before you can run other types of software.

Painting application A graphics application that is used to create and edit pictures and illustrations. Painting programmes produce a freehand, fine-art effect.

Portrait layout Work printed with the long edge of the paper vertical. The pages of books, magazines and newspapers are almost always printed in portrait layout.

Program A word used for the set of instructions that the computer carries out. See also **software** and **application.**

RAM Stands for random access memory. The RAM holds the information and instructions that are being used by the computer during your work sessions. It is completely cleared when you switch off the computer.

Record The information held in a database on a particular item. Each record consists of data entered into fields.

Relative cell reference In a spreadsheet formula a relative cell reference adjusts to its new location when the formula is copied to other cells.

Scroll bar Scroll bars are long bars with arrows at each end which are used in many applications. Scroll bars are used with the mouse to bring extra parts of documents into view.

Scrolling Bringing other parts of a document into view on the screen. Scrolling is necessary because software usually has more information to display than can be fitted on to a single screen.

Selecting Identifying certain parts of a file with a highlight so that the selected section can be deleted, moved or copied. Usually, both the mouse and the keyboard can be used to select text.

Spreadsheet A software application designed to deal with numerical information. Spreadsheets store numerical data in a grid of cells, and can perform a wide range of calculations upon these.

Software A word used for the set of instructions that the computer carries out. See also **program** and **application**.

Stand-alone computer A stand-alone is a computer that is a self-contained machine. It is not linked to other computers and works independently of them.

Word-processor A software application that is designed to deal with text-based information. Word-processing is one of the most common uses of IT. Practically any kind of text-based document can be created with a word-processor.

Answers to self-assessment tests

Answers to Unit 1

1	a	16	b	31	a	46	c
2	b	17	d	32	b	47	d
3	d	18	a	33	c	48	c
4	b	19	b	34	d	49	a
5	a	20	a	35	b	50	c
6	c	21	a	36	c	51	a
7	a	22	b	37	a	52	c
8	c	23	a	38	b	53	b
9	d	24	b	39	a	54	b
10	a	25	c	40	a	55	b
11	a	26	b	41	b	56	b
12	b	27	a	42	b	57	d
13	b	28	d	43	b	58	a
14	a	29	b	44	d	59	c
15	c	30	d	45	a	60	c

Answers to Unit 2

1	d	16	a	31	c	46	b
2	c	17	b	32	d	47	d
3	c	18	c	33	c	48	c
4	b	19	c	34	b	49	b
5	b	20	c	35	c	50	c
6	a	21	b	36	a	51	a
7	d	22	a	37	c	52	b
8	b	23	c	38	d	53	a
9	c	24	d	39	b	54	c
10	b	25	c	40	a	55	d
11	a	26	d	41	c	56	a
12	b	27	d	42	b	57	a
13	a	28	a	43	a	58	c
14	c	29	c	44	a	59	c
15	d	30	b	45	d	60	a

Answers to Unit 3

1	c	16	c	31	c	46	a
2	d	17	b	32	a	47	c
3	c	18	d	33	c	48	c
4	c	19	c	34	d	49	a
5	c	20	a	35	a	50	b
6	d	21	a	36	c	51	a
7	c	22	a	37	c	52	a
8	d	23	b	38	c	53	d
9	b	24	b	39	a	54	b
10	c	25	b	40	a	55	d
11	c	26	c	41	b	56	c
12	b	27	a	42	a	57	d
13	c	28	b	43	c	58	d
14	c	29	b	44	d	59	b
15	c	30	b	45	d	60	c

Answers to Unit 4

1	c	6	b	11	b	16	c
2	b	7	a	12	d	17	c
3	d	8	c	13	b	18	d
4	b	9	d	14	d	19	d
5	a	10	a	15	b	20	b

Further reading

Chapters 1, 2 and 3

Benson, S. (ed.) (1993), *A Handbook for Care Assistants*, Care Concern.

Eslays, J., Guest, V., Laurence, J. (1990), *Fundamentals of Health and Physical Education,* Heinemann.

First Aid Manual, 6th ed. (1992), Dorling Kindersley.

Murphy, E. (1992), *Healthy Living*, Churchill Livingstone.

Trickett, J. (1991), *The Prevention of Food Poisoning,* Stanley Thornes.

Tull, A. (1983), *Food and Nutrition*, O.U.P.

Williams, K. (1991), *A Practical Approach to Caring,* Pitman Publishing.

Chapters 4, 5 and 6

Argyle, M. (1987), *The Psychology of Happiness,* Methuen.

Argyle, M., and Henderson, M. (1985), *The Anatomy of Personal Relationships*, Penguin.

Berryman, J. et al (1991), *Developmental Psychology and You*, Routledge.

Bilton, T. et al (1987), *Introducing Sociology,* Macmillan.

Duck, S. (1992), *Human Relationships*, 2nd ed., Sage.

Goodman, N. (1992), *Introduction to Sociology,* Harper Perennial.

Haralambos, M. (ed.) (1986), *Sociology, a New Approach,* Causeway Press Ltd.

Hayes, N., and Orrell, S. (1993), *Psychology, an Introduction*, 2nd ed., Longman.

Joseph, M. (1990), *Sociology for Everyone*, Polity Press.

North, P. J. (1980), *People in Society*, Longman.

Worsley (ed.) (1992). *The New Introducing Sociology,* Penguin.

Chapters 7, 8 and 9

Ham, C. (1991), *The New National Health Service*, Radcliffe Medical Press.

Kohner, N. (1988), *Caring at Home*, Kings Fund.

Moore, S. (1993), *Social Welfare Alive*, Stanley Thornes.

Tossell, D., and Webb, R. (1994), *Inside the Caring Services*, Edward Arnold.

Whitfield, C. (ed.) (1990), *People Who Help*, Profile Productions Ltd.

Chapters 10, 11 and 12

Goodman, N. (1992), *Introduction to Sociology*, Harper Perennial.

Haralambos, M. (1986), *Sociology, a New Approach*, Causeway Press Ltd.

Hargie, O. et al (1987), *Social Skills in Interpersonal Communication,* 2nd ed., Routledge.

Joseph, M. (1990), *Sociology for Everyone*, Polity Press.

Moonie, N. (ed.) (1995), *Health and Social Care Advanced,* 2nd ed., Heinemann.

Pease, A. (1981), *Body Language*, Sheldon Press.

Icons for photocopying

Photocopy any of the range of icons below and paste on to your GNVQ assignments. This will enable you and your tutor to see at a glance those areas which have been covered in your evidence collection.

 Communication

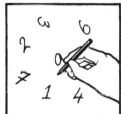 Application of number

 Information technology

 I did this on my own without help

 I did this with guidance

 Unit 1 Promoting health and well-being

 Unit 2 Influences on health and well-being

 Unit 3 Health and social care services

Unit 4
Communication
and interpersonal
relationships

Action
planning

Identify
information
needs

Monitoring

Identify
and use
sources

Evaluation

Synthesis

Command
of
language

Index

The page numbers in brackets refer to Fast Facts

HEINEMANN GNVQ

Health and Social Care Advanced 2nd edition

Now you have successfully completed your GNVQ Health and Social Care Intermediate award, you will be ready for further study or the world of work. Whichever route you intend to pursue, **Health and Social Care Advanced 2nd edition** will be of interest to you. It will develop your knowledge and help you understand the values that are important to people working in the caring fields; if you are continuing to an advanced award, you will find this book fully covers the 8 mandatory units.

By the same authors the Advanced Book offers you:

- starting points for evidence collection, together with help on grading your work

- times to reflect on your learning

- opportunities to apply the theory you have learnt to practical situations

- fast facts to help with revision

- self-assessment tasks to test understanding and to prepare you for external tests

- core skills – including chapters on the additional core skills of Working with Others and Improve own Learning.

Health and Social Care Advanced 2nd edition will give you an excellent base for further study, a broad understanding of the health and caring field and the skills you need to succeed in the world of work.

You can order Health and Social Care Advanced 2nd edition by filling in the form below and returning it to:
Orders Department, Heinemann Educational,
FREEPOST, PO Box 381, Oxford, OX2 8BR
Or place your order now by phoning
(01865) 314333

Contents

Equal Opportunities and Client Rights
Interpersonal Interaction in Health and Social Care
Physical Aspects of Health and Well-Being
Health and Social Well-Being: Psycho Social Aspects
The Structure and Development of Health and Social Care Services
Health and Social Care Practice
Education for Health and Social well-Being
Research Perspectives in Health and Social Care
Core Skills

Health and Social Care Advanced 2nd edition Order Form

Please accept this as my order for
Health and Social Care Advanced 2nd edition
435 45253 3   £16.99

Quantity [   ]   Value [   ]

- [ ] I enclose payment by cheque/postal order made payable to Heinemann Educational

- [ ] Credit card: [ ] Visa   [ ] Access   [ ] American Express   [ ] Diners

Credit Card Number [ ][ ][ ][ ][ ][ ][ ][ ][ ][ ][ ][ ][ ][ ][ ][ ]
Exp. Date [ ][ ][ ][ ][ ]

Name of cardholder...

Title (Mr/Mrs/Miss/Ms)..

Name..

Address*...

....

....Post code........................

Signed..Date ....

Tel. no...

* If paying by credit card, use address shown on your statement

For the purpose of the Data Protection Act 1984, Heinemann Educational is collecting this information on behalf of Reed International Books Limited.

F 508 GHS O